THE ELIZABETHAN UNDERWORLD

THE
ELIZABETHAN
UNDERWORLD

A collection of Tudor and early Stuart tracts and
ballads telling of the lives and misdoings of
vagabonds, thieves, rogues and cozeners, and giving
some account of the operation of the criminal law

The Text prepared with Notes and an Introduction by

A. V. JUDGES

Professor of the History of Education
University of London King's College

With 20 Illustrations

1965
OCTAGON BOOKS, INC.
NEW YORK

Published in the United States of America
1965 by Octagon Books Inc.

First published 1930
by George Routledge & Sons Ltd.
Reprinted (with a new preface) 1965
by Routledge & Kegan Paul Ltd.
Broadway House, 65-74 Carter Lane
London, E.C.4

Library of Congress Catalog Card No. 64-25620

Printed in Great Britain

CONTENTS

(An asterisk denotes that portions of the original have been omitted.)

CONTENTS

LIST OF ILLUSTRATIONS

vii

But now I demanding alms from door to door for God's sake, I found little remedy, for charity had then ascended up to heaven.

Lazarillo de Tormes, chap. III.

From hunger and cold who lives more free,
Or who more richly clad than we?
Our bellies are full, our flesh is warm,
And against pride our rags are a charm.
Enough is our feast, and for to-morrow
Let rich men care, we feel no sorrow.

RICHARD BROME, *A Jovial Crew*, Act. I.

Falstaff. Why, Hal, 'tis my vocation, Hal; 'tis no sin for a man to labour in his vocation. 1 *Henry IV*, Act I, sc. ii.

Clown. Nay, look you here. Here's one that for his bones is prettily stuffed. Here's fullams and gourds; here's tall men and low men; here trey-deuce-ace; passage comes apace.

Nobody and Somebody (c. 1592).

Spiegelberg. How you will stare! How you will open your eyes! to see signatures forged; dice loaded; locks picked, and strong boxes gutted;—all that you shall learn of Spiegelberg! The rascal deserves to be hanged on the first gallows that would rather starve than manipulate with his fingers.

SCHILLER, *The Robbers*, Act I, sc. ii (trans. Bohn.)

PREFACE TO THE SECOND EDITION

AFTER going out of print in 1934, this collection of material, which deals with life on the criminal fringe of a society already famous for us in the inexhaustible gusto of its other literary manifestations, comes back into circulation. The first edition, as I must now gratefully acknowledge, was set elegantly in type by a printer who indulged my every whim. A few slips and misprints have now been dealt with ; otherwise the new edition has called for little change. Thus the dubious etymology of the thieves' vocabulary has been left alone. Precision in scholarship is by no means compatible with the modernization of spelling and punctuation ; and it was not surprising that I ran into difficulty with the need for uniformity in the handling of a large number of cant expressions which offered no pretence at regularity in the originals.

The apology previously made for the inclusion of portions only (in some cases) of scarce tracts has to be repeated. I have thought of them all as social documents and have treated them accordingly. The purpose is not to make available definitive texts of early English ephemeral prints, but to reproduce as broadly as a single volume will allow the literary texture—much of it a kind of journalistic *collage*—assumed by the discovery by the Elizabethan age of the manners and customs of the rascals and tricksters who profited from its weaknesses.

A. V. Judges.

April 1964.

GYPSIES ON THE MARCH (Fifteenth Century).

INTRODUCTION

§1

IT is not always the social historian's good fortune to discover among the principal sources for his subject a body of material in which are combined the qualities of romantic fiction and close observation. And when this occurs he hardly knows whether to congratulate himself after all. For while it is satisfactory to be able to gather together the sweeping generalizations of those contemporary writers who were conscious of the existence of a social problem, and to savour the atmosphere of their discussions, the topics may have become too exciting both to themselves and their public for them to be able to restrain their imaginative impulses.

In their studies of rogue life and behaviour, the pamphleteers of the Elizabethan period broke several of the rules which ought to govern scientific observation. And such has been the literary success of their achievement that we love them for it. Who, after all, will presume to quarrel with a man who turns a reforming tract into a novel, even when he so far forgets himself as to exalt the character of the intended villain?

The tendency in literary criticism has been, on the whole, to overlook the historical value of these descriptive writings. Historians themselves have hardly glanced at them; and this is all the more surprising when we look back at the efforts of the great literary editors of the last two generations, men with the zeal and ability of Halliwell-Phillips, Grosart and Furnivall, to kindle a general interest in the low-life literature of the Elizabethan and Jacobean ages, and in particular to call attention to the wealth of material throwing light on the manifestations of crime, poverty and vagrancy in those spacious times. The administrative aspects of the poor law have, indeed, been subjected to close study. But when the uninstructed student sets out to gather information on the conditions of slum life within the towns, the system of criminal justice and the whole field of penal administration, including police activity and prison management, it is only to discover that there are large provinces of the social commonwealth of sixteenth and seventeenth century England that still await conscientious exploration.

This introductory essay makes no pretence to undertake so ambitious a project, and is offered merely to assist the reader to understand the background of the tracts and ballads in the light of our present knowledge of the times. Of the writers themselves, I have put what could conveniently be said within small compass into the notes at the end of the volume.[1]

The works here printed are those which I believe to be the most instructive among writings of their kind. In making the selection I was not unprepared to be influenced by considerations of readability and literary quality. Fortunately, no serious conflict as between the different criteria presented itself, and one can gain as genuine pleasure from the easy forthright styles of Harman and the author of the *Manifest Detection*, as from Greene's economically worded pen paintings and Dekker's golden sentences.

The authors of our tracts did not invent their subject, or even go out to seek it. It thrust itself upon them, as it did upon all intelligent and spirited observers. Moreover, most of them were men of experience. Copland had walked the streets as watchman within his London ward, and doubtless served his turn as constable; Harman had been on the commission of the peace in Kent, and his official dealings with his "rowsey rakehells" were many and varied; Greene, according to his own account, drifted into the society of London's underworld and learnt its tricks; Dekker found his natural playground as a youth in the streets and markets of the City; Fennor, though not himself a jail-bird, rubbed shoulders with the most unfortunate of his fellow-beings while waiting for release from a debtor's prison.

§2

Among the conclusions upon the matter of vagrancy and lawlessness made by sixteenth century writers, two seem to stand out as principal : first, that unemployment, extreme poverty, reckless, unsocial behaviour, organized robbery, are not phenomena common to all stages and periods of society, but have definite remediable causes here and now ; secondly,

---

[1] Much useful comment and criticism will be found in F. W. Chandler, *Literature of Roguery*, vol. I, F. Aydelotte, *Elizabethan Rogues and Vagabonds*, *The Cambridge History of English Literature*, vol. iii, ch. 5, vol. iv, ch. 16.

that unless measures—the publicist usually has his own recipe—be promptly taken, anarchy and rebellion will destroy the commonwealth. There are times when we are almost persuaded that the valiant beggar is the uncrowned king.   And when we turn from tracts and memorials to acts of government, the conviction is scarcely lessened.   Vagrants and suspicious persons found idly amusing themselves in a place in which they had no home or stake, were treated as enemies of the community. They were of a class ; they were feared, detested, pounced upon, scourged and pilloried ; they were often ruthlessly destroyed.   And still they came, tramping singly or in groups along the country highways, sneaking into barns and hovels on the fringes of the towns, adapting themselves to city life to swell the ranks of the criminal classes of London, Exeter, Bristol and Norwich, everywhere unsettling the common folk, and disturbing the conventions of an orderly régime.

Whatever exaggeration we may discover in panicky appeals for rigorous deeds, or read into official acts and regulations, it is clear that a problem of the first magnitude did exist, not only in the minds of justices and legislators, but also in actual fact.   All accounts affirm that the number of beggars was prodigious ; thieves abounded everywhere ; and in the unruly north their bands were still a menace to the villages after the borderland ceased to be a frontier.[1]   Figures giving the numbers of beggars and masterless men, and estimating the gallows' harvest of thieves are not lacking ; but few can be accepted without criticism,[2] so that quantitative judgment must be reserved until further work has been done upon the sessions rolls.   The remarks of an Italian visiting England at the end of the fifteenth century are often quoted. In spite, he says, of the severe laws and the extensive powers of the magistracy, " there is no country in the world where there are so many thieves and robbers as in England ; insomuch that few venture to go alone in the country, excepting in the middle of the day, and fewer still in the towns at night, and least of all in London ".[3]   Twenty years earlier Chief Justice Fortescue had a similar comparison to make. " There be . . .   more men hanged in England in a year for robbery and manslaughter than be hanged in France for such manner of crime

---

[1] *Acts of Privy Council*, 1615-16, 235-6.

[2] 72,000 rogues, etc., during Henry VIII's reign (or the last two years of it), Harrison, *Description of England*, ed. Furnivall, *Elizabethan England*, 246.   Three or four hundred hanged each year, Ibid.   13,000 masterless men apprehended in searches of 1569, Strype, *Annals* (1824) I, ii,346.   10,000 reported to be still at large, c. 1577, Harrison, *op. cit.*, 127. Beggars in London estimated at 1,000 or more in 1517, Aydelotte, *Eliz. Rogues*, app. A1 ; at 12,000 in 1594, *Ibid*, 4.   (Author discusses value of the figures.)

[3] *Italian Relation of England*, Camden Soc. (1847), 34.

in seven years. There is no man hanged in Scotland in seven year together for robbery ; and yet they be oftentimes hanged for larceny and ſtealing of goods in the absence of the owner thereof."[1] Robbers are recruited from the ranks of those who have fallen into poverty, he remarks ; as much, or more, deſtitution can be seen in France, but the people of that country have not the heart for violence or sedition. Both these writers speak of a time when conditions in England were ſtill unsettled in consequence of the civil wars, when forcible entries and the bribing of sheriffs and juries were so common as scarcely to excite remark. And it may be objeſted that a truer piſture could be obtained some years later when the " Tudor despotism " had been accepted after trial. Now it is precisely at the moment when Tudor efficiency and ſtrong government commenced to beſtow their benefits on England in other departments of public life that the figures of Autolycus and his disreputable associates are said to have begun to ſtalk the land.[2] The larger towns energetically organized syſtems of poor relief, and were followed at a discreet interval by the ſtate ; new vagabond aſts appeared on the ſtatute book ; composers of traſts, following More's example, sought for the roots of unemployment and deſtitution ; commissions enquired into the depopulation of rural areas ; country juſtices were ordered to look to the matter. When it is recalled that in other European countries during this period similar difficulties were faced by the authorities, and, insofar as poor law regulation was concerned, similar measures were adopted[3], we are forced to the conclusion that the improvements in the government of town and ſtate in the early sixteenth century accentuated an exiſting problem by causing men to set up higher ideals of public order and security. It was then only necessary that local causes should produce obvious, if but momentary, dislocations of the economic ſtruſture of society, for observers to be spurred into noticing the wide interval between the reality and their ideal, and into taking aſtion accordingly. This interpretation seems to fit moſt of the faſts in England, even if it cannot be so closely applied elsewhere.[4]

[1] *Governance of England*, ch. xiii.

[2] e.g. Harrison (c. 1577) : " It is not yet threescore years since this trade [vagabondage] began," *op. cit.*, 127. And see Ashley, *Economic Hiſtory*, I, 351ff.

[3] For Germany, Flanders, Switzerland, see Ashley, *op. cit.*, I, 340ff., also F. R. Salter, *Early Traſts on Poor Relief* ; for France, S. and B. Webb, *English Poor Law Hiſtory*, I, 33ff., A. Chevalley, *Thomas Deloney, le Roman de Métiers*, 215, and the same author's edition of *La vie généreuse des Mercelots*.

[4] On the nature of the new social idealism of mid sixteenth-century England, in some sense a reaſtion to medieval ways of thought, see J. W. Allen, *Political Thought in the Sixteenth Century*, chap. 3, " The Very and True Commonweal."

We know, of course, that many exacerbating causes of dislocation were active; and they would have been prominent enough in the history of the period had there been no publicists to bring them to our notice. Discharged retainers and serving-men, flung off by their employers when convention, if not necessity, called for the partial disbandment of the military personnel of the great households, made effective additions to the ranks of roguery. Servants of all descriptions seem to have found the vagrant's life an attractive one.

> *Cook.* The truth is, except the coachman and the footman, all serving-men are out of request.
> *Gnotho.* Nay, say not so, for you were never in more request than now, for requesting is but a kind of begging; for when you say, " I beseech your worship's charity ", 'tis all one as if you say, " I request it "; and in that kind of requesting I am sure serving-men were never in more request.[1]

The poorer servants of the state were also subject to vicissitudes of fortune. Inadequate provision for discharged soldiers left these turbulent and demoralized men to fend for themselves, and they frequently took the easy course. Such penniless vagrants were doubly dangerous; for unused, as many of them were, to the arts of peace, it was difficult to find means of assimilating them; and with their military training in mass discipline they responded readily to the invitation of any robber leader who could offer pillage. At the conclusion of each foreign campaign the troubles recurred. The homes for heroes were not in evidence[2]; the men were not apprenticed to any craft or skilled in husbandry; and so, set adrift at Plymouth or Southampton or some other port with a few shillings of discharge money, they either moved singly across the country with no definite objective, or proceeded in companies to one of the bigger towns, seeking to gather spoils by beggary or arms. On one occasion, at least, London was threatened with something like a siege. The expedition taken by Norris and Drake to Portugal in the summer of 1589, soon came back after having suffered great loss of life, and with no success to its credit. The returning soldiery was landed on the south coast. Each man kept his arms and uniform, and these he was expected to sell to make up the deficit in his pay. When large numbers of them drifted up to London, and a band

---

[1] Middleton and Rowley, *The Old Law* (1599), III, i.

[2] See quotation from *Grievous Groans for the Poor* (1622) in Eden, *State of the Poor* (1797), i, 154-5 ; S. and B. Webb, *English Poor Law History*, I, 80. It must not be thought that the returned soldier without means was a novel portent. He was a familiar problem to the authorities in the fourteenth century : Abram, *English Life and Manners in the Later Middle Ages*, 97.

of five hundred threatened to loot Bartholomew Fair, martial law was proclaimed. Two thousand City militiamen were called out on one occasion to scatter a horde which was menacing the capital. A proclamation of 24 August threatened all mariners, soldiers and masterless men who did not procure passports to their homes within two days with summary execution. It was at least six months before the panic abated.[1]

It seems probable that most of the beggars of the more redoubtable kind began their lives as soldiers, sailors or retainers. These, together with the " wild rogues ", or men born in the profession, and a sprinkling of " young shifting gentlemen, which oftentimes do bear more port than they are able to maintain ", formed the backbone of the ragged army, and insofar as it possessed any organization at all, they provided the nerves and sinews. They were feared by gentry and common people alike, because they had courage, resource and versatile talents, had often too a good address and plausible appearance, and knew how to stir up trouble in a district when it served their purpose. Joseph Hext, one of the Somerset justices, wrote a long account to a member of the Privy Council in 1596, describing the terrorism exercised by these people in his own county, where local juries, out of sympathy or fear, refused to bring indictments against them.

> I do not see how it is possible for the poor countryman to bear the burdens duly laid upon him, and the rapines of the infinite numbers of the wicked wandering idle people of the land ; so as men are driven to watch their sheep folds, their pastures, their woods, their cornfields, all things growing too too common. Others there be (and I fear me emboldened by the wandering people) that stick not to say boldly they must not starve, they will not starve. And this year there assembled eighty in a company, and took a cartload of cheese from one driving it to a fair, and dispersed it amongst them, for which some of them have endured long imprisonment and fine by the judgment of the good Lord Chief Justice[2] at our last Christmas sessions ; which may grow dangerous by the aid of such numbers as are abroad, especially in this time of dearth ; who no doubt animate them to all contempt both of noblemen and gentlemen, continually buzzing into their ears that the rich men have gotten all into their hands and will starve the poor. And I may justly say that the infinite numbers of the idle wandering poor and robbers of the land are the chiefest cause of the dearth, for, though they labour not, and yet they spend doubly as much as the labourer doth, for they lie idly in the ale-houses day and night, eating and drinking excessively. And within these three months I took a thief, that was executed this last assizes, that confessed unto me that he and two more lay in an ale-house three weeks in which time they ate twenty fat sheep, whereof they stole every night one, besides they break many a poor man's plough by stealing an ox or two from

---

[1] *Acts P.C.*, xvii, xviii, *passim* ; Cheyney, *Hist. of England from the Defeat of the Armada*, i, 183-5 ; Sharpe, *London and the Kingdom*, i, 547.

[2] Sir John Popham. See p. 507, note 1.

him. . . . I may justly say that the able men that are abroad seeking the spoil and confusion of the land are able, if they were reduced to good subjection, to give the greatest enemy her Majesty hath a strong battle; and as they are now they are so much strength unto the enemy; besides, the generation that daily springeth from them is like to be most wicked.[1]

The " upright-men " and " valiant beggars " commanded the respect of the other vagrants, and sometimes also their womenfolk and chattels.[2] There were, of course, large numbers of wanderers who lacked their ability and hardihood, professional beggars in the sense that they had no other means of regular subsistence, but harmless creatures many of them, who had taken to the vagrant life through misfortune. They had been turned out of their small tenement, perhaps, or become unsettled during one of the industrial depressions which caused unemployment in the clothing areas in 1528 and at recurring intervals until the long industrial decline in the last years of James I. It is impossible to estimate what percentage of the whole these martyrs to progress comprised; but it seems not unlikely, judging from the efforts made by English statesmen to prevent too rapid a revolution in the technique of farming and the forms of textile production, that throughout the whole period covered by the writings in this book the ranks of the unemployed wanderers were reinforced by a steady trickle of men and women somehow or other " left out " of the economic system.

Much has been written about the enclosing of fields, of the changes in farming methods, and of the uncharitableness of landlords, in their reactions upon the fortunes of the common folk. And it is noteworthy that it is during the years which see the enclosure of common lands and the conversion of arable fields to sheep pasture[3] bringing about the depopulation of considerable areas, that the greatest outcry against innovation is heard[4]. Revolutions in method such as these might, and certainly did, proceed unheard of when circumstances were favourable to the noiseless adjustment of the social mechanism. At other times the outcry was so vigorous that the incautious might easily be persuaded that catastrophic changes were in progress. It cannot safely be said even approximately how many small farmers and cottagers were com-

[1] Tawney and Power, *Tudor Economic Documents*, ii, 341-4.

[2] See below pp. 71-2, 105, 107.

[3] " Etranges et pourtant éternelles interdépendances de la littérature avec la vie économique : le roman picaresque en Angleterre et l'élevage du mouton ne sont pas sans rapports ! " A. Chevalley, *op. cit.*, 213.

[4] Enclosure commissions made enquiries into depopulation in 1517-19, 1548, 1566 and 1607. For a discussion of sixteenth century views upon agrarian change, and an account of its social effects, see R. H. Tawney, *The Agrarian Problem in the Sixteenth Century*.

pelled to leave their homes and start life afresh. One authority conjectures that the total number of displacements within the large area of central and southern England chiefly affected by the enclosure movement during our period was somewhere between thirty and fifty thousand souls.[1] This would give an average of two to three hundred a year. But we know that more than once within the space of a very few years the processes of eviction and displacement were accelerated, and that in certain cases whole villages were depopulated almost at a blow. It was not inevitable even then that the homeless peasantry should volunteer *en bloc* for the life of the roads. The industrial towns would absorb a small proportion, although the effort required to break down a local labour monopoly was always a considerable one ; others might settle down as artisans in one of the loosely spread manufacturing communities of the country districts, which were encroaching on the exclusive rights of the town producers ; a very few might acquire farmsteads elsewhere. The greater number in all likelihood simply squatted on a convenient stretch of waste, that is to say, they erected hovels or cottages on uncultivated land and resisted efforts at removal by the local authorities until they had established a sort of prescriptive right to be left alone.

Upon the less fortunate of these squatters and the homeless residue the diligent enquirer must fix his regard. It was a truism among composers of local government memorials that the chief nurseries of vagabondage, disorder and vice were to be found in the colonies of shacks and huts erected without licence on the commons, and in the isolated tippling houses, which occupied the same place as a social centre in the lives of the squatters as church and tavern did in the orthodox and respectable village community.

Before we turn to the administrative devices which a sorely troubled society erected or improved in the attempt to check the evils lightly touched upon above, reference must be made to two vagabond classes which have so far escaped mention. These are the decayed clerics, together with pseudo-clerics, and the gypsies. Neither group occupies a prominent position in the discussions of our pamphleteers, but it will not be out of place to bring together some of the fragmentary information which bears upon their doings.

In the first four decades of the sixteenth century the country roads were traversed and made picturesque by the figures of itinerant friars, pardoners and proctors. Upon the quality of the first of these it would

---

[1] Professor Gay's calculations. See discussions upon the value of the available statistics by A. H. Johnson, *Disappearance of the Small Landowner*, and R. H. Tawney, *op. cit.*

be rash to generalize. There were friars good and bad; men who earned the charity they begged, and worked hard to retain for their orders some of the popularity gained by the pious work of their predecessors; and men also against whom nothing too vile could be said. On the whole it may be affirmed that the friars were taking more out of the community than they were giving in return, and that the portraits painted a century before by Chaucer and Langland might be adapted with little modification to the majority of the friars with whom the public were now brought into contact. At length they passed out of sight—unpitied and unregretted, with the noble exception of those who elected to face the martyr's road to Tyburn gallows. When the suppression of the friaries was as yet unaccomplished, Clement VII sent a message to Wolsey urging moderation, but rather out of apprehension of tumult than from hope of reformation, for " they be as desperate beasts past shame that can lose nothing by clamors ".[1]

The pardoners too, a disreputable, shifty crew, received no mercy at the hands of the Reformation Parliament. Their livelihood ceased; their trade became an official category of vagrancy in England; and, as if in refutation of any suggestion that the severity of the English government towards them was a vulgar piece of Protestant display, the Council of Trent in 1562 banished the profession from Christendom for ever on the grounds that " no further hope can be entertained of amending " their ways. Pardoners, the English countertype of the indulgence-brokers who moved uneasily through the limelight of the first Reformation controversies in Germany, seem sometimes to have been confused here with proctors, i.e., collectors of charitable subscriptions. And not unnaturally; for promises were made by hospital collectors and others on similar missions which partook of the spiritual comforts offered by the Romish indulgence-sellers, and were exploited with more or less success according to the gullibility of the subscribers and the remoteness of the proctor from the controlling hand of his superiors. Although this kind of licensed begging was frowned upon by the authorities because of the abuses to which it gave rise,[2] the trade of the proctor and his impersonators did not cease to be profitable until long after the Henrician legislation. The king himself in 1544 gave instructions that collectors bearing his licence should seek alms of the charitable in churches, provided always that the said " collector nor his

---

[1] A. F. Pollard, *Wolsey*, 183, citing *L. P. Henry VIII*, 610. See too Abram, *Social Life in Fifteenth Century*, 114; Coulton, *Five Centuries of Religion*, Vol. II.

[2] See pp. 54, 81-2 below.

said deputy do not in any wise declare, show, or set forth any pardons or indulgences granted by the Bishop of Rome, or by colour or virtue of the same . . . take any money, alms ", etc.[1] And the practice was certainly allowed to continue until 1596 when we find Hext complaining bitterly of the " lewd proctors which carry the broad seal and the green seal in their bags " as a cover for their real trade of receiving stolen goods[2].

Proctors were not of necessity clerics. It would be safe to say that after the breach with Rome most of them were not. Whatever may have been the effect of the Reformation settlement on the general character of the parish clergy, it did unquestionably draw a harder line between ecclesiastical and lay vocations, and made a clean sweep of the borderland of minor orders which we are given to believe, had harboured many suspicious characters[3]. The precise effects upon beggary and thievery produced by the suppression of the monasteries have been a matter of argument ever since Cobbett advanced his thesis that the Reformation closed the door on a merry and contented England and forced the Tudor government to dragoon the poor. The question resolves itself into two parts. Did the cessation of monastic doles create a new vagrancy problem? Did the closing of the religious houses aggravate that problem by turning out numbers of the religious on to the roads to swell the ranks of those whom they had once comforted?

The answers which have been offered to the first part of the question have shown wide disagreement. It has been argued that the conventual foundations had checked destitution and crime by a humane and justly balanced system of poor relief. It has been claimed both by sixteenth century controversialists and by later writers that the alms giving of the monks, far from allaying mendicancy and its evils, positively created them by its indiscriminate nature. A third view, which is likely to hold the field for some time to come, is that the charity which was being dispensed as monastic alms on the eve of the dissolution was too small in amount to affect the situation one way or the other. According to the *Valor Ecclesiasticus*, the tenth-free alms (i.e., charities and doles given under the conditions of endowments) " constituted less than three per cent.[4] of the monastic budget, and most of these represented food for the poor on certain holidays and commemoration days ".

[1] Harl. MSS. 364, fo. 22, cited Aydelotte, 24-5 ; *A Supplication of the Poor Commons* (E.E.T.S, *Four Supplications*, 1871), 89.

[2] Tawney and Power, *Documents*, ii, 343.

[3] Benefit of clergy continued, but did not necessarily imply being in orders.

[4] Say £4,000 as an outside estimate.

" It is very difficult to believe ", continues Dr. Savine in his survey of the social activities of the monks[1], " that the taxed alms greatly exceeded the amount of the alms which were tenth-free." It has been calculated that the English monastic houses had an average distribution of one to every sixty square miles of the area of the country, " probably not as many as there were Hundreds, but slightly more than there now are of Petty Sessional Divisions "[2] ; they were not distributed upon the map according to the material needs of the people, and while some could give assistance to the extent of 30s. to 40s. a week, there were many others whose own income from all sources did not exceed the former amount. It can only have been at the kitchen doors of a few of the larger houses that scenes of riot and waste occurred. In such cases the abrupt displacement of the easy-going, if not overwhelmingly generous, occupants of the monastic buildings by a lay owner of the speculative land-agent type must have come as a blow to the customary recipients of the crumbs of good cheer, and caused heightened activity upon the roads. As a general rule, however, the social consequences of the suppression were slight.

But what of the dispossessed ? Did not the greedy monarch take their fat lands and pleasant cloisters unto himself, and reap a large fortune from their disposal ? He did, it is true. That is to say, he took the whole, and returned a part, in the form of an extension of secular endowments and a scheme of pensions for those expelled religious who were put on the waiting list for livings. The proportion returned to the beneficiaries may not have been a generous one,[3] but it was sufficient to provide against the extreme poverty which would have driven men to beggary. Even the friars, whose lack of worldly endowments precluded the creation of a pension fund, were accommodated somehow.[4]

One class among those who suffered were the monastic servants, in whom none of the scholars investigating the circumstances of the dissolution have shown much interest. While the old employers were slipped into bishoprics, cathedral chapters and country livings, there is no record of anything that was done to secure livelihoods for the personal valets, bakers, brewers, butlers, laundry-workers, cellarers, gardeners,

[1] *English Monasteries on the Eve of the Dissolution*, 265.

[2] Webb, *English Poor Law History*, i, 16.

[3] Mr. G. Baskerville in a paper contributed to *Essays in History presented to R. L. Poole*, 436ff., argues from a close examination of the individual fortunes that the recipients did quite well under the circumstances.

[4] Baskerville, *loc. cit.* It can hardly be doubted that the monastic dissolution had an indirect effect on the vagrancy situation by the hastening of enclosures and of the processes of eviction in certain areas.

and the rest of the army of subordinates which had waited on the monks. It would be interesting to know what proportion of them turned from their respectable careers to lives of lawlessness and deceit. Dr. Aydelotte speaks of the homeless monks who " swelled still further, after the dissolution of the monasteries, the ranks which they had helped to maintain before ". It would be nearer to the truth to say that any augmentation was due to the presence of domestic and garden retainers whose services were no longer required by the grantees of surrendered lands.[1] None would be less unwilling than these to spread disaffection on their travels.[2]

Of a very different quality were " the wretched, wily, wandering vagabonds calling and naming themselves Egyptians "[3], the effect of whose example upon true-born Englishmen the Tudor government was so anxious to check. They puzzled contemporaries even more than their successors puzzle us to-day. The early history of the gypsy race after the migration from India a thousand years ago has largely been reconstructed by the investigations of philologists. The true European gypsy seems to share a common ancestry with the *dom* of modern India, a vagrant " of low caste who gains his livelihood by singing and dancing ". The tribes accepted loan-words on their travels, passing first into Persia, where the " European " bands (the *Phen*) parted company with the " Asiatic " (the *Ben*) in the tenth century. Then the northernmost group entered Armenia, and moved onward towards the centre of the Byzantine empire, picking up such Christian names as Plato and Theophilus for their offspring on the way. Gypsies are found in Greece by the end of the eleventh century, men of the family of Ham, fortune-tellers and ventriloquists, " wandering and fugitive as though accursed by God ". The whole of the Balkan peninsula became a field for the exercising of their peculiar talents. But the advancing power of the Osmanlis, which overcame Constantinople itself in 1453, forced them onward. The *avant-garde* moved westward in 1417, reaching Hamburg

---

[1] Cardinal Gasquet puts the total number of dispossessed religious at about 8,000, " besides probably more than ten times that number who were their dependents or otherwise obtained a living in their service " [apparently excludes all tenants and labourers on agricultural estates], *Henry VIII and the English Monasteries*, 7th edn., 190. Dr. Savine is more cautious, and estimates the number of " monastic laymen " as four to five times that of the monks, i.e., about 35,000. See too R. H. Snape, *English Monastic Finances*, 12-18. We must not suppose that more than a small percentage took to the vagrant life.

[2] Burnet argues that the convicted clerks specially mentioned in the vagabond act of 1547 (1 Edward VI, C. 3) were chiefly ex-monks, *Hist. of Reformation*, 1865 edn., ii, 100. But the clause seems only to provide special procedure in the case of a man who can plead his clergy : he may not be in orders at all.

[3] p. 64 below.

before the end of the year.   In 1419 gypsies were in France, in 1422 in Rome.   The main body followed, and by 1440 western continental Europe was overrun.[1]   The turn of the century must have witnessed the first invasion of the British Isles,[2] and we find that as early as 1530[3] Parliament begins to legislate with exceptional severity against gypsy vagrants, as thieves and fortune-tellers.   Those who remain in the country are to suffer imprisonment and forfeiture of goods.   Twenty-four years later a felon's death is substituted for imprisonment for " Egyptians and other persons commonly called Egyptians ".[4]   But those who prefer the pursuit of an honest calling to banishment or death are free to abandon the wandering life without fear of injury from the state.   The Tudor legislators appear to have been troubled by the existence of native-born men and women who pretended to be gypsies and assumed the name and costume of the tribe.   That the bands of Egyptians attracted to their ranks men and women of English race in any considerable numbers is to be doubted, although cases are on record. There seems as yet to have been little of the pseudo-gypsydom which we know to-day.   But was a gypsy of a new generation, born in England still an Egyptian ? Technically, no.   He was an Englishman.   As such he may well have been able to avoid the penalties of the law. Troubled by this obstacle to the enforcement of the gypsy statutes, Parliament in 1562 tried to make the position clear by enacting that any man consorting with Egyptians and counterfeiting their speech and behaviour should be apprehended as a felon.[5]

The attractiveness of these people in the eyes of the wonder-loving countryfolk was enhanced by the " strangeness of their attire and garments ".   Dr. Andrew Borde, the first English man of letters to provide an informed discussion on their manners and language, wrote in 1547 : " The people of the country [Egypt] be swart and doth go disguised in their apparel contrary to other nations.   They be light-fingered and use picking ; they have little manner and evil lodging, and

[1] An interesting account of the early wanderings of the gypsy tribes, based on linguistic study, was given in a paper by Dr. John Sampson at the 1923 meeting of the British Assn. It is reprinted in the *Journal of the Gypsy Lore Society*, 3rd ser., ii, 156ff.

[2] But there was a tradition that they were known still earlier in Scotland under the name of Saracens, *N. and Q.*, 5th ser., ix, 511.

[3] 22 Henry VIII, c. 6.

[4] 1 and 2 Philip and Mary, c. 4.

[5] 5 Eliz., c. 20.   It is generally thought by philologists, following Borrow, that few of the cant words of the sixteenth century had any connection with Romany expressions.   But on the words *ken, lour* and some others see J. Sampson in a letter dealing with Henry Bradley's *Collected Papers*, in *Times Literary Supplement*, 21 June, 1928.

yet they be pleasant dancers ".[1] They danced for the villagers in the clothes they habitually wore, dressed like princes of Egypt, with wonderful head-coverings embroidered in gold. Caps such as these were worn in 1510 by mummers at court. Skelton's Elynour Rummynge (1517) has " clothes upon her head that weigh a sow of lead . . . like an Egyptian capped about, when she goeth out ". Rich clothes and rags surmounted by a cloak worn toga-fashion, hung about them in a fantastic medley, astonishing beholders of the big parties of men and women, many of them mounted on one beast, which moved along the country tracks.[2] Dekker, always equipped with curious information, describes the women as wearing " rags and patched filthy mantles uppermost, when the under-garments are handsome and in fashion ".[3] Trustworthy evidence as to their habits is hard to obtain. Neither Dekker nor Rid[4] appears to have first-hand knowledge of the people he describes. That they were feared by the authorities there is ample evidence to show. Parliament passed savage acts with the object of annihilating their bands, country justices sent in anxious letters to the Council, and all over the country village constables and churchwardens gave sixpences and shillings to gypsy leaders with Romany names such as Hearn and Gray and Jackson[5], as bribes to " avoid the parish ". Can it be that these groups of vagrants were able to resist attempts to break them up because the common people had accepted them, fowl-stealing and all, for the sake of their head-dresses and their dancing and their strange knowledge of good and evil ?

§3

It is not proposed to consider in detail the numerous exotic types of the urban underworld. The elaborate classifications presented by Dekker and other writers in the tracts included in this volume give a far more vivid picture of the life of the City's shady characters in street and ordinary and brothel than can be expected from any modern pen. It would not be correct, moreover, to think of the lower ranks of these City specialists as in any wide degree distinct in origin from the common

---

[1] First Book of the Introduction of Knowledge, of which chapter 38 is reproduced in J.G.L.S., N.S , i, 163ff.

[2] See H. T. Crofton in ibid, ii, 207ff.

[3] p. 345 below.

[4] Art of Juggling (1612): see note by H. T. Crofton in N. and Q., 5th ser., ix, 511.

[5] J. C. Cox in Derbyshire Archaeological Soc. Trans., i, 36, 39; T. W. Thompson in Journal of Gypsy Lore Society, 3rd ser., vii, 30. A considerable amount of scattered material in the pages of this journal now awaits the attention of the social historian.

vagrant. Many may have been London born ; but their parents must often have been migrants. For it is a curious paradox of sixteenth century social development that the towns, although the home of the more revolutionary changes of the age—in commerce, industry and political thought—yet preserved in their organization a truer perception than did the countryside of the medieval ideal : a place for Everyman, and Everyman in his place. London, a law unto itself, may have possessed less than the normal endowment of the peculiar social consciousness of the corporate town, which was aware of each citizen's existence, his pedigree, his capabilities and his relations with his fellows. But even London's own children were labelled and ticketed from birth ; they were known to their wards, and transgressed the laws of the community at their peril. Their birthplace had not yet reached proportions so vast that a Cockney might pass a day in the streets without meeting men and women who knew his name and circumstances. Immigrants were in a different case. They could lurk in the liberties without their existence being known, or camp out in a suburban slum, and no one the wiser. Need we be surprised that the authorities of both City and State firmly decided that London, like Alice, must be dissuaded by energetic measures from growing larger ? And every child knows that Alice went on growing.

The civic counterpart of the sturdy beggar was but a species—with an infinite number of varieties—of the genus *rogue*. We may remark that men like Harman and his imitators, to say nothing of Acts of Parliament, found it natural to analyse their human material under division headings which declared the present activities of the specimens noted, whether wild rogue, hooker or angler, hedge thief or foist[1], and not according to the walk in life which had, or should have been, followed. This, perhaps, indicates the accomplishment of the most important change in the history of the status of English roguery. At some point since the beginning of vagrancy legislation in the fourteenth century (in pursuance of which local justices had held their courts and recorded the names of their victims against their forsaken occupations)[2], the picaro became a professional, a professor of one of the crafts or mysteries[3] odious to all right thinkers of the commonwealth. " We get the impression ", say Mr. and Mrs. Webb, " as regards the hundred years that

[1] See the lengthy official catalogue in the vagabond act of 1572, 14 Eliz., c. 5, s. 5.

[2] B. H. Putnam, *The Enforcement of the Statutes of Labourers.*

[3] Notice the temptation, to which Greene and Rid succumbed, to equip the loose rogues' organisations with sets of rules, articles of indenture, etc.

succeeded the Black Death (1348-9), of a widespread dislocation of social relationships which amounted to an economic war."[1] Out of that struggle emerged the free companies of the English beggars. Boys and girls were born into roguery, and youths and young women drifted into it without ever learning the elements of husbandry or handicraft.

The significance of the change never seems to have occurred to those responsible for suggesting reforms. It was always tacitly assumed that reformation to a tidy, laborious, and maybe even virtuous, life could be accomplished by simple, if somewhat radical measures. Desperate individual cases were, of course, freely admitted to exist, and, it may be added, short work was needed to put an end to that existence. Where felony could not be proved, rescue work might partake of such variant devices as licensing to beg so that lost fortunes could be rehabilitated ; savage whippings and mutilations to teach the virtues of the honest life ; and the setting up of penitentiaries where the wild blood might be sobered quickly.

In this last order of treatment, which marks the first step in the development of the workhouse system of later days, there was at length manifested the genuine desire to reclaim by educating, reinforced by an equally strong belief that public services should where possible pay for themselves ; and with the first recognition by the legislature of the need for houses of correction in 1575[2], the time has already come for the abandonment of faith in the mid-century penal provisions, which could be efficacious only insofar as they inspired terror in a notoriously hard-bitten section of the community.

It would be out of place here to trace with any closeness the development of poor law policy in its faltering progress from the acts of the Reformation Parliament to the administrative decrees of the early Stuarts.[3] It is sufficient to say that the lead was taken by those who came in closest contact with destitution, the corporations of the larger industrial towns. These experimented with various methods of indoor and outdoor relief and came to two general conclusions. The first practically forced itself into their decisions. Properly organized relief

---

[1] *English Poor Law History*, i, 26. The Webbs contrast the savagery of the fourteenth and fifteenth century governmental enactments designed to frighten the idle and vicious into taking work with the promiscuous almsgiving of private institutions, which was nothing but unmerited indulgence—the whole constituting " a monstrous policy ".

[2] 18 Eliz., c. 3. It became obligatory in all counties in 1610 : 7 James I, c. 4.

[3] See the illuminating summary in Tawney, *Agrarian Problem in the Sixteenth Century*, 266ff., and the results of Miss E. Leonard's close investigations in her *Early History of Poor Relief*.

methods in a congested area could not be conducted out of voluntary subscriptions ; compulsory rating must be imposed. And so a new chapter in administrative history opened with the decision of the Common Council of London that from Michaelmas 1547, " citizens and inhabitants of the said City shall forthwith contribute and pay towards the sustentation, maintaining and finding of the said poor personages by the space of one whole year next ensuing the moiety . . . of one whole fifteen[th] ", and that weekly church collections should be discontinued.[1] The second conclusion touched the accommodation of the homeless poor. The ancient hospitals were usually inadequate even for the cherishing of the special cases they were designed to deal with, and the dissolution of collegiate foundations spelt disaster for many of them. What the more zealous of the municipal reformers now persuaded the authorities to accept was the principle that the town must assume complete responsibility for its own poor, feed them, house and discipline them (where necessary in a building provided for the purpose) and make plans for the education of the younger members of mendicant families. All beggars but those native to the town must be excluded from the system. The rules evolved by this process of reasoning in some cases went so far as to declare that no begging at all should be tolerated.[2]

Where local governments successfully found a way, the state laboriously followed. Groping after a form of compulsory assessment which might still preserve the colour of exhortation to voluntary works of pity, Parliament in 1563 enacted[3] that when a parishioner stubbornly refused to give the sum suggested by the collectors of a poor rate, and the bishop's remonstrances with him proved unavailing, he should be put under bond to meet the magistrates, who in their turn should charitably and gently persuade him. If this failed, he might go to prison. Two statutes[4] of the third decade of Elizabeth's reign made sundry changes, strengthening the compulsory character of assessment, defining the word " vagabond ", revising the penalties for those who merited this title, and for their reformation prescribing the adoption by towns and counties

[1] Guildhall Journal, xv, fo. 325b., printed Tawney and Power, Documents, ii, 305-6. Isolated instances of municipal rating occur, of course, earlier than this, but the amounts levied were trifling and the ends usually of a non-recurring nature. See E. Cannan, History of Local Rates in England, chaps. i and ii.

[2] See e.g. the case of Norwich, where there were said to have been more than two thousand beggars in 1570 on the eve of the inauguration of a new set of orders. Leonard, op. cit., 101ff.

[3] 5 Eliz., c. 3.

[4] 14 Eliz., c. 5 ; 18 Eliz., c. 6.

of stocks of working materials and houses of correction respectively, " to the intent that such as be already grown up in idleness, and so rogues at this present, may not have any just excuse in saying they cannot get any service or work ". In these enactments we have in all its important essentials the famous Elizabethan poor law which ruled the destinies of hundreds of thousands of poor people until the passing of the amending act of 1834. It assumed a somewhat gentler form in the legislation of 1597[1], which was in part reenacted with little change in 1601.[2]

In considering the growth of a national policy specially directed to the suppression of the more troublesome kinds of vagrants the investigator is apt to find his material intricately entangled with that relating to measures which concern a much larger body of men and women. The truth is that until the middle of the sixteenth century, about the time in fact when Harman was writing his *Caveat for Common Cursitors*, no very clear distinction was in practice drawn between different classes of persons seeking relief. One of the chief interest-bearing legacies of the policy enshrined in the early statutes of labourers was the assumption that unemployment itself was a kind of vice, practised only by those who challenged the prevailing order of society. Some men and women were obviously unfit for work. The rest must be driven back to it with the whip and the fear of the gallows, whether they were wandering workmen seeking to improve their condition or incorrigible rogues with no condition to improve. London, which led the way in the elaboration of municipal relief works, knew only two kinds of destitution as late as 1557 : " There is as great a difference between a poor man and a beggar as is between a true man and a thief "[3]—although five years previously beggary had been examined in its nature and manifestations and found to be practised by *three* distinguishable sorts, the " succourless poor child ", the " sick and impotent " and the " sturdy vagabond ".[4]

By degrees the principal corporate towns came to realize during the reign of Elizabeth that even if the erection of houses of correction for the last class was beyond their capacity, special provisions ought to be made for the relief and oversight of their own deserving cases ; and so we see the institution of industrial schools and apprenticeship schemes

[1] 39 Eliz., c. 3 and 4.
[2] 43 Eliz., c. 2.
[3] The Order of the Hospitals, qu. Leonard, *op. cit.*, 36.
[4] Petition to Privy Council, 1552, qu. Leonard, *op. cit.*, 32. The recognition of the hopelessness of mere beating had then forced the City to undertake the equipment of Bridewell as a " model " house of correction.

for the homeless child, new almshouses for the impotent, an organized out-relief for the harmless poor abiding in their own homes. For the most part the aldermen of England were content that the homeless able-bodied vagrant should continue to wander, so long as his itinerary excluded their own province of local government.

It may readily be imagined that the state, while approving and encouraging by special legislation the charitable works of towns and parishes, looked upon the problem of mendicancy from a somewhat different angle. Persuaded in the end to recognize the threefold classification of sturdy, impotent, and immature, it was naturally more concerned with a class of vagrants which menaced the public safety than with harmless folk who merely threatened the ratepayers' pockets. Charity for the deserving was a secondary consideration when compared with the need for spirited action against the impudent and seditious. How then were the sturdy vagrants to be disposed of? Even more important, how prevent their spontaneous generation in the uneasy foam of economic discontent?

The answer to the second question is to be found in the great body of social enactments within the appropriate volumes of the Statutes of the Realm, where may be discovered what is perhaps the most impressive documentation of any era of economic change in the source-books of history. " Throughout almost all the social legislation of the Tudor period we may see the England of the past erecting vain barriers against the England of the future ", remarks George Unwin in his admirable survey of economic conditions in Shakespeare's England.[1] To state the matter shortly, all that which was new and disturbing in agriculture and industry was discouraged, unless maybe it could pass through a net so designed that any innovation tending to greater differentiation between capital and labour, or likely to escape the paternal control of some superior authority, became entangled in the meshes. The governments of Elizabeth and James I, true to ancestral type, discouraged the extension of pasture-farming and the creation of large non-co-oper-ative estates, because experience showed that such procedure uprooted men from their holdings.[2] They tried to strengthen burghal supervision over the textile industry, and looked askance at the growing prosperity of extra-mural enterprize for the same reason. And if grown men and women could not always be checked in their exploitation of the

---

[1] *Studies in Economic History*, 315.

[2] Thus an act of 1589 (31 Eliz., c. 7) forbade the letting of cottages to labourers with less than four acres of land attached.

new possibilities of an age of expansion, at least their children might be preserved from the virus of competitive enterprize. The means adopted were a strict enforcement of the apprenticeship laws, and a veto upon the employment of the children of peasants in the towns.[1] The act of Elizabeth which tightened the regulation of town apprenticeship declared also that countrymen without industrial qualifications and without lands of the yearly value of £10 should and must be retained to serve in husbandry by the year. Persons of any age within this category who had the temerity to leave their parishes without a testimonial from a police officer or two householders ran the risk of being whipped as vagabonds. Even labour-saving inventions in the cloth industry were open to suspicion as solvents of a regimented harmony among the producers, and were suppressed by the same authority which could approve the use of innovations in the rising glass and hardware trades.

§4

Turning from prophylactic medicine to the surgery of cure it is tempting to seek for the key principle of the Tudor vagrancy legislation in its whipping clauses. But this would be a mistake. Consideration shows that physical punishment, although popular with arm-chair enthusiasts, was after all a mere device employed in shepherding an unruly flock. The essential idea is embodied in the magic word " settlement ". Now settlement has a special technical meaning among local government officers. In the first place, it can be used only with reference to people who live below an arbitrarily fixed level of subsistence. In the second place, it conveys the idea that a poor person can only " belong " to one or perhaps two of a limited number of localities. In the third place, it is endowed with a selective power in determining which of those localities shall for poor law purposes be considered the right one. Most authorities are agreed that the English law of settlement did not attain its full vigour and flavour until the passage of " An Act for the better relief of the poor of this Kingdom " in 1662,[2] and some are of the opinion that that year saw its birth. What the act really did was to make it possible that any person who received relief or seemed likely

---

[1] The Statute of Artificers (1563, 5 Eliz., c. 4) declared for a uniform apprenticeship of seven years for all the higher mysteries, barred the entrance to them to all but the sons of burgesses and owners of freehold, and closed the occupation of weaver to " fully three-quarters of the rural population ".

[2] 13 and 14 Charles II, c. 12.

to be a burden on the rates in the future should be summarily removed from a parish in which he had not yet sojourned forty days, to the last place in which he and his family were deemed to have lived for a period of that length. And, indeed, as the Webbs point out, it affected the ability of every person in the country, other than those who were property owners of a certain estate (" numbering fewer than one-tenth of the population "), to seek work in a new place or even to pay visits to friends. This was certainly something new; but it was novel only inasmuch as it extended the principle of the sixteenth century vagrancy acts, and it may even be argued that already between 1572 and 1597 a strict reading of statute law would have sanctioned the extrusion from a parish of any unemployed person who had not established a three-years settlement there. As early as 1388, when the first passport regulations were laid down in Parliament, the principle of settlement received statutory recognition, and we need not look only at the national poor law to see it observed. The Statute of Artificers (1563) has already been mentioned as a codification of the previous provisions made against the movement of labourers and artisans without credentials, and as an attempt to check the movement of dissatisfied countryfolk into the slums of the towns. A similar tendency can be discerned in much of the other Tudor legislation.[1]

In pre-Reformation times, for reasons perhaps connected with the existence of monastic charity, the mere act of begging was not regarded as the serious crime against society which it grew to become in the eyes of a later generation. It was a bad business, but within reason it must be tolerated. Nearly two hundred years before the suppression of the religious houses it was made a misdemeanour to give alms to an able-bodied vagrant,[2] and at the same time it was ordered that a wandering man or woman refusing work should be put in jail until he or she thought better of it. The stocks were substituted in 1388,[3] and after a series of vagabond acts, which were seemingly neglected by the responsible officials, had failed to improve matters, a statute[4] of 1495 specified a detention of three days and three nights in the stocks. The City of London had for some time previously had its own special treatment for

---

[1] A bill was introduced into the House of Commons (but failed to pass) in 1621 to prevent any person with less property than would produce forty shillings a year from *coming to dwell* in a corporate town. *Hist. MSS. Comm.*, Rep. iii, 22; *Commons Journals*, I, 596.

[2] Ordinance of Labourers, 1349.

[3] 12 Richard II, c. 3.

[4] 11 Henry VII, c. 2.

B

beggars. The privileged few[1] pursued their calling under supervision, wearing official badges ; the undesirables were expelled. Early in the sixteenth century the latter had the letter V (for *vagabond*) fastened on their breasts and were " driven throughout all Chepe with a basin ringing before them " ; they were also beaten at the cart's tail and flung out of the gates.[2] This last barbarous punishment, already by ancient custom inflicted by the virtuous London aldermen upon bawds and other female undesirables, commended itself to the legislature when in 1531 it looked for a stronger deterrent for the valiant rogue. The ensuing act[3], which confirmed the common practice of licensing beggars within specified limits, was passed at the time when it is generally agreed that beggars became a public menace. We may here take the opportunity of printing a quotation from this characteristic Tudor beggars' act.

> . . . and be it further enacted . . . that if any man or woman being whole and mighty in body and able to labour having no land, master, nor using any lawful merchandize, craft, or mystery, whereby he might get his living . . . be vagrant and can give none reckoning how he doth lawfully get his living, that then it shall be lawful to the constables and all other the King's officers, ministers, and subjects of every town, parish, and hamlet, to arrest the said vagabonds and idle persons and to bring them to any of the Justices of Peace of the same shire or liberty . . . and that every such Justice of Peace . . shall cause every such idle person so to him brought to be had to the next market town or other place where the said Justices of Peace . . . shall think most convenient, . . . and there to be tied to the end of a cart naked and be beaten with whips throughout the same market town or other place till his body be bloody by reason of such whipping ; and after such punishment and whipping had, the person so punished . . . shall be enjoined upon his oath to return forthwith without delay in the next and straight way to the place where he was born, or where he last dwelled before the same punishment by the space of three years, and there put himself to labour like as a true man oweth to do.

A second offence entailed the loss of one ear, a third offence the loss of that which remained.[4] It will be seen that the conventional three-years' settlement period is already established, but that no machinery yet exists for keeping track of the vagrants' movements while on the journey to the place to which he belongs. An act of 1536[5] gave more detailed instructions concerning the reception of the wanderer when he made his reappearance in his own parish, and offered a general indication of the classes of beggars, which might be deemed worthy of casual

[1] Perhaps *few* hardly gives the right impression. There were 1,000 badged beggars in London in 1517. Aydelotte, 61.

[2] Leonard, 25.

[3] 22 Henry VIII, c. 12.

[4] Section 4 of above act; applies to certain types of vagrant only.

[5] 27 Henry VIII, c. 25. All vagrants punished with the whip were to be given a certificate exempting them from further torment on the homeward march.

relief. At the same time no mitigation was made in the treatment of the able-bodied, whose third offence now became a felony to be visited with death. It would be interesting to discover how many beggars actually suffered as felons under this act; for the question immediately presents itself: How could past convictions, say in Suffolk and Essex, become known to the justices in Staffordshire? No clearing-house of criminal information existed, and an arrested person was unlikely to give damning evidence against himself.

The next statute concerning vagrants became law in 1547[1], and made a clean sweep of all preceding legislation. A new experiment was to be tried, since presumably the gallows had not been hung with their proper victims, and since there was nothing to prevent a man or woman, once having been returned to the place of birth or last residence, from setting off on a fresh pilgrimage. It was now declared that any vagrant could be offered work. Refusal, sustained before two magistrates, would enable the latter to " immediately cause the said loiterer to be marked with an hot iron in the breast the mark of a V, and adjudge the said person . . . to such presentor to be his slave . . . for the space of two years "; bread and butter eked out with " refuse of meat " to be his portion; " beating, chaining, or otherwise " the suggested means that might be adopted to coerce him to work. A second offence—if the servant were reclaimed—extended the period of slavery to life and authorized further branding; a third, as previously, would entail conviction as a felon. Children, youths, and girls, in like case, were to be forcibly apprenticed, and enslaved if they were caught after flight; they then ranked as personal property and could be devised by will.

It would seem that the brutality of this enslaving statute was dictated by panic, for there was then much unsettlement in the land. Two years later a reversion was made[2] to the whipping enactment of 1531, while the apprenticeship of beggars' children, though still obligatory, was freed from the taint of slavery. Any labourers refusing to work for a "reasonable wage " became automatically vagabonds and could be punished at the cart's tail. This remained the position until 1572, when heavier punishments were again decreed.[3] It is sometimes thought that the enslaving act of 1547 reached the high-water mark in a repressive series. But it did at least give a man two chances before

---

[1] 1 Edward VI, c. 3.

[2] 3 and 4 Edward, VI, c. 16.

[3] 14 Eliz., c. 5. For the enforcement of this act in Middlesex see Leonard, 70-1.

being strung up as a malefactor. He was now to have one clear chance only. ⌐Offence the first : whipping and the burning of a hole in the ear, *unless* some compassionate employer would take him into service. Offence the second : death as a felon, *unless* again an employer for the next two years could be found. Offence the third : death in any case, and no nonsense about benefit of clergy. ⌐The provisions of the act were condemned at the time as too severe, and were probably laxly enforced. It was no doubt extremely difficult to find willing employers for hardened vagabonds, and though such an obstacle to the performance of the spirit of the act was made theoretically less troublesome by a general provision in 1576 for the creation of public places of work, the law was now in danger of stultifying itself by its own rigidity. So in 1593 we observe a second return to ancient paths.[1] Vagabonds were now to be whipped again, as they were in 1531. But by this time the passport system had reached a fair state of organization, bridewells were raising their menacing silhouettes upon the sky-line, and the shepherding of the tramp population had ceased to be the concern only of county and parish officers. " An Act for the punishment of Rogues, Vagabonds and Sturdy Beggars "[2] in 1597 was again launched back on the returning pendulum, but the old exaggerated sweep had been diminished. Banishment or perpetual service in the galleys might now be reserved for dangerous rogues, and imposed at the discretion of quarter sessions. Those returning from banishment were to be hanged. All other vagrants must be whipped and despatched with papers to their place of settlement, that is, either of birth or last residence of twelve months.

We have reached the last of the important pre-Restoration acts defining the " passing on " system ; but one more must be mentioned in connection with roguery. That of 1597, although seemingly harsh, did not achieve its object. Rogues were duly banished to foreign lands. Preferring the land of their birth, they came back to create more mischief. The penalty for unauthorized return was death without benefit of clergy ; but who was to know that they were convicted incorrigibles if they chose to re-enter the kingdom by a port in another county ? Although not in principle abandoned, the punishment of transportation was given up in 1603-4 by an act[3] which brought back once again the devices of branding and setting rogues to labour. The second offence remained a felony matter, and in order that henceforward there should

[1] 35 Eliz., c. 7, ss. 6 and 7.
[2] 39 Eliz., c. 4.
[3] 1 James I, c. 7. It must be admitted that apart from this statute there is little evidence that the banishing clause of 39 Eliz. c. 4 was put into operation.

be no escape, the courts at the first conviction were to see that on the left shoulder " a great Roman R " was branded.

The natural inclination of justices was to class all but the most evilly disposed of their vagrants in the category deserving whipping. The branded class remained a select body ; and it is not known to what extent the revised penalty succeeded in intention. As the century progressed the general tendency appears to have worked in mitigation of the branding and hanging clauses ; but, as if to compensate for mercy shown in individual cases, the law was casting a wider net. We have noticed already that the Settlement Act of the Restoration made it a precarious thing for any but well-to-do people to pay visits away from home. In the same way the application of the term *vagrant* was stretched to cover practically all unauthorized travellers. The climax is said to have been reached during the Interregnum, in 1656, when it was decreed that all persons found wandering from their place of abode without business reasons or good and sufficient cause should be deemed vagrants under the act of 1597, and no mention is made of begging or soliciting.[1]

One of the more interesting achievements of recent historical enquiry has been the rediscovery of the elaborate system of central control built up by Elizabeth and her two successors for the supervision of local authorities in their work of relief and deterrence.[2] The Privy Council, which by the end of James I's reign was already being departmentalized in standing committees, acted as the supervising authority. The justices of the peace received administrative orders, took action as prescribed or as they thought fit, and sent in reports from time to time upon the success of their efforts. Admonition followed if their work fell below what was expected of them. We are only concerned with the doings of this " administrative hierarchy " insofar as they relate to disorderly persons. Action was of two kinds : the appointment of special *ad hoc* officers, and the round-up.

From time to time the Council, becoming convinced that desperate remedies were required for unusual situations, decided to reinforce the inadequate police system in selected parts of the kingdom with special officers ; and in accordance with administrative orders, provost-marshals would be appointed as officers with extraordinary powers in dealing with vagrants. They exercised a martial law against the non-respectable, with authority to hang vagabonds without proper common

[1] Firth and Rait, *Acts and Ordinances*, ii, 1098.
[2] See especially Leonard, *op. cit.*, chaps. 6, 8, 9, 10, 11.

law process.[1] More than once these officers were appointed in times of turbulence in London and the home counties. Soldiers might be called in in emergencies, as in 1615, when a squad of twelve infantrymen was drafted into Northumberland because several notorious malefactors had escaped from Newcastle jail and there was a band of sixteen or more thieves and outlaws at large, roaming the county and pillaging by night.[2]

The second method consisted less in helping than in co-ordinating the efforts of the civil magistrates[3]. Here the device employed was the organization of simultaneous searches. A small " privy search ", very thorough but local in extent, would round up unsuspecting criminals, vagrants and wanted men, for trial by special sessions of the peace. The law declared[4] that the round-up should be made four times a year ; but it was often found necessary to apply stimulants to the local magistrates in order to secure that searches should be made even at much longer intervals. In London and Middlesex the justices realized the value of concerted efforts, and we read of periods of intense activity in the arrangement of night searches in the slums and tenement warrens, and in the suburban bungalow towns beyond the City boundaries. For twenty years (1571-91) London enjoyed the services of a Recorder, William Fleetwood, who took an almost malicious delight in disturbing the quiet lives of the criminal orders, and in hounding them off in great batches to Tyburn. Several letters sent by him to Burghley relating his adventures are extant[5] and provide amusing if grim reading. When official business was slack he would make plans for a round-up, without requiring even a hint from the Council. On the day following the search the arrested persons would be summarily dealt with by Recorder and aldermen.

> . . . Upon Thursday at even her Majesty in her coach near Islington taking of the air, her Highness was environed with a number of rogues. One Mr. Stone, a footman, came in all haste to my Lord Mayor and after to me and told us of the same. I did the same night send warrants out into the said quarters and into Westminster and the Duchy[6] ; and in the morning I went abroad myself, and I took that day seventy-four rogues, whereof some were blind and yet great usurers and very rich ; and the same day towards night I sent for Mr. Harris and Mr. Smith and the governors of Bridewell and took all the names of the rogues and sent them from the Sessions Hall unto Bridewell, where they remained that night. Upon

[1] e.g., Proclamations 5 Nov., 1591, 9 Sept., 1598, 24 July, 1616.
[2] *Acts P. C.*, 1615-6, 235-6.
[3] Or the two methods might be combined : *ibid*, 693-6.
[4] 19 Henry VIII, c. 12.
[5] T. Wright, *Elizabeth and her Times*, *passim*.
[6] The precinct of the Savoy.

twelfth day in the forenoon the Master of the Rolls, myself and others received a charge before my Lords of the Council as touching rogues and masterless men and to have a privy search. The same day . . . I met the governors of Bridewell and so that afternoon we examined all the said rogues and gave them substantial payment. And the strongest we bestowed in the mill and the lighters. The rest we dismissed with a promise of double pay if we met with them again. Upon Sunday . . . I conferred with [the Dean of Westminster] touching Westminster and the Duchy, and then I took order for Southwark, Lambeth and Newington, from whence I received a shoal of forty rogues, men and women, and above. I bestowed them in Bridewell. I did the same afternoon peruse Paul's, where I took about twenty cloaked rogues that there use to keep standing. I placed them also in Bridewell. . . . Upon Friday morning at the Justice Hall there were brought in above a hundred lewd people taken in the privy search. The Masters of the Bridewell received them and immediately gave them punishment. This Saturday, after causes of conscience heard by my Lord Mayor and me, I dined and went to Paul's and in other places as well within the liberties as elsewhere, and I found not one rogue stirring. Amongst all these things I did note that we had not of London, Westminster, nor Southwark, nor yet Middlesex, nor Surrey, above twelve, and those we have taken order for. The residue for the most were of Wales, Salop, Chester, Somerset, Berks, Oxford and Essex; and that few or none of them had been about London three or four months. . . . The chief nursery of all these evil people is the Savoy and the brick kilns near Islington.[1]

Upon Friday last we sat at the Justice Hall at Newgate from 7 in the morning until 7 at night, where were condemned certain horse-stealers, cutpurses and suchlike to the number of ten, whereof nine were executed, and the tenth stayed by a means from the Court. These were executed upon Saturday in the morning. . . . The same day, my Lord Mayor being absent about the goods of the Spaniards, and also all my Lords the Justices of the Benches being also away, we few that were there did spend the same day about the searching out of sundry that were receptors of felons, where we found a great many as well in London, Westminster, Southwark, as in all other places about the same. Amongst our travels this one matter tumbled out of the way, that one Wotton, a gentleman-born and sometime a merchantman of good credit, who falling by time into decay kept an ale-house at Smart's Quay near Billingsgate, and after that, for some misdemeanour being put down, he reared up a new kind of life, and in the same house he procured all the cutpurses about this City to repair to his said house. There was a school-house set up to learn young boys to cut purses. There were hung up two devices; the one was a pocket, the other a purse. The pocket had in it certain counters and was hung about with hawks' bells and over the top did hang a little sacring-bell; and he that could take out a counter without any noise was allowed to be a *public foister*; and he that could take a piece of silver out of the purse without the noise of any of the bells, he was adjudged a *judicial nipper*. . . .
Memorandum: that in Wotton's house at Smart's Quay are written in a table various poesies, and among the rest one is this:
    Si spie sporte, si non spie, tunc steale.
Another is thus:
    Si spie, si non spie, Foyste, nyppe, lyfte, shave and spare not.[2]

[1] Fleetwood to Burghley, 14 Jan., 1582, Tawney and Power, *Documents*, ii, 335-6.
[2] The same to the same, *ibid*, ii, 337-9.

So much for the privy search. There are times when we hear of something much more ambitious. One of the defects of the privy search from the point of view of the justices was that the news of their progress got about too quickly. The alarm would be given, and over the borders of their jurisdiction would go the rag-tag and bob-tail of the population until the danger was passed. The notion suggested itself that a really widespread, synchronized search would produce good results, especially if the constables and watchmen could be reinforced by volunteers and banded together under captains. A whole county or group of counties could thus be beaten up systematically.[1] In times of general unrest circular letters to the shire towns would issue from the Privy Council. The searches ordered in 1571 affected eighteen counties at the least, and took place on agreed days at monthly intervals throughout the whole area concerned.[2] Those ordered during the years 1569-72 appear to be the most elaborately organized on record; but the practice continued to be revived spasmodically until the time of the Civil War. The numbers of victims captured in a single haul is sometimes surprising. The authorities of the North Riding, for example, secured a great rounding-up of 196 vagrants in the spring of 1596. In the quarter sessions of May there were brought to trial all those who were of full age to the number of 106, some of them being apparently gypsies and " feigning themselves to have knowledge in palmistry, physiognomy and other abused sciences, using certain disguised apparel and foreign speech ". All were condemned to death, and nine valiant men and aliens suffered execution forthwith; " the terror whereof so much appalled the residue of the condemned prisoners; and their children, which stood to behold the miserable end of their parents, did then cry out so piteously as had seldom been seen or heard, to the great sorrow and grief of all beholders ". The justices, moved with compassion, decided that bloodshed must go no further: the rest should be sent to their homes. A remarkable course was then decided upon. A royal pardon was obtained, and the whole band was entrusted to the care of one William Portington, who received instructions to set out on a tour of England, estimated to last over seven months, with the object of seeing the individuals under his charge to their respective homes. The party crossed the borders of Lancashire, and then we lose sight of

[1] Shropshire in 1571 employed 125 persons in a man-hunt of this kind.

[2] Strype gives a good account of the searches in the north in 1569, a year of insurrection. He understands the total number taken up throughout the nation to have been 13,000, although this is almost incredible he says. *Annals*, edn. 1824, I (ii), 295ff., 554ff.

it. Unless Portington excelled as a disciplinarian it is unlikely that he kept his crew together for many days.[1]

§5

We need not stay to consider the further development of the vagrancy laws nor dwell upon the tragi-comedy of their failure to accomplish the purposes for which they were originally designed. Whipping continued as a popular form of deterrence until well into the second half of the eighteenth century ; and then it suddenly declined, together with imprisonment, in the warm shadow of a new humanitarian sentiment. The system of " passing-on ", which of course failed in its real object, became more and more highly organized ; and, indeed, it may be said without exaggeration to have been during two centuries the most heavily thumbed chapter studied by public officers under the prevailing canon of the social sciences. No large class of the population seems to have benefited by this system unless perhaps it was the order of professional vagrants themselves, who we are not surprised to learn in 1781 will " rob their way from some distant province, and then be conveyed, together with their spoils, rich and jovial, at the expense of the country they have infested, and to any other place they may prefer occasionally, and to which perjury is the easy passport ".[2]

Without attempting to answer the question as to whether a more successful code might not have been devised, one may well stop to enquire whether a better job of the existing system could not conceivably have been made, had the personnel of restraint been efficiently organized. The most severe critic of Tudor statesmanship would hesitate to blame Burghley and his colleagues for failing to accomplish a root-and-branch reform of a scheme of local justice which was shirked by five or six later generations equipped with more experience, more science, and more leisure for such things. But a few trifling improvements in a police organization on whose shoulders stacks of statutes were piled at every fresh parliament of the sixteenth century, would have saved public authorities a vast deal of trouble in the years to come. New wine was poured too lavishly into old bottles, and it is to their credit that they bore so much of the strain. The three orders of officials designated

[1] *Archaelogia Cambrensis*, 4th ser., xi, 226ff. Portington, the conductor, is open to the suspicion of being a gypsy himself. *Journal of Gypsy Lore Soc.*, 3rd ser., vii, 36.

[2] Sir W. Young, *Observations*, p. 61, qu. Webb, *English Poor Law History*, i, 381.

by the circumstances of past history to deal administratively with the criminal classes were unpaid amateurs.[1]

First of these in dignity, if not in importance, must be placed the sheriffs of the counties, successors to an office which had in earlier times represented in all important matters the full majesty of the royal authority within the area of the shire. This omnicompetence had disappeared long before the sixteenth century. By the end of it the sheriff, who was now always appointed for one year only, had lost not only his chief financial functions—these were among the first to go—but his military leadership as well. He remained a collector of the prince's debts, and with the assistance of his paid under-sheriff, who did most of the office work, the chief police officer of his area. In this latter province lay the more considerable of his duties, and it is in his rôle of executioner of the sentences of the royal justices that we meet him most frequently in contemporary records.

It must not be imagined that this dignified personage was himself in the habit of arresting and hanging malefactors, or of knocking up reluctant householders with summonses for debt. Each sheriff employed a corps of bailiffs and petty officials to establish personal contact with the individuals whose names appear on the writs and assize rolls, and the principal remuneration of these underlings seems to have been derived from the exactions, both warranted and illicit, which they levied on their victims. It is vain to search for a complimentary picture of these ingenious ruffians. Blackstone, writing in the eighteenth century, uses studied moderation. They are " employed by the sheriffs on account of their adroitness and dexterity in hunting and seizing their prey. The sheriff being answerable for the misdemeanours of these bailiffs, they are therefore usually bound in an obligation with sureties for the due execution of their office, and thence are called *bound-bailiffs*, which the common people have corrupted into a much more homely appellation ".[2]

The two high sheriffs who acted jointly for London and Middlesex had a larger and more complicated machinery for the enforcement of their orders than had most of their colleagues. The London prisons, including the two Counters, required a considerable staff of keepers, out-door officers and catchpoles, and there were sundry other paid

---

[1] No authoritative history of English police administration exists, but much may be gleaned from the works on local government by Mr. and Mrs. Webb, and from C. A. Beard, *The Office of the Justice of the Peace.* See too F. W. Maitland, *Justice and Police.*

[2] I *Commentaries*, chap. ix.

subordinates with special duties, of whom it is sometimes difficult to say whether they were employed by the sheriffs or by the Lord Mayor and aldermen. From time to time we meet with officers called marshal-men attempting to keep order or making arrests. Sometimes they are clearly servants of the Marshalsea, a royal prison which, like most of the other London jails, seems to welcome all and sundry within its grim jaws. More often they are officers of the City or County, and on occasion they may even be the bandogs of the extraordinarily appointed provost-marshals. They acted as a kind of military police at times when the normal machinery proved too weak for an emergency, as when in 1592 there occurred one of those unsettling street riots in which incorrigible rogues, " artfully drawing in City apprentices to join them "[1], defied the constables and beadles and began to damage property. The affair began in Bermondsey Street and Blackfriars in an attempt to rescue a feltmonger's servant who had been arrested by a marshal-man of the Marshalsea prison. Retaliation followed in a manner which excited adverse comment.

> The said apprentices and masterless men (stated the official investigator) assembled themselves by occasion and pretence of their meeting at a play which besides the breach of the sabbath day giveth opportunity of committing these and suchlike disorders. The principal doers in this rude tumult I mean to punish to the example of others, wherein also it may please your Lordship to give me your direction if you shall advise upon anything meet to be done for the farther punishment of the said offenders. Hereof I thought meet to advertise your Lordship, which I am informed by the inhabitants of Southwark, men of best reputation among them, that the Knight Marshal's men in their serving of their warrants do not use themselves in that good discretion and moderate usage as were meet to be done in like cases, but after a most rough and violent manner provoking them by such hard dealing to contend with them, which otherwise would obey in all dutiful sort; as I understand they did in this case, where they entered the house where the warrant was to be served with a dagger drawn, affrighting the good wife who sat by the fire with a young infant in her arms, and afterwards, having taken the party and certain others and committed them to prison where they lay five days without making their answer; these mutinous apprentices assembled themselves in their disordered manner; the said Marshal's men, being within the Marshalsea, issued forth with their daggers drawn and with bastinadoes in their hands beating the people, whereof some came that way by chance but to gaze as the manner is, and afterwards drew their swords, whereby the tumult was rather incensed, and themselves endangered but that help came to prevent farther mischiefs.[2]

Like the sheriffs, the justices of the peace, who constitute the second of our three arms of the law, were chosen among the knights, esquires

[1] Compare the affrays of 1595 which occasioned the proclamation of martial law in London. Maitland, *History of London*, i, 278-9.

[2] Remembrancia, i, 662 ; Malone Soc., *Collections*, I (i), 70-3.

and gentlemen of the county in which they were required to serve. The number on the commission would vary from twenty to eighty according to the populousness of the county ; but the effective number fell short of the total by a good deal. Perhaps a quarter could be depended on for attendance at quarter sessions. Of the remainder some were old, or too occupied with national affairs ; others belonged to the order of " those that be drones and not bees ", as the Lord Keeper indignantly remarked in 1599 ; while there were some," pocket-justices ", who were in office " by countenance, and are idle and will not do anything, and as they do no ill so they do no good ; but others are evil and use their office to show their malice and revenge ".[1]

" It is such a form of subordinate government ", says Coke in his *Institutes*, " for the tranquillity and quiet of the realm, as no part of the Christian world hath the like." A remarkable system certainly, and a singularly happy expression of the English genius for getting important public services performed for nothing. Mr. Justice Shallow took his place on a bench composed of gentlemen possessing every kind of ability but that of the trained official. Enthusiasm was supposed to make up for lack of skill, and when all was said there were always competent lawyers in the service of the county from whom advice could be obtained.

In all the social experiments of the Tudors and early Stuarts it was the justice who bore the burden and heat of the day. Two hundred and ninety-three statutes were passed previous to 1603 bearing upon the duties of these humble magistrates, and the parliaments of Elizabeth had contributed a total of seventy-eight, " ranging in subject ", as Professor Cheyney drily observes, " from a law for the preservation of the spawn and fry of fish to one against fond and fantastical prophecies ".[2] In some localities the practising justices in the later years of Elizabeth had their hands full with the acts against recusants. Normally their two most exacting tasks were the enforcement of the poor law and the exercise of criminal jurisdiction. The civil justice they dispensed was inconsiderable, but on the criminal side their responsibilities were enormous. Acting as single units their powers were less extensive than those of a stipendiary magistrate to-day. They embraced a number of petty offences which could be tried summarily in the informal milieu of the dining-room or the market place. Drunkenness, petty theft, vagrancy and non-attendance at church were cases which could be dealt with in this manner, and the penalties included whipping and the

[1] J. Hawarde, *Les Reportes del Cases in Camera Stellata*, 106, 109, 160.
[2] *History of England*, ii, 321.

ftocks. More serious matters would often come before the neareft magiftrate for a preliminary hearing. If he were satisfied after examining the chief witnesses and cross-examining the accused that a case for a higher court exifted, he would order the matter to ftand over till quarter sessions. In the meantime the suspected person would either be bailed or remain a prisoner in the county jail. In his individual capacity the juftice can be described more accurately as a policeman or detective than a magiftrate. The preliminary hearing on an accusation of felony was not so much a trial as an interrogation designed to reveal the facts upon which a quarter session or assize case could be built up.[1] Sufficient evidence failing, the policeman transformed himself into a judge and gave a moderate sentence for the lesser crime, or, alternatively, dismissed the case. Thomas Harman without awareness of any unusual procedure tells us[2] that he hung up a " dumb " beggar by the wrifts until he confessed his fraud. Readers who care to turn to the incident will see that there was little of court-room decorum in the conduct of the enquiry.[3]

The officially conducted trial came later when those who were alleged to have committed serious offences were brought before the grand jury at quarter sessions. If an indictment were then presented the accused came immediately for trial before the bench of county juftices, and the sentence generally followed swiftly. The early seventeenth century muft have seen the quarter sessions magiftrates at the zenith of their power in criminal causes. Only in accusations of treason does it seem to have been obligatory to defer the trial for the royal juftices of oyer and terminer and jail delivery at the next assizes.[4] Capital punishments might be, and frequently were inflicted by the County bench. " In Devonshire in the midwinter sessions of 1598 out of sixty-five culprits who were tried eighteen were hung, thirteen flogged, seven acquitted, and seven on account of their claim to benefit of clergy branded and released."[5] Adding thirty-five who were condemned at the assizes, seventy-four men and women met their death in this county in this one year. This apportionment of trials for capital

[1] The written evidence and depositions were put in by the prosecution when the real trial came on. See p. 503, note 6.

[2] pp. 91-2.

[3] Two or more juftices acting in place of one had greater powers, but these extended into the adminiftrative rather than the judicial field.

[4] " Subject to the proviso that cases of difficulty muft be sent to the assizes. During the eighteenth century the cuftom sprang up of always sending to the assizes cases which might be capitally punished." Holdsworth, *Hiftory of English Law*, i, 293. See too J. Lifter, *Weft Riding Sessions Rolls*, xii-xiv.

[5] E. P. Cheyney, *Hiftory of England*, ii, 333, drawing upon sessions rolls.

offences between professional and amateur judges probably represents a common average.

In the text of the present collection the justice of the peace makes frequent appearances. It will be observed that it is the single justice that we meet most often. Working in close association with him in the detection of crime and the arrest of offenders, the constable enters even more frequently into the discussion. He is a worthy fellow, and merits our regard as the third arm of the police organization.

Of the constable there are two orders, the high and the petty. The former is the more exalted, but in practical affairs he is less important than his junior without whom local government must have fallen to pieces. The high constable acts, either singly or with a partner, as the senior officer of the hundred, an administrative unit which has by our time lost a great part of its original autonomy. Ideally he is an educated gentleman[1] with a local reputation, capable of keeping accounts —for the responsibility of raising county rates falls upon him—and of inspiring respect. He acts as the channel through which the orders of the magistrates pass to the village officers, over whom he is expected to have a general supervision. Infractions of the labour laws are reported to him, and he holds " sessions " with his colleagues of other hundreds to see that they are observed. He does much miscellaneous work at quarter sessions time. But apart from the occasional management of special searches for vagabonds he seems to be able to avoid dirtying his hands with criminal matters. And this is where the petty constable comes in.

> There dwells, and within call, if it please your worship,
> A potent monarch called the constable,
> That does command a citadel called the stocks ;
> Whose guards are certain files of rusty billmen.[2]

The nature of the authority of this official is shortly described in two of the notes to the text[3], and this is certainly not the place in which to enquire into his interesting historical antecedents. However democratic his origin in the remote past, by the end of the sixteenth century he has become the servant of the justices and the master of his parish or ward or leet division. He serves for a year, or until he can persuade the appointing authority to find a successor, and while in office he must keep order within his domain. It is impossible to withhold one's

[1] Bacon, *The Office of Constables, Works*, edn. 1854, i, 648ff.
[2] Massinger, *A New Way to Pay Old Debts*, I, i.
[3] p. 520, note 28 ; p. 521, note 1.

sympathy from this unfortunate person. All the unpleasant duties come his way, while churchwardens and overseers get the credit. Like the infantry lance-corporal he muſt earn unpopularity among those who perform " fatigues ", and he muſt go out in all weathers to see that the jobs are done. He is generally without social diſtinction, and is therefore despised by the officers above him. James Gyffon of Albury, evidently a superior specimen of his order, breaks into plaintive verses[1] on the hardships of his lot ; but he makes less than might be expected of the onerous task of the man who muſt come into personal contact with the rough people of the highways and ditches. Every ſtranger entering the village or ward is suspect, and will almoſt certainly commit some technical offence. If the new arrival is in any way disreputable and is allowed to ſtay, there will be complaints of begging or pilfering, or that a householder out of pity has taken an " unlawful inmate ", who, if a woman, muſt be chased away at once, or she is sure to be in labour before many days are out, and what an outcry will be heard in an indignant purse-tight parish then ! Licences to travel muſt be examined and countersigned ; tramps failing to account for themselves muſt be put in the ſtocks—and a watch set over them pending a magis-trate's enquiry, or they will find a means to escape with the wicked subtlety of their kind. And now and again there will be violent and humiliating encounters with the professional bullies of the road. " Whip-ping till the back be bloody "—to be performed personally by the conſtable—may even at times be a welcome task. And, finally, when a serious crime has been committed, there will be the need to raise the hue and cry.

> For the better apprehension of thieves and man-killers, there is an old law in England very well provided whereby it is ordered that, if he that is robbed, or any man complain and give warning of slaughter or murder committed, the conſtable of the village whereunto he cometh and crieth for succour is to raise the parish about him, and to search woods, groves, and all suspected houses and places, where the trespasser may be, or is supposed to lurk ; and not finding him there, he is to give warning unto the next conſtable, and so one conſtable, after search made, to advertise another from parish to parish, till they come to the same where the offender is harboured and found. It is also provided that, if any parish in this business do not her duty, but suffereth the thief (for the avoiding of trouble sake) in carrying him to the jail, if he should be apprehended, or other letting of their work to escape, the same parish is not only to make fine to the king, but also the same, with the whole hundred wherein it ſtandeth, to repay the party robbed his damages, and leave his eſtate harmless. Cer-tainly this is a good law : howbeit I have known of my own experience felons being taken to have escaped out of the ſtocks, being rescued by other

[1] pp. 488-90.

for want of watch and guard, that thieves have been let pass, because the covetous and greedy parishioners would neither take the pains nor be at the charge to carry them to prison, if it be far off ; that when hue and cry have been made even to the faces of some constables, they have said : " God restore your loss ! I have other business at this time ". And by such means the meaning of many a good law is left unexecuted, malefactors emboldened, and many a poor man turned out of that which he hath sweat and taken pains toward the maintenance of himself and his poor children and family.[1]

In the boroughs no essential variation from the country parish constable's duties was to be found. Local needs and traditional methods would be responsible for the development of peculiar functions, but there was a natural tendency to preserve supplementary officers for special tasks. In the towns, also, one is more conscious of the leet court as the creator of the constabular area.

London had its own organization and a highly differentiated police personnel, in which the unpaid constabulary played a smaller part than elsewhere. But it cannot be conceded that the City was any more fortunate than the provincial boroughs in its attempt to suppress the underworld. Much of the matter printed in this volume goes to show that criminal life in the metropolis offered opportunities for activities varied and interesting enough for a whole school of literature to be sustained upon it. The area covered by the City, by the suburbs in Surrey and Middlesex, and by the City of Westminster, was admittedly too vast for men even to formulate plans for the creation of a common authority which might grapple with the questions of law and order. The only body which pretended to exercise a general supervision was the Privy Council, and mighty as its influence undoubtedly was, it was powerless to shake the City of London's pride in its somewhat dubious privileges. Westminster was persuaded into reorganization by Lord Burghley, the High Steward of that city, in 1585, when an act[2] (subsequently renewed at intervals) was passed constituting a special court of burgesses whose duty it became to supervise all that pertained to the suppression of disorderly elements within its area. The spreading suburbs of the two cities continued to be ruled by the magistrates of the home counties under whose jurisdiction they fell. Within the municipal nucleus itself there was trouble and confusion, for even here no body of citizens was equipped with powers sufficiently extensive to bring all the streets under a common supervision.

[1] Wm. Harrison, *Description of England* (ed. Furnivall, *Elizabethan England*), p. 247. See below, p. 501, note 10.

[2] 27 Eliz., c. 17. The constitution is described by S. and B. Webb in *Manor and Borough*, ch. iv.

One of the gravest of police problems arose out of the existence within the City's limits of liberties or " bastard sanctuaries ". These areas had in pre-Tudor times been small exemplars of the class of ecclesiastical and lay franchises which by charter or prescription claimed independence of royal justice. They were once enclaves of a jurisdiction where the king's writ did not run, and as such afforded shelter for fugitive criminals and debtors. The Reformation statutes of Henry VIII, following upon a long sustained battle between an aggressive royal power and firmly entrenched privilege, had marked the collapse of ecclesiastical sanctuary and the triumph of the crown. Extra-regal privileges disappeared by degrees, but sanctuaries of a sort remained. First the old practice of compelling a sanctuary-man to abjure the realm was abolished on the curious grounds that the country thereby lost good men apt for the navy and the wars, and others who might disclose the knowledge of the commodities and secrets of the realm[1]. Sanctuary of the old type was already doomed, but some provision obviously had to be made for criminals and others who were now denied escape to the Continent or Ireland. An act of 1540[2] set up seven cities of refuge, among which Westminster, York and Manchester were numbered, for their reception. There were naturally protests from the cities of refuge against the dubious concession ; but the threat to their peace of mind was less perilous than would have been the case in earlier years, for the same act declared that sanctuary would no longer protect offenders who were accused of murder, robbery and certain other heinous felonies. Meanwhile ecclesiastical jurisdiction in general had been taken from the Bishop of Rome ; but this did not extinguish the immunities of all the old religious houses. The franchises in question were now vested in the crown, and the inmates continued, where they dared, to defy the local magistracy. London, as has been said, was peculiarly burdened. And Westminster suffered too. The Abbey was of course a special case, having traditional rights in sanctuary matters of the most considerable kind. As a " city of refuge " the Abbey precincts lost their statutory position with the rest in the first parliament of Edward VI, but this seems to have made no practical difference for a while.[3] Indeed, in

[1] 22 Henry VIII, c. 14. For Wolsey's earlier interest in the abuse see A. F. Pollard, *Wolsey*, p. 53 n.

[2] 32 Henry VIII, c. 12. Churches and churchyards were still left available for temporary refuge, but their hospitality was not of a generous nature ; and apparently a man could be starved out by his adversaries. In any case only forty days were allowed for church-sanctuary.

[3] See paper by Miss I. D. Thornley in *Tudor Studies*, ed. Seton-Watson, p. 204.

Mary's reign the sanctuary limits still harboured within themselves people guilty of the worst offences. Henry Machyn gives us a slight glimpse of the refugees in his diary[1] :

> The 6 day of December [1556] the abbot of Westminster went a procession with his convent. Before him went all the sanctuary men with cross-keys upon their garments, and after went three for murder. One was Lord Dacre's son of the north, was whipped with a sheet about him for killing of Master West, esquire, dwelling beside, . . . and another thief that did long to one of Master Comptroller . . . did kill Richard Egglyston, the Comptroller's tailor, and killed him in the Long Acres, the back-side Charing Cross ; and a boy that killed a big boy that sold papers and printed books, with hurling of a stone, and hit him under the ear in Westminster Hall.

The area of the Abbey remained as a bolt-hole for debtors and other fugitives even after the failure of the Marian system, though acting in defiance of royal authority. Closely linked with the Westminster sanctuary was the ecclesiastical foundation of St. Martin-le-Grand, which had been brought under the general supervision of the Abbey, " the one at the elbow of the City, the other in the very bowels ", as More declared when mapping out the criminal topography of London. With a possible competitor in Whitefriars, St. Martin's precinct became the most troublesome thorn in the side of the City police, for its immunities, a constant source of dispute even in the fourteenth century, were by no means weakened by the association with the Abbey. In 1548 the ecclesiastical buildings on the site fell to the Crown's disposal ; they were destroyed, and the site itself used in building a new residential quarter ; and this, with the tenements in the surrounding alleys, became popular with the foreigners who came to reinforce the existing population of artizans, metal-workers, makers of artificial jewellery and other gauds. In 1593 the aliens in St. Martin's liberty were numbered at 193, French, Dutch and German, a suspect crew whom we notice successfully resisting the efforts of the City to search workshops and segregate plague victims.[2]

Farther west, adjoining the Temple on the site of the old conventual buildings of the White Friars, there existed a debtors' stronghold. Whitefriars owed its present immunity to the same sequence of events as did St. Martin's. At the Reformation its jurisdiction went, not to the City magistrates, but to the king's nominees, Henry arguing, so it is reported, that " he was as well able to keep the liberties as the friars

[1] Camden Soc., 1848, p. 121.
[2] A. J. Kempe, *Historical Notices of St. Martin-le-Grand*, 1825, pp. 167ff.

INTRODUCTION

were ". The site became the property of private families, while jurisdiction of a petty nature was in the hands of justices of the peace who
were exempt from civic control.[1] Any privileges of sanctuary which
might still be held to remain were altogether abolished by statute[2] in
1623; but in practice the immunities of Whitefriars and other like
areas continued. The refugee from justice was now no longer sheltering
in that ghostly shadow of the Church's protection which had hovered
long after the friars had gone. But he found sanctuary just the same.
Lax justice allowed Whitefriars to keep its unofficial privileges and the
inmate would have observed no difference after 1623. Respectability
had departed some years before the end of Elizabeth's reign, but decent
folk could still penetrate its recesses. The Whitefriars private theatre
was drawing audiences to the old refectory hall in 1609, and remained
in being for ten or twelve years. It is not improbable that at the time
of Charles I's accession, the swarming undesirables of the tenement
houses had made the neighbourhood unsafe. Throughout the seventeenth century the liberty is mentioned in contemporary references as
the resort of debtors and " wanted " men and women. " Here they
formed a community of their own, adopted the language of pickpockets,
openly resisted the execution of every legal process, and extending their
cant terms to the place they lived in, new-named their precinct by the
well-known appellation of Alsatia, after the province which formed a
debatable land between Germany and France "[3]. Macaulay's description of Alsatia in his remarks on the state of England in 1685 is nearly
as famous as Scott's more imaginative chapters on the quarter in *The
Fortunes of Nigel*[4].

> Insolvents . . . were to be found in every dwelling, from cellar
> to garret. Of these a large proportion were knaves and libertines, and were
> followed to their asylum by women more abandoned than themselves. The
> civil power was unable to keep order in a district swarming with such inhabi-
> tants. Though the immunities legally (*sic*) belonging to the place extended
> only to cases of debt, cheats, false witnesses, forgers and highwaymen found

[1] References indicating the debatable character of the government of the Blackfriars
and Whitefriars liberties will be found in Chambers, *Elizabethan Stage*, ii, 477-8; further
discussion of the liberties within the walls and on the fringes of London in Miss E. Jeffries
Davis' article in *Tudor Studies*, 287-311.

[2] 21 James I, c. 28, s. 7. Already in 1608 a charter from James I gave the City jurisdiction in a modified form over Black- and Whitefriars; but this seems to have made little
difference.

[3] Wheatley and Cunningham, *London Past and Present*, iii, 503; and see *Acts P. C.*
1615-6, p. 153 for the difficulty experienced by the City in getting the liberties to contribute
their share in military charges, musters, etc.

[4] Chapters 16 and 17.

refuge there. For amidst a rabble so desperate no peace officer's life was in safety. At the cry of "Rescue", bullies with swords and cudgels, and termagant hags with spits and broomsticks, poured forth by hundreds; and the intruder was fortunate if he escaped back into Fleet Street, hustled, stripped and pumped upon. Even the warrant of the Chief Justice of England could not be executed without the help of a company of musketeers. Such relics of the darkest ages were to be found within a short walk of the chambers where Somers was studying history and law, of the chapel where Tillotson was preaching.[1]

In connection with the constable's duties, we must not forget that he had a responsibility for the good behaviour of parishioners. Suspicious behaviour and eccentric conduct generally, if not a technical offence at common law, was sufficiently serious to warrant detention and enquiry. One of the commonest causes of arrest in London was the misdemeanour of being out in the streets at night without legitimate business. One's very presence out of doors even on his own property after the conventional bed-time of the locality might get him into trouble, as we may discover from a case at Devizes.

> April 23 [1584]. This day Hugh Norryshe being taken in a search at midnight lying in his garden very suspiciously, and being commanded by the bailiffs and constables to go and lie in his house, refused so to do, but in very lewd and slanderous speeches abused the officers in calling of them knaves, with other opprobrious words, and not yielding himself to go with them, but as that they were forced to bear him, and the man being examined before Mr. Mayor and found culpable therein, was for his said contempt and abuses committed to the ward, and there to set by both the feet in the stocks.[2]

While the lay courts had considerable powers in the oversight of behaviour and morals, the chief supervision in this province was undertaken by the courts ecclesiastical, a system of tribunals over which the bishops and their officials presided, and whence they ruled the dioceses with the rod of excommunication. The methods here employed were much the same as those which had been followed on the eve of the Reformation and earlier[3]. The national prince, it is true, had outlawed the jurisdiction of the foreigner in ecclesiastical matters; but he was wise enough to leave the judicial activity of the Church almost unhindered by the temporal authority.

An energetic bishop could make his will felt; he could, indeed, on his triennial visitations review personally the whole moral life of

---

[1] Macaulay, *History*, edn. 1858, i, 364.

[2] *Annals of Devizes* (1555-1791), i, 87.

[3] The constitutional changes are discussed by Canon (later Bishop) Stubbs in his Historical Appendix (I) to the *Report of the Ecclesiastical Courts Commission*, 1883, C. 3760.

his charge, sitting in judgment in the court commonly presided over by the archdeacon, with his hand upon the throttle-valve of incipient crime. Presentations of misdoers could bring everything to light—from untidy surplices to incest and bigamy—in a list of offences ranging through ale-house-haunting, dicing and swearing by parsons and their flocks, being sick in church, failure to attend communion, tippling and the keeping of open shop at service-time on Sundays, malicious, contentious and uncharitable behaviour, usury, blasphemy, bawdry, parent-beating and notorious evil-living. A modern authority on the Church records of the Elizabethan age confesses to a kind of horror at the state of public and private life that they reveal. "When the criminal records of any defined area are consistently bad, and when no improvement is seen over a number of years, we can conclude that life in that area is stagnant and unwholesome." There is disclosed "a consistency of moral decay which can hardly be paralleled in English history—the general gloom is only lit up here and there by individual characters. . . . Praiseworthy injunction failed to produce reform . . . The bishops were avaricious, the parochial clergy fell far short of their calling, and the administration of local government was deplorably corrupt. Purity, honesty, fair dealing and justice do not flourish under such conditions ".[1]

The grimness of the picture conflicts oddly with the generally accepted notion of the pleasant, comfortable life of the English village in the sunny days of the great queen. Lest we travel too far towards a new pessimism, let it be admitted that many of the cases in the arch-deacons' courts were concerned with peccadillos of the lightest nature, and even with behaviour which nowadays would be regarded as reflecting a praiseworthy and independent spirit. That the innocent must sometimes have suffered cannot be doubted : for the procedure of the church courts was archaic and often dismally unjust to the accused. Shortly before the archdeacon's half-yearly visitation, the summoner would arrive in a parish. He would frequently be armed with articles of inquisition calculated to jog the minds of minister and churchwardens concerning the nature of the offences for which culprits might be forthcoming. The wardens, either from personal knowledge, or from information supplied by parishioners,[2] drew up bills of presentment against transgressors—they were themselves liable to punishment if

---

[1] W. P. M. Kennedy, *Parish Life under Elizabeth*, 149-51

[2] The presentment usually says "upon a fame". Compurgation sometimes had its practical value as the only way of clearing a name from this kind of slander.

they omitted a name—and offenders were summoned to the court to answer the *libellum,* or charge. If fortunate, the alleged evil-doer might compound with the summoner or the accuser before the date, but once the papers got into court he must attend and answer or be excommunicated. If he pleaded innocent he must answer the charge on oath, and perhaps be forced under examination to convict himself of a far more heinous crime. The old system of purgation, which had been abandoned by the common law courts for centuries, still persisted among the judicial methods of the canon law. It is to be presumed that if a man, even when innocent, failed to produce oath-helpers from among his neighbours, whether from lack of means to transport them or for other reasons, he would fail to ward off conviction[1], unless he could make an extraordinarily good case for himself under oath. Conviction was normally followed by the infliction of a penance, often of a public and humiliating nature. It could sometimes, though irregularly, be commuted for a money fine.[2] Failure to obey the court's instruction led to excommunication, either minor or major. The former debarred a man from attendance at church services—and therefore from marriage. His very entrance into a church caused the cessation of the service if one were in progress.[3] And somewhat unfairly the authorities could fine the excluded sinner for non-attendance. Thus even the lesser excommunication was a thing to be avoided.

The greater excommunicate was technically beyond the pale of society. Men were even presented at the archdeacon's court for conversing with him[4], for dealing with him at market. He could get no satisfaction in an action at law : his testimony was not admissable. When he died Christian burial was refused. There was therefore no conceivable inducement to remain in this position longer than could be helped. Yet absolution cost money in heavy fees ; and there were some men, governed by principles, or by pride, or by pig-headedness, who delayed in the necessary steps to have the excommunication lifted. Then the Church would shoot its last bolt. " He was turned over to the High Commission, where temporal punishments—mulct or incarceration—followed ecclesiastical methods. Or if at the end of forty days, an excommunicate person showed no signs of practical repentance

---

[1] But not always. See the case of Andrew Robinson in 1624. C. W. Foster, *History of Aisthorpe and Thorpe-in-the-Fallows*, p. 140.

[2] W. P. M. Kennedy, *Elizabethan Episcopal Administration*, I, cxxviii.

[3] W. Hale Hale, *Series of Precedents and Proceedings*, 1847, p. 198.

[4] Excommunications in theory automatically followed the action.

the ecclesiastical judge might apply to the bishop and procure against him the writ *De excommunicatio capiendo* ; but this was a dangerous and risky proceeding, as the temporal judges were contemptuous of, if not hostile to, the courts christian."[1]

The criminal procedure of the Church was effective in inducing fear, failing respect, among ordinary men ; but the very efficiency of its inquisitorial methods led to the abuses which discredited it. We can go back to Chaucer for a portrait of the type of official produced by the archideaconal jurisdiction. " Proctors, apparitors, registrars, and other scribes whose fees depended on citations and the drawing up of court proceedings, documents, or certificates, had ever interest in haling persons before the official. . . . Hence the system tended to create spies, of whom the chief were the apparitors, or summoners, and their underlings."[2] Moreover, if Greene is to be credited, there existed a class of perjured villains who posed as officials of the courts, and forced blackmail from the transgressors they smelt out.[3]

§6

The whole history of English criminal law and procedure in relation to social development calls for revision and explanation. On this difficult ground, beset with pitfalls for the incautious, any but the legal historian will hesitate to tread. It will be sufficient here to note the *schema* of punishments employed by Elizabethan justice in its dealings with the convicted criminal and misdemeanant, while omitting discussion of the means used to obtain conviction in the courts.

Sir James Fitzjames Stephen in his great work upon the criminal law rightly places privilege of clergy at the beginning of his analysis in the famous chapter on legal penalties.[4] The privilege, or benefit, claimed by men[5] of education convicted of felony exempted them from punishment by the lay courts ; that is to say, instead of having to face the inevitable penalty of death on the gallows they came under the jurisdiction of the bishops' courts and underwent a short term of

[1] Kennedy, *op. cit.*, I, cxxv, cxxvi.

[2] S. L. Ware, *The Elizabethan Parish*, 53, 54.

[3] See below pp. 139-40. For an able discussion of the whole question of criminal jurisdiction in the church courts, see S. A. Peyton, Introduction to *Churchwardens' Presentments in the Oxfordshire Peculiars* (Oxfordshire Record Society, 1928).

[4] *History of the Criminal Law of England*, i, ch. 13.

[5] Until the dissolution of the monasteries nuns were eligible. From that time until 1692 only men could claim the privilege. Pollock and Maitland, *History of Engl. Law*, I, 445.

imprisonment. Until the middle of the fourteenth century the privilege was restricted to clergymen in orders, and the trial normally took place in the ecclesiastical courts. Then by degrees, as the practice grew up of trying all accused persons (irrespective of the cloth of their coats) in the lay courts up to the stage of conviction or acquittal, the conventions governing admission of " clergy " were widened. " It seems ", says Professor Holdsworth, " to have been in consequence of the statute (*pro clero*, 1350) that the privilege was later extended to all who could read. But this extension is connected with the greater control assumed by royal courts over the conditions under which the privilege could be claimed."[1]

High treason and highway robbery were already exempted. Under the Tudors the state proceeded to extend the list of non-clergyable felonies. Murder committed in churches and on highways was added in 1512 ; piracy[2] in 1536, burglary accompanied by threats of violence in 1547 ; stealing from the person privily in 1565 ; and in the latter part of Elizabeth's reign, rape and abduction with intent to marry. Moreover, the layman pleading benefit of clergy had since 1489 been allowed only one chance. On the second conviction[3] he merited death without respite, having forfeited his rights. The procedure in court is explained by Sir Thomas Smith :

> Of him whom the twelve men pronounce guilty, the judge asketh what he can say for himself. If he can read he demandeth his clergy. . . . For which purpose the bishop must send one with authority under his seal to be judge in that matter in every jail delivery. If the condemned (*sic*) man demandeth to be admitted to his book, the judge commonly giveth him a Psalter, and turneth to what place he will. The prisoner readeth as well as he can, God knoweth sometime very slenderly ! Then he [the judge] asketh of the bishop's commissary: *Legit ut clericus*? The commissary must say *Legit* or *Non legit*[4], for these be words formal, and our men of law be very precise in their words formal. If he say *Legit*, the judge proceedeth no further to sentence of death ; if he say *Non*, the judge forthwith or the next day proceedeth to sentence.[5]

Before we contemptuously dismiss the pleading of clergy as a confusing legal anachronism, it is well to remember that it served an important function in mitigating a criminal code of excessive severity.

[1] Holdsworth, *History of English Law*, iii, 297.

[2] See Stephen, *Hist. Criminal Law*, i, 465.

[3] Established as such by the branding of the thumb (M for murder, T for theft) on the first conviction. 4 Henry VII, c. 14.

[4] The court may apparently challenge the ordinary's ruling. Holdsworth (*ibid*, iii, 298) on Hale.

[5] *De Republica Anglorum*, ii, 23.

On this ground Blackstone defended its survival as late as 1769. In Blackstone's day the laws of felony were even harsher than when Smith was writing, and the definition of clerical immunity from the death penalty had been hard put to it to extend protection to an equivalent degree.

It is arguable, of course, that benefit of clergy persisted in favour with lawyers and legislators because it made a class distinction of a sort. And it is noteworthy that while the officially recognized right of sanctuary, the poor man's last resort, perished with the Tudors, clergyable offences were only restricted to exclude the worst offences,[1] while from 1547[2] every peer of the realm, " though he cannot read ", must be regarded as to all intents and purposes in connection with a criminal trial equivalent to a " clerk convict ". The distinction between lettered and unlettered, such as it was, may be considered to have borne less heavily on members of the criminal class, who would be educated up to the tricks, than on the obscure wrongdoers of the countryside, men who were driven to commit crime for once in their lives by hunger or passion, only to learn the short sharp lesson on the next sessions day. It was in cases of theft that the law showed least mercy. Broadly speaking, theft involved hanging. Only on one of two grounds could a thief escape the penalty. Provided he had not committed his robbery from the person, from the person's premises, or by menaces on the highway— and when you consider the matter, few alternatives were left—the felon might, if sufficiently educated, plead his clergy. In the second case, the value of the object stolen might be computed at less than twelve pence,[3] and the offence would then be petty larceny, a felony which was not quite a felony, and merited whipping or the pillory or the stocks, or all of these combined.

Can we discern any movement of protest against the severity of the law in this matter of theft? Granted the general contentment with the operation of the clergy test, I think there was little uneasiness among the propertied classes about the operation of the penal code which protected their possessions. It was admitted, of course, that severity towards robbers and housebreakers cut both ways, that a thief might be as willing to hang for a sheep as for a goat, for a slit windpipe as

[1] But there existed what we cannot but regard as curious anomalies. One might for instance be hanged for stealing two shillings from a man's pocket, merely fined for the misdemeanour of beating him within an inch of his life.

[2] 1 Edward VI, c. 12.

[3] One was privileged to embezzle or convert up to forty shillings without endangering the neck.

for a stolen purse. But few to my knowledge appear to have urged a mitigation of penalties on common-sense grounds, unless we except Cardinal Pole, to whom the following remarks in debate with Lupset are attributed by Thomas Starkey.

> Methink, to descend to this part, the order of our law also in the punishment of theft is over-strait, and faileth much from good civility. For with us for every little theft a man is by and by hanged without mercy or pity; which meseemeth is again good nature and humanity, specially when they steal for necessity, without murder or manslaughter committed therein. . . . Better it were to find some way how the man might be brought to better order and frame.[1] . . . If the frailty of man fall thereunto, and specially to privy theft, as picking and stealing secretly, I would think it good that the felon should be take and put in some common work, as to labour in building the walls of cities and towns, or else in some magnifical work of the prince of the realm, which pain should be more grievous to them than death is reputed.[2]

Among the few who appealed publicly to humanitarian sentiment Thomas Dekker has an honourable place.

> Many lose their lives
> For scarce as much coin as will hide their palm :
> Which is most cruel. Those have vexed spirits
> Who pursue lives.[3]

and it is to be remarked that, although the work which has come down to us from this friendly critic of society is filled with references to scamps and ne'er-do-wells, he seldom takes satisfaction in the gallows' fate which the law reserves for them.

To the plain man of the jury-panel it was ridiculous to make the harsh distinction the law required between him who stole thirteen pence and his neighbour who stole eleven pence. The former might be a first offender, the latter a hardened criminal. Fortunately, however, for the cause of true justice, in cases of theft the jury appears generally to have been required to estimate the worth of the article stolen as well as to give its verdict as to guilt. Common sense often led to the giving of a true verdict on the question of guilt and a false verdict on the question of value. And there are cases on record of the most ridiculous under-valuation, as at the trial of a Halifax clothier[4] at the West Riding Sessions, where the indictment valued twenty-seven head of poultry at 18s. 11d., and the verdict found the prisoner guilty to the extent of 10d. He escaped with a whipping (and the poultry ?).

[1] Starkey's Life and Letters (ed. Herrtage) E.E.T.S, 1878, pp. 119-20.
[2] Ibid, p. 197. cf. More, Utopia, Everyman edn., p. 28.
[3] The Honest Whore (I), I, v.
[4] J. Lister, West Riding Sessions Rolls, p. 138 ; and see elsewhere in the same volume for similar instances.

The reference to Halifax should remind us that hanging by the neck, although the common penalty, was not the only method of ending the felon's life. Pirates caught in the Thames mouth, or tried in London, were tied up and left to drown in the high tides of Wapping. Halifax also retained an ancient local custom.

In the clothmaking district within its curious jurisdiction the thief caught in possession of stolen property—generally animals or rolls of cloth—suffered death in a unique manner and after an unusual process of trial. The gibbet-law of Halifax, which is supposed to have been a survival of the old custom of infangthef, was practised until 1650, when the last two victims of the ingenious guillotine which made such a remarkable impression on visitors to the town were beheaded. Sixteen jurors, selected by the four local constables, recorded in writing their verdict of the guilt of the accused ; and further, without the intervention of a magistrate, they gave their " determinate sentence ". " By the ancient custom and liberty of Halifax, whereof the memory of man is not to the contrary ", the felons " are to suffer death by having their heads severed and cut off their bodies at Halifax gibbet ". A victim of Halifax custom, we learn, is " forthwith beheaded on the next market day, . . . or else upon the same day that he is convicted, if market be then holden. The engine . . . is a square block of wood of the length of four foot and an half, which doth ride up and down in a slot, rabet or regalt, between two pieces of timber, that are framed and set upright, of five yards in height. In the nether end of the sliding block is an axe keyed or fastened with iron into the wood, which being drawn up to the top of the frame is there fastened with a wooden pin, . . . into the midst of which pin there is a long rope fastened that cometh down into the midst of the people, so that . . . every man there doth either take hold of the rope, or putteth his arm so near the same as he can get, in token that he is willing to see true justice executed ; and pulling the pin out in this manner, the head-block wherein the axe is fastened doth fall down with such violence that, if the neck of the transgressor were so big is that of a bull, it should be cut in sunder at a stroke, and roll from the body by an huge distance ". If a live beast had been stolen, it was tied to the pin and made to release the falling block.[1]

Special punishments intended to mark the public disapprobation of certain offences existed in but few instances. Harrison gives a list which

[1] Stephen, *Hist. Criminal Law*, i,265ff. a sixteenth century account in Harl. MSS. 785, 20, 10, qu. J. Lister, *Notes on Old Halifax*, 1906, p. 202 ; a similar account is given by Harrison.

includes the use of the pillory and the branding of·a P on the forehead in cases of perjury. " Many trespasses also are punished by the cutting off of one or both ears from the head of the offender, as the utterance of seditious words against the magistrates, fraymakers, petty robberies, etc. Rogues are burned through the ears ; carriers of sheep out of the land by the loss of their hands ; such as kill by poison are either boiled or scalded to death in lead or seething water.[1] Heretics are burned quick.[2] Harlots and their mates by carting, ducking, and doing of open penance in sheets are often put to rebuke." Harrison would have some sharper law for adulterers. " For what great smart is it to be turned out of hot sheet into a cold, or after a little washing in the water to be let loose again into their former trades ? Howbeit the dragging of some of them over the Thames between Lambeth and Westminster at the tail of a boat is a punishment that most terrifyeth them that are condemned thereto ; but this is inflicted upon them by none other than the knight marshal and that within the compass of his jurisdiction and limits only."[3] He would even have made them serve as galley-slaves ; for it was at this time that this form of punishment was coming into discussion.

The life which the Rector of Radwinter would have reserved for those of his flock who were loose in their morals the government considered as a possible one for reprieved convicts. On occasion the cells of the jails were combed for the purposes of war recruitment.[4] Transportation and the galleys offered possible variations in cases where the prince's prerogative of mercy was to be shown. The history of transportation hardly begins within our period : all the projects failed. But for the lack of success of the experimental galley flotillas which were from time to time set upon the sea, it is probable that the living death of galley-slavery would have become a normal penalty enforced upon hardy criminals reprieved from execution. Such a punishment, indeed, found its way into a statute in 1598, when the quarter sessions justices were given the alternative of sending incorrigible vagabonds of dangerous character into perpetual banishment or to the queen's galleys.[5] Chattel-slavery was not known to the common law ; but there can be no doubt

---

[1] Boiling to death for poisoning was a legal penalty only between 1530 and 1547. Three or four persons were thus executed. Stephen, *op. cit.*, i, 476.

[2] *Description of England*, ed. Furnivall, 241.

[3] *Ibid*, p. 242

[4] As for the Cadiz expedition, 1596, Cheyney, *Hist. of England*, ii, 49-50 ; for Mansfeld's army in 1624 (imprisoned debtors), H. G. R. Reade, *Sidelights on the Thirty Years' War*, i, 547.

[5] 39 Eliz., c. 4, s. 4.

that numbers of Englishmen, being slaves of the state, were sent to serve their periods as oarsmen on these ships. The Council apparently regarded itself as exercising leniency to death-deserving men in stipulating for this new punishment. At all events it provided a way out for the conscience of the assize judge when a doubt existed as to whether a convict ought to perish or be reprieved.[1] In 1586 an administrative commission was actually appointed for the decision of cases sent up from the counties[2], and the Recorder of London wrote to Burghley that at a gaol delivery at Newgate in that year no prisoners were executed, but all reprieves were sent before the commissioners.[3] At this time there is doubt as to whether the royal navy had more than one serviceable galley at its disposal ; but in 1601 and 1602, following Spinola's remarkable experiment of bringing some Spanish galleys up from the Mediterranean for the Dutch war, four more were built in England and ordered to be manned by felons. The men required were produced by the criminal courts ; but heavy were the complaints of the counties when it was found that £3 a year must be paid by the localities for the diet and support of each of their abandoned children while in the queen's penal ships. The galleys in question never, however, saw service on the seas, and the full complement of rowers cannot possibly have been long preserved.[4]

Yet three decades later Sir William Monson still regards galley-service as a suitable alternative to the house of correction, where " people are punished or pardoned as they are able to gratify their keepers ; . . . the rich buys his ease, the poor is threatened with cruelty, which has caused that desperateness in men towards their keepers that to be revenged they have slain them ". The galleys, on the other hand, would furnish sharp punishment and strict discipline. " The terror of galleys will make men avoid sloth and pilfering and apply themselves to labour and pains ; it will keep servants and apprentices in awe ; . . . it will save much blood that is lamentably spilt by execution of thieves and offenders, and more of this kingdom than any other. . . . And that they may be known from others, they must be shaved both head and face, and marked in the cheek with a hot iron, for men to take notice of them to be the king's labourers, for so they should be termed and not slaves."[5]

[1] Instructions of 1582 : Corbett, *Drake and the Tudor Navy*, i, 403.
[2] *Egerton Papers* (Camden Soc., 1840), p. 116.
[3] Wright, *Queen Elizabeth and her Times*, ii, 291.
[4] Hist. MSS. Comm., *Hatfield MSS.*, xii, 244 ; *Monson Naval Tracts* (1923), iv, 109.
[5] *Ibid*, iv, 106-7.

We need not be surprised that imprisonment has an exceedingly small place among punitive devices. The reason readily suggests itself. Prisons were absolutely necessary for the safe custody of accused persons awaiting trial. For the fulfilment of any other purpose they could only be regarded as expensive luxuries. A man or woman once convicted of crime was either unfitted to live or fit to be at large. Why institute penal servitude when the county jails were already full to overcrowding and, moreover, ravaged with pestilence? And so, in examining the statute book we find imprisonment rarely mentioned as a punishment until quite modern times. It was too exotic and gruesome a torment even for the hardened stomach of the Elizabethan age to tolerate.

Nevertheless the first bridewells, or houses of correction, were prisons of a sort. They restricted the liberty of the rogues and strumpets who were serving sentences therein; like the county jails they strove to " live of their own "; but unlike them they were cleanly kept and strictly managed under the supervision of the local magistrates. (The interiors of the jails proper never saw the face of a magistrate from one decade to another.) Yet " so little at the outset were [the bridewells] regarded as places of punishment, and so much as means of finding employment for the unemployed poor, that it was evidently not unusual about the middle of the seventeenth century, to give the inmates regular wages in return for their work ".[1] Unfortunately we have little knowledge of the working of these early workhouses, with the exception of the London Bridewell, the mother-house of them all. This abandoned royal palace[2], like the greater London prisons, was a warren of alleys, closes, wings and outbuildings, and while under the direct control of the City aldermen accommodated an average of two hundred inmates—not quite all of whom were confined as idle or disorderly. Workshops and apprenticeship schemes were planned or were in operation as early as 1557, twenty years before the Act of Parliament which enjoined the county authorities to erect houses of work. Operations began with two corn-mills turned by tread-engines which were manned by eighteen vagabonds undergoing reformation; a bakehouse; a clothworkers' room, to which the ladies of the town were shepherded after the preliminary whipping; and a smithy for nail-making. We read too of wool-card-making boy apprentices from Christ's Hospital, glove-making and fustian-weaving; also lime-burning and a dredging out of the Thames

[1] S. and B. Webb, *English Prisons under Local Government*, p. 13. A useful authority, which unhappily tells us little about prison conditions before the eighteenth century.

[2] See below p. 498, note 28.

waterway.   Just after the turn of the century the governors were beguiled into the adoption of a scheme for farming out the place as an industrial colony to a group of promoters at a rent of £300 a year.   This was not a step forward ; rather it was a relapse into the old-fashioned and questionable methods followed by those responsible for the great majority of the common jails.   Private enterprize has never succeeded in this particular department of social service.   In the case of Bridewell failure was evident almost at once ; and within a few months the four undertakers were forced to give up their ten-year lease and turn their relations and friends out of the tenements they had established within the palace.   Only sixty industrial inmates were left, and of these the young women had abandoned their work, discarded their neat blue liveries, and nightly entertained their gentlemen friends with crabs, lobsters and artichoke pies in the clerk's room.[1]   So Bridewell returned to public management.

Well would it have been for the reputation of the county jails and London prisons had private exploitation been excluded from them also. No critic has a good word to say of the jails or of the mercenary scamps their keepers.   Complaints were many, and both Hutton's *Black Dog of Newgate*[2] and Fennor's *Counter's Commonwealth*[3] voice the same grievances : cruelty, extortion, lack of public surveillance.   Newgate, a state prison and felon's ward, was one of the least well conducted ; and conditions in the Fleet and Counters, which were really compulsory boarding houses for debtors and persons committed for contempt of court, were paradisal compared with those of any common jail, Newgate included.   Yet the descriptions of life within a debtors' prison are sickening enough, and if it was no worse than at the time when John Howard made his great tour of inspection[4] in the eighteenth century, it was certainly no better.[5]   No public funds were available for the care and nourishment of prisoners[6] ; failing charity the poor man starved.

[1] See O'Donoghue, *Bridewell Hospital*, pp. 187-204.

[2] Below pp. 265-91.

[3] Below pp. 423-87.

[4] An abridgement of Howard's *State of the Prisons* (3rd. edn., 1784) is now available in the *Everyman Library*.   See section vii for London jails.

[5] Compare for example the management of the Fleet at the beginning of the seventeenth century in *The Œconomy of the Fleete* (Camden Soc. 1879, with valuable introduction by A. Jessopp) with that of the same prison a little more than a century later, as reported in Howell's *State Trials*, xvii, 298-310.

[6] An act of 1572 (14 Eliz., c. 5) authorized the raising of a small county allowance for poor prisoners, but in practice this was found only sufficient for the provision of bread to convicted felons awaiting their fate, who, since they had forfeited their worldly goods, were a first charge on the public.

" By the common law ", the Law Officers reported in 1765, " no prisoners being in prison on suspicion of having committed an offence have any legal right to support or maintenance from the sheriff or jailer."[1] The man with command over any moderate means was speedily ruined by the extortion of the jailers. " A broker takes forty in the hundred ", says Mynshul, " and is called unconscionable devil for it ; but these men think they may without danger to their souls wring £50 *per annum* (out of prisoners' afflictions and utterly undone states) for one nasty chamber, hung with cobweb lawn for the greater grace, and haunted with lice and rats for want of better company."[2] And the same author mentions the case of a jailer in a small prison who charged $\frac{1}{2}d.$ for a quart of water and sold bullocks' livers to the prisoner that he had begged for his dog.[3] It was a common practice to charge heavy fees for the knocking off of irons on the release of a prisoner, and if the victim were unable to meet in full the manifold charges he had incurred for food, drink, " unlocking of gates ", and sometimes even provision of light, he might stay within the walls, his body forfeit to the tipstaffs, until his bones were rotted with damp or he was carried off with jail-fever.[4]

On this dismal note it seems proper to make an end to these jottings on crime and punishment. Prison life, criminal justice, police methods before the nineteenth century, are all subjects which will repay a closer investigation than historians have yet thought it necessary to perform ; but the fittest enquiry will be that which seeks to trace through the centuries the development of criminal law as a form of specialized social control, and its adaptation to changes in the ethics of society. If this small collection may serve to make easier the investigator's task its most cherished function will be fulfilled. Apart from this hypothetical rôle I hope it may prove to be, in poor Luke Hutton's words, " both pithy, pleasant, and profitable for all readers ".

---

[1] Acts of Privy Council, George III, vol.iv, p. 172, qu, Webb, *English Prisons*, 9.

[2] Geoffrey Mynshul, *Essays and Characters of a Prison*, 1638 edn., p. 32.

[3] *Ibid*, pp. 38-9.

[4] See Bacon's remarks on the public danger of allowing foul air to stagnate in these places where is to be caught " the most pernicious infection next the plague " (*Sylva Sylvarum*, § 914).

¶A manifest detection of the moste vyle and detestable vse of Diceplay, and other practises lyke the same, a Myrrour very necessary for all yonge Gentilmen & others sodenly enabled by worldly abúdace, to loke in. Newly set forth for their behoufe.

¶Democritus.

Si te ris vous estes plus folz que ne ries
    de me veoir rire
De vous et de voz actes sont plus que mon
    rire plut dire
Tant ilya a vous redire et aulx plus sages
    de vous tous.
Qui est pleine fol qui ne rit de vous.

¶Fortune vient a point.

Plate I

[face p. lxiv

ℭ The hye way to the Spyttell hous,

ℭ Copland and the porter.

ℭ Who so hath lust, or wyll leaue his thryft
And wyll fynd, no better way nor shyft
Come this hye way, here to seke some rest
For it is ordeyned for eche vnthryfty gest.

Plate II

[face p. 1

Elizabethan Underworld

THE HIGHWAY TO THE SPITAL-HOUSE

By ROBERT COPLAND

[1535-6]

WHOSO hath lust, or will leave his thrift,
    And will find no better way nor shift,
Come this highway, here to seek some rest,
    For it is ordained for each unthrifty guest.

Prologue of Robert Copland,
Compiler and Printer of this Book.

To despise poor folk is not my appetite,
Nor such as live of very alms' deed,
But mine intent is only for to write
The misery of such as live in need
And all their life in idleness doth lead,
Whereby doth sue such inconvenience
    That they must end in meschant indigence.

Christ in this world right poverty did sue,
Giving us example to follow that degree,
Saying, *Beati pauperes spiritu,*
Beati mites, beati mundo corde[1] :
Blessed be they that poor in spirit be,
And ben clean in heart, and make therewith all,
    For they shall possess the realm celestial.

They be not poor that have necessity,
Except therewith they ben right well content ;
Nor they be not rich that have great plenty,
If that they think that they have competent
And ever pleased with that God hath them sent,
For surely it is our Lord's ordinance
    That each should be pleased with suffisance.

That man that hath more than sufficient
With goods at will, and daily doth increase,
And ever is bare, hungry and indigent,
Scraping and snudging without any cease,
Ever coveting ; the mind hath no peace,
But lyeth by rapine and usury
    And careth not how he cometh thereby,

C

Eke in distress doing no benefit,
Letting the poor die in great misery,
His neighbour in prison doth not visit,
Nor yet forgive small parcel of duty,
Weary travellers in the streets let lie,
The dead bodies without any burial;
   His goods his god a man may full well call.

Of such rich men reciteth the Gospel
Making likeness of impossibility,
Saying that more easily a great camel
May pass and go through a needle's eye
Than a rich man in Heaven for to be;
For whoso misuseth that God hath him sent
   With cursed Dives in Hell shall be brent.

These truant beggars, begging from place to place,
Nor yet these needy of all manner fashion,
These apprentices that do run from all grace,
These hired servants that keep no condition
Nor all that feign perfect devotion,
Nor many other living in needy covert,
   Though they lack good, be not poor of heart.

See ye not daily of all manner estate,
How in the law they traverse and conject,
How neighbours do fall at anger and debate;
'Tween man, wife, eke the life imperfect,
The father and child, from quietness abject;
And all that for good they may make each other smart,
   Which is a sign they be not poor of heart.

If that our prince do ask a subsidy,
From our enemies us to defend,
Or if our creditors demand their duty,
To confess poverty then we pretend.
But if our neighbour in aught us offend
Then we find money to play overthwart,
   Which is a token we be not poor at heart.

How many poor that have little in store
Is content with his small substance?
But ever they grudge and wish for more
To be promoted and have furtherance.
The very beggars for their pittance
From bag and staff are loath for to depart,
   Which is a token they be not poor at heart.

Of these two estates there be four degrees:
A rich rich, a poor poor, a rich poor also,
A poor, rich in all necessities.
The two can agree, but the other, no.
A proud heart, a beggar's purse thereto,
The rich purse and the poor spirit
   May well agree and be in one perfect.

Exhortation of the Compiler.

I pray all you which have enough, with grace,
For the love of God to do your charity,
And from the poor never turn your face,
For Christ saith, Whatever that he be
That to the least of Mine doth in the name of Me,
Unto Myself I do accept the deed,
   And for reward my realm they shall possede.

Finis.

   Here beginneth the casuality
   Of the entrance into hospitality.

To write of Sol in his exaltation,
   Of his solstice or declination,
Or in what sign, planet, or degree,
   As he in course is used for to be,
Scorpio, Pisces, or Sagittary,
   Or when the moon her way doth contrary,
Or her eclipse, her wane, or yet her full
   It were but lost for blockish brainès dull.
But plainly to say, even as the time was,
   About a fortnight after Hallowmas,
I chanced to come by a certain spital
   Where I thought best to tarry a little
And under the porch for to take succour
   To bide the passing of a stormy shower,
For it had snowen and frozen very strong,
   With great icicles on the evès long;
The sharp north wind hurled bitterly,
   And with black clouds darkèd was the sky,
Like as in winter some days be natural
   With frost and rain and storms over all:
So still I stood. As chanced to be,
   The porter of the house stood also by me
With whom I reasoned of many divers things
   Touching the course of all such weatherings;
And as we talked there gathered at the gate
   People as methought of very poor estate,
With bag and staff, both crooked, lame and blind,
   Scabby and scurvy, pock-eaten flesh and rind,
Lousy and scald, and peelèd like as apes,
   With scantly a rag for to cover their shapes,
Breechless, barefooted, all stinking with dirt
   With thousand of tatters, drabbling to the skirt,
Boys, girls, and luskish strong knaves,
   Diddering and daddering, leaning on their staves,
Saying, " Good master, for your mother's blessing,
   Give us a halfpenny towards our lodging!"
The porter said, " What need you to crave,
   That in the spital shall your lodging have?

Ye shall be entreated as ye ought to be,
For I am charged that daily to see.
The sisters shall do their observance
As of the house is the due ordinance."

Copland.

Porter (said I), God's blessing and our Lady
Have ye for speaking so courteously
To these poor folk, and God his soul pardon,
That for their sake made this foundation!
But, sir, I pray you, do ye lodge them all
That do ask lodging in this hospital?

Porter.

Forsooth, yea! We do all such folk in take
That do ask lodging for our Lord's sake,
And, indeed, it is our custom and use
Sometime to take in, and some to refuse.

Copland.

Then is it comen to every wight,
How they live all day, to lie here at night?
As losels, mighty beggars and vagabonds,
And truants that walk over the lands,
Michers, hedge-creepers, fillocks and lusks,
That all the summer keep ditches and busks,
Loitering and wandering from place to place,
And will not work, but the bypaths trace,
And live with haws, and hunt the blackberry,
And with hedge-breaking make themselves merry;
But in the winter they draw to the town,
And will do nothing but go up and down
And all for lodging that they have here at night?
Methinks that therein ye do no right,
Nor all such places of hospitality,
To comfort people of such iniquity.
But, sir, I pray you of your goodness and favour
Tell me which ye leave and which ye do succour.
For I have seen at sundry hospitals
That many have lain dead without the walls,
And for lack of succour have died wretchedly.
Unto your foundation I think contrary;
Much people resort here and have lodging;
And yet I marvel greatly of one thing,
That in the night so many lodge without:
For in the watch when that we go about
Under the stalls, in porches, and in doors,
I wot not whether they be thieves or whores
But surely, every night there is found
One or other lying by the pound,
In the sheep cots or in the hayloft,
And at Saint Bartholmew's church-door full oft,

And even here alway by this brick wall,
   We do them find, that do both chide and brawl
And like as beasts together they be throng,
   Both lame and sick and whole them among,
And in many corners where that we go,
   Whereof I wonder greatly that they do so;
But oft-times, when that they us see,
   They do run a great deal faster than we.

Porter.

Such folks be they that we do abject,
   We are not bound to have to them aspect.
Those be michers that live in truandise;
   Hospitality doth them alway despise.

Copland.

Sir, I pray you, who hath of you relief?

Porter.

Forsooth, they that be at such mischief
That for their living can do no labour,
   And have no friends to do them succour,
As old people, sick and impotent,
   Poor women in childbed, have here easement,
Weak men sore wounded by great violence,
   And sore men eaten with pox and pestilence,
And honest folk fallen in great poverty
   By mischance or other infirmity,
Wayfaring men and maimed soldiers
   Have their relief in this poor house of ours;
And all other which we seem good and plain
   Have here lodging for a night or twain,
Bedrid folk and such as cannot crave,
   In these places most relief they have,
And if they hap within our place to die
   Then are they buried well and honestly;
But not every unsick stubborn knave,
   For then we should over many have.

Copland.

How say you by these common beggars that cry
   Daily on the world, and in the highways lie
At Westminster and Saint Paul's,
   And in all streets they sit as desolate souls?
Methink it, it a very well done deed
   With devotion such people to feed.

Porter.

Where any giveth alms with good intent
   The reward cannot be no wise misspent.

Copland.

Yea, but sir, I will not lie, by my soul!
  As I walked to the church of Saint Paul,
There sat beggars, on each side the way two,
  As is seen daily they be wont to do;
Sir, one there was, a mighty stubborn slave,
  That for the other began to beg and crave:
" Now, master, in the way of your good speed,
  To us all four, behold where it is need,
And make this farthing worth a halfpenny
  For the five joys of our blessed Lady!
Now turn again for Saint Erasmus' sake,
  And on my bare knees here a vow I make,
Our Lady's psalter three times, even now;
  Now turn again, as God shall turn to you!
Now, master, do that no man did this day,
  On yon poor wretch that rotteth in the way:
Now, master, for Him that died on tree,
  Let us not die for lack of charity!"
Thus he prated, as he full well can,
  Till an honest serving-man
Came by the way, and by compassion
  Of his words did his devotion.
When he was gone a little from thence,
  I saw the beggar pull out eleven pence,
Saying to his fellows, " See what here is.
  Many a knave have I called master for this.
Let us go dine; this is a simple day.
  My master therewith shall I scantly pay."
Come these folks hither, good master porter?

Porter.

No, in sooth, this house is of no such supporter;
They have houses, and keep full ill jesting,
  And to them resort all the whole offspring,
In the Barbican,² and in Turnmill Street,
  In Houndsditch, and behind the Fleet
And in twenty places more than there,
  Where they make revel and gaudy cheer,
With *Fill the pot fill, and go fill me the can,*
  Here is my penny, and I am the gentleman.
And there they bide, and fill as doth a gull,
  And when that they have their heads full,
Then they fall out and make revelling,
  And in this wise make the drunken reckoning:
" Thou beggarly knave, bag nor staff hast thou none,
  But as I am fain daily to lend thee one,
Thou gettest it no more, though it lie and rot,
  Nor my long cloak, nor my new-patched coat."
This rule make they every day and night,
  Till, like as swine, they lie sleeping upright.
Some beggarly churls to whom they resort
  Be the maintainers of a great sort

Of mighty lubbers, and have them in service
  Some journeymen and some to their 'prentice,
And they walk to each market and fair
  And to all places where folk do repair,
By day on stilts or stooping on crutches
  And so dissimule as false loitering flowches,
With bloody clouts all about their leg,
  And plasters on their skin when they go beg.
Some counterfeit lepry, and other some
  Put soap in their mouth to make it scum,
And fall down as Saint Cornelys' evil.
  These deceits they use worse than any devil;
And when they be in their own company,
  They be as whole as either you or I.
But at the last, when sickness cometh indeed,
  Then to the spital-house must they come need.

Copland.

Ah, Jesu mercy! What man could conject
  The misery of such a wretched sect!
None honest man; but yet I you heartily pray,
  Tell me of other that come this way.
Come here any of those masterless men,
  That everywhere do go and run,
That have served the king beyond the sea,
  And now that they out of wages be
They must beg, or else go bribe and steal?
  Methink it is a great soul-heal
To help them, till they were purveyed
  Into some service; for, if they were arrayed,
Some of them were proper men and tall,
  And able to go whither they shall.

Porter.

That is truth; but they use one ill thing,
  For they do wear soldiers' clothing,
And so, begging, deceive folk over all,
  For they be vagabonds most in general,
And will abide no laborous subjection
  With honest persons, under correction;
For, when they be weary, they will run away
  And perchance carry with them what they may;
And so when a man would bring them to thrift,
  They will him rob and from his good[s] him lift.

Copland.

Though some so do, they do not all so,
  For some might chance well, as many one do.

Porter.

That is true; but it has been seen long agone
  That many have fared the worse for one;
And of these be two sorts most commonly
  The one of them liveth by open beggary,

Ragged and lousy, with bag, dish and staff,
  And ever haunteth among such riff-raff,
One time to this spital, another to that,
  Prowling and poaching to get somewhat
At every door, lumps of bread or meat;
  For, if the staff in his hand once catch heat,
Then farewell labour! and hath such delight
  That thrift and honesty from him is quit;
And in such misery they live day by day
  That of very need they must come this way.

Copland.

Of the other now; what is their estate?

Porter.

By my faith, nightingales of Newgate!
These be they that daily walks and jets,
  In their hose trussed round to their doublets,
And say, " Good masters, of your charity,
  Help us poor men that come from the sea!
From the *Bonaventure* we were cast to land,
  God it knows, as poorly as we stand."
And sometime they say that they were take in France,
  And had been there seven years in durance,
In Montreuil, in Brest, in Tournay or Terouenne,
  In Morlaix, in Clermont or in Hesdin3;
And to their countries they have far to gone,
  And among them all penny have they none.
" Now, good men's bodies," will they say then,
  " For God's sake help to keep us true men."
Or else they say, they have in prison been
  In Newgate, the King's Bench, or Marshalsea,
As many true men, taken by suspicion,
  And were quit by proclamation.
And if any ax what countrymen they be
  And, like your mastership, of the north, all three,
Or of Cheshire, or else nigh Cornwall,
  Or where they list for to gab and rail;
And may perchance the one is of London,
  The other of York and the third of Hampton.
And thus they loiter in every way and street,
  In towns and churches, whereas people meet,
In lanes and paths, and at each crossway,
  There they do prate, babble, lie and pray.
But if ye be cleanly and haply come alone,
  Your purse and clothing may fortune to be gone.
But at no door for bread, drink, nor pottage,
  Nor scoules of meat, nor no such baggage,
They none desire to put in bag nor male,
  But very white thread to sew good ale.
And when they have gotten what they may,
  Then to their lodging they do take their way

Into some alley, lane, or blind hostry,
  And to some corner, or house of bawdry
Whereas ben folk of their affinity,
  Brothels and other such as they be,
And there they meet and make their gaudy cheer,
  And put on their clothing and other gear,
Their swords and bucklers and their short daggers,
  And there they revel as unthrifty braggers
With horrible oaths, swearing as they were wood,
  Arms, nails, wounds, heart, soul and blood,
Death, foot, mass, flesh, bones, life and body,
  With all other words of blasphemy,
Boasting them all in deeds of their mischief,
  And thus they pass the time with dance, whore, pipe, thief.
The hangman shall lead the dance at the end,
  For none other ways they do not pretend.
And when that they can get nothing by begging,
  To maintain such life they fall to stealing;
And so this way they come at the last,
  Or on the gallows make a tumbling cast.

Copland.
More pity to see our own nation
  For to behave them on such fashion.
Surely there is an Act of Parliament,[4]
  That if any strong vagabond be hent,
To be set in a pair of stocks openly
  Certain days, with bread and water only,
And then to be banishèd from town to town;
  I think that Act is not put down.[5]
If it were execute as to my reason
  Men should not see within a little season
So many of them, nor idle slouches,
  And mighty beggars with their pokes and crutches;
But they be maintained by this naughty sect,
  That all this land is with them infect;
I mean these bawdy briberous knaves,
  That lodgeth them, that so polls and shaves.
It were alms that they were lookèd on
  For they be worse than any thief or felon.
But to our purpose; cometh not this way
  Of these rogers, that daily sing and pray
With *Ave regina,* or *De profundis,*
  Quem terra Ponthus and *Stella Maris?*
At every door where they foot and fridge,
  And say they come from Oxford and Cambridge,
And be poor scholars and have no manner thing,
  Nor also friends to keep them at learning,
And so do loiter for crust and crumb,
  With staff in hand and fist in bosom,
Passing time so by day and year,
  As in their legend I purpose shall appear
Another time, after my fantasy.

Porter.

Such folks of truth come here daily,
And ought of right this house for to use
In their age, for they fully do refuse
The time of virtuous exercise,
   Whereby they should unto honour arise.

Copland.

Sir, yet there is another company
   Of the same sect, that live more subtily,
And be in manner as master wardens,
   To whom these rogers obey as captains,
And be named clewners, as I hear say.

Porter.

   By my sooth, all false harlots be they,
And deceivers of people over all.
   In the country most of them we shall find.
They say that they come from the university,
   And in the schools have taken degree
Of priesthood, but friends have they none
   To give them any exhibition,
And how that they forth would pass
   To their country and sing their first mass,
And there pray for their benefactors,
   And serve God all times and hours,
And so they loiter in such rogations
   Seven or eight years, walking their stations,
And do but gull, and follow beggary,
   Feigning true-doing by hypocrisy,
As another time shall be showèd plain.
   But yet there is of a like manner train
Of false bribers, deceitful and fraudulent,
   That among people call themselves sapient.[6]
These ride about in many sundry wise,
   And in strange array do themselves disguise,
Sometime in manner of physician,
   And another time as a heathen man,
Counterfeiting their own tongue and speech,
   And hath a knave that doth him English teach,
With " Me non speak English, by my fait ;
   My servant speak you what me sayt "—
And maketh a manner of strange countenance,
   With admirations his fal[se]ness to advance ;
And when he cometh there as he would be
   Then will he feign marvellous gravity ;
And so, chanceth his hostess or his host
   To demand out of what strange land or coast
Cometh this gentleman—" Forsooth, hostess,
   This man was born in heathenness,"
Saith his servant, " and is a cunning man,
   For all the seven sciences surely he can,
And is sure in physic and palmistry,
   In augury, soothsaying and physiognomy,

So that he can right soon espy
  If any be disposed to malady,
And therefore can give such a medicine,
  That maketh all accesses to decline.
But surely if it were known that he
  Should meddle with any infirmity
Of common people, he might get him hate
  And lose the favour of every great estate.
Howbeit of charity yet now and then
  He will minister his cure on poor men.
No money he taketh, but all for God's love
  Which, by chance, ye shall see him prove."
Then saith he, " Qui, speak my hostess?
  Grande maladie make a great excess;
Dis infant rompre un grand postum,
  By Got, he à la mort tuk under thum."—
" What saith he? " saith the good wife.
  " Hostess, he sweareth by his soul and life
That this child is vexèd with a bag
  In his stomach, as great as he may wag;
So that two, or three days come about,
  It will choke him withouten doubt;
But then he saith, except ye have his rede,
  This child therewith will suddenly be dead."—
" Alas ! " quoth she, if she love it well,
  " Now, sweet master, give me your counsel.
For God's sake I ask it and our Lady
  And here is twenty shillings by and by."—
" Quid est? " saith he. " Forsooth, she doth offer
  Viginti solidi pour fournir votre coffre,
To do your help," saith this false servitor.—
  " Non, point d'argent ! " saith he. " Pardieu, je non cure."—
" He will no money, hostess, I you promit;
  For God's sake he doeth it each wight."
Then calleth he anon for his casket.
  That scantly is worth a rotten basket,
And taketh out a powder of experience,
  That a cart-load is not worth twopence,
And in a paper doth fair fold it up;
  Fasting three days, he biddeth that to sup.
Then for a space he taketh licence—
  God wot as yet he paid for none expense—
And so departeth. And on the next day
  One of his fellows will go the same way
To bolster the matter of his false beaupere.
  He sitteth down and maketh good cheer;
Which in likewise looketh on the child,
  Saying, " That heavenly Virgin undefiled,
Our Lady Mary ! preserve this child now !
  For it is sick, hostess, I tell it you,
For, or three days, but our Lord him save,
  I ensure you it will be in a grave."—

"Good sir," saith she, "alas, and well away!
Here was a gentleman e'en yesterday
That told the same access and disease."
"Hostess," saith he, "if that it would you please,
What manner man was it, I pray you tell?"—
"Good sir," she saith, "in sooth I know not well,
But English speech indeed he can none,
But is a Jew, his man told us each one."—
"Yea, *was*," saith he. "I know him well indeed;
I would I had spoke with him or he yede.
But hostess, in faith, took he anything?"—
"By my troth," saith she, "not one farthing!"—
"I wot," saith he, "but I marvel that he would,
But out of charity in such a mean household.
Do say so much, for if great estates it knew
His company then would they all eschew."—
"Good sir," saith she, "yet of your gentleness
Help this poor child of this said sickness.
And here is twenty shillings for your pain,
And your expense for a week or twain."—
"Well, hostess," saith he, "I will do more than that
For you, but I shall tell you what;
For my labour I shall ask nothing at all,
But for the drugs that occupy he shall,
The which be dear and very precious.
And surely I will never out of your house
Till he be whole as either you or I."
Then goeth his knave to a town to buy
These drugs that be not worth a turd;
And there they lie a fortnight at board
With these good folks and put them to cost;
Both meat and money clearly have they lost.
Yet, God wot, what waste they made and revel!
So at the last departeth this javel
With the money, and straight rideth he
Where the thief his fellow and divers others be;
And there they prate and make their avaunt
Of their deceits, and drink adieu taunt.
As they live, I pray God them amend,
Or as they be to bring them to an end:
For the spital is not for their estate,
Howbeit they come daily by the gate.

Copland.
A shrewd sort, by our Lady, and a cumbrous!
Jesus keep them out of every good man's house!
But cometh any pardoners this way?

Porter.
Yea, sir, they be our proctors,7 and fain they may,
Chiefly since their false popery was known,
And their bullish indulgence overthrown,
They be all nought; reckon each with other,
Subtlety is their father, and falsehood their mother,

For by letters they name them as they be:
  P a Pardoner; Clewner a C;
R a Roger; A an Aurium, and a Sapient, S.
  Thus they know each other doubtless.
But when their juggling oars do fail,
  They run ashore and here strike sail.

Copland.

By my sooth, I am weary to hear of their living
  Wherefore I pray you, if ye be pleasing,
Tell me shortly of all folk in general
  That come the highway to the hospital.

Porter.

It is tedious, but for your mind
  As nigh as I can I will show the kind,
Of every sort and which by likeliness
  To the Spital his way doth address.
But as for order, I promise none to keep
  For they do come as they were scattered sheep,
Wandering without reason, rule, or guide,
  And for other lodging do not provide.
But to our purpose; there cometh in this voyage
  They that toward God have no courage
And to his word give none advertance,
  Eke to father and mother do not reverence;
They that despise folk in adversity,
  They that seek strife and iniquity
They that for themself do keep nothing
  And such as hate other in their well-doing,
They may be sure, or ever they die,
  Lest they lack lodging, here for to lie.

Priests and clerks, that live viciously,
  Not caring how they should do their duty,
Unruly of manners and slack in learning,
  Ever at the ale-house for to sit bibbing,
Neglecting the obedience to them due,
  And unto Christ's flock take none anew,
But like as wolves that ravish the fold,
  These people do this right way hold.

Young heirs that enjoy their heritage,
  Ruling themself or they come of age,
Occupying unthrifty company,
  Spending up their patrimony
Whilst they be young and use dissolute plays;
  Of very need they must come these ways.

All such people as have little to spend,
  Wasting it till it be at an end;
And when they be sick and have nothing,
  Toward the Spital then they be coming.

They that have small lands and tenements,
  Wearing daily costly garments,
That at the last they must be fain
  To sell their rents themselves to sustain,
Which is a token of very experience,
  This way for to come by consequence.

Bailiffs, stewards, caters, and renters,
  Paymasters, creditors, and receivers
That be negligent to make reckonings,
  Delivering and trusting without writings,
Uncaring for to run in arrearage,
  By this way they must need make passage.

Landlords that do no reparations,
  But leave their lands in desolations,
Their housing unkept wind- and water-tight,
  Letting the principals rot downright,
And suffereth their tenants to run away;
  The way to our house we can them not deny.

They that sue in the court daily
  For little business, and spendeth largely
With great gifts, and yet their labour lost,
  This way they come to seek for their cost.

Farmers and husbandmen that be
  In great farms, and doth not oversee
Their husbandry, but letteth their corn rot,
  Their hay to must, their sheep die in the cot,
Their land untilled, undunged and unsown,
  Their meadows not defenced, and unmown,
Their fruit to perish, hanging on the trees,
  Their cattle scatter, and lose their honey-bees.

All young heirs, born in a rich estate,
  And would live still after the same rate,
Being young brethren of small possibility,
  Not having wherewith to maintain such degree,
But make shifts and borrow over all,
  Such trace prison to be their hospital.

Self-willed people that cannot be in rest,
  But in the law do ever writhe and wrest,
And will not fall to any agreement,
  Till in their necks is laid by judgment
The costs and charges, and so are made full bare;
  Lodging for such folk we do ever spare.

People that alway will be at distance,
  And on their neighbours ever take vengeance
Being avenging on every small wrong—
  From this way they cannot be long.

They that will meddle in every man's matter
  And of other folks' deeds doth alway clatter,
Maintaining their own saying to be true,
  And is not believed ; they cannot eschew
That they must needs come hitherward,
  For by much meddling their credence is marred.

Merchants that beyond the sea buy dear,
  And lend it good cheap when they be here,
And be never paid but by the law,
  Here have no bedding but lie on the straw.

They that sell good cheap in despite,
  Letting all their gains for to go quite,
Buying ware dear and sell for a little,
  They be very guests to lie in our Spital.

Craftsmen that do work day and night,
  Having great charge, and their gains light,
Wasting their tools an dcan them not renew,
  Full well may say, " Farewell, good thrift, adieu ! "
He that winneth much, and when he hath done,
  With waste and games spendeth it soon,
Leaving not wherewith again to begin,
  In this highway he hasteth to ryn.

He that hath a good occupation
  And will live on the courtly fashion
And to work or labour is weary,
  Weening for to live more easily,
Sometime doth make an unthrifty change,
  With bag and staff in our park to range.

Rufflers, and masterless men that cannot work,
  And sleepeth by day, and walketh in the dark,
And with delicates gladly doth feed,
  Swearing and cracking—an easy life to lead !—
With common women daily for to haunt,
  Making revel, and drink adieu taunt,
Saying, " Make we merry as long as we can,
  And drink apace ; the Devil pay the maltman !
Wine was not made for every haskard,
  But beer and ale for every dastard."
And when their money is gone and spent,
  Then this way is most convenient.

Taverners that keep bawdry and polling,
  Marring wine with brewing and rolling ;
Innholders that lodge whores and thieves,
  Seldom their getting anyway proves,
So by reason their gains be geason,
  This way they run many a season.

Bakers and brewers, that with musty grain
  Serve their customers, must take it again,
And many times have they no utterance,
  For their weights and measures is of no substance,
And lose both their credence and good,
  Come this way by all likelihood
For they do infect what should be man's food.

They that will be surety for every debt
  And will pay more than they of right be set,
For to be named a man liberal,
  And in manner he hath nothing at all;
Such foolish facers, when their good is spent,
  To the spital ward they run incontinent.

Young folk that wed or they be wise,
  And alway charges on their hand doth rise,
House-rent and children and every other thing,
  And can do nothing for to get their living,
And have no friends them for to sustain,
  To come this way at last they must be fain.

They that sell away their rents and lands
  And bestoweth it for to be merchants,
And adventureth till them have all lost,
  And turmoileth away from pillar to post,
And ever loseth all that they go about,
  Cometh this way among the other rout.

They that in hope to have their friends die
  Will do nothing, but live wantonly,
Trusting to have the treasure that is left;
  But many times it is them bereft,
And have nothing, and nothing can do,
  Such come this way with other too.

They that doth to other folks good deed,
  And hath themself of other folk more need,
And quencheth the fire of another place,
  And leaveth his own, that is in worse case
When that is brent, and wotteth not where to lie,
  To the spital then must he needs hie.

They that will not suffer their clothe[s] whole,
  But jag and cut them with many a hole,
And payeth more for making than it cost,
  When it is made the garment is but lost,
Patching them with colours like a fool;
  At last they be ruled after our school.

They that do make too much of their wives,
  Suffering them to be nought of their lives,
Letting them have overmuch of their will,
  Clothing them better than they can fulfil,

Letting them go to feasts, dances and plays,
  To every bridal, and do nothing on days,
And giveth them all the sovereignty,
  Must needs come this way, for they cannot pthe.[8]

Copland.

Come hither any of these woeful creatures,
  That be sore wounded and much woe endures
With a shrewd wife, and is never quiet,
  Because that she would have all her diet,
But brawl and chide, babble, cry and fight
  Ever uncontented both day and night?

Porter.

Come this way, quotha? Yes, I warrant you.
  Of them always come this way enow;
We have chambers purposely for them
  Or else they should be lodged in Bedlam.

Copland.

Marry! God forbid it should be as ye tell!

Porter.

By my good faith, the very devil of hell
I trow to my mind hath not much more pain.
  One were in a manner as good be slain,
For there is no joy, but ever anguish,
  On both sides they do always languish;
For the one goeth hither and the other thither,
  Both they spend, and lie nothing together,
So at the last of very necessity,
  Hither they come to ask lodging of me.

Copland.

I know it is the right fashion;
  A realm striving in itself goeth to desolation.
God amend all, I have heard what it is:
  Tell of some other, I am weary of this.

Porter.

All masters that let their servants play,
  Feeding them daintily day by day,
And doth clothe and pay them as they should be,
  Being negligent their work to oversee,
Suffering them waste and their good spill,
  In their presence to do their lewd will;
And all those that pay not their hire,
  Vengeance of God it doth desire;
These on both parts do each other wrong;
  This way they come with a great throng.

All such servants as be negligent
  In their service, and will not be content
To do their work, but slack their business,
  Bribe and convey from master and mistress,
Changing masters, and run from town to town,
  And are late rising, and between lie down,
Playing by night, and trifling by day,
  Of righteousness they do here stay.

Such folk as take on them great rent
  In soils for them inconvenient
Unto their faculty, and often do remove
  Enterprising that they cannot achieve,
Doing curious labours, and have small wage,
  Unto our house they come for hostage.

They that borrow on their garments and napery
  And do not fetch them again shortly,
But let them be worn and then pay the sum;
  Into our highway they be far come.

They that borrow, and purpose not to pay,
  Till in prison they spend all away
And do forswear that is their due;
  They that law for a debt untrue,
And receiveth money in another man's name
  Not being content to restore the same;
They that forget that to them is ought;
  They that strive with all folk for nought;
They that lend and set no time to pay,
  Reason will drive them to come this way.

Old folks that all their goods do give,
  Keeping nothing whereon to live,
And put from their house when they have need,
  Toward our house fast do they speed.
They that give children money to spend
  And causeth them not at their bidding attend,
But doth maintain them in their lewdness,
  And from sin will not them redress,
In idle wantonness suffering them to be,
  Nor teach them virtuous faculty
Are the cause that, when they be old,
  To take the way toward our household.

They that evermore have a delight
  To feed and make feasts at their appetite,
With costly dishes and dainty drink,
  Letting their stock evermore shrink
Making a great port, and be little worth,
  To come hither they come straight-forth.

They that take no heed to their household,
   But let their implements mould,
Their hangings rot, their napery unclean,
   Their furs and woollen not overseen,
Their vessel mar and their goods decay,
   Cannot choose but needs come this way.

Lechers, fornicators and advouterers,
   Incests, harlots, bawds, and bolsterers,
Apple-squires, enticers, and ravishers,
   These to our place have daily herbegers.

Copland.
No marvel of them, and happy they be
   If they do and in so honest degree ;
For surely their ending is fairest,
   If that with poverty they be suppressed,
For I do find written of advoutry,
   That these five sorrows ensueth thereby :
Ex istis penis patietur quisquis adulter ;
   Aut erit hic pauper, hic aut subito morietur,
Aut aliquid membrum casu vulnere perdet,
   Aut erit infamis per quod sit carcere vinctus.

Either they shall be poor, or die suddenly,
   Or lose by wound some member of the body,
Or to be slandered, to suffer sharp prison ;
   Therefore poverty is fairest by reason.
And yet beside that they be so beaten
   That with great pox their limbs be eaten.

How say ye by these horrid swearers,
   These blasphemers, and these God terrors,
Come there any this way to have succour ?

Porter.
Do they ? Yea, I warrant, every hour,
All rotten and torn, arms, heads and legs ;
   They are the most sort that anywhere begs
And be the people that most annoy us.

Copland.
   I believe well, for I find written thus :

*Vir multum jurans replebitur iniquitate, et a
domo ejus non recedet plaga.* Ecclesiasticus, xxii.9

A great swearer is full of iniquity,
   And from his house the plague shall never be.
In the commandments is written plain,
   " Thou shalt not take the name of God in vain " ;
For whoso doth use it customably
   The stroke of God cannot eschew truly.

But come none of these slothful folks hither
   That be so unlusty, so sluggish and lither,
That care not how the world doth go
   Neither holidays, nor working days also,
But lie in bed till all masses be done,
   Loitering their work till it pass noon,
And so enjoy to linger and to sleep,
   And to their living they take no manner keep?

         Porter.
These folks come in so great number,
   That all the ways they do encumber,
And with them doth come all these folk that spare
   To assay their friends for their own welfare
But follow their own mind alway,
   Nor to their friends in no case will obey,
And of their promises they be no more set by,
   But to this way they must them needs apply.

         Copland.
And how by these people so full of covetise,
   That all the world's good can them not suffice,
But by usury, rapine, and extortion,
   Do poll the poor folk of their portion?
And they that invent news by tyranny
   Upon poor men's lands fraudulently,
And like as wolves the sheep doth take and tease,
   For their own lucre, and to live in ease,
And day by day in every manner degree
   They do prolong their iniquity?

         Porter.
As for with them we have to do nothing
   Unto the law it is all belonging.
Howbeit, if they chance to be poor,
   Then often indeed they do come by our door.

         Copland.
But then I pray you how say ye by these
   That break this precept, *non furtum facies,*
Thieves and murderers, and these watchers of ways
   That rob and steal both by nights and days,
And that delight in murder and in theft,
   Whose conditions in no wise can be left—
Do not they ofttimes come hither by you?

         Porter.
Of them that cometh daily enow,
But they be led and commonly fast bound,
   Because their lodging may sooner be found,
And ben conveyed by men of charity,
   Where that they have hospitality,

And ben well kept and wrapped surely;
 And when time cometh that they must die,
They be buried aloft in the air,
 Because dogs shall not on their graves repair.

Copland.

Almighty Jesu of His mercy defend
 Every good man's child from such an end!
And how say ye by all these great drunkards,
 That sup all off by pots and tankards,
Till they be so drunk that they cannot stand?
 That is but little used in this land,
Except it be among Dutch folk or Flemings,
 For Englishmen know not of such reckonings.

Porter.

No do? Yes, yes. I assure you hardily
 They can do it as well as anybody
With double beer, be it wine or ale,
 They cease not till they can tell no right tale,
With *Quyxte quaxte, ic brynxte lief brore*
 An ortkyn, or an half beres, by Got's more.
Yea, rather than fail, drink it clean out,
 With *Fill the pot once again round about;*
Give us more drink for sparing of bread;
 Till their cups be wiser than their head.
And so sit they, and spend up all their thrift,
 And after come here; they have no other shift.

Copland.

How say ye by these folks full of ire
 That burn in wrath hotter than fire,
And never be quiet, but chide and brawl
 With wrath and anger, fretting hart and gall,
Wayward, wood, furious and fell;
 For where they be, quietness cannot dwell,
But alway strife, mistrust and great disease,
 And in no wise none man can them please.

Porter.

Hither they come, and I will tell you why:
 None can live by them well and quietly,
But with each one they fall out and make bate,
 Causing people them for to hate,
And will suffer them to dwell nowhere,
 But are fain for to remain here.

Copland.

It may well be so, for where is none agree,
 Neither thrift nor welfare cannot be.
But I trust it be not between man and wife
 Then it were pity and eke a sorry life

For where is no peace at bed, nor at board,
  I reckon their thrift is not worth a turd.
But of these people that ben so stout
  That in wealth and woe bear it so out
That pride will not suffer them for to fall,
  Methink this way they come not all!

Porter.

Oh, yes, yes, God wot, of them be not few,
  For here all day they assemble in a rew,
And here they crack, babble, and make great boast,
  And among all other would rule the roost,
With " Stand back, thou lewd villain, beggarly knave !
  I will that thou know my wife," and " I have
Spent more in a day with good honesty
  Than thou in thy life ever was like to be,
For I tell thee I have kept or now such report,
  That all my neighbours did to me resort,
And have or now kept a great household,
  And had enough of silver and of gold.
In all our parish none was better decked,
  And I think scorn for to be thus checked
Of such lewd persons, that never had good " ;
  And " Eke I am born of as good a blood
As any in this town, and a gentleman ;
  But if I had as much as I wist when
I should make a many of these poor carls to know
  What manner thing a gentleman is, I trow."

Copland.

Lo, here one may see that there is none worse
  Than is a proud heart and a beggar's purse,
Great boast and small roost—this is evident—
  For a proud heart will never be shent.
But, good porter, I pray you, be so kind
  To tell me of them out of mind.
As for the envious, I let them dwell,
  For their hospital is the deep pit of hell.

Porter.

How say ye by this lewd hypocrisy
  That is used so superstitiously ?
I cry God mercy, if I make any lie
  Of them that devout prayers seem to occupy,
As if God from the cross by them should be undone,
  And sit in the church till it be noon,
Never speaking in any folks' presence,
  But it soundeth to virtue and reverence.
Yet when they be moved to anger or wrath,
  I trow to my mind that other folk hath
Not half the spite, vengeance and rigour
  As they will have to their poor neighbour.
For some of them, if they might be a lord,
  Would hang another, they be of such discord,

And where they once take hatred or enmity,
  During their life have never charity :
And who that hath no charity nor love
  Can never please the Amity above ;
And so this way they be fain to come.

Copland.

I believe well; for truly there be some
That neither have love to one nor other ;
  For I ween if it were sister or brother
They would no more pity them nor rue
  (They be so fell) than on a thief or Jew.
For when ye think to have them most in reason,
  Then be their hearts full of deadly poison ;
And in their fury they be so violent,
  That they will bring one to an exigent,
And never pardon, nor no man forgive,
  Till their neighbour hath nothing on to live ;
And so they make by their own conscience
  Between God and the Devil no difference.
But hey, alas ! do none this way trace
  That do take wives of no small efficace,
Which cannot get, bestow, nor yet save,
  And to go gay they will spend and crave,
Making men ween that they love them alone,
  And be full false to them each one,
Spending their goods without any care,
  Without good gowns, but not of hoods bare ?

Porter.

They must come hither for they cannot choose,
  For they that will themself so use,
The one to get, and the other to spend,
  And when all is brought to an end,
Hither they come to have comfort.
  Sir, I beshrew all the whole sort.
Such genyfenyes keepeth many one low,
  Their husbands must obey as dog to bow.
Alas ! silly men, ye are ill at ease,
  These dainty housewives for to feed and please :
For so they sit and sew half an hour on a clout,
  Their whole day's work is patched out,
And so, by their trifling, and living nought
  With other means, they be hither brought.

Copland.

Well, good porter, I pray you let them alone,
  For happy is he that hath a good one.
I pray you show me of other guests,
  For against women I love no jests.
The shower is almost done, and I have far to go.
  Come none of these pedlars this way also,
With pack on back, with their bousy speech,
  Jagged and ragged, with broken hose and breech ?

Porter.

Enow, enow. *With bousy cove maund nase,*
  Tour the patrico in the darkman case,
Docked the dell for a copper make :
  His watch shall feng a prounce's nab-cheat.
Cyarum, by Solomon, and thou shalt peck my jere
  In thy gan ; for my watch it is nace gear ;
  or the bene bouse my watch hath a wyn.
  And thus they babble, till their thrift is thin,
I wot not what, with their babbling French,
  But out of the spital they have a party[10] stench.
And with them comes gatherers of cony-skins,
  That chop with laces, points, needles and pins.

Copland.

Come any mariners hither of Cock Lorel's[11] boat?

Porter.

  Every day they be alway afloat :
We must them receive and give them costs free :
  And also with them the fraternity
Of unthrifts, which do our house endue,
  And never fail with brethren alway new.
Also here is kept and holden in degree
  Within our house the orders eight time three
Of knaves only ; we can them not keep out
  They swarm as thick as bees in a rout ;
And chief of all that doth us encumber,
  The order of fools that be without number ;
For daily they make such press and cry
  That scant our house can them satisfy.

Copland.

Yet one thing I wonder that you do not tell ;
  Come there no women this way to dwell?

Porter.

Of all the sorts that be spoken of afore,
  I warrant women enow in store,
That we are weary of them. Every day
  They come so thick that they stop the way.
The sisterhood of drabs, sluts and callets
  To here resort, with their bagets and wallets,
And be partners of the confrérie
  Of the maintainers of ill husbandry.

Copland.

A lewd sort is of them, of a surety.
  Now, master porter, I thank you heartily
Of your good talking. I must take my leave.
  The shower is done, and it is toward eve.
Another time and at more leisure
  I will do for you as great a pleasure.

Porter.

There be a thousand more than I can tell;
    But at this time I bid you farewell.

L'Envoy of the Author.

Go little quire to every degree,
And on thy matter desire them to look,
Desiring them for to pardon me
That I am so bold to put them in my book.
To eschew vice I thee undertook,
Disdaining no matter of creature.
I were to blame if I them forsook;
None in this world of wealth can be sure.

Finis.

Imprinted at London in the Fleet-street at *The Rose Garland* by Robert Copland.

A Manifest Detection of the most vile and detestable use of Dice-play, and other practices like the same:

A mirror very necessary for all young gentlemen and others suddenly enabled by worldly abundance to look in. Newly set forth for their behoof.

[By Gilbert Walker (?)]

[1552]

GENTLE Reader, when you shall read this book, devised as a mean to show and set forth such naughty practices as hath been, and be peradventure yet used in houses of dice-play, think it not to be written in dispraise of offence of the honest, but for that, under colour and cloak of friendship, many young gentlemen be drawn to their undoing. And to the intent that such as have not yet fed of that sour-sweet or hungry bait (wherewith they at length unawares be choked), shall learn, not only to avoid the danger thereof by knowing their mischievous and most subtle practice, in getting a prey to spoil the same; but shall also by mean thereof see, as it were in a glass, the miserable ends that a sort of handsome gentlemen hath by this crafty and subtle device come to, imputing, for want of knowledge, their cause of misery to ill fortune. Thus, having in few words showed the effect of that which the book shall declare with some more circumstance, I bid you farewell.

The names of the dice :

A bale of barred cinque-deuces.

A bale of flat cinque-deuces.

A bale of flat sice-aces.

A bale of barred sice-aces.

A bale of barred cater-treys.

A bale of flat cater-treys.

A bale of fullams of the best making.

A bale of light graviers.

A bale of langrets contrary to the vantage.

A bale of gourds with as many high men as low men, for passage.

A bale of demies.

A bale of long dice for even and odd.

A bale of bristles.

A bale of direct contraries.

INTERLOCUTORS : *R.* and *M.*

R. speaketh :

HAPPILY as I roamed me in the church of Paul's now twenty days ago, looking for certain my companions that hither might have stalled a meeting, there walked up and down by me in the body of the church a gentleman, fair dressed in silks, gold, and jewels, with three or four servants in gay liveries, all 'broidered with sundry colours, attending upon him. I advised him well, as one that pleased me much for his proper personage, and more for the wearing of his gear, and he again, at each check made in our walking, cast earnest looks upon me, not such as by his hollow frownings and piercing aspect might pretend any malice or disdain, but rather should signify by his cheerful countenance that he noted in me something that liked him well, and could be content to take some occasion to embrace mine acquaintance. Anon, whiles I devised with myself what means I might make to understand his behaviour, and what sort he was of—for man's nature, as ye know, is in those things curious, specially in such as profess courting—he humbled himself far beneath my expectation, and began to speak first after this manner :

" Sir, it seemeth to me that we have both one errand hither, for I have marked you well now more than half an hour, stalking up and down alone, without any company, sometime with such heavy and uncheerful countenance as if ye had some hammers working in your head, and that breach of company had moved your patience. And I, for my part, what face soever I set on the matter, am not all in quiet ; for had all promises been kept, I should, or this hour, have seen a good piece of money told here upon the font, and as many indentures, obligations, and other writings sealed, as cost me twice forty shillings for the drawing and counsel. But as to me, let them that be a-cold blow the coals, for I am already on the sure side, and if I miss of my hold this way, I doubt not to pinch them as near by another shift ; though indeed I must confess that unkindness and breach of promise is so much against my nature that nothing can offend me more. And you, on the other side, if your grief in tarrying be the same that I take it, ye cannot do better than to make little of the matter, for ye seem to be a man that wadeth not so unadvisedly in the deep but that always ye be sure of an anchor-hold. And therefore let us by mine advice forget such idle griefs, and whiles noontide draweth on, talk of other matters that may quicken our spirits to make a merry dinner. Perchance this occasion may confirm a joyful acquaintance between us."

" Sir," quoth I, " as touching the cause of my long abiding here, it is not very great, neither is it tied to any such thrift as ye speak of, but lack of company will soon lead a man into a brown study."

" Well then," quoth he, " if your head be fraught with no heavier burden, it is an easy matter to lighten your load, for a little grief is soon forgotten. But I pray you, sir, long ye not to the Court? Methinks I have seen you ere now, and cannot call it home where it should be."

M. A good workman, by St. Mary! Now do I easily foresee, without any instruction further, whereto this matter tendeth. But yet tell what further talk had ye?

R. I told him I was yet but a raw courtier, as one that came from school not many months afore, and was now become servant to my Lord Chancellor of England; partly to see experience of things, the better to govern myself hereafter; and, chiefly, to have a staff to lean unto to defend mine own. And he again commended me much therein, declaring how divers notable persons, rashly by ignorance misguiding themselves, were suddenly shaken asunder, and fallen on the rocks of extreme penury; and how some other, even goodly wits, circumspectly working in all their doings, have, by want of such a leaning-stock, been overthrown with tyrants' power. " For which cause," quoth he, "like as I cannot but praise your wary working in this your first courting, so for my lord your master's sake you shall not lack the best that I may do for you. For, albeit that I am much beholden to all the Lords of the Council, as [one] whom they stick not at all times to take to their board, and use sometime for a companion at play, yet is he my singular good lord above all the rest. And, if I shall confess the truth, a great part of my living hath risen by his friendly preferment. And, though I say it myself, I am too old a courtier, and have seen too much, to bear nothing away; and, in case our acquaintance hold, and by daily company gather deep root, I shall now and then show you a lesson worth the learning; and to th' end hereafter each of us may be the bolder of the other, I pray you, if ye be not otherwise bespoken, take a capon with me at dinner. Though your fare be but homely and scant, yet a cup of good wine I can promise you, and all other lacks shall be supplied with a friendly welcome."

" I thank you, sir," quoth I. " Ye offer me more gentleness than I can deserve; but, since I have tarried all this while, I will abide the last hour, to prove how well my companions will hold their appointment ; and for that cause, I will forbear to trouble you till another time."

" Nay, not so," quoth he.   " Yet had I rather spend twenty pounds than that my lord your master should know but that the worst groom of his stable is as dear to me as any kinsman I have.   And therefore lay all excuses aside, and shape yourself to keep me company for one dinner, while your man and mine shall walk here together till twelve of the clock ; and, if your friends happen to come hither, he shall bring them home to us.   I love to see gentlemen swarm and cleave together like burrs."

M.   How then ?   Went ye home together ?

R.   What else ?   Would ye have me forsake so gentle a friend, and so necessary acquaintance ?

M.   Go to.   Say on.   Lo, how gentle lambs are led to the slaughter-man's fold !   How soon reckless youth falleth in snare of crafty dealing !

R.   Soon after, we came home to his house.   The table was fair spread with diaper cloths ; the cupboard garnished with much goodly plate.   And last of all came forth the gentlewoman his wife, clothed in silks and embroidered works ; the attire of her head broidered with gold and pearl ; a carcanet about her neck, agreeable thereto, with a flower of diamonds pendant thereat, and many fair rings on her finger.   " Bess," quoth he, " bid this gentleman welcome."   And with that she courteously kissed me ; and, after, moved communication of my name, my natural country, what time my father died, and whether I were married yet or not, always powdering our talk with such pretty devices, that I saw not a woman in all my life whose fashions and entertainment I liked better.

The goodman, in the mean season, had been in the kitchen, and suddenly returning, and breaking our talk, somewhat sharply blamed his wife that the dinner was no further forward.   And whiles she withdrew her from us, by like to put things in a good readiness, " Come on," quoth he, " you shall see my house the while.   It is not like your large country houses.   Rooms, ye wot, in London be strait, but yet the furniture of them be costly enough ; and victuals be here at such high prices, that much money is soon consumed, specially with them that maintain an idle household.   Nevertheless, assure yourself that no man is welcomer than you to such cheer as ye find."   And, consequently, bringing me through divers well-trimmed chambers, the worst of them apparelled with verdures, some with rich cloth of Arras, all with beds, chairs and cushions of silk and gold, of sundry colours, suitably wrought,

" Lo, here," quoth he, " a poor man's lodging ; which if ye think it may do you any pleasure—for the inns of London be the worſt of England —take your choice, and heartily welcome, reserving but one for my lord my wife's cousin, whom I dare not disappoint, leſt haply he should lour, and make the house too hot for us."

I gave him thanks, as meet it was I should, neither yet refusing his gentle offer—for, indeed, mine own lodging is somewhat loathsome, and peſtered with company—nor yet embracing it, because hitherto I had not by any means deserved so great a pleasure.

So down we came again into the parlour, and found there divers gentlemen, all ſtrangers to me. And what should I say more, but to dinner we went.

M. Let me hear, then, what matters were moved at dinner-time, and how ye passed the afternoon till the company brake up and sundered themselves.

R. That can I readily tell you. I have not yet forgotten it, since done it was so late. As touching our fare, though partridge and quail were no dainties, and wines of sundry grapes flowed abundantly, yet spare I to speak thereto, because ye have demanded a contrary queſtion. So soon as we had well victualled ourselves, I wot not how, but easily it came to pass that we talked of news, namely, of Boulogne, how hardly it was won,[1] what policy then was practised to get it, and what case the soldiers had in the siege of it, insomuch that the leaſt progress the king maketh into the inland parts of the realm, dislodgeth more of his train, and leaveth them to their own provision, with less relief of victuals than had the worſt unwaged adventurer there. From this the goodman led us to talk of home pleasures, enlarging the beauties of peace and London paſtimes, and made so jolly a discourse thereof, that, to my judgment, he seemed skilful in all things.

" Methinks," quoth he, " such simple fare as this, taken in peace, without fear and danger of gunshot, is better than a prince's purveyance in war, where each morsel he eateth shall bring with it a present fear of sudden mischance or violent hoſtility. And though that in the open camp none might have more familiar access to the nobility than here at home, yet, for my part, I thank God, I have no cause to complain either, because of their gentleness ; no usher keeps the door between me and them when I come to visit them, or that the greateſt princes refuse not sometimes to hallow my poor table and house with their person ; which— be it spoken without boaſt, or imbraiding—doth sometime coſt me twenty pounds a day. I am sure that some of this company do remember what a brave company of lords supped with me the laſt term, and I think how ye have heard how some of them got an hundred pounds or two by their coming."

With this and that like talk, consumed was our dinner. And, after the table was removed, in came one of the waiters with a fair silver bowl, full of dice and cards.

" Now maſters," quoth the goodman, " who is so disposed, fall to. Here is my twenty pounds. Win it and wear it."

Then each man chose his game. Some kept the goodman company at the hazard, some matched themselves at a new game called " primero."

M. And what did you the while?

R. They egged me to have made one at dice, and told me it was a shame for a gentleman not to keep gentlemen company for his twenty or forty crowns. Nevertheless, because I alleged ignorance, the gentlewoman said I should not sit idle, all the reſt being occupied, and so we two fell to sant, five games a crown.

M. And how sped you in the end?

R. In good faith, I passed not for the loss of twenty or forty shillings for acquaintance, and so much I think it coſt me ; and then I left off. Marry, the dice-players ſtuck well by it, and made very fresh play, saving one or two that were clean shriven, and had no more money to lose. In the end, when I should take my leave to depart, I could not by any means be suffered so to break company, unless I would deliver the gentlewoman a ring, for a gage of my return to supper. And so I did. And, to tell you all in a few words, I have haunted none other since I got that acquaintance. My meat and drink and lodging is every way so delicate, that I make no haſte to change it.

M. And what ! pay you nothing for it? Have ye not an ordinary charge for your meals?

R. None at all. But this device we have, that every player, at the firſt hand he draweth, payeth a crown to the box by way of a relief towards the house charges.

M. Ye may fare well of that price at the ſtark ſtaring ſtews.

R. In good faith, and methink it an easy burthen for him that will put his forty pounds in adventure to pay the tribute of a crown and fare well for it, whose chance is to lose a hundred crowns or two, would never have spared one to make a new ſtock withal, and whose hap is to win, were a very churl to be a niggard of so little.

M. Is every man a player there, or do some go scot-free?

R. Whoso liſteth not to put much in hazard playeth at mumchance

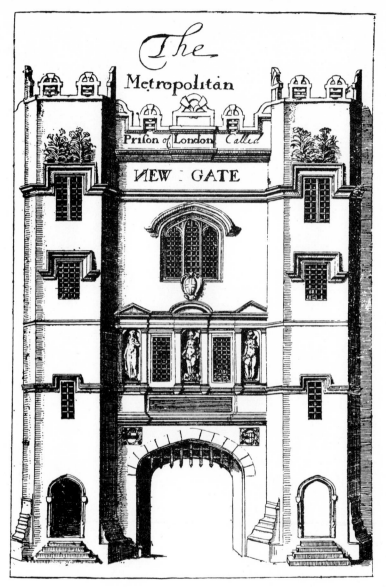

Plate III
NEWGATE IN 1650.

[*face p. 32*

Plate IV.
CARD AND DICE BOXES OF THE SIXTEENTH AND SEVENTEENTH CENTURIES.

[face p. 33

for his crown with some one or other : so some goeth free, and some
be at double charge ; for always we have respect that the house be
relieved, and it standeth so much the more with good reason, because
that besides the great charges of victuals, and great attendance of the
servants, and great spoil of napery and household stuff, the goodman
also looseth his twenty or forty pounds to keep us company.

M. And what do you the whiles ? I am sure ye be not yet so
cunning as to keep such workmen company.

R. And why not, I pray you ? Is it so hard a thing to tell twenty,
or to remember two or three chances ? But yet indeed I play little
myself, unless it be at the cards. Otherwise I am the goodman's half
for the most part, and join both our lucks together.

M. How sped ye there for the most part ?

R. Not always as well so I would wish. I will be plain with you,
as with my friend : it hath cost me forty pounds within this sennight.
But I vouchsafe my loss the better, I had such fair play for it ; and who
would not hazard twenty pound among such quiet company, where no
man gives a foul word ? At one good hand a man may chance, as I
have often seen, to make his forty pound a hundred ; and I have seen
a man begin to play with five hundred mark lands, and once yet, ere the
year went about, would have sold land if he had it.

M. Perchance so too.

R. But his luck was too bad ; the like falleth scarcely once in a
hundred years.

M. That is but one doctor's opinion. I see it betide every day,
though not in this so large a proportion. And because I see you so raw
in these things, that ye account that for most unfeigned friendship, where
most deceit is meant, and, being already given to play, may in a few days
come further behind than all your travail of your latter years can overtake again ; I can neither forbear thee, for the zeal I bear unto you, or
the hatred I bear to the occupation, to make you understand some parts
of the sleights and falsehoods that are commonly practised at dice and
cards ; opening and overturning the things, not so that I would learn
you to put the same in use, but open their wicked snares.

R. I thank you for your gentle offer. I would be glad to know the
worst, lest haply I should fall in such crafty company. But yonder at
my lodging cometh none but men of worship, some mounted upon mules
fair trapped, some upon fine hackneys with foot-cloths ; all such as, I
dare say, would not practise a point of legerdemain for an hundred
pound.

D

M.   Well, as to that, there lay a straw, till anon that the matter lead us to speak more of it.   And in the mean season, let this be sufficient ; that so soon as ye began your declaration of the first acquaintance in Paul's, I felt aforehand the hooks were laid to pick your purse withal.

R.   Wist I that, I would from henceforth stand in doubt of mine own hands, the matter hath such appearance of honesty.

M.   Well, hearken to me awhile.   There is no man, I am sure, that hath experience in the world, and by reading of histories conferreth our time to the days of our elders, but will easily grant, that, as time hath grown and gathered increase by running, so wit, first planted in a few, hath in time taken so many roots, that in every corner ye may find new branches budding and issuing from the same.   For proof whereof, to speak of one thing among many that at this time may serve our purpose, although the Greek and Latin histories be full of notable examples of good princes that utterly exiled dicing out of their seigniories and countries, or at the least held them as infamed persons ; yet find I not that in these our forefathers' days, any the like sleight and crafty deceit was practised in play, as now is common in every corner.   Yea, and he, namely Hodge Setter,[2] whose surname witnesseth what opinion man had of him, though forty years agone was thought peerless in crafty play, and had, as they say, neither mate nor fellow, yet now towards his death was so far behind some younger men in that knowledge, that I myself have known more than twenty that could make him a fool, and cannot suffer him to have the name of a workman in that faculty.

And it is not yet twenty years agone since all that sought their living that way, as then were few in number—scarcely so many as were able to maintain a good fray—so were they much of Hodge Setter's estate, the next door to a beggar.   Now, such is the misery of our time, or such is the licentious outrage of idle misgoverned persons, that of only dicers a man might have half an army, the greatest number so gaily beseen and so full of money, that they bash not to insinuate themselves into the company of the highest, and look for a good hour to creep into a gentleman's room of the Privy Chamber.   And hereof you may right well assure yourself, that if their cost were not exceeding great, it were not possible by the only help thereof to lead so sumptuous a life as they do, always shining like blazing stars in their apparel, by night taverning with [s]trumpets, by day spoiling gentlemen of their inheritance.   And to speak all at once, like as all good and liberal sciences had a rude beginning, and by the industry of good men, being augmented by little and by little, at last grew to a just perfection ; so this detestable privy robbery, from a few and deceitful rules is in few years grown to the body of an art, and hath his peculiar terms, and thereof as great a multitude applied to it, as hath grammar or logic, or any other of the approved sciences.

Neither let this seem strange unto you, because the thing is not commonly known, for this faculty hath one condition of juggling, that if the sleight be once discovered, marred is all the market. The first precept thereof is to be as secret in working as he that keepeth a man company from London to Maidenhead, and makes good cheer by the way, to the end in the thicket to turn his prick upwards, and cast a weaver's knot on both his thumbs behind him. And they, to the intent that ever in all companies they may talk familiarly in all appearance, and yet so covertly indeed that their purpose may not be espied, they call their worthy art by a new-found name, calling themselves *cheators*,[3] and the dice *cheaters*, borrowing the term from among our lawyers, with whom all such casuals as fall unto the lord at the holding his leets, as waifs, strays and suchlike, be called *cheats*, as are accustomably said to be escheated to the lord's use.

R. Trow ye, then, that they have any affinity with our men of law?

M. Never with those that be honest. Marry! with such as be ambidexters, and use to play on both the hands, they have a great league; so have they also with all kind of people that from a good order of civility are fallen, and resolved, as it were, from the hardness of virtuous living, to the delicacy and softness of uncareful idleness and gainful deceit; for gain and ease be the only pricks that they shoot at. But [by] what right or honest means they might acquire it, that part never cometh in question among them. And hereof it riseth that, like as law, when the term is truly considered, signifieth an ordinance of good men established for the commonwealth to repress all vicious living, so these cheaters turned the cat in the pan, giving to divers vile patching shifts an honest and godly title, calling it by the name of a *law*; because, by a multitude of hateful rules, a multitude of dregs and draff (as it were all good learning) govern and rule their idle bodies, to the destruction of the good labouring people. And this is the cause that divers crafty sleights, devised only for guile, hold up the name of a law, ordained, ye wot, to maintain plain dealing. Thus give they their own conveyance the name of cheating law; so do they other terms, as sacking law, high law, figging law, and suchlike.

R. What mean ye hereby? Have ye spoken broad English all this while, and now begin to choke me with mysteries and quaint terms?

M. No, not for that. But always ye muſt consider that a carpenter hath many terms, familiar enough to his 'prentices, that other folk underſtand not at all ; and so have the cheaters, not without great need, for a falsehood, once detećted, can never compass the desired effećt. Neither is it possible to make you grope the bottom of their art, unless I acquaint you with some of their terms. Therefore note this at the firſt, that sacking law signifieth whoredom ; high law, robbery ; figging law, pickpurse craft.

R. But what is this to the purpose ; or what have cheaters to do with whores or thieves ?

M. As much as with their very entire friend, that hold all of one corporation. For the firſt and original ground of cheating is a counterfeit countenance in all things, a ſtudy to seem to be, and not to be indeed ; and because no great deceit can be wrought but where special truſt goeth before, therefore the cheater, when he pitcheth his hay to purchase his profit, enforceth all his wits to win credit and opinion of honeſty and uprightness. Who hath a great[er] outward show of simplicity than the pickpurse, or what woman will seem so fervent in love as will the common harlot? So, as I told you before, the foundation of all those sorts of people is nothing else but mere simulation and bearing in hand. And like as they spring all from one root, so tend they all to one end : idly to live by rape and ravin, devouring the fruit of other men's labours. All the odds between them be in the mean ećtions, that lead towards the end and fixed purpose.[4]

R. I am almoſt weary of my trade already to hear that our gay gameſters are so ſtrongly allied with thieves and pickpurses. But I pray you proceed, and let me hear what sundry shifts of deceit they have to meet all well together at the close.

M. That is more than I promised you at the beginning, and more than I intend to perform at this time ; for every of them keepeth as great schools in their own faculty as the cheaters do ; and if I should make an open discourse of every wrinkle they have to cover and work deceit withal, I should speak of more sundry quaint conveyances than be rocks in Milford Haven to defend the ships from the boiſterous rage of the weather. But I will firſt go forward with that I have in hand, and by the way, as occasion shall serve, so touch the reſt that ye may see their workmanship, as it were afar off more than half a kenning. The cheater, for the moſt part, never receiveth his scholar, to whom he will discover the secret of his art, but such one as before he had from some wealth and plenty of things made so bare, and brought to such misery, that he will refuse no labour, nor leave no ſtone unturned, to pick up a penny underneath. And this he doth not but upon a great skill. For, like as it is an old proverb and a true, that he muſt needs go whom the Devil driveth, so is there not such a devil to force a man to an extreme refuge as is necessity and want, specially where it hath proceeded of abundance. Therefore the cheater, using necessity for a great part of persuasion, when he hath sucked this needy companion so dry that there remaineth no hope to press any drop of further gain from him, taketh some occasion to show him a glimpse of his faculty. And if, haply, he find him eagle-eyed, and diligent to mark, anon shapeth him in such a fashion, as that he will raise a new gain by him, and, withal, somewhat relieve his urgent poverty. Then, walking aside into some solitary place, he maketh the firſt way to his purpose after this, or the like, manner :

" I am sure it is not yet out of your remembrance how late it is since ye firſt fell into my company ; how great loss ye had at play before we entered in any acquaintance, and how little profit redounded unto me since ye firſt haunted my house. Neither can ye forget, on the other side, how friendly I have entertained you in every condition, making my house, my servants, my horses, mine apparel, and other things whatsoever I had, rather common to us both than private to myself. And now I perceive that of a youthful wantonness and, as it were, a childish oversight, ye have suddenly brought yourself, unawares to me, so far under the hatches, and are shaken with lavish dispense, that ye cannot find the way to rise again, and bear any sail among men, as heretofore you have done. Which thing, whiles I deeply consider with myself, I cannot but lament much your negligence, and, more, the harm that is like to ensue upon it. For, firſt, your friends being, as I have heard, many in number, and all of worship, shall conceive such inward grief of your unthriftiness, that not one will vouchsafe a gentle plaſter to quench the malice of this fretting corsie that penury hath applied ; and I, again, because my hap was to have you in my house, and to gain a little of other men's leavings, shall be counted the cause of your undoing, and slandered for taking a few feathers out of the neſt when other had ſtolen the birds already. For which causes, and specially to help you to maintain yourself like a gentleman, as hitherto of yourself ye have been able, I can be content to put you in a good way, so as, treading the ſteps that I shall appoint you, neither shall ye need to run to your friends for succour, and all men shall be glad to use you for a companion. But wiſt I that I should find you crafting with me in any point, and void of that fidelity and secretness, some sparks whereof I have noted in your nature, assure yourself that I would never make you privy to the matter, but give you over to your own provision, perchance to end your life with infamy and wretchedness."

The young man, that lately flowed in plenty and pleasures, and now was pinched to the quick with lack of all things, humbled himself anon to be wholly at his devotion, and gave him a thousand thanks for his great kindness. Then forth goeth the cheater, and further says:

"Though your experience in the world be not so great as mine, yet am I sure ye see that no man is able to live an honest man unless he have some privy way to help himself withal, more than the world is witness of. Think you the noblemen could do as they do, if in this hard world they should maintain so great a port only upon their rent? Think you the lawyers could be such purchasers[5] if their pleas were short, and all their judgments, justice and conscience? Suppose ye that offices would be so dearly bought, and the buyers so soon enriched, if they counted not pillage an honest point of purchase? Could merchants, without lies, false making their wares, and selling them by a crooked light, to deceive the chapman in the thread or colour, grow so soon rich and to a baron's possessions, and make all their posterity gentlemen? What will ye more? Whoso hath not some awkward way to help himself, but followeth his nose, as they say, always straight forward, may well hold up the head for a year or two, but the [third] he must needs sink and gather the wind into beggars' haven. Therefore mine advice shall be, that ye beat all your wits, and spare not to break your brains always to save and help one. Your acquaintance, I know, is great amongst your countrymen, such as be rich and full of money, nevertheless, more simple than that they know what good may be done in play, and better it is that each man of them smart a little, than you to live in lack. Therefore seek them out busily at their lodgings; but always bear them in hand that ye met them by chance. Then will it not be hard to call them hither to take part of a supper; and, having them once within the house doors, doubt ye not but they shall have a blow at one pastime or other, that shall lighten their purses homeward. Myself will lend you money to keep them company, and, nevertheless, make you partaker of the gain. And, to the end ye shall not be ignorant by what means I will compass the matter, come, on go we unto my closet, and I shall give you a lesson worth the learning." Then bringeth he forth a great box with dice, and first teacheth him to know a langret.

R. A God's name, what ſtuff is it? I have often heard men talk of false dice,[6] but I never yet heard so dainty a name given them.

M. So much the sooner may ye be deceived. But suffer me a while, and break not my talk, and I shall paint you anon a proper kind of pulling.

" Lo, here," saith the cheater to this young novice, " a well-favoured die, that seemeth good and square ; yet is the forehead longer on the cater and trey than any other way, and therefore holdeth the name of a langret. Such be also called barred cater-treys, because commonly, the longer end will, of his own sway, draw downwards, and turn up to the eye sice, cinque, deuce, or ace. The principal use of them is at novem quinque. So long as a pair of barred cater-treys be walking on the board, so long can ye caſt neither 5 nor 9, unless it be, by a great mischance, that the roughness of the board, or some other ſtay, force them to ſtay and run againſt their kind ; for without cater-trey ye wot that 5 nor 9 can never fall."[7]

R. By this reason, he that hath the firſt dice is like always to ſtrip and rob all the table about !

M. True it is, were there not another help. And for the purpose an odd man is at hand, called a flat cater-trey, and none other number. The granting that trey or cater be always one upon the one die, if there is no chance upon the other die but may serve to make 5 or 9, and so caſt forth and lose all. " Therefore," saith the maſter, " mark well your flat, and learn to know him surely when he runneth on the board. The whiles he is abroad, ye forbear to caſt at much ; and, keeping this rule to avoid suspeċtion, because I am known for a player, ye shall see me bring all the gain into your hands."

R. But what shift have they to bring the flat in and out ?

M. A jolly fine shift, that properly is called foiſting ; and it is nothing else but a sleight to carry easily within the hand as often as the foiſter liſt. So that when either he or his partner shall caſt the dice, the flat comes not abroad till he have made a great hand and won as much as him liſt. Otherwise the flat is ever on, unless at few times that, of purpose, he suffer the silly souls to caſt in a hand or two to give them courage to continue their play, and live in hope of winning.

R. This gear seemeth very ſtrange unto me, and it sinketh not yet into my brain how a man might carry so many dice in one hand, and chop them and change them so often, and the thing not espied.

M. So jugglers' conveyance seemeth to exceed the compass of reason till ye know the feat. But what is it that labour overcometh not ?

And true it is, to foist finely and readily, and with the same hand to tell money to and fro, is a thing hardly learned, and asketh a bold spirit and long experience, though it be one of the first he learned. But to return to the purpose. If haply this young scholar have not so ready and so skilful an eye to discern the flat at every time that he is foisted in—for use maketh mastery, as well in this as in other things—then partly to help this ignorance withal, and partly to teach the young cock to crow, all after the cheaters' kind, the old cole instructeth the young in the terms of his art after this manner :

" Ye know that this outrageous swearing and quarrelling that some use in play, giveth occasion to many to forbear, that else would adventure much money at it ; for this we have a device amongst us, that rather we relent and give place to a wrong, than we would cause the play, by strife, to cause any company to break. Neither have we any oaths in use but lightly these : ' of honesty,' ' of truth,' ' by salt,' ' [St.] Martin ' ; which, when we use them affirmatively, we mean always directly the contrary. As for example : If haply I say unto you, when the dice cometh to your hands, ' Of honesty, cast at all,' my meaning is, that ye shall cast at the board, or else at very little. If, when a thing is offered in gage, I swear by St. Martin I think it fine gold, then mean I the contrary, that it is but copper. And like as it is a gentle and old proverb, ' Let losers have their words,' so, by the way, take forth this lesson, ever to show gentleness to the silly souls, and creep if ye can into their very bosoms. For harder it is to hold them when ye have them, than for the first time to take them up. For these young wits be so light, and so wavering, that it requireth great travail to make them always dance after one pipe. But to follow that we have in hand : be they young, be they old, that falleth into our laps, and be ignorant of our art, we call them all by the name of a *cousin*, as men that we make as much of as if they were of our kin indeed. The greatest wisdom of our faculty resteth in this point, diligently to foresee to make the cousin sweat, that is, to have a will to keep play and company, and always to beware that we cause him not [to] smoke, lest that having any feel or savour of guile intended against him, he slip the collar as it were a hound, and shake us off for ever. And whensoever ye take up a cousin, be sure, as near as ye can, to know aforehand what store of bit he hath in his buy, that is, what money he hath in his purse, and whether it be in great cogs or in small, that is, gold or silver ; and at what game he will soonest stoop, that we may feed him with his own humour, and have cauls ready for him ; for thousands there be that will not play a groat at novem, and yet will lose a hundred pound at the hazard ; and he that will not stoop a dodkin at the dice, perchance at cards will spend God's cope ; therefore they must be provided for every way.

"Generally, your fine cheats, though they be good made both in the King's Bench and in the Marshalsea, yet Bird, in Holborn, is the finest workman. Acquaint yourself with him, and let him make you a bale or two of squariers of sundry sizes, some less, some more, to throw into the first play, till ye perceive what your company is ; then have in a readiness, to be foisted in when time shall be, your fine cheats of all sorts. Be sure to have in store of such as these be : a bale of barred cinque-deuces, [and] flat cinque-deuces, a bale of barred sice-aces and flat sice-aces, a bale of barred cater-treys and flat cater-treys ; the advantage whereof is all on the one side, and consisteth in the forging.[8] Provide also a bale or two of fullams, for they have great use at the hazard ; and, though they be square outward, yet being within at the corner with lead or other ponderous matter stopped, minister as great an advantage as any of the rest. Ye must also be furnished with high men and low men for a mumchance and for passage.[9] Yea, and a long die for even and odd is good to strike a small stroke withal, for a crown or two, or the price of a dinner. As for gourds and bristle dice [these] be now too gross a practice to be put in use ; light graviers there be, demies, contraries, and of all sorts, forged clean against the apparent vantage, which have special and sundry uses.

"But it is enough at this time to put you in a remembrance what tools ye must prepare to make you a workman. Hereafter, at more leisure, I shall instruct you of the several uses of them all, and in the mean season take with you also this lesson : that when fine squariers only be stirring, there rests a great help in cogging ; that is, when the undermost die standeth dead by the weighty fall of his fellow, so that if 6 be my chance, and 10 yours, grant that, upon the die, I cog and keep always an ace, deuce, or trey, I may perhaps soon cast 6, but never 10. And there be divers kind of cogging, but of all other the Spanish cog bears the bell, and seldom raiseth any smoke."

"Gramercy," saith the scholar, and now thinketh he himself so ripely instructed, that though he be not yet able to beguile others, yet he supposeth himself sufficiently armed against all falsehood that might be wrought to bring him to an afterdeal, and little seeth he the while how many other ends remain, how many points there be in slippery cheaters' science, that he shall not yet be skilful enough to tag in their kind, perchance in four or five years' practice.

R.   Why, have they any deeper reaches to lift a man out of his saddle, and rid him of his money, than ye have opened already?

M.   Alas! this is but a warning, and, as it were, the shaking of a rod to a young boy to scare him from places of peril.   All that I have told you yet, or that I have minded to tell you, 'greeth not to the purpose to make you skilful in cheaters' occupation.   For as soon would I teach you the next way to Tyburn as to learn you the practice of it!   Only my meaning is to make you see as far into it as should a cobbler into a tanner's faculty; to know whether his leather be well liquored, and well and workmanly dressed or not.   And, like as I would not wish a cobbler a currier, lest two sundry occupations running together into one, might, perhaps, make a lewd London medley in our shoes, the one using false-hood in working, the other facing and lying in uttering; so seek I to avoid, that ye should not both be a courtier, in whom a little honest, moderate play is tolerable, and, withal, a cheater, that with all honesty hath made an undefensible dormant defiance.   For, even this new-nurtured novice, notwithstanding he is received into the college of these double dealers, and is become so good a scholar that he knoweth readily his flats and bars, and hath been snapper with the old cole at two or three deep strokes; yea, and though he have learned to verse, and lay in the reason well favouredly, to make the cousin stoop all the cogs in his buy, yet if he once wax slow in seeking out cousins, and be proud of his new thrift, and so goodly a passage to recover his old losses, the knap of the case, the goodman of the house calleth secretly unto him the third person, for the most part a man that might be warden of his company, and talketh with him after this manner:

"Here is a young man in my house, if ye know him, that hath been one of the sweetest cousins alive, so long as he was able to make a groat. Now at the last, I wot not how he came by it, he hath gotten some know-ledge, and talks a great deal more than he can in deed.   Marry! a langret he knoweth metely well, and that is all his skill.   I made much of him all this month, because he hath great acquaintance of men of the country, and specially the cloth-men of the west parts;[10] and, at the beginning, would every day fill the case with jolly fat cousins.   And, albeit he had no knowledge to work any feat himself, yet did I use him always honestly, and gave him his whole snap, to the end he should be painful and diligent to take the cousins up, and bring them to the blow. Now waxen is he so proud of his gain, because he hath gotten a new chain, fire-new apparel, and some store of bit, that I cannot get him once out of the door to go about anything.   'Take some pains yourself,' saith he, ' and bring some of your own cousins home, or else let all alone for me.' Thus if ye see that nothing mars him, but that he is too fat, and might we make him once lean again, as he was within this month, then should we see the hungry whoreson trudge. There should not be ſtirring a cousin in any quarter but he would wind him ſtraight. Therefore come you in anon, like a ſtranger, and [ye] shall see him take you up roundly. If ye lack contraries, to crossbite him withal, I shall lend you a pair of the same size that his cheats be."

R. Is there no more fidelity among them? Can they not be content, one false knave to be true to his fellow, though they conspire to rob all other men?

M. Nothing less! Did not I warn you in the beginning, that the end of the science is mere deceit? And would ye have themselves, againſt their kind, to work contrary to their profession? Nay, they be ever so like themselves, that, when all other deceits fail, look which of them in play gets any ſtore of money into his hands, he will every foot, as he draweth a hand, be figging more or less, and rather than fail, cram it and hide it in his hose, to make his gain greateſt. Then when they fall to the division of the gain, and the money that the cousin hath loſt is not forthcoming, nor will be confessed among them, it is a world to hear what rule they make, and how the one imbraideth the other with dishoneſty, as if there were some honeſty to be found among them. What should I then speak of swearing and ſtaring, were they always as liberal of alms as they be of oaths! I had rather bring a beggar to have the reward of a cheater, than to the beſt alms-knight's room that the King gives at Windsor. But these ſtorms never fall but in secret councils within themselves, and then peradventure the ſtronger part will ſtrip the weaker out of his clothes rather than he should flock away with the ſtuff and make them louts to labour for his lucre.

R. Then is it but folly to recover my losses in yonder company. And, if there cannot be one faithful couple found in the whole band, how might *I* hope, that am but a ſtranger, to win an unfeigned friend amongſt them?

M. As for in that case, never speak more of the matter, and be as sure as ye are of your creed that all the friendly entertainment ye have at your lodging is for no other end but for to persuade you to play, and bring you to loss. Neither was it any better than falsehood in fellow-ship, when the goodman got you to be half, and seemed unwillingly to lose both your moneys.

R. By these means, either muſt I utterly forbear to hazard anything at the dice, or live in doubt, and suspected of my friend, whensoever I fall to play.

M.   No question thereof !   For the contagion of cheating is now so universal that they swarm in every quarter, and therefore ye cannot be in safety from deceit, unless ye shun the company of hazarders, as a man would fly a scorpion.

R.   Then am I sufficiently lessoned for the purpose.   But, because at the first our talk matched dice and cards together, like a couple of friends that draw both in a yoke, I pray you, is there much craft at cards as ye have rehearsed at the dice ?

M.   Altogether, I would not give a point to choose ; they have such a sleight in sorting and shuffling of the cards, that play at what game ye will, all is lost aforehand.   If two be confederated to beguile the third, the thing is compassed with the more ease than if one be but alone. Yet are there many ways to deceive.   Primero, now, as it hath most use in Court, so is there most deceit in it.   Some play upon the prick[11] ; some pinch the cards privily with their nails ; some turn up the corners ; some mark them with fine spots of ink.   One fine trick brought in a Spaniard ; a finer than this invented an Italian, and won much money with it by our doctors, and yet, at the last, they were both over-reached by new sleights devised here at home.   At trump, sant, and such other like, cutting at the neck is a great vantage, so is cutting by a bum card (finely) under and over, stealing the stock of the decarded cards, if their broad laws be forced aforehand.   At decoy, they draw easily twenty hands together, and play all upon assurance when to win or lose.   Other helps I have heard of besides : as, to set the cousin upon the bench with a great looking-glass behind him on the wall, wherein the cheater might always see what cards were in his hand.[12]   Sometimes they work by signs made by some of the lookers-on.   Wherefore methinks this, among the rest, proceeded of a fine invention : A gamester, after he had been oftentimes bitten among the cheaters, and after much loss, grew very suspicious in his play, that he could not suffer any of the sitters-by to be privy to his game.   For this the cheaters devised a new shift.   A woman should sit sewing beside him, and by the shift, or slow drawing her needle, give a token to the cheater what was the cousin's game. So that, a few examples instead of infinite, that might be rehearsed, this one universal conclusion may be gathered, that, give you to play, and yield yourself to loss.

R.   I feel well that if a man happen to put his money in hazard, the odds is great that he shall rise a loser.   But many men are so continent of their hands, that nothing can cause them to put aught in adventure ; and some, again, be unskilful, that lack of [c]unning forceth them to forbear.

M. I grant you well both. But, nevertheless, I never yet saw man so hard to be vanquished, but they would make him stoop at one law or other.   And for that purpose, their first travail is, after that they have taken up the cousin, and made him somewhat sweat, to seek by all means they can to understand his nature, and whereunto he is inclined. If they find he taketh pleasure in the company of females, then seek they to strike him at the sacking law.   And take this always for a maxim, that all the bawds in a country be of the cheaters' familiar acquaintance. Therefore it shall not be hard, at all times, to provide for this amorous knight a lewd, lecherous lady to keep him loving company.   Then fall they to banqueting, to minstrels, masking ; and much is the cost that the silly cousin shall be at in jewels, apparel, and otherwise.   He shall not once get a grant to have scarcely a lick at this dainty lady's lips ; and ever anon she layeth in this reason : for her sake to put his twenty or forty crowns in adventure.   " Ye wot not," saith she, " what may be a woman's luck."   If he refuse it, Lord ! how unkindly she taketh the matter, and cannot be reconciled with less than a gown, or a kirtle of silk, which commonly is a reward unto her by knap of the case, and the cut-throats, his complices, to whom the matter is put in daying.[13] Yea, and the more is, if haply they perceive that he esteemed not bruised ware, but is enamoured with virginity, they have a fine cast, within an hour's warning, to make Joan[14] Silverpin as good a maid as if she had never come at stews, nor opened to any man her quiver.   The mystery thereof ye shall understand by this my tale, which I myself saw put in experience.

A young roisterly gentleman, desiring a maiden make to content his wanton lust, resorted to a bawd, and promised her good wages to provide him a maid against the next day.   He declared unto her that he took more pleasure in virginity than beauty, but if both came together the pleasure was much the more thankful, and her reward should be the better.   This Mother Bawd undertook to serve his turn according to his desire, and having at home a well-painted, mannerly harlot, as good a maid as Fletcher's mare, that bare three great foals, went in the morning to the apothecary's for half a pint of sweet water, that commonly is called surfling water, or clinker-device, and on the way homeward turned into a nobleman's house to visit his cook, an old acquaintance of hers.   Uneath had she set her feet within the kitchen, and set down her glass, the more handsomely to warm her afore the range, but anon the cook had taken her in his arms, and whiles they wreſtled, more for manner's sake of the light than for any squeamish business, had she been behind the door, down fell the glass and spilt was the water. " Out, alas ! " quoth the woman.—" Quiet yourself," quoth the cook, " let us go into the buttery to breakfaſt, and I will buy you a new glass, and pay for the filling."

Away they went out of the kitchen ; and the boy, that turned a couple of spits, delighting with the savour of the water, let firſt one spit ſtand, and after another, always with one hand taking up the water as it dropped from the board by him, and washed his eyes, his mouth, and all his face withal. Soon after that this liquor was with the heat of the fire dried, and soaked up in the boy's face, down came the cook again into the kitchen, and finding the breaſt of the capon all burnt for lack of turning, caught up a great baſting-ſtick to beat the turnspit. And, haply caſting a sour look upon him, espied the boy's mouth and eyes drawn so together and closed, that neither had he left an eye to look withal, and scarcely might ye turn your little finger in his mouth. The cook, abashed with the sudden change, ran about the house half out of his wit, and cried, " The kitchen-boy is taken. He can neither see nor speak." And so the poor boy, with his ſtarched face, continued more than half an hour a wondering-ſtock to all the house, till a man of experience bade bathe his face with hot fat beef broth, whereby, forthwith, he was reſtored to as wide a mouth, and as open eyes as he had before.

R. A good miracle, and soon wrought. If maids be so easy to make, no marvel it is we have such ſtore in London. But forth, I pray you, with your purpose. When whoredom hath no place, what other shifts have they to raise their thrift upon ?

M. A hundred more than I can rehearse ; but moſt commonly one of these that follow. If it be winter season, when masking is moſt in use, then, missing of their cheaped helps, they spare not for coſt of the dearer. Therefore, firſt do they hire, in one place or other, a suit of right masking apparel, and after, invite divers gueſts to a supper— all such as be then of eſtimation, to give them credit by their acquain- tance, or such as they think will be liberal, to hazard some thing in a mumchance. By which means they assure themselves at the leaſt to have the supper shot-free, perchance, to win twenty pounds, about. And, howsoever the common people eſteem the thing, I am clean out of doubt that the more half of your gay masques in London are grounded upon such cheating crafts, and tend only the pulling and robbing of the King's subjects.

Another jolly shift, and for the subtle invention and fineness of wit exceedeth far all the rest, is the barnard's law,[15] which, to be exactly practised, asketh four persons at the least, each of them to play a long several part by himself.

The first is the taker-up, of a skilful man in all things, who hath by long travail conned, without the book, a hundred reasons to insinuate himself into a man's acquaintance. Talk of matters in law : and he hath plenty of cases at his fingers' ends that he hath seen tried and ruled in every of the King's courts. Speak of grazing and husbandry : no man knoweth more shires than he ; no man knoweth better when to raise a gain, and how the abuses and overture of prices might be redressed.[16] Finally, enter into what discourse of things they list, were it into a broom-man's faculty, he knoweth what gain they have for old boots and shoes, and whence their gain cometh. Yea, and it shall escape him hard, but that ere your talk break off, he will be your countryman at least, and, peradventure, either of kin, or ally, or some sole sib unto you—if your reach surmount not his too far. In case he bring to pass that ye be glad of his acquaintance, and content with his company, played is the chief of his part, and he giveth place to the principal player, the barnard. Nevertheless, he lightly hath in his company a man of more worship than himself, that hath the countenance of a possessioner of land, and he is called the verser ; and though it be a very hard thing to be a perfect taker-up, and as it were, a man universally practised in all accidents of a man's life, yet doth the barnard go so far beyond him in cunning, as doth the sun's summer brightness exceed the glimmering light of the winter stars.

This body's most common practice is to come stumbling into your company like some rich farmer of the country, a stranger to you all, that had been at some market town thereabouts, buying and selling, and there tippled so much malmsey, that he had never a ready word in his mouth, and is so careless for his money that out he throweth an hundred or two of old angels upon the board's end, and, standing somewhat aloof, calleth for a pot of ale, and saith, " Masters, I am somewhat bold with you. I pray you be not aggrieved that I drink my drink by you," and minister such idle drunken talk, that the verser, who counterfeiteth the gentleman, cometh stoutly and sits at your elbow, praying you to call him [the barnard] near to laugh at his folly. Between them two the matter shall be so workmanly conveyed, and so finely argued, that

out cometh a pair of old cards, whereat the barnard teacheth the verser
a new game, that he supposeth cost him two pots of ale for the learning
not past an hour or two before. The first wager is drink, the next
twopence, or a groat, and lastly, to make the tale short, they use the
matter so that he that hath eighty years of his back, and never played
for a groat in his life, cannot refuse to be the verser's half, and consequently, at one cutting of the cards, to lose all they play for, be it an
hundred pound.

And if, perhaps, when the money is lost, the cousin begins to smoke,
and swear that the drunken knave shall not get his money so, then
standeth the rubber at the door, and draweth his sword, and picketh
a quarrel to his own shadow, if he lack an ostler or a tapster or some other
to fall out withal; that, whiles the street and company gather to the
fray, as the manner is, the barnard steals away with all the stuff, and
picks him to one blind tavern or other, such as before is appointed
among them, and there abideth the coming of his companions to make
an equal portion of the gain. And whensoever these shifts may not
take place, then lead they the cousin to the gaze of an interlude, or the
bear-baiting at Paris Garden,[17] or some other place of throng, where,
by [a] fine-fingered fig-boy, a grounded disciple of James Ellis,[18] picked
shall be his purse, and his money lost in a moment. Or else they run
to the last refuge of all, and, by a knot of lusty companions of the high
law, not only shake the harmless body out of all his clothes, but bind
him or bob him to boot, that less had been his harm to have stooped
low at the first, and so to have stopped their greedy mouths, than to
save himself so long, and in the end to be fleeced as bare as a new-born
sheep, and perchance so far from his friends, that he shall be forced to
trip on his ten toes homeward, for lack of a hackney to ride on, and beg
for his charges on the way.

R. Now speak ye indeed of a ready way to thrift, but it hath an
ill-favoured success many times.

M. I wot what you mean. You think they come home by Tyburn
or St. Thomas of Waterings;[19] and so they do indeed, but nothing so
soon as a man would suppose. They be but petty figgers and unlessoned
lads that have such ready passage to the gallows. The old thieves go
through with their vices (?) well twenty or thirty years together, and be
seldom taken or 'tainted, specially that fig bodies that have a goodly
corporation for the relief. Their craft, of all others, requireth most
sleight, and hath marvellous plenty of terms and strange language;
and therefore no man can attain to be a workman thereat, till he have

had a good time of schooling, and by that means do not only know each other well, but they be subject to an order such as the elders shall prescribe. No man so sturdy to practise his feat but in the place appointed, nor for any cause once to put his foot in another's walk! Some two or three hath Paul's Church in charge; other hath Westminster Hall in term-time; divers Cheapside with the flesh and fish shambles; some the Borough and bear-baiting; some the Court; and part follow markets and fairs in the country with pedlars' foot-packs; and generally to all places of assembly. Some of them are certainly 'pointed, as it were, by their wardens to keep the haunt, with commission but a short while, and to interchange their places as order shall be made, to avoid suspicion. By occasion whereof, whensoever any stroke is workmanly stricken, though it were at Newcastle, the rest of the fig-boys that keeps resident in London, can forthwith prognosticate by whom the worthy feat was wrought; and one great provision they have, that is a sovran salve at all times of need; a treasurer they choose in some blind corner, a trusty secret friend; that whensoever there cometh any jewels, plate, or such gear to their share, the present sale whereof might chance to discover the matter, the same is committed into his hands in pledge as it were of money lent, and he taketh a bill of sale in default of repayment, as if all things were done by good faith and plain dealing. So that whensoever he shall seek to make money of his gages, at the end of two or three months, if any question arise how he came by them, he showeth anon a fair bill of sale for his discharge, from John a Knock or John a Stile, a man that never was, never shall be, found. And such theft by this occasion is ever mannerly covered.

Another help they have, that of every purse that is cleanly conveyed, a rateable portion is duly delivered into the treasurer's hands, to the use, that whensoever by some misadventure any of them happen to be taken and laid in prison, this common stock may serve to satisfy the party grieved, and to make friends to save them from hanging.

Now have ye a calendar, as it were, to put you in remembrance of these chief points and practices of cheating; enough, I suppose, to serve for a warning that ye withdraw yourself from yonder costly company, wherein, if my experience may serve to give you occasion to eschew such evils, I shall be glad of this our happy meeting.

R. Yes, doubt ye not thereof but that this talk hath wrought already such effects in me, that, though I live a hundred years, I shall not lightly fall into the cheaters' snares. But because ye spake of the principal points, whereby I conceive that yet some small sparks remain untouched, I pray you put me out of doubt thereof ; and then, on God's name, ye shall gladly depart with as many thanks as if ye had disbursed a large sum of money for redemption of my land, and saved it from selling. For had not forewarning come, the merchant and I muſt within a few days have coped together, as did my bed-fellow but now the laſt week ; whose losses I pity so much the more, as that now I underſtand by what cheatery it was won.

M. The feat of losing is easily learned, and, as I told you in the beginning that the cheaters beat and busy their brains only about fraud and subtlety, so can it not be chosen but give themselves over all to that purpose, and muſt every day forge out one new point of knavery or other to deceive the simple withal. As of late I knew a young gentleman so wary in his doings, that neither by dice or cards, nor by damosels of dalliance, nor of the ways afore rehearsed, could be made ſtoop one penny out of his purse. For this the cheater [who] consulted with the lewd lady, in this case devised that she should dally with the gentle-man and, playing with his chain, should find the mean to keep it awhile, till they might fig a link or two to make a like by. Done it was anon, and within a few days after, another made of copper, equal in length to that. At the ;entleman's next returning to the house, the damosel dallied so long with the chain, sometime putting it about her neck, and sometimes about his, that in the end she foiſted the copper chain in the other's place, and thereby robbed him of better than forty pounds.

This and the like shifts I forbear to remember, sooner because the deceit reſteth not in any slight practice at dice and cards ; nevertheless, because cheaters were the firſt inventors as well of this as of all other falsehood in fellowship, that now daily is put in use at all manner of games : as when one man loſt, not many years ago, an hundred pound land at shooting, by occasion that some that shot with him on his side were booty fellows againſt him ; another was rid of his six hundred pounds at tennis in a week by the fraud of his ſtopper. Methink they cannot be better rewarded than sent home to the place they come from.

And, since cheaters were the firſt authors thereof, let them also bear the blame. And, having disclosed unto you, as briefly as I can, the principal practice of the cheaters' crafty faculty, and other workmen of their alliance, I will bid you farewell for this time.

THE

Fraternity of Vagabonds.

As well of ruffling vagabonds as of beggarly, of women
as of men, of girls as of boys,

with

their proper names and qualities.

With a description of the crafty company of

Cozeners and Shifters.

[Whereunto also is adjoined

the Twenty=five Orders of Knaves,

otherwise called

a Quartern of Knaves.

Confirmed for ever by Cock Lorel.]

[by John Awdeley]

[1561]

The Upright-man speaketh :

Our brotherhood of vagabonds,
  If you would know where dwell.
In Gravesend barge which seldom stands,
  The talk will show right well.

Cock Lorel[1] answereth :

Some orders of my knaves also
  In that barge shall ye find :
For nowhere shall ye walk, I trow,
  But ye shall see their kind.

The Printer to the Reader.

This brotherhood of vagabonds,
To show that there be such indeed,
Both juſtices and men of lands,
Will teſtify it if it need.
   For at a Sessions as they sat,
   By chance a vagabond was got.

Who promised if they would him spare,
And keep his name from knowledge then,
He would as ſtrange a thing declare,
As ever they knew since they were men.
   " But if my fellows do know," said he,
   " That thus I did, they would kill me."

They granting him this his requeſt,
He did declare as here is read,
Both names and ſtates of moſt and leaſt,
Of this their vagabonds' brotherhood.
   Which at the requeſt of a worshipful man
   I have set it forth as well as I can.

Finis.

The

Fraternity of Vagabonds

both ruffling and beggarly,

Men and Women, Boys and Girls,

with

their proper names and qualities.

Whereunto are adjoined

the Company of Cozeners and Shifters.

An Abram-man.[2]

AN abram-man is he that walketh bare-armed, and bare-legged, and feigneth himself mad, and carryeth a pack of wool, or a stick with bacon on it, or suchlike toy, and nameth himself Poor Tom.

A Ruffler.

A ruffler goeth with a weapon to seek service, saying he hath been a servitor in the wars, and beggeth for his relief. But his chiefest trade is to rob poor wayfaring men and market women.

A Prigman.

A prigman goeth with a stick in his hand like an idle person. His property is to steal clothes of the hedge, which they call storing of the rogueman; or else filch poultry, carrying them to the ale-house, which they call the bousing inn, and there sit playing at cards and dice, till that is spent which they have so filched.

A Whip-jack.

A whip-jack is one, that by colour of a counterfeit licence (which they call a gybe, and the seals they call jarks) doth use to beg like a mariner; but his chiefest trade is to rob booths in a fair, or to pilfer ware from stalls, which they call heaving of the booth.

A Frater.

A frater goeth with a like licence to beg for some spital-house or hospital. Their prey is commonly upon poor women as they go and come to the markets.

A Queer-bird.

A queer-bird is one that came lately out of prison and goeth to seek service. He is commonly a stealer of horses, which they term a prigger of palfreys.

An Upright-man.

An upright-man is one that goeth with the truncheon of a staff, which staff they call a filchman. This man is of so much authority that, meeting with any of his profession, he may call them to account, and command a share or snap unto himself of all that they have gained by their trade in one month. And if he do them wrong, they have no remedy against him, no, though he beat them, as he useth commonly to do. He may also command any of their women, which they call doxies, to serve his turn. He hath the chief place at any market walk and other assemblies, and is not of any to be controlled.

A Curtal.

A curtal is much like to the upright-man, but his authority is not fully so great. He useth commonly to go with a short cloak, like to grey friars, and his woman with him in like livery, which he calleth his altham, if she be his wife, and if she be his harlot, she is called his doxy.

A Palliard.

A palliard is he that goeth in a patched cloak ; and his doxy goeth in like apparel.

An Irish Toyle.

An Irish toyle is he that carrieth his ware in his wallet, as laces, pins, points and suchlike. He useth to show no wares until he have his alms ; and if the goodman and wife be not in the way, he procureth of the children or servants a fleece of wool, or the worth of twelve pence of some other thing, for a pennyworth of his wares.

A Jarkman.[3]

A jarkman is he that can write and read, and sometime speak Latin. He useth to make counterfeit licences which they call gybes, and sets to seals, in their language called jarks.

A Swigman.

A swigman goeth with a pedlar's pack.

A Washman.

A washman is called a palliard, but not of the right making. He useth to lie in the highway with lame or sore legs or arms to beg. These men the right palliards will oftentimes spoil, but they dare not complain. They be bitten with spickworts and sometime with ratsbane.

A Tinkard.

A tinkard leaveth his bag a sweating at the ale-house, which they term their bousing inn, and in the mean season goeth abroad a begging.

A Wild Rogue.

A Wild Rogue is he that hath no abiding place, but by his colour of going abroad to beg is commonly to seek some kinsman of his, and all that be of his corporation be properly called rogues.

A Kitchin Co.

A kitchin co is called an idle runagate boy.

A Kitchin Morts.

A kitchin morts is a girl ; she is brought at her full age to the upright-man to be broken, and so she is called a doxy, until she come to the honour of an altham.

Doxies.

Note especially all which go abroad working laces and shirt-strings. They name them doxies.

A Patriarch Co.[4]

A patriarch co doth make marriages, and that is until death depart the married folk, which is after this sort : when they come to a dead horse or any dead cattle, then they shake hands and so depart, every one of them a several way.

The Company of Cozeners and Shifters.

A Courtesy-man.

A courtesy-man is one that walketh about the back lanes in London in the day-time, and sometime in the broad streets in the night-season, and when he meeteth some handsome young man cleanly apparelled, or some other honest citizen, he maketh humble salutations and low courtesy, and showeth him that he hath a word or two to speak with his mastership. This child can behave himself mannerly, for he will desire him that he talketh withal to take the upper hand, and show him much reverence, and at last like his familiar acquaintance will put on his cap, and walk side by side, and talk on this fashion :

" Oh, sir, you seem to be a man, and one that favoureth men, and therefore I am the more bolder to break my mind unto your good mastership. Thus it is, sir, there is a certain of us (though I say it, both tall and handsome men of their hands) which have come lately from the wars, and, as God knoweth, have nothing to take to, being both masterless and moneyless, and knowing no way whereby to earn one penny. And further, whereas we have been wealthily brought up, and we also have been had in good estimation, we are ashamed now to declare our misery, and to fall a craving as common beggars, and as for to steal and rob, God is our record, it striketh us to the heart to think of such a mischief, that ever any handsome man should fall into such a danger for this worldly trash. Which if we had to suffice our want and necessity, we should never seek thus shamefastly to crave on such good pitiful men as you seem to be, neither yet so dangerously to hazard our lives for so vile a thing. Therefore, good sir, as you seem to be a handsome man yourself, and also such a one as pitieth the miserable case of handsome men, as now your eyes and countenance showeth to have some pity upon this my miserable complaint ; so in God's cause I require your mastership, and in the behalf of my poor afflicted fellows, which, though here in sight, they cry not with me to you, yet, wheresoever they be, I am sure they cry unto God to move the hearts of some good men to show forth their liberality in this behalf. All which, and I with them, crave now the same request at your good mastership's hand."

With these or suchlike words he frameth his talk. Now if the party, which he thus talketh withal, proffereth him a penny or twopence, he taketh it, but very scornfully, and at last speaketh on this sort :

" Well sir, your good will is not to be refused. But yet you shall understand, good sir, that this is nothing for them, for whom I do thus shamefastly entreat. Alas sir, it is not a groat or twelve pence I speak for, being such a company of servitors as we have been : yet nevertheless, God forbid I should not receive your gentle offer at this time, hoping hereafter through your good motions to some such like good gentleman as you be, that I, or some of my fellows in my place, shall find the more liberality."

These kind of idle vagabonds will go commonly well apparelled without any weapon, and in place where they meet together, as at their hostelries or other places, they will bear the port of right good gentlemen, and some are the more trusted, but commonly they pay them with stealing a pair of sheets or coverlet, and so take their farewell early in the morning, before the master or dame be stirring.

A Cheater or Fingerer.

These commonly be such kind of idle vagabonds as scarcely a man shall discern, they go so gorgeously, sometime with waiting men and sometime without. Their trade is to walk in such places whereas gentlemen and other worshipful citizens do resort, as at Paul's,[5] or at Christ's Hospital,[6] and sometime at the Royal Exchange.[7] These have very many acquaintances, yea, and for the most part will acquaint themselves with every man and feign a society in one place or other. But chiefly they will seek their acquaintance of such (which they have learned by diligent enquiring where they resort) as have received some portion of money of their friends, as young gentlemen which are sent to London to study the laws, or else some young merchantman or other kind of occupier, whose friends hath given them a stock of money to occupy withal. When they have thus found out such a prey, they will find the means by their familiarity as very courteously to bid him to breakfast at one place or other, where they are best acquainted, and closely among themselves will appoint one of their fraternity, which they call a fingerer, an old beaten child, not only in such deceits, but also such a one as by his age is painted out with grey hairs, wrinkled face, crooked back, and most commonly lame, as it might seem, with age ; yea, and such a one as to show a simplicity shall wear a homely cloak and hat scarce worth sixpence. This nimble-fingered knight, being appointed to this place, cometh in as one not known of these cheaters, but as unawares shall sit down at the end of the board where they sit, and call for his penny pot of wine, or a pint of ale, as the place serveth.   Thus, sitting as it were alone, mumbling on a crust or some such thing, these other younkers will find some kind of merry talk with him, sometimes questioning where he dwelleth, and sometimes enquiring what trade he useth, which commonly he telleth them he useth husbandry. And talking thus merrily, at last they ask him, " How sayest thou, father, wilt thou play for thy breakfast with one of us, that we may have some pastime as we sit ? "

This old carl, making it strange at the first, saith : " My masters, Ich am an old man and half blind, and can skill of very few games, yet for that you seem to be such good gentlemen as to proffer to play for that of which you had no part, but only I myself, and therefore of right Ich am worthy to pay for it, I shall with all my heart fulfil your request " : and so falleth to play, sometime at cards, and sometime at dice ; which, through his counterfeit simplicity in the play, sometimes overcounteth himself, or playeth sometimes against his will, so as he would not, and then counterfeiteth to be angry, and falleth to swearing, and so, losing that, proffereth to play for a shilling or two.   The other thereat having good sport, seeming to mock him, falleth again to play, and so by their legerdemain and counterfeiting winneth each of them a shilling or twain, and at last whispereth the young man in the ear to play with him also, that each one might have a fling at him.

This young man, for company, falleth again to play also with the said fingerer, and winneth as the other did ; which, when he had lost a noble or six shillings, maketh as though he had lost all his money, and falleth a entreating for part thereof again to bring him home, which the other knowing his mind and intent, stoutly denyeth, and jesteth and scoffeth at him.   This fingerer, seeming then to be in a rage, desireth them, as they are true gentlemen, to tarry till he fetcheth more store of money, or else to point some place where they may meet.   They, seeming greedy hereof, promiseth faithfully and clappeth hands so to meet.   They, thus tickling the young man in the ear, willeth him to make as much money as he can, and they will make as much as they can, and consent as though they will play booty against him.   But in the end they so use the matter, that both the young man loseth his part, and, as it seemeth to him, they losing theirs also, and so maketh as though they would fall together by the ears with this fingerer, which by one wile or other at last conveyeth himself away, and they, as it were raging like mad bedlams, one runneth one way, another another way, leaving the loser indeed all alone.   Thus these cheaters at their accustomed hostelries meet closely together, and there receive each one his part of this their vile spoil.

Of this fraternity there be that be called helpers, which commonly haunt taverns or ale-houses, and cometh in as men not acquainted with none in the company, but spying them at any game will bid them God-speed and God-be-at-their-game, and will so place himself that he will show his fellow by signs and tokens, without speech commonly, but sometime with far-fetched words, what cards he hath in his hand, and how he may play against him. And those between them both getteth money out of the other's purse.

A Ring-faller.

A ring-faller is he that getteth fair copper rings, some made like signets and some after other fashions, very fair gilded, and walketh up and down the streets, till he spyeth some man of the country, or some other simple body whom he thinketh he may deceive, and so goeth a little before him or them, and letteth fall one of these rings, which, when the party that cometh after spyeth and taketh it up, he having an eye backward, cryeth, "Half part!" The party that taketh it up, thinking it to be of great value, profferth him some money for his part, which he not fully denyeth, but willeth him to come into some ale-house or tavern, and there they will commune upon the matter. Which, when they come in and are set in some solitary place (as commonly they call for such a place), there he desireth the party that found the ring to show it him. When he seeth it, he falleth a entreating the party that found it, and desireth him to take money for his part, and telleth him that if ever he may do him any friendship hereafter he shall command him, for he maketh as though he were very desirous to have it. The simple man, seeing him so importune upon it, thinketh the ring to be of great value, and so is the more loather to part from it. At last this ring-faller asketh him what he will give him for his part, "For," saith he, "seeing you will not let me have the ring, allow me my part, and take you the ring." The other asketh what he counteth the ring to be worth, he answereth, "Five or six pound."—"No," saith he, "it is not so much worth."—"Well," saith this ring-faller, "let me have it, and I will allow you forty shillings for your part." The other party, standing in a doubt and looking on the ring, asketh if he will give the money out of hand. The other answereth, he hath not so much ready money about him, but he will go fetch so much for him, if he will go with him.　　The other, that found the ring, thinking he meaneth truly, beginneth to proffer him twenty shillings for his part, sometimes more or less, which he very scornfully refuseth at the first, and still entreateth that he might have the ring, which maketh the other more fonder of it, and desireth him to take the money for his part, and so proffereth him money.　　This ring-faller seeing the money, maketh it very strange, and first questioneth with him where he dwelleth, and asketh him what is his name, and telleth him that he seemeth to be an honest man, and therefore he will do somewhat for friendship's sake, hoping to have as friendly a pleasure at his hand hereafter, and so proffereth him for twenty shillings more he should have the ring.　　At last, with entreaty on both parts, he giveth the ring-faller the money and so departeth, thinking he hath gotten a very great jewel.

These kind of deceiving vagabonds have other practices with their rings, as sometimes to come to buy wares of men's 'prentices, and sometimes of the masters, and when he hath agreed of the price, he saith he hath not so much money about him, but pulleth of one of these rings off from his fingers, and proffereth to leave it in pawn till his master or his friends hath seen it, so promising to bring the money.　　The seller, thinking he meaneth truly, letteth him go, and never seeth him after, till perhaps at Tyburn or suchlike place.

There is another kind of these ring-choppers, which commonly carry about them a fair gold ring indeed, and these have other counterfeit rings made so like this gold ring, as ye shall not perceive the contrary, till it be brought to the touchstone.　　This child will come to borrow money of the right gold ring.　　The party mistrusting the ring not to be good, goeth to the goldsmith with the party that hath the ring and tryeth it whether it be good gold, and also weigheth it to know how much it is worth.　　The goldsmith tryeth it to be good gold, and also to have his full weight like gold, and warrenteth the party which shall lend the money that the ring is worth so much money, according to the weight. This younker, coming home with the party which shall lend the money, and having the gold ring again, putteth up the gold ring, and pulleth out a counterfeit ring very like the same, and so delivereth it to the party which lendeth the money, they thinking it to be the same which they tried, and so delivereth the money or sometimes wares, and thus vilely be deceived.[8]

A CAVEAT OR WARNING FOR COMMON CURSITORS, VULGARLY CALLED VAGABONDS,

SET FORTH BY THOMAS HARMAN, ESQUIRE, FOR THE UTILITY AND PROFIT
OF HIS NATURAL COUNTRY.

[1566]

To the Right Honourable and my singular good lady, Elizabeth, Countess of Shrewsbury,[1] Thomas Harman wisheth all joy and perfect felicity, here and in the world to come.

AS of ancient and long time there hath been, and is now at this present, many good, godly, profitable laws and acts made and set forth in this most noble and flourishing realm for the relief, succour, comfort and sustentation of the poor, needy, impotent and miserable creatures being and inhabiting in all parts of the same ; so is there, Right Honourable and mine especial good lady, most wholesome statutes, ordinances, and necessary laws, made, set forth and published, for the extreme punishment of all vagrants and sturdy vagabonds, as passeth through and by all parts of this famous isle, most idly and wickedly ; and I well by good experience, understanding and considering your most tender, pitiful, gentle, and noble nature, not only having a vigilant and merciful eye to your poor, indigent, and feeble parishioners ; yea, not only in the parish where your honour most happily doth dwell, but also in others environing or nigh adjoining to the same ; as also abundantly pouring out daily your ardent and bountiful charity upon all such as cometh for relief unto your luckly gates ; I thought it good, necessary, and my bounden duty, to acquaint your goodness with the abominable, wicked, and detestable behaviour of all these rowsey, ragged rabblement of rakehells, that—under the pretence of great misery, diseases, and other innumerable calamities which they feign—through great hypocrisy do win and gain great alms in all places where they wilily wander, to the utter deluding of the good givers, deceiving and impoverishing of all such poor householders, both sick and sore, as neither can or may walk abroad for relief and comfort (where, indeed, most mercy is to be showed). And for that I, most honourable lady, being placed as a poor gentleman, have kept a house these twenty years, whereunto poverty daily hath and doth repair, not without some relief, as my poor calling and hability may and doth extend, I have of late years gathered a great suspicion that all should not be well, and, as the proverb saith : " Something lurk and lay hid that did not plainly appear." For I, having more occasion, through sickness, to tarry and remain at home than I have been accustomed, do, by my there abiding, talk and confer daily with many of these wily wanderers of both sorts, as well men and women, as boys and girls, by whom I have gathered and understand their deep dissimulation and detestable dealing, being marvellous subtle and crafty in their kind, for not one amongst twenty will discover, either declare their scelerous secrets. Yet with fair flattering words, money, and good cheer, I have attained to the type by such as the meanest of them hath wandered these thirteen years, and most sixteen and some twenty and upward, and not without faithful promise made unto them never to discover their names or anything they showed me. For they would all say, if the upright-men should understand thereof, they should not be only grievously beaten, but put in danger of their lives, by the said upright-men.

There was a few years since a small brief² set forth of some zealous man to his country, of whom I know not, that made a little show of their names and usage, and gave a glimpsing light, not sufficient to persuade of their peevish, pelting, and picking practices, but well worthy of praise. But, good madam, with no less travail than good will, I have repaired and rigged the ship of knowledge, and have hoist up the sails of good fortune, that she may safely pass about and through all parts of this noble realm, and there make port sale of her wished wares, to the confusion of their drowsy demeanour and unlawful language, pilfering picking, wily wandering, and liking lechery of all these rabblement of rascals that ranges about all the coasts of the same, so that their undecent, doleful dealing and execrable exercises may appear to all, as it were in a glass, that thereby the Justices and shrieves may in their circuits be more vigilant to punish these malefactors, and the constables, bailiffs and borsholders, setting aside all fear, sloth, and pity, may be more circumspect in executing the charge given them by the aforesaid Justices. Then will no more this rascal rabblement range about the country ; then greater relief may be showed to the poverty of each parish ; then shall we keep our horses in our pastures unstolen ; then our linen clothes shall and may lie safely on our hedges untouched ; then shall we not have our clothes and linen hooked out at our windows as well by day as by night ; then shall we not have our houses broken up in the night, as of late one of my neighbours had, and two great bucks of clothes stolen out, and most of the same fine linen ; then shall we safely keep our pigs and poultry from pilfering ; then shall we surely pass by the highways leading to markets and fairs unharmed ; then shall our shops and booths be unpicked and spoiled ; then shall these uncomely companies be dispersed and set to labour for their living, or hastily hang for their demerits ; then shall it encourage a great number of gentlemen and others, seeing this security, to set up houses and keep hospitality in the country, to the comfort of their neighbours, relief of the poor, and to the amendment of the commonwealth ; then shall not sin and wickedness so much abound among us ; then will God's wrath be much the more pacified towards us ; then shall we not taste of so many and sundry plagues, as now daily reigneth over us ; and then shall this famous empire be in more wealth and better flourish, to the inestimable joy and comfort of the Queen's most excellent Majesty, whom God of His infinite goodness, to His great glory, long and many years make most prosperously to reign over us, to the great felicity of all the peers and nobles, and to the unspeakable joy, relief, and quietness of mind of all her faithful commons and subjects.

Now, methinketh, I see how these peevish, perverse, and pestilent people begin to fret, fume, swear, and stare at this my book, their life being laid open and apparently painted out, that their confusion and end draweth on apace. Whereas indeed, if it be well weighed, it is set forth for their singular profit and commodity, for the sure safeguard of their lives here in this world, that they shorten not the same before their time, and that by their true labour and good life, in the world to come they may save their souls, that Christ, the second Person in [the] Trinity, hath so dearly bought with His most precious blood. So that hereby I shall do them more good than they could have devised for themselves. For behold, their life being so manifest wicked and so apparently known, the honourable will abhor them, the worshipful will reject them, the yeomen will sharply taunt them, the husbandmen utterly defy them, the labouring men bluntly chide them, the women with a loud exclamation wonder at them, and all children with clapping hands cry out at them.

I many times musing with myself at these mischievous mislivers, marvelled when they took their original and beginning ; how long they have exercised their execrable wandering about. I thought it meet to confer with a very old man that I was well acquainted with, whose wit and memory is marvellous for his years, being about the age of fourscore, what he knew when he was young of these lousy loiterers. And he showed me, that when he was young he waited upon a man of much worship in Kent, who died immediately after the laſt Duke of Buckingham was beheaded.[3] At his burial[4] there was such a number of beggars, besides poor householders dwelling thereabouts, that uneath they might lie or ſtand about the house. Then was there prepared for them a great and a large barn, and a great fat ox sod out in frumenty for them, with bread and drink abundantly to furnish out the premises ; and every person had twopence, for such was the dole. When night approached, the poor householders repaired home to their houses : the other wayfaring bold beggars remained all night in the barn ; and the same barn being searched with light in the night by this old man (and then young), with others, they told seven score persons of men, every of them having his woman, except it were two women that lay alone together for some especial cause. Thus having their makes to make merry withal, the burial was turned to bousing and belly-cheer, mourning to mirth, faſting to feaſting, prayer to paſtime and pressing of paps, and lamenting to lechery.

So that it may appear this uncomely company hath had a long continuance, but then nothing given so much to pilfering, picking, and spoiling ; and, as far as I can learn or underſtand by the examination of a number of them, their language—which they term pedlars' French or canting—began but within these thirty years, little above ; and that the firſt inventor thereof was hanged, all save the head ; for that is the final end of them all, or else to die of some filthy and horrible diseases. But much harm is done in the mean space by their continuance, as some ten, twelve and sixteen years [are gone] before they be consumed, and the number of them doth daily renew. I hope their sin is now at the higheſt ; and that as short and as speedy a redress will be for these, as hath been of late years for the wretched, wily, wandering vagabonds calling and naming themselves Egyptians,[5] deeply dissembling and long hiding and covering their deep, deceitful praĉtices, feeding the rude common people, wholly addiĉted and given to novelties, toys, and new inventions ; delighting them with the ſtrangeness of the attire of their heads, and praĉtising palmiſtry to such as would know their fortunes ; and, to be short, all thieves and whores, as I may well write, as some have had true experience, a number can well witness, and a great sort hath well felt it. And now, thanks be to God, through wholesome laws, and the due execution thereof, all be dispersed, banished, and the memory of them clean extinguished ; that when they be once named hereafter, our children will much marvel what kind of people they were. And so, I trust, shall shortly happen of these. For what thing doth chiefly cause these rowsey rakehells thus to continue and daily increase ? Surely a number of wicked persons that keep tippling houses in all shires where they have succour and relief ; and whatsoever they bring, they are sure to receive money for the same, for they sell good pennyworths. The buyers have the greatest gain. Yea, if they have neither money nor ware, they will be trusted ; their credit is much. I have taken a note of a good many of them, and will send their names and dwelling-places to such Justices as dwelleth near or next unto them, that they by their good wisdoms may displace the same, and authorise such as have honesty. I will not blot my book with their names, because they be resident. But as for this fleeting fellowship, I have truly set forth the most part of them that be doers at this present, with their names that they be known by.[6] Also, I have placed in the end thereof their lewd language, calling the same pedlars' French or canting.[7] And now shall I end my prologue, making true declaration, Right Honourable Lady, as they shall fall in order of their untimely trifling time, lewd life, and pernicious practices, trusting that the same shall neither trouble or abash your most tender, timorous, and pitiful nature, to think the small meed should grow unto you for such alms so given. For God, our merciful and most loving Father, well knoweth your hearts and good intent. The giver never wanteth his reward, according to the saying of St. Augustine : " As there is, neither shall be, any sin unpunished, even so shall there not be any good deed unrewarded." But how comfortably speaketh Christ our Saviour unto us in His Gospel : " Give ye, and it shall be given you again." Behold farther, good madam, that for a cup of cold water Christ hath promised a good reward. Now St. Austin properly declareth why Christ speaketh of cold water, because the poorest man that is shall not excuse himself from that charitable work, lest he would, peradventure, say that he hath neither wood, pot, nor pan to warm any water with. See farther what God speaketh in the mouth of His prophet Isaiah : " Break thy bread to him that is a hungered." He saith not give him a whole loaf, for peradventure the poor man hath it not to give : then let him give a piece. This much is said, because the poor that hath it should not be excused : now how much more then the rich ? Thus you see, good madam, for your treasure here dispersed, where need and lack is, it shall be heaped up abundantly for you in Heaven, where neither rust or moth shall corrupt

E

or destroy the same. Unto which triumphant place, after many good, happy, and fortunate years prosperously here dispended, you may for ever and ever there most joyfully remain. Amen.

Finis.

THE EPISTLE TO THE READER

Although, good reader, I write in plain terms—and not so plainly as truly—concerning the matter, meaning honestly to all men, and wish them as much good as to mine own heart, yet, as there hath been, so there is now, and hereafter will be, curious heads to find faults. Wherefore I thought it necessary, now at this second impression, to acquaint thee with a great fault, as some taketh it,[8] but none as I mean it, calling these vagabonds *cursitors* in the entitling of my book, as runners or rangers about the country, derived of this Latin word, *curro*. Neither do I write it *cooresetores*, with a double *oo*, or *cowresetors*, with a *w*, which hath another signification. Is there no diversity between a *gardein* and a *garden*, *maynteynaunce* and *maintenance*, *streytes* and *stretes*? Those that have understanding know there is a great difference. Who is so ignorant by these days as knoweth not the meaning of a *vagabond*? And if an idle loiterer should be so called of any man, would not he think it both odious and reproachful? Will he not shun the name? Yea, and whereas he may and dare, with bent brows will revenge that name of ignominy. Yet this plain name *vagabond* is derived, as others be, of Latin words, and now use makes it common to all men. But let us look back four hundred years sithence, and let us see whether this plain word *vagabond* was used or no.[9] I believe not : and why? Because I read of no such name in the old statutes of this realm, unless it be in the margent of the book, or in the Table, which in the collection and printing was set in. But these were then the common names of these lewd loiterers: *faitours*, *Roberdsmen*, *draw-latches*, and *valiant beggars*. If I should have used such words, or the same order of writing as this realm used in King Henry the Third or Edward the First's time— Oh, what a gross barbarous fellow have we here ! His writing is both homely and dark, that we had need to have an interpreter. Yet then it was very well, and in short season a great change we see. Well, this delicate age shall have his time on the other side. Eloquence have I none ; I never was acquainted with the Muses ; I never tasted of Helicon.

But according to my plain order, I have set forth this work, simply and truly, with such usual words and terms as is among us well known and frequented. So that, as the proverb saith, " Although truth be blamed, it shall never be shamed." Well, good reader, I mean not to be tedious unto thee, but have added five or six more tales, because some of them were done while my book was first in the press. And, as I trust I have deserved no rebuke for my good will, even so I desire no praise for my pain, cost, and travail. But faithfully for the profit and benefit of my country I have done it, that the whole body of the realm may see and understand their lewd life and pernicious practices, that all may speedily help to amend that is amiss. Amen say all with me.

Finis.

Chapter I

A Ruffler

The ruffler, because he is first in degree of this odious order, and is so called in a statute[10] made for the punishment of vagabonds in the twenty-seventh year of King Henry the Eighth, late of most famous memory, he shall be first placed, as the worthiest of this unruly rabblement. And he is so called when he goeth first abroad. Either he hath served in the wars, or else he hath been a serving-man ; and, weary of well-doing, shaking off all pain, doth choose him this idle life, and wretchedly wanders about the most shires of this realm. And with stout audacity demandeth where he thinketh he may be bold, and circumspect enough as he seeth cause to ask charity, ruefully and lamentably, that it would make a flinty heart to relent, and pity his miserable estate, how he hath been maimed and bruised in the wars ; and, peradventure, some will show you some outward wound, which he got at some drunken fray, either halting of some privy wound festered with a filthy fiery flankard. For be well assured that the hardiest soldiers be either slain or maimed, either and they escape all hazards, and return home again. If they be without relief of their friends, they will surely desperately rob and steal, and either shortly be hanged or miserably die in prison. For they be so much ashamed and disdain to beg or ask charity, that rather they will as desperately fight for to live and maintain themselves, as manfully and valiantly they ventured themselves in the Prince's quarrel.   Now these rufflers, the outcasts of serving-men, when begging or craving fails, then they pick and pilfer from other inferior beggars that they meet by the way, as rogues, palliards, morts, and doxies.   Yea, if they meet with a woman alone riding to the market, either old man or boy, that he well knoweth will not resist, such they filch and spoil.   These rufflers, after a year or two at the farthest, become upright-men, unless they be prevented by twined hemp.

I had of late years an old man to my tenant, who customably a great time went twice in the week to London, either with fruit or with pease-cods, when time served therefore.   And as he was coming homeward on Blackheath, at the end thereof next to Shooters Hill, he overtook two rufflers, the one mannerly waiting on the other, as one had been the master, and the other the man or servant, carrying his master's cloak.   This old man was very glad that he might have their company over the hill, because that day he had made a good market ; for he had seven shillings in his purse, and an old angel, which this poor man had thought had not been in his purse, for he willed his wife overnight to take out the same angel, and lay it up until his coming home again; and he verily thought that his wife had so done, which indeed forgot to do it.   Thus, after salutations had, this master ruffler entered into communication with this simple old man, who, riding softly beside them, commoned of many matters.   Thus feeding this old man with pleasant talk, until they were on the top of the hill, where these rufflers might well behold the coast about them clear, quickly steps unto this poor man, and taketh hold of his horse bridle, and leadeth him into the wood, and demandeth of him what and how much money he had in his purse.

" Now, by my troth," quoth this old man, " you are a merry gentle-man.   I know you mean not to take away anything from me, but rather to give me some if I should ask it of you."

By and by this servant thief casteth the cloak that he carried on his arm about this poor man's face, that he should not mark or view them, with sharp words to deliver quickly that he had, and to confess truly what was in his purse.   This poor man, then all abashed, yielded, and confessed that he had but just seven shillings in his purse.   And the truth is he knew of no more.   This old angel was fallen out of a little purse into the bottom of a great purse.   Now, this seven shillings in white money they quickly found, thinking indeed that there had been no more ; yet farther groping and searching, found this old angel. And with great admiration, this gentleman thief began to bless him,

saying, " Good Lord, what a world is this ! How may," quoth he,
" a man believe or trust in the same ? See you not," quoth he. " This
old knave told me that he had but seven shillings, and here is more by
an angel. What an old knave and a false knave have we here ! " quoth
this ruffler. " Our Lord have mercy on us ! Will this world never be
better ? "—and therewith went their way, and left the old man in the
wood, doing him no more harm. But sorrowfully sighing this old man,
returning home, declared his misadventure, with all the words and
circumstances above showed. Whereat for the time was great laughing,
and this poor man for his losses among his loving neighbours well
considered in the end.

CHAPTER II

A UPRIGHT-MAN

A upright-man, the second in sect of this unseemly sort, must be next
placed. Of these ranging rabblement of rascals, some be serving-men,
artificers, and labouring men traded up in husbandry. These, not
minding to get their living with the sweat of their face, but casting of
all pain, will wander, after their wicked manner, through the most
shires of this realm :—as Somersetshire, Wiltshire, Berkshire, Oxfordshire, Hertfordshire, Middlesex, Essex, Suffolk, Norfolk, Sussex, Surrey
and Kent, as the chief and best shires of relief. Yea, not without punishment by stocks, whippings, and imprisonment, in most of these places
abovesaid. Yet, notwithstanding they have so good liking in their
lewd, lecherous loiterings, that full quickly all their punishments is
forgotten. And repentance is never thought upon until they climb
three trees with a ladder.

These unruly rascals, in their roiling, disperse themselves into
several companies, as occasion serveth, sometime more and sometime
less. As, if they repair to a poor husbandman's house, he will go alone,
or one with him, and stoutly demand his charity, either showing how
he hath served in the wars, and there maimed, either that he seeketh
service, and sayeth that he would be glad to take pain for his living,
although he meaneth nothing less. If he be offered any meat or drink,
he utterly refuseth scornfully, and will nought but money ; and if he
espy young pigs or poultry, he well noteth the place, and then the next
night, or shortly after, he will be sure to have some of them, which

they bring to their stalling kens, which is their tippling houses, as well known to them, according to the old proverb, as the beggar knows his dish. For, you must understand, every tippling ale-house will neither receive them or their wares, but some certain houses in every shire, especially for that purpose, where they shall be better welcome to them than honester men. For by such have they most gain, and shall be conveyed either into some loft out of the way, or other secret corner not common to any other. And thither repair at accustomed times their harlots, which they term morts and doxies,—not with empty hands. For they be as skilful in picking, rifling, and filching as the upright-men, and nothing inferior to them in all kind of wickedness, as in other places hereafter they shall be touched. At these foresaid pelting, peevish places and unmannerly meetings, oh, how the pots walk about! Their talking tongues talk at large. They boll and bouse one to another, and for the time bousing belly-cheer. And after their roisting recreation, if there be not room enough in the house, they have clean straw in some barn or backhouse near adjoining, where they couch comely together, and it were dog and bitch. And he that is hardest may have his choice, unless for a little good manner. Some will take their own that they have made promise unto, until they be out of sight, and then, according to the old adage, out of mind.

Yet these upright-men stand so much upon their reputation, as they will in no case have their women walk with them, but separate themselves for a time, a month or more, and meet at fairs, or great markets, where they meet to pilfer and steal from stalls, shops, or booths. At these fairs the upright-men use commonly to lie and linger in highways, by-lanes, some pretty way or distance from the place, by which ways they be assured that company passeth still to and fro. And there they will demand, with cap in hand and comely courtesy, the devotion and charity of the people. They have been much lately whipped at fairs. If they ask at a stout yeoman's or farmer's house his charity, they will go strong as three or four in a company; where, for fear more than good will, they often have relief. They seldom or never pass by a Justice's house, but have by-ways, unless he dwell alone, and but weakly manned. Thither will they also go strong, after a sly, subtle sort, as with their arms bound up with kercher or list, having wrapped about the same filthy cloths, either their legs in such manner be wrapped, halting downright; not unprovided of good cudgels, which they carry to sustain them, and, as they feign, to keep dogs from them, when they come to such good gentlemen's houses.

If any search be made, or they suspected for pilfering clothes off hedges, or breaking of houses, which they commonly do when the owners be either at the market, church, or other ways occupied about their business,—either rob some silly man or woman by the highway, as many times they do,—then they hie them into woods, great thickets, and other rough corners, where they lie lurking three or four days together, and have meat and drink brought them by their morts and doxies. And while they thus lie hidden in covert, in the night they be not idle, neither, as the common saying is, well occupied. For then, as the wily fox, creeping out of his den, seeketh his prey for poultry, so do these for linen and anything else worth money that lieth about or near a house, as sometimes a whole buck of clothes, carried away at a time. When they have a greater booty than they may carry away quickly to their stalling kens, as is abovesaid, they will hide the same for a three days in some thick covert, and in the night time carry the same, like good water-spaniels, to their foresaid houses. To whom they will discover where or in what places they had the same, where the marks shall be picked out clean, and conveyed craftily far off to sell. If the man or woman of the house want money themselves ; if these upright-men have neither money nor wares, at these houses they shall be trusted for their victuals, and it amount to twenty or thirty shillings. Yea, if it fortune any of these upright-men to be taken, either suspected, or charged with felony or petty bribery, done at such a time or such a place, he will say he was in his host's house. And if the man or wife of that house be examined by an officer, they boldly vouch, that they lodged him such a time, whereby the truth cannot appear.

And if they chance to be retained into service, through their lamentable words, with any wealthy man, they will tarry but a small time, either robbing his master or some of his fellows. And some of them useth this policy, that, although they travel into all these shires above-said, yet will they have good credit especially in one shire, where at divers good farmers' houses they be well known, where they work a month in a place or more, and will for that time behave themselves very honestly and painfully, and may at any time, for their good usage, have work of them. And to these at a dead lift, or last refuge, they may safely repair unto, and be welcome, when in other places, for a knack of knavery that they have played, they dare not tarry.

These upright-men will seldom or never want ; for what is gotten by any mort, or doxy, if it please him, he doth command the same. And if he meet any beggar, whether he be sturdy or impotent, he will demand of him, whether ever he was ſtalled to the rogue or no. If he say he was, he will know of whom, and his name that ſtalled him. And if he be not learnedly able to show him the whole circumſtance thereof, he will spoil him of his money, either of his beſt garment, if it be worth any money, and have him to the bousing ken, which is to some tippling house next adjoining, and layeth there to gage the beſt thing that he hath for twenty pence or two shillings. This man obeyeth for fear of beating. Then doth this upright-man call for a gage of bouse, which is a quart pot of drink, and pours the same upon his peld pate, adding these words : " I, G. P., do ſtall thee, W. T., to the rogue, and that from henceforth it shall be lawful for thee to cant "—that is, to ask or beg—" for thy living in all places." Here you see that the upright-man is of great authority. For all sorts of beggars are obedient to his heſts, and sur-mounteth all others in pilfering and ſtealing.

I lately had ſtanding in my well-house, which ſtandeth on the back-side of my house, a great cauldron of copper, being then full of water, having in the same half a dozen of pewter dishes, well marked, and ſtamped with the cognizance of my arms, which, being well noted when they were taken out, were set aside, the water poured out, and my cauldron taken away, being of such bigness that one man, unless he were of great ſtrength, was not able far to carry the same. Notwithſtanding, the same was one night within this two years conveyed more than half a mile from my house, into a common or heath, and there beſtowed in a great fir-bush. I then immediately the next day sent one of my men to London, and there gave warning in Southwark, Kent Street, and Barmesey Street,[11] to all the tinkers there dwelling, that if any such cauldron came thither to be sold, the bringer thereof should be ſtayed ; and promised twenty shillings for a reward. I gave also intelligence to the watermen that kept the ferries, that no such vessel should be either conveyed to London or into Essex, promising the like reward to have underſtanding thereof. This my doing was well underſtand in many places about, and that the fear of espying so troubled the conscience of the ſtealer, that my cauldron lay untouched in the thick fir-bush more than half a year after, which, by a great chance, was found by hunters for conies ; for one chanced to run into the same bush where my cauldron was, and being perceived, one thruſt his ſtaff into the same bush, and hit my cauldron a great blow, the sound whereof did cause the man to think and hope that there was some great treasure hidden, whereby he thought to be the better while he lived ; and in farther searching he found my cauldron. So had I the same again unlooked for.

CHAPTER III

A HOOKER, OR ANGLER

These hookers, or anglers, be perilous and most wicked knaves, and be derived or proceed forth from the upright-men. They commonly go in frieze jerkins and gallyslops, pointed beneath the knee. These, when they practise their pilfering, it is all by night ; for, as they walk a day-times from house to house to demand charity, they vigilantly mark where or in what place they may attain to their prey, casting their eyes up to every window, well noting what they see there, whether apparel or linen, hanging near unto the said windows, and that will they be sure to have the next night following. For they customably carry with them a staff of five or six foot long, in which, within one inch of the top thereof, is a little hole bored through, in which hole they put an iron hook, and with the same they will pluck unto them quickly anything that they may reach therewith, which hook in the day-time they covertly carry about them, and is never seen or taken out till they come to the place where they work their feat. Such have I seen at my house, and have oft talked with them and have handled their staves, not then understanding to what use or intent they served, although I had and perceived by their talk and behaviour great likelihood of evil suspicion in them. They will either lean upon their staff, to hide the hole thereof, when they talk with you, or hold their hand upon the hole. And what stuff, either woollen or linen, they thus hook out, they never carry the same forthwith to their stalling kens, but hides the same a three days in some secret corner, and after conveys the same to their houses abovesaid, where their host or hostess giveth them money for the same, but half the value that it is worth, or else their doxies shall afar off sell the same at the like houses. I was credibly informed that a hooker came to a farmer's house in the dead of the night, and putting back a draw window of a low chamber, the bed standing hard by the said window, in which lay three persons (a man and two big boys), this hooker with his staff plucked off their garments which lay upon them to keep them warm, with the coverlet and sheet, and left them lying asleep naked saving their shirts, and had away all clean, and never could understand where it became. I verily suppose that when they were well waked with cold, they surely thought that Robin Goodfellow, according to the old saying, had been with them that night.

Chapter IV

A Rogue

A rogue is neither so ſtout or hardy as the upright-man. Many of them will go faintly and look piteously when they see, either meet any person ; having a kercher, as white as my shoes, tied about their head, with a short ſtaff in their hand, halting, although they need not, requiring alms of such as they meet, or to what house they shall come. But you may easily perceive by their colour that they carry both health and hypocrisy about them, whereby they get gain, when others want that cannot feign and dissemble. Others there be that walk ſturdily about the country, and feigneth to seek a brother or kinsman of his, dwelling within some part of the shire. Either that he hath a letter to deliver to some honeſt householder, dwelling out of another shire, and will show you the same fair sealed, with the superscription to the party he speaketh of, because you shall not think him to run idly about the country ; either have they this shift : they will carry a certificate or passport about them from some Juſtice of the Peace, with his hand and seal unto the same, how he hath been whipped and punished for a vagabond according to the laws of this realm, and that he muſt return to T——, where he was born or laſt dwelt, by a certain day limited in the same, which shall be a good long day. And all this feigned, because without fear they would wickedly wander, and will renew the same where or when it pleaseth them ; for they have of their affinity that can write and read.

These also will pick and ſteal as the upright-men, and hath their women and meetings at places appointed, and nothing to them inferior in all kind of knavery. There be of these rogues curtals, wearing short cloaks, that will change their apparel as occasion serveth. And their end is either hanging, which they call trining in their language, or die miserably of the pox.

There was not long sithence two rogues that always did associate themselves together, and would never separate themselves, unless it were for some especial causes, for they were sworn brothers, and were both of one age, and much like of favour. These two, travelling into Eaſt Kent, resorted unto an ale-house there, being wearied with travelling, saluting with short courtesy, when they came into the house, such as they saw sitting there, in which company was the parson of the parish ;

and, calling for a pot of the best ale, sat down at the table's end : the liquor liked them so well, that they had pot upon pot, and sometime, for a little good manner, would drink and offer the cup to such as they best fancied ; and, to be short, they sat out all the company, for each man departed home about their business. When they had well refreshed themselves, then these rowsey rogues requested the goodman of the house with his wife to sit down and drink with them, of whom they inquired what priest the same was, and where he dwelt. Then they, feigning that they had an uncle a priest, and that he should dwell in these parts, which by all presumptions it should be he, and that they came of purpose to speak with him, but, because they had not seen him sithence they were six years old, they durst not be bold to take acquaintance of him until they were farther instructed of the truth, and began to enquire of his name, and how long he had dwelt there, and how far his house was off from the place they were in. The good wife of the house, thinking them honest men without deceit, because they so far enquired of their kinsman, was but of a good zealous natural intent, showed them cheerfully that he was an honest man and well beloved in the parish, and of good wealth, and had been there resident fifteen years at the least.

"But," saith she, " are you both brothers ? "—" Yea surely," said they ; " we have been both in one belly, and were twins."—" Mercy, God ! " quoth this foolish woman ; " It may well be, for ye be not much unlike,"—and went unto her hall window, calling these young men unto her, and looking out thereat, pointed with her finger and showed them the house standing alone, no house near the same by almost a quarter of a mile. " That," said she, " is your uncle's house."—" Nay," saith one of them, " he is not only my uncle, but also my godfather." —" It may well be," quoth she. " Nature will bind him to be the better unto you."—" Well," quoth they, " we be weary, and mean not to trouble our uncle to-night. But tomorrow, God willing, we will see him and do our duty. But, I pray you, doth our uncle occupy husbandry ? What company hath he in his house ? "—" Alas ! " saith she, " but one old woman and a boy. He hath no occupying at all. Tush," quoth this good wife, " you be madmen. Go to him this night, for he hath better lodging for you than I have, and yet I speak foolishly against my own profit, for by your tarrying here I should gain the more by you."

" Now, by my troth," quoth one of them, " we thank you, good hostess, for your wholesome counsel and we mean to do as you will us.

We will pause awhile, and by that time it will be almost night. And, I pray you, give us a reckoning." So, mannerly paying for that they took, bade their host and hostess farewell, with taking leave of the cup, marched merrily out of the doors towards this parson's house, viewed the same well round about, and passed by two bowshots off into a young wood, where they lay consulting what they should do until midnight.

Quoth one of them, of sharper wit and subtler than the other, to his fellow, " Thou seest that this house is stone-walled about, and that we cannot well break in, in any part thereof. Thou seest also that the windows be thick of mullions, that there is no creeping in between. Wherefore we must of necessity use some policy, when strength will not serve. I have a horse-lock here about me," saith he ; " and this I hope shall serve our turn."

So when it was about twelve of the clock, they came to the house and lurked near unto his chamber window. The dog of the house barked a good, that with the noise this priest waketh out of his sleep, and began to cough and hem. Then one of these rogues steps forth nearer the window and maketh a rueful and pitiful noise, requiring for Christ sake some relief, that was both hungry and thirsty, and was like to lie without the doors all night and starve for cold, unless he were relieved by him with some small piece of money. " Where dwellest thou ? " quoth this parson.—" Alas ! sir," saith this rogue, " I have small dwelling, and have come out of my way. And I should now," saith he, " go to any town now at this time of night, they would set me in the stocks and punish me."—" Well," quoth this pitiful parson, " away from my house, either lie in some of my out-houses until the morning. And hold ! Here is a couple of pence for thee."—" A God reward you ! " quoth this rogue ; " and in Heaven may you find it ! " The parson openeth his window, and thrusteth out his arm to give his alms to this rogue that came whining to receive it, and quickly taketh hold of his hand, and calleth his fellow to him, which was ready at hand with the horse-lock, and clappeth the same about the wrist of his arm, that the mullions standing so close together for strength, that for his life he could not pluck in his arm again, and made him believe, unless he would at the least give them three pounds, they would smite off his arm from the body. So that this poor parson, in fear to lose his hand, called up his old woman that lay in the loft over him, and willed her to take out all the money he had, which was four marks, which he said was all the money in his house, for he had lent six pounds to one of his neighbours not four days before.

"Well," quoth they, "Master Parson, if you have no more, upon this condition we will take off the lock, that you will drink twelve pence for our sakes to-morrow at the ale-house where we found you, and thank the good wife for the good cheer she made us."

He promised faithfully that he would so do. So they took off the lock, and went their way so far ere it was day, that the parson could never have any understanding more of them. Now this parson, sorrowfully slumbering that night between fear and hope, thought it was but folly to make two sorrows of one. He used contentation for his remedy, not forgetting in the morning to perform his promise, but went betimes to his neighbour that kept tippling, and asked angrily where the same two men were that drank with her yesterday. "Which two men?" quoth this good wife. "The strangers that came in when I was at your house with my neighbours yesterday."—"What! your nephews?" quoth she. "My nephews?" quoth this parson; "I trow thou art mad."—"Nay, by God!" quoth this good wife, "as sober as you. For they told me faithfully that you were their uncle. But, in faith, are you not so indeed? For, by my troth, they are strangers to me. I never saw them before."—"Oh, out upon them!" quoth the parson; "they be false thieves, and this night they compelled me to give them all the money in my house."—"Benedicite!" quoth this good wife, "and have they so indeed? As I shall answer before God, one of them told me besides that you were godfather to him, and that he trusted to have your blessing before he departed."—"What! did he?" quoth this parson; "a halter bless him for me!"—"Methinketh, by the mass, by your countenance you looked so wildly when you came in," quoth this good wife, "that something was amiss."—"I use not to jest," quoth this parson, "when I speak so earnestly."—"Why, all your sorrows go with it!" quoth this good wife. "And sit down here, and I will fill a fresh pot of ale shall make you merry again."—"Yea," saith this parson, "fill in, and give me some meat. For they made me swear and promise them faithfully that I should drink twelve pence with you this day."—"What! did they?" quoth she; "Now, by the Marymass, they be merry knaves. I warrant you they mean to buy no land with your money. But how could they come into you in the night, your doors being shut fast? Your house is very strong." Then this parson showed her all the whole circumstance, how he gave them his alms out at the window: they made such lamentable cry that it pitied him at the heart; for he saw but one when he put out his hand at the window.

" Be ruled by me," quoth this good wife. " Wherein ? " quoth
this parson. " By my troth, never speak more of it. When they shall
understand of it in the parish, they will but laugh you to scorn."—" Why,
then," quoth this parson, " the Devil go with it." And there an end.

CHAPTER V

A WILD ROGUE

A wild rogue is he that is born a rogue. He is a more subtle and
more given by nature to all kind of knavery than the other, as beastly
begotten in barn or bushes, and from his infancy traded up in treachery ;
yea, and before ripeness of years doth permit, wallowing in lewd lechery—
but that is counted amongst them no sin. For this is their custom,
that when they meet in barn at night, every one getteth a make to lie
withal, and there chance to be twenty in a company, as there is sometime
more and sometime less. For to one man that goeth abroad, there are
at the least two women, which never make it strange when they be called,
although she never knew him before. Then, when the day doth appear,
he rouses him up, and shakes his ears, and away wandering where he
may get ought to the hurt of others. Yet before he skippeth out of his
couch and departeth from his darling, if he like her well, he will appoint
her where to meet shortly after, with a warning to work warily for some
cheats, that their meeting might be the merrier.

Not long sithence, a wild rogue chanced to meet a poor neighbour
of mine, who for honesty and good nature surmounteth many. This
poor man, riding homeward from London, where he had made his
market, this rogue demanded a penny for God's sake, to keep him a
true man. This simple man, beholding him well, and saw he was of
tall personage with a good quarterstaff in his hand, it much pitied him,
as he said, to see him want ; for he was well able to serve his prince in
the wars. Thus, being moved with pity, and looked in his purse to
find out a penny ; and, in looking for the same, he plucked out eight
shillings in white money, and raked therein to find a single penny ; and
at the last finding one, doth offer the same to this wild rogue. But he,
seeing so much money in this simple man's hand, being stricken to the
heart with a covetous desire, bid him forthwith deliver all that he had,
or else he would with his staff beat out his brains. For it was not a
penny would now quench his thirst, seeing so much as he did. Thus,

swallowing his spittle greedily down, [he] spoiled this poor man of all the money that he had, and leapt over the hedge into a thick wood, and went his way as merrily as this good simple man came home sorrowfully. I, once rebuking a wild rogue because he went idly about, he showed me that he was a beggar by inheritance. His grandfather was a beggar, his father was one, and he must needs be one by good reason.

Chapter VI

A Prigger of Prancers

A prigger of prancers be horse-stealers ; for to prig signifieth in their language to steal, and a prancer is a horse. So being put together, the matter is plain. These go commonly in jerkins of leather, or of white frieze, and carry little wands in their hands, and will walk through grounds and pastures, to search and see horses meet for their purpose. And if they chance to be met and asked by the owners of the ground what they make there, they feign straight that they have lost their way, and desire to be instructed the best way to such a place. These will also repair to gentlemen's houses and ask their charity, and will offer their service. And if you ask them what they can do, they will say that they can keep two or three geldings, and wait upon a gentleman. These have also their women, that, walking from them in other places, mark where and what they see abroad, and showeth these priggers thereof when they meet, which is within a week or two. And look, where they steal anything, they convey the same at the least three score miles off or more.

There was a gentleman, a very friend of mine, riding from London homeward into Kent, having within three miles of his house business, alighted off his horse, and his man also, in a pretty village, where divers houses were, and looked about him where he might have a convenient person to walk his horse, because he would speak with a farmer that dwelt on the back-side of the said village, little above a quarter of a mile from the place where he lighted, and had his man to wait upon him, as it was meet for his calling. Espying a prigger there standing, thinking the same to dwell there, charging this pretty prigging person to walk his horse well, and that they might not stand still for taking of cold, and at his return, which he said should not be long, he would give him a penny to drink, and so went about his business.

This pelting prigger, proud of his prey, walketh his horse up and down till he saw the gentleman out of sight, and leaps him into the saddle, and away he goeth amain. This gentleman returning, and finding not his horses, sent his man to the one end of the village, and he went himself unto the other end, and enquired as he went for his horses that were walked, and began somewhat to suspect, because neither he nor his man could see nor find him. Then this gentleman diligently enquired of three or four town dwellers there whether any such person [had been seen], declaring his stature, age, apparel, with so many lineaments of his body as he could call to remembrance. And *una voce* all said that no such man dwelt in their street, neither in the parish, that they knew of. But some did well remember that such a one they saw there lurking and huggering two hours before the gentleman came thither, and a stranger to them. " I had thought," quoth this gentleman, " he had here dwelled,"—and marched home mannerly in his boots. Far from the place he dwelt not. I suppose at his coming home he sent such ways as he suspected or thought meet to search for this prigger, but hitherto he never heard any tidings again of his palfreys. I had the best gelding stolen out of my pasture that I had, amongst others, while this book was first a printing.

Chapter VII

A Palliard

These palliards be called also clapperdudgeons. These go with patched cloaks, and have their morts with them, which they call wives. And if he go to one house to ask his alms, his wife shall go to another ; for what they get, as bread, cheese, malt and wool, they sell the same for ready money ; for so they get more and if they went together. Although they be thus divided in the day, yet they meet jump at night. If they chance to come to some gentleman's house standing alone, and be demanded whether they be man and wife, and if he perceive that any doubteth thereof, he showeth them a testimonial with the minister's name, and others of the same parish, naming a parish in some shire far distant from the place where he showeth the same. This writing he carryeth to salve that sore. There be many Irishmen[12] that go about with counterfeit licences. And if they perceive you will straitly examine them, they will immediately say they can speak no English.

Farther, understand for truth that the worst and wickedest of all this beastly generation are scarce comparable to these prating palliards. All for the most part of these will either lay to their legs an herb called spearwort, either arsenic, which is called ratsbane. The nature of this spearwort will raise a great blister in a night upon the soundest part of his body. And if the same be taken away, it will dry up again and no harm. But this arsenic will so poison the same leg or sore, that it will ever after be incurable.[13] This do they for gain and to be pitied. The most of these that walk about be Welshmen.

CHAPTER VIII

A FRATER

Some of these fraters will carry black boxes at their girdle, wherein they have a brief of the Queen's Majesty's letters patents, given to such a poor spital-house for the relief of the poor there, which brief is a copy of the letters patents, and utterly feigned if it be in paper or in parchment without the great seal.[14] Also, if the same brief be in print, it is also of authority. For the printers will see and well understand, before it come in press, that the same is lawful. Also, I am credibly informed that the chief proctors of many of these houses, that seldom travel abroad themselves, but have their factors to gather for them, which look very slenderly to the impotent and miserable creatures committed to their charge, and die for want of cherishing; whereas they and their wives are well crammed and clothed, and will have of the best. And the founders of every such house, or the chief of the parish where they be, would better see unto these proctors, that they might do their duty : they should be well spoken of here, and in the world to come abundantly therefore rewarded.

I had of late an honest man, and of good wealth, repaired to my house to common with me about certain affairs. I invited the same to dinner, and, dinner being done, I demanded of him some news of these parts where he dwelt. " Thanks be to God, sir," saith he ; " all is well and good now."—" Now ! " quoth I, " this same ' now ' declareth that some things of late hath not been well."—" Yes, sir," quoth he, " the matter is not great. I had thought I should have been well beaten within this seventh night."—" How so ? " quoth I.

" Marry, sir," said he, " I am Constable for fault of a better, and was commanded by the Justice to watch. The watch being set, I took an honest man, one of my neighbours, with me, and went up to the end of the town as far as the spital-house, at which house I heard a great noise, and, drawing near, stood close under the wall, and this was at one of the clock after midnight." Where he heard swearing, prating, and wagers laying, and the pot apace walking, and forty pence gaged upon a match of wrestling, pitching of the bar, and casting of the sledge. And out they go, in a fustian fume, into the back-side, where was a great axle-tree, and there fell to pitching of the bar, being three to three. The moon did shine bright, the Constable with his neighbour might see and behold all that was done ; and how the wife of the house was roasting of a pig, while her guests were in their match. At the last they could not agree upon a cast, and fell at words, and from words to blows. The Constable with his fellow runs unto them to part them, and in the parting licks a dry blow or two. Then the noise increased. The Constable would have had them to the stocks. The wife of the house runs out with her goodman to entreat the Constable for her guests, and leaves the pig at the fire alone. In cometh two or three of the next neighbours, being waked with this noise, and into the house they come, and find none therein, but the pig well roasted, and carrieth the same away with them, spit and all, with such bread and drink also as stood upon the table.

When the goodman and the goodwife of the house had entreated and pacified the Constable, showing unto him that they were proctors and factors all of spital-houses, and that they tarried there but to break their fast, and would ride away immediately after, for they had far to go, and therefore meant to ride so early. And, coming into their house again, finding the pig with bread and drink all gone, made a great exclamation, for they knew not who had the same.

The Constable returning, and hearing the lamentable words of the good wife, how she had lost both meat and drink, and saw it was so indeed, he laughed in his sleeve, and commanded her to dress no more at unlawful hours for any guests. For he thought it better bestowed upon those smell-feasts his poor neighbours than upon such sturdy lubbers. The next morning betimes the spit and pots were set at the spital-house door for the owner. Thus were these factors beguiled of their breakfast, and one of them had well beaten another. " And, by my troth," quoth this Constable, " I was glad when I was well rid of them."—" Why," quoth I, " could they cast the bar and sledge well ? "—

" I will tell you, sir," quoth he. " You know there hath been many games this summer. I think verily that if some of these lubbers had been there, and practised amongst others, I believe they would have carried away the best games. For they were so strong and sturdy, that I was not able to stand in their hands."—" Well," quoth I, " at these games you speak of, both legs and arms be tried."—" Yea," quoth this officer, " they be wicked men. I have seen some of them sithence with clouts bound about their legs, and halting with their staff in their hands. Wherefore some of them, by God, be nought all."

CHAPTER IX

A ABRAM-MAN

These abram-men be those that feign themselves to have been mad, and have been kept either in Bethlem[15] or in some other prison a good time, and not one amongst twenty that ever came in prison for any such cause. Yet will they say how piteously and most extremely they have been beaten and dealt withal. Some of these be merry and very pleasant ; they will dance and sing. Some others be as cold and reasonable to talk withal. These beg money. Either when they come at farmers' houses, they will demand bacon, either cheese, or wool, or anything that is worth money. And if they espy small company within, they will with fierce countenance demand somewhat. Where for fear the maids will give them largely, to be rid of them.

If they may conveniently come by any cheat, they will pick and steal, as the upright-man or rogue, poultry or linen. And all women that wander be at their commandment. Of all that ever I saw of this kind, one naming himself Stradling is the craftiest and most dissemblingest knave. He is able with his tongue and usage to deceive and abuse the wisest man that is. And surely for the proportion of his body, with every member thereunto appertaining, it cannot be amended. But as the proverb is, God hath done His part. This Stradling saith he was the Lord Stourton's man ; and when he was executed, for very pensiveness of mind he fell out of his wit, and so continued a year after and more[16] ; and that with the very grief and fear, he was taken with a marvellous palsy, that both head and hands will shake when he talketh with any and that apace or fast, whereby he is much pitied, and getteth greatly. And if I had not demanded of others, both men and women, that commonly walketh as he doth, and known by them his deep dissimulation, I never had underſtand the same. And thus I end with these kind of vagabonds.

CHAPTER X

A FRESH-WATER MARINER OR WHIPJACK

These fresh-water mariners, their ships were drowned in the plain of Salisbury. These kind of caterpillars counterfeit great losses on the sea. These be some weſtern men, and moſt be Irishmen. These will run about the country with a counterfeit licence, feigning either shipwreck, or spoiled by pirates, near the coaſt of Cornwall or Devonshire, and set aland at some haven town there, having a large and formal writing, as is abovesaid, with the names and seals of such men of worship at the leaſt four or five, as dwelleth near or next to the place where they feign their landing. And near to those shires will they not beg, until they come into Wiltshire, Hampshire, Berkshire, Oxfordshire, Hertfordshire, Middlesex, and so to London, and down by the river to seek for their ship and goods that they never had. Then pass they through Surrey, Sussex, by the sea-coaſts, and so into Kent, demanding alms to bring them home to their country.

Sometime they counterfeit the seal of the Admiralty.[17] I have divers times taken away from them their licences, of both sorts, with such money as they have gathered, and have confiscated the same to the poverty nigh adjoining to me. And they will not be long without another. For at any good town they will renew the same. Once with much threatening and fair promises, I required to know of one company, who made their licence? And they swear that they bought the same at Portsmouth of a mariner there, and it coſt them two shillings. With such warrants to be so good and effeċtual, that if any of the beſt men of law, or learned, about London, should peruse the same, they were able to find no fault therewith, but would assuredly allow the same.

Chapter XI

A Counterfeit Crank

These that do counterfeit the crank be young knaves and young harlots, that deeply dissemble the falling sickness. For the crank in their language is the falling evil. I have seen some of these with fair writings testimonial, with the names and seals of some men of worship in Shropshire[18] and in other shires far off, that I have well known, and have taken the same from them. Many of these do go without writings, and will go half naked, and look most piteously. And if any clothes be given them, they immediately sell the same, for wear it they will not, because they would be the more pitied, and wear filthy cloths on their heads, and never go without a piece of white soap about them, which, if they see cause or present gain, they will privily convey the same into their mouth, and so work the same there, that they will foam as it were a boar, and marvellously for a time torment themselves. And thus deceive they the common people, and gain much. These have commonly their harlots as the other.

Upon Allhallow Day in the morning last, *Anno Domini* 1566, or my book was half printed,[19] I mean the first impression, there came early in the morning a counterfeit crank under my lodging at the White-friars,[20] within the cloister in a little yard or court, whereabouts lay two or three great ladies, being without the liberties of London, whereby he hoped for the greater gain. This crank there lamentably lamenting and pitifully crying to be relieved, declared to divers there his painful and miserable disease. I being risen and not half ready, heard his doleful words and rueful moanings ; hearing him name the falling sickness, thought assuredly to myself that he was a deep dissembler. So, coming out at a sudden, and beholding his ugly and irksome attire, his loathsome and horrible countenance, it made me in a marvellous perplexity what to think of him, whether it were feigned or truth. For after this manner went he : He was naked from the waist upward, saving he had a old jerkin of leather patched, and that was loose about him, that all his body lay out bare. A filthy foul cloth he wear on his head, being cut for the purpose, having a narrow place to put out his face, with a bauer made to truss up his beard, and a string that tied the same down close about his neck ; with an old felt hat which he still carried in his hand to receive the charity and devotion of the people, for that would he hold out from him ; having his face from the eyes downward, all smeared with fresh blood, as though he had new fallen, and been tormented with his painful pangs ; his jerkin being all berayed with dirt and mire, and his hat and hosen also, as though he had wallowed in the mire. Surely the sight was monſtrous and terrible ! I called him unto me, and demanded of him what he ailed. " Ah, good maſter," quoth he, " I have the grievous and painful disease called the falling sickness."—" Why," quoth I, " how cometh thy jerkin, hose and hat so berayed with dirt and mire, and thy skin also ? " " Ah, good maſter, I fell down on the back-side here in the foul lane hard by the waterside ; and there I lay almoſt all night, and have bled almoſt all the blood out in my body." It rained that morning very faſt ; and, while I was thus talking with him, a honeſt poor woman that dwelt thereby brought him a fair linen cloth, and bid him wipe his face therewith ; and there being a tub ſtanding full of rain-water, offered to give him some in a dish that he might make himself clean. He refuseth the same. " Why doſt thou so ? " quoth I. " Ah, sir," saith he, " if I should wash myself, I should fall to bleeding afresh again, and then I should not ſtop myself." These words made me the more to suspeċt him.

Then I asked of him where he was born, what his name was, how long he had this disease, and what time he had been here about London, and in what place. " Sir," saith he, " I was born at Leiceſter. My name is Nicholas Jennings ; and I have had this falling sickness eight years, and I can get no remedy for the same ; for I have it by kind. My father had it, and my friends before me ; and I have been these two years here about London, and a year and a half in Bethlem."—" Why ? Waſt thou out of thy wits ? " quoth I. " Yea, sir, that I was."—" What is the keeper's name of the house ? "—" His name is," quoth he, " John Smith."—" Then," quoth I, " he muſt underſtand of thy disease. If thou hadſt the same for the time thou waſt there, he knoweth it well." —" Yea, not only he, but all the house beside," quoth this crank ; " for I came thence but within this fortnight."

I had ſtand so long reasoning the matter with him that I was acold, and went into my chamber and made me ready, and commanded my servant to repair to Bethlem, and bring me true word from the keeper there whether any such man hath been with him as a prisoner having the disease aforesaid, and gave him a note of his name and the keeper's also. My servant, returning to my lodging, did assure me that neither was there ever any such man there, neither yet any keeper of any such name. But he that was there keeper,[21] he sent me his name in writing, affirming that he letteth no man depart from him unless he be fet away by his friends, and that none that came from him beggeth about the City.

Then I sent for the printer of this book, and showed him of this dissembling crank, and how I had sent to Bethlem to understand the truth, and what answer I received again, requiring him that I might have some servant of his to watch him faithfully that day, that I might understand trustily to what place he would repair at night unto; and thither I promised to go myself to see their order, and that I would have him to associate me thither.

He gladly granted to my request, and sent two boys, that both diligently and vigilantly accomplished the charge given them, and found the same crank about the Temple, whereabout the most part of the day he begged, unless it were about twelve of the clock he went on the back-side of Clement's Inn without Temple Bar. There is a lane that goeth into the fields. There he renewed his face again with fresh blood, which he carried about him in a bladder, and daubed on fresh dirt upon his jerkin, hat and hosen; and so came back again unto the Temple, and sometime to the waterside, and begged of all that passed by. The boys beheld how some gave groats, some sixpence, some gave more. For he looked so ugly and irksomely, that every one pitied his miserable case that beheld him. To be short, there he passed all the day till night approached. And when it began to be somewhat dark, he went to the waterside, and took a sculler, and was set over the water into St. George's Fields,[22] contrary to my expectation; for I had thought he would have gone into Holborn, or to St. Giles in the Field. But these boys, with Argus' and lynxes' eyes, set sure watch upon him, and the one took a boat and followed him, and the other went back to tell his master.

The boy that so followed him by water, had no money to pay for his boat hire, but laid his penner and his inkhorn to gage for a penny. And by that time the boy was set over, his master, with all celerity, had taken a boat and followed him apace. Now had they still a sight of the crank, which crossed over the fields towards Newington,[23] and thither he went, and by that time they came thither it was very dark. The printer had there no acquaintance, neither any kind of weapon about him; neither knew he how far the crank would go, because he then suspected that they dogged him of purpose. He there stayed him, and called for the Constable, which came forth diligently to inquire what the matter was. This zealous printer charged this officer with him as a malefactor and a dissembling vagabond. The Constable would have laid him all night in the cage that stood in the street. " Nay," saith this pitiful printer, " I pray you have him into your house. For this is like to be a cold night, and he is naked. You keep a victualling house. Let him be well cherished this night, for he is well able to pay for the same. I know well his gains hath been great to-day, and your house is a sufficient prison for the time, and we will there search him."

The Constable agreed thereunto. They had him in, and caused him to wash himself. That done, they demanded what money he had about him. Saith this crank, " So God help me, I have but twelve pence," and plucked out the same of a little purse. " Why, have you no more ? " quoth they. " No," saith this crank, " as God shall save my soul at the day of judgment."—" We must see more," quoth they, and began to strip him. Then he plucked out another purse, wherein was forty pence. " Tush," saith this printer, " I must see more." Saith this crank, " I pray God I be damned both body and soul if I have any more." " No," saith this printer, " Thou false knave ; here is my boy that did watch thee all this day, and saw when such men gave thee pieces of sixpence, groats, and other money. And yet thou hast showed us none but small money." When this crank heard this, and the boy vowing it to his face, he relented, and plucked out another purse, wherein was eight shillings and odd money. So had they in the whole that he had begged that day 13s. 3½d. Then they stripped him stark naked ; and as many as saw him said they never saw a handsomer man, with a yellow flaxen beard, and fair-skinned, without any spot or grief. Then the good wife of the house fet her goodman's old cloak, and caused the same to be cast about him, because the sight should not abash her shamefast maidens, neither loath her squeamish sight.

Thus he set him down at the chimney's end, and called for a pot of beer, and drank off a quart at a draft, and called for another, and so the third, that one had been sufficient for any reasonable man, the drink was so strong. I myself the next morning tasted thereof. But let the reader judge what and how much he would have drunk and he had been out of fear ! Then when they had thus wrung water out of a flint in spoiling him of his evil-gotten goods, his passing pence, and fleeting trash, the printer with this officer were in jolly jealousy,[24] and devised to search a barn for some rogues and upright-men, a quarter of a mile from the house, that stood alone in the fields, and went out about their business, leaving this crank alone with his wife and maidens. This crafty crank, espying all gone, requested the good wife that he might go out on the back-side to make water, and to exonerate his paunch. She bade him draw the latch of the door and go out, neither thinking or mistrusting he would have gone away naked. But, to conclude, when he was out, he cast away the cloak, and, as naked as ever he was born, he ran away[25] over the fields to his own house, as he afterwards said.

Now the next morning betimes, I went unto Newington, to understand what was done, because I had word or it was day that there my printer was. And at my coming thither I heard the whole circumstance, as I above have written. And I, seeing the matter so fall out, took order with the chief of the parish that this 13s. 3½d. might the next day be equally distributed by their good discretions to the poverty of the same parish,[26] whereof this crafty crank had part himself, for he had both house and wife in the same parish, as after you shall hear. But this lewd loiterer could not lay his bones to labour, having got once the taste of this lewd lazy life, for all this fair admonition, but devised other subtle sleights to maintain his idle living, and so craftily clothed himself in mariners' apparel, and associated himself with another of his companions. They, having both mariners' apparel, went abroad to ask charity of the people, feigning they had lost their ship with all their goods by casualty on the seas, wherewith they gained much. This crafty crank, fearing to be mistrusted, fell to another kind of begging, as bad or worse, and apparelled himself very well with a fair black frieze coat, a new pair of white hose, a fine felt hat on his head, a shirt of Flanders work esteemed to be worth sixteen shillings ; and upon New Year's Day came again into the Whitefriars to beg.

The printer, having occasion to go that ways, not thinking of this crank, by chance met with him, who asked his charity for God's sake. The printer, viewing him well, did mistrust him to be the counterfeit crank which deceived him upon Allhallow Day at night, demanded of whence he was, and what was his name. " Forsooth," saith he, " my name is Nicholas Jennings, and I came from Leicester to seek work, and I am a hat-maker by my occupation, and all my money is spent ; and if I could get money to pay for my lodging this night, I would seek work to-morrow amongst the hatters."

The printer, perceiving his deep dissimulation, putting his hand into his purse, seeming to give him some money, and with fair allusions brought him into the street, where he charged the Constable with him, affirming him to be the counterfeit crank that ran away upon Allhallow Day last. The Constable being very loath to meddle with him, but the printer knowing him and his deep deceit, desired he might be brought before the Deputy of the ward,[27] which straight was accomplished, which when he came before the Deputy, he demanded of him whence he was, and what was his name. He answered as before he did unto the printer. The Deputy asked the printer what he would lay unto his charge. He answered and alleged him to be a vagabond and deep deceiver of the people, and the counterfeit crank that ran away upon Allhallow Day last from the Constable of Newington and him, and requested him earnestly to send him to ward. The Deputy, thinking him to be deceived, but nevertheless laid his commandment upon him, so that the printer should bear his charges if he could not justify it. He agreed thereunto. And so he and the Constable went to carry him to the Counter. And as they were going under Ludgate, this crafty crank took his heels and ran down the hill as fast as he could drive, the Constable and the printer after him as fast as they could. But the printer of the twain being lighter of foot, overtook him at Fleet Bridge, and with strong hand carried him to the Counter, and safely delivered him.

In the morrow, the printer sent his boy that stripped him upon Allhallow Day at night to view him, because he would be sure, which boy knew him very well. This crank confessed unto the Deputy that he had hosted the night before in Kent Street in Southwark, at the sign of *The Cock*, which thing to be true, the printer sent to know, and found him a liar; but further enquiring, at length found out his habitation, dwelling in Master Hill's rents, having a pretty house, well stuffed, with a fair joint-table, and a fair cupboard garnished with pewter, having an old ancient woman to his wife. The printer being sure thereof, repaired unto the Counter, and rebuked him for his beastly behaviour, and told him of his false feigning, willed him to confess it, and ask forgiveness. He perceived him to know his deep dissimulation, relented, and confessed all his deceit; and so remaining in the Counter three days, was removed to Bridewell, where he was stripped stark naked, and his ugly attire put upon him before the masters thereof, who wondered greatly at his dissimulation. For which offence he stood upon the pillory in Cheapside, both in his ugly and handsome attire; and after that went in the mill while his ugly picture was a drawing; and then was whipped at a cart's tail through London, and his displayed banner carried before him unto his own door, and so back to Bridewell again, and there remained for a time, and at length let at liberty, on that condition he would prove an honest man, and labour truly to get his living. And his picture remaineth in Bridewell for a monument.[28]

Chapter XII

A Dummerer

These dummerers are lewd and most subtle people. The most part of these are Welshmen, and will never speak, unless they have extreme punishment, but will gape, and with a marvellous force will hold down their tongues doubled, groaning for your charity, and holding up their hands full piteously, so that with their deep dissimulation they get very much. There are of these many, and but one that I understand of hath lost his tongue indeed. Having on a time occasion to ride to Dartford, to speak with a priest there, who maketh all kind of conserves very well, and useth stilling of waters, and, repairing to his house, I found a dummerer at his door, and the priest himself perusing his licence under the seals and hands of certain worshipful men, which priest had thought the same to be good and effectual. I, taking the same writing, and reading it over, and noting the seals, found one of the seals like unto a seal that I had about me, which seal I bought besides Charing Cross, that I was out of doubt it was none of those gentlemen's seals that had subscribed ; and, having understanding before of their peevish practices, made me to conceive that all was forged and nought.

I made the more haste home ; for well I wist that he would and must of force pass through the parish where I dwelt ; for there was no other way for him. And coming homeward, I found them in the town, according to my expectation, where they were stayed. For there was a palliard associate with the dummerer and partaker of his gains, which palliard I saw not at Dartford. The stayers of them was a gentleman called Chayne, and a servant of my Lord Keeper's called Wostestowe, which was the chief causer of the staying of them, being a surgeon, and cunning in his science, had seen the like practices, and, as he said, had caused one to speak afore that was dumb. It was my chance to come at the beginning of the matter.

" Sir," quoth this surgeon, " I am bold here to utter some part of my cunning. I trust," quoth he, " you shall see a miracle wrought anon. For I once," quoth he, " made a dumb man to speak."

Quoth I, " You are well met, and somewhat you have prevented me. For I had thought to have done no less or they had passed this town. For I well know their writing is feigned, and they deep dissemblers."

The surgeon made him gape, and we could see but half a tongue. I required the surgeon to put his finger in his mouth, and to pull out his tongue, and so he did, notwithstanding he held strongly a pretty while. At the length he plucked out the same, to the great admiration of many that stood by. Yet when we saw his tongue, he would neither speak nor yet could hear.

Quoth I to the surgeon, " Knit two of his fingers together, and thrust a stick between them, and rub the same up and down a little while, and for my life he speaketh by and by."

" Sir," quoth this surgeon, " I pray you let me practise another way."

I was well contented to see the same. He had him into a house, and tied a halter about the wrists of his hands, and hoisted him up over a beam, and there did let him hang a good while. At the length, for very pain he required for God's sake to let him down. So he that was both deaf and dumb could in short time both hear and speak. Then I took that money I could find in his purse, and distributed the same to the poor people dwelling there, which was fifteen pence halfpenny, being all that we could find. That done, and this merry miracle madly made, I sent them with my servant to the next Justice, where they preached on the pillory for want of a pulpit, and were well whipped, and none did bewail them.

CHAPTER XIII

A DRUNKEN TINKER

These drunken tinkers, called also priggs, be beastly people, and these young knaves be the worst. These never go without their doxies, and if their women have anything about them, as apparel or linen, that is worth the selling, they lay the same to gage, or sell it outright, for bene bouse at their bousing ken. And full soon will they be weary of them, and have a new. When they happen on work at any good house, their doxies linger aloof, and tarry for them in some corner ; and if he tarryeth long from her, then she knoweth he hath work, and walketh near, and sitteth down by him. For besides money he looketh for meat and drink for doing his dame pleasure. For if she have three or four holes in a pan, he will make as many more for speedy gain. And if he see any old kettle, chafer, or pewter dish abroad in the yard where he worketh, he quickly snappeth the same up, and into the budget it goeth round. Thus they live with deceit.

I was credibly informed by such as could well tell, that one of these tippling tinkers with his dog robbed by the highway four palliards and two rogues, six persons together, and took from them above four pound in ready money, and hid him after in a thick wood a day or two, and so escaped untaken. Thus with picking and stealing, mingled with a little work for a colour, they pass their time.

Chapter XIV

A Swadder or Pedlar

These swadders and pedlars be not all evil, but of an indifferent behaviour. These stand in great awe of the upright-men, for they have often both wares and money of them. But forasmuch as they seek gain unlawfully against the laws and statutes of this noble realm, they are well worthy to be registered among the number of vagabonds. And undoubtedly I have had some of them brought before me, when I was in Commission of the Peace, as malefactors, for bribering and stealing. And now of late it is a great practice of the upright-man, when he hath gotten a booty, to bestow the same upon a packful of wares, and so goeth a time for his pleasure, because he would live without suspicion.

Chapter XV

A Jarkman and a Patrico

Forasmuch as these two names, a jarkman and a patrico, be in the old brief of vagabonds,[29] and set forth as two kinds of evil-doers, you shall understand that a jarkman hath his name of a jark, which is a seal in their language, as one should make writings and set seals for licences and passports. And for truth there is none that goeth about the country of them that can either write so good and fair a hand, either indite so learnedly, as I have seen and handled a number of them, but have the same made in good towns where they come; as what can not be had for money? As the proverb saith, *Omnia venalia Romae*. And many hath confessed the same to me.

Now, also, there is a patrico, and not a patriarcho, which in their language is a priest that should make marriages till death did depart. But they have none such, I am well assured. For I put you out of doubt that not one amongst a hundred of them are married; for they take lechery for no sin, but natural fellowship and good liking, love: so that I will not blot my book with these two that be not.

CHAPTER XVI

A DEMANDER FOR GLIMMER

These demanders for glimmer be for the most part women; for glimmer, in their language, is fire. These go with feigned licences and counterfeited writings, having the hands and seals of such gentlemen as dwelleth near to the place where they feign themselves to have been burnt, and their goods consumed with fire. They will most lamentably demand your charity, and will quickly shed salt tears, they be so tender-hearted. They will never beg in that shire where their losses (as they say) was. Some of these go with slates at their backs (which is a sheet to lie in a nights). The upright-men be very familiar with these kind of women, and one of them helps another.

A demander for glimmer came unto a good town in Kent, to ask the charity of the people, having a feigned licence about her, that declared her misfortune by fire, done in Somersetshire; walking with a wallet on her shoulders, wherein she put the devotion of such as had no money to give her, that is to say, malt, wool, bacon, bread, and cheese. And always, as the same was full, so was it ready money to her, when she emptied the same, wheresoever she travelled. This harlot was, as they term it, snout-fair, and had an upright-man or two always attending on her watch (which is on her person), and yet so circumspect, that they would never be seen in her company in any good town, unless it were in small villages where tippling houses were, either travelling together by the highways. But the truth is, by report, she would weekly be worth six or seven shillings with her begging and bitchery.

This glimmering mort, repairing to an inn in the said town, where dwelt a widow of fifty winter old of good wealth—but she had an unthrifty son, whom she used as a chamberlain to attend guests when they repaired to her house. This amorous man, beholding with ardent eyes this glimmering glancer, was presently piteously pierced to the heart, and lewdly longed to be clothed under her livery, and, bestowing a few fond words with her, understood straight that she would be easily persuaded to liking lechery, and, as a man mazed, mused how to attain to his purpose, for he had no money. Yet, considering with himself that wares would be welcome where money wanted, he went with a wanion to his mother's chamber, and there seeking about for odd ends, at length found a little whistle of silver that his mother did use customably to wear on, and had forgot the same for haste that morning, and offers the same closely to this mannerly Marian, that if she would meet him on the back-side of the town and courteously kiss him without constraint, she should be mistress thereof, and it wear much better.

"Well," saith she, " you *are* a wanton "; and beholding the whistle, was farther in love therewith than ravished with his person, and agreed to meet him presently, and to accomplish his fond fancy. To be short and not tedious, a quarter of a mile from the town, he merely took measure of her under a bawdy bush. So she gave him that she had not, and he received that he could not, and, taking leave of each other with a courteous kiss, she pleasantly passed forth on her journey, and this untoward lickerous chamberlain repaired homeward.

But or these two turtles took their leave, the good wife missed her whistle, and sent one of her maidens into her chamber for the same, and being long sought for, none could be found. Her mistress hearing that, diligent search was made for the same, and that it was taken away, began to suspect her unblessed babe, and demanded of her maidens whether none of them saw her son in her chamber that morning. And one of them answered that she saw him not there, but coming from thence. Then had she enough, for well she wist that he had the same, and sent for him, but he could not be found. Then she caused her ostler, in whom she had better affiance in for his truth,—and yet not one amongst twenty of them but have well left their honesty, as I hear a great sort say—to come unto her, which attended to know her pleasure. " Go, seek out," saith she, " my untoward son, and bid him come speak with me."—" I saw him go out," saith he, " half an hour sithence on the back-side. I had thought you had sent him of your arrant."—" I sent him not," quoth she. " Go, look him out."

This hollow ostler took his staff in his neck, and trudged out apace that way he saw him before go, and had some understanding, by one of the maidens, that his mistress had her whistle stolen and suspected her son. And he had not gone far but that he espied him coming homeward alone, and, meeting him, axed where he had been.

" Where have I been ? " quoth he, and began to smile.

" Now, by the mass, thou haſt been at some bawdy banquet."

" Thou haſt even told truth," quoth this chamberlain.

" Surely," quoth this oſtler, " thou hadſt the same woman that begged at our house to-day, for the harms she had by fire. Where is she ? " quoth he.

" She is almoſt a mile by this time," quoth this chamberlain.

" Where is my miſtress's whiſtle ? " quoth this oſtler. " For I am well assured that thou hadſt it, and I fear me thou haſt given it to that harlot."

" Why, is it missed ? " quoth this chamberlain.

" Yea," quoth this oſtler, and showed him all the whole circumſtance, what was both said and thought on him for the thing.

" Well, I will tell thee," quoth this chamberlain. " I will be plain with thee. I had it indeed, and have given the same to this woman, and I pray thee make the beſt of it, and help now to excuse the matter. And yet surely, and thou wouldſt take so much pain for me as to over-take her, for she goeth but softly, and is not yet far off, and take the same from her, and I am ever thine assured friend."

" Why, then, go with me," quoth this oſtler.

" Nay, in faith," quoth this chamberlain. " What is freer than a gift ? And I had pretty paſtime for the same."

" Hadſt thou so ? " quoth this oſtler. " Now, by the mass, and I will have some too, or I will lie in the duſt or I come again." Passing with haſte to overtake this paramour, within a mile from the place where he departed he overtook her, having an upright-man in her company, a ſtrong and a ſturdy vagabond. Somewhat amazed was this oſtler to see one familiarly in her company, for he had well hoped to have had some delicate dalliance, as his fellow had. But, seeing the matter so fall out, and being of good courage, and thinking to himself that one true man was better than two false knaves, and being on the highway, thought upon help, if need had been, by such as had passed to and fro, demanded fiercely the whiſtle that she had even now of his fellow.

" Why, husband," quoth she, " can you suffer this wretch to slander your wife ? "

" Avaunt varlet ! " quoth this upright-man, and lets drive with all his force at this oſtler, and after half a dozen blows, he ſtrikes his ſtaff out of his hand, and as this oſtler ſtepped back to have taken up his ſtaff again, his glimmering mort flings a great ſtone at him, and ſtruck

¶A Caueat oʒ Warening,

FOR COMMEN CVRSE-

TORS VVLGARELY CALLED

Uagabones, ſet foʒth by Thomas harman.
Eſquiere, foʒ the vtilite and pʒoffyt of his naturall
Cuntrey. Augmented and inlarged by the fyʒſt authoʒ here of.
Anno Domini. M. D. LXVII.

¶ *Vewed, examined and allowed, according vnto the*
Queenes Mareſtyes Iniunctions.

¶ Impʒinted at London in Fleteſtrete at the ſigne of the
Falcon, by *Wyllia n Gryffith*, and are to be ſold at his ſhoppe in
Saynt Dunſtones Churche parde. in the Weſt.
Anno Domini. 1 5 6 7.

Plate V.

[*face p. 96*

Plate VI.

NICHOLAS JENNINGS IN TWO ROLES.

These two pictures lively set out
One body and soul.   God send him more grace !
This monstrous dissembler, a crank all about,
Uncomely coveting, of each to embrace
Money or wares, as he made his race ;
And sometime a mariner, and a serving-man,
Or else an artificer, as he would feign then.
Such shifts he used, being well tried,
Abandoning labour, till he was espied.
Condign punishment for his dissimulation
He surely received, with much exclamation.

[*face p. 97*

him on the head that down he falls, with the blood about his ears, and while he lay th[u]s amazed, the upright-man snatches away his purse, wherein he had money of his mistress's as well as of his own, and there let him lie, and went away with speed that they were never heard of more.

When this dry-beaten ostler was come to himself, he faintly wandereth home, and creepeth in to his couch, and rests his idle head. His mistress heard that he was come in, and laid him down on his bed, repaired straight unto him, and ask[s] him what he ailed, and what the cause was of his so sudden lying on his bed.

" What is the cause ? " quoth this ostler. " Your whistle, your whistle ! "—speaking the same piteously three or four times.

" Why, fool," quoth his mistress, " take no care for that, for I do not greatly weigh it ; it was worth but three shillings fourpence."

" I would it had been burnt for four years agone."

" I pray thee, why so ? " quoth his mistress. " I think thou art mad."

" Nay, not yet," quoth this ostler ; " but I have been madly handled."

" Why, what is the matter ? " quoth his mistress, and was more desirous to know the case.

" And you will forgive my fellow and me, I will show you. Or else I will never do it."

She made him presently faithful promise that she would.

" Then," saith he, " send for your son home again, which is ashamed to look you in the face."

" I agree thereto," saith she.

" Well, then," quoth this ostler, " Your son hath given the same mort that begged here for the burning of her house, a whistle, and you have given her five shillings in money, and I have given her ten shillings of my own."

" Why, how so ? " quoth she.

Then he sadly showed her of his mishap, with all the circumstance that you have heard before, and how his purse was taken away, and fifteen shillings in the same, whereof five shillings was her money, and ten shillings his own money.

" Is this true ? " quoth his mistress.

" Ay, by my troth," quoth this ostler, " and nothing grieves me so much, neither my beating, neither the loss of my money, as doth my evil and wretched luck ! "

" Why, what is the matter ? " quoth his mistress.

F

" Your son," saith this ostler, " had some cheer and pastime for that whistle, for he lay with her, and I have been well beaten, and have had my purse taken from me.   And you know your son is merry and pleasant, and can keep no great counsel.   And then shall I be mocked and laughed to scorn in all places when they shall hear how I have been served."

" Now, out upon you, knaves both ! " quoth his mistress, and laughs out the matter ; for she well saw it would not otherwise prevail.

CHAPTER XVII

A BAWDY-BASKET

These bawdy-baskets be also women, and go with baskets and cap-cases on their arms, wherein they have laces, pins, needles, white inkle, and round silk girdles of all colours.   These will buy conyskins, and steal linen clothes off on hedges.   And for their trifles they will procure of maiden-servants, when their mistress or dame is out of the way, either some good piece of beef, bacon, or cheese, that shall be worth twelvepence, for twopence of their toys.   And as they walk by the way, they often gain some money with their instrument by such as they suddenly meet withal.   The upright-men have good acquaintance with these, and will help and relieve them when they want.   Thus they trade their lives in lewd loathsome lechery.   Amongst them all is but one honest woman, and she is of good years.   Her name is Joan Messenger.   I have had good proof of her, as I have learned by the true report of divers.

There came to my gate the last summer, *Anno Domini* 1566, a very miserable man, and much deformed, as burnt in the face, blear-eyed, and lame of one of his legs, that he went with a crutch.   I axed him where he was born, and where he dwelt last, and showed him that thither he must repair and be relieved, and not to range about the country ; and seeing some cause of charity, I caused him to have meat and drink, and when he had drunk, I demanded of him whether he was never spoiled of the upright-man or rogue.

" Yes, that I have," quoth he ; " and not this seven years, for so long I have gone abroad, I had not so much taken from me, and so evil handled, as I was within these four days."

" Why, how so ? " quoth I.

" In good faith, sir," quoth he, " I chanced to meet with one of these bawdy-baskets which had an upright-man in her company, and as I would have passed quietly by her, ' Man,' saith she unto her make, ' do you not see this ill-favoured, windshaken knave ? ' ' Yes,' quoth the upright-man. ' What say you to him ? ' ' This knave oweth me two shillings for wares that he had of me, half a year ago, I think it well.' Saith this upright-man, ' Sirrah,' saith he, ' pay your debts.' Saith this poor man, ' I owe her none ; neither did I ever bargain with her for anything, and as I am advised I never saw her before in all my life.' ' Mercy, God ! ' quoth she, ' what a lying knave is this ! And he will not pay you, husband, beat him surely.' And the upright-man gave me three or four blows on my back and shoulders, and would have beat me worse and I had not given him all the money in my purse ; and, in good faith, for very fear, I was fain to give him fourteen pence, which was all the money that I had. ' Why,' saith this bawdy-basket, ' haſt thou no more ? Then thou oweſt me ten pence ſtill ; and, be well assured that I will be paid the next time I meet with thee.' And so they let me pass by them. I pray God save and bless me, and all other in my case, from such wicked persons," quoth this poor man.

" Why, whither went they then ? " quoth I.

" Into Eaſt Kent, for I met with them on this side of Rocheſter. I have divers times been attempted, but I never loſt much before. I thank God there came ſtill company by afore this unhappy time."

" Well," quoth I, " thank God of all, and repair home into thy native country."

Chapter XVIII

A Autem-Mort

These autem-morts be married women, as there be but a few. For autem in their language is a church. So she is a wife married at the church. And they be as chaſte as a cow I have, that goeth to bull every moon, with what bull she careth not. These walk moſt times from their husband's company a month and more together, being associate with another as honeſt as herself. These will pilfer clothes of hedges. Some of them go with children of ten or twelve years of age. If time and place serve for their purpose, they will send them into some house at the window, to steal and rob, which they call in their language, milling of the ken ; and will go with wallets on their shoulders and slates at their backs.

There is one of these autem-morts, she is now a widow, of fifty years old. Her name is Alice Milson. She goeth about with a couple of great boys ; the youngest of them is fast upon twenty years of age. And these two do lie with her every night, and she lieth in the midst. She saith that they be her children, that betelled be babes born of such abominable belly.

Chapter XIX

A Walking Mort

These walking morts be not married. These for their unhappy years doth go as a autem-mort, and will say their husbands died either at Newhaven,[30] Ireland, or in some service of the Prince. These make laces upon staves, and purses, that they carry in their hands, and white valance for beds. Many of these hath had and have children. When these get ought, either with begging, bitchery, or bribery, as money or apparel, they are quickly shaken out of all by the upright-men, that they are in a marvellous fear to carry anything about them that is of any value. Wherefore, this policy they use : they leave their money now with one and then with another trusty householders, either with the goodman or goodwife, sometime in one shire, and then in another, as they travel. This have I known, that four or five shillings, yea, ten shillings, left in a place, and the same will they come for again within one quarter of a year, or sometime not in half a year ; and all this is to little purpose, for all their peevish policy ; for when they buy them linen or garments, it is taken away from them, and worse given them, or none at all.

The last summer, *Anno Domini* 1566, being in familiar talk with a walking mort that came to my gate, I learned by her what I could, and I thought I had gathered as much for my purpose as I desired. I began to rebuke her for her lewd life and beastly behaviour, declaring to her what punishment was prepared and heaped up for her in the world to come for her filthy living and wretched conversation.

" God help ! " quoth she, " how should I live ? None will take me into service. But I labour in harvest-time honestly."

" I think but a while with honesty," quoth I.

" Shall I tell you? " quoth she. " The best of us all may be amended. But yet, I thank God, I did one good deed within this twelve months."

" Wherein ? " quoth I.

Saith she, " I would not have it spoken of again."

" If it be meet and necessary," quoth I, " it shall lie under my feet."

" What mean you by that ? " quoth she.

" I mean," quoth I, " to hide the same, and never to discover it to any."

" Well," quoth she, and began to laugh as much as she could, and swear by the mass that if I disclosed the same to any, she would never more tell me anything. " The last summer," quoth she, " I was great with child, and I travelled into East Kent by the sea-coast, for I lusted marvellously after oysters and mussels, and gathered many, and in the place where I found them, I opened them and ate them still. At the last, in seeking more, I reached after one, and stepped into a hole and fell in into the waist, and there did stick, and I had been drowned if the tide had come, and espying a man a good way off, I cried as much as I could for help. I was alone. He heard me, and repaired as fast to me as he might, and finding me there fast sticking, I required for God's sake his help. And whether it was with striving and forcing myself out, or for joy I had of his coming to me, I had a great colour in my face, and looked red and well-coloured. And, to be plain with you, he liked me so well as he said that I should there lie still, and I would not grant him that he might lie with me. And, by my troth, I wist not what to answer, I was in such a perplexity. For I knew the man well. He had a very honest woman to his wife, and was of some wealth ; and, on the other side, if I were not holp out, I should there have perished, and I granted him that I would obey to his will. Then he plucked me out. And because there was no convenient place near hand, I required him that I might go wash myself, and make me somewhat cleanly, and I would come to his house and lodge all night in his barn, whither he might repair to me, and accomplish his desire. ' But let it not be,' quoth he, ' before nine of the clock at night for then there will be small stirring.' ' And I may repair to the town,' quoth she, ' to warm and dry myself ' ; for this was about two of the clock in the afternoon. ' Do so,' quoth he ; ' for I must be busy to look out my cattle hereby before I can come home.' So I went away from him, and glad was I."

" And why so ? " quoth I.

" Because," quoth she, " his wife, my good dame, is my very friend, and I am much beholden to her. And she hath done me so much good or this, that I were loath now to harm her any way."

" Why," quoth I, " what and it had been any other man, and not your good dame's husband ? "

" The matter had been the less," quoth she.

" Tell me, I pray thee," quoth I, " who was the father of thy child ? "

She studied a while, and said that it had a father.

" But what was he ? " quoth I.

" Now, by my troth, I know not," quoth she. " You bring me out of my matter, so you do."

" Well, say on," quoth I.

" Then I departed straight to the town, and came to my dame's house, and showed her of my misfortune, also of her husband's usage in all points, and that I showed her the same for good will, and bid her take better heed to her husband, and to herself. So she gave me great thanks, and made me good cheer, and bid me in any case that I should be ready at the barn at that time and hour we had appointed. ' For I know well,' quoth this good wife, ' my husband will not break with thee. And one thing I warn thee, that thou give me a watchword aloud when he goeth about to have his pleasure of thee, and that shall be " Fie, for shame, fie," and I will be hard by you with help. But I charge thee, keep this secret until all be finished. And hold,' saith this good wife ; ' here is one of my petticoats I give thee.' ' I thank you, good dame,' quoth I, ' and I warrant you I will be true and trusty unto you.' So my dame left me setting by a good fire with meat and drink ; and with the oysters I brought with me, I had great cheer. She went straight and repaired unto her gossips dwelling thereby, and, as I did after understand, she made her moan to them, what a naughty, lewd, lecherous husband she had, and how that she could not have his company for harlots, and that she was in fear to take some filthy disease of him, he was so common a man, having little respect whom he had to do withal. ' And,' quoth she, ' now here is one at my house, a poor woman that goeth about the country, that he would have had to do withal. Wherefore, good neighbours and loving gossips, as you love me, and as you would have help at my hand another time, devise some remedy to make my husband a good man, that I may live in some surety without disease, and that he may save his soul that God so dearly bought.' After she had told her tale, they cast their piercing eyes all upon her. But one ftout dame amongft the reft had these words : ' As your patient bearing of troubles, your honeft behaviour among us your neighbours, your tender and pitiful heart to the poor of the parish, doth move us to lament your case, so the unsatiable carnality of your faithless husband doth inftigate and ftir us to devise and invent some speedy redress for your case and the amendment of his life. Wherefore, this is my counsel, and you will be advertised by me, for I say to you all, unless it be this good wife, who is chiefly touched in this matter, I have the next cause ; for he was in hand with me not long ago, and company had not been present, which was by a marvellous chance, he had, I think, forced me. For often he hath been tempting with me, and yet have I sharply said him nay. Therefore, let us assemble secretly into the place where he hath appointed to meet this gillot that is at your house, and lurk privily in some corner till he begin to go about his business. And then me-thought I heard you say even now that you had a watchword, at which word we will all ftep forth, being five of us besides you, for you shall be none because it is your husband, but get you to bed at your accuftomed hour. And we will carry each of us a good birchen rod in our laps, and we will all be muffled for knowing. And see that you go home and acquaint that walking mort with the matter ; for we muft have her help to hold, for always four muft hold and two lay on.' ' Alas ! ' saith this good wife, ' he is too ftrong for you all. I would be loath for my sake you should receive harm at his hand.' ' Fear you not,' quoth these ftout women. ' Let her not give the watchword until his hosen be about his legs. And I trow we all will be with him to bring before he shall have leisure to pluck them up again.' They all with one voice agreed to the matter, that the way she had devised was the beft. So this good wife repaired home. But before she departed from her gossips, she showed them at what hour they should privily come in on the back-side, and where to tarry their good hour. So by the time she came in, it was almoft night, and found the walking mort ftill sitting by the fire, and declared to her all this new devise abovesaid, which promised faithfully to fulfil to her small power as much as they had devised. Within a quarter of an hour after, in cometh the goodman, who said that he was about his cattle. ' Why, what have we here, wife, setting by the fire ? And if she have eat and drunk, send her into the barn to her lodging for this night, for she troubleth the house.' ' Even as you will, husband,' saith his wife. ' You know she cometh once in two years into these quarters. Away,' saith this good wife, ' to your lodging ! ' ' Yes, good dame,' saith she, ' as faft as I can.' Thus, by looking one on the other, each knew other's mind, and so departed to her comely couch.

" The goodman of the house shrugged him for joy, thinking to himself, ' I will make some pastime with you anon ' ; and, calling to his wife for his supper, set him down, and was very pleasant, and drank to his wife, and fell to his mammerings, and munched apace, nothing understanding of the banquet that was a preparing for him after supper, and, according to the proverb, that sweet meat will have sour sauce. Thus, when he was well refreshed, his spirits being revived, entered into familiar talk with his wife of many matters, how well he had spent that day to both their profits, saying some of his cattle were like to have been drowned in the ditches, driving others of his neighbours' cattle out that were in his pastures, and mending his fences that were broken down. Thus profitably he had consumed the day, nothing talking of his helping out of the walking mort out of the mire, neither of his request nor yet of her promise. Thus feeding her with friendly fantasies, consumed two hours and more. Then feigning how he would see in what case his horse were in and how they were dressed, repaired covertly into the barn, whereas his friendly foes lurked privily, unless it were this mannerly mort, that comely couched on a bottle of straw. ' What, are you come ? ' quoth she. ' By the mass, I would not for a hundred pound that my dame should know that you were here, either any else of your house.' ' No, I warrant thee,' saith this goodman, ' they be all safe and fast enough at their work, and I will be at mine anon ' ; and lay down by her, and straight would have had to do with her. ' Nay, fie,' saith she, ' I like not this order. If ye lie with me, you shall surely untruss you and put down your hosen, for that way is most easiest and best.' ' Sayest thou so ? ' quoth he, ' Now, by my troth, agreed.' And when he had untrussed himself and put down, he began to assault the unsatiable fort. ' Why,' quoth she, that was without shame, saving for her promise, ' And are you not ashamed ? ' ' Never a whit,' saith he. ' Lie down quickly.' ' Now, fie, for shame, fie,' saith she aloud, which was the watchword. At the which word, these five furious, sturdy, muffled gossips flings out, and takes sure hold of this betrayed person, some plucking his hosen down lower, and binding the same fast about his feet ; then binding his hands, and knitting a handkercher about his eyes, that he should not see. And when they had made him sure and fast, then they laid him on until they were windless. ' Be good,' saith this mort, ' unto my master, for the passion of God ! ' and laid on as fast as the rest, and still ceased not to cry upon them to be merciful unto him, and yet laid on apace. And when they had well beaten him, that the blood braſt plentifully out in moſt places, they let him lie ſtill bound—with this exhortation, that he should from that time forth know his wife from other men's, and that this punishment was but a flea-biting in respeſt of that which should follow, if he amended not his manners. Thus leaving him bluſtering, blowing, and foaming for pain, and melancholy that he neither might or could be revenged of them, they vanished away, and had this mort with them, and safely conveyed her out of the town. Soon after cometh into the barn one of the goodman's boys, to fet some hay for his horse ; and finding his maſter lying faſt bound and grievously beaten with rods, was suddenly abashed and would have run out again to have called for help. But his maſter bade him come unto him and unbind him ; ' and make no words,' quoth he, ' of this. I will be revenged well enough.' Yet notwithſtanding, after better advice, the matter being unhoneſt, he thought it meeter to let the same pass, and not, as the proverb saith, to awake the sleeping dog. And, by my troth," quoth this walking mort, " I come now from that place, and was never there sithence this part was played, which is somewhat more than a year. And I hear a very good report of him now, that he loveth his wife well, and useth himself very honeſtly. And was not this a good aſt, now ? How say you ? "

" It was prettily handled," quoth I. " And is here all ? "

" Yea," quoth she, " here is the end."

Chapter XX

A Doxy

These doxies be broken and spoiled of their maidenhead by the upright-men, and then they have their name of doxies, and not afore. And afterward she is common and indifferent for any that will use her, as *homo* is a common name to all men. Such as be fair and somewhat handsome, keep company with the walking morts, and are ready always for the upright-men, and are chiefly maintained by them, for others shall be spoiled for their sakes. The other inferior sort will resort to noblemen's places, and gentlemen's houses, ſtanding at the gate, either lurking on the back-side about back-houses, either in hedgerows, or some other thicket, expecting their prey, which is for the uncomely company of some courteous guest, of whom they be refreshed with meat and some money, where exchange is made, ware for ware. This bread and meat they use to carry in their great hosen; so that these beastly bribering breeches serve many times for bawdy purposes.

I chanced, not long sithence, familiarly to common with a doxy that came to my gate, and surely a pleasant harlot, and not so pleasant as witty, and not so witty as void of all grace and goodness. I found by her talk that she had passed her time lewdly eighteen years in walking about. I thought this a necessary instrument to attain some knowledge by. And before I would grope her mind, I made her both to eat and drink well. That done, I made her faithful promise to give her some money if she would open and discover to me such questions as I would demand of her, and never to bewray her, neither to disclose her name.

" And you should," saith she, " I were undone."

" Fear not that," quoth I. " But, I pray thee," quoth I, " say nothing but truth."

" I will not," saith she.

" Then first tell me," quoth I, " how many upright-men and rogues dost thou know, or hast thou known and been conversant with, and what their names be ? "

She paused awhile, and said, " Why do you ask me, or wherefore ? "

" For nothing else," as I said, " but that I would know them when they came to my gate."

" Now, by my troth," quoth she, " then are ye never the near, for all mine acquaintance for the most part are dead."

" Dead ! " quoth I, " how died they ? For want of cherishing, or of painful diseases ? "

Then she sighed, and said they were hanged.

" What, all ? " quoth I, " And so many walk abroad, as I daily see ! "

" By my troth," quoth she, " I know not past six or seven by their names "—and named the same to me.

" When were they hanged ? " quoth I.

" Some seven years agone, some three years, and some within this fortnight "—and declared the place where they were executed, which I knew well to be true by the report of others.

" Why," quoth I, " did not this sorrowful and fearful sight much grieve thee, and for thy time long and evil spent ? "

" I was sorry," quoth she, " by the mass. For some of them were good loving men. For I lacked not when they had it, and they wanted not when I had it, and divers of them I never did forsake, until the gallows departed us."

" O merciful God ! " quoth I, and began to bless me.

" Why bless ye ? " quoth she. " Alas ! good gentleman, every one must have a living."

Other matters I talked of. But this now may suffice to show the reader, as it were in a glass, the bold beastly life of these doxies. For such as hath gone any time abroad will never forsake their trade, to die therefore. I have had good proof thereof. There is one, a notorious harlot of this affinity called Bess Bottomly. She hath but one hand, and she hath murdered two children at the least.

Chapter XXI

A Dell

A dell is a young wench, able for generation, and not yet known or broken by the upright-man. These go abroad young, either by the death of their parents and nobody to look unto them, or else by some sharp mistress that they serve do run away out of service ; either she is naturally born one, and then she is a wild dell. These are broken very young. When they have been lain withal by the upright-man, then they be doxies, and no dells. These wild dells, being traded up with their monstrous mothers, must of necessity be as evil, or worse, than their parents, for neither we gather grapes from green briars, neither figs from thistles. But such buds, such blossoms, such evil seed sown, will worse being grown.

Chapter XXII

A Kinchin Mort

A kinchin mort is a little girl. The morts their mothers carries them at their backs in their slates, which is their sheets, and brings them up savagely, till they grow to be ripe : and soon ripe, soon rotten.

Chapter XXIII

A Kinchin Co

A kinchin co is a young boy, traden up to such peevish purposes as you have heard of other young imps before, that when he groweth unto years, he is better to hang than to draw forth.

Chapter XXIV

Their Usage in the Night

Now I think it not unnecessary to make the reader understand how and in what manner they lodge a nights in barns or back-houses, and of their usage there, forasmuch as I have acquainted them with their order and practices a day times. The arch and chief walkers, that hath walked a long time, whose experience is great because of their continuing practise, I mean all morts and doxies, for their handsomeness and diligence for making of their couches. The men never trouble themselves with that thing, but takes the same to be the duty of the wife. And she shuffles up a quantity of straw or hay into some pretty corner of the barn where she may conveniently lie, and well shaketh the same, making the head somewhat high, and drives the same upon the sides and feet like a bed : then she layeth her wallet, or some other little pack of rags or scrip under her head in the straw, to bear up the same, and layeth her petti-coat or cloak upon and over the straw, so made like a bed, and that serveth for the blanket. Then she layeth her slate (which is her sheet) upon that. And she have no sheet, as few of them go without, then she spreadeth some large clouts or rags over the same, and maketh her ready, and layeth her drousily down. Many will pluck off their smocks, and lay the same upon them instead of their upper sheet, and all her other pelt and trash upon her also ; and many lyeth in their smocks. And if the rest of her clothes in cold weather be not sufficient to keep her warm, then she taketh straw or hay to perform the matter. The other sort, that have not slates, but tumble down and couch a hogshead in their clothes, these be still lousy, and shall never be without vermin, unless they put off their clothes, and lie as is above said. If the upright-man come in where they lie, he hath his choice, and creepeth in close by his doxy. The rogue hath his leavings. If the morts or doxies lie or be lodged in some farmer's barn, and the door be either locked or made fast to them, then will not the upright-man press to come in, unless it be in barns and out-houses standing alone, or some distance from houses which be commonly known to them, as St. Quinten's, " Three Cranes of the Vintry,"[31] St. Tybbes, and Knapsbery. These four be within one mile compass near unto London. Then have you four more in Middlesex : " Draw the Pudding out of the Fire " in Harrow-on-the-Hill parish, " The Cross Keys " in Cranford parish, St. Julian's in Thistleworth[32] parish, " The House of Pity " in Northall[33] parish. These are their chief houses near about London, where commonly they resort unto for lodging, and may repair thither freely at all times. Sometime shall come in some rogue, some picking knave, a nimble prig. He walketh in softly a nights, when they be at their rest, and plucketh off as many garments as be ought worth that he may come by, and worth money, and may easily carry the same, and runneth away with the same with great celerity, and maketh port-sale at some convenient place of theirs, that some be soon ready in the morning, for want of their casters and togmans ; where instead of blessing is cursing ; in place of praying, pestilent prating with odious oaths and terrible threatenings.

The upright-men have given all these nicknames to the places above-said. Yet have we two notable places in Kent, not far from London. The one is between Deptford and Rotherhithe, called the King's Barn, standing alone, that they haunt commonly ; the other is Ketbroke,[34] standing by Blackheath, half a mile from any house. There will they boldly draw the latch of the door, and go in when the goodman with his family be at supper, and sit down without leave, and eat and drink with them, and either lie in the hall by the fire all night, or in the barn, if there be no room in the house for them. If the door be either bolted or locked, if it be not opened unto them when they will, they will break the same open to his farther cost. And in this barn sometime do lie forty upright-men with their doxies together at one time. And this must the poor farmer suffer, or else they threaten him to burn him and all that he hath.

THE NAMES OF THE UPRIGHT-MEN, ROGUES, AND PALLIARDS.

Here followeth the unruly rabblement of rascals, and the most notorious and wickedest walkers that are living now at this present, with their true names as they be called and known by. And, although I set and place here but three orders, yet, good reader, understand that all the others abovenamed are derived and come out from the upright-men and rogues. Concerning the number of morts and doxies, it is superfluous to write of them. I could well have done it, but the number of them is great, and would ask a large volume.

Upright-Men

A.
Anthony Heymer.
Anthony Jackson.

B.
Burfet.
Brian Medcalfe.

C.
Core the Cuckold.
Christopher Cooke.

D.
Dowzabell (skilful in fence).
David Coke.
Dick Glover.
Dick Abryſtowe.
David Edwardes.
David Holland.
David Jones.

E.
Edmund Dun (a singing man).
Edward Skinner (alias Ned Skinner).
Edward Browne.

F.
Follentine Hylles.
Ferdinando Angell.
Francis Daughton.

G.
Griffin.
Great John Graye.
George Marrinar.
George Hutchinson.

H.
Harry Hylles (alias Harry Godepar).
Harry Agglyntine.
Harry Smyth (he drivelleth when he speaketh.)
Harry Jonson.

I.
James Barnard.
John Myllar.
John Walchman.
John Jones.
John Teddar.
John Braye.
John Cutter.
John Bell.
John Stephens.
John Graye.
John Whyte.
John Rewe.
John Mores.
John a Farnando.
John Newman.
John Wyn (alias Williams).

John a Pycons.
John Thomas.
John Arter.
John Palmer (alias Tod).
John Geoffrey.
John Goddard.
John Graye the little.
John Graye the great.
John Williams the longer.
John Horwood (a maker of wells; he will take half his bargain in hand, and when he hath wrought two or three days, he runneth away with his earneſt).
John Peter.
John Porter.
John Appowes.
John Arter.
John Bates.
John Comes.
John Chyles (alias great Chyles).
John Levet (he maketh taps and faussets).
John Lovedall (a master of fence).

John Lovedale.
John Mekes.
John Appowell.
John Chapell.
John Griffen.
John Mason.
John Humphrey (with the lame hand).
John Stradling (with the shaking head).
John Frank.
John Baker.
John Bascafeld.

K.

L.

Leonard Just.
Long Greene.
Laurence Ladd.
Laurence Marshall.

M.

N.

Nicholas Wilson.
Ned Barington.
Ned Wetherdon.
Ned Holmes.

O.

P.

Philip Greene.

Q.

R.

Robert Gravener.
Robert Gerse.
Robert King.
Robert Egerton.
Robert Bell (brother to John Bell).
Robert Maple.
Robert Langton.
Robin Bell.
Robin Toppe.
Robert Brownswerd (he weareth his hair long).
Robert Curtis.
Richard Brymmysh.
Richard Justice.
Richard Barton.
Richard Constance.
Richard Thomas.
Richard Cadman.
Richard Scategood.
Richard Apryce.
Richard Walker.
Richard Coper.

S.

Stephen Nevet.

T.

Thomas Bullock.
Thomas Cutter.
Thomas Garret.
Thomas Newton.

Thomas Webb.
Thomas Graye (his toes be gone).
Tom Bodel.
Thomas Wast.
Thomas Dawson (alias Thomas Jacklin).
Thomas Basset.
Thomas Marchant.
Thomas Web.
Thomas Awefeld.
Thomas Gybbins.
Thomas Lacon.
Thomas Bate.
Thomas Allen.

V.

W.

Well-arrayed Richard.
William Chamborne.
William Pannell.
William Morgan.
William Belson.
William Ebes.
William Garret.
William Robinson.
William Umberville.
William Davids.
Will Pen.
William Jones.
Will Powell.
William Clarke.
Walter Wirral.
William Browne.
Walter Martin.
William Grace.
William Pickering.

Rogues

A.

Archie Douglas (a Scot)

B.

Black Dick.

C.

D.

Dick Durram.

David Dew Nevet (a counterfeit crank).

E.

Edward Ellis.

Edward Anseley.

F.

G.

George Belberby.

Goodman.

Gerard Gybbin (a counterfeit crank).

H.

Harry Walles (with the little mouth).

Humphrey Ward.

Harry Mason.

I.

John Warren.

John Donne (with one leg).

John Elson.

John Raynoles (Irishman).

John Harris.

James Monkaster (a counterfeit crank).

John Dewe.

John Crew (with one arm).

John Browne (great stammerer).

L.

Little Dick.

Little Robin.

Lambert Rose.

M.

More (burnt in the hand).

N.

Nicholas Adams (a great stammerer).

Nicholas Crispin.

Nicholas Blunt (alias Nicholas Jennings, a counterfeit crank).

Nicholas Lynch.

R.

Richard Brewton.

Richard Horwood (well near eighty years old ; he will bite a sixpenny nail

asunder with his teeth ; and a bawdy drunkard).

Richard Crane (he carryeth a kinchin co at his back).

Richard Jones.

Ralph Ketley.

Robert Harrison.

S.

Simon King.

T.

Thomas Paske.

Thomas Bere.

Thomas Shawnean (Irishman).

Thomas Smith (with the scald skin).

W.

William Carew.

William Wastfield.

Wilson.

William Jinks (with a white beard, a lusty and strong man ; he runneth about the country to seek work, with a big boy his son carrying his tools as a dauber or plasterer, but little work serveth him).

Palliards

B.
Bashford.

D.
Dick Sehan (Irish).
David Powell.
David Jones (a coun-
terfeit crank).

E.
Edward   Hayward
(hath his mort fol-
lowing him, which
feigned the crank).
Edward Lewes (a
dummerer).

H.
Hugh Jones.

I.
John Perse (a coun-
terfeit crank).
John Davids.

John Harrison.
John Carew.
James Lane (with one
eye ; Irish).
John Fisher.
John Dewe.
John Gylford (Irish ;
with a counter-
feit licence).

L.
Laurence (with the
great leg).

N.
Nicholas Newton (car-
rieth a feigned
licence).
Nicholas Decase.

P.
Prestove.

R.
Robert Lackley.
Robert Canloke.
Richard Hilton[35] (car-
rieth two kinchin-
morts about him).
Richard Thomas.

S.
Soth Gard.
Swanders.

T.
Thomas Edwards.
Thomas Davids.

W.
William Thomas.
William Coper with
the hare-lip.
Will Pettyt (beareth
a kinchin-mort at
his back).
William Bowmer.

There is above an hundred of Irishmen and women that wander about to beg for their living, that hath come over within these two years. They say they have been burned and spoiled by the Earl of Desmond, and report well of the Earl of Ormonde.[36]

All these above written for the most part walk about Essex, Middlesex, Sussex, Surrey, and Kent. Then let the reader judge what number walks in other shires ; I fear me too great a number, if they be well understand.

Here followeth their pelting speech :

Here I set before the good reader the lewd, lousy language of these loitering lusks and lazy lorels, wherewith they buy and sell the common people as they pass through the country ; which language they term pedlars' French, a unknown tongue only but to these bold, beastly, bawdy beggars and vain vagabonds, being half mingled with English when it is familiarly talked. And first placing things by their proper names as an introduction to this peevish speech :

nab, a head.

nab-cheat, a hat or cap.

glaziers, eyes.

a smelling-cheat, a nose.

gan, a mouth.

a prattling-cheat, a tongue.

crashing-cheats, teeth.

hearing-cheats, ears.

fambles, hands.

a fambling-cheat, a ring on thy hand.

quarroms, a body.

prat, a buttock.

stamps, legs.

a caster, a cloak.

a togman, a coat.

a commission, a shirt.

drawers, hosen.

stampers, shoes.

a muffling-cheat, a napkin.

a belly-cheat, an apron.

duds, clothes.

a lag of duds, a buck of clothes.

a slate or slates, a sheet or sheets.

libbege, a bed.

bung, a purse.

lour, money.

mint, gold.

a bord, a shilling.

half-a-bord, sixpence.

flag, a groat.

a win, a penny.

a make, a halfpenny.

bouse, drink.

bene, good.

beneship, very good.

queer, nought.

a gage, a quart pot.

a skew, a cup.

pannam, bread.

cassan, cheese.

yarrum, milk.

lap, buttermilk or whey.

peck, meat.

poplars, porridge.

ruff-peck, bacon.

a grunting-cheat or a patrico's kinchin, a pig.

a cackling-cheat, a cock or capon.

a margery-prater, a hen.

a Roger or tib of the buttery, a goose.

a quacking-cheat or a redshank, a drake or duck.

grannam, corn.

a lowing-cheat, a cow.

a bleating-cheat, a calf or sheep.

a prancer, a horse.

autem, a church.

Solomon, a altar or mass.

patrico, a priest.

nosegent, a nun.

a gybe, a writing.

a jark, a seal.

a ken, a house.

a stalling-ken, a house that will receive stolen ware.

a bousing ken, a ale-house.

a libken, a house to lie in.
a libbege, a bed.
glimmer, fire.
rome-bouse, wine.
lage, water.
a skipper, a barn.
Strummel, straw.
a gentry cove's ken, a noble or gentleman's house.
a jigger, a door.
bufe, a dog.
the lightmans, the day.
the darkmans, the night.
Rome-vill, London.
dewse-a-vill, the country.
rome-mort, the Queen.
a gentry cove, a noble or gentleman.
a gentry mort, a noble or gentlewoman.
the Queer Cuffin, the Justice of Peace.
the harman-beck, the constable.
the harmans, the stocks.
queer-ken, a prison-house.
queer cramp-rings, bolts or fetters.
trining, hanging.
chats, the gallows.
the high-pad, the highway.
the ruffmans, the woods or bushes.
a smelling-cheat, a garden or orchard.

crassing-cheats, apples, pears, or any other fruit.
to filch, to beat, to strike, to rob.
to nip a bung, to cut a purse.
to scour the cramp-rings, to wear bolts or fetters.
to heave a bough, to rob or rifle a booth.
to cly the jerk, to be whipped.
to cut benely, to speak gently.
to cut bene whids, to speak, or give good words.
to cut queer whids, to give evil words or evil language.
to cut, to say.
to tour, to see.
to bouse, to drink.
to maund, to ask or require.
to stall, to make or ordain.
to cant, to speak.
to mill a ken, to rob a house.
to prig, to ride.
to dup the jigger, to open the door.
to couch a hogshead, to lie down and sleep.
to niggle, to have to do with a woman carnally.
Stow you, hold your peace.
bing a waste, go you hence.
to the Ruffian, to the Devil.
the Ruffian cly thee, the Devil take thee.

The upright-cove canteth to the rogue.
The upright-man speaketh to the rogue.

UPRIGHT-MAN. *Bene lightmans to thy quarroms! In what libken hast thou libbed in this darkmans, whether in a libbege or in the strummel?*

Good-morrow to thy body! In what house hast thou lain in all night, whether in a bed or in the straw?

ROGUE. *I couched a hogshead in a skipper this darkmans.*

I laid me down to sleep in a barn this night.

UPRIGHT-MAN. *I tour the strummel trine upon thy nab-cheat and togman.*

I see the straw hang upon thy cap and coat.

ROGUE. *I say by the Solomon I will lage it off with a gage of bene bouse. Then cut to my nose watch.*

I swear by the mass I will wash it off with a quart of good drink. Then say to me what thou wilt.

MAN. *Why, hast thou any lour in thy bung to bouse?*

Why, hast thou any money in thy purse to drink?

ROGUE. *But a flag, a win, and a make.*

But a groat, a penny, and a halfpenny.

MAN. *Why, where is the ken that hath the bene bouse?*

Where is the house that hath good drink?

ROGUE. *A bene-mort hereby at the sign of the Prancer.*

A goodwife hereby at the sign of the Horse.

MAN. *I cut it is queer bouse. I boused a flag the last darkmans.*

I say it is small and naughty drink. I drank a groat there the last night.

ROGUE. *But bouse there a bord, and thou shalt have beneship.*

But drink there a shilling, and thou shalt have very good.

Tour ye. Yonder is the ken. Dup the jigger and maund that is beneship.

See you. Yonder is the house. Open the door and ask for the best.

MAN. *This bouse is as beneship as rome-bouse.*

This drink is as good as wine.

Now I tour that bene bouse makes nase nabs.

Now I see that good drink makes a drunken head.

Maund of this mort what bene peck is in her ken.

Ask of this wife what good meat she hath in her house.

ROGUE. *She hath a cackling-cheat, a grunting-cheat, ruff-peck, cassan, and poplar of yarrum.*

She hath a hen, a pig, bacon, cheese, and milk-porridge.

MAN. *That is beneship to our watch.*

That is very good for us.

[ROGUE]. *Now we have well boused, let us strike some cheat.*

Now we have well drunk, let us steal something.

[MAN]. *Yonder dwelleth a queer cuffin. It were beneship to mill him.*
Yonder dwelleth a hoggish and churlish man. It were very well done to rob him.

ROGUE. *Now bing we a waste to the high-pad ; the ruffmans is by.*
Nay, let us go hence to the highway ; the woods is at hand.

MAN. *So may we happen on the harmans, and cly the jerk, or to the queer-ken and scour queer cramp-rings, and so to trining on the chats.*
So we may chance to set in the stocks, either be whipped, either had to prison-house, and there be shackled with bolts and fetters, and then to hang on the gallows.

[ROGUE]. *Gerry gan !! the Ruffian cly thee !*
A turd in thy mouth ! the Devil take thee !

MAN. *What ! Stow your bene, cove, and cut benat whids ! And bing we to Rome-vill, to nip a bung. So shall we have lour for the bousing ken. And when we bing back to the dewse-a-vill, we will filch some duds off the ruffmans, or mill the ken for a lag of duds.*
What ! Hold your peace, good fellow, and speak better words ! And go we to London, to cut a purse. Then shall we have money for the ale-house. And when we come back again into the country, we will steal some linen clothes off some hedges, or rob some house for a buck of clothes.

By this little ye may wholly and fully understand their untoward talk and pelting speech, mingled without measure. And as they have begun of late to devise some new terms for certain things, so will they in time alter this, and devise as evil or worse. This language now being known and spread abroad, yet one thing more I will add unto, not meaning to English the same, because I learned the same of a shameless doxy. But for the phrase of speech I set it forth only.

There was a proud patrico and a nosegent. He took his jockam in his famble, and a wapping he went ; he docked the dell ; he prig to prance ; he binged a waste into the darkmans ; he filched the cove without any filchman.

While[37] this second impression was in printing, it fortuned that Nicholas Blunt, who called himself Nicholas Jennings, a counterfeit crank, that is spoken of in this book, was found begging in the White-friars on New Year's Day last past, *Anno Domini* 1567 [-8] and committed unto a officer, who carried him unto the Deputy of the ward, which committed him unto the Counter; and as the Constable and another would have carried him thither, this counterfeit crank ran away, but one lighter of foot than the other overtook him, and so leading him to the counter, where he remained three days, and from thence to Bridewell, where before the Master he had this disguised apparel put upon him, which was monstrous to behold, and after stood in Cheapside with the same apparel on a scaffold.

A stocks to stay sure, and safely detain
  Lazy lewd loiterers, that laws do offend,
Impudent persons, thus punished with pain,
  Hardly for all this, do mean to amend.[38]

Fetters or shackles serve to make fast
Male malefactors that on mischief do muse,
  Until the learned laws do quit or do cast
Such subtle searchers as all evil do use.
  A whip is a whisker that will wrest out blood,
Of back and of body, beaten right well.
  Of all the other it doth the most good;
Experience teacheth, and they can well tell.
  O doleful day! now death draweth near,
His bitter sting doth pierce me to the heart.
  I take my leave of all that be here,
Now piteously playing this tragical part.
  Neither stripes nor teachings in time could convert;
Wherefore an ensample let me to you be,
  And all that be present, now pray you for me.
This counterfeit crank, now view and behold,
  Placed in pillory, as all may well see.
This was he, as you have heard the tale told,
  Before recorded with great subtlety,
Abused many with his impiety,
  His loathsome attire, in most ugly manner,
Was through London carried with displayed banner.

Thus I conclude my bold beggars' book,
That all estates most plainly may see,
As in a glass well polished to look,
Their double demeanour in each degree;
Their lives, their language, their names as they be,
That with this warning their minds may be warned
To amend their misdeeds, and so live unharmed.

Finis.

A NOTABLE DISCOVERY OF COZENAGE

By Robert Greene

[1591]

*To the young gentlemen, merchants, apprentices, farmers, and plain
countrymen, health.*

DIOGENES, Gentlemen, from a counterfeit coiner of money, became
a current corrector of manners, as absolute in the one, as dissolute
in the other. Time refineth men's affects, and their humours grow
different by the distinction of age. Poor Ovid that amorously writ in
his youth the art of love, complained in his exile amongst the Getae of
his wanton follies; and Socrates' age was virtuous though his prime
was licentious. So, Gentlemen, my younger years had uncertain
thoughts, but now my ripe days calls on to repentant deeds, and I sorrow
as much to see others wilful, as I delighted once to be wanton. The
odd madcaps I have been mate to, not as companion, but as a spy to
have an insight into their knaveries, that seeing their trains I might
eschew their snares, those mad fellows I learned at last to loath, by their
own graceless villainies; and what I saw in them to their confusion
I can forewarn in others to my country's commodity. None could
decipher tyrannism better than Aristippus; not that his nature was
cruel, but that he was nurtured with Dionysius. The simple swain that
cuts the lapidary's stones, can distinguish a ruby from a diamond only
by his labour. Though I have not practised their deceits, yet conversing
by fortune and talking upon purpose with such copesmates, hath given
me light into their conceits, and I can decipher their qualities, though I
utterly mislike of their practices. To be brief, Gentlemen, I have seen
the world and rounded it, though not with travel, yet with experience,
and I cry out with Solomon, *Omnia sub sole vanitas*. I have smiled with
the Italian, and worn the viper's head in my hand, and yet stopped his
venom. I have eaten Spanish myrobalans, and yet am nothing the more
metamorphosed. France, Germany, Poland, Denmark, I know them
all, yet not affected to any in the form of my life; only I am English-
born, and I have English thoughts, not a devil incarnate because I am

Italianate, but hating the pride of Italy, because I know their peevishness. Yet in all these countries where I have travelled, I have not seen more excess of vanity than we Englishmen practise through vainglory: for as our wits be as ripe as any, so our wills are more ready than they all to put in effect any of their licentious abuses. Yet amongst the rest, letting ordinary sins pass, because custom hath almost made them a law, I will only speak of two such notable abuses, which the practitioners of them shadow with the name of arts, as never have been heard of in any age before. The first and chief is called the art of cony-catching; the second, the art of crossbiting; two such pestilent and prejudicial practices, as of late have been the ruin of infinite persons, and the subversion and overthrow of many merchants, farmers and honest-minded yeomen. The first is a deceit at cards, which, growing by enormity into a cozenage, is able to draw (by the subtle show thereof) a man of great judgment to consent to his own confusion. Yet, Gentlemen, when you shall read this book, written faithfully to discover these cozening practices, think I go not about to disprove or disallow the most ancient and honest pastime or recreation of card-play, for thus much I know by reading: when the city of Thebes was besieged by them of Lacedaemonia, being girt within strong fenced walls, and having men enough, and able to rebate the enemy, they found no inconvenience of force to breed their ensuing bane but famine, in that, when victuals waxed scant, hunger would either make them yield by a fainting composition, or a miserable death. Whereupon to weary the foe with wintering at the siege, the Thebans devised this policy: they found out the method of cards and dice, and so busied their brains with the pleasantness of that new invention, passing away the time with strange recreations and pastimes, beguiling hunger with the delight of the new sports, and eating but every third day and playing two, so their frugal sparing of victuals kept them from famine, the city from sacking, and raised the foe from a mortal siege. Thus was the use of cards and dice first invented, and since amongst princes highly esteemed, and allowed in all commonwealths, as a necessary recreation for the mind. But as in time and malice of man's nature hatcheth abuse, so good things by ill wits are wrested to the worse, and so in cards; for from an honest recreation it is grown to a prejudicial practice and most high degree of cozenage, as shall be discovered in my *Art of Cony-catching*; for not only simple swains, whose wits is in their hands, but young gentlemen and merchants, are all caught like conies in the hay, and so led like lambs to their confusion.

The poor man that cometh to the Term to try his right, and layeth his land to mortgage to get some crowns in his purse to see his lawyer, is drawn in by these devilish cony-catchers, that at one cut at cards loseth all his money, by which means, he, his wife and children, is brought to utter ruin and misery. The poor 'prentice, whose honeſt mind aimeth only at his maſter's profits, by these peſtilent vipers of the common-wealth is smoothly enticed to the hazard of this game at cards, and robbed of his maſter's money, which forceth him ofttimes either to run away, or bankrupt all, to the overthrow of some honeſt and wealthy citizen. Seeing then such a dangerous enormity groweth by them to the discredit of the eſtate of England, I would wish the Juſtices appointed as severe censors of such fatal mischiefs, to show themselves *patres patriæ*, by weeding out such worms as eat away the sap of the tree, and rooting this base degree of cozeners out of so peaceable and prosperous a country, for of all devilish praſtices this is the moſt prejudicial. The high-lawyer that challengeth a purse by the highway side, the foiſt, the nip, the ſtale, the snap—I mean the pickpockets and cutpurses—are nothing so dangerous to meet withal as these cozening cony-catchers. The cheaters that with their false dice make a hand and ſtrike in at hazard or passage with their dice of advantage, are nothing so dangerous as these base-minded caterpillars. For they have their vies and their revies upon the poor cony's back, till they so ferret-beat him, that they leave him neither hair on his skin nor hole to harbour in. There was before this, many years ago,[1] a praſtice put in use by such shifting companions, which was called the barnard's law, wherein, as in the art of cony-catching, four persons were required to perform their cozening commodity : the taker-up, the verser, the barnard and the rutter ; and the manner of it indeed was thus. The taker-up seemeth a skilful man in all things, who hath by long travail learned without book a thousand policies to insinuate himself into a man's acquaintance. Talk of matters in law, he hath plenty of cases at his fingers' ends, and he hath seen, and tried, and ruled in the King's courts. Speak of grazing and hus-bandry, no man knoweth more shires than he, nor better which way to raise a gainful commodity, and how the abuses and overture of prices might be redressed.[2] Finally, enter into what discourse they liſt, were it into a broom-man's faculty, he knoweth what gains they have for old boots and shoes ; yea, and it shall scape him hardly, but that ere your talk break off, he will be your countryman at leaſt, and, peradventure either of kin, ally or some ſtale sib to you, if your reach far surmount not his. In case he bring to pass that you be glad of his acquaintance, then doth he carry you to the taverns, and with him goes the verser, a man of more worship than the taker-up, and he hath the countenance of a landed man.   As they are set, comes in the barnard ſtumbling into your company, like some aged farmer of the country, a ſtranger unto you all, that had been at some market town thereabout, buying and selling, and there tippled so much malmsy that he had never a ready word in his mouth, and is so careless of his money that out he throweth some forty angels on the board's end, and, ſtanding somewhat aloof, calleth for a pint of wine, and saith, "Maſters, I am somewhat bold with you; I pray you be not grieved if I drink my drink by you"; and thus miniſters such idle drunken talk that the verser, who counter-feited the landed man, comes and draws more near to the plain honeſt-dealing man, and prayeth him to call the barnard more near to laugh at his folly.   Between them two the matter shall be so workmanly conveyed and finely argued that out cometh an old pair of cards, whereat the barnard teacheth the verser a new game, that he says coſt him for the learning two pots of ale not two hours ago.   The firſt wager is drink, the next twopence or a groat, and laſtly, to be brief, they use the matter so, that he that were an hundred year old and never played in his life for a penny, cannot refuse to be the verser's half, and consequently, at one game at cards he loseth all they play for, be it a hundred pound. And if perhaps, when the money is loſt (to use their word of art), the poor countryman begin to smoke them and swears the drunken knave shall not get his money so, then ſtandeth the rutter at the door and draweth his sword and picketh a quarrel at his own shadow, if he lack an oſtler or a tapſter or some other to brabble with, that while the ſtreet and company gather to the fray, as the manner is, the barnard ſteals away with all the coin, and gets him to one blind tavern or other, where these cozeners had appointed to meet.

Thus, Gentlemen, I have glanced at the barnard's law, which though you may perceive it to be a prejudicial insinuating cozenage, yet is the art of cony-catching so far beyond it in subtlety, as the Devil is more honeſt than the holieſt angel: for so unlikely is it for the poor cony to lose, that might he pawn his ſtake to a pound, he would lay it that he cannot be crossbitten in the cut at cards, as you shall perceive by my present discovery.   Yet, Gentlemen, am I sore threatened by the hackſters of that filthy faculty that if I set their praſtices in print, they will cut off that hand that writes the pamphlet; but how I fear their bravados, you shall perceive by my plain painting out of them; yea, so little do I eſteem such base-minded braggards that, were it not I hope of their amendment, I would in a schedule set down the names of such cozening cony-catchers.

Well, leaving them and their course of life to the honourable and the worshipful of the land to be censors of with justice, have about for a blow at the art of crossbiting. I mean not crossbiters at dice, when the cheater with a langret, cut contrary to the vantage, will crossbite a barred cater-trey; nor I mean not when a broking knave crossbiteth a gentleman with a bad commodity; nor when the foist, the pickpocket (sir, reverence I mean), is crossbitten by the snap, and so, smoked for his purchase; nor when the nip, which the common people call a cutpurse, hath a crossbite by some bribing officer, who, threatening to carry him to prison, takes away all the money, and lets him slip without any punishment; but I mean a more dishonourable art, when a base rogue, either keepeth a whore as his friend, or marries one to be his maintainer, and with her not only crossbites men of good calling, but especially poor ignorant country farmers, who, God wot, be by them led like sheep to the slaughter. Thus, gentle readers, have I given you a light in brief what I mean to prosecute at large, and so with an humble suit to all Justices, that they will seek to root out these two roguish arts, I commit you to the Almighty.

Yours, Rob. Greene.

THE ART OF CONY-CATCHING

THERE be requisite effectually to act the art of cony-catching three several parties, the setter, the verser, and the barnacle. The nature of the setter is to draw any person familiarly to drink with him, which person they call the cony, and their method is according to the man they aim at. If a gentleman, merchant or apprentice, the cony is the more easily caught, in that they are soon induced to play, and therefore I omit the circumstance which they use in catching of them. And for because the poor country farmer or yeoman is the mark which they most of all shoot at, who they know comes not empty to the Term, I will discover the means they put in practice to bring in some honest, simple and ignorant men to their purpose.

The cony-catchers, apparelled like honest civil gentlemen or good fellows, with a smooth face, as if butter would not melt in their mouths, after dinner when the clients are come from Westminster Hall and are at leisure to walk up and down Paul's, Fleet Street, Holborn, the Strand, and such common haunted places, where these cozening companions attend only to spy out a prey; who, as soon as they see a plain country fellow, well and cleanly apparelled, either in a coat of homespun russet, or of frieze, as the time requires, and a side-pouch at his side—" There is a cony," saith one.   At that word out flies the setter, and overtaking the man, begins to salute him thus : " Sir, God save you, you are welcome to London !   How doth all our good friends in the country ?   I hope they be all in health ? "   The countryman, seeing a man so courteous he knows not, half in a brown study at this strange salutation, perhaps makes him this answer : " Sir, all our friends in the country are well, thanks be to God ; but truly I know you not.   You must pardon me." " Why sir," saith the setter, guessing by his tongue what countryman he is, " are you not such a countryman ? "   If he say, " Yes," then he creeps upon him closely.   If he say, " No," then straight the setter comes over him thus : " In good sooth, sir, I know you by your face and have been in your company before.   I pray you, if without offence, let me crave your name and the place of your abode."   The simple man straight tells him where he dwells, his name and who be his next neighbours, and what gentlemen dwell about him.   After he hath learned all of him, then he comes over his fallows kindly : " Sir, though I have been somewhat bold to be inquisitive of your name, yet hold me excused, for I took you for a friend of mine, but since by mistaking I have made you slack your business, we'll drink a quart of wine or a pot of ale together."   If the fool be so ready as to go, then the cony is caught ; but if he smack the setter, and smells a rat by his clawing, and will not drink with him, then away goes the setter, and discourseth to the verser the name of the man, the parish he dwells in, and what gentlemen are his near neighbours.   With that, away goes he, and, crossing the man at some turning, meets him full in the face, and greets him thus :

" What, Goodman Barton, how fare all our friends about you ? You are well met.   I have the wine for you.   You are welcome to town." The poor countryman hearing himself named by a man he knows not, marvels, and answers that he knows him not, and craves pardon.

" Not me, Goodman Barton, have you forgot me ?   Why, I am such a man's kinsman, your neighbour not far off.   How doth this or that good gentleman, my friend ?   Good Lord, that I should be out of your remembrance.   I have been at your house divers times."

" Indeed, sir," saith the farmer, " are you such a man's kinsman ? Surely, sir, if you had not challenged acquaintance of me, I should never have known you. I have clean forgot you, but I know the good gentleman your cousin well; he is my very good neighbour."

" And for his sake," saith the verser, " we'll drink afore we part."

Haply the man thanks him, and to the wine or ale they go; then, ere they part, they make him a cony and so ferret-claw him at cards, that they leave him as bare of money as an ape of a tail. Thus have the filthy fellows their subtle fetches to draw on poor men to fall into their cozening practices. Thus, like consuming moths of the commonwealth, they prey upon the ignorance of such plain souls, as measure all by their own honesty, not regarding either conscience, or the fatal revenge that's threatened for such idle and licentious persons, but do employ all their wits to overthrow such as with their handy thrift satisfy their hearty thirst; they preferring cozenage before labour, and choosing an idle practice before any honest form of good living. Well, to the method again of taking up their conies : If the poor countryman smoke them still, and will not stoop unto either of their lures, then one, either the verser, or the setter, or some of their crew—for there is a general fraternity betwixt them—steppeth before the cony as he goeth, and letteth drop twelvepence in the highway, that of force the cony must see it. The countryman, spying the shilling, maketh not dainty, for *quis nisi mentis inops oblatum respuit aurum ?* but stoopeth very mannerly and taketh it up. Then one of the cony-catchers behind crieth, " Half part ! " and so challengeth half of his finding. The countryman, content, offereth to change the money. " Nay, faith ! friend," saith the verser, " 'tis ill luck to keep found money ; we'll go spend it in a pottle of wine, or in a breakfast " (*dinner* or *supper*—as the time of day requires). If the cony say he will not, then answers the verser, " Spend my part." If still the cony refuse, he taketh half and away.

If they spy the countryman to be of a having and covetous mind, then have they a further policy to draw him on. Another that knoweth the place of his abode, meeteth him and saith, " Sir, well met ! I have run hastily to overtake you. I pray you, dwell you not in Derbyshire, in *such a village*? "—" Yes, marry! do I, friend," saith the cony. Then replies the verser, " truly, sir, I have a suit to you ; I am going out of town, and must send a letter to the parson of your parish. You shall not refuse to do a stranger such a favour as to carry it him. Haply, as men may in time meet, it may lie in my lot to do you as good a turn, and for your pains I will give you twelvepence. The poor cony in mere simplicity saith, " Sir, I'll do so much for you with all my heart. Where is your letter ? "—" I have it not, good sir, ready written ; but may I entreat you to step into some tavern or alehouse. We'll drink the while, and I will write but a line or two." At this the cony stoops, and for greediness of the money, and upon courtesy goes with the setter unto the tavern. As they walk they meet the verser, and then they all three go into the tavern together.

See, Gentlemen, what great logicians these cony-catchers be, that have such rhetorical persuasions to induce the poor countryman to his confusion, and what variety of villainy they have to strip the poor farmer of his money. Well, imagine the cony is in the tavern. Then sits down the verser, and saith to the setter, " What, sirrah, wilt thou give me a quart of wine, or shall I give thee one ? "

" We'll drink a pint," saith the setter, " and play a game at cards for it, respecting more the sport than the loss."

" Content," quoth the verser. " Go call for a pair." And while he is gone to fetch them, he saith to the cony, " You shall see me fetch over my young master for a quart of wine finely ; but this you must do for me : when I cut the cards, as I will not cut above five off, mark then of all the greatest pack which is undermost, and when I bid you call a card for me, name that, and you shall see, we'll make him pay for a quart of wine straight."

" Truly," saith the cony, " I am no great player at cards, and I do not well understand your meaning."

" Why," saith he, " It is thus : I will play at mumchance, or decoy, that he shall shuffle the cards, and I will cut. Now, either of us must call a card. You shall call for me, and he for himself, and whose card comes first wins. Therefore, when I have cut the cards, then mark the nethermost of the greatest heap, that I set upon the cards which I cut off, and always call that for me."

" Oh now," saith the cony, " I understand you. Let me alone, I warrant I'll fit your turn."

With that in comes the setter with his cards and asketh at what game they shall play. " Why," saith the verser, " at a new game called mumchance, that hath no policy nor knavery, but plain as a pikestaff. You shall shuffle and I'll cut. You shall call a card, and this honest man, a stranger almost to us both, shall call another for me, and which of our cards comes first, shall win."

" Content," saith the setter, " for that's but mere hazard." And so he shuffles the cards, and the verser cuts off some four cards, and then, taking up the heap to set upon them, giveth the cony a glance of the bottom card of that heap and saith, " Now, sir, call for me."

The cony, to blind the setter's eyes, asketh as though he were not made privy to the game : "What shall I call ? "[3]

"What card ? " saith the verser. "Why, what you will, either heart, spade, club or diamond, cote-card or other."

"Oh, is it so ? " saith the cony. "Why then, you shall have the four of hearts," which was the card he had a glance of ; and saith the setter (holding the cards in his hand, and turning up the uppermost card, as if he knew not well the game) " I'll have the knave of trumps."

"Nay," saith the verser, "there is no trump ; you may call what card you will."

"Then," saith he, "I'll have the ten of spades." With that he draws, and the four of hearts comes first.

"Well," saith the setter, " 'tis but hazard ; mine might have come as well as yours ; five is up, I fear not the set." So they shuffle and cut, but the verser wins.

"Well," saith the setter, " no butter will cleave on my bread. What ! not one draught among five. Drawer, a fresh pint. I'll have another bout with you."

"But, sir, I believe," saith he to the cony, " you see some card, that it goes so cross on my side."

"I ? " saith the cony. "Nay, I hope you think not so of me ; 'tis but hazard and chance, for I am but a mere stranger unto the game. As I am an honest man, I never saw it before."

Thus this simple cony closeth up smoothly to take the verser's part, only for greediness to have him win the wine.

"Well," answers the setter, "then I'll have one cast more." And to it they go, but he loseth all, and beginneth to chafe in this manner : "Were it not," quoth he, "that I care not for a quart of wine, I could swear as many oaths for anger, as there be hairs on my head. Why should not my luck be as good as yours, and fortune favour me as well as you ? What ! Not one called card in ten cuts ? I'll foreswear the game for ever."

"What ! chafe not, man," saith the verser, "seeing we have your quart of wine, I'll show you the game " ; and with that, discourseth all to him, as if he knew it not.

The setter, as simply as if the knave were ignorant, saith, "Ay, marry ! I think so ; you must needs win when he knows what card to call. I might have played long enough before I had got a set."

"Truly," says the cony, " 'tis a pretty game, for 'tis not possible for him to lose that cuts the cards. I warrant the other that shuffles may lose St. Peter's cope if he had it. Well, I'll carry this home with me into the country, and win many a pot of ale with it."

" A fresh pint," saith the verser, " and then we'll away. But seeing, sir, you are going homeward, I'll learn you a trick worth the noting, that you shall win many a pot with in the winter nights." With that he culls out the four knaves, and pricks one in the top, one in the midst, and one in the bottom. " Now sir," saith he, " you see these three knaves apparently. Thrust them down with your hand, and cut where you will, and, though they be so far asunder, I'll make them all come together."

" I pray you, let's see that trick," saith the cony ; " methinks it should be impossible."

So the verser draws, and all the three knaves comes in one heap. This he doth once or twice ; then the cony wonders at it, and offers him a pint of wine to teach it him.

" Nay," saith the verser, " I'll do it for thanks, and therefore mark me where you have taken out the four knaves, lay two together above and draw up one of them that it may be seen, then prick the other in the midst, and the third in the bottom, so when any cuts, cut he never so warily, three knaves must of force come together, for the bottom knave is cut to lie upon both the upper knaves."

" Ay, marry," saith the setter, " but then the three knaves you showed come not together."

" Truth," saith the verser, " but one among a thousand mark not it ; it requires a quick eye, a sharp wit, and a reaching head to spy at the first."

" Now gramercy, sir, for this trick," saith the cony, " I'll domineer with this amongst my neighbours."

Thus doth the verser and the setter feign friendship to the cony, offering him no show of cozenage, nor once to draw him in for a pint of wine, the more to shadow their villainy. But now begins the sport. As thus they sit tippling, comes the barnacle and thrusts open the door, looking into the room where they are, and as one bashful steppeth back again and saith, " I cry you mercy, gentlemen, I thought a friend of mine had been here ; pardon my boldness."

" No harm," saith the verser, " I pray you drink a cup of wine with us and welcome."

So in comes the barnacle and, taking the cup, drinks to the cony, and then saith, " What ! at cards gentlemen ? Were it not I should be

(a)

(b)

Plate VII.

(a) At the gallows foot.
(b) Nicholas Jennings in the pillory.

[face p. 128

A
Notable Difcouery of Coofenage.

Now daily practifed by fundry lewd per-
fons , called Connie-catchers, and
Croffe-byters.

Plainely laying open thofe pernitious fleights that hath brought many ignorant men to confufion.

*Written for the general benefit of all Gentlemen, Citizens, Aprentifes, Countrey Farmers
and yeomen, that may hap to fall into the company of fuch coofening companions.*

With a delightfull difcourfe of the coofnage of Colliers.

Nafcintur pro patria.   By R. Greene, Maifter of Arts.

LONDON
Printed by Thomas Scarlet for Thomas Nelfon.
1 5 9 2.

Plate VIII.

[*face p. 129*]

offensive to the company, I would play for a pint till my friend come that I look for."

"Why sir," saith the verser, "if you will sit down you shall be taken up for a quart of wine."

"With all my heart," saith the barnacle. "What will you play at, at primero, prima-vista, cent, one-and-thirty, new cut, or what shall be the game?"

"Sir," saith the verser, "I am but an ignorant man at cards, and I see you have them at your fingers' end. I will play with you at a game wherein can be no deceit; it is called mumchance at cards, and it is thus: you shall shuffle the cards, and I will cut, you shall call one, and this honest country yeoman shall call a card for me, and which of our cards comes first shall win. Here you see is no deceit, and this I'll play."

"No, truly," saith the cony, "methinks there can be no great craft in this."

"Well," saith the barnacle, "for a pint of wine, have at you." So they play as before, five up, and the verser wins. "This is hard luck," saith the barnacle, "and I believe the honest man spies some card in the bottom, and therefore I'll make this, always to prick the bottom card."

"Content," saith the verser; and the cony, to cloak the matter, saith, "Sir, you offer me injury to think that I can call a card, when I neither touch them, shuffle, cut, nor draw them."

"Ah sir," saith the barnacle, "give losers leave to speak." Well, to it they go again, and then the barnacle, knowing the game best, by chopping a card wins two of the five, but lets the verser win the set; then in a chafe he sweareth 'tis but his ill luck, and he can see no deceit in it, and therefore he will play twelvepence a cut. The verser is content, and wins two or three shillings of the barnacle. Whereat he chafes, and saith, "I came hither in an ill hour; but I will win my money again, or lose all in my purse." With that he draws out a purse with some three or four pound, and claps it on the board. The verser asketh the cony secretly by signs if he will be his half; he says "Ay," and straight seeks for his purse. Well, the barnacle shuffles the cards thoroughly, and the verser cuts as before. The barnacle, when he hath drawn one card, saith, "I'll either win something or lose something; therefore I'll vie and revie every card at my pleasure, till either yours or mine come out, and therefore twelvepence upon this card; my card comes first for twelvepence." "No," saith the verser. "Ay," saith

G

the cony, " and I durſt hold twelvepence more." " Why, I hold you,"
saith the barnacle.   And so they vie and revie till some ten shillings be
on the ſtake.   And then next comes forth the verser's card, that the
cony called, and so the barnacle loseth.

Well, this flesheth the cony ; the sweetness of gain maketh him
frolic, and no man is more ready to vie and revie than he.   Thus for
three or four times the barnacle loseth, at laſt to whet on the cony, he
ſtriketh his chopped card and winneth a good ſtake.   " Away with the
witch ! " cries the barnacle, " I hope the cards will turn at laſt."   " Ay,
much," thinketh the cony, " 'twas but a chance that you asked so right,
to ask one of the five that was cut off ; I am sure there was forty to one
on my side, and I'll have you on the lurch anon."   So ſtill they vie and
revie, and for once that the barnacle wins, the cony gets five.   At laſt
when they mean to shave the cony clean of all his coin, the barnacle
chafeth, and upon a pawn borroweth some money of the tapſter, and
swears he will vie it to the uttermoſt.   Then thus he chops his card
to crossbite the cony : he firſt looks on the bottom card, and shuffles
often, but ſtill keeping that bottom card, which he knows, to be uppermoſt ; then sets he down the cards, and the verser to encourage the
cony, cut[s] off but three cards, whereof the barnacle's card muſt needs
be the uppermoſt ; then shows he the bottom card of the other heap
cut off to the cony, and sets it upon the barnacle's card which he knows,
so that of force the card that was laid uppermoſt muſt come forth firſt,
and then the barnacle calls that card.   They draw a card, and then the
barnacle vies, and the countryman vies upon him ; for this is the law,
as often as one vies or revies, the other muſt see it, else he loseth the
ſtake.   Well, at laſt the barnacle plies it so, that perhaps he vies more
money than the cony hath in his purse.   The cony, upon this, knowing
his card is the third or fourth card, and that he hath forty to one againſt
the barnacle, pawns his rings, if he have any, his sword, his cloak, or
else what he hath about him, to maintain the vie ; and when he laughs
in his sleeve, thinking he hath fleeced the barnacle of all, then the barnacle's card comes forth, and ſtrikes such a cold humour unto his heart
that he sits as a man in a trance, not knowing what to do, and sighing
while his heart is ready to break, thinking on the money that he hath
loſt.

Perhaps the man is very simple and patient, and, whatsoever he
thinks, for fear goes his way quiet with his loss (while the cony-catchers
laugh and divide the spoil), and being out of the doors, poor man, goes
to his lodging with a heavy heart, pensive and sorrowful, but too late,

for perhaps his state did depend on that money, and so he, his wife, his children and his family, are brought to extreme misery.

Another, perhaps, more hardy and subtle, smokes the cony-catchers, and smelleth cozenage, and saith they shall not have his money so. But they answer him with braves, and though he bring them before an officer, yet the knaves are so favoured, that the man never recovers his money, and yet he is let slip unpunished. Thus are the poor conies robbed by these base-minded caterpillars; thus are serving-men oft enticed to play, and lose all; thus are 'prentices induced to be conies, and so are cozened of their masters' money; yea, young gentlemen, merchants and others, are fetched in by these damnable rakehells, a plague as ill as Hell, which is present loss of money, and ensuing misery. A lamentable case in England, when such vipers are suffered to breed, and are not cut off with the sword of justice! This enormity is not only in London, but now generally dispersed through all England, in every shire, city and town of any receipt, and many complaints are heard of their egregious cozenage. The poor farmer, simply going about his business or unto his attorney's chamber, is catched up and cozened of all. The serving-man sent with his lord's treasure, loseth oft-times most part to these worms of the commonwealth. The 'prentice, having his master's money in charge, is spoiled by them, and from an honest servant either driven to run away, or to live in discredit for ever. The gentleman loseth his land, the merchant his stock, and all to these abominable cony-catchers, whose means is as ill as their living, for they are all either wedded to whores, or so addicted to whores, that what they get from honest men they spend in bawdy-houses among harlots, and consume it as vainly as they get it villainously. Their ears are of adamant, as pitiless as they are treacherous, for be the man never so poor, they will not return him one penny of his loss.

I remember a merry jest done of late to a Welshman, who, being a mere stranger in London, and not well acquainted with the English tongue, yet chanced amongst certain cony-catchers, who espying the gentleman to have money, they so dealt with him, that what by signs and broken English, they got him in for a cony, and fleeced him of every penny that he had, and of his sword, at last the man smoked them, and drew his dagger upon them at Ludgate (for thereabouts they had catched him), and would have stabbed one of them for his money. People came and stopped him, and the rather because they could not understand him, though he had a card in one hand and his dagger in the other, and said, as well as he could, " a card, a card, mon Dieu."

In the meanwhile the cony-catchers were got into Paul's, and so away. The Welshman followed them, seeking them there up and down in the church, still with his naked dagger and the card in his hand, and the gentlemen marvelled what he meant thereby.   At last one of his countrymen met him, and enquired the cause of his choler ; and then he told him how he was cozened at cards, and robbed of all his money, but as his loss was voluntary, so his seeking them was mere vanity, for they were stepped into some blind ale-house to divide the shares.

Near to St. Edmundsbury in Suffolk, there dwelt an honest man, a shoemaker, that having some twenty marks in his purse, long a gathering and nearly kept, came to the market to buy a dicker of hides, and by chance fell among cony-catchers, whose names I omit, because I hope of their amendment.   This plain countryman, drawn in by these former devices, was made a cony, and so straight stripped of all his twenty mark, to his utter undoing.   The knaves 'scaped, and he went home a sorrowful man.   Shortly after, one of these cony-catchers was taken for a suspected person, and laid in Bury jail.   The sessions coming and he produced to the bar, it was the fortune of this poor shoemaker to be there, who spying this rogue to be arraigned, was glad and said nothing unto him, but looked what would be the issue of his appearance.   At the last he was brought before the Justices, where he was examined of his life and, being demanded what occupation he was, said none.

" What profession then are you of ?   How live you ? "

" Marry," quoth he, " I am a gentleman, and live of my friends."

" Nay, that is a lie," quoth the poor shoemaker.   " Under correction of the worshipful of the bench, you have a trade, and are by your art a cony-catcher."

" A cony-catcher," said one of the Justices, and smiled.   " What is he, a warrener, fellow?   Whose warren keepeth he, canst thou tell ? "

" Nay sir, your worship mistaketh me," quoth the shoemaker. " He is not a warrener, but a cony-catcher."

The bench, that never heard this name before, smiled, attributing the name to the man's simplicity, thought he meant a warrener ; which the shoemaker spying, answered, that some conies this fellow catched were worth twenty mark apiece.   " And for proof," quoth he, " I am one of them " ; and so discoursed the whole order of the art and the baseness of the cozening ; whereupon the Justices looking into his life, appointed him to be whipped, and the shoemaker desired that he might give him his payment, which was granted. When he came to his punishment, the shoemaker laughed, saying, " 'Tis a mad world when poor conies are able to beat their catchers." But he lent him so friendly lashes, that almost he made him pay an ounce of blood for every pound of silver.

Thus we see how the generation of these vipers increase[s], to the confusion of many honest men, whose practices to my poor power I have discovered, and set out, with the villainous sleights they use to entrap the simple. Yet have they cloaks for the rain, and shadows for their villainies, calling it by the name of *art* or *law* : as cony-catching art, or cony-catching law. And hereof it riseth, that like as law,[4] when the term is truly considered, signifieth the ordinance of good men, established for the commonwealth, to repress all vicious living, so these cony-catchers turn the cat in the pan, giving to divers vile patching shifts, an honest and godly title, calling it by the name of a *law*, because by a multitude of hateful rules, as it were in good learning, they exercise their villainies to the destruction of sundry honest persons. Hereupon they give their false conveyance the name of cony-catching law, as there be also other laws, as high law, sacking law, figging law, cheating law and barnard's law. If you marvel at these mysteries and quaint words, consider, as the carpenter hath many terms familiar enough to his 'prentices, that other understand not at all, so have the cony-catchers ; not without great cause, for a falsehood once detected, can never compass the desired effect. Therefore will I presently acquaint you with the signification of the terms in a table ; but leaving them till time and place.

Coming down Turnmill Street[5] the other day, I met one whom I suspected a cony-catcher. I drew him on to the tavern, and after a cup of wine or two, I talked with him of the manner of his life, and told him I was sorry for his friends' sake that he took so bad a course, as to live upon the spoil of poor men, and specially to deserve the name of cony-catching, dissuading him from that base kind of life, that was so ignominious in the world, and so loathsome in the sight of God.

" Tut, sir," quoth he, calling me by my name, " as my religion is small, so my devotion is less. I leave God to be disputed on by divines. The two ends I aim at are gain and ease ; but by what honest gains I may get, never comes within the compass of my thoughts. Though[6] your experience in travel be great, yet in home matters mine be more. Yea, I am sure you are not so ignorant, but you know that few men can live uprightly, unless he have some pretty way, more than the world is witness to, to help him withal. Think you some lawyers could be such purchasers, if all their pleas were short, and their proceedings justice and conscience ; that offices would be so dearly bought, and the buyers so soon enriched, if they counted not pillage an honest kind of purchase ; or do you think that men of handy trades make all their commodities without falsehood, when so many of them are become daily purchasers ? Nay, what will you more ; whoso hath not some sinister way to help himself, but followeth his nose always straight forward, may well hold up the head for a year or two, but the third he must needs sink, and gather the wind into beggars' haven ? Therefore, sir, cease to persuade me to the contrary, for my resolution is to beat my wits and spare not to busy my brains to save and help me, by what means soever I care not, so I may avoid the danger of the law."

Whereupon, seeing this cony-catcher resolved in his form of life, leaving him to his lewdness, I went away, wondering at the baseness of their minds, that would spend their time in such detestable sort. But no marvel, for they are given up into a reprobate sense and are in religion mere atheists, as they are in trade flat dissemblers. If I should spend many sheets in deciphering their shifts, it were frivolous, in that they be many and full of variety, for every day they invent new tricks and such quaint devices as are secret, yet passing dangerous, that if a man had Argus' eyes, he could scant pry into the bottom of their practices.

Thus for the benefit of my country I have briefly discovered the law of cony-catching, desiring all justices, if such cozeners light in their precinct, even to use *summum jus* against them, because it is the basest of all villainies ; and that London 'prentices, if they chance in such cony-catchers' company, may teach them "London law," that is, to defend the poor men that are wronged, and learn the caterpillars the highway to Newgate, where, if Hind[7] favour them with the heaviest irons in all the house and give them his unkindest entertainment, no doubt his other petty sins shall be half pardoned for his labour. But I would it might be their fortune to happen into Nobles Northward in Whitechapel ; there, in faith, Round Robin, his deputy, would make them, like wretches, feel the weight of his heaviest fetters. And so desiring both honourable and worshipful, as well justices, as other officers, and all estates, from the prince to the beggar, to rest professed enemies to these base-minded cony-catchers, I take my leave.

Nascimur pro patria.

A TABLE OF THE WORDS OF ART, USED IN THE EFFECTING THESE BASE
VILLAINIES

*Wherein is discovered the nature of every term, being proper to none but
to the professors thereof*

1 *High law* (robbing by the highway side).
2 *Sacking law* (lechery).
3 *Cheating law* (play at false dice).
4 *Crossbiting law* (cozenage by whores).
5 *Cony-catching law* (cozenage by cards).
6 *Versing law* (cozenage by false gold).
7 *Figging law* (cutting of purses and picking of pockets).
8 *Barnard's law* (a drunken cozenage by cards).

These are the eight laws of villainy, leading the highway to infamy.

IN HIGH LAW.

The thief is called a *high lawyer* ;
He that setteth the watch, a *scrippet* ;
He that ſtandeth to watch, an *oak* ;
He that is robbed, the *martin* ;
When he yieldeth, *ſtooping*.

IN SACKING LAW.

The bawd, if it be a woman, a *pander*
The bawd, if a man, an *apple-squire* ;
The whore, a *commodity* ;
The whore-house, a *trugging-place*.

IN CHEATING LAW.

Pardon me, Gentlemen, for although no man could better than
myself discover this law and his terms, and the name of their cheats,
barred dice, flats, forgers, langrets, gourds, demies, and many other,
with their nature, and the crosses and contraries to them upon advantage,
yet for some special reasons herein I will be silent.[8]

IN CROSSBITING LAW.

The whore, the *traffic* ;
The man that is brought in, the *simpler* ;
The villains that take them, the *crossbiters*.

In Cony-catching Law.

> The party that taketh up the cony, the *setter*;
> He that playeth the game, the *verser*;
> He that is cozened, the *cony*;
> He that comes in to them, the *barnacle*;
> The money that is won, *purchase*.

In Versing Law.

> He that bringeth him in, the *verser* ;
> The poor countryman, the *cousin* ;
> And the drunkard that comes in, the *suffier*.

In Figging Law.

> The cutpurse, a *nip* ;
> He that is half with him, the *snap* ;
> The knife, the *cuttle-bung* ;
> The pickpocket, a *foin* ;
> He that faceth the man, the *stale* ;
> Taking the purse, *drawing* ;
> Spying of him, *smoking* ;
> The purse, the *bung* ;
> The money, the *shells* ;
> The act doing, *striking*.

In Barnard's Law.

> He that fetcheth the man, the *taker* ;
> He that is taken, the *cousin* ;
> The landed man, the *verser* ;
> The drunken man, the *barnard* ;
> And he that makes the fray, the *rutter*.

Cum multis aliis quæ nunc præscribere longum est.

These quaint terms do these base arts use to shadow their villainy withal ; for, *multa latent quæ non patent*, obscuring their filthy crafts with these fair colours, that the ignorant may not espy what their subtlety is ; but their end will be like their beginning, hatched with Cain, and consumed with Judas. And so, bidding them adieu to the Devil, and you farewell to God, I end. And now to the art of crossbiting.

THE ART OF CROSSBITING

THE crossbiting law is a public profession of shameless cozenage, mixed with incestuous whoredoms, as ill as was practised in Gomorrah or Sodom, though not after the same unnatural manner. For the method of their mischievous art (with blushing cheeks and trembling heart let it be spoken) is, that these villainous vipers, unworthy the name of men, base rogues—yet why do I term them so well—being outcasts from God, vipers of the world and an excremental reversion of sin, doth consent, nay constrain their wives to yield the use of their bodies to other men, that, taking them together, he may crossbite the party of all the crowns he can presently make. And that the world may see their monstrous practices, I will briefly set down the manner.

They have sundry preys that they call " simplers," which are men fondly and wantonly given, whom for a penalty of their lust, they fleece of all that ever they have ; some merchants, 'prentices, serving-men, gentlemen, yeomen, farmers and all degrees. And this is their form : there are resident in London and the suburbs certain men attired like gentlemen, brave fellows, but basely minded, who living in want, as their last refuge, fall unto this crossbiting law, and to maintain themselves either marry with some stale whore, or else forsooth keep one as their friend ; and these persons be commonly men of the eight laws before rehearsed, either high-lawyers, versers, nips, cony-catchers, or such of the like fraternity. These, when their other trades fail—as the cheater when he has no cousin to grime with his stop dice, or the high-lawyer, when he hath no set match to ride about, and the nip when there is no term, fair, nor time of great assembly—then to maintain the main chance, they use the benefit of their wives or friends to the crossbiting of such as lust after their filthy enormities. Some simple men are drawn on by subtle means, which never intended such a bad matter.

In summer evenings and in the winter nights, these traffics, these common trulls I mean, walk abroad either in the fields or streets that are commonly haunted, as stales to draw men into hell, and afar off, as attending apple-squires, certain crossbiters stand aloof, as if they knew them not. Now so many men, so many affections ! Some unruly mates that place their content in lust, letting slip the liberty of their eyes on their painted faces, feed upon their unchaste beauties, till their hearts be set on fire. Then come they to these minions, and court them with many sweet words. Alas, their loves needs no long suits, for they are forthwith entertained, and either they go to the tavern to seal up the match with a pottle of hippocras, or straight she carries him to some bad place, and there picks his pocket, or else the crossbiters comes swearing in, and so outface the dismayed companion, that, rather than he would be brought in question, he would disburse all that he hath present. But this is but an easy cozenage.

Some other, meeting with one of that profession in the street, will question if she will drink with him a pint of wine. Their trade is never to refuse, and if for manners they do, it is but once ; and then, scarce shall they be warm in the room, but in comes a terrible fellow with a side hair and a fearful beard, as though he were one of Polyphemus' cut, and he comes frowning in and saith : " What hast thou to do, base knave, to carry my sister (or my wife) to the tavern : by His 'Ounds, you whore, 'tis some of your companions. I will have you both before the Justice, Deputy, or Constable, to be examined."

The poor serving-man, apprentice, farmer, or whatsoever he is, seeing such a terrible huff-snuff, swearing with his dagger in his hand, is fearful both of him and to be brought in trouble, and therefore speaks kindly and courteously unto him, and desires him to be content, he meant no harm. The whore, that hath tears at command, falls a weeping, and cries him mercy. At this submission of them both he triumphs like a braggard, and will take no compassion. Yet at last, through entreaty of other his companions coming in as strangers, he is pacified with some forty shillings, and the poor man goes sorrowful away, sighing out that which Solomon hath in his proverbs : *A shameless woman hath honey in her lips, and her throat as sweet as honey, her throat as soft as oil : but the end of her is more bitter than aloes, and her tongue is more sharp than a two-edged sword, her feet go unto death, and her steps lead unto Hell.*

Again these trulls, when they have got in a novice, then straight they pick his purse, and then have they their crossbiters ready, to whom they convey the money and so offer themselves to be searched. But the poor man is so outfaced by these crossbiting ruffians that he is glad to go away content with his loss ; yet are these easy practices. Oh, might the justices send out spials in the night ! They should see how these streetwalkers will jet in rich guarded gowns, quaint periwigs, ruffs of the largest size, quarter- and half-deep, gloried richly with blue starch, their cheeks dyed with surfling water—thus are they tricked up, and either walk like stales up and down the streets, or stand like the devil's *Si quis*[9] at a tavern or ale-house, as if who should say :

" If any be so minded to satisfy his filthy lust, to lend me his purse, and the Devil his soul, let him come in and be welcome."

Now, sir, comes by a country farmer, walking from his inn to perform some business and, seeing such a gorgeous damsel, he, wondering at such a brave wench, stands staring her on the face, or perhaps doth but cast a glance, and bid her good speed, as plain simple swains have their lusty humours as well as others.

The trull, straight beginning her exordium with a smile, saith: " How now, my friend ! What want you ? Would you speak with anybody here ? "

If the fellow have any bold spirit, perhaps he will offer the wine, and then he is caught. 'Tis enough. In he goes, and they are chambered. Then sends she for her husband, or her friend, and there either the farmer's pocket is stripped, or else the crossbiters fall upon him, and threaten him with Bridewell[10] and the law. Then, for fear, he gives them all in his purse, and makes them some bill to pay a sum of money at a certain day.

If the poor farmer be bashful, and passeth by one of these shameless strumpets, then will she verse it with him, and claim acquaintance of him, and, by some policy or other, fall aboard on him, and carry him into some house or other. If he but enter in at the doors with her (though the poor farmer never kissed her), yet then the crossbiters, like vultures, will prey upon his purse, and rob him of every penny. If there be any young gentleman that is a novice and hath not seen their trains, to him will some common filth, that never knew love, feign an ardent and honest affection, till she and her crossbiters have versed him to the beggars' estate.

Ah, gentlemen, merchants, yeomen and farmers, let this to you all, and to every degree else, be a caveat to warn you from lust, that your inordinate desire be not a mean to impoverish your purses, discredit your good names, condemn your souls, but also that your wealth got with the sweat of your brows, or left by your parents as a patrimony, shall be a prey to those cozening crossbiters ! Some fond men are so far in with these detestable trugs that they consume what they have upon them, and find nothing but a Neapolitan favour for their labour. Read the seventh of Solomon's proverbs, and there at large view the description of a shameless and impudent courtesan.

Yet is there another kind of crossbiting which is most pestilent, and that is this. There lives about this town certain householders, yet mere shifters and cozeners, who, learning some insight in the Civil

Law, walk abroad like apparitors, summoners and informers, being none at all, either in office or credit ; and they go spying about where any merchant, or merchant's 'prentice, citizen, wealthy farmer, or other of credit, either accompany with any woman familiarly, or else hath gotten some maid with child (as men's natures be prone to sin) ; ſtraight they come over his fallows thus : They send for him to a tavern, and there open the matter unto him, which they have cunningly learned out, telling him he muſt be presented to the Arches,[11] and the citation shall be peremptorily served in his parish church. The party, afraid to have his credit cracked with the worshipful of the City and the reſt of his neighbours, and grieving highly his wife should hear of it, ſtraight takes composition with this cozener for some twenty marks. Nay, I heard of forty pound crossbitten at one time. And then the cozening informer, or crossbiter, promiseth to wipe him out of the book and discharge him from the matter, when it was neither known nor presented. So go they to the woman, and fetch her off if she be married, and, though they have this gross sum, yet oft-times they crossbite her for more. Nay, thus do they fear citizens, 'prentices and farmers, that they find but anyway suspicious of the like fault. The crossbiting bawds, for no better can I term them, in that for lucre they conceal the sin and smother up luſt, do not only enrich themselves mightily thereby, but also discredit, hinder and prejudice the Court of the Arches and the officers belonging to the same. There are some poor blind patches of that faculty, that have their tenements purchased and their plate on the board very solemnly, who only get their gains by crossbiting, as is afore rehearsed. But (leaving them to the deep insight of such as be appointed with juſtice to correct vice) again to the crew of my former crossbiters, whose fee-simple to live upon is nothing but the following of common, dishoneſt and idle trulls, and thereby maintain themselves brave, and the ſtrumpets in handsome furniture. And to end this art with an English demonſtration, I'll tell you a pretty tale of late performed in Bishopsgate Street :

There was there five traffics, pretty, but common housewives, that ſtood faſt by a tavern door, looking if some prey would pass by for their purpose. Anon the eldeſt of them, and moſt experienced in that law, called Mall B., spied a maſter of a ship coming along.

" Here is a simpler," quoth she, " I'll verse him, or hang me. Sir," said she, " good even. What, are you so liberal to beſtow on three good wenches that are dry, a pint of wine ? "

" In faith, fair women," quoth he, " I was never niggard for so much ":

and with that he takes one of them by the hand, and carries them all into the tavern. There he bestowed cheer and hippocras upon them, drinking hard till the shot came to a noble, so that they three, carousing to the gentleman, made him somewhat tipsy, and then *et Venus in vinis, ignis in igne fuit!* Well, night grew on, and he would away, but this Mistress Mall B. stopped his journey thus :

" Gentleman," quoth she, " this undeserved favour of yours makes us so deeply beholden to you, that our ability is not able anyway to make sufficient satisfaction ; yet, to show us kind in what we can, you shall not deny me this request, to see my simple house before you go."

The gentleman, a little whittled, consented, and went with them. So the shot was paid, and away they go : Without the tavern door stood two of their husbands, J. B. and J. R., and they were made privy to the practice. Home goes the gentleman with these lusty housewives, stumbling. At last he was welcome to Mistress Mall's house, and one of the three went into a chamber, and got to bed, whose name was A. B. After they had chatted a while, the gentleman would have been gone, but she told him that, before he went, he should see all the rooms of her house, and so led him up into the chamber where the party lay in bed.

" Who is here ? " said the gentleman.

" Marry," saith Mall, " a good pretty wench, sir ; and if you be not well, lie down by her ; you can take no harm of her."

Drunkenness desires lust ; and so the gentleman begins to dally ; and away goes she with the candle ! And at last he put off his clothes and went to bed. Yet he was not so drunk, but he could after a while remember his money, and, feeling for his purse, all was gone, and three links of his whistle broken off. The sum that was in his purse was in gold and silver twenty nobles. As thus he was in a maze, though his head were well laden, in comes J. B., the goodman of the house, and two other with him, and speaking somewhat loud.

" Peace, husband," quoth she, " there is one in bed, speak not so loud."

" In bed ? " saith he, " Gog's Nownes ! I'll go see."

" And so will I," saith the other.

" You shall not," saith his wife, but strove against him ; but up goes he, and his crossbiters with him, and, seeing the gentleman in bed, out with his dagger, and asked what base villain it was that there sought to dishonest his wife. Well, he sent one of them for a constable, and made the gentleman rise, who, half drunk, yet had that remembrance to speak fair and to entreat him to keep his credit. But no entreaty could serve, but to the Counter he must, and the constable must be sent for.   Yet, at the last, one of them entreated that the gentleman might be honestly used, and carried to a tavern to talk of the matter till a constable come.

"Tut !" saith J. B.   " I will have law upon him."

But the base crossbiter at last stooped, and to the tavern they go, where the gentleman laid his whistle to pawn for money, and there bestowed as much of them as came to ten shillings, and sat drinking and talking until the next morrow. By that the gentleman had stolen a nap, and waking, it was daylight, and then, seeing himself compassed with these crossbiters, and remembering his night's work, soberly smiling, asked them if they knew what he was. They answered: " Not well."

"Why then," quoth he, " you base cozening rogues ! You shall ere we part " : and with that drawing his sword, kept them into the chamber, desiring that the constable might be sent for.

But this brave of his could not dismay Mistress Mall ; for she had bidden a sharper brunt before—witness the time of her martyrdom, when upon her shoulders was engraven the history of her whorish qualities.[12] But she replying, swore, sith he was so lusty, her husband should not put it up by no means.

" I will tell thee, thou base crossbiting bawd," quoth he, " and you cozening companions, I serve a nobleman, and for my credit with him, I refer me to the penalty he will impose on you ; for, by God, I will make you an example to all crossbiters ere I end with you ! I tell you, villains, I serve —— " ; and with that he named his lord.

When the guilty whores and cozeners heard of his credit and service, they began humbly to entreat him to be good to them.

" Then," quoth he, " first deliver me my money."

They upon that gladly gave him all, and restored the links of his chain. When he had all, he smiled, and sware afresh that he would torment them for all this, that the severity of their punishment might be a caveat to others to beware of the like cozenage, and upon that knocked with his foot and said he would not let them go till he had a constable.   Then in general they humbled themselves, so recompensing the party, that he agreed to pass over the matter, conditionally beside, that they would pay the sixteen shillings he had spent in charges, which they also performed.   The gentleman stepped his way, and said : " You may see the old proverb fulfilled : *Fallere fallentem non est fraus.*"

Thus have I deciphered an odious practise, not worthy to be named. And now, wishing all, of what estate soever, to beware of filthy lust and such damnable stales as draws men on to inordinate desires, and rather to spend their coin amongst honest company, than to bequeath it to such base crossbiters as prey upon men, like ravens upon dead carcases, I end with this prayer, that crossbiting and cony-catching may be as little known in England, as the eating of swines' flesh was amongst the Jews. Farewell!

Nascimur pro patria.

Finis.

A PLEASANT DISCOVERY OF THE COZENAGE OF COLLIERS

ALTHOUGH, courteous readers, I did not put in amongst the laws of cozening, the law of legering, which is a deceit wherewith colliers abuse the commonwealth in having unlawful sacks,[12a] yet take it for a petty kind of craft or mystery, as prejudicial to the poor as any of the other two. For I omitted divers other devilish vices : as the nature of the lift, the black art, and the curbing law, which is the filchers and thieves that come into houses or shops and lift away anything ; or picklocks, or hookers at windows, though they be as species and branches to the table before rehearsed. But, leaving them, again to our law of legering.

Know, therefore, that there be inhabiting in and about London, certain caterpillars (colliers, I should say) that term themselves, among themselves, by the name of legers, who, for that the honourable the Lord Mayor of the City of London and his officers look straightly to the measuring of coals, do (to prevent the execution of his justice) plant themselves in and about the suburbs of London, as Shoreditch, Whitechapel, Southwark and such places, and there they have a house or yard that hath a back gate, because it is the more convenient for their cozening purpose, and the reason is this : the leger (the crafty collier, I mean) riseth very early in the morning, and either goeth towards Croydon, Whetstone, Greenwich or Romford, and there meeteth the country colliers, who bring coals to serve the market. There, in a forestalling manner, this leger bargaineth with the country collier for his coals, and payeth for them nineteen shillings or twenty at the most, but commonly fifteen and sixteen. And there is in the load thirty-six sacks ; so that they pay for every couple about fourteenpence.

Now, having bought his coals, every sack containing full four bushels, he carryeth the country collier home to his legering place, and there at the back gate causeth him to unload and, as they say, shoot the coals down. As soon as the country collier hath despatched and is gone, then the leger, who hath three or four hired men under him, bringeth forth his own sacks, which be long and narrow, holding at the most not three bushels, so that they gain in the change of every sack a bushel for their pains. Tush! yet this were somewhat to be borne withal, although the gain is monstrous; but this sufficeth not, for they fill not these sacks full by far, but put into them some two bushels and a half, laying in the mouth of the sack certain great coals, which they call fillers, to make the sack show fair, although the rest be small willow-coals, and half dross. When they have thus, not filled their sacks, but thrust coals into them, that which they lay uppermost is best filled, to make the greater show. Then [they have] a tall, sturdy knave, that is all ragged, and dirty on his legs, as though he came out of the country, for they dirty their hose and shoes on purpose to make themselves seem country colliers. Thus with two sacks apiece they either go out at the back gate, or steal out at the street side, and so go up and down the suburbs and sell their coals, in summer for fourteen and sixteenpence a couple, and in winter for eighteen or twenty. The poor cooks and other citizens that buy them think they be country colliers that have left some coals of their load and would gladly have money, supposing (as the statute is) they be good and lawful sacks, are thus cozened by the legers and have but two bushels and a half for four bushels, and yet are extremely racked in the price, which is not only a great hinderance to her Majesty's poor commons, but greatly prejudicial to the master-colliers, that bring true sacks and measure out of the country. Then consider, gentle readers, what kind of cozenage these legers use, that make of thirty sacks some fifty-six, which I have seen, for I have set down with my pen how many turns they have made of a load, and they make twenty-eight, every turn being two sacks, so that they have got an intolerable gains by their false measure.

I could not be silent, seeing this abuse, but thought to reveal it for my country's commodity, and to give light to the worshipful justices, and other her Majesty's officers in Middlesex, Surrey and elsewhere, to look to such a gross cozenage as, contrary to a direct statute, doth defraud and impoverish her Majesty's poor commons. Well may the honourable and worshipful of London flourish, who carefully look to the country coals, and if they find not four bushels in every sack, do sell them to the poor as forfeit, and distribute the money to them that have need, burning the sack and honouring, or rather dishonouring, the pillory with the colliers' dirty faces! And well may the honourable and worshipful of the suburbs prosper, if they look in justice to these legers who deserve more punishment than the statute appoints for them, which is whipping at a cart's tail, or, with favour, the pillory!

A plain discovery

For fuel or firing being a thing necessary in a commonwealth, and charcoal used more than any other, the poor, not able to buy by the load, are fain to get in their fire by the sack, and so are greatly cozened by the retail. Seeing therefore the careful laws her Majesty hath appointed for the wealth of her commons and succour of the poor, I would humbly entreat all her Majesty's officers, to look into the life of these legers, and to root them out, that the poor feel not the burden of their inconscionable gains. I heard with my ears a poor woman of Shoreditch, who had bought coals of a leger, with weeping tears complain and rail against him in the street, in her rough eloquence calling him " cozening knave," and saying: " 'Tis no marvel, villain (quoth she), if men compare you colliers to the Devil, seeing your consciences are worser than the Devil's; for he takes none but those souls whom God hates; and you undo the poor whom God loves."

"What is the matter, good wife," quoth I, "that you use such invective words against the collier?"

"A collier, sir!" saith she. "He is a thief and a robber of the common people. I'll tell you, sir: I bought of a country collier two sacks for thirteenpence, and I bought of this knave three sacks, which cost me twenty-two pence. And, sir, when I measured both their sacks, I had more in the two sacks by three pecks, than I had in the three. I would," quoth she, " the justices would look into this abuse, and that my neighbours would join with me in a supplication, and, by God, I would kneel before the Queen, and entreat that such cozening colliers might not only be punished with the bare pillory (for they have such black faces that no man knows them again, and so are they careless), but that they might leave their ears behind them for a forfeit; and if that would not mend them, that Bull[13] with a fair halter might root them out of the world, that live in the world by such gross and dishonest cozenage."

The collier, hearing this, went smiling away, because he knew his life was not looked into, and the woman wept for anger that she had not some one by that might with justice revenge her quarrel.

There be also certain colliers that bring coals to London in barges, and they be called gripers. To these comes the leger, and bargains with him for his coals, and sells by retail with the like cozenage of sacks as I rehearsed before. But these mad legers, not content with this monstrous gain, do besides mix among their other sacks of coals store of shruff dust and small coal to their great advantage. And, for proof hereof, I will recite you a matter of truth, lately performed by a cook's wife upon a cozening collier.

How a cook's wife in London did lately serve a collier for his cozenage.

It chanced this summer that a load of coals came forth of Kent to Billingsgate, and a leger bought them, who thinking to deceive the citizens as he did those in the suburbs, furnished himself with a couple of sacks, and comes up St. Mary Hill[14] to sell them. A cook's wife bargained with the collier and bought his coals, and they agreed upon fourteenpence for the couple ; which being done, he carried the coals into the house and shot them. And when the wife saw them, and perceiving there was scarce five bushels for eight, she calls a little girl to her, and bade her go for the constable ; " For thou cozening rogue," quoth she, speaking to the collier, " I will teach thee how thou shalt cozen me with thy false sacks, whatsoever thou dost to others, and I will have thee before my Lord Mayor." With that she caught a spit in her hand and swore if he offered to stir she would therewith broach him ; at which words the collier was amazed, and the fear of the pillory put him in such a fright that he said he would go to his boat, and return again to answer whatsoever she durst object against him. " And for pledge hereof," quoth the collier, " keep my sacks, your money, and the coals also." Whereupon the woman let him go ; but as soon as the collier was out of doors, it was needless to bid him run, for down he gets to his boat, and away he thrusts from Billingsgate, and so immediately went down to Wapping, and never after durst return to the cook's wife to demand either money, sacks or coals.

How a flaxwife and her neighbours used a cozening collier.

Now, Gentlemen, by your leave, and hear a merry jest : There was in the suburbs of London a flaxwife that wanted coals, and, seeing a leger come by with a couple of sacks, that had before deceived her in like sort, cheaped, bargained and bought them, and so went in with her to shoot them in her coalhouse. As soon as she saw her coals, she easily guessed there was scarce six bushels; yet, dissembling the matter, she paid him for them, and bade him bring her two sacks more. The collier went his way, and in the meantime the flaxwife measured the coals, and there was just five bushels and a peck. Hereupon she called to her neighbours, being a company of women, that before time had also been pinched in their coals, and showed them the cozenage, and desired their aid to her in tormenting the collier, which they promised to perform. And thus it fell out: She conveyed them into a back room (some sixteen of them), every one having a good cudgel under her apron.

Straight comes the collier and saith: " Mistress, here be your coals."

" Welcome, good collier," quoth she. " I pray thee follow me into the back-side, and shoot them in another room."

The collier was content, and went with her. But as soon as he was in the good wife locked the door, and the collier, seeing such a troop of wives in the room, was amazed, yet said: " God speed you all, shrews ! "

" Welcome," quoth one jolly dame, being appointed by them all to give sentence against him ; who, so soon as the collier had shot his sacks, said: " Sirrah collier, know that we are here all assembled as a grand jury, to determine of thy villainies, for selling us false sacks of coals, and know that thou art here indicted upon cozenage. Therefore, hold up thy hand at the bar, and either say, ' guilty ' or ' not guilty,' and by whom thou wilt be tried, for thou must receive condign punishment for the same ere thou depart."

The collier, who thought they had but jested, smiled and said : " Come on. Which of you shall be my judge ? "

" Marry," quoth one jolly dame, " that is I ; and, by God, you knave, you shall find I will pronounce sentence against you severely, if you be found guilty."

When the collier saw they were in earnest, he said : " Come, come ; open the door and let me go."

With that five or six started up and fell upon the collier and gave unto him half a score of sound lambacks with their cudgels and bade him speak more reverently to their principal. The collier, feeling it smart, was afraid, and thought mirth and courtesy would be the best mean to make amends for his villainy, and therefore said he would be tried by the verdict of the smock.[15] Upon this, they panelled a jury, and the flaxwife gave evidence ; and, because this unaccustomed jury required witness, she measured the coals before the collier's face, upon which he was found guilty, and she that sat as principal to give judgment upon him, began as followeth :

" Collier, thou art condemned here, by proof, of flat cozenage, and I am now appointed in conscience to give sentence against thee, being not only moved thereunto because of this poor woman, but also for the general commodity of my country ; and therefore this is my sentence : We have no pillory for thee, nor cart to whip thee at ; but here I do award that thou shalt have as many bastinados as thy bones will bear, and then to be turned out of doors without sacks or money." This sentence being pronounced, she rose up, and gave no respite of time for the execution ; but, according to the sentence before expressed, all the women fell upon him, beating him extremely, among whom he lent some lusty buffets. But might overcomes right, and therefore *Ne Hercules contra duos.* The women so crushed him, that he was not able to lift his hands to his head, and so with a broken pate or two he was paid, and, like Jack Drum, fair and orderly thrust out of doors.

This was the reward that the collier had, and I pray God all such colliers may be so served, and that good wives, when they buy such sacks, may give them such payments, and that the honourable and worshipful of this land may look into this gross abuse of colliers, as well for charity sake, as also for the benefit of the poor. And so, wishing colliers to amend their deceitful and disordered dealings herein, I end.

Finis.

THE SECOND PART OF CONY-CATCHING

By Robert Greene

[1591]

A TABLE OF THE LAWS CONTAINED IN THIS SECOND PART

1. *Black art* (picking of locks).
2. *Curbing law* (hooking at windows).
3. *Vincent's law* (cozenage at bowls).
4. *Prigging law* (horse-stealing).
5. *Lifting law* (stealing of any parcels).

The discovery of the words of art used in these laws

IN BLACK ART.

The gains gotten, *pelfry.*
The picklock is called a *charm.*
He that watcheth, a *stand.*
Their engines, *wresters.*
Picking the lock, *farcing.*

IN CURBING LAW.

He that hooks, the *curber.*
He that watcheth, the *warp.*
The hook, the *curb.*
The goods, *snappings.*
The gin to open the window, the *tricker.*

IN LIFTING LAW.

He that first stealeth, the *lift.*
He that receives it, the *marker.*
He that standeth without and carries it away, the *santar.*
The goods gotten, *garbage.*

IN VINCENT'S LAW.

They which play booty, the *bankers*.
He that betteth, the *gripe*.
He that is cozened, the *vincent*.
Gains gotten, *termage*.

IN PRIGGING LAW.

The horse-stealer, the *prigger*.
The horse, the *prancer*.
The tolling-place, *All Hallows'*.
The toller, the *rifler*.
The sureties, *quitteries*.[1]

For the *foist* and the *nip*, as in the first book.[2]

To all young gentlemen, merchants, citizens, apprentices, yeomen, and plain country farmers, health.

WHEN Scaevola, Gentlemen, saw his native city besieged by Porsenna, and that Rome, the mistress of the world, was ready to be mastered by a professed foe to the public estate, he entered boldly into the enemy's camp, and in the tent of the king, taking him for the king, slew the king's secretary; whereupon condemned, brought to the fire, he thrust his right hand into the flame, burning it off voluntary, because it was so unfortunate to miss the fatal stab he had intended to his country's enemies, and then with an honourable resolution, breathed out this: *Mallem non esse quam non prodesse patria.* This instance of Scaevola greatly hath emboldened me to think no pains nor danger too great that groweth to the benefit of my country; and though I cannot, as he, manage with my courtlax, nor attempt to unleaguer Porsenna, yet with my pen I will endeavour to display the nature and secrets of divers cozenages more prejudicial to England than the invasion of Porsenna was to Rome. For when that valiant king saw the resolution of Scaevola, as one dismayed at the honour of his thoughts, he sorrowed so brave a man had so desperately lost his hand, and thereupon grew friends with the Romans. But, Gentlemen, these cony-catchers, these vultures, these fatal harpies, that putrify with their infections this flourishing estate of England, as if they had their consciences sealed with a hot iron, and that as men delivered up into a reprobate sense, grace were utterly exiled from their hearts ; so with the deaf adder they not only stop their ears against the voice of the charmer, but dissolutely, without any spark of remorse, stand upon their bravados, and openly in words and actions maintain their palpable and manifest cozenages, swearing by no less than their enemies' blood, even by God Himself, that they will make a massacre of his bones, and cut off my right hand for penning down their abominable practices. But alas for them, poor snakes ! Words are wind, and looks but glances : every thunder-clap hath not a bolt, nor every cony-catcher's oath an execution. I live still, and I live to display their villainies, which, Gentlemen, you shall see set down in most ample manner in this small treatise.

But here, by the way, give me leave to answer an objection that some inferred against me ; which was, that I showed no eloquent phrases, nor fine figurative conveyance in my first book, as I had done in other of my works, to which I reply that τo $\pi\rho\acute{\epsilon}\pi o\nu$ a certain decorum is to be kept in every thing, and not to apply a high style in a base subject, beside the faculty is so odious, and the men so servile and slavish-minded, that I should dishonour that high mystery of eloquence, and derogate from the dignity of our English tongue, either to employ any figure or bestow one choice English word upon such disdained rakehells as those cony-catchers. Therefore, humbly I crave pardon, and desire I may write basely of such base wretches, who live only to live dishonestly. For they seek the spoil and ruin of all, and like drones eat away what others labour for.

I have set down divers other laws untouched in the first, as their vincent's law, a notable cozenage at bowls, when certain idle companions stand and make bets, being compacted with the bowlers, who look like honest-minded citizens, either to win or lose, as their watchword shall appoint ; then the prigger, or horse-stealer, with all his gins belonging to his trade, and their subtle cautels to amend the statute[3] ; next, the curbing law, which some call but too basely hookers, who either dive in at windows, or else with a hook, which they call a curb, do fetch out whatsoever, either apparel, linen or woollen, that be left abroad. Beside I can set down the subtlety of the black art, which is picking of locks, a cozenage as prejudicial as any of the rest ; and the nature of the lift, which is he that stealeth any parcels, and slyly taketh them away. This, Gentlemen, have I searched out for your commodities, that I might lay open to the world the villainy of these cozening caterpillars, who are

not only abhorred of men, but hated of God, living idly to themselves
and odiously to the world.   They be those foolish children that Solomon
speaks of, that feeds themselves fat with iniquity, those untamed heifers,
that will not brook[4] the yoke of labour, but get their livings by the painful thrift of other men's hands.   I cannot better compare them than
unto vipers, who while they live are hated and shunned of all men as
most prejudicial creatures ; they feed upon hemlock and aconiton, and
such fatal and empoisoned herbs ; but the learned apothecaries takes
them, cuts off their heads, and after they be embowelled of their flesh,
they make the most precious mithridate.[5]   So these cony-catchers,
foists, nips, priggers, and lifts, while they live are most improfitable
members of the commonwealth ; they glut themselves as vipers upon
the most loathsome and detestable sins, seeking after folly with greediness, never doing anything that is good, till they be trussed up at Tyburn ;
and then is a most wholesome mithridate made of them, for by their
deaths others are forewarned for falling into the like enormities.   And
as the gangrena is a disease incurable by the censure of the surgeons,
unless the member where it is fixed be cut off, so this untoward generation of loose libertines can by no wholesome counsels nor advised
persuasions be dissuaded from their loathsome kind of life, till by death
they be fatally and finally cut off from the commonwealth, whereof
spake Ovid well in his *Metamorphoses* :[6]

Inmedicabile vulnus,
Ense recidendum, est ne pars sincera trahatur.

Sith then, this cursed crew, these Machiavellians—that neither
care for God nor Devil, but set, with the epicures, gain, and ease, their
summum bonum—cannot be called to any honest course of living, if the
honourable and worshipful of this land look into their lives, and cut off
such upstarting suckers that consume the sap from the root of the tree,
they shall neither lose their reward in Heaven, nor pass over any day
wherein there will not be many faithful prayers of the poor exhibited
for their prosperous success and welfare—so deeply are these monstrous
cozeners hated in the commonwealth. Thus, Gentlemen, I have
discovered in brief what I mean to prosecute at large : though not
eloquently, yet so effectually, that, if you be not altogether careless,
it may redound to your commodity : forewarned, forearmed : burnt
children dread the fire ; and such as neither counsel, nor other men's
harms may make to beware, are worthy to live long, and still by the loss.
But hoping these secrets I have set abroach, and my labours I have

taken in searching out those base villainies, shall not be only taken with thanks, but applied with care, I take my leave with this farewell. God either confound, or convert, such base-minded cozeners.

Yours, R. G.

A Tale of a Nip.

I WILL tell you, Gentlemen, a pleasant tale of a most singular, experienced, and approved nip, and yet I will not name any, although I could discourse of one that is *magister in artibus*, both a nip and a foist and a crossbiter. But I will tell you a merry jig of a notable nip, named . . . . No more of that if you love me! Who, taking a proper youth, by St. Davy, to his 'prentice, to teach him the order of striking and foisting, so well instructed him in his mystery that he could as well skill of a cuttle-bung as a barber of a razor, and, being of a prompt wit, knew his places, persons, and circumstances, as if he had been a moral philosopher.

The old colt, this grand cutpurse—by St. Laurence, let that suffice—did, as the tale was told to me, supply Mannering's place at the burial of the old Lady Rich,[7] and coming thither very devout to hear the sermon, thrust with his apprentice amidst the throng, and lighted upon a rich parson in Essex, not far off from Rochford Hundred. The priest was faced afore with velvet, and had a good bung, which, the nip espying, began to jostle the priest very hard at the entrance of the door, and his apprentice struck the strings, and took his bung clear. The priest little suspecting it, fell to his prayers, and yet, for all his other meditations, he felt for his purse, which, when he missed, he fetched a great sigh, and said, " Lord have mercy upon me."—" What ail you, sir ? " said one that stood by. " Nothing," said the priest, " but I think upon the sins of the people " ; and so passed it over with silence. Well, it so fell out that when the bung came to sharing, the 'prentice and his master fell out, and the master controlled him and said, " Art not my 'prentice, and hast not bound thyself to me for three years ? Is not thy gettings my gains ? Then why dost thou stand upon the snap ? "—" Why," says the 'prentice, " brag you so of my years ! Shall I be made a slave because I am bound to you ? No, no ! I can quittance my indenture when I list."[8] His master in a great rage asked how.—" Marry ! " says the 'prentice : " I will nip a bung, or draw a pocket, openly, and so be taken, arraigned and condemned ; and then

Bull shall cancel my indentures at Tyburn,[9] and so I will not serve you a day after." At this, his master laughed and was glad for further advantage to yield the bucklers to his 'prentice, and to become friends. For approving the truth of this, myself conferred with the priest, and he told me thus much.

THE DISCOVERY OF THE PRIGGING LAW, OR NATURE OF HORSE-STEALING

To the effecting of this base villainy of prigging, or horse-stealing, there must of necessity be two at the least, and that is the prigger and the marter. The prigger is he that steals the horse, and the marter is he that receives him, and chops and changeth him away in any fair, mart, or other place where any good rent for horses is. And their method is thus : The prigger, if he be a lance-man, that is, one that is already horsed, then he hath more followers with him, and they ride like gentlemen, and commonly in the form of drovers, and so, coming into pasture grounds or enclosures, as if they meant to survey for cattle, do take an especial and perfect view, where prancers or horses be, that are of worth, and whether they have horse-locks or no. Then lie they hovering about till fit opportunity serve, and in the night they take him or them away ; and are skilful in the black art, for picking open the trammels or locks and so make haste till they be out of those quarters. Now if the priggers steal a horse in Yorkshire, commonly they have vent for him in Surrey, Kent, or Sussex, and their marters that receive them at his hand, chops them away in some blind fairs after they have kept them a month or two, till the hue and cry[10] be ceased and passed over. Now if their horse be of any great value, and sore sought after, and so branded or ear-marked that they can hardly sell him without extreme danger, either they brand him with a cross-brand upon the former, or take away his ear-mark, and so keep him at hard-meat till he be whole, or else sell him in Cornwall or Wales, if he be in Cumberland, Lincolnshire, Norfolk or Suffolk. But this is if the horse be of great value and worthy the keeping. Marry ! if he be only coloured and without brands, they will straight spot him by sundry policies, and in a black horse, mark saddle-spots, or star him in the forehead, and change his tail, which secrets I omit, lest I should give too great a light to others to practise such lewd villainies.

But again to our lance-men priggers, who, as before I said, cry with the lapwing farthest from their nest, and from their place of residence, where their most abode is.   Furthest from thence they steal their horses, and then in another quarter as far off, they make sale of them by the marter's means, without it be some base prigger that steals of mere necessity, and, beside, is a trailer.   The trailer is one that goeth on foot, but meanly attired like some plain gran of the country, walking in a pair of boots without spurs, or else without boots ; having a long staff on his neck, and a black buckram bag at his back, like some poor client that had some writing in it ; and there he hath his saddle, bridle and spurs, stirrups and stirrup-leathers, so quaintly and artificially made that it may be put in the slop of a man's hose ; for his saddle is made without any tree, yet hath it cantle and bolsters, only wrought artificially of cloth and bombast, with folds to wrap up in a short room : his stirrups are made with vices and gins, that one may put them in a pair of gloves, and so are his spurs, and then a little white leather headstall and reins, with a small Scottish brake or snaffle, all so featly formed that, as I said before, they may be put in a buckram bag.   Now, this trailer he bestrides the horse which he priggeth, and saddles and bridles him as orderly as if he were his own, and then carryeth him far from the place of his breed, and there sells him.

    " Oh ! " will some man say, " it is easier to steal a horse than to sell him, considering that her Majesty and the honourable Privy Council hath in the last act of Parliament made a strict statute for horse-stealing and the sale of horses, whose proviso is this : that no man may buy a horse untolled, nor the toll be taken without lawful witnesses that the party that selleth the horse is the true owner of him, upon their oath and special knowledge, and that who buyeth a horse without this certificate or proof shall be within the nature of felony, as well as the party that stealeth him."[1]

    To this I answer, that there is no act, statute, nor law so strict conveyed but there be straight found starting-holes to avoid it, as in this. The prigger, when he hath stolen a horse, and hath agreed with his marter, or with any other his confederate, or with an honest person, to sell his horse, bringeth to the toller, which they call the rifler, two honest men, either aparelled like citizens or plain country yeomen, and they not only affirm, but offer to depose, that they know the horse to be his, upon their proper knowledge, although perhaps they never saw man nor horse before, and these perjured knaves be commonly old knights of the post, that are foisted off from being taken for bail at the

King's Bench or other places, and seeing for open perjuries they are refused, there they take that course of life, and are wrongly called querries. But it were necessary, and very much expedient for the commonwealth, that such base rogues should be looked into, and be punished as well with the pillory, as the other with the halter. And thus have I revealed the nature of priggers, or horse-stealers, briefly, which if it may profit, I have my desire, but that I may recreate your minds with a pleasant history, mark the sequel.

A pleasant story of a horse-stealer.

Not far from T[ru]ro in Cornwall, a certain prigger, a horse-stealer, being a lance-man, surveying the pastures thereabouts, spied a fair black horse without any white spot at all about him. The horse was fair and lusty, well proportioned, of a high crest, of a lusty countenance, well buttocked, and strongly trussed, which set the prigger's teeth a water to have him. Well, he knew the hardest hap was but a halter, and therefore he ventured fair, and stole away the prancer ; and, seeing his stomach was so good as his limbs, he kept him well, and by his policy seared him in the forehead, and made him spotted in the back, as if he had been saddle-bitten, and gave him a mark in both ears, whereas he had but a mark in one.

Dealing thus with his horse, after a quarter of a year, that all hurly-burly was past for the horse, he came riding to T[ru]ro to the market, and there offered him to be sold. The gentleman that lost the horse was there present, and looking on him with other gentlemen, liked him passing well, and commended him, insomuch that he bet the price of him, bargained, and bought him. And so when he was tolled, and the horse-stealer clapped him good luck : " Well, my friend," quoth the gentleman, " I like the horse the better, in that once I lost one, as like him as might be, but mine wanted these saddle spots and this star in the forehead."—" It may be so, sir," said the prigger. And so the gentleman and he parted. The next day after, he caused a letter to be made, and sent the gentleman word that he had his horse again that he lost, only he had given him a mark or two, and for that he was well rewarded, having twenty mark for his labour. The gentleman, hearing how he was cozened by a horse-stealer, and not only robbed, but mocked, let it pass till he might conveniently meet with him to revenge it.

It fortuned, not long after, that this lance-man prigger was brought to T[ru]ro jail for some such matter, and indeed it was about a mare that he had ſtolen. But as knaves have friends, especially when they are well moneyed, he found divers that spake for him, and who said it was the firſt fault, and the party plaintiff gave but slender evidence againſt him, so that the judge spake favourably in his behalf. The gentleman as then sat on the bench, and, calling to mind the prigger's countenance, how he had ſtolen his horse and mocked him, remembered he had the letter in his pocket that he sent him, and therefore, rising up, spake in his behalf, and highly commended the man, and desired the judges for one fault he might not be caſt away.

" And, besides, may it please you," quoth he, " I had this morning a certificate of his honeſty and good behaviour sent me " ; and with that he delivered them the letter, and the Judge, with the reſt of the bench, smiled at this conceit, and asked the fellow if he never ſtole horse from that gentleman.

" No," quoth the prigger, " I know him not. Your honours miſtakes me."

Said the gentleman, " He did borrow a black horse of me, and marked him with a ſtar in the forehead, and asked twenty mark of me for his labour " ; and so discoursed the whole matter. Whereupon the queſt went upon him, and condemned him, and so the prigger went to Heaven in a ſtring, as many of his faculty had done before.

THE VINCENT'S LAW, WITH THE DISCOVERY THEREOF

THE vincent's law is a common deceit or cozenage used in bowling-alleys, amongſt the baser sort of people that commonly haunt such lewd and unlawful places. For, although I will not discommend altogether the nature of bowling, if the time, place, person, and such necessary circumstances be observed, yet, as it is now used, praⳄised and suffered, it groweth altogether to the maintenance of unthrifts, that idly and disorderly make that recreation a cozenage.

Now the manner and form of their device is thus affeⳄed : the bawkers—for so the common haunters of the alley are termed—apparelled like very honeſt and subſtantial citizens, come to bowl, as though rather they did it for sport than gains, and under that colour of carelessness, do shadow their pretended knavery. Well, to bowls they go, and then there resort of all sorts of people to behold them, some simple men brought in of purpose by some cozening companions to be ſtripped of his crowns ; others, gentlemen, or merchants, that delighted with the sport, stand there as beholders to pass away the time. Amongst these are certain old soakers, which are lookers-on, and listen for bets, either even or odd, and these are called gripes. And these fellows will refuse no lay, if the odds may grow to their advantage. For the gripes and the bawkers are confederate, and their fortune at play ever sorts according as the gripes have placed their bets, for the bawker, he marketh how the lays goes, and so throws his casting. So that note this : the bowlers cast ever booty, and doth win or lose as the bet of the gripe leadeth them ; for suppose seven be up for the game, and the one hath three and the other none, then the vincent—for that is the simple man that stands by, and not acquainted with their cozenage, nor doth so much as once imagine that the bawkers, that carry the countenance of honest substantial men, would by any means, or for any gains, be persuaded to play booty—well, this vincent (for so the cozeners or gripes please to term him), seeing three to none, beginneth to offer odds on that side that is fairest to win. " What odds ? " says the gripe.—" Three to one," says the vincent.—" No," says the gripe, " it is more." And with that they come to four for none. Then the vincent offers to lay four to one. " I take six to one," says the gripe.—" I lay it," says the vincent ; and so they make a bet of some six crowns, shillings, or pence, as the vincent is of ability to lay, and thus will sundry take their odds of him. Well, then the bawkers go forward with their bowls, and win another cast, which is five. Then the vincent grows proud, and thinks, both by the odds and goodness of the play, that it is impossible for his side to lose, and therefore takes and lays bets freely. Then the bawkers' fortune begins to change, and perhaps they come to three for five ; and still, as their luck changes, diversity of bets grows on, till at last it comes to five and five ; and then the gripe comes upon the vincent and offers him odds, which, if the vincent take, he loseth all, for upon what side the gripe lays, that side ever wins, how great soever the odds be at the first in the contrary part, so that the cozenage grows in playing booty, for the gripe and the bawker meet together at night, and there they share whatsoever termage they have gotten—for so they call the money that the poor vincent loseth unto them. Now, to shadow the matter the more, the bawker that wins and is aforehand with the game, will lay frankly that he shall win, and will bet hard, and lay great odds—but with whom ? Either with them which play with him, that are as crafty knaves as himself, or else with the gripe : and this makes the vincent stoop to the blow, and to lose all the money in his purse. Besides, if any honest men that holds themselves skilful in bowling, offer to play any set match against these common bawkers, if they fear to have the worse, or suspect the others' play to be better than theirs, then they have a trick in watering of the alley, to give such a moisture to the bank, that he that offers to strike a bowl with a shore,[12] shall never hit it whilst he lives, because the moisture of the bank hinders the proportion of his aiming.

Divers other practices there are in bowling, tending unto cozenage, but the greatest is booty, and therefore would I wish all men that are careful of their coin, to beware of such cozeners, and none to come in such places, where a haunt of such hell-rakers are resident, and not in any wise to stoop to their bets, lest he be made a vincent, for so manifest and palpable is their cozenage that I have seen men stone-blind offer to lay bets frankly, although they can see a bowl no more than a post, but only hearing who plays, and how the old gripes make their lays. Seeing then as the game is abused to a deceit, that is made for an honest recreation, let this little be a caveat for men to have an insight into their knavery.

For the foist and the nip, as in the first book

[CONY-CATCHING]

THE professors of this law, being somewhat dashed, and their trade greatly impoverished, by the late editions of their secret villainies, seek not a new means of life, but a new method how to fetch in their conies and to play their pranks; for as grievous is it for them to let slip a country farmer come to the Term,[13] that is well apparelled, and in a dirty pair of boots (for that is a token of his new coming up), and a full purse, as it was for the boys of Athens to let Diogenes pass by without a hiss. But the countrymen, having had partly a caveat for their cozenage, fear their favourable speeches and their courteous salutations, as deadly as the Greeks did the whistle of Polyphemus.

The cony-catcher now no sooner cometh in company, and calleth for a pair of cards, but straight the poor cony smokes him, and says: " Masters, I bought a book of late for a groat, that warns me of card-play, lest I fall among cony-catchers."

" What, dost thou think us to be such ? " says the verser.

" No, Gentlemen," says the cony, " you may be men of honest disposition, but yet, pardon me, I have forsworn cards ever since I read it."

At this reply, God wot, I have many a cozening curse at these cony-catchers' hands, but I solemnly stick to the old proverb : the fox, the more he is cursed, the better he fares. But yet I will discover some of their newest devices, for these caterpillars resemble the sirens, who, sitting with their watching eyes upon the rocks to allure sea-passengers, to their extreme prejudice, sound out most heavenly melody in such pleasing chords, that whoso listens to their harmony, lends his ear unto his own bane and ruin ; but if any wary Ulysses pass by and stop his ears against their enchantments, then have they most delightful jewels to show him, as glorious objects, to inveigle his eye with such pleasant vanities that, coming more nigh to behold them, they may dash their ship against a rock and so utterly perish.   So these cony-catchers, for that I smoked them in my last book, and laid open their plots and policies, wherewith they drew poor conies into their hay, seeking, with the orators, *benevolentiam captare,* and as they use rhetorical tropes and figures, the better to draw their hearers with the delight of variety, so these moths of the commonwealth apply their wits to wrap in wealthy farmers with strange and uncouth conceits.   Tush, it was so easy for the setter to take up a cony before I discovered their cozenage, that one stigmatical shameless companion amongst the rest would in a bravery wear parsley in his hat, and said, he wanted but *aqua vitæ* to take a cony with ; but since, he hath looked upon his feet, and veiled his plumes with the peacock, and swears by all the shoes in his shop I shall be the next man he means to kill, for spoiling of his occupation.   But I laugh at his bravados, and though he speaks with his eunuch's voice, and wears a long sword like a morris-pike, were it not I think he would, with Bathyllus, hang himself at my invective, his name should be set down, with the nature of his follies.   But let him call himself home from this course of life, and this cozenage, and I shall be content to shadow what he is with pardon. But from this digression again to the double diligence of these cony-catchers, whose new sleights, because you shall the more easily perceive, I will tell you a story pleasant and worth the noting.[14]

A pleasant tale of a horse, how at Uxbridge he cozened a cony-catcher, and had like to brought him to his neck-verse.[15]

It fortuned that, not long since, certain cony-catchers met by hap a pranker or horse-stealer at Uxbridge, who took up his inn where those honest crew lodged, and, as one vice follows another, was as ready to have a cast at cards as he had a hazard at a horse.   The cony-catchers who supped with him, feeling him pliant to receive the blow, began to lay the plot how they might make him stoop all the money in his purse,

THE
SECOND

and laſt part of Conny-catching.

With new additions containing many merry tales of
all lawes worth the reading, becauſe they are worthy to be remembred.

Diſcourſing ſtrange cunning in Cooſnage, which if you reade without laughing, Ile giue you my cap for a Noble.

Mallem noneſſe quam non prodeſſe patrie.

R. G.

LONDON.
Printed by Iohn Wolfe for William Wright.
1592

Plate IX.

[*face p. 160*

THIRDE

and laſt Part of Conny-
catching.

WITH THE NEW DEVISED
knaui/h Art of Foole-taking.

The like Coſenages and Villenies neuer before diſcouered.

By R. G.

Imprinted at London by *Thomas Scarlet* for
Cutberd Burbie, and are to be ſolde at his ſhoppe in the
Poultrie, by S. Mildreds Church. 1592.

Plate X.

[*face p. 161*

and so for a pint of wine drew him in at cards by degrees. As these rakehells do, *lento gradu*, measure all things by minutes, he fell from wine to money, and from pence to pounds, that he was stripped of all that ever he had, as well crowns, apparel, as jewels ; that at last to maintain the main, and to check vies with revies, he laid his horse in the hazard and lost him.

When the prigger had smoked the game, and perceived he was bitten of all the bite in his bung, and turned to walk penniless in Mark Lane, as the proverb is, he began to chafe, and to swear, and to rap out Gog's Nowns—and pronouns !—while at voluntary he had sworn through the eight parts of speech in the accidence, avowing they had cozened him both of his money and horse. Whereupon the gross ass, more hardy than wise, understanding the cony-catchers were gone, went to the Constable and made hue and cry[16] after them, saying they had robbed him of his horse. At this the headboroughs followed amain, and by chance met with another hue and cry that came for him that had stolen, which hue and cry was served upon the horse-stealer.

And at that time, as far as I can either conjecture or calculate, the cony-catchers were taken suspicious for the same horse, and the rather for that they were found loose livers, and could yield no honest method or means of their maintenance. Upon this, for the horse they were apprehended, and bound over to the sessions at Westminster, to answer what might be objected against them in her Majesty's behalf. Well, the horse-stealer brake from his keepers, and got away, but the rest of the rascal crew, the cony-catchers I mean, were brought to the place of judgment, and there, like valiant youths, they thrust twelve men into a corner, who found them guiltless for the fact, but if great favour had not been shown, they had been condemned, and burnt in the ears for rogues.[17] Thus the horse-stealer made hue and cry after the cony-catchers ; and the man that had lost the horse, he pursued the horse-stealer, so that a double hue and cry passed on both sides, but the cony-catchers had the worse ; for what they got in the bridle they lost in the saddle, what they cozened at cards had like to cost them their necks at the sessions, so that, when they were free and acquitted, one of the cony-catchers in a merry vein said, he had catched many conies, but now a horse had like to caught him : " And so deeply," quoth he, " that *Miserere mei* had like to have been my best matins."

Thus we may see, *fallere fallentem non est fraus* : every deceit hath his due : he that maketh a trap falleth into the snare himself ; and such as covet to cozen all are crossed themselves oftentimes almost to the

H

cross, and that is the next neighbour to the gallows. Well, Gentlemen, thus have I bewrayed much and got little thanks, I mean of the dishonest sort, but I hope such as measure virtue by her honours will judge of me as I deserve. Marry! the goodmen cony-catchers, those base excrements of dishonesty, report they have got one . . . —I will not bewray his name,[18] but a scholar they say he is—to make an invective against me, in that he is a favourer of those base reprobates. But let them, him, and all know, the proudest peasant of them all dare not lift his plumes in disparagement of my credit, for, if he do, I will for revenge only appoint the jakes-farmers of London, who shall case them in their filthy vessels, and carry them as dung to manure the barren places of Tyburn. And so for cony-catchers an end.

A DISCOURSE, OR RATHER DISCOVERY, OF A NIP AND THE FOIST, LAYING OPEN THE NATURE OF THE CUTPURSE AND PICKPOCKET

Now Gentlemen, merchants, farmers, and termers, yea, whatsoever he be that useth to carry money about him, let him attentively hear what a piece of new-found philosophy I will lay open to you, whose opinions, principles, aphorisms, if you carefully note and retain in memory, [may] perhaps save some crowns in your purse ere the year pass ; and therefore thus. The nip and the foist, although their subject is one which they work on, that is, a well-lined purse, yet their manner is different, for the nip useth his knife, and the foist his hand ; the one cutting the purse, the other drawing the pocket. But of these two scurvy trades, the foist holdeth himself of the highest degree, and therefore they term themselves gentlemen foists, and so much disdain to be called cutpurses as the honest man that lives by his hand or occupation, insomuch that the foist refuseth even to wear a knife about him to cut his meat withal, lest he might be suspected to grow into the nature of the nip. Yet, as I said before, is their subject and haunt both alike, for their gains lies by all places of resort and assemblies, therefore their chief walks is Paul's, Westminster, the Exchange,[19] plays, bear-garden,[20] running at tilt, the Lord Mayor's day, any festival meetings, frays, shootings, or great fairs. To be short, wheresoever is any extraordinary resort of people, there the nip and the foist have fittest opportunity to show their juggling agility.

Commonly, when they spy a farmer or merchant whom they suspect to be well moneyed, they follow him hard until they see him draw his purse, then spying in what place he puts it up, the ftall, or shadow, being with the foift or nip, meets the man at some ftrait turn, and joftles him so hard that the man, marvelling, and perhaps quarrelling with him, the whilft the foift hath his purse, and bids him farewell. In Paul's, especially in the term-time, between ten and eleven, then is their hours and there they walk, and, perhaps, if there be great press, ftrike a ftroke in the middle walk, but that is upon some plain man that ftands gazing about, having never seen the church before ; but their chiefeft time is at divine service, when men devoutly given do go up to hear either a sermon, or else the harmony of the choir and the organs. There the nip and the foift, as devoutly as if he were some zealous person, ftandeth soberly, with his eyes elevated to Heaven, when his hand is either on the purse or in the pocket, surveying every corner of it for coin. Then, when the service is done, and the people press away, he thrufteth amidft the throng, and there worketh his villainy. So likewise in the markets, they note how every one putteth up his purse, and there, either in a great press, or while the party is cheapening of meat, the foift is in their pocket, and the nip hath the purse by the ftrings, or sometimes cuts out the bottom, for they have ftill their ftalls following them, who thrufteth or joftleth him or her whom the foift is about to draw. So likewise at plays, the nip ftandeth there leaning like some mannerly gentleman againft the door as men go in, and there finding talk with some of his companions, spyeth what every man hath in his purse, and where, in what place, and in which sleeve or pocket he puts the bung, and, according to that, so he worketh, either where the thruft is great within, or else as they come out at the doors. But suppose that the foift is smoked, and the man misseth his purse, and apprehendeth him for it, then ftraight, he either conveyeth it to his ftall, or else droppeth the bung, and with a great brave he defyeth his accuser ; and though the purse be found at his feet, yet because he hath it not about him, he comes not within compass of life.[21]

Thus have they their shifts for the law, and yet at laft so long the pitcher goeth to the brook that it cometh broken home ; and so long the foifts put their villainy in practise that weftward they go, and there solemnly make a rehearsal sermon at Tyburn.[22] But again, to the places of resort, Weftminfter,[23] ay, marry, that is their chiefeft place that brings in their profit ; the term-time is their harveft, and therefore, like provident husbandmen, they take time while time serves, and make hay while the sun shines, following their clients, for they are at the Hall very early, and there work like bees, haunting every court, as the Exchecquer Chamber, the Star Chamber, the King's Bench, Common Pleas, and every place where the poor client ſtandeth to hear his lawyer handle his matter, for the poor man is so busied with his causes, and so careful to see his counsel, and to ply his attorney, that he thinketh leaſt of his purse. But the foiſt or nip, he watcheth, and, seeing the client draw his purse to pay some charges or fees necessary for the court, marketh where he putteth it, and then when he thruſteth into the throng, either to answer for himself, or to ſtand by his counsellor to put him in mind of his cause, the foiſt draws his pocket and leaves the poor client penniless. This do they in all courts, and go disguised like serving-men, wringing the simple people by this juggling subtlety. Well might, therefore, the honourable and worshipful of those courts do, to take order for such vile and base-minded cutpurses, that as the law hath provided death for them, if they be taken, so they might be rooted out, especially from Weſtminſter, where the poor clients are undone by such roguish catchers.

It boots not to tell their course at every remove of her Majeſty, when the people flock together, nor at Bartholomew Fair,[24] on the Queen's day at the Tilt-yard,[25] and at all other places of assembly ; for let this suffice, at any great press of people or meeting, there the foiſt and the nip is in his kingdom. Therefore let all men take this caveat, that when they walk abroad amid any of the forenamed places, or like assemblies, that they take great care for their purse, how they place it, and not leave it careless in their pockets or hose, for the foiſt is so nimble-handed, that he exceeds the juggler for agility, and hath his legerdemain as perfectly. Therefore an exquisite foiſt muſt have three properties that a good surgeon should have, and that is, an eagle's eye, a lady's hand, and a lion's heart ; an eagle's eye, to spy out a purchase, to have a quick insight where the bung lies, and then a lion's heart, not to fear what the end will be, and then a lady's hand to be little and nimble, the better and the more easy to dive into any man's pocket.

These are the perfect properties of a foiſt. But you muſt note that there be diversities of this kind of people, for there be city nips, and country nips which haunt from fair to fair, and never come in London, unless it be at Bartholomew Fair, or some other great and extraordinary assemblies. Now there is a mortal hate between the country foiſt and the city foiſt : for if the city foiſt spy one of the country foiſts in London, ſtraight he seeks by some means to smoke him ; and so the country nip, if he spy a city nip in any fair, then he smokes him ſtraight, and brings him in danger, if he flee not away the more speedily.   Beside, there be women foiſts and women nips, but the woman foiſt is the moſt dangerous, for commonly there is some old bawd or snout-fair ſtrumpet, who inveigleth either some ignorant man, or some young youth to folly ; she hath ſtraight her hand in the pocket, and so foiſts him of all that he hath. But let all men take heed of such common harlots, who either sit in the ſtreets in evenings, or else dwell in bawdy-houses, and are pliant to every man's lure.   Such are always foiſts and pickpockets, and seek the spoil of all such as meddle with them, and, in cozening of such base-minded lechers as give themselves to such lewd company, are worthy of whatsoever befalls, and sometimes they catch such a Spanish pip, that they have no more hair on their heads than on their nails.

But, leaving such ſtrumpets to their souls' confusion and bodies' correction in Bridewell, again to our nips and foiſts, who have a kind of fraternity or brotherhood amongſt them,[26] having a hall or place of meeting, where they confer of weighty matters touching their workmanship, for they are provident in that every one of them hath some truſty friend whom he calleth his treasurer, and with him he lays up some rateable portion of every purse he draws, that when need requires, and he is brought in danger, he may have money to make composition with the party.   But of late there hath been a great scourge fallen among them ; for now if a purse be drawn of any great value, ſtraight the party maketh friends to some one or other of the Council, or other inferior her Majeſty's Juſtices, and then they send out warrants, if they cannot learn who the foiſt is, to the keepers of Newgate, that take up all the nips and foiſts about the City,[27] and let them lie there while the money be re-answered unto the party, so that some pay three pound, nay, five pound at a time, according as the same loss did amount unto, which doth greatly impoverish their trade, and is likewise an hindrance to their figging law.

Therefore about such causes grow their meetings, for they have a kind of corporation, as having wardens of their company, and a hall. I remember their hall was once about Bishopsgate, near unto Fisher's Folly,[28] but because it was a noted place, they have removed it to Kent Street,[29] and as far as I can learn, it is kept at one Laurence Pickering's house, one that hath been, if he be not ſtill, a notable foiſt.   A man of good calling he is, and well allied, brother-in-law to Bull the hangman.[30] There keep they their feaſts and weekly meetings fit for their company.

Thus have I partly set down the nature of the foist, and the nip, with their special haunts, as a caveat to all estates to beware of such wicked persons, who are as prejudicial unto the commonwealth, as any other faculty whatsoever; and although they be by the great discretion of the Judges and Justices daily trussed up, yet still there springeth up young, that grow in time to bear fruit fit for the gallows. Let then every man be as careful as possibly he may, and by this caveat take heed of his purse, for the prey makes the thief, and there an end.

A merry tale, how a miller had his purse cut in Newgate Market.

It fortuned that a nip and his stall, drinking at the *Three Tuns* in Newgate Market,[31] sitting in one of the rooms next to the street, they might perceive where a meal-man stood selling of meal, and had a large bag by his side, where by conjecture was some store of money. The old cole, the old cutpurse I mean, spying this, was delighted with the show of so glorious an object, for a full purse is as pleasing to a cutpurse eye, as the curious physiognomy of Venus was to the amorous god of war; and, entering to a merry vein, as one that counted that purchase his own, discovered it to the novice and bade him go and nip it. The young toward scholar, although perhaps he had strucken some few strokes before, yet seeing no great press of people, and the meal-man's hand often upon his bag, as if he had in times past smoked some of their faculty, was half afraid, and doubted of his own experience, and so refused to do it.

"Away, villain!" said the old nip. "Art thou faint-hearted? Belongs it to our trade to despair? If thou wilt only do common work, and not make experience of some hard matters to attempt, thou wilt never be master of thine occupation. Therefore try thy wits and do it."

At this the young stripling stalks me out of the tavern, and feeling if his cuttle-bung were glib and of a good edge, went to this meal-man to enter combat hand to hand with his purse. But, seeing the meal-man's eye was still abroad, and for want of other sport that he played with his purse, he was afraid to trust either to his wit or fortune, and therefore went back again without any act achieved.

"How now!" saith the old nip, "what hast thou done?"

"Nothing," quoth he. "The knave is so wary, that it is unpossible to get any purchase there, for he stands playing with his purse, for want of other exercise."

At this his fellow looks out and smiles, making this reply: "And

doſt thou count it impossible to have the meal-man's bung ? Lend me
thy knife, for mine is left at home, and thou shalt see me ſtrike it ſtraight,
and I will show thee a method, how perhaps hereafter to do the like by
my example, and to make thee a good scholar. And therefore go with
me, and do as I shall inſtruct thee. Begin but a feigned quarrel, and
when I give thee a watchword, then throw flour in my face, and, if I do
miss his purse, let me be hanged for my labour."

With that he gave him certain principles to observe, and then paid
for the wine, and out they went together. As soon as they were come
unto the meal-man, the old nip began to jeſt with the other about the
miller's sack, and the other replied as knavishly. At laſt the elder called
the younger rogue.

" Rogue ! thou swain," quoth he, " doſt thou, or dareſt thou dishonour me with such a base title ? " And with that, taking a whole
handful of meal out of the sack, threw it full in the old nip's neck, and
his breaſt, and then ran his way.

He, being thus duſted with meal, entreated the meal-man to wipe
it out of his neck, and ſtooped down his head. The meal-man, laughing
to see him so rayed and whited, was willing to shake off the meal, and
the whilſt he was busy about that, the nip had ſtrucken the purse and done
his feat, and both courteously thanked the meal-man, and closely went
away with his purchase. The poor man, thinking little of this cheat,
began again to play with his purse ſtrings, and suspected nothing till
he had sold a peck of meal, and offered for to change money, and then
he found his purse bottomless, which ſtruck such a quandary to his
ſtomach as if in a froſty morning he had drunk a draught of small-beer
next his heart. He began then to exclaim againſt such villains, and
called to mind how in shaking the duſt out of the gentleman's neck, he
shaked his money out of his purse, and so the poor meal-man fetched
a great sigh, knit up his sack and went sorrowing home.

A kind conceit of a foiſt performed in Paul's.

While I was writing this discovery of foiſting, and was desirous of
any intelligence that might be given me, a gentleman, a friend of mine,
reported unto me this pleasant tale of a foiſt, and as I well remember
it grew to this effect :

There walked in the middle walk a plain country farmer, a man of
good wealth, who had a well-lined purse, only barely thruſt up in a
round slop, which a crew of foiſts having perceived, their hearts were

set on fire to have it, and every one had a fling at him, but all in vain, for he kept his hand close in his pocket, and his purse fast in his fist like a subtle churl, that either had been forewarned of Paul's, or else had aforetime smoked some of that faculty. Well, howsoever it was impossible to do any good with him, he was so wary. The foists spying this, strained their wits to the highest string how to compass this bung, yet could not all their politic conceits fetch the farmer over, for jostle him, chat with him, offer to shake him by the hand, all would not serve to get his hand out of his pocket. At last one of the crew, that for his skill might have been doctorate in his mystery, amongst them all chose out a good foist, one of a nimble hand and great agility, and said to the rest thus :

" Masters, it shall not be said such a base peasant shall slip away from such a crew of gentlemen-foists as we are, and not have his purse drawn, and therefore this time I'll play the stall myself, and if I hit him not home, count me for a bungler for ever " ; and so left them and went to the farmer and walked directly before him and next him three or four turns. At last, standing still, he cried, " Alas, honest man, help me. I am not well " ; and with that sunk down suddenly in a swoon. The poor farmer, seeing a proper young gentleman, as he thought, fall dead afore him, stepped to him, held him in his arms, rubbed him and chafed him.

At this, there gathered a great multitude of people about him, and the whilst the foist drew the farmer's purse and away. By that the other thought the feat was done, he began to come something to himself again, and so half staggering, stumbled out of Paul's, and went after the crew where they had appointed to meet, and there boasted of his wit and experience.

The farmer, little suspecting this villainy, thrust his hand into his pocket and missed his purse, searched for it, but lining and shells and all was gone, which made the countryman in a great maze, that he stood still in a dump so long that a gentleman, perceiving it, asked what he ailed.

" What ail I, sir ? " quoth he. " Truly I am thinking how men may long as well as women."

" Why dost thou conjecture that, honest man ? " quoth he.

" Marry ! sir," answers the farmer. " The gentleman even now that swooned here, I warrant him breeds his wife's child, for the cause of his sudden qualm, that he fell down dead, grew of longing ! "

The gentleman demanded how he knew that.

" Well enough, sir," quoth he, " and he hath his longing too, for the poor man longed for my purse, and thanks be to God he hath it with him."

At this all the hearers laughed, but not so merrily as the foist and his fellows, that then were sharing his money.

A quaint conceit of a cutler and a cutpurse.[32]

A nip, having by fortune lost his cuttle-bung, or having not one fit for his purpose, went to a cunning cutler to have a new made, and prescribed the cutler such a method and form to make his knife, and the fashion to be strong, giving such a charge of the fineness of the temper and setting of the edge, that the cutler wondered what the gentleman would do with it.   Yet, because he offered so largely for the making of it, the cutler was silent and made few questions, only he appointed [him] the time to come for it, and that was three days after.   Well, the time being expired, the gentleman-nip came, and, seeing his knife, liked it passing well, and gave him his money with advantage.   The cutler desirous to know to what use he would put it, said to the cutpurse thus :

" Sir," quoth he, " I have made many knives in my days, and yet I never saw any of this form, fashion, temper, or edge, and therefore, if without offence, I pray you tell me how or to what will you use it ? "

While thus he stood talking with the nip, *he*, spying the purse in his apron, had cut it passing cunningly, and then, having his purchase close in his hand, made answer : " In faith, my friend, to dissemble is a folly.   'Tis to cut a purse withal, and I hope to have good handsel."

" You are a merry gentleman," quoth the cutler.

" I tell true," quoth the cutpurse, and away he goes.

No sooner was he gone from the stall, but there came another and bought a knife, and should have single money[33] again.   The cutler, thinking to put his hand in his bag, thrust it quite through at the bottom. All his money was gone, and the purse cut.   Perceiving this, and remembering how the man prayed he might have good handsel, he fetched a great sigh, and said :

" Now I see : he that makes a snare, first falls into it himself.   I made a knife to cut other men's purses, and mine is the first handsel. Well, revenge is fallen upon me, but I hope the rope will fall upon him." And so he smoothed up the matter to himself, lest men should laugh at his strange fortune.

THE DISCOVERY OF THE LIFTING LAW

THE lift is he that ſtealeth or prowleth any plate, jewels, bolts of satin, velvet, or such parcels from any place, by a sleight conveyance under his cloak, or so secretly that it may not be espied. Of lifts there be divers kinds as their natures be different, some base rogues, that lift, when they come into ale-houses, quart pots, platters, cloaks, swords, or any such paltry trash which commonly is called pilfering or petu-lacery, for, under the colour of spending two or three pots of ale, they lift away anything that cometh within the compass of their reach, having a fine and nimble agility of the hand, as the foiſt had.

These are the common and rascal sort of lifts ; but the higher degrees and gentlemen-lifts have to the performance of their faculty three parties of necessity, the lift, the marker and the santar. The lift, attired in the form of a civil country gentleman, comes with the marker into some mercer's shop, haberdasher's, goldsmith's, or any such place where any particular parcels of worth are to be conveyed, and there he calls to see a bolt of satin, velvet, or any such commodity, and, not liking the pile, colour, or brack, he calls for more, and the whiles he begins to resolve which of them moſt fitly may be lifted, and what garbage (for so he calls the goods ſtolen) may be moſt easily conveyed. Then he calls to the mercer's man and says, " Sirrah, reach me that piece of velvet or satin, or that jewel, chain, or piece of plate " ; and whilſt the fellow turns his back, he commits his garbage to the marker ; for note, the lift is without his cloak, in his doublet and hose, to avoid the more suspicion. The marker, which is the receiver of the lift's luggage, give a wink to the santar, that walks before the window, and then, the santar going by in great haſte, the marker calls him and says, " Sir, a word with you. I have a message to do unto you from a very friend of yours, and the errand is of some importance."

" Truly, sir," says the santar, " I have very urgent business in hand, and as at this time I cannot ſtay . . . ."

" But one word, and no more," says the marker. And then he delivers him whatsoever the lift hath conveyed unto him ; and then the santar goes his way, who never came within the shop, and is a man unknown to them all.

Suppose he is smoked, and his lifting looked into, then are they upon their pantofles, because there is nothing found about them. They defy the world for their honeſty, because they be as dishoneſt as any in the world, and swear, as God shall judge them, they never saw the parcel

loſt.   But oaths with them are like wind out of a bellows, which being
cool kindleth fire ; so their vows are without conscience, and so they
call for revenge.   Therefore, let this be a caveat to all occupations,
sciences and myſteries that they beware of the gentleman-lift, and to
have an eye to such as cheapen their wares, and not, when they call to
see new ſtuff, to leave the old behind them, for the fingers of lifts are
formed of adamant[34] : though they touch not, yet they have virtue
attractive to draw any pelf to them, as the adamant doth the iron.

But yet these lifts have a subtle shift to blind the world, for this
close kind of cozenage they have when they want money : One of them
apparels himself like a country farmer, and with a memorandum drawn
in some legal form, comes to the chamber of some counsellor or Ser-
jeant-at-Law, with his marker and his santar, and there tells the lawyer
his case and desires his counsel, the whilſt the marker and the santar
lay the platform for any rapier, dagger, cloak, gown, or any other parcel
of worth that is in the withdrawing or outer chamber, and as soon as
they have it they go their way.   Then when the lawyer hath given his
opinion of the case the lift requires, then he puts in some demur or
blind, and says he will have his cause better discovered, and then he
will come to his worship again.   So, taking his leave without his ten
shillings fee, he goes his ways to share what his companions had gotten.
The like method they use with scriveners, for coming by the shop, and,
seeing any garbage worth the lifting, one ſtarteth in to have an obligation
or bill made in haſte, and, while the scrivener is busy, the lift bringeth
the marker to the blow, and so the luggage is carried away.   Now,
these lifts have their special receivers of their ſtolen goods, which are
two sundry parties : either some notorious bawds, in whose houses they
lie, and they keep commonly tapping-houses, and have young trugs in
their house, which are consorts to these lifts, and love them so dear that
they never leave them till they come to the gallows ; or else they be
brokers, a kind of idle sort of lewd livers, as pernicious as the lift, for
they receive at their hands whatsoever garbage is conveyed, be it linen,
woollen, plate, jewels, and this they do by a bill of sale, making the bill
in the name of John a' Nokes or John a' Stiles, so that they shadow the
lift, and yet keep themselves without the danger of the law.   Thus are
these brokers and bawds, as it were, efficient causes of the lifter's villainy,
for, were it not their alluring speeches and their secret consellings, the
lift, for want of receivers should be fain to take a new course of life, or
else be continually driven into great extremes for selling his garbage.
And thus much briefly for the nature of the lift.

THE DISCOVERY OF THE CURBING LAW

THE curber, which the common people call the hooker, is he that with a curb, as they term it, or hook, doth pull out of a window any loose linen cloth, apparel, or else any other household stuff whatsoever, which stolen parcels they in their art call snappings. To the performance of this law there be required duly two persons, the curber and the warp. The curber, his office is to spy in the day-time fit places where his trade may be practised at night, and, coming unto any window, if it be open, then he hath his purpose ; if shut, then growing into the nature of the black art, [he] hath his trickers, which are engines of iron, so cunningly wrought, that he will cut a bar of iron in two with them so easily, that scarcely shall the standers-by hear him. Then, when he hath the window open and spies any fat snappings worth the curbing, then straight he sets the warp to watch, who hath a long cloak to cover whatsoever he gets. Then doth the other thrust in a long hook some nine foot in length, which he calleth a curb, that hath at the end a crook, with three tines turned contrary, so that 'tis unpossible to miss, if there be any snappings abroad. Now this long hook they call a curb, and, because you shall not wonder how they carry it for being spied, know this, that it is made with joints like an angle-rod, and can be conveyed into the form of a truncheon, and worn in the hand like a walking staff until they come to their purpose, and then they let it out at the length, and hook or curb whatsoever is loose and within the reach ; and then he conveys it to the warp, and from thence, as they list, their snappings go to the broker or to the bawd, and there they have as ready money for it, as merchants have for their ware in the Exchange. Beside, there is a diver, which is the very nature of the curber, for as he puts in a hook, so the other puts in at the window some little figging boy, who plays his part notably ; and perhaps the youth is so well instructed, that he is a scholar in the black art, and can pick a lock if it be not too cross-warded, and deliver to the diver what snappings he finds in the chamber. Thus you hear what the curber doth, and the diver, and what inconvenience grows to many by their base villainies. Therefore I wish all men-servants and maids to be careful for their masters' commodities, and to leave no loose ends abroad, especially in chambers where windows open to the street, lest the curber take them as snappings, and convey them to the cozening broker. Let this suffice ; and now I will recreate your wits with a merry tale or two.

Of a curber, and how cunningly he was taken.

It fortuned of late that a curber and his warp went walking in the dead of the night to spy out some window open for their purpose, and by chance came by a nobleman's house about London, and saw the window of the porter's lodge open, and looking in, spied fat snappings, and bade his warp watch carefully, for there would be purchase, and, with that, took his curb, and thrust it into the chamber. And the porter, lying in his bed, was awake and saw all, and so was his bedfellow that was yeoman of the wine-cellar. The porter stole out of his bed to see what would be done.

The first snapping the curber light on was his livery-coat. As he was drawing it unto the window, the porter easily lifted it off, and so the curber drew his hook in vain, the whilst his bedfellow stole out of the chamber, and raised up two or three more, and went about to take them. But still the rogue plied his business, and lighted on a gown, that he used to sit in in the porter's lodge, and warily drew it, but when it came to the window, the porter drew it off so lightly, that the hooker perceived it not. Then, when he saw his curb would take no hold, he swore and chafed and told the warp he had hold of two good snaps, and yet missed them both, and that the fault was in the curb. Then he fell to sharping and hammering of the hook, to make it hold better, and in again he thrusts it, and lights upon a pair of buff hose; but when he had drawn them to the window, the porter took them off again, which made the curber almost mad, and swore he thought the Devil was abroad to-night, he had such hard fortune.

" Nay," says the yeoman of the cellar, " there is three abroad, and we are come to fetch you and your hooks to Hell."

So they apprehended these base rogues and carried them into the porter's lodge, and made that their prison. In the morning a crew of gentlemen in the houses, sat for judges—in that they would not trouble their Lord with such filthy caterpillars—and by them they were found guilty, and condemned to abide forty blows apiece with a bastinado, which they had solemnly paid, and so went away without any further damage.

Of the subtlety of a curber in cozening a maid.

A merry jest and as subtle was reported to me of a cunning curber, who had apparelled himself marvellous brave, like some good well-favoured young gentleman, and, instead of a man, had his warp to wait upon him.   This smoothfaced rogue comes into Moorfields,[35] and caused his man to carry a pottle of hippocras under his cloak, and there had learned out, amongst others that was drying of clothes, of a very well-favoured maid that was there with her flasket of linen, what her master was, where she dwelt, and what her name.   Having gotten this intelligence, to this maid he goes, courteously salutes her, and after some pretty chat, tells her how he saw her sundry times at her master's door, and was so besotted with her beauty, that he had made inquiry what her qualities were, which by the neighbours he generally heard to be so virtuous, that his desire was the more inflamed, and thereupon in sign of good will, and in further acquaintance, he had brought her a pottle of hippocras.   The maid, seeing him a good proper man, took it very kindly, and thanked him, and so they drunk the wine, and, after a little lovers' prattle, for that time they parted.

The maid's heart was set on fire that a gentleman was become a suitor to her, and she began to think better of herself than ever she did before, and waxed so proud that her other suitors were counted too base for her, and there might be none welcome but this new-come gentleman her lover.   Well, divers times they appointed meetings, that they grew very familiar, and he oftentimes would come to her master's house, when all but she and her fellow maids were in bed, so that he and the warp his man did almost know every corner of the house.   It fortuned that so long he dallied, that at length he meant earnest, but not to marry the maid, whatsoever he had done else, and coming into the fields to her on a washing day, saw a mighty deal of fine linen, worth twenty pound as he conjectured.   Whereupon he thought this night to set down his rest, and therefore he was very pleasant with his lover, and told her that that night after her master and mistress were in bed, he would come, and bring a bottle of sack with him and drink with her.   The maid, glad at these news, promised to sit up for him ; and so they parted till about ten o'clock at night, when he came, and brought his man with him, and one other curber with his tools, who should stand without the doors.   To be brief, welcome he came, and so welcome as a man might be to a maid.   He, that had more mind to spy the clothes than to look on her favour, at last perceived them in a parlour that stood to the streetward, and there would the maid have had him sit.   " No, sweeting," quoth he, " it is too near the street.   We can neither laugh nor be merry, but every one that passeth by must hear us."   Upon that they removed into another room, and pleasant they were, and tippled the sack round till all was out, and the gentleman swore that he would have another pottle, and so sent his man, who told the other curber, that stood without, where the window was he should work at, and away goes he for more sack and brings it very orderly, and then to their cups they fall again, while the curber without had not left one rag of linen behind.   Late it grew, and the morning began to wax grey, and away goes this curber and his man, leaving the maid very pleasant with his flattering promises until such time as, poor soul, she went into the parlour, and missed all her mistress' linen.   Then what a sorrowful heart she had I refer to them that have grieved at the like loss.

THE DISCOVERY OF THE BLACK ART

THE black art is picking of locks ; and to this busy trade two persons are required, the charm and the stand.   The charm is he that doth the feat, and the stand is he that watcheth.   There be more that do belong to the burglary for conveying away the goods, but only two are employed about the lock.   The charm hath many keys and wrests, which they call picklocks, and for every sundry fashion they have a sundry term ; but I am ignorant of their words of art, and therefore I omit them : only this, they have such cunning in opening a lock, that they will undo the hardest lock though never so well warded, even while a man may turn his back.   Some have their instruments from Italy, made of steel ; some are made here by smiths, that are partakers in their villainous occupations.   But, howsoever, well may it be called the black art, for the Devil cannot do better than they in their faculty.

I once saw the experience of it myself, for, being in the Counter upon commandment, there came in a famous fellow in the black art, as strong in that quality as Samson.   The party now is dead, and by fortune died in his bed.   I, hearing that he was a charm, began to enter familiarity with him, and to have an insight into his art.   After some acquaintance he told me much, and one day, being in my chamber, I showed him my desk, and asked him if he could pick that little lock that was so well warded, and too little, as I thought, for any of his gins.

" Why, sir," says he, " I am so experienced in the black art, that if I do but blow upon the lock, it shall fly open ; and therefore let me come to your desk, and do but turn five times about, and you shall see my cunning."   With that I did as he bade me, and ere I had turned five times, his hand was rifling in my desk very orderly.   I wondered at it, and thought verily that the Devil and his dam was in his fingers. Much discommodity grows by this black art in shops and noblemen's houses for their plate. Therefore are they most severely to be looked into by the honourable and worshipful of England. And to end this discourse as pleasantly as the rest, I will rehearse you a true tale done by a most worshipful knight in Lancashire against a tinker that professed the black art.

A true and merry tale of a knight and a tinker that was a picklock.

Not far off from Bolton-in-the-moors, there dwelled an ancient knight, who for courtesy and hospitality was famous in those parts. Divers of his tenants, making repair to his house, offered divers complaints to him, how their locks were picked in the night, and divers of them utterly undone by that means ; and who it should be they could not tell, only they suspected a tinker, that went about the country, and in all places did spend very lavishly. The knight willingly heard what they exhibited, and promised both redress and revenge, if he or they could learn out the man.

It chanced not long after their complaints, but this jolly tinker, so expert in the black art, came by the house of this knight, as the old gentleman was walking before the gate, and cried for work. The knight, straight conjecturing this should be that famous rogue that did so much hurt to his tenants, called in and asked if they had any work for the tinker. The cook answered, there was three or four old kettles to mend.

"Come in, tinker." So this fellow came in, laid down his budget and fell to his work. "A black jack of beer for the tinker," says the knight. "I know tinkers have dry souls." The tinker he was pleasant and thanked him humbly. The knight sat down with him and fell a ransacking his budget, and asked wherefore this tool served and wherefore that. The tinker told him all. At last as he tumbled among his old brass, the knight spied three or four bunches of picklocks. He turned them over quickly as though he had not seen them, and said : "Well, tinker, I warrant thou art a passing cunning fellow and well skilled in thine occupation by the store of thy tools thou hast in thy budget."

"In faith, if it please your worship," quoth he, "I am, thanks be to God, my craft's master."

" Ay, so much I perceive that thou art a passing cunning fellow," quoth the knight. " Therefore let us have a fresh jack of beer, and that of the best and strongest, for the tinker."

Thus he passed away the time pleasantly, and when he had done his work, he asked what he would have for his pains.

" But two shillings—of your worship," quoth the tinker.

" Two shillings ? " says the knight. " Alas, tinker, it is too little! For I see by thy tools thou art a passing cunning workman. Hold, there is two shillings. Come in. Thou shalt drink a cup of wine before thou goest. But I pray thee tell me, which way travellest thou ? "

" Faith, sir," quoth the tinker, " all is one to me. I am not much out of my way wheresoever I go ; but now I am going to Lancaster."

" I pray thee, tinker," then quoth the knight, " carry me a letter to the jailer, for I sent in a felon thither the other day and I would send word to the jailer he should take no bail for him."

" Marry, that I will, in most dutiful manner," quoth he, " and much more for your worship than that."

" Give him a cup of wine," quoth the knight. " And sirrah (speaking to his clerk) make a letter to the jailer." But then he whispered to him and bade him make a *mittimus*[36] to send the tinker to prison.

The clerk answered, he knew not his name.

" I'll make him tell it thee himself," says the knight ; " and therefore fall you to your pen."

The clerk began to write his *mittimus*, and the knight began to ask what countryman he was, where he dwelt, what was his name. The tinker told him all, and the clerk set it in with this proviso to the jailer, that he should keep him fast bolted, or else he would break away. As soon as the *mittimus* was made, sealed and subscribed in form of a letter, the knight took it, and delivered it to the tinker, and said, " Give this to the chief jailer of Lancaster ; and here is two shillings more for thy labour."

So the tinker took the letter and the money, and with many a cap and knee thanked the old knight and departed, and made haste till he came at Lancaster, and stayed not in the town so much as to taste one cup of nappy ale before he came to the jailer, and to him very briefly he delivered his letter. The jailer took it and read it, and smiled a good, and said :

" Tinker, thou art welcome for such a knight's sake. He bids me give thee the best entertainment I may."

"Ay, sir," quoth the tinker, "the knight loves me well; but, I pray you, hath the courteous gentleman remembered such a poor man as I?"

"Ay, marry, doth he, tinker. And, therefore, sirrah," quoth he to one of his men, "take the tinker into the lowest ward; clap a strong pair of bolts on his heels, and a basil of twenty-eight pound weight. And then, sirrah, see if your picklocks will serve the turn to bail you hence!"

At this the tinker was blank, but yet he thought the jailer had but jested. But, when he heard the *mittimus*, his heart was cold, and had not a word to say; his conscience accused him. And there he lay while the next sessions, and was hanged at Lancaster, and all his skill in the black art could not serve him.

Finis

THE THIRD AND LAST PART OF CONY-CATCHING

By Robert Greene

[1592]

To all such as have received either pleasure or profit by the two former
published books of this argument, and to all beside that desire to know
the wonderful sly devices of this hellish crew of cony-catchers.

IN the time of King Henry the Fourth, as our English chroniclers have
kept in remembrance, lived diverse sturdy and loose companions in
sundry places about the City of London, who gave themselves to no
good course of life, but because the time was somewhat troublesome,
watched diligently, when by the least occasion of mutiny offered, they
might prey upon the goods of honest citizens, and so by their spoil
enrich themselves. At that time likewise lived a worthy gentleman,
whose many very famous deeds (whereof I am sorry I may here make
no rehearsal, because neither time nor occasion will permit me) renown
his name to all ensuing posterities ; he being called Sir Richard Whittington, the founder of Whittington College[1] in London, and one that
bear the office of Lord Mayor of this City three several times. This
worthy man, well noting the dangerous disposition of that idle kind of
people, took such good and discreet order (after he had sent divers of
them to serve in the king's wars, and they, loath to do so well, returned
to their former vomit) that in no place of or about London they might
have lodging or entertainment, except they applied themselves to such
honest trades and exercises as might witness their maintaining was by
true and honest means. If any to the contrary were found, they were
in justice so sharply proceeded against, as the most hurtful and dangerous
enemies to the commonwealth.

In this quiet and most blissful time of peace, when all men, in course
of life, should show themselves most thankful for so great a benefit,
this famous City is pestered with the like or rather worse kind of people,
that bear outward show of civil, honest, and gentlemanlike disposition,
but in very deed their behaviour is most infamous to be spoken of. And
as now by their close villainies they cheat, cozen, prig, lift, nip, and
suchlike tricks, now used in their cony-catching trade, to the hurt and

undoing of many an honest citizen, and other : so if God should in justice be angry with us, as our wickedness hath well deserved, and, as the Lord forfend, our peace should be molested as in former time, even as they did, so will these be the first in seeking domestical spoil and ruin ; yea, so they may have it, it skils not how they come by it. God raise such another as was worthy Whittington, that in time may bridle the headstrong course of this hellish crew, and force them live as becometh honest subjects, or else to abide the reward due to their looseness.

By reading this little treatise ensuing, you shall see to what marvellous subtle policies these deceivers have attained, and how daily they practise strange drifts for their purpose. I say no more, but, if all these fore-warnings may be regarded, to the benefit of the well-minded, and just control of these careless wretches, it is all I desire, and no more than I hope to see.

Yours in all he may,

R.G.

THE THIRD AND LAST PART OF CONY-CATCHING, WITH THE NEW-DEVISED KNAVISH ART OF FOOL-TAKING.

BEING by chance invited to supper, where were present divers, both of worship and good account, as occasion served for intercourse of talk, the present treacheries and wicked devices of the world was called in question. Amongst other most hateful, and well worthy repre-hension, the wondrous villainies of loose and lewd persons, that bear the shape of men, yet are monsters in condition was specially remembered and not only they, but their complices, their confederates, their base-natured women and close compactors were noted ; namely, such as term themselves cony-catchers, crossbiters, with their appertaining names to their several cozening qualities, as already is made known to to the world by two several imprinted books,[2] by means whereof the present kind of conference was occasioned.

Quoth a gentleman sitting at the table, whose deep step into age deciphered his experience, and whose gravity in speech reported his discretion ; quoth he : " By the two published books of cony-catching I have seen divers things whereof I was before ignorant. Notwithstanding, had I been acquainted with the author, I could have given him such notes of notorious matters that way intenting as in neither of the pamphlets are the like set down. Beside, they are so necessary to be known, as they will both forearm any man against such treacherous vipers, and forewarn the simpler sort from conversing with them."

The gentleman being known to be within Commission of the Peace, and that what he spake of either came to him by examinations, or by riding in the circuits as other like officers do, was entreated by one man above the rest, as his leisure served him, to acquaint him with those notes, and he would so bring it to pass as the writer of the other two books should have the sight of them, and if their quantity would serve, that he should publish them as a third, and more necessary, part than the former were.

The gentleman replied : " All such notes as I speak are not of mine own knowledge. Yet from such men have I received them, as I dare assure their truth ; and but that by naming men wronged by such mates, more displeasure would ensue than were expedient, I could set down both time, place and parties. But the certainty shall suffice without any such offence. As for such as shall see their injuries discovered, and, biting the lip, say to themselves, ' Thus was I made a cony ', their names being shadowed, they have no cause of anger, in that the example of their honest simplicity beguiled may shield a number more endangered from tasting the like. And, seeing you have promised to make them known to the author of the former two books, you shall the sooner obtain your request ; assuring him thus much upon my credit and honesty, that no one untruth is in the notes, but every one credible, and to be justified, if need serve."

Within a fortnight or thereabout afterward, the gentleman performed his promise, in several papers sent the notes, which here are in our book compiled together. When thou hast read, say, if ever thou heardest more notable villainies discovered. And if thou or thy friends receive any good by them, as it cannot be but they will make a number more careful of themselves, thank the honest gentleman for his notes, and the writer that published both the other and these for general example.

A pleasant tale how an honest substantial citizen was made a cony, and simply entertained a knave that carried away his goods very politicly.

What laws are used among this hellish crew, what words and terms they give themselves and their copesmates, are at large set down in the former two books. Let it suffice ye then in this, to read the simple true discourses of such as have by extraordinary cunning and treachery been deceived, and remembering their subtle means there, and sly practices here, be prepared against the reaches of any such companions.

Not long since, a crew of cony-catchers meeting together, and in conference laying down such courses as they severally should take to shun suspect, and return a common benefit among them, the carders received their charge, the dicers theirs, the hangers-about-the-Court theirs, the followers of sermons theirs, and so the rest to their offices; but one of them especially, who at their wonted meetings, when report was made how every purchase was gotten, and by what policy each one prevailed, this fellow in a kind of priding scorn, would usually say:

"In faith, masters, these things are prettily done—common sleights, expressing no deep reach of wit. And I wonder men are so simple to be so beguiled. I would fain see some rare artificial feat indeed, that some admiration and fame might ensue the doing thereof. I promise ye, I disdain these base and petty paltries, and, may my fortune jump with my resolution, ye shall hear, my boys, within a day or two, that I will accomplish a rare stratagem indeed, of more value than forty of yours, and, when it is done, shall carry some credit with it!"

They, wondering at his words, desired to see the success of them, and so, dispersing themselves as they were accustomed, left this frolic fellow pondering on his affairs. A citizen's house in London, which he had diligently eyed and aimed at for a fortnight's space, was the place wherein he must perform this exploit; and, having learned one of the servant-maid's name of the house, as also where she was born and her kindred, upon a Sunday in the afternoon, when it was her turn to attend on her master and mistress to the garden in Finsbury Fields, to regard the children while they sported about, this crafty mate, having duly watched their coming forth, and seeing that they intended to go down St. Laurence Lane,³ stepped before them, ever casting an eye back, lest they should turn some contrary way. But, their following still fitting his own desire, near unto the conduit in Aldermanbury he crossed the way and came unto the maid, and kissing her said: "Cousin Margaret, I am very glad to see you well. My uncle your father, and all your friends in the country are in good health, God be praised!"

The maid, hearing herself named, and not knowing the man, modestly blushed, which he perceiving, held way on with her amongst her fellow apprentices, and thus began again: "I see, cousin, you know me not, and I do not greatly blame you, it is so long since you came forth of the country; but I am such a one's son"—naming her uncle right, and his son's name, which she very well remembered, but had not seen him in eleven years. Then, taking forth a bowed groat, and an old penny bowed, he gave it her as being sent from her uncle and aunt, whom he termed to be his father and mother. " Withal," quoth he, " I have a gammon of bacon and a cheese from my uncle your father, which are sent to your master and mistress, which I received of the carrier, because my uncle enjoined me to deliver them, when I must entreat your mistress that at Whitsuntide next she will give you leave to come down into the country." The maid, thinking simply all he said was true, and as they, so far from their parents, are not only glad to hear of their welfare, but also rejoice to see any of their kindred, so this poor maid, well knowing her uncle had a son so named as he called himself, and thinking from a boy, as he was at her leaving the country, he was now grown such a proper handsome young man, was not a little joyful to see him. Beside, she seemed proud that her kinsman was so neat a youth, and so she held on questioning with him about her friends, he soothing each matter so cunningly, as the maid was confidently persuaded of him.

In this time, one of the children stepped to her mother and said, " Our Marget, mother, hath a fine cousin come out of the country, and he hath a cheese for my father and you." Whereon she, looking back, said : " Maid, is that your kinsman ? "—" Yea forsooth, mistress," quoth she, " my uncle's son, whom I left a little one when I came forth of the country."

The wily treacher, being master of his trade, would not let slip this opportunity, but courteously stepping to the mistress—who, loving her maid well, because indeed she had been a very good servant, and from her first coming to London had dwelt with her, told her husband thereof —coined such a smooth tale unto them both, fronting it with the gammon of bacon and the cheese sent from their maid's father, and hoping they would give her leave at Whitsuntide to visit the country, as they with very kind words entertained him, inviting him the next night to supper, when he promised to bring with him the gammon of bacon and the cheese. Then, framing an excuse of certain business in the town, for that time he took his leave of the master and mistress and his new cousin Margaret, who gave many a look after him, poor wench, as he went, joying in her thoughts to have such a kinsman.

On the morrow he prepared a good gammon of bacon, which he closed up in a soiled linen cloth, and sewed an old card upon it, whereon he wrote a superscription unto the master of the maid, and at what sign it was to be delivered, and afterward scraped some of the letters half out, that it might seem they had been rubbed out in the carriage. A good cheese he prepared likewise, with inscription accordingly on it, that it could not be discerned but that some unskilful writer in the country had done it, both by the gross proportion of the letters, as also the bad orthography, which amongst plain husbandmen is very common, in that they have no better instruction. So, hiring a porter to carry them, between five and six in the evening he comes to the citizen's house, and entering the shop, receives them of the porter, whom the honest-meaning citizen would have paid for his pains, but this his maid's new-found cousin said he was satisfied already, and so, straining courtesy, would not permit him.

Well, up are carried the bacon and the cheese, where God knows Margaret was not a little busy to have all things fine and neat against her cousin's coming up. Her mistress likewise, as one well affecting her servant, had provided very good cheer, set all her plate on the cupboard for show, and beautified the house with cushions, carpets, stools, and other devices of needlework, as at such times divers will do, to have the better report made of their credit amongst their servant's friends in the country, albeit at this time, God wot, it turned to their own after-sorrowing. The master of the house, to delay the time while supper was ready, he likewise shows this dissembler his shop, who, seeing things fadge so pat to his purpose, could question of this sort, and that well enough I warrant you, to discern the best from the worst and their appointed places, purposing a further reach than the honest citizen dreamed of. And to be plain with ye, such was this occupier's trade, as, though I may not name it, yet thus much I dare utter, that the worst thing he could carry away, was worth about twenty nobles, because he dealt altogether in whole and great sale, which made this companion forge this kindred and acquaintance, for an hundred pound or twain was the very least he aimed at.

At length the mistress sends word supper is on the table, whereupon up he conducts his guest, and, after divers welcomes, as also thanks for the cheese and bacon, to the table they sit, where, let it suffice, he wanted no ordinary good fare, wine and other knacks, besides much talk of the country, how much his friends were beholden for his cousin Margaret, to whom by her mistress' leave he drank twice or thrice, and she, poor soul, doing the like again to him, with remembrance of her father and other kindred, which he still smoothed very cunningly. Countenance of talk made them careless of the time, which slipped from them faster than they were aware of, nor did the deceiver hasten his departing, because he expected what indeed followed, which was, that, being past ten of the clock, and he feigning his lodging to be at St. Giles in the Field, was entreated both by the goodman and his wife, to take a bed there for that night. For fashion sake, though very glad of this offer, he said he would not trouble them, but, giving them many thanks, would to his lodging, though it were further. But wonderful it was to see how earnest the honest citizen and his wife laboured to persuade him, that was more willing to stay than they could be to bid him, and what dissembled willingness of departure he used on the other side, to cover the secret villainy intended. Well, at the length, with much ado, he is contented to stay, when Margaret and her mistress presently stirred to make ready his bed, which the more to the honest man's hard hap, but all the better for this artificial cony-catcher, was in the same room where they supped, being commonly called their hall, and there indeed stood a very fair bed, as in such sightly rooms it may easily be thought citizens use not to have anything mean or simple.

The mistress, lest her guest should imagine she disturbed him, suffered all the plate to stand still on the cupboard, and when she perceived his bed was warmed, and everything else according to her mind, she and her husband, bidding him good night, took themselves to their chamber, which was on the same floor, but inward, having another chamber between them and the hall, where the maids and children had their lodging. So, desiring him to call for anything he wanted, and charging Margaret to look it should be so, to bed are they gone ; when the apprentices having brought up the keys of the street door, and left them in their master's chamber as they were wont to do, after they had said prayers, their evening exercise, to bed go they likewise, which was in a garret backward over their master's chamber. None are now up but poor Margaret and her counterfeit cousin, whom she, loath to offend with long talk, because it waxed late, after some few more speeches, about their parents and friends in the country, she, seeing him laid in bed, and all such things by him as she deemed needful, with a low courtesy I warrant ye commits him to his quiet, and so went to bed to her fellows the maidservants.

Well did this hypocrite perceive the keys of the doors carried into the goodman's chamber, whereof he, being not a little glad, thought now they would imagine all things sure, and therefore doubtless sleep the sounder. As for the keys, he needed no help of them, because such as he go never unprovided of instruments fitting their trade, and so at this time was this notable treacher.

In the dead time of the night, when sound sleep makes the ear unapt to hear the very least noise, he forsaketh his bed, and, having gotten all the plate bound up together in his cloak, goeth down into the shop, where, well remembering both the place and parcels, maketh up his pack with some twenty pounds' worth of goods more. Then fettling to his engine, he getteth the door off the hinges, and being forth, lifteth close to again, and so departs, meeting within a dozen paces, three or four of his companions that lurked thereabouts for the purpose. Their word for knowing each other, as is said, was *quest*, and this villain's comfortable news to them was *twag*, signifying he had sped. Each takes a fleece for easier carriage, and so away to bell-brow, which, as I have heard is, as they interpret it, the house of a thief-receiver, without which they can do nothing ; and this house with an apt porter to it, stands ready for them all hours of the night. Too many such are there in London, the masters whereof bear countenance of honest substantial men, but all their living is gotten in this order. The end of such, though they 'scape awhile, will be sailing westward in a cart to Tyburn. Imagine these villains there in their jollity, the one reporting point by point his cunning deceit, and the other, fitting his humour, extolling the deed with no mean commendations.

But, returning to the honest citizen, who, finding in the morning how dearly he paid for a gammon of bacon and a cheese, and how his kind courtesy was thus treacherously requited, blames the poor maid, as innocent herein as himself, and imprisoning her, thinking so to regain his own, grief with ill cherishing there shortens her life. And thus ensueth one hard hap upon another, to the great grief both of master and mistress, when the truth was known, that they so wronged their honest servant. How it may forewarn others I leave to your own opinions, that see what extraordinary devices are nowadays to beguile the simple and honest liberal-minded.

Of a notable knave, who for his cunning deceiving a gentleman of his purse, scorned the name of a cony-catcher, and would needs be termed a fool-taker, as master and beginner of that new-found art.

A crew of these wicked companions being one day met together in Paul's Church, as that is a usual place of their assembly, both to deter-mine on their drifts, as also to speed of many a booty, seeing no likelihood of a good afternoon (so they term it either forenoon or after- when ought is to be done), some dispersed themselves to the plays, other to the bowling-alleys, and not past two or three stayed in the church.

Quoth one of them, " I have vowed not to depart, but something or other I'll have before I go. My mind gives me that this place yet will yield us all our suppers this night."

The other, holding like opinion with him, there likewise walked up and down, looking when occasion would serve for some cash.   At length they espied a gentleman toward the law entering in at the little north door, and a country client going with him in very hard talk, the gentle-man holding his gown open with his arms on either side as very many do, gave sight of a fair purple velvet purse, which was half put under his girdle, which I warrant you the resolute fellow that would not depart without something, had quickly espied. " A game," quoth he to his fellows. " Mark the stand "; and so, separating themselves, walked aloof, the gentleman going to the nether step of the stairs that ascend up into the choir, and there he walked still with his client.   Oft this crew of mates met together, and said there was no hope of nipping the bung because he held open his gown so wide, and walked in such an open place. " Base knaves," quoth the frolic fellow, " if I say I will have it, I must have it, though he that owns[4] it had sworn the contrary." Then, looking aside, he spied his trug, or quean, coming up the church. " Away," quoth he to the other.   " Go look you for some other purchase; this wench and I are sufficient for this."

They go ; he lessons the drab in this sort, that she should go to the gentleman, whose name she very well knew, in that she had holpen to cozen him once before, and, pretending to be sent to him from one he was well acquainted with for his counsel, should give him his fee for avoiding suspicion, and so frame some wrong done her, as well enough she could. When her mate, taking occasion as it served, would work the mean, she should strike, and so they both prevail. The quean, well inured with such courses, because she was one of the most skilful in that profession, walked up and down alone in the gentleman's sight, that he might discern she stayed to speak with him, and as he turned toward her, he saw her take money out of her purse, whereby he gathered some benefit was toward him ; which made him the sooner despatch his other client, when she, stepping to him, told such a tale of commenda-tions from his very friend, that had sent her to him, as she said, that he entertained her very kindly, and giving him his fee, which before her face he put up into his purse, and thrust it under his girdle again, she proceeded to a very sound discourse, whereto he listened with no little attention.

The time serving fit for the fellow's purpose, he came behind the gentleman, and, as many times one friend will familiarly with another, clap his hands over his eyes to make him guess who he is, so did this companion, holding his hands fast over the gentleman's eyes, said, " Who am I ? " twice or thrice, in which time the drab had gotten the purse and put it up. The gentleman, thinking it had been some merry friend of his, reckoned the names of three or four, when, letting him go, the crafty knave, dissembling a bashful shame of what he had done, said :

" By my troth, sir, I cry ye mercy. As I came in at the church door, I took ye for such a one (naming a man), a very friend of mine, whom you very much resemble. I beseech ye, be not angry ; it was very boldly done of me, but in penance of my fault, so please ye to accept it, I will bestow a gallon or two of wine on ye " ; and so laboured him earnestly to go with him to the tavern, still alleging his sorrow for mistaking him.

The gentleman, little suspecting how Who-am-I ? had handled him, seeing how sorry he was, and seeming to be a man of no such base condition, took all in good part, saying, " No harm, sir, to take one for another, a fault wherein any man may easily err " ; and so excusing the acceptation of his wine, because he was busy there with a gentlewoman his friend.

The treacher with a courtesy departed, and the drab, having what she would, shortening her tale (he desiring her to come to his chamber the next morning) went to the place where her copesmate and she met, and not long after, divers other of the crew, who, hearing in what manner this act was performed, smiled a good thereat, that she had both got the gentleman's purse, her own money again, and his advice for just nothing. He that had done this tall exploit, in a place so open in view, so hardly to be come by, and on a man that made no mean esteem of his wit, bids his fellows keep the worthless name of a cony-catcher to themselves ; for he henceforth would be termed a fool-taker, and such as could imitate this quaint example of his, which he would set down as an entrance into that art, should not think scorn to become his scholars.

Night drawing on apace, the gentleman returned home, not all this while missing his purse, but being set at supper, his wife entreated a pint of sack, which he minding to send for, drew to his purse, and seeing it gone, what strange looks, besides sighs, were between him and his wife, I leave to your supposing. And blame them not ; for, as I have heard, there was seven pound in gold, beside thirty shillings and odd white money in the purse. But in the midſt of his grief, he remembered him that said, " Who am I ? " Wherewith he brake forth into a great laughter, the cause whereof his wife being desirous to know, he declared all that passed between him and the deceiver, as also how soon afterward the quean abbreviated her discourse and followed. " So by troth wife," quoth he, " between Who-am-I ? and the drab, my purse is gone." Let his loss teach others to look better to theirs.

Another tale of a cozening companion who would needs try his cunning in this new-invented art, and how by his knavery at one inſtant he beguiled half a dozen and more.

Of late time there hath a certain base kind of trade been used, who, though divers poor men, and doubtless honeſt, apply themselves to, only to relieve their need, yet are there some notorious varlets do the same, being compaſted with such kind of people as this present treatise manifeſteth to the world, and, what with outward simplicity on the one side, and cunning close treachery on the other, divers honeſt citizens and day-labouring men, that resort to such places as I am to speak of, only for recreation as opportunity serveth, have been of late sundry times deceived of their purses. This trade, or rather unsufferable loitering quality, in singing of ballads and songs at the doors of such houses where plays are used, as also in open markets and other places of this City, where is moſt resort ; which is nothing else but a sly fetch to draw many together, who, liſtening unto an harmless ditty, afterward walk home to their houses with heavy hearts. From such as are hereof true witnesses to their coſt, do I deliver this example.

A subtle fellow, belike emboldened by acquaintance with the former deceit, or else being but a beginner to praſtise the same, calling certain of his companions together, would try whether he could attain to be maſter of his art or no, by taking a great many of fools with one train. But let his intent and what else beside remain to abide the censure after the matter is heard, and come to Gracious Street,[5] where this villainous prank was performed. A roguing mate, and such another with him, were there got upon a ſtall singing of ballads, which belike was some pretty toy, for very many gathered about to hear it, and divers buying, as their affeſtions served, drew to their purses and paid the singers for them. The sly mate and his fellows, who were dispersed among them that ſtood to hear the songs, well noted where every man that bought put up his purse again, and to such as would not buy, counterfeit warning was sundry times given by the rogue and his associate, to beware of the cutpurse, and look to their purses, which made them often feel where their purses were, either in sleeve, hose, or at girdle, to know whether they were safe or no.

Thus the crafty copesmates were acquainted with what they moſt desired, and as they were scattered, by shouldering, thruſting, feigning to let fall something, and other wily tricks fit for their purpose, here one loſt his purse, there another had his pocket picked, and, to say all in brief, at one inſtant, upon the complaint of one or two that saw their purses were gone, eight more in the same company found themselves in like predicament. Some angry, others sorrowful, and all greatly discontented, looking about them, knew not who to suspeſt or challenge, in that the villains themselves that had thus beguiled them, made show that they had suſtained like loss. But one angry fellow, more impatient than all the reſt, he falls upon the ballad-singer, and, beating him with his fiſts well favouredly, says, if he had not liſtened his singing, he had not loſt his purse, and therefore would not be otherwise persuaded, but that they two and the cutpurses were compaſted together. The reſt that had loſt their purses likewise, and saw that so ma[n]y complain together, they jump in opinion with the other fellow, and begin to tug and hale the ballad singers, when, one after one, the false knaves began to shrink away with the purses. By means of some officer then being there present, the two rogues were had before a Juſtice, and upon his discreet examination made,[6] it was found, that they and the cutpurses were compaſted together, and that by this unsuspeſted villainy, they had deceived many. The fine fool-taker himself, with one or two more of that company, was not long after apprehended, when I doubt not but they had their reward answerable to their deserving ; for I hear of their journey weſtward, but not of their return. Let this forewarn those that liſten singing in the ſtreets.

Of a crafty mate that brought two young men unto a tavern, where, departing with a cup, he left them to pay both for the wine and cup.

A friend of mine sent me this note, and assuring me the truth thereof, I thought necessary to set it down amongſt the reſt, both for the honeſt simplicity on the one side, and moſt cunning knavery used on the other ; and thus it was.

Two young men of familiar acquaintance, who delighted much in music, because themselves therein were somewhat expert, as on the virginals, bandore, lute and suchlike, were one evening at a common inn of this town, as I have heard, where the one of them showed his skill on the virginals, to the no little contentment of the hearers. Now, as divers guests of the house came into the room to listen, so among the rest entered an artificial cony-catcher, who, as occasion served, in the time of ceasing between the several toys and fancies he played, very much commended his cunning, quick hand, and such qualities praise-worthy in such a professor. The time being come when these young men craved leave to depart, this politic varlet, stepping to them, desired that they would accept a quart of wine at his hand, which he would most gladly he would bestow upon them. Besides, if it liked him that played on the virginals to instruct, he would help him to so good a place, as happily might advantage him for ever.

These kind words, delivered with such honest outward show, caused the young men, whose thoughts were free from any other opinion than to be as truly and plainly dealt withal as themselves meant, accepted his offer, because he that played on the virginals was desirous to have some good place of service, and hereupon to the tavern they go, and being set, the wily companion calleth for two pints of wine, a pint of white, and a pint of claret, casting his cloak upon the table, and falling to his former communication of preferring the young man. The wine is brought, and two cups withal, as is the usual manner. When drinking to them of the one pint, they pledge him, not unthankful for his gentle-ness. After some time spent in talk, and, as he perceived, fit for his purpose, he takes the other cup, and tastes the other pint of wine, where-with he finding fault, that it drank somewhat hard, said, that rose-water and sugar would do no harm; whereupon he leaves his seat, saying he was well acquainted with one of the servants of the house, of whom he could have twopennyworth of rose-water for a penny, and so of sugar likewise, wherefore he would step to the bar unto him. So, taking the cup in his hand, he did, the young men never thinking on any such treachery as ensued, in that he seemed an honest man, and beside left his cloak lying on the table by them.

No more returns the younker with rose-water and sugar, but, stepping out of doors, unseen of any, goes away roundly with the cup. The young men, not a little wondering at his long tarrying, by the coming of the servants to see what they wanted, who took no regard of his sudden departure, find themselves there left, not only to pay for the wine, but for the cup also, being rashly supposed by the master and his servants to be copartners with the treacherous villain. But their honest behaviour well known, as also their simplicity too much abused, well witnessed their innocency; notwithstanding they were fain to pay for the cup, as afterward they did, having nothing towards their charge but a thread-bare cloak not worth two shillings. Take heed how you drink wine with any such companions.

Of an honest householder which was cunningly deceived by a subtle companion that came to hire a chamber for his master.

Not far from Charing Cross dwelleth an honest young man, who being not long since married, and having more rooms in his house than himself occupieth, either for term-time, or the Court lying so near, as divers do, to make a reasonable commodity, and to ease house-rent, which, as the world goeth now in none of the cheapest, letteth forth a chamber or two, according as it may be spared. In an evening but a while since, came one in the manner of a serving-man to this man and his wife, and he must needs have a chamber for his master, offering so largely, as the bargain was soon concluded between them. His intent was to have fingered some booty in the house, as by the sequel it may be likeliest gathered. But, belike no fit thing lying abroad, or he better regarded than haply he would be, his expectation that way was frustrate. Yet as a resolute cony-catcher indeed, that scorneth to attempt without some success, and rather will prey upon small commodity than return to his fellows disgraced with a lost labour, he summons his wits together, and by a smooth tale overreached both the man and his wife. He tells them that his master was a captain late come from the sea, and had costly apparel to bring thither, which, for more easy carriage, he entreats them lend him a sheet to bind it up in. They suspecting no ill, because he required their boy should go with him to help him carry the stuff, the good wife steps unto her chest, where her linen lay finely sweetened with roseleaves and lavender, and lends him a very good sheet indeed.

This success made him bold to venture a little further, and then he tells them his master had a great deal of broken sugar and fine spices, that lay negligently abroad in his lodging as it was brought from the ship, all which he was assured his master would bestow on them, so he could devise how to get it brought thither.

These liberal promises, prevailing with them that lightly believed, and withal were somewhat covetous of the sugar and spices. The woman

A DISPVTATION,

Betweene a Hee Conny-catcher, and a

Shee Conny-catcher, whether a Theefe or a Whoore, is
moſt hurtſull in Couſonage, to the Common-wealth.

DISCOVERING THE SECRET VILLA-

nies of alluring Strumpets.

With the Conuerſion of an Engliſh Courtizen, reformed
this preſent yeare, 1592.

Reade, laugh, and learne.

Naſcimur pro patria.

R. G.

Imprinted at London, by A. I. for T. G. and are to be ſolde at
the Weſt ende of Paules. 1592.

Plate XI.

[face p. 192

The Blacke Dogge of Newgate:

both pithie and profitable
for all Readers.

Vide, Lege, Caue.

Time fhall'trie the trueth.
by Luke Hutton

Imprinted at London by *G. Simfon* and *W. White.*

Plate XII.

[*face p. 193*

demanded if a couple of pillow-beres would not serve to bring the sugar and spices in. " Yes, marry," quoth he, " so the sugar may best be kept by itself, and the spices by themselves. And," quoth he, " because there are many crafty knaves abroad "—grieving that any should be craftier than himself—" and in the evening the linen might quickly be snatched from the boy." For the more safety, he would carry the sheet and pillow-beres himself, and within an hour or little more, return with the boy again, because he would have all things ready before his master came, who, as he said, was attending on the Council at the Court.

The man and his wife, crediting his smooth speeches, sends their boy with him, and so along toward Ivy Bridge[7] go they. The cony-catcher, seeing himself at free liberty, that he had gotten a very good sheet, and two fine pillow-beres, steps to the wall, as though he would make water, bidding the boy go fair and softly on before. The boy, doubting nothing, did as he willed him, when presently he stepped into some house hard by fit to entertain him. And never since was he, his master, the sugar, spices, or the linen heard of. Many have been in this manner deceived, as I hear. Let this then give them warning to beware of any such unprofitable guests.

Of one that came to buy a knife and made first proof of his trade on him that sold it.

One of the cunning nips about the town came unto a poor cutler to have a cuttle made according unto his own mind, and not above three inches would he have both the knife and the haft in length ; yet of such pure metal, as possible may be. Albeit the poor man never made the like before, yet, being promised four times the value of his stuff and pains, he was contented to do this, and the day being come that he should deliver it, the party came, who, liking it exceedingly, gave him the money promised, which the poor man gladly put up into his purse, that hung at a buttonhole of his waistcoat before his breast, smiling that he was so well paid for so small a trifle. The party perceiving his merry countenance, and imagining he guessed for what purpose the knife was, said, " Honest man, whereat smile you ? "—" By my troth, sir," quoth the cutler, " I smile at your knife, because I never made one so little before ; and, were it not offensive unto you, I would request to know to what use you will put it to."—" Wilt thou keep my counsel ? " quoth the nip. " Yea on mine honesty," quoth the cutler. " Then hearken

I

in thy ear," said the nip, and so rounding with him, cut the poor man's purse that hung at his bosom, he never feeling when he did it. " With this knife," quoth the nip, " mean I to cut a purse."—" Marry, God forbid ! " quoth the cutler : " I cannot think you to be such a kind of man. I see you love to jeſt " ; and so they parted.

The poor man, not so wise as to remember his own purse, when by such a warning he might have taken the offender doing the deed, but rather proud, as it were, that his money was so easily earned, walks to the ale-house, which was within a house or two of his own, and, finding there three or four of his neighbours, with whom he began to jeſt very pleasantly, swears by cock and pie he would spend a whole groat upon them, for he had gotten it and more clearly by a good bargain that morning.

Though it was no marvel to see him so liberal, because indeed he was a good companion, yet they were loath to put him unto such coſt, Notwithſtanding he would needs do it, and so far as promise ſtretched, was presently filled in and set upon the board. In the drinking time often he wished to meet with more such cuſtomers as he had done that morning, and commended him for a very honeſt gentleman, I warrant you. At length, when the reckoning was to be paid, he draws to his purse, where, finding nothing left but a piece of the ſtring in the button-hole, I leave to your judgment whether he was now as sorry as he was merry before.

Blank and all amort sits the poor cutler, and with such a pitiful countenance as his neighbours did not a little admire his solemn altera-tion, and, desirous to know the cause thereof, from point to point he discourseth the whole manner of the tragedy, never naming his new cuſtomer, but with such a far-fetched sigh, as soul and body would have parted in sunder. And in midſt of all his grief, he brake forth into these terms :

" I'll believe a man the better by his word while I know him. The knife was bought to cut a purse indeed, and I thank him for it he made the firſt proof of the edge with me."

The neighbours grieving for his loss, yet smiling at his folly to be so overreached, were fain to pay the groat the cutler called in, because he had no other money about him, and spent as much more beside to drive away his heaviness.

This tale, because it was somewhat misreported before,[8] upon talk had with the poor cutler himself, is set down now in true form and manner how it was done. Therefore is there no offence offered, when by better consideration, a thing may be enlarged or amended, or at least the note be better confirmed.

Let the poor cutler's mishap example others, that they brag not over-hastily of gain easily gotten, lest they chance to pay as dearly for it as he did.

Of a young nip that cunningly beguiled an ancient professor of that trade, and his quean with him at a play.

A good fellow that was newly entered into the nipping craft, and had not as yet attained to any acquaintance with the chief and cunning masters of that trade, in the Christmas holidays last came to see a play at the *Bull within Bishopsgate,*[9] there to take his benefit as time and place would permit him. Not long had he stayed in the press, but he had gotten a young man's purse out of his pocket, which when he had, he stepped into the stable to take out the money, and to convey away the purse. But looking on his commodity he found nothing therein but white counters, a thimble and a broken threepence, which belike the fellow that ought it, had done of purpose to deceive the cutpurse withal, or else had played at the cards for counters, and so carried his winnings about him till his next sitting to play. Somewhat displeased to be so overtaken, he looked aside, and spied a lusty youth entering at the door, and his drab with him. This fellow he had heard to be one of the finest nippers about the town, and ever carried his quean with him, for conveyance when the stratagem was performed. He puts up the counters into the purse again, and follows close to see some piece of their service. Among a company of seemly men was this lusty companion and his minion gotten, where both they might best behold the play, and work for advantage, and ever this young nip was next to him, to mark when he should attempt any exploit, standing as it were more than half between the cunning nip and his drab, only to learn some part of their skill. In short time the deed was performed, but how, the young nip could not easily discern, only he felt him shift his hand toward his trug, to convey the purse to her, but she, being somewhat mindful of the play, because a merriment was then on the stage, gave no regard, whereby, thinking he had pulled her by the coat, he twitched the young nip by the cloak, who, taking advantage of this offer, put down his hand and received the purse of him. Then, counting it discourtesy to let him lose all his labour, he softly plucked the quean by the coat, which she feeling, and imagining it had been her companion's hand, received of him the first purse with the white counters in it. Then, fearing lest his stay should hinder him, and seeing the other intended to have more purses ere he departed, away goes the young nip with the purse he got so easily, wherein, as I have heard, was thirty-seven shillings and odd money, which did so much content him, as that he had beguiled so ancient a stander in that profession. What the other thought when he found the purse, and could not guess how he was cozened, I leave to your censures. Only this makes me smile, that one false knave can beguile another, which bids honest men look the better to their purses.

How a gentleman was craftily deceived of a chain of gold and his purse, in Paul's Church in London.

A gentleman of the country, who, as I have heard since the time of his mishap, whereof I am now to speak, had about half a year before buried his wife, and, belike thinking well of some other gentlewoman, whom he meant to make account of as his second choice, upon good hope or otherwise persuaded, he came up to London to provide himself of such necessaries as the country is not usually stored withal. Besides silks, velvets, cambrics and suchlike, he bought a chain of gold that cost him fifty-seven pounds and odd money, whereof, because he would have the maidenhead or first wearing himself, he presently put it on in the goldsmith's shop, and so walked therewith about London as his occasions served. But let not the gentleman be offended, who, if this book come to his hands, can best avouch the truth of this discourse, if hereby the way I blame his rash pride, or simple credulity; for between the one and other, the chain he paid so dear for about ten of the clock in the morning, the cony-catchers the same day ere night shared amongst them, a matter whereat he may well grieve, and I be sorry, in respect he is my very good friend. But to the purpose. This gentleman walking in Paul's, with his chain fair glittering about his neck, talking with his man about some business, was well viewed and regarded by a crew of cony-catchers, whose teeth watered at his goodly chain, yet knew not how to come by it, hanging as it did, and therefore entered into secret conspiration among themselves, if they could not come by all the chain, yet how they might make it lighter by half a score pounds at the least. Still had they their eyes on the honest gentleman, who little doubted any such treason intended against his so late bought bargain; and they, having laid their plot, each one to be assistant in this enterprise, saw when the gentleman dismissed his servant to go about such affairs as he had appointed him, himself still walking there up and down the middle aisle.

One of these mates, that stood most on his cunning in these exploits, followed the serving-man forth of the church calling him by divers names, as John, Thomas, William, etc., as though he had known his right name, but could not hit on it. Which whether he did or no I know not, but well I wot the serving-man turned back again, and seeing him that called him seemed a gentleman, booted and cloaked after the newest fashion, came with his hat in his hand to him, saying, " Sir, do ye call me ? "—" Marry do I, my friend," quoth the other, " dost not thou serve such a gentleman ? "—and named one as himself pleased. " No, truly, sir," answered the serving-man. " I know not any such gentleman as you speak of."—" By my troth," replied the cony-catcher, " I am assured I knew thee and thy master, though now I cannot suddenly remember myself." The serving-man, fearing no harm, yet fitting the humour of this treacherous companion, told right his master's name whom he served, and that his master was even then walking in Paul's. " O' God's will," quoth the cony-catcher, repeating his master's name, " a very honest gentleman. Of such a place is he not ? " naming a shire of the country—for he must know both name, country, and some-times what gentlemen dwell near the party that is to be overreached, ere he can proceed. " No indeed sir," answered the serving-man, with such reverence as it had been to an honest gentleman indeed. " My master is of such a place, a mile from such a town, and hard by such a knight's house." By which report the deceiver was half instructed, because, though he was ignorant of the fellow's master, yet well he knew the country and the knight named. So craving pardon that he had mistaken him, he returns again into the church, and the serving-man trudgeth about his assigned business.

Being come to the rest of the crew, he appoints one of them, whom he knew to be expert indeed, to take this matter in hand, for himself might not do it, lest the serving-man should return and know him. He schooled the rest likewise what every man should do when the pinch came, and, changing his cloak with one of his fellows, walked by himself attending the feat. And everyone being as ready, the appointed fellow makes his sally forth, and, coming to the gentleman, calling him by his name, gives him the courtesy and embrace, likewise thanking him for good cheer he had at his house, which he did with such seemly behaviour and protestation, as the gentleman, thinking the other to be no less, used like action of kindness to him. Now as country gentlemen have many visitors both with near-dwelling neighbours and friends that journey from far, whom they can hardly remember, but some principal one that serves as countenance to the other ; so he, not discrediting the cunning mate's words, who ſtill at every point alleged his kindred to the knight, neighbour to the gentleman, which the poor serving-man had, doubting no ill, revealed before, and that both there and at his own house in hawking-time with that knight and other gentlemen of the country he had liberally taſted his kindness ; desiring pardon that he had forgotten him, and offered him the courtesy of the City.   The cony-catcher excused himself for that time, saying, at their next meeting he would beſtow it on him.   Then, seeming to have espied his chain, and commending the fairness and workmanship thereof, says : " I pray ye, sir, take a little counsel of a friend.   It may be you will return thanks for it.   I wonder," quoth he, " you dare wear such a coſtly jewel so open in sight, which is even but a bait to entice bad men to adventure time and place for it, and nowhere sooner than in this city, where, I may say to you, are such a number of cony-catchers, cozeners and such like, that a man can scarcely keep any thing from them, they have so many reaches and sleights to beguile withal ; which a very especial friend of mine found too true not many days since."

Hereupon he told a very solemn tale of villainies and knaveries in his own profession, whereby he reported his friend had loſt a watch of gold ; showing how closely his friend wore it in his bosom, and how ſtrangely it was gotten from him, that the gentleman by that discourse waxed half afraid of his chain, and giving him many thanks for this good warning, presently takes the chain from about his neck, and tying it up faſt in a handkerchief, put it up into his sleeve, saying : " If the cony-catcher get it here, let him not spare it."

Not a little did the treacher smile in his sleeve, hearing the rash security but indeed simplicity of the gentleman, and no sooner saw he it put up, but presently he counted it sure his own, by the assiſtance of his complices, that lay in an ambuscado for the purpose.   With embraces and courtesies on either side, the cony-catcher departs, leaving the gentleman walking there ſtill.   Whereat the crew were not a little offended that he ſtill kept in the church, and would not go abroad. Well, at length, belike remembering some business, the gentleman, taking leave of another that talked with him, haſted to go forth at the furtheſt weſt door of Paul's, which he that had talked with him, and gave him such counsel, perceiving, hied out of the other door, and got to the entrance ere he came forth, the reſt following the gentleman at an inch. As he was ſtepping out, the other ſtepped in, and let fall a key, having his hat so low over his eyes that he could not well discern his face, and, ſtooping to take up the key, kept the gentleman from going backward or forward, by reason his leg was over the threshold. The foremoſt cony-catcher behind, pretending a quarrel unto him that ſtooped, rapping out an oath, and drawing his dagger, said, " Do I meet the villain? Nay, he shall not 'scape me now," and so made offer to ſtrike him.

The gentleman at his ſtanding up, seeing it was he that gave him so good counsel, and pretended himself his very friend, but never imagining this train was made for him, ſtepped in his defence, when the other following tripped up his heels ; so that he and his counseller were down together, and two more upon them, ſtriking with their daggers very eagerly. Marry, indeed the gentleman had moſt of the blows, and both his handkercher with the chain, and also his purse with three and fifty shillings in it, were taken out of his pocket in this ſtruggling, even by the man that himself defended.

It was marvellous to behold how, not regarding the villain's words uttered before in the church, nor thinking upon the charge about him, which after he had thus treacherously loſt unwittingly, he ſtands pacifying them that were not discontented but only to beguile him. But they, vowing that they would presently go for their weapons, and so to the field, told the gentleman he laboured but in vain, for fight they muſt and would, and so, going down by Paul's Chain,[10] left the gentleman made a cony going up toward Fleet Street, sorry for his new counseller and friend, and wishing him good luck in the fight ; which indeed was with nothing but wine pots, for joy of their late-gotten booty. Near to St. Dunſtan's Church, the gentleman remembered himself, and feeling his pocket so light, had suddenly more grief at his heart than ever happen[ed] to him or any man again. Back he comes to see if he could espy any of them, but they were far enough from him. God send him better hap when he goes next a wooing, and that this his loss may be a warning to others !

How a cunning knave got a trunk well-ſtuffed with linen and certain parcels of plate out of a citizen's house, and how the maſter of the house holp the deceiver to carry away his own goods.

Within the City of London dwelleth a worthy man who hath very great dealing in his trade, and his shop very well frequented with customers, had such a shrewd mischance of late by a cony-catcher, as may well serve for an example to others lest they have the like.

A cunning villain, that had long time haunted this citizen's house, and gotten many a cheat which he carried away safely, made it his custom when he wanted money, to help himself ever where he had sped so often. Divers things he had which were never missed, especially such as appertained to the citizen's trade, but when any were found wanting, they could not devise which way they were gone, so politically this fellow always behaved himself. Well knew he what times of greatest business this citizen had in his trade, and when the shop is most stored with chapmen. Then would he step up the stairs (for there was and is another door to the house besides that which entereth into the shop), and what was next hand came ever away with. One time above the rest, in an evening about Candlemass, when daylight shuts in about six of the clock, he watched to do some feat in the house, and seeing the mistress go forth with her maid, the goodman and his folks very busy in the shop, up the stairs he goes as he was wont to do, and lifting up the latch of the hall portal door, saw nobody near to trouble him, when stepping into the next chamber, where the citizen and his wife usually lay, at the bed's feet there stood a handsome trunk, wherein was very good linen, a fair gilt salt, two silver French bowls for wine, two silver drinking pots, a stone jug covered with silver, and a dozen of silver spoons. This trunk he brings to the stairs' head, and, making fast the door again, draws it down the steps so softly as he could, for it was so big and heavy, as he could not easily carry it. Having it out at the door, unseen of any neighbour or anybody else, he stood struggling with it to lift it up on the stall, which by reason of the weight troubled him very much.

The goodman coming forth of his shop, to bid a customer or two farewell, made the fellow afraid he should now be taken for all together, but, calling his wits together to escape if he could, he stood gazing up at the sign belonging to the house, as though he were desirous to know what sign it was, which the citizen perceiving, came to him and asked him what he sought for.

" I look for the sign of the *Blue Bell*, sir," quoth the fellow, " where a gentleman having taken a chamber for this term-time hath sent me hither with this his trunk of apparel."

Quoth the citizen, " I know no such sign in this street, but in the next (naming it) there is such a one indeed, and there dwelleth one that letteth forth chambers to gentlemen."

" Truly sir," quoth the fellow, " that's the house I should go to. I pray you, sir, lend me your hand but to help the trunk on my back, for I, thinking to ease me a while upon your ſtall, set it short, and now I can hardly get it up again."

The citizen, not knowing his own trunk, but indeed never thinking on any such notable deceit, helps him up with the trunk, and so sends him away roundly with his own goods. When the trunk was missed, I leave to your conceits what household grief there was on all sides, especially the goodman himself, who, remembering how he helped the fellow up with a trunk, perceived that hereby he had beguiled himself, and loſt more than in haſte he should recover again. How this may admonish others I leave to the judgment of the indifferent opinion, that see when honeſt meaning is so craftily beleaguered as good fore-sight muſt be used to prevent such dangers.

How a broker was cunningly overreached by as crafty a knave as himself, and brought in danger of the gallows.

It has been used as a common byword : *a crafty knave needeth no broker*, whereby it should appear that there can hardly be a craftier knave than a broker. Suspend your judgments till you have heard this discourse ensuing, and then, as you please, censure both the one and the other.

A lady of the country sent up a servant whom she might well put in truſt, to provide her of a gown answerable to such direćtions as she had given him, which was of good price, as may appear by the outside and lace, whereto doubtless was every other thing agreeable. For the tailor had seventeen yards of the beſt black satin could be got for money, and so much gold lace, beside spangles, as valued thirteen pound. What else was beside, I know not, but let it suffice thus much was loſt, and therefore let us to the manner how.

The satin and the lace being brought to the tailor that should make the gown, and spread abroad on the shop-board to be measured, certain good fellows of the cony-catching profession chanced to go by, who, seeing so rich lace, and so excellent good satin, began to commune with themselves how they might make some purchase of what they had seen. And quickly it was to be done, or not at all. As ever in a crew of this quality, there is some one more ingenious and politic than the reſt, or at leaſtwise that covets to make himself more famous than the reſt, so this inſtant was there one in this company that did swear his cunning should deeply deceive him, but he would have both the lace and satin. When having laid the plot with his companions, how and which way their help might stand him in stead, this way they proceeded.

Well noted they the serving-man that stood in the shop with the tailor, and gathered by his diligent attendance that he had some charge of the gown there to be made. Wherefore by him must they work their treachery intended, and use him as an instrument to beguile himself. One of them sitting on a seat near the tailor's stall could easily hear the talk that passed between the serving-man and the tailor, where among other communication, it was concluded that the gown should be made of the self-same fashion in every point, as another lady's was, who then lay in the City ; and that measure being taken by her, the same would fitly serve the lady for whom the gown was to be made. Now the serving-man intended to go speak with the lady, and upon a token agreed between them (which he carelessly spake so loud that the cony-catcher heard it), he would as her leisure served, certify the tailor, and he should bring the stuff with him, to have the lady's opinion both of the one and the other.

The serving-man being gone about his affairs, the subtle mate that had listened to all their talk acquaints his fellows both with the determination and token appointed for the tailor's coming to the lady. The guide and leader to all the rest for villainy—though there was no one but was better skilled in such matters than honesty—he appoints that one of them should go to the tavern, which was not far off, and laying two faggots on the fire in a room by himself, and a quart of wine filled, for countenance of the treachery. Another of that crew should give attendance on him, as if he were his master, being bareheaded, and " Sir " humbly answering at every word. To the tavern goes this counterfeit gentleman, and his servant waiting on him, where everything was performed as is before rehearsed, when the master-knave, calling the drawer, demanded if there dwelt near at hand a skilful tailor, that could make a suit of velvet for himself. Marry, it was to be done with very great speed !

The drawer named the tailor that we now speak of, and upon the drawer's commending his cunning, the man in all haste was sent for, to a gentleman for whom he must make a suit of velvet forthwith. Upon talk had of the stuff, how much was to be bought of everything appertaining thereto, he must immediately take measure of this counterfeit gentleman, because he knew not when to return that way again. Afterward they would go to the mercer's.

As the tailor was taking measure on him bareheaded, as if he had been a substantial gentleman indeed, the crafty mate had cunningly gotten his purse out of his pocket, at the one string whereof was fastened a little key, and at the other his signet ring. This booty he was sure of already, whether he should get anything else or no of the mischief intended. Stepping to the window, he cuts the ring from the purse, and by his supposed man, rounding him in the ear, sends it to the plotlayer of this knavery, minding to train the tailor along with him, as it were to the mercer's, while he the meantime took order for the other matter.

Afterward, speaking aloud to his man, " Sirrah," quoth he, " despatch what I bade you, and about four of the clock meet me in Paul's. By that time I hope the tailor and I shall have despatched." To Cheapside goeth the honest tailor with this notorious dissembler, not missing his purse for the space of two hours after, in less than half which time the satin and gold lace was gotten likewise by the other villain from the tailor's house in this order.

Being sure the tailor should be kept absent, he sends another mate home to his house, who abused his servants with this device : that the lady's man had met their master abroad, and had sent him to the other lady to take measure of her, and, lest they should delay the time too long, he was sent for the satin and lace, declaring the token appointed, and withal giving their master's signet ring for better confirmation of his message. The servants could do no less than deliver it, being commanded, as they supposed, by so credible testimony. Neither did the leisure of any one serve to go with the messenger, who seemed an honest young gentleman, and carried no cause of distrust in his countenance. Wherefore they delivered him the lace and satin, folded up together as it was, and desired him to will their master to make some speed home, both for cutting out of work and other occasions.

To a broker fit for their purpose goes this deceiver with the satin lace, who, knowing well they could not come honestly by it, nor anything else he bought of that crew, as often before he had dealt much with them, either gave them not so much as they would have, or at least as they judged they could have in another place, for which the ringleader of this cozenage vowed in his mind to be revenged on the broker. The master-knave, who had spent two hours and more in vain with the tailor, and would not like of any velvet he saw, when he perceived that he missed his purse, and could not devise how or where he had lost it, showed himself very sorry for his mishap, and said in the morning he would send the velvet home to his house, for he knew where to speed of better than any he had seen in the shops. Home goes the tailor very sadly, where he was entertained with a greater mischance, for there was the lady's serving-man, swearing and stamping that he had not seen their master since the morning they parted, neither had he sent for the satin and lace, but, when the servants justified their innocency, beguiled both with the true token rehearsed, and their master's signet ring, it exceedeth my cunning to set down answerable words to this exceeding grief and amazement on either part, but most of all the honest tailor, who sped the better by the broker's wilfulness, as afterward it happened, which made him the better brook the loss of his purse. That night all means were used that could be, both to the mercer's, broker's, goldsmith's, goldfiner's, and such like, where haply such things do come to be sold. But all was in vain. The only help came by the inventer of this villainy, who scant sleeping all night, in regard of the broker's extreme gaining, both by him, and those of his profession. The next morning he came by the tailor's house, at what time he espied him with the lady's serving-man, coming forth of the doors ; and into the tavern he went to report what a mishap he had upon the sending for him thither the day before.

As he was but newly entered his sad discourse, in comes the party offended with the broker, and having heard all, whereof none could make better report than himself, he takes the tailor and serving-man aside, and pretending great grief for both their causes, demands what they would think him worthy of that could help them to their good again. On condition to meet with such a friend, offer was made of five pound, and after sundry speeches passing between them alone, he, seeming that he would work the recovery thereof by art, and they promising not to disclose the man that did them good, he drew forth a little book out of his bosom, whether it were Latin or English it skilled not, for he could not read a word on it. Then desiring them to spare him alone a while, they should perceive what he would do for them. Their hearts encouraged with some good hope, kept all his words secret to themselves ; and not long had they sitten absent out of the room, but he called them in again, and seeming as though he had been a scholar indeed, said he found by his figure that a broker in such a place had their goods lost, and in such a place of the house they should find it, bidding them go thither with all speed, and as they found his words, so (with reserving to themselves how they came to knowledge thereof) to meet him there again in the evening, and reward him as he had deserved.

Away in haste goes the tailor and the serving-man, and entering the house with the constable, found them in the place where he that revealed it, knew the broker alway laid such gotten goods. Of their joy again I leave you to conjecture, and think you see the broker with a good pair of bolts on his heels, ready to take his farewell of the world in a halter, when time shall serve. The counterfeit cunning man, and artificial cony-catcher, as I heard, was paid his five pound that night. Thus one crafty knave beguiled another. Let each take heed of dealing with any such kind of people.

Finis.

A DISPUTATION BETWEEN A HE-CONY-CATCHER AND A SHE-CONY-CATCHER

By Robert Greene

[1592]

To all gentlemen, merchants, apprentices, and country farmers, health.

GENTLEMEN, countrymen, and kind friends, for so I value all that are honest and enemies of bad actions, although in my books of cony-catching I have discovered divers forms of cozenings, and painted out both the sacking and crossbiting laws, which strumpets use, to the destruction of the simple, yet, willing to search all the substance, as I have glanced at the shadow, and to enter into the nature of villainy, as I have broached up the secrets of vice, I have thought good to publish this dialogue of disputation between a he-cony-catcher and a she-cony-catcher, whether of them are most prejudicial to the commonwealth, discoursing the base qualities of them both, and discovering the inconvenience that grows to men, through the lightness of inconstant wantons, who, being wholly given to the spoil, seek the ruin of such as light into their company. In this dialogue, loving countrymen, shall you find what prejudice ensues by haunting of whore-houses, what dangers grows by dallying with common harlots, what inconvenience follows the inordinate pleasures of unchaste libertines, not only by their consuming of their wealth, and impoverishment of their goods and lands, but to the great endangering of their health. For in conversing with them they aim not simply at the loss of goods, and blemish of their good names, but they fish for diseases, sickness, sores incurable, ulcers bursting out of the joints, and salt rheums, which by the humour of that villainy, leapt from Naples into France, and from France into the bowels of England; which makes many cry out in their bones, whilst Goodman Surgeon laughs in his purse; a thing to be feared as deadly while men live, as Hell is to be dreaded after death, for it not only infecteth the body, consumeth the soul, and waste[th] wealth and worship, but engraves a perpetual shame in the forehead of the party so abused. Whereof Master Huggins hath well written in his *Mirror of Magistrates*, in the person of Mempricius, exclaiming against harlots. The verses be these :[1]

> Eschew vile Venus' toys ; she cuts off age :
> And learn this lesson oft, and tell thy friend,
> By pox, death sudden, begging, harlots end.

Besides, I have here laid open the wily wisdom of overwise courtezans, that with their cunning can draw on, not only poor novices, but such as hold themselves masters of their occupation. What flatteries they use to bewitch, what sweet words to inveigle, what simple holiness to entrap, what amorous glances, what smirking œillades, what cringing curtsies, what stretching " adios," following a man like a bloodhound, with their eyes white, laying out of hair, what frouncing of tresses, what paintings, what ruffs, cuffs and braveries, and all to betray the eyes of the innocent novice, whom when they have drawn on to the bent of their bow, they strip like the prodigal child, and turn out of doors like an outcast of the world ! The crocodile hath not more tears, Proteus more shape, Janus more faces, the hieria[2] more sundry tunes to entrap the passengers, than our English courtezans—to be plain, our English whores—to set on fire the hearts of lascivious and gazing strangers. These common, or rather consuming, strumpets, whose throats are softer than oil, and yet whose steps lead unto death. They have their ruffians to rifle, when they cannot fetch over with other cunning, their crossbiters attending upon them, their foists, their bufts, their nips, and suchlike. Being waited on by these villains, as by ordinary servants, so that who thinks himself wise enough to escape their flatteries, him they crossbite ; who holds himself to rule, to be bitten with a counterfeit apparitor, him they rifle ; if he be not so to be versed upon, they have a foist or a nip upon him, and so sting him to the quick. Thus he that meddles with pitch cannot but be defiled, and he that acquainteth himself or converseth with any of these cony-catching strumpets, cannot but by some way or other be brought to confusion. For either he must hazard his soul, blemish his good name, lose his goods, light upon diseases, or at the least have been tied to the humour of an harlot, whose quiver is open to every arrow, who likes all that have fat purses, and loves none that are destitute of pence. I remember a monk *in diebus illis* writ his opinion of the end of an adulterer thus :

> *Quatuor his casibus sine dubio cadet adulter,*
> *Aut hic pauper erit, aut hic subito morietur,*
> *Aut cadet in causum qua debet judice vinci,*
> *Aut aliquod membrum casu vel crimine perdet,*

Which I Englished thus :

> *He that to harlots' lures do yield him thrall,*
> *Through sour misfortune to bad end shall fall :*
> *Or sudden death, or beggary shall him chance,*
> *Or guilt before a judge his shame enhance :*
> *Or else by fault or fortune he shall leese,*
> *Some member sure escape from one of these.*

Seeing then such inconvenience grows from the caterpillars of the commonwealth, and that a multitude of the monsters here about London, particularly and generally abroad in England, to the great overthrow of many simple men that are inveigled by their flatteries, I thought good not only to discover their villainies in a dialogue, but also to manifest by an example how prejudicial their life is to the state of the land, that such as are warned by an instance, may learn and look before they leap. To that end, kind countrymen, I have set down at the end of the disputation the wonderful life of a courtezan ; not a fiction, but a truth of one that yet lives, but[4] now in another form repentant ; in the discourse of whose life, you shall see how dangerous such trulls be to all estates that be so simple as to trust their feigned subtleties. Here shall parents learn how hurtful it is to cocker up their youth in their follies, and have a deep insight how to bridle their daughters, if they see them anyways grow wantons. Wishing therefore my labours may be a caveat to my countrymen to avoid the company of such cozening courtezans,

Farewell !

R.G.

A DISPUTATION BETWEEN LAURENCE, A FOIST, AND FAIR NAN, A TRAFFIC, WHETHER A WHORE OR A THIEF IS MOST PREJUDICIAL.

Laurence[5]. Fair Nan, well met ! What news about your Vine Court[6] that you look so blithe ? Your cherry cheeks discovers your good fare, and your brave apparel bewrays a fat purse. Is Fortune now a late grown so favourable to foists, that your husband hath lighted on some large purchase, or hath your smooth looks linked in some young novice to sweat for a favour all the bite in his bung, and to leave himself as many crowns as thou hast good conditions, and then he shall be one of Pierce Penilesse fraternity[7]? How is it, sweet wench? Goes the world on wheels, that you tread so daintily on your tiptoes?

Nan. Why, Laurence, are you pleasant or peevish that you quip with such brief girds? Think you a quartern-wind cannot make a quick sail, that easy lifts cannot make heavy burthens, that women have not wiles to compass crowns as well as men; yes, and more, for though they be not so ftrong in the fifts, they be more ripe in their wits, and 'tis by wit that I live and will live, in despite of that peevish scholar, that thought with his cony-catching books to have crossbit our trade. Doft thou marvel to see me thus brisked? Fair wenches cannot want favours, while the world is so full of amorous fools. Where can such girls as myself be blemished with a threadbare coat, as long as country farmers have full purses, and wanton citizens pockets full of pence?

Laur. Truth, if fortune so favour thy husband, that he be neither smoked nor cloyed, for I am sure all thy bravery comes by his nipping, foifting and lifting.

Nan. In faith, sir, no! Did I get no more by mine own wit than I reap by his purchase, I might both go bare and penniless the whole year. But mine eyes are ftalls, and my hands lime-twigs, else were I not worthy the name of a she-cony-catcher. Circe had never more charms, Calypso more enchantment, the sirens more subtle tunes, than I have crafty sleights to inveigle a cony and fetch in a country farmer. Laurence, believe me, you men are but fools, your gettings is uncertain, and yet you ftill fish for the gallows. Though by some great chance you light upon a good bung, yet you faft a great while after; whereas we mad wenches have our tenants—for so I call every simple lecher and amorous fox—as well out of term as in term to bring us our rents. Alas! were not my wits and my wanton pranks more profitable than my husband's foifting, we might often go to bed supperless for want of surfeiting, and yet, I dare swear, my husband gets a hundred pounds a year by bungs.

Laur. Why, Nan, are you grown so ftiff, to think that your fair looks can get as much as our nimble fingers, or that your sacking can gain as much as our foifting? No, no, Nan, you are two bows down the wind. Our foift will get more than twenty the proudeft wenches in all London.

Nan. Lie a little further and give me some room. What, Laurence, your tongue is too lavish ; all ſtands upon proof, and sith I have leisure and you no great business, as being now when Paul's is shut up, and all purchases and conies in their burrows, let us to the tavern and take a room to ourselves, and there, for the price of our suppers, I will prove that women, I mean of our faculty, a traffic, or, as base knaves term us, ſtrumpets, are more subtle, more dangerous in the commonwealth, and more full of wiles to get crowns, than the cunningeſt foiſt, nip, lift, prags, or whatsoever that lives at this day.

Laur. Content. But who shall be moderator in our controversies, sith in disputing *pro* and *contra* betwixt ourselves, it is but your Yea and my Nay, and so neither of us will yield to other's victories.

Nan. Truſt me Laurence ; I am so assured of the conqueſt, offering so in the ſtrength of mine own arguments, that when I have reasoned, I will refer it to your judgment and censure.

Laur. And truſt me as I am an honeſt man, I will be indifferent.

Nan. Oh swear not so deeply, but firſt let me hear what you can say for yourself.

Laur. What ? Why more, Nan, than can be painted out in a great volume ; but briefly this : I need not describe the laws of villainy, because R. G. hath so amply penned them down in the *Firſt Part of Cony-catching*,[8] that though I be one of the faculty, yet I cannot discover more than he hath laid open.

Therefore firſt to the gentleman-foiſt. I pray you what finer quality, what art is more excellent, either to try the ripeness of the wit, or the agility of the hand, than that for him that will be maſter of his trade muſt pass the proudeſt juggler alive the points of legerdemain ; he muſt have an eye to spy the bung, or purse, and then a heart to dare to attempt it—for this by the way, he that fears the gallows shall never be good thief while he lives. He muſt as the cat watch for a mouse, and walk Paul's, Weſtminſter, the Exchange, and such common-haunted places, and there have a curious eye to the person, whether he be gentle-man, citizen, or farmer, and note, either where his bung lies, whether in his hose or pockets, and then dog the party into a press where his ſtall with heaving and shoving shall so moleſt him, that he shall not feel when we ſtrip him of his bung, although it be never so faſt or cunningly couched about him. What poor farmer almoſt can come to plead his case at the bar, to attend upon his lawyer's at the bench, but, look he never so narrowly to it, we have his purse, wherein sometime there is fat purchase, twenty or thirty pounds. And I pray you, how long would one of your traffics be earning so much with your chamber work? Besides, in fairs and markets, and in the circuits after judges, what infinite money is gotten from honeſt-meaning men, that either busy about their necessary affairs, or carelessly looking to their crowns, light amongſt us that be foiſts? Tush, we dissemble in show, we go so neat in apparel, so orderly in outward appearance, some like lawyers' clerks, others like serving-men, that attended there about their maſters' business, that we are hardly smoked, versing upon all men with kind courtesies and fair words, and yet being so warily watchful, that a good purse cannot be put up in a fair, but we sigh if we share it not amongſt us. And though the books of cony-catching hath somewhat hindered us, and brought many brave foiſts to the halter, yet some of our country farmers, nay, of our gentlemen and citizens, are so careless in a throng of people, that they show us the prey, and so draw on a thief, and bequeath us their purses, whether we will or no, for who loves wine so ill, that he will not eat grapes if they fall into his mouth, and who is so base, that if he see a pocket fair before him, will not foiſt in if he may, or, if foiſting will not serve, use his knife and nip; for, although there be some foiſts that will not use their knives, yet I hold him not a perfect workman or maſter of his myſtery, that will not cut a purse as well as foiſt a pocket, and hazard any limb for so sweet a gain as gold. How answer you me this brief objection, Nan? Can you compare with either our cunning to get our gains in purchase?

Nan. And have you no ſtronger arguments, Goodman Laurence, to argue your excellency in villainy but this? Then in faith put up your pipes, and give me leave to speak. Your choplogic hath no great subtlety, for simple you reason of foiſting, and appropriate that to yourselves, to you men I mean, as though there were not women foiſts and nips as neat in that trade as you, of as good an eye, as fine and nimble a hand, and of as resolute a heart, yes Laurence, and your good miſtresses in that myſtery, for we without like suspicion can pass in your walks under the colour of simplicity to Weſtminſter, with a paper in our hand, as if we were diſtressed women that had some supplication to put up to the judges, or some bill of information to deliver to our lawyers, when, God wot, we shuffle in for a bung as well as the best of you all, yea, as yourself, Laurence, though you be called King of Cutpurses, for though they smoke you, they will hardly mistrust us, and suppose our stomach stand against it to foist, yet who can better play the stall or the shadow than we, for in a thrust or throng, if we shove hard, who is he that will not favour a woman, and in giving place to us, give you free passage for his purse? Again, in the market, when every wife hath almost her hand on her bung, and that they cry, " Beware the cutpurse and cony-catchers ! " then I as fast as the best, with my hand-basket as mannerly as if I were to buy great store of butter and eggs for provision of my house, do exclaim against them with my hand on my purse, and say the world is bad when a woman cannot walk safely to market for fear of these villainous cutpurses, whenas the first bung I come to, I either nip or foist, or else stall another while he hath strucken, despatched, and gone. Now I pray you, gentle sir, wherein are we inferior to you in foisting? And yet this is nothing to the purpose, for it is one of our most simplest shifts. But yet I pray you, what think you when a farmer, gentleman, or citizen, come to the term? Perhaps he is wary of his purse, and watch him never so warily, yet he will never be brought to the blow. Is it not possible for us to pinch him ere he pass, he that is most chary of his crowns abroad, and will cry, " 'Ware the cony-catchers," will not be afraid to drink a pint of wine with a pretty wench, and perhaps go to a trugging house to ferry out one for his purpose. Then with what cunning we can feed the simple fop, with what fair words, sweet kisses, feigned sighs, as if at that instant we fell in love with him that we never saw before ! If we meet him in an evening in the street, if the farmer or other whatsoever be not so forward as to motion some courtesy to us, we straight insinuate into his company, and claim acquaintance of him by some means or other, and if his mind be set for lust, and the Devil drive him on to match himself with some dishonest wanton, then let him look to his purse, for if he do but kiss me in the street, I'll have his purse for a farewell, although he never commit any other act at all. I speak not this only by myself, Laurence, for there be a hundred in London more cunning than myself in this kind of cony-catching. But if he come into a house, then let our trade alone to verse upon him, for first we feign ourselves hungry, for the benefit of the house, although our bellies were never so full, and no doubt the good pander or bawd she comes forth like a sober matron, and sets store of cates on the table, and then I fall aboard on them, and though I can eat little, yet I make havoc of all. And let him be sure every dish is well sauced, for he shall pay for a pippin-pie that cost in the market fourpence, at one of the trugging-houses eighteenpence. Tush ! what is dainty if it be not dear bought, and yet he must come off for crowns besides, and when I see him draw to his purse, I note the putting up of it well, and ere we part, that world goes hard if I foist him not of all that he hath. And then, suppose the worst, that he miss it, am I so simply acquainted or badly provided, that I have not a friend, which with a few terrible oaths and countenance set, as if he were the proudest soldado that ever bare arms against Don John of Austria, will face him quite out of his money, and make him walk like a woodcock homeward by weeping cross, and so buy repentance with all the crowns in his purse ? How say you to this, Laurence, whether are women-foists inferior to you in ordinary cozenage or no.

Laur.   Excellently well reasoned, Nan.   Thou hast told me wonders, but, wench, though you be wily and strike often, your blows are not so big as ours.

Nan.   Oh, but note the subject of our disputation, and that is this : which are more subtle and dangerous in the commonwealth, and to that I argue.

Laur.   Ay, and beshrew me, but you reason quaintly.   Yet will I prove your wits are not so ripe as ours, nor so ready to reach into the subtleties of kind cozenage, and though you appropriate to yourself the excellency of cony-catching, and that you do it with more art than we men do, because of your painted flatteries and sugared words, that you flourish rhetorically like nets to catch fools, yet will I manifest with a merry instance a feat done by a foist, that exceeded any that ever was done by any mad wench in England.

A pleasant tale of a country farmer, that took it in scorn to have his purse cut or drawn from him, and how a foist served him.

It was told me for a truth that not long since, here in London, there lay a country farmer, with divers of his neighbours, about law matters, amongst whom, one of them going to Westminster Hall, was by a foist stripped of all the pence in his purse, and, coming home, made great complaint of his misfortune. Some lamented his loss, and others exclaimed against the cutpurses, but this farmer he laughed loudly at the matter, and said such fools as could not keep their purses no surer were well served. " And for my part," quoth he, " I so much scorn the cutpurses, that I would thank him heartily that would take pains to foist mine."—" Well," says his neighbour, " then you may thank me, sith my harms learns you to beware. But if it be true that many things fall out between the cup and the lip, you know not what hands Fortune may light in your own lap."—" Tush," quoth the farmer. " Here's forty pounds in this purse in gold. The proudest cutpurse in England win it and wear it." As thus he boasted, there stood a subtle foist by and heard all, smiling to himself at the folly of the proud farmer, and vowed to have his purse or venture his neck for it, and so went home and bewrayed it to a crew of his companions, who taking it in dudgeon that they should be put down by a peasant, met either at Laurence Pickering's[9] or at Lambeth. Let the blackamoor take heed I name him not, lest an honourable neighbour of his frown at it, but, wheresoever they met, they held a convocation, and both consulted and concluded all by a general consent to bend all their wits to be possessors of this farmer's bung ; and for the execution of this their vow, they haunted about the inn where he lay, and dogged him into divers places, both to Westminster Hall and other places, and yet could never light upon it. He was so watchful and smoked them so narrowly, that all their travail was in vain, at last one of them fled to a more cunning policy, and went and learned the man's name and where he dwelt, and then hied him to the Counter and entered an action against him of trespass, damages two hundred pounds.[10] When he had thus done, he feed two sergeants, and carried them down with him to the man's lodging, wishing them not to arrest him till he commanded them. Well agreed they were, and down to the farmer's lodging they came, where were a crew of foists, whom he had made privy to the end of his practice, stood waiting. But he took no knowledge at all of them, but walked up and down. The farmer came out and went to Paul's. The cutpurse bade stay, and would not yet suffer the officers to meddle with him, till he came into the west end of Paul's Churchyard, and there he willed them to do their office, and they, stepping to the farmer, arrested him. The farmer amazed, being amongst his neighbours, asked the sergeant at whose suit he was troubled.

" At whose suit soever it be," said one of the cutpurses that stood by, " you are wronged, honest man, for he hath arrested you here in a place of privilege, where the Sheriffs nor the officers have nothing to do with you, and therefore you are unwise if you obey him."[11]

" Tush," says another cutpurse, " though the man were so simple of himself, yet shall he not offer the Church so much wrong, as by yielding to the mace, to imbolish Paul's liberty, and therefore I will take his part." And with that he drew his sword.

Another took the man and haled him away. The officer, he stuck hard to him, and said he was his true prisoner, and cried "Clubs!"[12] The 'prentices arose, and there was a great hurly-burly, for they took the officer's part, so that the poor farmer was mightily turmoiled amongst them, and almost haled in pieces. Whilst thus the strife was, one of the foists had taken his purse away, and was gone, and the officer carried the man away to a tavern, for he swore he knew no such man, nor any man that he was indebted to. As then they sat drinking of a quart of wine, the foist that had caused him to be arrested, sent a note by a porter to the officer that he should release the farmer, for he had mistaken the man ; which note the officer showed him, and bade him pay his fees and go his ways. The poor countryman was content with that, and put his hand in his pocket to feel for his purse, and, God wot, there was none, which made his heart far more cold than the arrest did, and with that, fetching a great sigh he said :

" Alas ! masters, I am undone ! My purse in this fray is taken out of my pocket and ten pounds in gold in it besides white money."

" Indeed," said the sergeant, " commonly in such brawls the cut-purses be busy, and I pray God the quarrel was not made upon purpose by the pickpockets."

" Well," says his neighbour, " who shall smile at you now ? The other day when I lost my purse you laughed at me."

The farmer brook all, and sat malcontent, and borrowed money of his neighbours to pay the sergeant, and had a [y]earning I believe ever after to brave the cutpurse.

How say you to this, Mistress Nan ? Was it not well done ? What choice-witted wench of your faculty, or the foist, hath ever done the like ? Tush ! Nan. If we begin once to apply our wits, all your inventions are follies towards ours.

Nan. You say good, Goodman Laurence, as though your subtleties were sudden as women's are. Come but to the old proverb, and I put you down : 'Tis as hard to find a hare without a meuse, as a woman without a scuse ; and that wit that can devise a cunning lie, can plot the intent of deep villainies. I grant this fetch of the foist was pretty, but nothing in respect of that we wantons can compass. And, therefore, to quit your tale with another, hear what a mad wench of my profession did alate to one of your faculty.

A passing pleasant tale how a whore cony-catched a foiſt.

There came out of the country a foiſt, to try his experience here in
Weſtminſter Hall, and ſtruck a hand or two, but the devil a snap he
would give to our citizen-foiſts, but wrought warily, and could not be
fetched off by no means ; and yet it was known he had some twenty
pounds about him ; but he had planted it so cunningly in his doublet,
that it was sure enough for finding. Although the city foiſt[s] laid all
the plots they could, as well by discovering him to the jailers as other-
ways, yet he was so politic that they could not verse upon him by any
means, which grieved them so, that one day at a dinner they held a
council amongſt themselves how to cozen him, but in vain ; till at laſt
a good wench that sat by undertook it, so they would swear to let her
have all that he had. They confirmed it solemnly, and she put it in
practice thus : She subtly insinuated herself into this foiſt's company,
who seeing her a pretty wench, began, after twice meeting, to wax
familiar with her, and to queſtion about a night's lodging. After a
little nice loving and bidding, she was content for her supper and what
else he would of courtesy beſtow upon her, for she held it scorn, she said,
to set a salary price on her body. The foiſt was glad of this, and yet
he would not truſt her, so that he put no more but ten shillings in his
pocket ; but he had above twenty pounds twilted in his doublet. Well,
to be short, supper-time came, and thither comes my gentle foiſt, who
making good cheer, was so eager of his game, that he would ſtraight to
bed by the leave of Dame Bawd, who had her fee too ; and there he lay
till about midnight, when three of four old hackſters whom she had
provided upon purpose came to the door and rapped luſtily.

" Who is there ? " says the bawd, looking out of the window.

Marry, say they, such a Juſtice, and named one about the City that
is a mortal enemy to cutpurses—" who is come to search your house
for a Jesuit and other suspected persons."

" Alas ! sir," says she ; " I have none here."

" Well," quoth they, " ope the door."

" I will," says she, and with that she came into the foiſt's chamber,
who heard all this, and was afraid it was some search for him, so that he
desired the bawd to help him that he might not be seen.

" Why then," quoth she, " ſtep into this closet."

He whipped in haſtily, and never remembered his clothes. She
locked him in safe, and then let in the crew of rakehells, who, making
as though they searched every chamber, came at laſt into that where

his leman lay, and asked her what she was. She, as if she had been afraid, desired their worships to be good to her. She was a poor country maid come up to the term.

" And who is that," quoth they, " that was in bed with you ? "

" None forsooth ! " says she.

" No ? " says one. " That is a lie. Here is the print of two ; and, besides, wheresoever the fox is, here is his skin, for this is his doublet and hose."

Then down she falls upon her knees, and says, indeed it was her husband.

" Your husband ? " quoth they. " Nay, that cannot be so, minion, for why then would you have denied him at the first." With that one of them turned to the bawd, and did question with her what he was and where he was.

" Truly, sir," says she, " they came to my house, and said they were man and wife, and for my part I know them for no other, and he, being afraid, is indeed, to confess the truth, shut up in the closet."

" No doubt, if it please your worships," says one rakehell, " I warrant you he is some notable cutpurse or pickpocket, that is afraid to show his face. Come and open the closet, and let us look on him."

" Nay sir," says she. " Not for to-night, I beseech your worship ; carry no man out of my house, I will give my word he shall be forthcoming to-morrow morning."

" Your word, Dame Bawd," says one. " 'Tis not worth a straw. You, housewife, that says ye are his wife, ye shall go with us ; and for him, that we may be sure he may not start, I'll take his doublet, hose and cloak, and tomorrow I'll send them to him by one of my men. Were there a thousand pounds in them, there shall not be a penny diminished."

The whore kneeled down on her knees and feigned to cry pitifully, and desired the Justice, which was one of her companions, not to carry her to prison.

" Yes, housewife," quoth he, " your mate and you shall not tarry together in one house, that you may make your tales all one. And therefore bring her away. And after ye, Dame Bawd ! See you lend him no other clothes, for I will send his in the morning betimes ; and come you with him to answer for lodging him."

" I will, sir," says she. And so away goes the wench and her companions laughing, and left the bawd and the foist. As soon as the bawd thought good, she unlocked the closet, and cursed the time that ever they came in her house. " Now," quoth she, " here will be a fair ado.

How will you answer for yourself? I fear me I shall be in danger of the cart."

" Well," quoth he, " to be short, I would not for forty pounds come afore the Justice."

" Marry, no more would I," quoth she. " Let me shift if you were conveyed hence, but I have not a rag of man's apparel in the house."

" Why," quoth he, " seeing it is early morning, lend me a blanket to put about me, and I will 'scape to a friend's house of mine."

" Then leave me a pawn," quoth the bawd.

" Alas ! I have none," says he, " but this ring on my finger."

" Why that," quoth she ; " or tarry while the Justice comes."

So he gave it her, took the blanket and went his ways, whither I know not, but to some friend's house of his. Thus was this wily foist by the wit of a subtle wench cunningly stripped of all that he had, and turned to grass to get more fat.

How say you to this device, Laurence? Was it not excellent? What think you of a woman's wit if it can work such wonders ?

Laur. Marry, I think my mother was wiser than all the honest women of the parish besides.

Nan. Why then, belike she was of our faculty, and a matron of my profession, nimble of her hands, quick of tongue and light of her tail, I should have put in, sir reverence ; but a foul word is good enough for a filthy knave.

Laur. I am glad you are so pleasant, Nan. You were not so merry when you went to Dunstable. But, indeed, I must needs confess that women-foists, if they be careful in their trades, are, though not so common yet more dangerous than men-foists. Women have quick wits, as they have short heels, and they can get with pleasure what we fish for with danger. But now, giving you the bucklers at this weapon, let me have a blow with you at another.

Nan. But before you induce any more arguments, by your leave in a little by talk. You know, Laurence, that, though you can foist, nip, prig, lift, curb, and use the black art, yet you cannot crossbite without the help of a woman, which crossbiting nowadays is grown to a marvellous profitable exercise ; for some cowardly knaves that, for fear of the gallows, leave nipping and foisting, become crossbites, knowing there is no danger therein but a little punishment, at the most the pillory, and *that* is saved with a little *unguentum aureum*. As for example, Jack Rhodes is now a reformed man, whatsoever he hath been in his youth. Now in his latter days he is grown a corrector of vice, for whomsoever he takes suspicious with his wife, I warrant you he sets a sure fine on head, though he hath nothing for his money but a bare kiss. And in this art we poor wenches are your surest props and stay. If you will not believe me, ask poor A. B. in Turnmill Street[13] what a saucy signor there is, whose purblind eyes can scarcely discern a louse from a flea, and yet he hath such insight into the mystical trade of crossbiting, that he can furnish his board with a hundred pounds' worth of plate. I doubt the sand-eyed ass will kick like a western pug if I rub him on the gall. But tis' no matter if he find himself touched, and stir, although he boasts of the chief of the clergy's favour. Yet I'll so set his name out, that the boys at Smithfield Bars[14] shall chalk him on the back for a crossbite. Tush, you men are fops in fetching novices over the coals. Hearken to me, Laurence. I'll tell thee a wonder.

Not far off from Hogsdon,[15] perhaps it *was* there—and if you think I lie, ask Master Richard Chot, and Master Richard Strong, two honest gentlemen, that can witness as well as I this proof of a woman's wit—there dwelt here sometimes a good ancient matron, that had a fair wench to her daughter, as young and tender as a morrow-mass priest's leman. Her she set out to sale in her youth, and drew on sundry to be suitors to her daughter, some wooers, and some speeders. Yet none married her, but of her beauty they made a profit, and inveigled all, till they had spent upon her what they had, and then, forsooth, she and her young pigeon turn them out of doors like prodigal children. She was acquainted with Dutch and French, Italian and Spaniard, as well as English, and at last, as so often the pitcher goes to the brook that it comes broken home, my fair daughter was hit on the master-vein and gotten with child. Now the mother, to colour this matter to save her daughter's marriage, begins to wear a cushion under her own kirtle, and to feign herself with child, but let her daughter pass as though she ailed nothing. When the forty weeks were come, and that my young mistress must needs cry out forsooth, this old B. had gotten housewives answerable to herself, and so brought her daughter to bed, and let her go up and down the house ; and the old crone lay in childbed as though she had been delivered, and said the child was hers, and so saved her daughter's 'scape. Was not this a witty wonder, Master Laurence, wrought by an old witch, to have a child in her age, and make a young whore seem

an honeſt virgin ? Tush ! this is little to the purpose. If I should
recite all, how many she had cozened under the pretence of marriage !
Well, poor plain signor, see, you were not ſtiff enough for her, although
it coſt you many crowns and the loss of your service. I'll say no more.
Perhaps she will amend her manners.

Ah, Laurence, how like you of this gear ? In crossbiting we put
you down ; for God wot it is little looked to in and about London,
and yet I may say to thee, many a good citizen is crossbit in the year
by odd walkers abroad. I heard some named the other day as I was
drinking at the *Swan* in Lambeth Marsh[16]—But let them alone. 'Tis
a foul bird that defiles the own neſt, and it were a shame for me to speak
againſt any good wenches or boon companions, that by their wits can
wreſt money from a churl. I fear me R. G. will name them too soon in
his *Black Book*. A peſtilence on him ! They say he hath there set
down my husband's pedigree, and yours too, Laurence. If he do it,
I fear me your brother-in-law Bull is like to be troubled with you both.[17]

Laur. I know not what to say to him, Nan. Hath plagued me
already. I hope he hath done with me. And yet I heard say he would
have about at my nine-holes. But, leaving him as an enemy of our
trade, again to our disputation. I cannot deny, Nan, but you have set
down ſtrange precedents of women's prejudicial wits, but yet, though
you be crossbites, foiſts and nips, yet you are not good lifts, which is
a great help to our faculty, to filch a bolt of satin or velvet.

Nan. Stay thee a word. I thought thou hadſt spoken of R. B. of
Long Lane and his wife. Take heed. They be parlous folks, and
greatly acquainted with keepers and jailers. Therefore meddle not
you with them ; for I hear say, R. G. hath sworn, in despite of the
Brazil ſtaff, to tell such a foul tale of him in his *Black Book*, that it will
coſt him a dangerous joint.

Laur. Nan, Nan, let R. G. beware ! For had not an ill fortune
fallen to one of R. B. his friends, he could take little harm.

Nan. Who is that, Laurence ?

Laur. Nay, I will not name him.

Nan. Why then I prithee what misfortune befell him ?

Laur. Marry, Nan, he was ſtrangely washed alate by a French barber, and had all the hair of his face miraculously shaven off by the scythe of God's vengeance, insomuch that some said he had that he had not, but, as hap was, howsoever his hair fell off, it ſtood him in some ſtead when the brawl was alate, for if he had not caſt off his beard, and so being unknown, it had coſt him some knocks, but it fell out to the beſt.

Nan. The more hard fortune that he had such ill hap. But haſty journeys breed dangerous sweats, and the physicians call it the Ale Peria.[18] Yet omitting all this, again to where you left.

Laur. You have almoſt brought me out of my matter. But I was talking about the lift, commending what a good quality it was, and how hurtful it was, seeing we praċtise it in mercers' shops, with haberdashers of small wares, haberdashers of hats and caps, amongſt merchant tailors for hose and doublets, and in such places, getting much gains by lifting, when there is no good purchase abroad by foiſting.

Nan. Suppose you are good at the lift, who be more cunning than we women, in that we are more truſted, for they little suspeċt us, and we have as close conveyance as you men. Though you have cloaks, we have skirts of gowns, hand-baskets, the crowns of our hats, our placards, and for a need, false bags under our smocks, wherein we can convey more closely than you.

Laur. I know not where to touch you, you are so witty in your answers, and have so many ſtarting-holes. But let me be pleasant with you a little. What say you to prigging or horse-ſtealing? I hope you never had experience in that faculty.

Nan. Alas, simple sot! Yes, and more shift to shun the gallows than you.

Laur. Why 'tis impossible.

Nan. In faith, sir, no. And for proof I will put you down with a ſtory of a mad merry little dapper fine wench, who at Spilsby Fair[19] had three horse of her own or another man's to sell. As she, her husband, and another good fellow walked them up and down the fair, the owner came and apprehended them all, and clapped them in prison. The jailer not keeping them close prisoners, but letting them lie all in a chamber, by her wit she so instructed them in a formal tale, that she saved all their lives thus. Being brought the next morrow after their apprehension before the Justices, they examined the men how they came by those horses, and they confessed they met her with them, but where she had them they knew not. Then was my pretty piece brought in, who, being a handsome trull, blushed as if she had been full of grace, and, being demanded where she had the horses, made this answer :

" May it please your worships, this man being my husband, playing the unthrift as many more have done, was absent from me for a quarter of a year, which grieved me not a little ; insomuch that, desirous to see him, and having intelligence he would be at Spilsby Fair, I went thither even for pure love of him on foot, and, being within some ten miles of the town, I waxed passing weary and rested me often and grew very faint. At last there came riding by me a serving-man in a blue coat, with three horses tied one at another's tail, which he led, as I guessed, to sell at the fair. The serving-man, seeing me so tired, took pity on me, and asked me if I would ride on one of his empty horses, for his own would not bear double. I thanked him heartily, and at the next hill got up, and rode till we came to a town within three miles of Spilsby, where the serving-man alighted at a house, and bade me ride on afore, and he would presently overtake me. Well, forward I rode half a mile, and looking behind me could see nobody. So, being alone, my heart began to rise, and I to think on my husband. As I had rid a little farther, looking down a lane, I saw two men coming lustily up as if they were weary, and marking them earnestly, I saw one of them was my husband, which made my heart as light as before it was sad. So staying for them, after a little unkind greeting betwixt us, for I chid him for his unthriftiness, he asked me where I had the horse, and I told him how courteously the serving-man had used me. ' Why then ' says he, ' stay for him.'—' Nay,' quoth I, ' let's ride on, and get you two up on the empty horses, for he will overtake us ere we come at the town. He rides on a stout lusty young gelding.' So forward we went, and looked often behind us ; but our serving-man came not. At last we coming to Spilsby alighted, and broke our fast, and tied our horses at the door, that if he passed by, seeing them, he might call in. After we had broke our fast, thinking he had gone some other way, we went into the horse fair, and there walked our horses up and down to meet with the serving-man, not for the intent to sell them. Now may it please your worship, whether he had ſtolen the horses from this honeſt man or no, I know not. But alas! simply I brought them to the horse fair, to let him that delivered me them have them again, for I hope your worships doth imagine, if I had ſtolen them as it is suspeċted, I would never have brought them into so public a place to sell. Yet if the law be any way dangerous for the foolish deed, because I know not the serving-man, it is I muſt bide the punishment, and as guiltless as any here."

And so, making a low curtsy, she ended, the Juſtice holding up his hand and wondering at the woman's wit, that had cleared her husband and his friend, and saved herself without compass of law. How like you of this, Laurence? Cannot we wenches prig well?

Laur. By God, Nan! I think I shall be fain to give you the bucklers.

Nan. Alas! good Laurence, thou art no logician. Thou canſt not reason for thyself, nor haſt no witty arguments to draw me to an exigent. And therefore give me leave at large to reason for this supper. Remember the subjeċt of our disputation is this positive queſtion, whether whores or thieves are moſt prejudicial to the commonwealth. Alas! you poor thieves do only ſteal and purloin from men, and the harm you do is to imbolish men's goods, and bring them to poverty. This is the only end of men's thievery, and the greateſt prejudice that grows from robbing or filching. So much do we by our theft, and more by our lechery, for what is the end of whoredom but consuming of goods and beggary, and, besides, perpetual infamy? We bring young youths to ruin and utter deſtruċtion. I pray you, Laurence, whether had a merchant's son, having wealthy parents, better light upon a whore than a cutpurse, the one only taking his money, the other bringing him to utter confusion; for if the foiſt light upon him, or the cony-catcher, he loseth at the moſt some hundred pounds; but if he fall into the company of a whore, she flatters him, she inveigles him, she bewitcheth him, that he spareth neither goods nor lands to content her, that is only in love with his coin. If he be married, he forsakes his wife, leaves his children, despiseth his friends, only to satisfy his luſt with the love of a base whore, who, when he hath spent all upon her and he brought to beggary, beateth him out like the prodigal child, and for a small reward, brings him, if to the faireſt end, to beg, if to the second, to the gallows, or at the laſt and worſt, to the pox, or as prejudicial diseases.

I pray you, Laurence, when any of you come to your confession at Tyburn, what is your laſt sermon that you make?—that you were brought to that wicked and shameful end by following of harlots. For to that end do you steal, to maintain whores, and to content their bad humours. Oh, Laurence! enter into your own thoughts, and think what the fair words of a wanton will do, what the smiles of a strumpet will drive a man to act, into what jeopardy a man will thrust himself for her that he loves, although for his sweet villainy he be brought to loathsome leprosy. Tush, Laurence, they say the pox came from Naples, some from Spain, some from France, but wheresoever it first grew, it is so surely now rooted in England, that by S. (*Syth*) it may better be called a *morbus Anglicus* than *Gallicus*! And I hope you will grant all these French favours grew from whores. Besides in my high loving, or rather creeping, I mean where men and women do rob together, there always the woman is most bloody, for she always urgeth unto death, and, though the men would only satisfy themselves with the party's coin, yet she endeth her theft in blood, murdering parties, so deeply as she is malicious.

I hope, gentle Laurence, you cannot contradict these reasons : they be so openly manifestly probable. For mine own part, I hope you do not imagine but I have had some friends besides poor George my husband. Alas! he knows it, and is content like an honest simple suffragan, to be co-rival with a number of other good companions ; and I have made many a good man, I mean a man that hath a household, for the love of me to go home and beat his poor wife, when, God wot, I mock him for the money he spent, and he had nothing for his pence but the waste beleavings of other's beastly labours. Laurence, Laurence, if concubines could inveigle Solomon, if Delilah could betray Samson, then wonder not if we, more nice in our wickedness than a thousand such Delilahs, can seduce poor young novices to their utter destructions ! Search the jails. There you shall hear complaints of whores. Look into the spitals and hospitals. There you shall see men diseased of the French marbles, giving instruction to others that are said to beware of whores. Be an auditor or ear-witness at the death of any thief, and his last testament is, " Take heed of a whore." I dare scarce speak of Bridewell, because my shoulders tremble at the name of it, I have so often deserved it. Yet look but in there, and you shall hear poor men with their hands in their pigeon-holes cry, " Oh fie upon whores ! " when Fowler[20] gives them the terrible lash. Examine beggars that lie lame by the highway, and they say they came to that misery by whores ; some threadbare citizens that from merchants and other good trades grow to be base informers and knights of the post, cry out when they dine with Duke Humphrey[21]. " Oh what wickedness comes from whores ! " 'Prentices that runs from their masters, cries out upon whores. Tush, Laurence ! What enormities proceeds more in the commonwealth than from whoredom ? But sith 'tis almost supper-time, and mirth is the friend to digestion, I mean a little to be pleasant. I pray you how many bad profits again grows from whores ? Bridewell would have very few tenants, the hospital would want patients, and the surgeons much work ; the apothecaries would have surfling water and potato roots lie dead on their hands, the painters could not despatch and make away their vermilion, if tallow-faced whores used it not for their cheeks. How should Sir John's broadsmen do, if we were not ?[22] Why, Laurence, the Galley would be moored and the Blue Boar so lean that he would not be man's meat, if we of the trade were not to supply his wants ! Do you think in conscience the Peacock could burnish his fair tail, were it not the whore of Babylon and suchlike makes him lusty with crowns ? No, no, though the Talbot hath bitten some at the game, yet new fresh huntsmen shake the she-crew out of the couples. What should I say more, Laurence ? The suburbs should have a great miss of us, and Shoreditch would complain to Dame Anne a Cleare,[23] if we of the sisterhood should not uphold her jollity. Who is that Laurence comes in to hear our talk ?

[*Laur.*] Oh 'tis the boy, Nan, that tells us supper is ready.

[*Nan.*] Why then, Laurence, what say you to me ? Have I not proved that in foisting and nipping we excel you ; that there is none so great inconvenience in the commonwealth as grows from whores, first for the corrupting of youth, infecting of age, for breeding of brawls, whereof ensues murder, insomuch that the ruin of many men comes from us, and the fall of many youths of good hope, if they were not seduced by us, do proclaim at Tyburn that we be the means of their misery ? You men-thieves touch the body and wealth ; but we ruin the soul, and endanger that which is more precious than the world's treasure. You make work only for the gallows ; we both for the gallows and the Devil, ay, and for the surgeon too, that some lives like loathsome lazars, and die with the French marbles. Whereupon I conclude that I have won the supper.

Laur. I confess it, Nan, for thou hast told me such wondrous villainies, as I thought never could have been in women, I mean of your profession. Why, you are crocodiles when you weep, basilisks when

K

you smile, serpents when you devise, and the Devil's chiefest brokers to bring the world to destruction. And so, Nan, let's sit down to our meat and be merry.

Thus, countrymen, you have heard the disputation between these two cozening companions, wherein I have shaked out the notable villainy of whores, although Mistress Nan, this good oratress, hath sworn to wear a long Hamburg knife to stab me, and all the crew have protested my death, and to prove they meant good earnest, they beleaguered me about in the *St. John's Head within Ludgate*[24], being at supper. There were some fourteen or fifteen of them met, and thought to have made that the fatal night of my overthrow, but that the courteous citizens and apprentices took my part, and so two or three of them were carried to the Counter, although a gentleman in my company was sore hurt.[25] I cannot deny but they begin to waste away about London, and Tyburn, since the setting out of my book, hath eaten up many of them ; and I will plague them to the extremity. Let them do what they dare with their Bilbao blades ! I fear them not. And to give them their last adieu, look shortly countrymen for a pamphlet against them, called *The Black Book*, containing four new laws never spoken of yet : the creeping law of petty thieves, that rob about the suburbs ; the limiting law, discoursing the orders of such as follow judges in their circuits, and go about from fair to fair ; the jugging law, wherein I will set out the disorders at nine-holes and rifling, how they are only for the benefit of the cutpurses ; the stripping law, wherein I will lay open the lewd abuses of sundry jailers in England. Beside, you shall see there what houses there be about the suburbs and town's end, that are receivers of cutpurses' stolen goods, lifts, and such like. And, lastly, look for a bead-roll or catalogue of all the names of the foists, nips, lifts and priggers, in and about London. And although some say I dare not do it, yet I will shortly set it abroach, and whosoever I name or touch, if he think himself grieved, I will answer him before the Honourable Privy Council.

THE CONVERSION OF AN ENGLISH COURTEZAN.

Sith to discover my parentage would double the grief of my living parents, and revive in them the memory of my great amiss, and that my untoward fall would be a dishonour to the house from whence I came ; sith to manifest the place of my birth would be a blemish, through my beaſtly life so badly misled, to the shire where I was born ; sith to discourse my name, might be holden a blot in my kindred's brow, to have a sinew in their ſtock of so little grace, I will conceal my parents, kin and country, and shroud my name with silence, leſt envy might taunt others for my wantonness. Know, therefore, I was born about three score miles from London, of honeſt and wealthy parents, who had many children, but I their only daughter, and therefore the jewel wherein they moſt delighted, and more, the youngeſt of all, and therefore the more favoured ; for being gotten in the waning of my parents' age, they doted on me above the reſt, and so set their hearts the more on fire. I was the faireſt of all, and yet not more beautiful than I was witty, insomuch that, being a pretty parrot, I had such quaint conceits and witty words in my mouth, that the neighbours said, I was too soon wise to be long old. Would to God, either the proverb had been authentical, or their sayings prophecies ! Then had I, by death in my nonage, buried many blemishes that my riper years brought me to. For the extreme love of my parents was the very efficient cause of my follies, resembling herein the nature of the ape, that ever killeth that young one which he loveth moſt, with embracing it too fervently. So my father and mother, but she moſt of all, although he too much, so cockered me up in my wantonness, that my wit grew to the worſt, and I waxed upward with the ill weeds. Whatsoever I did, were it never so bad, might not be found fault withal. My father would smile at it and say, 'twas but the trick of a child ; and my mother allowed of my unhappy parts, alluding to this profane and old proverb : an untoward girl makes a good woman.

But now I find, in sparing the rod, they hated the child ; that overkind fathers make unruly daughters. Had they bent the wand while it had been green, it would have been pliant ; but I, ill-grown in my years, am almoſt remediless. The hawk that is moſt perfeѐt for the flight and will, seldom proveth haggard ; and children that are virtuously nurtured in youth, will be honeſtly natured in age. Fie upon such as say, " Young saints, old devils " ! It is no doubt a devilish and damnable saying ; for what is not bent in the cradle, will hardly be bowed in the saddle. Myself am an inſtance, who after I grew to be six years old, was set to school, where I profited so much that I writ and read excellently well, played upon the virginals, lute and cithern, and could sing prick-song at the firſt sight ; insomuch as by that time I was twelve years old, I was holden for the moſt fair and beſt qualitied young girl in all that country ; but, with this, bewailed of my well-wishers, in that my parents suffered me to be so wanton.

But they so tenderly affected me, and were so blinded with my excellent qualities, that they had no insight into my ensuing follies. For I, growing to be thirteen year old, feeling the rein of liberty loose on mine own neck, began with the wanton heifer to aim at mine own will, and to measure content by the sweetness of mine own thoughts, insomuch that, pride creeping on, I began to prank myself with the proudest, and to hold it in disdain that any in the parish should exceed me in bravery. As my apparel was costly, so I grew to be licentious, and to delight to be looked on, so that I haunted and frequented all feasts and weddings, and other places of merry meetings, where, as I was gazed on of many, so I spared no glances to surview all with a curious eye-favour. I observed Ovid's rule right : *Spectatum veniunt, veniunt spectentur ut ipsæ.*[26]

I went to see and be seen, and decked myself in the highest degree of bravery, holding it a glory when I was waited on with many eyes, to make censure of my birth. Beside, I was an ordinary dancer, and grew in that quality so famous, that I was noted as the chiefest thereat in all the country. Yea, and to soothe me up in these follies, my parents took a pride in my dancing, which afterward proved my overthrow, and their heartbreaking.

Thus as an unbridled colt, I carelessly led forth my youth, and wantonly spent the flower of my years, holding such maidens as were modest, fools, and such as were not as wilfully wanton as myself, puppies, ill brought up and without manners. Growing on in years, as tide nor time tarrieth no man, I began to wax passion-proud, and think her not worthy to live that was not a little in love, that as divers young men began to favour me for my beauty, so I began to censure of some of them partially, and to delight in the multitude of many wooers, being ready to fall from the tree before I was come to the perfection of a blossom, which an uncle of mine seeing, who was my mother's brother, as careful of my welfare as nigh to me in kin, finding fit opportunity to talk with me, gave me this wholesome exhortation.

A watchword to wanton maidens.

" Cousin, I see the fairest hawk hath oftentimes the sickest feathers, that the hottest day hath the most sharpest thunders, the brightest sun, the most sudden shower, and the youngest virgins, the most dangerous fortunes. I speak as a kinsman, and wish as a friend. The blossom of a maiden's youth, such as yourself, hath attending upon it many frosts to nip it, and many cares to consume it, so that if it be not carefully looked unto, it will perish before it come to any perfection.

" A virgin's honour consisteth not only in the gifts of nature, as to be fair and beautiful. Though they be favours that grace maidens much, for as they be glistering, so they be momentary, ready to be worn with every winter's blast, and parched with every summer's sun, there is no face so fair, but the least mole, the slenderest scar, the smallest brunt of sickness will quickly blemish.

" Beauty, cousin, as it flourisheth in youth, so it fadeth in age : it is but a folly that feedeth man's eye, a painting that Nature lends for a time, and men allow on for a while, insomuch that such as only aim at your fair looks, tie but their loves to an apprenticeship of beauty, which broken, either with cares, misfortune or years, their destinies are at liberty, and they begin to loath you, and like of others.

> *Forma bonum fragile est ; quantumque accedit ad annos,*
> *Fit minor ; et spatio carpitur ipsa suo.*[27]

" Then cousin, stand not too much on such a slippery glory, that is as brittle as glass ; be not proud of beauty's painting, that, hatched by time, perisheth in short time. Neither are women the more admirable of wise men for their gay apparel, though fools are fed with guards ; for a woman's ornaments is the excellency of her virtues ; and her inward good qualities, are of far more worth than her outward braveries. Embroidered hair, bracelets, silks, rich attire and such trash do rather bring the name of a young maid in question, than add to her fame any title of honour.

" The Vestal Virgins were not reverenced of the senators for their curious clothing, but for their chastity. Cornelia was not famoused for ornaments of gold, but for excellent virtues. Superfluity in apparel showeth rather lightness of mind, than it importeth any other inward good quality ; and men judge of maidens' rareness by the modesty of their raiment, holding it rather garish than glorious to be tricked up in superfluous and exceeding braveries. Neither, cousin, is it seemly for maids to jet abroad, or to frequent too much company.

" For she that is looked on by many, cannot choose but be hardly spoken of by some ; for report hath a blister on her tongue, and maidens' actions are narrowly measured. Therefore would not the ancient Romans suffer their daughters to go any further than their mothers' looks guided them. And therefore Diana is painted with a tortoise under her feet, meaning that a maid should not be a straggler, but, like the snail, carry her house on her head, and keep at home at her work, so to keep her name without blemish, and her virtues from the slander of envy.

"A maid that hazards herself in much company may venture the freedom of her heart by the folly of her eye, for so long the pot goes to the water, that it comes broken home ; and such as look much muſt needs like at laſt. The fly dallies with a flame, but at length she burneth : flax and fire put together will kindle. A maid in company of young men shall be conſtrained to liſten to the wanton allurements of many cunning speeches. If she hath not either with Ulysses taſted of moly, or ſtopped her ears warily, she may either be enticed with the sirens, or enchanted by Circes. Youth is apt to yield to sweet persuasions, and therefore, cousin, think nothing more dangerous than to gad abroad. Neither, cousin, do I allow this wanton dancing in young virgins. 'Tis more commendation for them to moderate their manners than to measure their feet, and better to hear nothing than to liſten unto unreverent music. Silence is a precious jewel, and nothing so much worth as a countenance full of chaſtity ; light behaviour is a sign of lewd thoughts, and men will say, there goes a wanton that will not want one, if a place and person were agreeable to her desires. If a maiden's honour be blemished, or her honeſty called in queſtion, she is half deflowered, and therefore had maidens need to be chary, leſt envy report them for unchaſte.

"Cousin, I speak this generally, which if you apply particularly to yourself, you shall find in time my words were well said."

I gave him slender thanks, but with such a frump that he perceived how light I made of his counsel ; which he perceiving, shaked his head, and with tears in his eyes departed. But I, whom wanton desires had drawn in delight, ſtill presumed in my former follies, and gave myself either to gad abroad, or else at home to read dissolute pamphlets, which bred in me many ill-affeĉted wishes, so that I gave leave to love and luſt to enter into the centre of my heart, where they harboured till they wrought my final and fatal prejudice.

Thus leading my life loosely, and being soothed up with the applause of my too kind and loving parents, I had many of every degree that made love unto me, as well for my beauty, as for the hope of wealth that my father would beſtow upon me. Sundry suitors I had, and I allowed of all, though I particularly granted love to none, yielding them friendly favours, as being proud I had more wooers than any maid in the parish beside. Amongſt the reſt there was a wealthy farmer that wished me well, a man of some forty years of age, one too worthy for one of so little worth as myself, and him my father, mother, and other friends would have had me match myself withal. But I, that had had the reins of liberty too long in mine own hands, refused him and would not be ruled by their persuasions, and though my mother with tears entreated me to consider of mine own estate, and how well I sped if I wedded with him, yet carelessly I despised her counsel, and flatly made answer that I would none of him. Which, though it pinched my parents at the quick, yet rather than they would displease me, they left me in mine own liberty to love. Many there were beside him, men's sons of no mean worth, that were wooers unto me, but in vain. Either my fortune or destiny drove me to a worser end, for I refused them all, and, with the beetle, refusing to light on the sweetest flowers all day, nestled at night in a cow-shard.

It fortuned that, as many sought to win me, so amongst the rest there was an odd companion that dwelt with a gentleman hard by, a fellow of small reputation, and of no living; neither had he any excellent qualities but thrumming on the gittern. But of pleasant disposition he was, and could gawl out many quaint and ribaldrous jigs and songs, and so was favoured of the foolish sect for his foppery. This shifting companion, suitable to myself in vanity, would ofttimes be jesting with me, and I so long dallying with him, that I began deeply—Oh, let me blush at this confession !—to fall in love with him, and so construed of all his actions, that I consented to mine own overthrow. For as smoke will hardly be concealed, so love will not be long smothered, but will bewray her own secrets; which was manifest in me, who in my sporting with him, so bewrayed my affection, that he, spying I favoured him, began to strike when the iron was hot, and to take opportunity by the forehead, and one day, finding me in a merry vein, began to question with me of love, which although at the first I slenderly denied him, yet at last I granted, so that not only I agreed to plight him my faith, but that night meeting to have farther talk, I lasciviously consented that he cropped the flower of my virginity. When thus I was spoiled by such a base companion, I gave myself to content his humour, and to satisfy the sweet of mine own wanton desires. Oh, hear let me breathe and with tears bewail the beginning of my miseries, and to exclaim against the folly of my parents, who, by too much favouring me in my vanity in my tender youth, laid the first plot of my ensuing repentance ! Had they with due correction chastised my wantonness, and suppressed my foolish will with their grave advice, they had made me more virtuous and themselves less sorrowful. A father's frown is a bridle to the child, and a mother's check is a stay to the stubborn daughter. Oh, had my parents in overloving me not hated me, I had not at this time cause to complain ! Oh, had my father regarded the saying of the wise man, I had not been thus woebegone !

If thy daughter be not shamefast hold her straightly ; lest she abuse herself through overmuch liberty.

Take heed of her that hath an unshamefast eye ; and marvel not if she trespass against thee.[28]

The daughter maketh the father to watch secretly, and the carefulness he hath for her taketh away his sleep :

In her virginity, lest she should be deflowered in her father's house.

If therefore thy daughter be unshamefast in her youth, keep her straightly; lest she cause thine enemies to laugh thee to scorn, and make thee a common talk in the city, and defame thee among the people, and bring thee to public shame.[29]

Had my parents with care considered of this holy counsel, and levelled my life by the loadstone of virtue, had they looked narrowly into the faults of my youth, and bent the tree while it was a wand, and taught the hound while he was a puppy, this blemish had never befortuned me, nor so great dishonour had not befallen them. Then, by my example, let all parents take heed, lest in loving their children too tenderly, they subvert them utterly ; lest in manuring the ground too much with the unskilful husbandman, it wax too fat, and bring forth more weeds than flowers ; lest cockering their children under their wings without correction, they make them careless, and bring them to destruction : as their nurture is in youth, so will their nature grow in age. If the palm-tree be suppressed while it is a scion, it will contrary to nature be crooked when it is a tree.

> *Quo semel est imbuta recens servabit odorem.*
> *Testa diu.*

If then virtue be to be engrafted in youth, lest they prove obstinate in age, reform your children betimes both with correction and counsel. So shall you that are parents glory in the honour of their good endeavours. But, leaving this digression, again to the looseness of mine own life, who now having lost the glory of my youth, and suffered such a base slave to possess it, which many men of worth had desired to enjoy, I waxed bold in sin and grew shameless, insomuch he could not desire so much as I did grant, whereupon, seeing he durst not reveal it to my father to demand me in marriage, he resolved to carry me away secretly, and therefore wished me to provide for myself, and to furnish me every way both with money and apparel, hoping, as he said, that after we were departed, and my father saw we were married, and that no means was to amend it, he would give his free consent, and use us as kindly, and deal with us as liberally as if we had matched with his good will. I, that was apt to any ill, agreed to this, and so wrought the matter, that he carried me away into a strange place, and then using me a while as his wife, when our money began to wax low, he resolved secretly to go into the country where my father dwelt, to hear not only how my father took my departure, but what hope we had of his ensuing favour. Although I was loath to be left alone in a strange place, yet I was willing to hear from my friends, who no doubt conceived much heart-sorrow for my unhappy fortunes ; so that I parted with a few tears, and enjoined him to make all the haste he might to return. He being gone, as the eagles always resort where the carrion is, so the bruit being spread abroad of my beauty, and that at such an inn lay such a fair young gentlewoman, there resorted thither many brave youthful gentlemen and cutting companions, that, tickled with lust, aimed at the possession of my favour, and by sundry means sought to have a sight of me, which I easily granted to all, as a woman that counted it a glory to be wondered at by many men's eyes, insomuch that coming amongst them, I set their hearts more and more on fire, that there rose divers brawls who should be most in my company. Being thus haunted by such a troop of lusty rufflers, I began to find mine own folly, that had placed my first affection so loosely, and therefore began as deeply to loath him that was departed, as erst I liked him when he was present, vowing in myself, though he had the spoil of my virginity, yet never after should he triumph in the possession of my favour, and therefore began I to affection these new-come guests, and one above the rest, who was a brave young gentleman, and no less addicted unto me than I devoted unto him ; for daily he courted me with amorous sonnets and curious proud letters, and sent me jewels, and all that I might grace him with the name of my servant. I returned him as loving lines at last, and so contented his lusting desire, that secretly, and unknown to all the rest, I made him sundry nights my bedfellow, where I so bewitched him with sweet words, that the man began deeply to dote upon me, insomuch that, selling some portion of land that he had, he put it into ready money, and providing horse and all things convenient, carried me

secretly away, almost as far as the Bath. This was my second choice
and my second shame.

Thus I went forward in wickedness, and delighted in change, having
left mine old love to look after some other mate more fit for my³⁰ purpose.
How he took my departure when he returned, I little cared, for now I
had my content, a gentleman, young, lusty, and endued with good
qualities, and one that loved me more tenderly than himself. Thus
lived this new entertained friend and I together unmarried, yet as man
and wife for a while, so lovingly, as was to his content and my credit,
but as the tiger, though for a while she hide her claws, yet at last she will
reveal her cruelty, and as the *agnus castus* leaf, when it looks most dry is
then most full of moisture, so women's wantonness is not qualified by
their wariness, nor do their chariness for a month warrant their chastity
for ever ; which I proved true, for my supposed husband, being every
way a man of worth, could not so covertly hide himself in the country,
though a stranger, but that he fell in acquaintance with many brave
gentlemen, whom he brought home to his lodging, not only to honour
them with his liberal courtesy, but also to see me, being proud if any
man of worth applauded my beauty. Alas, poor gentleman ! Too much
bewitched by the wiliness of a woman, had he deemed my heart to be
a harbour for every new desire, or mine eye a suitor to every new face,
he would not have been so fond as to have brought his companions into
my company, but rather would have mewed me up as a hen, to have
kept that several to himself by force which he could not retain by kindness. But the honest-minded novice little suspected my change, although
I, God wot, placed my delight in nothing more than the desire of new
choice, which fell out thus :

Amongst the rest of the gentlemen that kept him company, there was
one that was his most familiar, and he reposed more trust and confidence
in him than in all the rest. This gentleman began to be deeply enamoured
of me, and showed it by many signs which I easily perceived, and I,
whose ear was pliant to every sweet word, and who so allowed of all that
were beautiful, affected him no less, so that, love prevailing above
friendship, he broke the matter with me, and made not many suits in
vain before he obtained his purpose, for he had what he wished, and I
had what contented me. I will not confess that any of the rest had
some seldom favours, but this gentleman was my second self, and I
loved him more for the time at the heel, than the other at the heart, so
that though the other youth bare the charges and was made Sir Pay-for-all,
yet this new friend was he that was master of my affections, which

kindness betwixt us was so unwisely cloaked that in short time it was manifest to all our familiars, which made my supposed husband to sigh and others to smile. But he that was hit with the horn was pinched at the heart ; yet so extreme was the affection he bare to me, that he had rather conceal his grief than any way make me discontent, so that he smothered his sorrow with patience, and brooked the injury with silence, till our loves grew so broad before, that it was a wonder to the world. Whereupon one day at dinner, I being very pleasant with his chosen friend and my choice lover, I know not how, but either by fortune, or it may be some set match, there was by a gentleman there present a question popped in about women's passions, and their mutability in affection, so that the controversy was defended, *pro* and *contra*. Which arguments, whether a woman might have a second friend or no, at last it was concluded, that love and lordship brooks no fellowship, and therefore none so base-minded to bear a rival. Hereupon arose a question about friends that were put in trust, how it was a high point of treason for one to betray another, especially in love, insomuch that one gentleman at the board protested by a solemn oath, that if any friend of his, made privy and favoured with the sight of his mistress whom he loved, whether it were his wife or no, should secretly seek to encroach into his room and offer him that dishonour to partake his love, he would not use any other revenge, but at the next greeting stab him with his poynado, though he were condemned to death for the action.

All this fitted for the humour of my supposed husband, and struck both me and my friend into a quandary, but I scornfully jested at it, whenas my husband, taking the ball before it fell to the ground, began to make a long discourse what faithless friends they were that would fail in love, especially where a resolved trust of the party beloved was committed unto them, and hereupon, to make the matter more credulous, and to quip my folly, and to taunt the baseness of his friend's mind, that, so he might with courtesy both warn us of our wantonness, and reclaim us from ill, he promised to tell a pleasant story, performed, as he said, not long since in England, and it was to this effect :

A pleasant discourse, how a wife wanton by her husband's gentle warning became to be a modest matron.

There was a gentleman, to give him his due, an esquire, here in England, that was married to a young gentlewoman, fair and of a modest behaviour, virtuous in her looks, howsoever she was in her thoughts,

and one that every way with her dutiful endeavour and outward appearance of honesty did breed her husband's content, insomuch that the
gentleman so deeply affected her, as he counted all those hours ill spent
which he passed not away in her company, besotting so himself in the
beauty of his wife, that his only care was to have her every way delighted.
Living thus pleasantly together, he had one special friend amongst the
rest, whom he so dearly affected, as ever Damon did his Pythias, Pylades
his Orestes, or Titus his Gisippus. He unfolded all his secrets in his
bosom, and what passion he had in his mind that either joyed him or
perplexed him, he revealed unto his friend, and directed his actions
according to the sequel of his counsels, so that they were two bodies
and one soul. This gentleman, for all the inward favour shown him
by his faithful friend, could not so withstand the force of fancy, but he
grew enamoured of his friend's wife, whom he courted with many
sweet words and fair promises, charms that are able to enchant almost
the chastest ears, and so subtly couched his arguments, discovered
such love in his eyes, and such sorrow in his looks, that despair seemed
to sit in his face, and swore that, if she granted not him *le don du merci*,
the end of a lover's sighs then would present his heart as a tragic sacrifice
to the sight of his cruel mistress. The gentlewoman, waxing pitiful,
as women are kind-hearted and are loath gentlemen should die for love,
after a few excuses, let him dub her husband knight of the forked order,
and so, to satisfy his humour, made forfeit of her own honour.

Thus these two lovers continued by a great space in such pleasures
as unchaste wantons count their felicity, having continually fit opportunity to exercise their wicked purpose, sith the gentleman himself
did give them free liberty to love, neither suspecting his wife, or suspecting his friend. At last, as such traitorous abuses will burst forth,
it fell so out, that a maid who had been an old servant in the house,
began to grow suspicious that there was too much familiarity between
her mistress and her master's friend, and upon this watched them divers
times so narrowly, that at last she found them more private than either
agreed with her master's honour or her own honesty, and thereupon
revealed it one day unto her master. He, little credulous of the light
behaviour of his wife, blamed the maid, and bade her take heed lest
she sought to blemish her virtues with slander, whom he loved more
tenderly than his own life. The maid replied, that she spake not of
envy to him, but of mere love she bare unto him, and the rather that
he might shadow such a fault in time, and by some means prevent it,
lest if others should note it as well as she, his wife's good name and his

friend's should be called in question. At these wise words, spoken by
so base a drug as his maid, the gentleman waxed astonished and listened
to her discourse, wishing her to discover how she knew or was so privy
to the folly of her mistress, or by what means he might have assured
proof of it. She told him that to her, her own eyes were witnesses,
for she saw them unlawfully together. " And please it you, sir," quoth
she, " to feign yourself to go from home, and then in the back-house
to keep you secret, I will let you see as much as I have manifested unto
you." Upon this the master agreed, and warned his maid not so much
as to make it known to any of her fellows. Within a day or two after,
the gentleman said he would go a hunting and so rise very early, and,
causing his men to couple up his hounds, left his wife in bed and went
abroad. As soon as he was gone a mile from the house, he commanded
his men to ride afore and to start the hare and follow the chase, " and
we will come fair and softly after." They, obeying their master's charge,
went their ways, and he returned by a back way to his house, and went
secretly to the place where his maid and he had appointed. In the
meantime, the mistress, thinking her husband safe with his hounds,
sent for her friend to her bedchamber, by a trusty servant of hers, in
whom she assured that was a secret pander in such affairs, and the
gentleman was not slack to come, but, making all the haste he could,
came and went into the chamber, asking for the master of the house
very familiarly. The old maid noting all this, as soon as she knew them
together, went and called her master and carried him up by a secret
pair of stairs to her mistress' chamber door, where, peeping in at a place
that the maid before had made for the purpose, he saw more than he
looked for, and so much as pinched him at the very heart, causing him
to accuse his wife for a strumpet, and his friend for a traitor. Yet, for
all this, valuing his own honour more than their dishonesty, thinking
if he should make an uproar, he should but aim at his own discredit,
and cause himself to be a laughing game to his enemies, he concealed
his sorrow with silence, and taking the maid apart, charged her to keep
all secret, whatsoever she had seen, even as she esteemed of her own
life, for if she did bewray it to any, he himself would with his sword
make an end of her days, and with that, putting his hand in his sleeve,
gave the poor maid six angels to buy her a new gown. The wench,
glad of this gift, swore solemnly to tread it underfoot, and, sith it pleased
him to conceal it, never to reveal it as long as she lived.

Upon this they parted, she to her drudgery, and he to the field to
his men, where, after he had killed the hare, he returned home, and

finding his friend in the garden, that in his absence had been grafting horns in the chimneys, and entertained him with his wonted familiarity, and showed no bad countenance to his wife, but dissembled all his thoughts to the full. As soon as dinner was done, and that he was gotten solitary by himself, he began to determine of revenge, but not as every man would have done, how to have brought his wife to shame, and her love to confusion, but he busied his brains how he might reserve his honour inviolate, reclaim his wife, and keep his friend, meditating a long time how he might bring all this to pass. At last a humour fell into his head, how cunningly to compass all three, and therefore he went and got him[31] certain slips, which are counterfeit pieces of money, being brass and covered over with silver, which the common people call slips. Having furnished himself with these, he put them in his purse, and at night went to bed as he was wont to do, yet not using the kind familiarity that he accustomed, notwithstanding he abstained not from the use of her body, but knew his wife as aforetimes, and every time he committed the act with her, he laid the next morning in the window a slip, where he was sure she might find it, and so many times as it pleased him to be carnally pleasant with his wife, so many slips he still laid down upon her cushnet.

This he used for the space of a fortnight, till at last, his wife finding every day a slip, or sometime more or less, wondered how they came there, and examining her waiting-maids, none of them could tell her anything touching them. Whereupon she thought to question with her husband about it, but being out of her remembrance, the next morning as he and she lay dallying in bed, it came into her mind, and she asked her husband if he laid those slips on her cushnet, that she of late found there, having never seen any before.

" Ay, marry, did I," quoth he, " and I have laid them there upon special reason, and it is this. Ever since I have been married to thee, I have deemed thee honest, and therefore used and honoured thee as my wife, parting coequal favours betwixt us as true loves, but alate finding the contrary, and with these eyes seeing thee play the whore with my friend, in whom I did repose all my trust, I sought not, as many would have done, to have revenged in blood, but for the safety of mine own honour, which otherwise would have been blemished by thy dishonesty, I have been silent, and have neither wronged my quon-dam friend, nor abused thee, but still do hold bed with thee, that the world should not suspect anything ; and to quench the desire of lust I do use thy body, but not so lovingly as I would a wife, but carelessly as I would a strumpet, and, therefore, even as to a whore, so I give thee hire, which is for every time a slip, a counterfeit coin, which is good enough for such a slippery wanton, that will wrong her husband that loved her so tenderly. And thus will I use thee for the safety of mine own honour, till I have assured proof that thou becomest honest."

And thus, with tears in his eyes, and his heart ready to burst with sighs, he was silent, when his wife, stricken with remorse of conscience, leaping out of her bed in her smock, humbly confessing all, craved pardon, promising if he should pardon this offence which was new begun in her, she would become a new reformed woman, and never after so much as in thought, give him any occasion of suspicion of jealousy. The patient husband, not willing to urge his wife, took her at her word, and told her that when he found her so reclaimed, he would, as afore he had done, use her lovingly and as his wife, but till he was so persuaded of her honesty, he would pay her still slips for his pleasure, charging her not to reveal any thing to his friend, or to make it known to him that he was privy to their loves.

Thus the debate ended, I guess in some kind greeting, and the gentleman went abroad to see his pastures, leaving his wife in bed full of sorrow and almost renting her heart asunder with sighs.

As soon as he was walked abroad, the gentleman his friend came to the house and asked for the goodman. The pander that was privy to all their practices, said that his master was gone abroad to see his pastures, but his mistress was in bed. "Why then," says he, "I will go and raise her up." So coming into the chamber and kissing her, meaning as he was wont to have used other accustomed dalliance, she desired him to abstain, with broken sighs and her eyes full of tears. He, wondering what should make her thus discontent, asked her what was the cause of her sorrow, protesting with a solemn oath that if any had done her injury, he would revenge it, were it with hazard of his life. She then told him, scarce being able to speak for weeping, that she had a suit to move him in, which if he granted unto her, she would hold him in love and affection without change next her husband for ever. He promised to do whatsoever it were. "Then," says she, "swear upon a Bible you will do it without exception." With that he took a Bible that lay in the window and swore that whatsoever she requested him to do, were it to the loss of his life, he would without exception perform it. Then she, holding down her head and blushing, began thus:

"I need not," quoth she, "make manifest how grossly and grievously you and I have both offended God, and wronged the honest gentleman my husband and your friend, he putting a special trust in us both, and assuring such earnest affiance in your unfeigned friendship, that he even committeth me, his wife, his love, his second life, into your bosom. This love have I requited with inconstancy, in playing the harlot. That faith that he reposeth in you, have you returned with treachery and falsehood, in abusing mine honesty and his honour. Now a remorse of conscience toucheth me for my sins, that I heartily repent, and vow ever hereafter to live only to my husband, and therefore my suit is to you, that from henceforth you shall never so much as motion any dishonest question unto me, nor seek any unlawful pleasure or conversing at my hands. This is my suit, and hereunto I have sworn you, which oath if you observe as a faithful gentleman, I will conceal from my husband what is past, and rest in honest sort your faithful friend for ever."

At this she burst afresh into tears, and uttered such sighs, that he thought for very grief her heart would have clave asunder. The gentleman, astonied at this strange metamorphosis of his mistress, sat a good while in a maze, and at last taking her by the hand, made this reply :

" So God help me, fair sweeting, I am glad of this motion, and wondrous joyful that God hath put such honest thoughts into your mind, and hath made you the means to reclaim me from my folly. I feel no less remorse than you do, in wronging so honest a friend as your husband, but this is the frailness of man, and therefore to make amends, I protest anew, never hereafter so much as in thought, as to motion you of dishonesty. Only I crave you be silent."

She promised that, and so they ended. And so for that time they parted. At noon the gentleman came home and cheerfully saluted his wife and asked if dinner were ready, and sent for his friend, using him wonderfully familiarly, giving him no occasion of mistrust, and so pleasantly they passed away the day together. At night when his wife and he went to bed, she told him all, what had passed between her and his friend, and how she had bound him with an oath, and that he voluntarily of himself swore as much, being heartily sorry that he had so deeply offended so kind a friend. The gentleman commended her wit, and found her afterward a reclaimed woman, she living so honestly that she never gave him any occasion of mistrust. Thus the wise gentleman reclaimed with silence a wanton wife, and retained an assured friend.

At this pleasant tale all the board was at a mutiny, and they said the gentleman did passing wisely that wrought so cunningly for the safety of his own honour, but highly exclaiming against such a friend as would to his friend offer such villainy, all condemning her that would be false to so loving a husband. Thus they did diversely descant and passed away dinner. But this tale wrought little effect in me, for as one past grace, I delighted in change. But the gentleman that was his familiar, and my paramour, was so touched, that never after he would touch me dishonestly, but reclaimed himself, abstained from me and became true to his friend. I wondering that according to his wonted custom he did not seek my company, he and I being one day in the chamber alone, and he in his dumps, I began to dally with him, and to ask him why he was so strange, and used not his accustomed favours to me. He solemnly made answer that, though he had played the fool in setting his fancy upon another man's wife, and in wronging his friend, yet his conscience was now touched with remorse, and ever since he heard the tale afore rehearsed, he had vowed in himself never to do my husband the like wrong again. " My husband ? " quoth I. " He is none of mine. He hath brought me from my friends and keeps me here unmarried, and therefore am I as free for you as for him " ; and thus began to grow clamorous, because I was debarred of my lust.

The gentleman seeing me shameless, wished me to be silent, and said : " Although you be but his friend, yet he hold you as dear as his wife, and therefore I will not abuse him, neither would I wish you to be familiar with any other, seeing you have a friend that loves you so tenderly."

Much good counsel he gave me, but all in vain, for I scorned it, and began to hate him, and resolved both to be rid of him and my supposed husband ; for, falling in another familiar of my husband's, I so inveigled him with sweet words, that I caused him to make a piece of money to steal me away, and so carry me to London, where I had not lived long with him, ere he, seeing my light behaviour, left me to the world, and to shift for myself. Here by my example may you note the inconstant life of courtezans and common harlots, who, after they have lost their honesty, care not who grow into their favour, nor what villainy they commit. They fancy all as long as crowns last, and only aim at pleasure and ease. They cleave like caterpillars to the tree, and consume the fruit where they fall ; they be vultures that prey on men alive, and like the serpent sting the bosom wherein they are nourished. I may best discourse their nature, because I was one of their profession, but now, being metamorphosed, I hold it meritorious for me to warn women from being such wantons, and to give a caveat to men, lest they addict themselves to such straggling strumpets, as love none, though they like all, but affectionate only for profit, and when he hath spent all, they beat him out of doors with the prodigal child. But stopping here, till occasion serve me fitter to discover the manner of courtezans, to myself, who now being brought to London, and left here at random, was not such a house-dove while any friend stayed with me, but that I had visit some houses in London that could harbour as honest a woman as myself, whenas, therefore, I was left to myself, I removed my lodging, and gat me into one of those houses of good hospitality whereunto persons resort, commonly called a trugging-house, or to be plain, a whore-house, where I gave myself to entertain all companions, sitting or standing at the door like a stale, to allure or draw in wanton passengers, refusing none that would with his purse purchase me to be his, to satisfy the disordinate desire of his filthy lust. Now I began not to respect personage, good qualities, to the gracious favour of the man, when eye had no respect of person, for the oldest lecher was as welcome as the youngest lover, so he brought meat in his mouth ; otherwise I pronounce[d] against him, *Si nihil attuleris, ibis, Homere foras.*[32]

I waxed thus in this hell of voluptuousness daily worse and worse, yet having as they term it, a respect to the main chance, as near as I could to avoid diseases, and to keep myself brave in apparel, although I paid a kind of tribute to the bawd, according as the number and benefit of my companions did exceed ; but never could I be brought to be a pickpocket or thievish by any of their persuasions, although I wanted daily no instructions to allure me to that villainy, for I think nature had wrought in me a contrary humour, otherwise my bad nurture, and conversing with such bad company had brought me to it. Marry, in all their vices I carried a brazen face and was shameless, for what ruffian was there in London that would utter more desperate oaths than I in mine anger, what to spet, quaff or carouse more devilishly, or rather damnably, than myself, and for beastly communication Messalina of Rome might have been waiting-maid. Besides, I grew so grafted in sin, that *consueto peccandi tollebat sensum peccati,* custom of sin took away the feeling of the sin, for I so accustomably use myself to all kind of vice, that I accounted swearing no sin. Whoredom—why, I smile at that, and could profanely say, that it was a sin which God laughed at. Gluttony I held good-fellowship, and wrath, honour and resolution. I despised God, nay, in my conscience I might easily have been persuaded there was no God. I contemned the preachers, and when any wished me to reform my life, I bade away with the Puritan ; and if any young woman refused to be as vicious every way as myself, I would then say : " Gip, fine soul, a young saint will prove an old devil." I never would go to the church and sermons. I utterly refused, holding them as needless tales told in a pulpit. I would not bend mine ears to the hearing of any good discourse, but still delighted in jangling ditties of ribaldry.

Thus to the grief of my friends, hazard of my soul, and consuming of my body, I spent a year or two in this base and bad kind of life, subject to the whistle of every desperate ruffian, till on a time, there resorted to our house a clothier, a proper young man, who by fortune, coming first to drink, espying me, asked me if I would drink with him. There needed no great entreaty, foras then I wanted company, and so clapped me down by him, and began very pleasantly then to welcome him. The man being of himself modest and honest, noted my personage, and judicially reasoned of my strumpetlike behaviour, and inwardly, as after he reported unto me, grieved that so foul properties were hidden in so good a proportion, and that such rare wit and excellent beauty was blemished with whoredom's base deformity, insomuch that he began to think well of me, and to wish that I were as honest as I was beautiful. Again, see how God wrought for my conversion ! Since I gave myself to my loose kind of life, I never liked any so well as him, insomuch that I began to judge of every part, and methought he was the properest man that ever I saw. Thus we sat both amorous of other, I lasciviously, and he honestly. At last he questioned with me what countrywoman I was, and why, being so proper a woman, I would beseem to dwell or lie in a base ale-house, especially in one that had a bad name. I warrant you he wanted no knavish reply to fit him, for I told him the house was as honest as his mother's. Marry, if there were in it a good wench or two, that would pleasure their friends at a need, I guess by his nose what porridge he loved, and that he hated none such. Well, seeing me in that voice, he said little, but shaked his head, paid for the beer and went his way, only taking his leave of me with a kiss, which methought was the sweetest that ever was given me. As soon as he was gone, I began to think what a handsome man he was, and wished that he would come and take a night's lodging with me, sitting in a dump to think of the quaintness of his personage, till other companions came in, that shaked me out of that melancholy.   But as soon again as I was secret to myself, he came into my remembrance.

Passing over thus a day or two, this clothier came again to our house, whose sight cheered me up, for that spying him out at a casement, I ran down the ſtairs and met him at the door, and heartily welcomed him, and asked him if he would drink.

" I come for that purpose," says he ; " but I will drink no more below but in a chamber."

" Marry, sir," quoth I, " you shall " ; and so brought him into the faireſt room.

In there sitting there together drinking, at laſt the clothier fell to kissing and other dalliance, wherein he found me not coy.   At laſt told me that he would willingly have his pleasure of me, but the room was too lightsome, for of all things in the world, he could not in such actions away with a light chamber.   I consented unto him, and brought him into a room more dark, but ſtill he said it was too light.   Then I carried him into a farther chamber, where, drawing a buckram curtain afore the window, and closing the curtains of the bed, I asked him, smiling, if that were close enough.

" No, sweet love," says he.   " The curtain is thin, and not broad enough for the window.   Peradventure some watching eye may espy us.   My heart misdoubts, and my credit is my life.   Good love if thou haſt a more close room than this, bring me to it."

" Why then," quoth I, " follow me " ; and with that I brought him into a back loft, where ſtood a little bed only appointed to lodge suspicious persons, so dark that at noondays it was impossible for any man to see his own hands.   " How now, sir ? " quoth I.   " Is not this dark enough ? "

He, sitting him down on the bed-side, fetched a deep sigh, and said indifferent, " So so, but there is a glimpse of light in at the tiles.   Somebody may by fortune see us."

" In faith, no," quoth I, " none but God."

" God ? " says he.   " Why, can God see us here ? "

" Good sir," quoth I, " why I hope you are not so simple, but God's eyes are so clear and penetrating, that they can pierce through walls of brass, and that were we enclosed never so secretly, yet we are manifeſtly seen to Him."

" And alas ! " quoth he, " sweet love, if God see us, shall we not be more ashamed to do such a filthy act before Him than before men ? I am sure thou art not so shameless but thou wouldſt blush and be afraid to have the meanest commoner in London see thee in the action of thy filthy lust. And dost thou not shame more to have God, the Maker of all things, see thee, who revengeth sin with death, He whose eyes are clearer than the sun, who is the searcher of the heart, and holdeth vengeance in His hands to punish sinners? Consider, sweet love, that if man and wife would be ashamed to have any of their friends see them in the act of generation, or performing the rights of marriage which is lawful and allowed before God, yet for modesty do it in the most covert they may, then how impudent or graceless should we be, to fulfil our filthy lust before the eyes of the Almighty, who is greater than all kings or princes on the earth. Oh, let us tremble that we but once durst have such wanton communication in the hearing of His Divine Majesty, who pronounceth damnation for such as give themselves over to adultery. It is not possible, saith the Lord, for any whore-master or lascivious wanton to enter into the kingdom of God. For such sins whole cities have sunk, kingdoms have been destroyed; and though God suffereth such wicked livers to escape for a while, yet at length he payeth home, in this world with beggary, shame, diseases, or infamy, and in the other life, with perpetual damnation. Weigh but the inconvenience that grows through thy loose life. Thou art hated of all that are good, despised of the virtuous, and only well thought of of reprobates, rascals, ruffians, and such as the world hates, subject to their lust, and gaining thy living at the hands of every diseased lecher. Oh, what a miserable trade of life is thine, that livest of the vomit of sin, in hunting after maladies! But suppose: while thou art young, thou art favoured of thy companions; when thou waxest old, and that thy beauty is vaded, then thou shalt be loathed and despised, even of them that professed most love unto thee. Then, good sister, call to mind the baseness of thy life, the heinous outrage of thy sin, that God doth punish it with the rigour of His justice. Oh, thou art made beautiful, fair, and well-formed! And wilt thou then by thy filthy lust make thy body, which, if thou be honest, is the Temple of God, the habitation of the Devil? Consider this, and call to God for mercy, and amend thy life. Leave this house, and I will become thy faithful friend in all honesty, and use thee as mine own sister."

At this, such a remorse of conscience, such a fearful terror of my sin struck into my mind, that I kneeled down at his feet, and with tears besought him he would help me out of that misery—for his exhortation had caused in me a loathing of my wicked life—and I would not only become a reformed woman, but hold him as dear as my father that

gave me life ; whereupon he kissed me with tears, and so we went
down together, where we had further communication, and presently
he provided me another lodging, where I not only used myself so honestly,
but also was so penitent, every day in tears for my former folly, that he
took me to his wife, and how I have lived since and loathed filthy lust,
I refer myself to the Majesty of God, who knoweth the secrets of all
hearts.

Thus, countrymen, I have published the conversion of an English
courtezan, which, if any way it be profitable either to forewarn youth,
or withdraw bad persons to goodness, I have the whole end of my desire,
only craving every father would bring up his children with careful
nurture, and every young woman respect the honour of her virginity.

But amongst all these blithe and merry jests, a little by your leave !
if it be no farther than Fetter Lane. Oh take heed ! that's too nigh the
Temple. What then ! I will draw as near the sign of the *White Hart*
as I can, and breathing myself by the bottle ale-house, I'll tell you a
merry jest, how a cony-catcher was used.

*A merry tale taken not far from Fetter Lane end, of a new-found cony-
catcher, that was cony-catched himself.*

So it fell out, that a gentleman was sick and purblind, and went to
a good honest man's house to sojourn, and taking up his chamber, grew
so sick, that the goodman of the house hired a woman to keep and attend
day and night upon the gentleman. This poor woman, having a good
conscience, was careful of his welfare and looked to his diet, which was
so slender, that the man, although sick, was almost famished, so that
the woman would no longer stay, but bade his host provide him of some
other to watch with him, sith it grieved her to see a man lie and starve
for want of food, especially being set on the score for meat and drink,
in the space of a fortnight, four pounds.

The goodman of the house at last, hearing how that poor woman
did find fault with his scoring, the gentleman not only put her out of
doors without wages, but would have arrested her for taking away his
good name, and defaming and slandering him, and with that, calling
one of his neighbours to him, said, " Neighbour, whereas such a bad-
tongued woman hath reported to my discredit that the gentleman that
lies sick in my house wants meat, and yet runs very much on the score,
I pray you judge by his diet whether he be famished or no. First in

the morning, he hath a caudle next his heart, half an hour after that, a quart of sugar sops, half an hour after that, a neck of mutton in broth, half an hour after that, chickens in sorrel sops, and an hour after that, a joint of roaſt meat for his dinner. Now, neighbour, having this provision, you may judge whether he be spoiled for lack of meat or no, and to what great charges his diet will arise." Whereas in truth, the poor gentleman would have been glad of the leaſt of these, for he could get none at all, but the cozening knave thought to verse upon him, and one day, seeing money came not briefly to the gentleman, took some of his apparel, his cloak I guess, and pawned it for forty shillings, whereas, God wot, all he ate in that time was not worth a crown.

Well, the gentleman seeing how the knave went about to cony-catch him, and that he had taken his cloak, smothered all for revenge, and watched opportunity to do it ; and on a time, seeing the goodman out, borrowed a cloak far better than his own of the boy, saying that he would go to a friend of his to fetch money for his maſter and discharge the house. The boy lending it him, away walks the gentleman, though weak after this great diet, and never came at the tailor's house to answer him cloak or money. And thus was he cony-catched himself, that thought to have versed upon another.

Finis.

THE
BLACK BOOK'S
MESSENGER.

Laying open the Life and Death

of *Ned Browne,* one of the most notable Cutpurses,
Crossbiters, and Cony-catchers, that
ever lived in England.

Herein he telleth very plea-

santly in his own person such strange pranks and
monstrous villainies by him and his consorts
performed, as the like was yet never
heard of in any of the former
books of cony-
catching.

Read and be warned. Laugh as you like.
Judge as you find.

Nascimur pro Patria.

by R[OBERT] G[REENE.]

1592

To the courteous reader, health.

GENTLEMEN, I know you have long expected the coming forth of my *Black Book*, which I long have promised, and which I had many days since finished, had not sickness hindered my intent. Nevertheless, be assured it is the first thing I mean to publish after I am recovered. This *Messenger* to my *Black Book* I commit to your courteous censures, being written before I fell sick, which I thought good in the meantime to send you as a fairing, discoursing Ned Browne's villainies, which are too many to be described in my *Black Book*.

I had thought to have joined with this treatise a pithy discourse of the repentance of a cony-catcher lately executed out of Newgate, yet forasmuch as the method of the one is so far differing from the other, I altered my opinion, and the rather for that the one died resolute and desperate, the other penitent and passionate. For the cony-catcher's repentance, which shall shortly be published, it contains a passion of great importance. First, how he was given over from all grace and godliness, and seemed to have no spark of the fear of God in him ; yet, nevertheless, through the wonderful working of God's spirit, even in the dungeon at Newgate the night before he died, he so repented him from the bottom of his heart, that it may well beseem parents to have it for their children, masters for their servants, and to be perused of every honest person with great regard.

And for Ned Browne, of whom my *Messenger* makes report, he was a man infamous for his bad course of life and well known about London. He was in outward show a gentlemanlike companion, attired very brave, and to shadow his villainy the more would nominate himself to be a marshal-man,[1] who when he had nipped a bung or cut a good purse, he would steal over in to the Low Countries, there to taste three or four stoups of Rhenish wine, and then come over forsooth a brave soldier. But at last he leapt at a daisy for his loose kind of life. And therefore imagine you now see him in his own person, standing in a great bay window with a halter about his neck ready to be hanged, desperately pronouncing this his whole course of life, and confesseth as followeth.

Yours in all courtesy,

R.G.

A table of the words of art lately devised by Ned Browne and his associates to crossbite the old phrases used in the manner of cony-catching.

He that draws the fish to the bait, *the beater.*
The tavern where they go, *the bush.*
The fool that is caught, *the bird.*
Cony-catching to be called *bat-fowling.*
The wine to be called *the shrap.*
The cards to be called *the lime-twigs.*
The fetching in a cony, *beating the bush.*
The good ass if he be won : *ſtooping to the lure.*
If he keep aloof : *a haggard.*
The verser in cony-catching is called *the retriever.*
And the barnacle *the pot-hunter.*

THE LIFE AND DEATH OF NED BROWNE, A NOTABLE CUTPURSE AND CONY-CATCHER.

IF you think, Gentlemen, to hear a repentant man speak, or to tell a large tale of his penitent sorrows, ye are deceived. For as I have ever lived lewdly, so I mean to end my life as resolutely, and not by a cowardly confession to attempt the hope of a pardon. Yet, in that I was famous in my life for my villainies, I will at my death profess myself as notable, by discoursing to you all merrily the manner and method of my knaveries, which, if you hear without laughing, then after my death call me base knave, and never have me in remembrance.

Know therefore, Gentlemen, that my parents were honest, of good report and no little esteem amongst their neighbours, and sought (if good nurture and education would have served) to have made me an honest man. But as one selfsame ground brings forth flowers and thistles, so of a sound stock proved an untoward scion ; and of a virtuous father, a most vicious son. It boots little to rehearse the petty sins of my nonage, as disobedience to my parents, contempt of good counsel, despising of mine elders, filching, pettilashery, and such trifling toys. But with these follies I inured myself, till, waxing in years, I grew into greater villainies. For when I came to eighteen years old, what sin was it that I would not commit with greediness, what attempt so bad, that I would not endeavour to execute ! Cutting of purses, stealing of horses, lifting, picking of locks, and all other notable cozenages. Why, I held them excellent qualities, and accounted him unworthy to live, that could not, or durst not, live by such damnable practices. Yet, as sin too openly manifested to the eye of the magistrate is either sore revenged or soon cut off, so I, to prevent that, had a net wherein to dance, and divers shadows to colour my knaveries withal, as I would title myself with the name of a fencer, and make gentlemen believe that I picked a living out by that mystery, whereas, God wot, I had no other fence but with my short knife and a pair of purse strings, and with them in troth many a bout have I had in my time in troth. Oh, what a simple oath was this to confirm a man's credit withal ! Why, I see the halter will make a man holy, for whilst God suffered me to flourish, I scorned to disgrace my mouth with so small an oath as *In faith* ; but I rent God in pieces, swearing and forswearing by every part of his body, that such as heard me rather trembled at mine oaths, than feared my braves, and yet for courage and resolution I refer myself to all them that have ever heard of my name.

Thus animated to do wickedness, I fell to take delight in the company of harlots, amongst whom, as I spent what I got, so I suffered not them I was acquainted withal to feather their nests, but would at my pleasure strip them of all that they had. What bad woman was there about London, whose champion I would not be for a few crowns, to fight, swear, and stare in her behalf, to the abuse of any that should do justice upon her ! I still had one or two in store to crossbite withal, which I used as snares to trap simple men in. For if I took but one suspiciously in her company, straight I versed upon him, and crossbit him for all the money in his purse. By the way, sith sorrow cannot help to save me, let me tell you a merry jest how once I crossbit a maltman, that would needs be so wanton, as when he had shut his malt to have a wench, and thus the jest fell out.

A pleasant tale how Ned Browne crossbit a maltman.

This *senex fornicator*, this old lecher, using continually into White-chapel, had a haunt into Petticoat Lane to a trugging-house there, and fell into great familiarity with a good wench that was a friend of mine, who one day revealed unto me how she was well thought on by a malt-man, a wealthy old churl, and that ordinarily twice a week he did visit her, and therefore bade me plot some means to fetch him over for some crowns. I was not to seek for a quick invention, and resolved at his coming to crossbite him, which was, as luck served, the next day. Monsieur the maltman, coming according to his custom, was no sooner secretly shut in the chamber with the wench, but I came stepping in with a terrible look, swearing as if I meant to have challenged the earth to have opened and swallowed me quick, and presently fell upon her and beat her. Then I turned to the maltman, and lent him a blow or two, for he would take no more. He was a stout stiff old tough churl, and then I railed upon them both, and objected to him how long he had kept my wife, how my neighbours could tell me of it, how the Lane thought ill of me for suffering it, and now that I had myself taken them together, I would make both him and her smart for it before we parted.

The old fox that knew the ox by the horn, was subtle enough to spy a pad in the straw, and to see that we went about to crossbite him, wherefore he stood stiff, and denied all, and although the whore cunningly on her knees weeping did confess it, yet the maltman faced her down, and said she was an honest woman for all him, and that this was but a cozenage compacted between her and me to verse and crossbite him for some piece of money for amends, but, sith he knew himself clear, he would never grant to pay one penny.

I was straight in mine oaths, and braved him with sending for the constable, but in vain. All our policies could not draw one cross from this crafty old carl, till I, gathering my wits together, came over his fallows thus. I kept him still in the chamber, and sent, as though I had sent for the constable, for a friend of mine, an ancient cozener, and one that had a long time been a knight of the post. Marry, he had a fair cloak and a damask coat, that served him to bail men withal. To this perjured companion I sent to come as a constable, to make the maltman stoop, who, ready to execute any villainy that I should plot, came speedily like an ancient wealthy citizen, and, taking the office of a constable in hand, began very sternly to examine the matter, and to deal indifferently, rather favouring the maltman than me. But I complained how long he had kept my wife. He answered, I lied, and that it was a cozenage to crossbite him of his money. Mas. Constable cunningly made this reply to us both :

" My friends, this matter is bad, and truly I cannot in conscience but look into it. For you, Browne, you complain how he hath abused your wife a long time, and she partly confesseth as much. He, who seems to be an honest man, and of some countenance amongst his neighbours, forswears it, and saith it is but a device to strip him of his money. I know not whom to believe, and therefore this is my best course because the one of you shall not laugh the other to scorn. I'll send you all three to the Counter, so to answer it before some justice that may take examination of the matter."

The maltman, loath to go to prison, and yet unwilling to part from any pence, said he was willing to answer the matter before any man of worship, but he desired the constable to favour him that he might not go to ward, and he would send for a brewer a friend of his to be his bail.

" In faith," says this cunning old cozener, " you offer like an honest man, but I cannot stay so long till he be sent for, but if you mean, as you protest, to answer the matter, then leave some pawn, and I will let you go whither you will while tomorrow, and then come to my house here hard by at a grocer's shop, and you and I will go before a justice, and then clear yourself as you may." The maltman, taking this crafty knave to be some substantial citizen, thanked him for his friendship and gave him a seal-ring that he wore on his forefinger, promising the next morning to meet him at his house.

As soon as my friend had the ring, away walks he, and while we stood brabbling together, he went to the brewer's house with whom this maltman traded and delivered the brewer the ring as a token from the maltman, saying he was in trouble, and that he desired him by that token to send him ten pound. The brewer, seeing an ancient citizen bringing the message, and knowing the maltman's ring, stood upon no terms, sith he knew his chapman would and was able to answer it again if it were a brace of hundred pounds, delivered him the money without any more ado ; which ten pound at night we shared betwixt us, and left the maltman to talk with the brewer about the repayment. Tush, this was one of my ordinary shifts, for I was holden in my time the most famous crossbiter in all London.

Well, at length as wedding and hanging comes by destiny, I would, to avoid the speech of the world, be married forsooth, and keep a house. But, Gentlemen, I hope you that hear me talk of marriage, do presently imagine that sure she was some virtuous matron that I chose out. Shall I say, my conscience, she was a little snout-fair, but the commonest harlot and hackster that ever made fray under the shadow of Coleman Hedge.[3] Wedded to this trull, what villainy could I devise but she would put in practice, and yet, though she could foist a pocket well, and get me some pence, and lift now and then for a need, and with the lightness of her heels bring me in some crowns, yet I waxed weary, and stuck to the old proverb, that change of pasture makes fat calves. I thought that in living with me two years she lived a year too long, and therefore, casting mine eye on a pretty wench, a man's wife well known about London, I fell in love with her, and that so deeply that I broke the matter to her husband, that I loved his wife, and must needs have her, and confirmed it with many oaths, that if he did not consent to it, I would be his death. Whereupon her husband, a kind knave, and one every way as base a companion as myself, agreed to me, and we bet a bargain, that I should have his wife, and he should have mine, conditionally that I should give him five pounds to boot, which I promised, though he never had it. So we, like two good horse-coursers, made a chop and change, and swapped up a roguish bargain, and so he married my wife and I his. Thus, Gentlemen, did I neither fear God nor His laws, nor regarded honesty, manhood, or conscience.

But these be trifles and venial sins. Now, sir, let me boast of myself a little, in that I came to the credit of a high lawyer, and with my sword freebooted abroad in the country like a cavalier on horse-back, wherein

I did excel for subtlety. For I had first for myself an artificial hair, and a beard so naturally made, that I could talk, dine, and sup in it, and yet it should never be spied. I will tell you there rests no greater villainy than in this practice, for I have robbed a man in the morning, and come to the same inn and baited, yea, and dined with him the same day ; and for my horse that he might not be known I could ride him one part of the day like a goodly gelding with a large tail hanging to his fetlocks, and the other part of the day I could make him a cut, for I had an artificial tail so cunningly counterfeited, that the ostler when he dressed him could not perceive it. By these policies I little cared for hues and cries, but straight with disguising myself would outslip them all, and as for my cloak, it was tarmosind, as they do term it, made with two outsides that I could turn it how I list, for howsoever I wore it the right side still seemed to be outward. I remember how prettily once I served a priest, and because one death dischargeth all, and is as good as a general pardon, hear how I served him.

A merry tale how Ned Browne used a priest.

I chanced as I rode into Berkshire to light in the company of a fat priest that had hanging at his saddle-bow a cap-case well stuffed with crowns that he went to pay for the purchase of some lands. Falling in talk with him, as communication will grow betwixt travellers, I behaved myself so demurely that he took me for a very honest man, and was glad of my company, although ere we parted it cost him very dear. And amongst other chat he questioned me if I would sell my horse— for he was a fair large gelding well spread and foreheaded, and so easily and swiftly paced, that I could well ride him seven mile an hour. I made him answer that I was loath to part from my gelding, and so shaped him a slight reply, but before we came at our bait he was so in love with him that I might say him no nay, so that when we came at our inn and were at dinner together we swapped a bargain. I had the priest's, and twenty nobles to boot, for mine.

Well, as soon as we had changed I got me into the stable, and there secretly I knit a hair about the horse fetlock so straight upon the vein that he began a little to check of that foot, so that when he was brought forth the horse began to halt ; which the priest espying, marvelled at it, and began to accuse me that I had deceived him.

" Well," quoth I, " 'Tis nothing but a blood, and as soon as he is warm he will go well, and if in riding you like him not, for twenty shillings loss, I'll change with you at night."

The priest was glad of this, and caused his saddle to be set on my gelding, and so, having his cap-case on the saddle pommel, rode on his way, and I with him. But still his horse halted, and by that time we were two miles out of the town he halted right down. At which the priest chafed, and I said I wondered at it, and thought he was pricked, bade him alight, and I would see what he ailed, and wished him to get up of my horse that I had of him for a mile or two, and I would ride of his, to try if I could drive him from his halt. The priest thanked me, and was sorrowful, and I, feeling about his foot cracked the hair asunder, and when I had done, got up on him, smiling to myself to see the cap-case hang so mannerly before me, and, putting spurs to the horse, made him give way a little, but being somewhat stiff, he halted for half a mile, and then began to fall into his old pace, which the priest spying, said : " Methinks my gelding begins to leave his halting."

" Ay, marry, doth he Master Parson," quoth I, " I warrant you he'll gallop too fast for you to overtake. And so, good priest, farewell, and take no thought for the carriage of your cap-case."

With that I put spurs to him lustily, and away flung I like the wind. The parson called to me, and said he hoped that I was but in jest, but he found it in earnest, for he never had his horse nor his cap-case after.

Gentlemen, this is but a jest to a number of villainies that I have acted, so graceless hath my life been. The most expert and skilful alchemist never took more pains in experience of his metals, the physician in his simples, the mechanical man in the mystery of his occupation, than I have done in plotting precepts, rules, axioms and principles, how smoothly and neatly to foist a pocket, or nip a bung.

It were too tedious to hold you with tales of the wonders I have acted, seeing almost they be numberless, or to make report how desperately I did execute them, either without fear of God, dread of the law, or love to my country. For I was so resolutely, or rather reprobately given, that I held death only as nature's due, and howsoever ignominiously it might happen unto me, that I little regarded. Which careless disdain to die, made me thrust myself into every brawl, quarrel and other bad action whatsoever, running headlong into all mischief, neither respecting the end, nor foreseeing the danger, and that secure life hath brought me to this dishonourable death.

But what should I stand here preaching? I lived wantonly, and therefore let me end merrily, and tell you two or three of my mad pranks and so bid you farewell. Amongst the rest I remember once walking up and down Smithfield, very quaintly attired in a fustian doublet and buff hose, both laid down with gold lace, a silk stock and a new cloak. I traced up and down very solemnly, as having never a cross to bless me withal, where being in my dumps there happened to me this accident following.

A pleasant tale how Ned Browne kissed a gentlewoman and cut her purse.

Thus, Gentlemen, being in my dumps, I saw a brave country gentlewoman coming along from St. Bartholomew's in a satin gown, and four men attending upon her. By her side she had hanging a marvellous rich purse embroidered, and not so fair without but it seemed to be as well lined within. At this my teeth watered, and, as the prey makes the thief, so necessity and the sight of such a fair purse began to muster a thousand inventions in my head how to come by it. To go by her and nip it I could not, because she had so many men attending on her: to watch her into a press, that was in vain, for, going towards St. John's Street, I guessed her about to take horse to ride home, because all her men were booted. Thus perplexed for this purse, and yet not so much for the bung as the shells, I at last resolutely vowed in myself to have it, though I stretched a halter for it. And so, casting in my head how to bring my fine mistress to the blow, at last I performed it thus. She standing and talking a while with a gentleman, I stepped before her and leaned at the bar till I saw her leave him, and then stalking towards her very stoutly as if I had been some young cavalier or captain, I met her, and courteously saluted her, and not only greeted her, but, as if I had been acquainted with her, I gave her a kiss, and so in taking acquaintance closing very familiarly to her I cut her purse. The gentlewoman seeing me so brave, used me kindly, and blushing said, she knew me not. " Are you not, mistress," quoth I, " such a gentlewoman, and such a man's wife ? "—" No truly sir," quoth she, " you mistake me."—" Then I cry you mercy," quoth I, " and am sorry that I was so saucily bold."— " There is no harm done, sir," said she, " because there is no offence taken." And so we parted, I with a good bung, and my gentlewoman with a kiss, which I dare safely swear, she bought as dear as ever she did thing in her life, for what I found in the purse that I keep to myself.

L

Thus did I plot devices in my head how to profit myself, though it were to the utter undoing of any one. I was the first that invented the letting fall of the key, which had like to cost me dear, but it is all one, as good then as now. And thus it was.

How Ned Browne let fall a key.

Walking up and down Paul's, I saw where a nobleman's brother in England came with certain gentlemen his friends in at the west door, and how he put up his purse, as having bought some thing in the Churchyard. I, having an eagle's eye, spied a good bung containing many shells as I guessed, carelessly put up into his sleeve, which drave me straight into a mutiny with myself how to come by it. I looked about me if I could see any of my fellow friends walking there, and straight I found out three or four trusty foists with whom I talked and conferred about this purse. We all concluded it was necessary to have it, so we could plot a means how to catch it. At last I set down the course thus : As soon as the throng grew great, and that there was jostling in Paul's for room, I stepped before the gentleman and let fall a key, which stooping to take up, I stayed the gentleman that he was fain to thrust by me, while in the press two of my friends foisted his purse, and away they went withal, and in it there was some twenty pound in gold. Presently, putting his hand in his pocket for his handkercher, he missed his purse, and suspected that he that let fall the key had it ; but suppositions are vain, and so was his thinking, seeing he knew me not, for till this day he never set eye of his purse.

There are a number of my companions yet living in England, who, being men for all companies, will by once conversing with a man, so draw him to them, that he shall think nothing in the world too dear for them, and never be able to part from them, until he hath spent all he hath.

If he be lasciviously addicted, they have Aretine's tables[4] at their fingers' ends, to feed him on with new kind of filthiness ; they will come in with Rous, the French painter, and what an usual vein in bawdry he had ! Not a whore or quean about the town but they know, and can tell you her marks, and where and with whom she hosts.

If they see you covetously bent, they will tell you wonders of the philosophers' stone, and make you believe they can make gold of goose-grease ; only you must be at some two or three hundred pounds' cost, or such trifling matter, to help to set up their stills, and then you need not care where you beg your bread, for they will make you do little better if you follow their prescriptions.

Discourse with them of countries, they will set you on fire with travelling.   Yea, what place is it they will not swear they have been in, and, I warrant you, tell such a sound tale, as if it were all Gospel they spake.   Not a corner in France but they can describe.   Venice?   Why it is nothing; for they have intelligence from it every hour, and at every word will come in with *Strado Curtizano*, and tell you such miracles of Madame Padilia and Romana Imperia,[5] that you will be mad till you be out of England.   And if he see you are caught with that bait, he will make as though he would leave you, and feign business about the Court, or that such a nobleman sent for him, when you will rather consent to rob all your friends, than be severed from him one hour. If you request his company to travel, he will say :

" In faith, I cannot tell.   I would sooner spend my life in your company than in any man's in England, but at this time I am not so provided of money as I would.   Therefore I can make you no promise. And if a man should adventure upon such a journey without money, it were miserable and base, and no man will care for us."

" Tut, money? " say you, like a liberal young master.   " Take no care for that, for I have so much land, and I will sell it.   My credit is so much, and I will use it.   I have the keeping of a cousin's chamber of mine, which is an old counsellor, and he this vacation time is gone down into the country.   We will break up his study, rifle his chests, dive into the bottom of his bags, but we will have to serve our turn. Rather than fail, we will sell his books, pawn his bedding and hangings, and make riddance of all his household stuff to set us packing."

To this he listens a little, and says : " These are some hopes yet." But if he should go with you, and you have money and he none, you will domineer over him at your pleasure, and then he were well set up to leave such possibilities in England, and be made a slave in another country !   With that you offer to part halves with him, or put all you have into his custody, before he should think you meant otherwise than well with him.   He takes you at your offer, and promiseth to husband it so for you, that you shall spend with the best and yet not waste so much as you do.   Which makes you (meaning simply) put him in trust and give him the purse.   Then all a boon voyage into the Low Countries you trudge, so to travel up into Italy, but *per varios casus et*[6] *tot discrimina rerum*, in a town of garrison he leaves you, runs away with your money, and makes you glad to betake yourself to provant, and to be a gentleman of a company. If he fear you will make after him, he will change his name, and if there be any better gentleman than other in the country where he sojourns, his name he will borrow, and creep into his kindred, or it shall cost him a fall, and make him pay sweetly for it in the end, if he take not the better heed. Thus will he be sure to have one ass or other afoot on whom he may prey, and ever to have new inventions to keep himself in pleasing.

There is no art but he will have a superficial sight into, and put down every man with talk, and, when he hath uttered the most he can, makes men believe that he knows ten times more than he will put into their heads, which are secrets not to be made common to every one.

He will persuade you he hath twenty receipts of love powders ; that he can frame a ring with such a quaint device, that if a wench put it on her finger, she shall not choose but follow you up and down the streets.

If you have an enemy that you would fain be rid of, he'll teach you to poison him with your very looks ; to stand on the top of Paul's with a burning-glass in your hand, and cast the sun with such a force on a man's face that walks under, that it shall strike him stark dead more violently than lightning ; to fill a letter full of needles, which shall be laid after such a mathematical order, that when he opens it to whom it is sent, they shall all spring up and fly into his body as forcibly as if they had been blown up with gunpowder, or sent from a caliver's mouth like small shot.

To conclude, he will have such probable reasons to procure belief to his lies, such a smooth tongue to deliver them, and set them forth with such a grace, that a very wise man he should be that did not swallow the gudgeon at his hands.

In this sort have I known sundry young gentlemen of England trained forth to their own destruction, which makes me the more willing to forewarn other of such base companions.

Wherefore, for the rooting out of these sly insinuating mothworms, that eat men out of their substance unseen, and are the decay of the forwardest gentlemen and best wits, it were to be wished that Amasis' law were revived, who ordained that every man at the year's end should give account to the magistrate how he lived, and he that did not so, or could not make an account of an honest life, to be put to death as a felon without favour or pardon.[7]

Ye have about London, that, to the disgrace of gentlemen, live gentlemen-like of themselves, having neither money nor land, nor any lawful means to maintain them ; some by play, and they go a mumming into the country all Christmas time with false dice, or, if there be any place where gentlemen or merchants frequent in the city or town corporate, thither will they, either disguised like young merchants or substantial citizens, and draw them all dry that ever deal with them.

There are some do nothing but walk up and down Paul's, or come to men's shops to buy wares, with budgets of writings under their arms, and these will talk with any man about their suits in law, and discourse unto them how these and these men's bonds they have for money, that are the chiefest dealers in London, Norwich, Bristol and suchlike places, and complain that they cannot get one penny. " Why, if such a man doth owe it you," will some man say that knows him, " I durst buy the debt of you, let me get it of him as I can."—" Oh," saith my budget-man, " I have his hand and seal to show. Look here else." And with that plucks out a counterfeit bond, as all his other writings are, and reads it to him. Whereupon, for half in half they presently compound, and after he hath that ten pound paid him for his bond of twenty, besides the forfeiture, or so forth. He says, " Faith, these lawyers drink me as dry as a sieve, and I have money to pay at such a day, and I doubt I shall not be able to compass it. Here are all the leases and evidences of my land lying in such a shire. Could you lend me forty pound on them till the next term, or for some six months, and it shall then be repaid with interest, or I'll forfeit my whole inheritance, which is better worth than a hundred marks a year."

The wealthy gentleman, or young novice, that hath store of crowns lying by him, greedy of such a bargain, thinking, perhaps, by one clause or other to defeat him of all he hath, lends him money, and takes a fair statute merchant of his lands before a judge.[8] But when all comes to all, he hath no more land in England than a younger brother's inheritance, nor doth any such great occupier as he feigneth know him, much less owe him any money ; whereby my covetous master is cheated forty or fifty pound thick at one clap.

Not unlike to these are they that, coming to ordinaries about the Exchange, where merchants do table for the most part, will say they have two or three ships of coals new come from Newcastle, and wish they could light on a good chapman, that would deal for them altogether. " What's your price ? " saith one. " What's your price ? " saith another. He holds them at the first at a very high rate, and sets a good face on it, as though he had such traffic indeed, but afterward comes down so low, that every man strives who shall give him earnest first, and ere he be aware, he hath forty shillings clapped in his hand, to assure the bargain to some one of them. He puts it up quietly, and bids them enquire for him at such a sign and place, where he never came, signifying also his name, when in troth he is but a cozening companion, and no such man to be found. Thus goes he clear away with forty shillings in his purse for nothing, and they unlike to see him any more.

A merry jest how Ned Browne's wife was crossbitten in her own art.

But here note, gentlemen, though I have done many sleights, and crossbitten sundry persons, yet so long goes the pitcher to the water, that at length it comes broken home. Which proverb I have seen verified. For I remember once that I, supposing to crossbite a gentleman who had some ten pound in his sleeve, left my wife to perform the accident, who in the end was crossbitten herself. And thus it fell out. She compacted with a hooker, whom some call a curber, and having before bargained with the gentleman to tell her tales in her ear all night, he came according to promise, who, having supped and going to bed, was advised by my wife to lay his clothes in the window, where the hooker's crome might crossbite them from him, yet secretly intending before in the night-time to steal his money forth of his sleeve. They, being in bed together, slept soundly; yet such was his chance, that he suddenly wakened long before her, and, being sore troubled with a lask, rose up and made a double use of his chamber-pot. That done, he intended to throw it forth at the window, which the better to perform, he first removed his clothes from thence; at which instant the spring of the window rose up of the own accord. This suddenly amazed him so, that he leapt back, leaving the chamber-pot still standing in the window, fearing that the Devil had been at hand. By and by he espied a fair iron crome come marching in at the window, which, instead of the doublet and hose he sought for, suddenly took hold of that homely service in the member vessel, and so plucked goodman jordan with all his contents down pat on the curber's pate. Never was gentle angler so dressed, for his face, his head, and his neck were all besmeared with the soft Sir Reverence, so as he stunk worse than a jakes-farmer. The gentleman, hearing one cry out, and seeing his mess of altogether so strangely taken away, began to take heart to him, and looking out perceived the curber lie almost brained, almost drowned, and well near poisoned therewith; whereat, laughing heartily to himself, he put on his own clothes, and got him secretly away, laying my wife's clothes in the same place, which the gentle angler soon after took.   But never could she get them again till this day.

This, Gentlemen, was my course of life, and thus I got much by villainy, and spent it amongst whores as carelessly.   I seldom or never listened to the admonition of my friends, neither did the fall of other men learn me to beware, and therefore am I brought now to this end. Yet little did I think to have laid my bones in France.   I thought, indeed, that Tyburn would at last have shaked me by the neck.   But having done villainy in England, this was always my course, to slip over into the Low Countries, and there for a while play the soldier, and partly that was the cause of my coming hither.   For, growing odious in and about London, for my filching, lifting, nipping, foisting and crossbiting, that everyone held me in contempt and almost disdained my company, I resolved to come over into France, by bearing arms to win some credit, determining with myself to become a true man. But as men, though they change countries, alter not their minds, so, given over by God into a reprobate sense, I had no feeling of goodness, but with the dog fell to my old vomit, and here most wickedly I have committed sacrilege, robbed a church, and done other mischievous pranks, for which justly I am condemned and must suffer death : whereby I learn that revenge deferred is not quittanced ; that though God suffer the wicked for a time, yet He pays home at length.   For while I lasciviously led a careless life, if my friends warned me of it, I scoffed at them, and if they told me of the gallows, I would swear it was my destiny, and now I have proved myself no liar : yet must I die more basely, and be hanged out at a window.

O countrymen and Gentlemen, I have held you long, as good at the first as at the last.   Take then this for a farewell : Trust not in your own wits, for they will become too wilful oft, and so deceive you.   Boast not in strength, nor stand not on your manhood, so to maintain quarrels ; for the end of brawling is confusion.   But use your courage in defence of your country, and then fear not to die ; for the bullet is an honourable death. Beware of whores, for they be the sirens that draw men on to destruction ; their sweet words are enchantments, their eyes allure, and their beauties bewitch.   Oh, take heed of their persuasions, for they be crocodiles, that when they weep, destroy.   Truth is honourable, and better is it to be a poor honest man, than a rich and wealthy thief.   For the fairest end is the gallows ; and what a shame is it to a man's friends, when he dies so basely !   Scorn not labour, Gentlemen, nor hold not any course of life bad or servile, that is profitable and honest, lest in giving yourselves over to idleness, and having no yearly maintenance, you fall into many prejudicial mischiefs. Contemn not the virtuous counsel of a friend, despise not the hearing of God's ministers, scoff not at the magistrates ; but fear God, honour your Prince, and love your country. Then God will bless you, as I hope He will do me, for all my manifold offences. And so, Lord, into thy hands I commit my spirit.——And with that he himself sprung out at the window and died.

Here, by the way, you shall understand, that, going over into France, he near unto Aix robbed a church, and was therefore condemned, and, having no gallows by, they hanged him out at a window, fastening the rope about the bar. And thus this Ned Browne died miserably, that all his life time had been full of mischief and villainy, slightly at his death regarding the state of his soul. But note a wonderful judgment of God showed upon him after his death. His body being taken down and buried without the town, it is verified that in the night-time there came a company of wolves, and tore him out of his grave, and ate him up, whereas there lay many soldiers buried and many dead carcases, that they might have preyed on to have filled their hungry paunches. But the judgments of God, as they are just, so they are inscrutable. Yet thus much we may conjecture, that as he was one that delighted in rapine and stealth in his life, so at his death the ravenous wolves devoured him, and plucked him out of his grave, as a man not worthy to be admitted to the honour of any burial. Thus have I set down the life and death of Ned Browne, a famous cutpurse and cony-catcher, by whose example, if any be profited, I have the desired end of my labour.

Finis.

THE BLACK DOG OF NEWGATE

both pithy and profitable for all readers

By LUKE HUTTON

[1596?]

TO THE HONOURABLE SIR JOHN POPHAM, KNIGHT, Lord Chief Justice of England[1] : all increase of honour and happiness.

TWO reasons, my honourable good Lord, me especially moved to dedicate this book to your Honour. The first, for I held it my duty, to certify you of the notable abuses daily committed by a great number of very bad fellows, who under the colour of office and service, do mightily abuse both justice and Justices ; which in this book is largely discovered. The next, for your Honour being thereof certified, such bad fellows shall be the sooner looked into, and their outrages qualified ; so that the sooner by you the like mischiefs may be prevented. What I have done, is in love and zeal ; both which I doubt not but they will excuse my boldness. And so the work be acceptable in your good opinion, I will not regard the malice of the threatening cony-catcher[s], who hath sworn, if I publish this book, they will do me what mischief they can.[2] But how little I regard their windy words, they may well perceive by my proceedings. If this work had been worth a talent, it should have been your Honour's: and being a poor man's mite, I desire it may be acceptable. And if hereafter I shall be better able, your Honour shall not fail but find me ready to do your Honour service, even to the uttermost of my power. Thus, assuring myself safe shielded with your favour, to whom I present this book, desiring you to take the full view of this Black Dog of Newgate,[3] I humbly and in all duty cease to be tedious ; praying to the Almighty to lengthen long your days, with increase of all virtue and honour, and after this life, to send you to everlasting happiness, and joys endless. *Amen.*

To do your Honour service whilst he liveth,

LUKE HUTTON.

To the Reader.

GENTLE readers, for my *Repentance* was so welcome, and so much the better because it was mine, in some part to satisfy your courtesies, I thought it my part to present you with thanks, and more, with my second labour ; which, albeit it be both my especial cost and travail, yet it is yours : and so I may say, for you are willing to pay the price of the *Black Dog of Newgate*. Marvel not, Gentlemen, that you pay so dear for a dog, indeed a cur. I wish you all well, and though three half-pence be a dog's price, yet if you, according to my poesy, accept my pen and paper, it will countervail the charge of sixpence. You have known me better if you ever knew me, and never worse if you now know me. But, for I have read some books of philosophy, I thought it best to be myself ; not as I was, for I hope you are otherwise persuaded, but as I am, and so to live or die. But for it is no better than the Black Dog of Newgate, I desire you not to think your time ill-bestowed in the reading, nor the price great which you gave for it. When you have perused it, if you like it not, say : the Dog came from Newgate ; hang him up ! and rend the paper in pieces ; and I will be your debtor a work of better acceptance. Yet let me give you to understand by the way that this Dog, and many dogs of his kind, have I known a great while, and if I had not had great occasion, I would never have bestowed so much time in deciphering a cur. Nay, more ! That you shall not think this Dog nor any of his kind to be as they have been, the murderers and utter undoing at the least of an infinite number, to be shadowed by the name of servant at Newgate, at this time I thought good faithfully to give you to understand, that he who was ever able to keep a good dog, and how[4] to make choice of his servants in Newgate, did in my sight thrust this Dog by the head and shoulders out of Newgate, making choice of men instead of dogs. And more I dare say : never shall a cur in shape of man commit the like abuses during his time in Newgate.[5] No more for the Dog of Newgate, but for this dog of mine with me still, well, I will never do you ill. So to your content, as I wish, I leave you and me to my better content when God will.

For ever fare you well !

LUKE HUTTON.

THE BLACK DOG OF NEWGATE:

Both pithy, pleasant, and profitable for all readers.

WHEN as black Titan with his dusky robe,
    Had Tellus clouded with his curtains' night,
Fair Phoebus, peering underneath earth's globe,
    With wingèd steeds hence takes his course aright,
Titan he leaves to bear imperial sway,
    Commanding night as Phoebus did the day.

The fiery chariot passeth underground;
    With Titan's mantle all the earth is spread,
And wreaths of jet about his temples bound.
    Earth's cell coal-black sweet Morpheus calls to bed:
No time to walk, to sport, to game, to see:
    I did obey that must commanded be.

Laid in my bed, I gan for to recount
    A thousand things which had been in my time;
My birth, my youth, my woes which all surmount
    My life, my loss, my liberty, my crime.
Then where I was unto my mind recalling,
    Methought earth gaped and I to hell was falling.

Amidst these fears that all my senses cumber,
    Care closed my eyes and sorrow wrung my heart:
Oppressed with grief mine eyelids gan to slumber;
    But born to woes must of more woes have part:
A thousand furies to my heart appearing,
    Their ugly shapes torments my soul with fearing.

Thus lay I long, beholding Hell and devils,
    Aghast with mazes, almost dead in fears;
Not knowing how to rid me from the evils
    They show in action, and in looks appears.
One antic monster, hideous, foul, and grim,
    Me most appalled, and most I looked at him.

Thought I: At last I will cry out for aid—
    Bouning to cry, near dead, affright with fear,
I heard a voice, which like an angel said,
    " Hutton, be bold; for thou shalt see and hear
Men devils, devils men, one both, both all deluding;
    World's evils wrack then, sheeps' cloth wolves' prey concluding."[6]

Hearing a voice my heart was much revived,
  Noting the words I did some courage take.
But sudden joys hath sudden woes achieved :
  A sudden noise this hellish crew did make,
Threatening by shows as though they would devour
  My life and soul, subdued by terror's power.

Thought checked my mind, fears, senses, all amazing,
  Hell broken loose, eye's visions, Furies affrighting,
Subdued earth's powers, uprears, heart's insight a gazing.
  Terror of mind with hope cries, fears faint arighting—
Help me o'erquelled. Waking with dread, I espied
  Graced gracious Minerva, who thus to my outcry replied :

" Fear not at all, nor faint thou with beholding,
  But light thy lamp and take thy pen in hand.
Write what thou sees[t], thy visions all unfolding :
  I will direct, and let thee understand
What all these hell-hounds shadow by appearing.
  View thou their worst, and then write of their fearing."

Subdued by worths which did all words exceed,
  Ravished with joys such feature to behold,
Abjecting fear, my glutted eyes I feed
  Upon her brightness, which all harms controlled.
Glimpse of her brightness senses all-endearing,
  Legions of devils could no more fright with fearing.

I preased myself to take the hardest steel,
  And from the flint I bett forth sparks of fire ;
Kindling the lint, my ready match I feel :
  Yielding my lamp the light of my desire
Soon spied Minerva, with laurel crowned and bays,
  Mirror divine, feature of worthless praise.

Before her feet submissively I fell,
  Pardon I craved, fearing I was too bold.
" Rise up," quoth she, " and view these hags of hell ;
  For divers secrets must thy pen unfold :
Make true record what shall be showed to thee,
  For these are they which world's deceivers be.

" I'll cleanse thine eyes, lest vapours do offend,
  I'll clear thy wits and give a pleasing muse ;
The deafest ear shall to thy talk attend :
  The work so worthy thou may not rebuke.
Newgate's black dog with pen and ink depaint :
  Curs of this kind shall thereby have restraint.

" Not for my sake do thou what I require,
  But for his sake,"—and with that word me shows
A fair old man, whose tears foretold desire,
  And in a mantle mourner-like he goes,
His veins like azure, his hair as white as wool,
  Tresses before, behind a bare smooth skull.

" And this is Time," Minerva thus replied,
  " Which mourns to see these hell-hounds, Time's abusing,
How thousands in their ravening jaws have died ;
  Slaughtering lambs, yet to the world excusing
Offence with colour, shadowing mighty evils
  By name of service : and yet incarnate devils.

" No more," quoth she, " but take thee to thy pen :
  Resolve the wise that they have been deceived.
Many black dogs have walked in shapes of men,
  And with deceits have commonwealth aggrieved :
His form and lineaments to the world disclose,
  That this black dog be known where'er he goes."

My muse gan blush, dreading to undertake
  So great a task. But Time again replied :
" Fear not at all ! Time doth the motion make.
  Unmask this beast : let him no longer hide
Himself in shrouds, who makes of sin a scoff.
  World's great'st admire whenas his vizard's off."

" Time," then said I, " fair Time, I will not use
  Longer delay, but satisfy thy will,
So Time will answer for my harmless muse,
  Who wanteth worth to nigh Parnassus' hill."
" Be brief," quoth Time. With that I took my pen,
  Obeying Time, without offence to men.

Then did I fix mine eye upon this beast
  Who did appear first in the shape of man,
Homely attired, of wonders not the least.
  A broom-man's song to sing this dog began,
From street to street trudgeth along this groom
  As if he would serve all the world with broom.

But in a trice he did transform his shape,
  Which broke a treble horror to my heart.
A Cerberus, nay, worse, he thrice at wide did gape,
  His ears all snakes, curling, they will not part ;
Coal-black his hue, like torches glow his eyes,
  His breath doth poison, smoke from his nostrils flies.

His countenance ghastly, fearful, grim, and pale,
  His foamy mouth still gapeth for his prey ;
With tiger's teeth he spares none to assail,
  His lips hell-gates, o'erpainted with decay,
His tongue the clapper, sounding woeful knell,
  Tolling poor men to ring a peal in hell.

Like sepulchre his throat is hollow made,
  Devouring all whom danger makes a prey,
Bribery his hand, spoil of the poor his trade,
  His fingers talons, seizing to betray ;
And with his arms he foldeth men in woes :
  Destruction still the path where'er he goes.

Methought his breast was all of burning brass
 Through which there grew a heart of hardest steel;
His belly huge like scalding furnace was,
 His thighs both like unto a fiery wheel,
His legs were long, one foot like to a hind,
 The other foot a hound's of bloody kind.

And in this shape I saw the monster walk
 About the streets, most fearful to behold.
But more to tell since I began to talk:
 Here is the tale which Time would fain have told.
Upon a sudden rushed this cur on me,
 As though my life his evening prey should be.

Within his clutches did he sieze me fast,
 And bear me straight into black Pluto's cell.
When there I came, he me in Limbo cast,
 A Stygian lake, the dungeon of deep hell.
But first my legs he lock'd in iron bolt
 As if poor I had been some wanton colt.

And then began with basest terms to braid,
 And then he threats as though he would me kill,
And then he dances for he me betrayed,
 And then speaks fair as though he meant no ill;
Then like Medusa doth he shake his locks,
 And then he threatens me with iron stocks.

At last he left me in that irksome den,
 Where was no day, for there was ever night.
" Woe's me," thought I, " the abject of all men,
 Clouded in care, quite banished from light;
Robbed of the sky, the stars, the day, the sun:
 This dog, this devil hath all my joys undone."

Surpressed with anguish, sorrow, grief and woe,
 Methought I heard a noise of iron chains,
Which din did torment and affright me so,
 That all my senses studied what it means.
But by and by, which did me comfort more,
 There came a man which opened Limbo's door.

All lean he was, and feeble too, God knows:
 Upon his arm he bear a bunch of keys.
With candlelight about the cell he goes,
 Who roughly said, " Sir, lie you at your ease? "
Swearing an oath that I did lie too soft,
 Who lay on ground, and thus he at me scoffed.

To see a man of feature, form and shape,
 · It did me good, and partly fears exiled;
But when I heard him gibe me like an ape,
 Then did I think that I was thrice beguiled.
Yet would I venture to this man to speak:
 Into discourses thus I gan to break:

" Ay me ! poor wretch ! that knows not where I am,
    Nor for what cause I am brought to this place ;
Bound for the slaughter, lying like a lamb,
    The butchers mean to kill within a space :
My griefs are more than can my tougue express.
    Ay me ! woe's me, that can find no redress !

" Yet, if thou be as thou dost seem, a man—
    And so thou art, if I do not mistake—
Do not increase, if so release thou can,
    The cruel tortures which me woeful make ;
And tell me first who thou thyself may'st be,
    That art a man, and yet dost gibe at me."

Seeing the fears which did my heart possess,
    Viewing the tears that trickled from mine eyes,
He answered thus : " A man, I must confess,
    I am myself, that here condemnèd lies,
And by the law adjudged I am to die.
    But now the keeper of these keys am I.

" This house is Newgate," gently he replied ;
    " And this place, Limbo, wherein now thou art.
Until thou pay a fine here must you bide,
    With all these bolts which do aggrieve thy heart.
No other place may here provided be,
    Till thou content the keeper with a fee."

With that he turned as though he would away.
    " Sweet, bide awhile," I did him so entreat.
Quoth he, " My friend, I can no longer stay.
    Yet what you want, if you will drink or eat,
Or have a fire, or candle by you burn,
    Say what you need, and I will serve your turn."

Quoth I, " Dear friend, then help me to a fire,
    Let me have candle for to give me light ;
Nor meat nor drink do I wish or desire,
    But only grant me gracious in thy sight,
And say what monster was it placed me here
    Who hath me almost lifeless made with fear."

" Nay peace," quoth he, " for there begins a tale,
    Rest now content and time will tell thee more ;
To strive in fetters it will small avail :
    Seek first to ease thy legs, which will grow sore.
When bolts are off, we will that matter handle."
    So he departed, leaving me a candle.

Away he went, and leaves me to my woes,
    And being gone I could not choose but think
That he was kind, though first unkind in shows,
    Who offered me both fire, bread and drink,
Leaving a candle by me for to burn :
    It eased my grief and left me less to mourn.

Joying to see, who whilom had no sight,
   I reached the candle which by burning ſtands,
But I, unworthy comfort of the light,
   A rat doth rob the candle from my hands ;
And then a hundred rats all sally forth
   As if they would convoy their prize of worth.

In vain I ſtrive to reobtain what's loſt ;
   My woes are now as woes at firſt began ;
With change of griefs my perplexed soul is tossed ;
   To see the end, I did bethink me then
How Time had promised secrets to disclose.
   So I expeĉt the worſt of hellish foes.

Whilſt thus I lay in irons underground,
   I heard a man that beggèd for release,
And in a chain of iron was he bound,
   Whose clattering noise filled full my heart with grief,
Begging one penny to buy a hundred bread,
   Hungered and ſtarved, for want of food nigh dead.

" Woe's me," thought I, " for thee so bound in chains !
   Woe's me for them thou begs for to suſtain !
Woe's me for all whose want all woes contains !
   Woe's me for me that in your woes complain !
Woe's me ! woe's you ! and woe is to us all !
   Woe to that dog made me to woe a thrall ! "

Whilſt thus I languish, I on sudden hear
   An uncouth noise which did approach my den.
Liſtening, unto the door I laid mine ear,
   And then I knew the voices were of men.
Still in nearness drew they more and more :
   At laſt I heard them opening Limbo's door.

In firſt there came the man that gave me light,
   And next the dog who brought me to that place ;
Another with a club appeared in sight
   Three weaponless, as though they moaned my case.
Fainting for fear I knew not what to say,
   Expeĉting then performance of decay.

But now this dog is in another shape,
   In every point proportioned as a man.
My heart did throb not knowing how to 'scape ;
   But to entreat this cur I thus began :
" Fair friend," quoth I, " if so thy will may be
   To ease my grief, I'll give thee any fee."

With that he grinned, and thus he made reply :
   " Thou art a villain worthy of this place.
Thy fault is such that thou shalt surely die.
   I will not pity thee in any case :
Such as thou art too many everywhere,
   But I will seek in time to have them here."

When he named *time*, then I on Time did think.
    But more he says : " If thou have any coin
To pay for ease, I will a little wink,
    And bolts' releasement with discharge I'll join
Of this close prison to some other ward,
    Paying thy fine, or else release is hard."

Like as the child doth kiss the rod for fear,
    Nor yet dare whimper though it have been beat,
So with smooth looks this dog approach I near.
    Before the Devil a candle do I set,
Treating him fair with fairest words maybe,
    Bidding him ask, he shall have gold of me.

" Why then," quoth he, " thy speeches please me well—
    Partners," quoth he, " strike off his irons all."
Then up we went as one should clime from hell,
    Until I came into a loathsome hall.
When there I came, they set me on a block :
    With punch and hammer my irons off they knock.

No marvel though, whilst they my legs untied,
    Mine eyes did surfeit, drunk with woes beholding.
Bolts, shackles, collars, and iron shears I spied,
    Thumb-stalls, waist-bands, torture's grief unfolding.
But whilst the ease of legs my sorrows calms,
    " Room," quoth a wretch, " for me with widow's alms ! "

" Take off these curtals," did another cry ;
    And on his knees he fell before this cur.
Who to his sorrowing made a dog's reply :
    " Down to thy ward, and do not make this stir !
What now I know, if I had known before,
    Instead of these light chains thou shouldst have more."

With that the poor man was thrust out of sight,
    And I, all-fearing, feared with fear of fears.
My irons off I went, as go I might,
    Unto this dog in whom all devils appears.
With golden angel I this cur presented.
    Saith he, " One more, else am I not contented."

Wonder it was to see a fiend of hell
    To thirst for angels of the fairest hue,
But devils are devils, and they would all o'erquell.
    Man's life and soul this dog seeks to subdue.
His mouth to stop, angels I gave him two,
    Yielding perforce as I perforce must do.

And then he left me in the partners' hall :
    The grate doth open and this dog out goes.
Thousand sorrows hold my heart in thrall ;
    Yet there I am not by myself in woes.
Hereon, o'erplunged with deep heart's grief-cries,
    I live a life thrice worse than he that dies.

Another sorry soul without a rag,
　　Hurkling for cold, in whom all want appears,
At laſt gan speak as if he meant to brag,
　　And thus he says: " Here have I been nine years.
Tell you of woes, when you my woes have seen,
　　And yet have many men more woeful been."

With that I rose and to this poor man went,
　　In hope to learn some novels by his talk.
Approaching him amidſt his discontent,
　　He asked me if so I pleased to walk.
" And if you will, then follow up these ſtairs,
　　To walk and talk deceiveth time of cares."

I followed him as he that in a wood
　　Hath loſt himself, and knows no way he takes.
And in diſtress I thought conferring good:
　　New woes with old juſt mixture consort makes.
And though the place do nought but discord sound,
　　My soul for his our discords concord found.

At firſt he gently took me by the hand,
　　And bids me welcome as I were his gueſt.
" You are a prisoner, I do understand.
　　And hither welcome are both bad and best.
Men of all sorts come for offending hither,
　　And being here, here bide they altogether."

And then he did begin thus to discourse:
　　" Cease to lament with vain-displaying tears.
Thyself dissolved to mopes gains no remorse:
　　Here none regards, though all thy mournings hears.
If under earth the devils can prove a hell,
　　Theirs is not like to this, where wretches dwell.

" See.　In yon hall are divers sorts of men.
　　Some weep, some wail, some mourn, some wring their hands,
Some curse, some swear, and some blaspheming."　Then
　　My heart did faint, my head-hair upright ſtands.
" O Lord," thought I, " this house will rend in sunder.
　　Or else there can be no hell this hell under."

Thus wondering, I on sudden did espy
　　One all in black came ſtumbling up the ſtairs.
" Who's yon ? " I asked.　And thus he made reply:
　　" Yon is the man doth mitigate our cares.
He preacheth Chriſt, and doth God's word deliver
　　To all diſtressed, to comfort men for ever."

Then drew I near to see what might betide,
　　Or what the sequel was of that I saw,
Expecting good would follow such a guide,
　　As preachèd Chriſt and taught a God to know.
A hundred cluſtered nighing the pulpit near
　　As if they longed the gospel for to hear.

" What's this," quoth I, " that now I do behold ?
    The hags of hell and Satan's impious limbs !
Some deeper secret doth this sight unfold,
    Than I can guess. This sight my senses dims."
Straight of my friend I askèd by and by
    What it might be ; who made me this reply :

" Yon men which thou beholds so pale and wan,
    Who whiles look up, and whiles look down again,
Are all condemned, and they must die each man.
    Judgment is given that cord shall stop their breath
For heinous facts—as murder, theft and treason.
    Unworthy life ! To die law thought it reason."

The sermon ended, the men condemned to die,
    Taking their leaves of their acquainted friends,
With sorry looks, pacing their steps, they ply
    Down to a hall where for them there attends
A man of office who, to daunt life's hopes,
    Doth cord their hands and scarf their necks with ropes.

Thus roped and corded, they descend the stairs :
    Newgate's black dog bestirs to play his part,
And does not cease for to augment their cares,
    Willing the carman to set near his cart.
Which done, these men, with fear of death o'erhanging,
    Bound to the cart are carried to be hanged.

This rueful sight, yet end to their doomed sorrows,
    Makes me aghast and forces me bethink.
Woe unto woe ! And so from woeful'st borrows
    A swame of grief. And then I sounding sink.
But by Time's aid I did revive again.
    Might I have died it would be lesser pain !

For now again the dog afresh assaults me,
    As if my spoil were next to be enacted ;
And like a subtle cur in speeches halts he
    With thousand sleighty wiles, old shifts compacted,
Charging me oft with that I never did :
    In his smooth'st looks are cruel bitings hid.

I spake him fair, as if I had offended.
    He treats me foul, who never did him ill.
He plays the gripe one Tityus intended
    To tire his heart, yet never hath his fill.
Even so this dog doth tire and prey on me,
    Till quite consumed my golden angels be.

Then woeful want did make me oft complain ;
    Hunger and cold do pinch me at the heart.
Then am I thrust out of my bed again,
    And from my chamber must I needs depart
To lowest wards to lie among the boards,
    Which nought but filth and noisome smell affords.

Midst forty men, surprised with care and grief,
   I lie me down on boards as hard as cannel.
No bed nor bolster may afford relief,
   For worse than dogs lie we in that foul kennel.
What might I think but sure, assure me then
   That metamorphosed we were beasts, not men.

Grief upon grief did still oppress my mind;
   Yet had I score compartners in my woe.
No ease but anguish my distresses find.
   Here lies a man his last life's breath doth blow,
And ere the sorry man be fully dead,
   The rats do prey upon his face and head.

Whilst that I languish in my woes, appears
   Time in his mantle, looking fresh and blithe.
Yet whiles his eyes did shed some drops of tears,
   Wherewith he seemed as he would whet his scythe.
Quoth Time, " By me shall sorrows be appeased.
   And now's the time thou shalt of cares be eased."

I did present this book which I had writ
   Into Time's hands, who took it and perused it.
" Yea," said Time, " thou must discover yet
   Who this dog is, who else will be excused.
For all be I so cleared thine eyes to see him,
   So may not others. Yet Time would have all fly him.

" And for thy verses covertly disclose
   The secret's sense and yet doth shadow truth,
Explain this black dog, who he is, in prose,
   For more apparent than thy poem showeth.
Truth needs no colours. Then this dog by kind
   Make known before, as he is known behind.

" My scythe," quoth Time, " is now prepared to cut :
   There is no scythe but Time's shall longer dure.
Newgate's black dog must Time to silence put.
   I'll break his teeth and make his biting sure.
The shapes of men on dogs of cruel kind,
   Time shall confound, that bear so bad a mind.

" Have thou no doubt but Time shall set thee free ;
   And yet hereafter learn thou to beware
Of this black dog, and do his dangers flee.
   Give others warning lest they fall their share.
Say to the world, when thou art freed from hell,
   Newgate's black dog thou saw and knew too well.

" And for thy poem draws to a conclusion,
   Time's pleasure is that thou this dog express,
In shape, in nature man, yet men's confusion ;
   A madding cur who doth from kind regress,
A mother's son, and most for to be wondered,
   Of mothers' sons this dog has spoiled a hundred.

In lowly sort complain to highest powers.
   (Truth will be heard and truth must not be hid.)
With foxlike wiles this dog poor souls devours.
   This dog of men decipher I thee bid.
And though there be curs many of his kind,
   Say but the truth, and yet leave nought behind."

When Time had said, I from my fears awake.
   Yet had I writ what premises contains.
'Twas no illusion moved me this poem make,
   But griefs endured and woes my heart sustained,
Grief, care and woe my silly heart do clog,
   Fettered to shame by this cur, Newgate's dog.

Now as I have described him in some sort,
   As he is fearful unto all him see,
His devilish practices now I will report,
   And set them down as wicked as they be.
Here ends my poem Newgate's black dog to name.
   Now read the rest and then commend or blame.

Finis.

A DIALOGUE

betwixt the Author and one Zawny, who was a prisoner in Newgate, and perfectly acquainted with matters touching the discovery of the superlative degree of cony-catching : pithy, pleasant, and profitable for all the readers hereof.

[AUTHOR]

ZAWNY, I have many times been in hand with thee to give me some notes upon thy knowledge, as concerning the notable abuses committed by a sort of dissolute fellows, who are in very deed the worst members in a commonwealth. I mean infamous cony-catching knaves, who continually seek the spoil of others to enrich themselves. And now is the time thy help will do me some pleasure ; for at the request of a very friend I was moved to write something of worth, whereupon I made choice of the Black Dog of Newgate to be a subject to write upon. Wherein I could not choose—divers strong reasons especially moving thereunto—but in that title shadow the knavery, villainy, robbery and cony-catching committed daily by divers, who in the name of service and office, were as it were attendants at Newgate. Again, I did choose to give my book that title, as well to satisfy some who yet think there is some spirit about that prison in the likeness of a Black Dog ; of which fond imagination to put them out of doubt, I thought good to give them to understand that indeed there is no such matter. The third reason was, for I being in Newgate a prisoner, and overthrown by these kind of bad people with their cony-catching in most vile and wicked manner, insomuch that, whilst I there languished in great extremity, I did both hear and see many outragious injuries by them committed on divers sorts of people. The premises considered, I do entreat thee to let me have thy help to set down some of their villainies committed in thy knowledge, and I will not be slack to present this book, being finished, into their godly hands, who will assuredly give them condign punishment, as also provide that the like mischiefs shall never be any more put in practice by any notable villains.

[ZAWNY]

Indeed you say well, and I agree. But yet you know I am a poor man, and am a prisoner. Again, it is ill meddling with edge tools. As you comprehend them in the name of a dog, so if they be angry, they will bite, and play the devil in their likeness. They have parlous heads, ſtore of money, and some good friends ; all which I want. Neither will I name any. But if their knaveries were known, it would be thought the gallows as fit for these cony-catchers as Newgate is for me, who am rather kept in to bribe them, than to answer any offence I have committed. Yet, seeing you have begun well, I would wish you end no worse ; and for my part, tell you one of their knaveries, and I'll tell another. So that ere we have done, if we tell all, the cony-catcher will think we have told too much. But by your leave, a word. I will name no man, for if they should be named, their friends would be angry : and more than that, I rather wish their amendment than their public infamy. Of which motion, if you like, begin when you will, and when you are weary, reſt you, and I will go on with it : for our matter being all one, no doubt our conclusion will be to the like effeċt.

[AUTHOR]

Godly, wise, honourable, worshipful and gentle reader, know firſt there be an infinite number of this seċt and company of cony-catchers, therefore it were an endless piece of work to name them all. But for I know too many of them, and have likewise paid for my acquaintance with them, it may be expeċted I should name some of them, which for the inconvenience might thereby ensue, I thought good to crave your patience on that behalf, assuring you that they are easy enough to be known by their colours : but what wicked parts they have performed, I will not fail but make manifeſt.

Therefore, firſt I desire you to imagine that these fellows (these cony-catchers, I would say) do promise to the world great matters— as for example : They will undertake, if a man be robbed by the way, they will help the party offended to his money again, or to the thieves at the leaſt. Likewise, if a purse be cut, a house broken, a piece of plate ſtole, they will promise the like. Marry ! to further this good piece of service, they muſt have a warrant procured from some juſtice at the leaſt, that by the said general warrant they may take up all suspeċted persons[7]. Which being obtained, then mark how notably therewith

they play the knaves, how shamefully they abuse the Justices who
granted the warrant, and how notoriously they abuse a great sort of
poor men, who neither the warrant mentioneth, nor the party aggrieved
in any wise thought to molest or trouble. And for they shadow all
their villainies under colour of some especial warrant, let it suffice thee
to read the sequel, and then judge of their abuses as they deserve.

Now first will I begin with their petty practices in their lewd actions.
Say there is a man or two robbed by the highway not far from London.
The rumour hereof being bruited in the City, these fellows will be sure
to have intelligence with the first ; in what manner the men were robbed,
how much money they lost, and where they dwell. The reason is this :
The cony-catchers have always abroad some odd fellows which are
inquisitors of purpose, who always what they hear rumoured, they
presently come and certify their good masters cony-catchers, of all,
whatsoever, how, where, and when, this robbery was committed. Presently away goes E.H. or N.S. or some of that sect, and inquires out the
party that was robbed ; with whom, if H. or S. hap to meet withal,
some occasion shall presently be found to intrude themselves into the
company of them [who] be robbed. And after some circumstances,
the cony-catcher begins to tell of a strange robbery committed in such
a place, saying it was shamefully done : and withal, they will cast some
words afar off, as who should say in effect: " If I be not deceived, I know
the thieves, and it may be that if I might speak with him or them that
were robbed, haply I should direct them how they might take the villains."

All this while the cony-catcher taketh no notice of them that were
robbed, neither doth the cony-catcher make any show that they knew
any such matter to be done to any in the company.

Now the poor men that were robbed, hearing their smooth speeches,
one of them begins very heavily to shape his tale in this, or suchlike
manner : " My honest friend, I know too well that such a robbery was
done, and in very deed I was the man was robbed in such a place, and
at such a time as you speak of. I beseech you, good friend, stand me
in what stead you may. And if you can help me again to my money,
or to take the thieves, I will not only think myself greatly beholden to
you, but I will also please you to your content. I am a poor man ; I
pray you do me what pleasure you may, good sir, I beseech you." These
and suchlike speeches he useth.

The cony-catcher presently joineth issues with him, and with much
cunning he tempereth his talk. To be short, he offereth all the pleasure

he can do him. " But," quoth he, " you know I am a stranger unto you, and I know not whether you will use me well or no. It may be, when I have done you good, you will lightly reward me. But I'll tell you what I'll do : Give me but forty shillings in hand to bear my charges the time I may search for them, and if I do not deserve it, I will restore it again, and lose all my labour. If you like of this motion, so it is : if not, I will not deal in your matter hot nor cold."

When the man that was robbed heareth him so brief, yet loath to part company on the sudden, he entreateth to know the cony-catcher's name, and where he dwelleth. To this question another of the cony-catcher's companions maketh this reply :

" Honest man, you need not doubt of his good meaning towards you. This is such a one as may do you pleasure, if he please to undertake it." Then he roundeth the man in the ear, and telleth him his name is E. H., and that he knoweth all the thieves about London, and that he hath done more good in helping men to their own than can be devised to be done by a hundred others, praising him for a wonderful good member in a commonwealth : further, certifying the part where this E. H. dwelleth, and with an oath whispering, he wisheth him to give him some 20s., and then agree what he shall give him more when the thieves be taken, making many protestations that he need not to misdoubt of E. H. his honest dealing with him in any respect.

Presently the poor man putteth his hand into his pocket, and out he pulls an angel. Then saith he : " Master H., I have heard of you before, and for I have heard nothing but well of you, I am the willinger to deal with you. Truly here is an angel for you, and I will give you a gallon of wine at the tavern. And if you do me good in this matter, I will give you 20s. more. Then with some entreaty he desireth him to take it in good part, and so giveth him the money.

The cony-catcher taketh the money very quaintly, as though he would refuse it, but in the end he pockets it up, and is willing to go to the tavern, where, after the drinking a gallon or two of wine, they conclude of the former matter. And E. H. will out of hand get the thieves into Newgate. And so much he promiseth to perform upon his honest fidelity, not letting to say, if he do it not he dare be hanged for it.

Then the day is appointed when within a week the party robbed shall come to Newgate to know what news ; and for that time they part, the honest man to his home or about his business, the cony-catchers to some other odd place about their knavery, where they laugh at the cony, devising how to get him in for more money, never intending to do anything in the matter which they have undertaken for the honest man, whose angel they drink merrily.

Now we will leave this man for a while to his business of more profit, and I will proceed with the cony-catchers for their practices.

These cony-catchers are never idle : and therefore it followeth next, to let you understand of a notable piece of service the said H. and S. played with a friend of mine.

It happened my friend being some time in question, could not miss but he must needs have acquaintance with these odd shavers ; and thus it fell out : My friend being in a tavern drinking with some of his acquaintance, whilst they were drinking together, in comes H. S., who presently used great courtesy to my friend. But, to be short, they took full survey of his weapons, his good cloak and neat apparel, which was enough for them to imagine that my friend had store of money. Whereupon they asked if he would give them a pottle of wine, which he willingly granted : and so, after one pottle, he gave them another. The reckoning paid, and the company ready to depart, quoth S. to E. H. : " I pray you hark in your ear." Presently he whispereth : " Thus it is : my fellow hath a warrant to take you. Therefore in kindness I wish you to draw to your purse, and give him an angel to drink, and I will undertake he shall not see you at this time."

My friend hearing his tale tend to a cony-catching effect, he begins to swear they are cony-catching knaves, and they shall not wrong him in any respect.

To be short, the cony-catcher sends for a constable, and charges the party aforesaid with felony. The constable, knowing them to be in office—but not to be such bad fellows—he presently apprehendeth the party ; which done, the cony-catchers, seeing the prisoner in safe keeping, disfurnished of his weapons, they presently require the prisoner of the constable, and they will be his discharge : which the constable did, thinking no less than they were right honest men.

Now mark what followed. As these two knaves were a bringing this party charged with felony to Newgate, one of them offereth yet for 20s. to set him free : of which, when the party had considered, knowing though he were clear of that he was charged, yet if he lay in prison till the Sessions, it would be greater charges, when he was on Newgate stairs ready to go into the jail, he was content to leave his cloak, that money he had in his purse, and his weapons which were in the constable's hand, pawn for the 20s. which the cony-catchers took, and discharged the prisoner without any more to do.

Not long after, the aforesaid cony-catchers meet with this their cony of 20s. price, and another, who was known to be, as they term him, " a good fellow about the town," in his company.

And where meet they but in a tavern not far without Bishopsgate, where these two poor conies had spoken for supper? Amidst their good cheer, in comes H. and S., bidding them be merry with their fare. One of these two being an odd fellow and in dread of these cony-catchers, knowing them very perfectly, set on the best face he could, and bade them welcome, entreating them to sit down and do as they did; of which proffer the cony-catchers accepted willingly, and sat down with them and ate and drunk merrily. Supper being ended, the reckoning was called for, the shot paid, and all things discharged; the conies would fain have been gone.

" Nay ! " quoth N. S., for of the two he was the grimmer knave and had most skill to talk; " I must let you know that which indeed I am sorry to do. Yet if you will do yourselves good, you may use us well, and we will not use you amiss. To be short, thus it is : Such a man was robbed within this week, and he hath got out a warrant for you two by name. He hath lost ten pounds Now, if you will restore the money, and bestow 20s. on us two to drink for our pains, we will undertake to satisfy the party and be your discharge. If not, we have a warrant, and you must answer it at Newgate. This back-reckoning is something sharp, but there is no remedy ; either pay so much money, or else must a constable be sent for, and so to Newgate as round as a hoop."

To be short, this was the conclusion : The conies paid down £11, every penny, whereof ten pound was to be paid to the man in the moon ! for I dare take it upon my death, neither of these conies did offend any such man in manner as these knaves had charged them.

ZAWNY.

By your leave a word : all this while you have not concluded what became of the first cony these odd shavers met with. I pray you be brief, and let us hear how he was ended withal ; and then you shall hear me tell you of wonders, if these be held to be but of moment.

AUTHOR.

Well then, to the first cony again. At his time appointed, he cometh to the wise man of Newgate, to inquire what is done in his matter ; and at Newgate the cony findeth his odd acquaintance with E. H., who at the first sight hath the time of the day for him, much courtesies ;

but to the tavern they muſt to debate the matter, where they muſt have a pottle of the beſt. Whilſt the wine is a filling, the cony-catcher showeth what great pain he hath taken to come by the thieves, and how hardly they missed of them. But for it is beſt to use few words, the cony-catcher from one day to another ſtill driveth off the cony, who is ſtill in hope that the cony-catcher meaneth good faith, whereas, indeed, he never made account what faith was. So to be short, if the thieves robbed him of some five or six pound, he hath got, or he find where he is, a dry shaving as much as forty or fifty shillings more.

I tell thee, Zawny, methinks these are notable villainies, and pity they should not be punished, who live by no other means but praſtising such pranks as these be !

Again this is a general rule to the cony-catcher, that when or where he meets with such a one as hath been at any time committed to Newgate, if that fellow have good apparel on his back, the cony-catcher taketh acquaintance of him and a quart of wine they muſt needs drink. When the reckoning comes to payment, the cony-catcher hath brought no money from home that day ; so by the other's drawing of his purse to pay for the wine, he knoweth what lining is in it. Then, if he have money, the cony-catcher is in hand with him for a bribe, some odd crown or an angel to drink. If the man be in any fault, fearing the worſt, he will not ſtand with him for a trifle. If he be in no fault, perhaps he tells : " In faith, you are deceived in me. I am not he you take me for." And so parteth, and giveth him nothing.

Presently the cony-catcher useth all means to know where he lies ; which, when he hath done, within a night or two away goes this knave with some old warrant to the conſtable of that Liberty, craving his aid to apprehend a bad fellow who is thought to have done much mischief. But for a surety he avoucheth him for an arrant thief, and that he hath been in Newgate. Upon these speeches the conſtable goes with this H. where the poor man lies, and apprehends him and conveys him to Newgate, laying some Juſtice's commandment on him—where he lies till the Sessions, unless he come off roundly with a bribe to the cony-catcher. But say the cony-catcher be miſtaken in this fellow's purse, and that he have not so much as he supposed : yet the cony-catcher is so ſtrong of faith that he will not believe the contrary. So by this means the poor man lieth in prison till he be quite a beggar, without releasement till the proclamation at the Sessions, at which time he is not worth the ground he goes on, neither knoweth he, being utterly overthrown, how to have any remedy, which is pitiful and lamentable.

ZAWNY.

I muse you should account of these trifling matters, whereas, indeed, they are nothing in respect of the prizes they have played. And if you will give me leave a little, I will come something nearer the cony-catcher than you have yet done.

AUTHOR.

I pray thee do. Yet I must needs tell thee I have been too near the cony-catcher ; and what I have spoken of him, it is not only with grief but with sorrow to my heart, and anguish of soul that these outrages should be committed, to the utter undoing of so many : as within this thirty years have been ; for so long did I hear one of these villains vaunt he had been in office about Newgate. And what I have done or said on this behalf, with my life and death I am ready to make proof of it, that it is true. This mind I bear, that the Devil should have his due of these knaves ; and I hold it my duty to reveal whatsoever is to the good of a commonwealth : and so I will, though the cony-catcher swear to give me a cut in the leg for my labour. And now, Zawny, I pray thee go forward.

[ZAWNY.]

Gentlemen, though I want eloquence, yet you shall see I have a rolling tongue, deep knowledge, and am a rare fellow to bewray many matters touching cony-catching.

Master Green, God be with thee ! for if thou hadst been alive,[8] knowing what I know, thou wouldst as well have made work as matter, but for my part I am a plain fellow, and what I know I will not be mealy-mouthed, but blab I wist, and out it must, nay, and out it shall ; for as the comedian[9] said I, *plenus rimarum sum.*

I know twenty and twenty of these fine cony-catchers, who learn of the fencers to double a blow, knowing what belongs to the button and the bob. Yet for the author hath only used four letters for two names, let them stand ; and when I name E. he must think Zawny can see whilst there is an eye in his head. " H." is *aspirationis nota,* and no letter indeed ; therefore I care not if this cony-catching H. were wiped out of the letters-row to hang on the gallows,[10] who is fitter to be a cipher to make up a number at Tyburn, than to be a man of so bad condition. As for a pottle of wine, he cares not who he hanged so he may have if it be but the wine. N. is the first of the second name the author useth. No knave, I warrant you ! And as for S., if he be in some sort a knave to be proved, he will be contented. Nay, he must in spite of his teeth disgest the name of a cony-catcher, for by that art, being not worth one groat a year, he is able by his fine wit to maintain himself in his satin doublet, velvet hose, his hat lined with velvet, his silk stock, his rapier and dagger gilt, his golden brooch, and all things correspondent as might seem a man both of wit and living.

And now I, according to my promise to the author, will have a cast at these fine cony-catchers, and I will not slander them in any wise, but speak the truth unto death. If I say more than I will prove, I will never bid you trust Zawny again.

Not long since, at a tilting upon triumph on the Coronation Day, many good subjects with joy assembled the place of triumph, as well rejoicing to see the Queen's most excellent Majesty, as also to see the tilting performed by sundry noble and right honourable personages.[11]

Amongst the rest, there comes a woman with six pounds in her purse, which the cutpurse met withal, she as it seemed having more mind on the pleasures of the present day and time than she had of her purse.

The jousts ended for that day, the woman thinking all had been well, takes her way homeward with a friend of hers. Yet by the way this good woman must needs drink with her friend a pint of wine. But here was the mischief; when the wine was to be paid for, the woman missed her purse, and looking on the strings, with a cold heart she might perceive her purse was cut away. Her friend, to comfort her, bade her take no thought, for he knew a man would help her to her purse again. " And," saith he, " we will presently go to him, for I know where he dwells."

The woman thanked her friend for his courteous offer, and away they go to E. H. his house, where they found him; to whom they brake the matter wholly how it was, desiring his help. Presently he had them in the wind, and bade them welcome, promising that if they would content him for his pains he would do her good, asking her what she would willingly bestow to have her money again. At the first word she offered him forty shillings. All this was well, and they agree to meet the next day about Whitehall, where they shall have answer to their content. And so, after they had drunk a quart of wine at the tavern, for that night they parted.

The next day, according to promise, they met, and this E. H. had in his company a man, who he said was a constable, but whether he said truly or no I will not say; but to the matter. They appoint the woman to go to a friend's house hard by, and she should hear more anon. Away went she, as they had appointed her, and away go they to look for cutpurses.

I warrant you they sought not long but here they met with a cutpurse, whom they take by the sleeve ; and there they meet with another as good a cutpurse as the former ; and so they take at the least a dozen cutpurses. Which when they have done, the cony-catcher begins to rail mightily, swearing they shall some of them be hanged. But to prison they shall all go, unless this money be had again—showing a warrant, or a piece of paper at the least ; which is sufficient to " bear the cony-catcher harmless," as he saith.

Now the cutpurses, though they be all clear of this matter, yet they begin to quake for fear, offering rather than they will go to prison, they will make up the money, so that E. H. will promise to give it them again when the cutpurse shall be known, who cut the purse indeed. This motion the cony-catcher liketh indifferently ; and so of these dozen of cutpurses, he taketh of some more, and of some less, that the sum is largely made up ; which done, they are all discharged. Marry, they must have some twenty shillings overplus for their pains and kindness showed to the cutpurses !—all which is granted.

To be short, no cutpurse scaped their hands, but he paid a share, so that there was gathered the first day at the least ten pounds amongst cutpurses, and the next day this E. H. met with the cutpurse who cut the purse indeed, of whom he took the money, with the vantage, and let him go without answering the matter. And to conclude, the woman had four pound of her money again, and so the matter was no more spoken of.

I think this was a piece of knavery, if you talk of knavery, and yet this is no knavery in respect of that I will show you in this next discovery of their cony-catching.

At the term-time, these fellows H. and S. have had great booties by their practices in this art, and this is their manner :

In the morning away they go to Westminster Hall,[12] where they know the cutpurse will be about his business ; but the cony-catchers are not without a couple who are their consorts ; who, as soon as they come to the Hall, thrust in amongst the thickest, and there they listen to hear if any purse were cut that day.

Likewise the cony-catchers, they take their standings, one of them at the waterside, the other in some close place, at another gate : so that lightly a cutpurse cannot come out of the Hall but one of them shall spy him, and take him by the sleeve.   If the cutpurse have done anything, word is presently brought to the tavern, whither the cony and the cony-catcher are gone to drink.   Now if it be some small sum, the cony-catcher showeth the cony a good countenance ; but if it be a large sum, as six pounds or upwards, the cony-catcher, dissembling his intent, will not ſtay but the drinking a pottle of wine.

The cutpurse entreats their company, and offereth both wine and a breakfaſt ; but all is in vain ; the cony-catcher will not tarry, swearing a great oath, he is sorry that it was his chance to see this cony or cutpurse this day, for there is a mischief done, and he fears some will smoke for it.   At this the cutpurse is afeared, but he for that time 'scapeth their fingers, for the cony-catcher will tarry no longer.

Now the cony-catcher sendeth presently one of his company to seek out the party who had his purse cut, which he performeth with diligence, and meeting with him, he tells the party that he heard he loſt his purse at Weſtminſter, and if he will be advised by him, he will help him to the moſt of his money again.

This honeſt man, glad to have part again of his money, offereth at the firſt word the one half to have the other, assuring this odd fellow for certainty that he loſt ten pounds.

" Well," saith this factor for the cony-catcher, " if your leisure will serve to go with me, I will bring you to one doth partly know who cut your purse.   Therefore it is your way to follow his counsel, and I warrant you my life for it but you shall have your desire."

Hereat the honeſt man is glad, and willingly goeth along with him to a place where he knoweth E. H. abideth his coming.   Now being met, the wise man of Newgate begins at the firſt dash to tell them whereabout they come, even in as ample manner as if the man who had his purse cut had told the tale himself.

No marvel though the countryman do wonder a while at the matter, but in the end telleth him it is so indeed, and according to the firſt motion they agree, which is the one half for the other, the countryman willing to refer the matter wholly to this cony-catcher's discretion.

Then away goes the countryman with H. the cony-catcher to a Juſtice, to whom he signifieth in every respect how his purse was cut, desiring of the Juſtice a warrant to take up all suspected persons ; of which motion the Juſtice, intending to do juſtice, grants his warrant, and gives it to H., willing him to certify him what shall be done on that behalf, as the warrant intendeth.

This warrant obtained, the cony-catcher is as pleasant as a pie.

Taking his leave of the Justice, away goes the countryman, and his good friends with him, and to the tavern straight, where they spend some time in drinking a pottle of the best wine, which the countryman must pay for; which done, H. taketh his leave of his client, promising him not to be slack in his business; which done, they part, the countryman to his lodging or as his occasion serveth, and the cony-catcher about his faculty.

Now woe to the cutpurses! For as H. happeneth to meet with them, they must to Newgate, showing warrant sufficient for a greater matter. But you must take notice that of a dozen or sixteen cutpurses who he hath apprehended, he is sure enough that he which cut the purse indeed shall be none of them.

This honest company of cutpurses being all in Newgate, H. goes presently and certifies the Justice, what a sort of notable thieves he hath taken, desiring the Justice to send for them at his pleasure, to examine them about the countryman's purse, assuring the Justice that they are cunning thieves, and that he dare lay his life they will confess nothing; which indeed the Justice findeth true; for they, being examined, will confess as much as ne'er a whit.

To Newgate away they go again, where they make all means to H. to stand their friend, showing their innocency. Yet rather than they will lie in prison, one offereth ten shillings, another twenty shillings, some more, some less, as they are of ability; offering, farther, to give, besides the sum, everyone something to H. for his good word to the Justice, that they may be set at liberty.

Now the cony-catcher hath the matter as he would wish it; and, taking their money first, he presently goes to the Justice and certifieth him that these which he hath apprehended did none of them cut the purse; and for he hath gotten knowledge who did, he desireth that they may be bailed. The Justice, glad to hear the truth is known, is willing to set them at liberty, which upon their bail he granteth. Of this money the countryman hath never a penny, and all these cutpurses are set at liberty. Which done, H. seeketh diligently for the cutpurse, who did the matter indeed; with whom, when he meeteth, he spareth not to tell him how sore the Justice is against him, and how earnestly the countryman will pursue the law; and, further, he sweareth that some of them who were in Newgate told the Justice plainly that he cut the purse.

This peal rings nothing well in the cutpurse's ears, who can find no favour—but to Newgate. Yet, upon entreaty made by the cutpurse,

M

the cony-catcher promiseth that for his part he will do him any good he can, wishing the cutpurse, as he is wise enough, so it were good for him to hold his own, and confess nothing to the Justice, what proof soever come against him, and in so doing it may lie in his power to do him good ; telling him, further, that the man who lost the money, though he be sore bent against him, yet he will partly be ruled by him.

Well, to Newgate marcheth this H. with his cutpurse, where he, to welcome him for all his fair words, he clappeth on his legs a good pair of bolts and shackles ; which done, he sendeth for the countryman, and telleth him of these good tidings, how the thief is taken, and how he hath used him.

The next way they take is to the Justice, to whom H. signifieth how the case standeth, railing mightily against the cutpurse, even in the worst manner he can devise ; saying, it will be evidently proved that he cut the purse, and none but he. Further, he requesteth that the cut-purse may be examined.   The cutpurse is sent for, who to every question the Justice can demand, having taken out his lesson (*Confess and be hanged*), hath his answer ready, so that there can be no advantage taken by his examination.

The Justice returneth him to Newgate again to abide till the next Sessions, requiring the party to be bound to give evidence against him. But the countryman, dwelling far from London, and it being long to the next Law-day, allegeth he can not be in the City at that time, for he is a poor man, and hath great occasion of business, so that he cannot be there to give evidence, neither can he say, if he would, any thing against that party ; for, so far as he can remember, he never saw that fellow before in his life.   Yet H. promiseth that it will be proved against the cutpurse.   So the countryman and H. take their leaves of the Justice, making show as though they would come again, though it be no part of H. his meaning.   H. goeth straight to Newgate, where he falls in hand with the cutpurse, swearing unto him by his honesty that he hath laboured the party who had his purse cut to take his money again, and not to give evidence against him, answering him with many oaths that if he may have his money again, he will presently go out of the town. The cutpurse, taking H. his hand, that no man shall give evidence against him at the Sessions, doth presently send abroad to his friends for the money ; which, as soon as it cometh, he delivereth to H. and withal a large overplus, because he will be sure of H. his favour.

This done, H. goes to the countryman, and tells him he got no more but six or seven pound, of which, if he will accept, and proceed no further

against the party, he hath it to pay him.   Marry! he will not be known
to the countryman, but that he had that money of some friends of the
cutpurse's, who upon the former condition is willing it should be paid;
if not, to have his money again.   The countryman, having haste out of
the City, is glad to take it.   Out of which sum, if it be seven pounds,
H. must have half; so that the poor man of ten pounds hath but three
pound, ten shillings, whereas the cony-catcher by this account hath got
at one hand and another very near forty mark.   The money shared,
the countryman takes horse, and away he rides.   Again, H. his mouth
is stopped, and the next Sessions the cutpurse is quit by proclamation,
no man being there to give evidence against him.

AUTHOR.

Oh! wonderful piece of villainy!   Zawny, I will trouble thee no
further.   Thou hast told enough, and I will tell no more.   Who hears
but this which is already spoken, will hold these knaves for execrable
varlets.   So for this time I will commend thee to thy other business,
wishing thy liberty, as I do my own.   And if thou have occasion, command me to do thee good, if it lie in my power.

ZAWNY.

Sir, I thank you for your courteous offer.   But yet I must tell you,
I could tell twenty such pranks as these are, which these cony-catching
fellows have played; but indeed they keep one order almost, in performing them all.   But since you think here is enough, I will say no
more, and so fare you well!

AUTHOR.

Thus have you heard, gentle reader, how at large this Black Dog
is deciphered; which, dog as he is, is worthy of your general hate.
But for I have with pains concluded my book under that title, I will
not request you according to the old proverb, *love me, love my hound*:
but only, love me, and hang my dog, for he is not worthy so good a name
as a hound.   And so, wishing you all well, I conclude.

Finis.

Luke Hutton's Lamentation,

which he wrote the day before his death, being condemned to be hanged at York for his robberies and trespasses committed thereabouts.

To the tune of *Wandering and Wavering*.

I AM a poor prisoner condemnèd to die ;
    Ah, woe is me, woe is me, for my great folly !
Fast fettered in irons in place where I lie.
    Be warned, young wantons, hemp passeth green holly.
My parents were of good degree,
By whom I would not rulèd be.
    Lord Jesus, forgive me ; with mercy relieve¹ me ;
    Receive, O sweet Saviour, my spirit unto thee.

My name is Hutton ; yea, Luke of bad life,
    Ah, woe is me ! etc.
Which on the highway did rob man and wife ;
    Be warned, etc.
Enticed by many a graceless mate,
Whose counsel I repent too late.
    Lord Jesus, forgive me, etc.

Not twenty years old, alas ! was I
    Ah, woe is me ! etc.
When I began this felony,
    Be warned, etc.
With me went still twelve yeomen tall,
Which I did my Twelve Apostles call.
    Lord Jesus, forgive me, etc.

There was no squire or baron bold,
    Ah, woe is me ! etc.
That rode by the way with silver and gold,
    Be warned, etc.
But I and my apostles gay
Would lighten their load as they went away.
    Lord Jesus, forgive me, etc.

This news procured my kinsfolk's grief,
    Ah, woe is me ! etc.
That hearing I was a famous thief,
    Be warned, etc.
They wept, they wailed, they wrung their hands,
That thus I should hazard life and lands.
    Lord Jesus, forgive me, etc.

They made me a jailer a little before,
    Ah, woe is me! etc.
To keep in prison offenders sore;
    Be warned, etc.
But such a jailer was never before;
I went and let them out every one.
    Lord Jesus, forgive me, etc.

I wist this sorrow sore grievèd me,
    Ah, woe is me! etc.
Such proper men should hangèd be.
    Be warned, etc.
My office then I did defy,
And ran away for company.
    Lord Jesus, forgive me, etc.

Three years I lived upon the spoil,
    Ah, woe is me! etc.
Giving many an earl the foil;
    Be warned, etc.
Yet did I never kill man nor wife,
Though lewdly long I led my life.
    Lord Jesus, forgive me, etc.

But all too bad my deeds have been,
    Ah, woe is me! etc.
Offending my Country and my good Queen;
    Be warned, etc.
All men in Yorkshire talk of me;
A stronger thief there could not be.
    Lord Jesus, forgive me, etc.

Upon St. Luke's Day was I born,
    Ah, woe is me! etc.
Who want of Grace hath made me scorn.
    Be warned, etc.
In honour of my birthday then
I robbed in bravery nineteen men.
    Lord Jesus, forgive me, etc.

The country were to hear this wrong
    Ah, woe is me! etc.
With hues and cries pursued me long.
    Be warned, etc.
Though long I 'scaped, yet lo, at the last,
At London I was in Newgate cast.
    Lord Jesus, forgive me, etc.

Where I did lie with grievèd mind
    Ah, woe is me! etc.
Although my keeper was gentle and kind.
    Be warned, etc.
Yet was he not so kind as I,
To let me go at liberty.
    Lord Jesus, forgive me, etc.

At laſt the Sheriff of Yorkshire came,[2]
    Ah, woe is me! etc.
And in a warrant he had my name.
    Be warned, etc.
Quoth he, " At York thou muſt be tried ;
With me, therefore, hence muſt thou ride."
    Lord Jesus, forgive me, etc.

Like pangs of death his words did sound,
    Ah, woe is me ! etc.
My hands and arms full faſt he bound.
    Be warned, etc.
" Good sir," quoth I, " I had rather ſtay ;
I have no heart to ride that way."
    Lord Jesus, forgive me, etc.

When no entreaty would prevail
    Ah, woe is me! etc.
I called for wine, beer and ale ;
    Be warned, etc.
And when my heart was in woeful case,
I drank to my friends with a smiling face.
    Lord Jesus, forgive me, etc.

With clubs and ſtaves I was guarded then :
    Ah, woe is me! etc.
I never before had such waiting-men.
    Be warned, etc.
If they had ridden before me amain,
Beshrew me if I had called them again.
    Lord Jesus, forgive me, etc.

And when unto York that I was come,
    Ah, woe is me! etc.
Each one on me did caſt his doom.
    Be warned, etc.
And whilst you live, this sentence note :
Evil men can never have good report.
    Lord Jesus, forgive me, etc.

Before the Judges then I was brought ;
    Ah, woe is me ! etc.
But sure I had a careful thought.
    Be warned, etc.
Nine-score indictments and seventeen
Against me there were read and seen.
    Lord Jesus, forgive me, etc.

And each of those were felony found,
    Ah, woe is me! etc.
Which did my heart with sorrow wound ;
    Be warned, etc.
What should I herein longer ſtay,
For this I was condemned that day.
    Lord Jesus, forgive me, etc.

My death each hour I did attend,
    Ah, woe is me! etc.
In prayers and tears my time I did spend,
    Be warned, etc.
And all my loving friends that day
I did entreat for me to pray.
    Lord Jesus, forgive me, etc.

I have deservèd death long since :
    Ah, woe is me! etc.
A viler sinner lived not than I,
    Be warned, etc.
On friends I hoped [my] life to save ;
But I am fitted for the grave.
    Lord Jesus, forgive me, etc.

Adieu, my loving friends each one,
    Ah, woe is me, woe is me, for my great folly !
Think on me, Lords, when I am gone.
    Be warned, young wantons, hemp passeth green holly.
When on the ladder you do me view,
Think I am nearer heaven than you.
    Lord Jesus, forgive me, ; with mercy relieve me ;
    Receive, O sweet Saviour, my spirit unto thee.
                 L. HUTTON.

FINIS

The Last Will and Testament

OF LAURENCE LUCIFER

The Old Bachelor of Limbo

ALIAS

Dick Devil-Barn, the Griping Farmer of Kent

BEING THE FINAL PORTION OF

THE BLACK BOOK

BY

THOMAS MIDDLETON (?)

1604.

IN the name of Beelzebub, Amen.

I Laurence Lucifer, *alias* Dick Devil-Barn, sick in soul but not in body, being in perfect health to wicked memory, do constitute and ordain this my last Will and Testament irrevocable as long as the world shall be trampled on by villainy.

Imprimis, I Laurence Lucifer bequeath my soul to Hell, and my body to the earth amongst you all. Divide me and share me equally, but with as much wrangling as you can, I pray. And it will be the better if you go to law for me.

As touching my worldly-wicked goods, I give and bequeath them in most villainous order following :

First, I constitute and ordain Lieutenant Prig-beard[1], Archpander of England, my sole heir of all such lands, closes, and gaps, as lie within the bounds of my gift. Beside I have certain houses, tenements and withdrawing-rooms in Shoreditch, Turnbold Street, Whitefriars and Westminster[2], which I freely give and bequeath to the aforesaid Lieutenant and the base heirs truly begot of his villainous body ; with this proviso, that he sell none of the land when he lacks money, nor make away any of the houses to impair and weaken the stock, no, not so much as to alter the property of any of them (which is to make them honest against their wills), but to train and muster all his wits upon the Mile End of his mazard,[3] rather to fortify the territories of Turnbold Street and enrich the county of Picthatch[4], with all his vicious endeavours, golden enticements and damnable practices. And, Lieutenant, thou must dive, as thou usest to do, into landed novices, who have only wit to be lickerish and no more, that so their tenants, trotting up to London with their quarterages, they may pay them their rent ; but thou and thy college shall receive the money.

Let no young wriggle-eyed damosel, if her years have struck twelve once, be left unassaulted, but it must be thy office to lay hard siege to her honesty, and to try if the walls of her maidenhead may be scaled with a ladder of angels. For one acre of such wenches will bring in more at year's end than an hundred acres of the best-harrowed land between Deptford and Dover. And take this for a note by the way : You must never walk without your deuce or deuce-ace of drabs after your boot-heels ; for when you are abroad you know not what use you may have for them. And lastly, if you be well feed by some riotous gallant, you must practise, as indeed you do, to wind out a wanton velvet cap and bodkin from the tangles of her shop, teaching her—you know how—to cast a cuckold's mist before the eyes of her husband, which is, telling him she must see her cousin, new-come to town, or that she goes to a woman's labour, when thou knowest she goes to none but her own ; and, being set out of the shop, with her man afore her to quench the jealousy of her husband, she by thy instructions shall turn the honest simple fellow off at the next turning and give him leave to see *The Merry Devil of Edmonton*[5] or *A Woman Killed with Kindness*[6], when his mistress is going to the same murder ! Thousand of such inventions, practices, and devices, I stuff thy trade withal ; beside the luxurious meetings at taverns, ten-pound suppers, and fifteen-pound reckonings, made up afterwards with riotous eggs and muscadine. All these female vomits and adulterous surfeits I give and bequeath to thee, which I hope thou wilt put in practice with all expedition after my decease. And to that end I ordain thee wholly and solely my only absolute, excellent, villainous heir.

Item, I give and bequeath to you, Gregory Gauntlet, high thief on horseback, all such sums of money that are nothing due to you, and to receive them in, whether the parties are willing to pay you or no. You need not make many words with them but only these two : " Stand and deliver ! " And therefore a true thief cannot choose but be wise, because he is a man of so very few words.

I need not instruct you, I think, Gregory, about the politic searching of crafty carriers' packs, or ripping up the bowels of wide boots and cloak-bags. I do not doubt but you have already exercised them all. But one thing I especially charge you of, the neglect of which makes many of your religion tender their wine-pipes at Tyburn at least three months before their day : that if you chance to rob a virtuous townsman on horseback, with his wife upon a pillion behind him, you presently speak them fair to walk a turn or two at one side, where, binding them both together like man and wife, arm in arm, very lovingly, be sure you tie them hard enough, for fear they break the bonds of matrimony ; which if it should fall out so, the matter would be sore upon your necks the next Sessions after, because your negligent tying was the cause of that breach between them.

Now as for your Welsh hue and cry (the only net to catch thieves in), I know you avoid well enough, because you can shift both your beards and your towns well. But for your better disguising henceforward, I will fit you with a beard-maker of mine own, one that makes all the false hairs for my devils, and all the periwigs that are worn by old courtiers, who take it for a pride in their bald days to wear yellow curls on their foreheads, when one may almoſt see the sun go to bed through the chinks of their faces.

Moreover, Gregory, because I know thee toward enough, and thy arms full of feats, I make thee Keeper of Coombe Park[7], Sergeant of Salisbury Plain, Warden of the Standing Place, Conſtable of all Heaths, Holes, Highways and Cony-groves, hoping that thou wilt execute these places and offices as truly as Derrick[8] will execute his place and office at Tyburn.

I give and bequeath to thee, Dick Dog-man, Grand Catchpole, over and above thy barebone fees, that will scarce hang wicked flesh on thy back, all such lurches, gripes, and squeezes, as may be wrung out by the fiſt of extortion.

And because I take pity on thee, waiting so long as thou useſt to do, ere thou canſt land one fare at the Counter, watching sometimes ten hours together in an ale-house, ever and anon peeping forth and sampling thy nose with the red lattice[9], let him whosoever that falleth into thy clutches at night pay well for thy ſtanding all day. And, cousin Richard, when thou haſt caught him in the mouse-trap of thy Liberty with the cheese of thy office, the wire of thy hard fiſt being clapped down upon his shoulders, and the back of his eſtate almoſt broken to pieces, then call the cluſter of thy fellow-vermins together, and sit in triumph with thy prisoner at the upper end of a tavern-table, where, under the colour of showing him favour, as you term it, in waiting for bail, thou and thy Counter-leech may swallow down six gallons of Charnico, and then begin to chafe that he makes you ſtay so long before Peter Bail[10] comes. And here it will not be amiss if you call in more wine-suckers and damn as many gallons again. For you know your prisoner's ransom will pay for all—this is, if the party be flush now, and would not have his credit coppered with a scurvy counter.[11]

Another kind of reſt you have, which is called shoe-penny, that is, when you will be paid for every ſtride you take, and if the channel be dangerous and rough, you will not ſtep over under a noble—a very excellent lurch to get up the price of your legs, between Paul's Chain and Ludgate.

But that which likes me beyond measure is the villainous nature of that arreſt which I may fitly term by the name of cog-shoulder, when you clap a' both sides like old Rowse in Cornewell[12], and receive double-fee both from creditor and debtor, swearing by the poſt of your office to shoulder-clap the party the firſt time he lights upon the lime-twigs of your Liberty ; when for a little usurers' oil you allow him free passage to walk by the wicked precinct of your noses, and yet you will pimple your souls with oaths, till you make them as well-favoured as your faces, and swear he never came within the verge of your eyelids. Nay, more, if the creditor were present to see him arrested on the one side, and the party you wot on over the way at the other side, you have such quaint shifts, pretty hindrances and lawyer-like d lays ere you will set forward, that in the meantime he may make himself away in some by-alley, or rush into the bowels of some tavern or drinking school ; or, if neither, you will find talk with some shark-shift by the way, and give him the marks of the party, who will presently start before you, give the debtor intelligence, and so a rotten fig for the catchpole ! A most witty, smooth and damnable conveyance ! Many such running devices breed in the reins of your offices beside. I leave to speak of your unmerciful dragging a gentleman through Fleet Street, to the utter confusion of his white feather, and the lamentable spattering of his pearl-colour silk stockings, especially when some six of your black dogs of Newgate are upon him at once. Therefore, sweet cousin Richard —for you are the nearest kinsman I have—I give and bequeath to you no more than you have already ; for you are so well gorged and stuffed with that, that one spoonful of villainy more would overlay your stomach quite, and, I fear me, make you kick up all the rest.

Item, I give and bequeath to you, Benedick Bottomless, most deep cutpurse, all the benefit of pageant days, great market days, ballad-places, but especially the sixpenny rooms in playhouses, to cut, dive, or nim, with as much speed, art, and dexterity, as may be handled by honest rogues of the quality. Nay, you shall not stick, Benedick, to give a shave of your office at Paul's Cross in the sermon time. But thou hold'st it a thing thou may'st do by law, to cut a purse in Westminster Hall ! True, Benedick ; but be sure the Law is on that side thou cut'st it on.

Item, I give and bequeath to you old Bias, *alias* Humphrey Hollowbank, true cheating bowler and lurcher, the one-half of all bets, cunning hooks, subtleties and cross-lays, that are ventured upon the landing of your bowl, and the safe arriving at the haven of the mistress, if it chance to pass all the dangerous rocks and rubs of the alley, and be not choked in the sand, like a merchant's ship, before it comes half-way home, which is none of your fault, you'll say and swear, although in your own turned conscience you know that you threw it about three yards short out of hand, upon very set purpose.

Moreover, Humphrey, I give you the lurching of all young novices, citizens' sons, and country gentlemen, that are hooked in by the winning of one twelvepenny game at first, lost upon policy, to be cheated of twelve pounds' worth a' bets afterward. And, old Bias, because thou art now and then smelt out for a cozener, I would have thee sometimes go disguised in honest apparel, and so, drawing in amongst bunglers and ketlers under the plain frieze of simplicity, thou mayest finely couch the wrought velvet of knavery.

Item, I give and bequeath to your cousin-german here, Francis Finger-false, Deputy of Dicing-houses, all cunning lifts, shifts and couches, that ever were, are, and shall be invented, from this hour of eleven o'clock upon Black Monday, until it smite twelve o'clock at doomsday! And this I know, Francis : if you do endure to excel, as I know you do, and will truly practise falsely, you may live more gallanter far upon three dice, than many of your foolish heirs about London upon their hundred acres.

But turning my legacy to you-ward, Barnabe Burning-glass,[13] Arch-tobacco-taker of England in ordinaries, upon stages both common and private, and, lastly, in the lodging of your drab and mistress ; I am not a little proud, I can tell you, Barnabe, that you dance after my pipe so long ; and, for all counterblasts[14] and tobacco-Nashes[15], which some call railers, you are not blown away, nor your fiery thirst quenched with the small penny-ale of their contradictions, but still suck that dug of damnation with a long nipple, still burning that rare phœnix of Phlegethon, tobacco, that from her ashes, burnt and knocked out, may arise another pipeful. Therefore I give and bequeath to thee a breath of all religions save the true one, and tasting of all countries save his own ; a brain well-sooted, where the Muses hang up in the smoke like red herrings. And look how the narrow alley of thy pipe shows in the inside ! So shall all the pipes through thy body. Besides I give and bequeath to thy lungs, as smooth as jet, and just of the same colour, that, when thou art closed in thy grave, the worms may be consumed with them, and take them for black-puddings.

Lastly, not least, I give and bequeath to thee Pierce Pennilesse[16], exceeding poor scholar, that hath made clean shoes in both Universities and been a pitiful batteler all thy lifetime, full often heard with this lamentable cry at the buttery-hatch : " Ho, Launcelot ! a cue of bread and a cue of beer ! "—never passing beyond the confines of a farthing, nor once munching commons, but only upon gaudy-days. To thee, most miserable Pierce, o'erpierced through and through with misery,

I bequeath the tithe of all vaulting-houses, the tenth denier of each *Heigh pass ! Come aloft !*[17]—beside the playing in and out of all wenches at thy pleasure, which I know as thou mayest use it, will be such a fluent pension that thou shalt never have need to write *Supplication* again.

Now, for the especial trust and confidence I have in both you Mihell Moneygod, usurer, and Leonard Lavender, broker or pawn-lender, I make you two my full Executors, to the true disposing of all these my hellish intents, wealthy villainies, and most pernicious damnable legacies.

And now, kinsmen and friends, wind about me. My breath begins to cool, and all my powers to freeze. And I can say no more to you, nephews, than I have said—only this : I leave you all, like ratsbane, to poison the realm. And, I pray, be all of you as arrant villains as you can be. And so farewell ! Be all hanged ; and come down to me as soon as you can.

This said, he departed to his molten kingdom, the wind risse, the bottom of the chair fell out, the scrivener fell flat upon his nose. And here is the end of a harmless moral.

Finis.

An Episode taken from

THE BELLMAN OF LONDON

By Thomas Dekker

1608

WHO would not rather sit at the foot of a hill, tending a flock of sheep, than at the helm of authority, controlling the stubborn and unruly multitude? Better it is in the solitary woods, and in the wild fields, to be a man amongst beasts than in the midst of a peopled city to be a beast among men. In the homely village art thou more safe than in a fortified castle; the stings of envy, nor the bullets of treason, are never shot through those thin walls; sound healths are drunk out of the wholesome wooden dish, when the cup of gold boils over with poison. The country cottage is neither battered down by the cannon in time of war, nor pestered with clamorous suits in time of peace. The fall of cedars, that tumble from the tops of kingdoms, the ruin of great houses, that bury families in their overthrow, and the noise of shipwrecks, that beget even shrieks in the heart of cities, never send their terrors thither. That place stands as safe from the shock of such violent storms as the bay-tree does from lightning.

The admiration of these beauties made me so enamoured, and so really in love with the inheritor of them, that the flames of my affection were, in their burning, only carried thither. So that instead of paved streets, I trod the unbeaten paths of the fields. The ranks of trees were to me as great buildings; lambs and skipping kids were as my merry companions; the clear fountain, as my cups of wine, roots and herbs, as the table of an ordinary; the dialogues of birds, as the scenes of a play; and the open empty meadows, as the proud and populous city. Thus did I wish to live, thus to die. And, having wandered long, like a Timonist[1], hating men because they dishonoured their creation, at length Fortune led me by the hand into a place, so curiously built by nature, as if it had been the palace where she purposed none should lie but herself. It was a grove set thick with trees, which grew in such order that they made a perfect circle; insomuch that I stood in fear it was kept by fairies, and that I was brought into it by enchantment. The branches of the trees, like so many hands, reached over one to another and in their embracements held so fast together that their boughs made a goodly green roof, which, being touched by the wind, it was a pleasure to behold so large a ceiling to move. Upon every branch sat a consort of singers, so that every tree showed like a music-room. The floor of this summer-house was paved all over with yellow field-flowers, and with white and red daisies, upon which the sun casting but a wanton eye, you would have sworn the one had been nails of gold, and the other, studs of enamelled silver. Amazed I was when I did but look into this little paradise, and afraid to enter, doubting whether it were some hallowed ground or no, for I could find no path that directed me to it; neither the foot of any man nor the hoof of any beast had beaten down the grass; for the blades of it stood so high and so even, as if their lengths had been given them by one measure. The melody which the birds made, and the variety of all sorts of fruits which the trees promised, with the pretty and harmless murmuring of a shallow stream, running in windings through the midst of it (whose noise went like a chime of bells, charming the eyes to sleep), put me in mind of that garden whereof our great-grandsire was the keeper. I even wept for sorrow to think he should be so foolish as to be driven from a place of such happiness; and blamed him in my mind for leaving such a precedent behind him, because by his fall we lost his felicity, and by his frailty all men are now apt to undo themselves and their posterity, through the enticements of women.

Into this grove, therefore, at last I did venture, resolving to make it the temple where my thoughts should spend themselves in fruitful contemplation. I purposed to divide the day into Acts, as if the ground had been a stage and that the life which there I meant to lead should have been but as a play. Some of my hours should have run out in speculation of the admirable workmanship of Heaven and of the orders which the celestial bodies are governed by. Some of my hours should have carried me up and down the earth and have shown unto me the qualities and proportions of the creatures that breed upon it. At another time would I have written satires against the impiety of the world; at another, I would have chanted roundelays in honour of the country life. The rest of my time should have fetched in provision for my body. These were appointed to be my Acts in this goodly theatre, the music between were the singers of the wood, the audience, such as Orpheus played unto, and those were mountains and trees, who, unless the whispering winds troubled them with their noise, would have been very attentive.

But whilst I was setting forth to run this goal, behold, casting up mine eye, I espied afar off certain clouds of smoke, whose vapours ascended up so black and thick into the element, as if the sighs of Hell had burst the bowels of the earth, and were flying up toward Heaven, to pull down more vengeance. Before I saw this, I believed that this place had been free from all resort. Desirous, therefore, to learn who they were that neighboured so nigh, and in a solitary wood, that stood so far from inhabited buildings, I stepped forward and came to the place, which, what by nature and what by art, was so fenced about with trees, quickset hedges, and bushes, which were grown so high that, but for the smoke, it was not possible to imagine how a house could there be builded. There was but one path leading to it, which, after much searching and many turnings, being found, boldly went I on, and arrived at a homely cottage. The very door of it put me in mind of that poor inn of good Baucis and Philæmon, where a god was a guest; for it was so low that even a dwarf might have seemed a tall man entering into it, so much would it have made him stoop.

This house stood not like great men's places, always shut, but wide open, as if Bounty had been the porter, and, being within, it seemed Hospitality dwelt there, and had given you welcome. For there was a table ready covered with fair linen; nut-brown round trenchers lay in good order, with bread and salt keeping their state in the middle of the board. The room itself was not sumptuous, but handsome; of indifferent bigness, but not very large. The windows were spread with herbs, the chimney dressed up with green boughs, and the floor strewed with bulrushes, as if some lass were there that morn to be married: but neither saw I any bride or bridegroom, nor heard I any music. Only in the next room (which was the kitchen, and into which I went) was there as much stirring, as commonly is to be seen in a booth upon the first day of the opening of a fair. Some sat turning of spits, and the place, being all smoky, made me think on Hell, for the joints of meat lay as if they had been broiling in the infernal fire; the turn-spits, who were poor tattered greasy fellows, looking like so many he-devils, some were basting, and seemed like fiends pouring scalding oil upon the damned; others were mincing of pie-meat, and showed like hangmen cutting up of quarters, whilst another whose eyes glowed with the heat of the fire, stood poking in at the mouth of an oven, torturing souls, as it were, in the furnace of Lucifer. There was such chopping of herbs, such tossing of ladles, such plucking of geese, such scalding of pigs, such singing, such scolding, such laughing, such swearing, such running to and fro, as if Pluto had that day bidden all his friends to a feaſt, and that these had been the cooks that dressed the dinner.

At the laſt, espying an old nimble-tongued beldam, who seemed to have the command of the place, to her I ſtepped, and in fair terms requeſted to know the name of the dwelling, why this great cheer was provided, and who were the gueſts ; for as yet I saw nobody but this band of the Black Guard. Inſtead of her tongue, her eyes, that had ſtarted back a good way into her head, as if they durſt not look out, made me an answer. I perceived by her very countenance that I was not welcome, which afterwards she confirmed in words, telling me the place was not for me, the feaſt was for others, and that I muſt inſtantly be gone, for that a ſtrange kind of people were that day to be merry there. No rhetoric that I could use had power to win her to discover who these gueſts should be, till, at the length, a bribe prevailing more than a parley, she told me I should be a specʧator of the comedy in hand, and in a private gallery behold all the acʧors, upon condition I would sit quietly and say nothing ; and for that purpose was I conveyed into an upper loft where unseen I might, through a wooden lattice that had the prospecʧt of the dining-room, both see and hear all that was to be done or spoken.

There lay I like a scout to discover the coming of the expecʧted enemy, who was to set upon this good cheer, and to batter down the walls of hot pies and paſties. Mine eyes even ached with ſtaring towards the door, to spy when these ſtates should enter, ducking down with their heads, like so many geese going into a barn. At length, with bag and baggage, they came dropping in one after another, sometimes three in a company, sometimes five, now more, now less, till, in the end, the great hall was so full that it swarmed with them. I know you wonder, and have longing thoughts to know what generation this is that lived in this hospitable familiarity ; but let me tell you, they are a people for whom the world cares not, neither care they for the world. They are all freemen, yet scorn to live in cities ; great travellers they are, and yet never from home ; poor they are, and yet have their diet from the beſt men's tables. They are neither old serving-men (for all I say they are poor) that have been courtiers, and are now paſt carrying of cloak-bags ; nor young gallants that have served in the Low Countries, albeit many of them go upon wooden legs ; nor hungry scholars, that all their life time have kept a wrangling in the schools, and in the end are glad to teach children their hornbooks : neither are they decayed poets, whose wits, like a fool's land, hold out but a twelvemonth, and then they live upon the scraps of other men's invention ; no, nor players they be, who out of an ambition to wear the best jerkin in a strolling company, or to act great parts, forsake the stately, and our more than Roman, City stages to travel upon the hard hoof from village to village for cheese and buttermilk ; neither are they any of those terrible noises, with threadbare cloaks, that live by red lattices and ivy-bushes[2], having authority to thrust into any man's room, only speaking but this, " Will you have any music ? " Neither are they citizens that have been blown up (without gunpowder), and by that means have been free of the grate at Ludgate[3] some five times. No, no, this is a ging of good fellows in whom there is more brotherhood. This is a crew that is not the Damned Crew, for *they* walk in satin ; but this is the *Ragged Regiment*. Villains they are by birth, varlets by education, knaves by profession, beggars by the statute, and rogues by Act of Parliament. They are the idle drones of a country, the caterpillars of a commonwealth, and the Egyptian lice of a kingdom. And albeit that at other times their attire was fitting to their trade of living, yet now were they all in handsome clean linen, because this was one of their quarter-dinners ; for you must understand that (as afterward I learned by intelligence) they hold these solemn meetings in four several seasons of the year at least, and in several places to avoid discovery.

The whole assembly being thus gathered together, one amongst the rest, who took upon him a seniority over the rest, charged every man to answer to his name, to see if the jury were full : the Bill, by which he meant to call them being a double jug of ale—that had the spirit of *aqua-vitæ* in it, it smelt so strong—and that he held in his hand ; another standing by with a toast, nutmeg, and ginger, ready to cry *Vous avez* as they were called, and all that were in the room having single pots by the ears, which like pistols were charged to go off so soon as ever they heard their names. This ceremony being set abroach, an oyez was made. But he that was *rector chori*, the captain of the tatterdemalions, spying one to march under his colours that had never before served in these lousy wars, paused awhile (after he had taken his first draught, to taste the dexterity of the liquor), and then began, justice-like, to examine this younger brother upon Interrogatories.

The first question he demanded, was, if he were stalled to the rogue or no. The poor Hungarian answered, yes, he was. Then was he asked by whom he was stalled, and where, and in what manner of compliment it was done ; to which question the novice having not so much beggarly knowledge as might make a learned reply, forthwith did the wicked elder command the young Slavonians[4] that stood about him to disfurnish him, that was so unskilful in the rudiments of roguery, of his best garment, and to carry it presently to the bousing ken (that was to say, to the tap-house), and there to pawn it for so much strong ale as could be ventured upon it. Thus the chief ragamuffin gave in charge ; the rest obeyed and did so ; whilst the other suffered himself to be stripped, and durst not resist their base authority.

This done, the grand signor called for a gage of bouse, which belike signified a quart of drink, for presently, a pot of ale being put into his hand, he made the young squire kneel down, and, pouring the full pot on his pate, uttered these words : *I, ——, do stall thee, ——, to the rogue, by virtue of this sovereign English liquor, so that henceforth it shall be lawful for thee to cant, that is to say, to be a vagabond and beg, and to speak that pedlar's French, or that canting language, which is to be found among none but beggars.* With that, the stalled gentleman rose, all the rest in the room hanging upon him for joy, like so many dogs about a bear, and leaping about him with shouts like so many madmen.

But a silence being proclaimed, all were hushed, whilst he that played the master-devil's part amongst these hell-hounds, after a shrug or two given, thus began to speak to him that was new-entered into the damned fraternity :

" Brother beggar," quoth he, " because thou art yet but a mere freshman in our college, I charge thee to hang thine ears to my lips, and to learn the orders of our house which thou must observe, upon pain either to be beaten with our cudgels the next time thou art met, or else to be stripped out of any garments that are worth the taking from thee. First, therefore, being no better than a plain ordinary rogue, marry, in time thou mayest rise to more preferment amongst us. Thou art not to wander up and down all countries, but to walk only, like an underkeeper of a forest, in that quarter which is allotted unto thee. Thou art likewise to give way to any of us that have borne all the offices of the wallet before thee, and, upon holding up a finger, to avoid any town or country village, where thou seest we are foraging to victual our army that march along with us. For, my poor *vigliacco*, thou must know that there are degrees of superiority and inferiority in our society, as there are in the proudest company.

" We have amongst us some eighteen or nineteen several offices for men, and about seven or eight for women.[5] The chiefest of us are

called upright-men, (Ay, my dear sunburnt brother, if all those that
are the chiefeſt men in other companies were upright-men too, what
good dealing would there be in all occupations !) ; the next ace, rufflers.
Then have we anglers, but they seldom catch fish, till they go up weſtward for flounders.   Then are there rogues (the livery thou thyself
now weareſt).   Next are wild rogues ; then priggers ; then palliards ;
then fraters; then Tom of Bedlam's band of madcaps, otherwise called
Poor Tom's flock of wild-geese, whom here thou seeſt by his black
and blue naked arms to be a man beaten to the world ; and those wild-
geese, or hare-brains, are called abram-men.   In the next squadron
march our brave whip-jacks.   At the tail of them come crawling our
counterfeit cranks.   In another troop are gabbling dummerers.   Then
curtals follow at their heels ; and they bring along with them ſtrange
engineers, called Irish toyles.   After whom follow the swigmen, the
jarkmen, the patricoes, and laſt the kinchin coes.   These are the tattered
regiments that make up our main army.   The victuallers to the camp
are women, and of those some are glimmerers, some bawdy-baskets,
some autem-morts ;   others walking morts ; some dopers,[6] others are
dells.   The laſt and leaſt are called kinchin morts.   With all which
comrades, thou shalt in thy beggarly peregrination meet, converse, and
be drunk, and in a short time know their natures and roguish conditions
without the help of a tutor."

At these words the victuals came smoking into the hall to be set
upon the board ; whereupon the whole swarm squatted down, being
as uncivil in manners, as unhandsome in apparel ; only the upright-men
and rufflers had the grain of the board given them, and sat at upper end
of the table.   The reſt took their trenchers as they happed into their
hands, yet so that every knave had his quean close by his side.

The table being thus furnished both with gueſts and meat, inſtead
of grace every one drew out a knife, rapped out a round oath and cried,
" Proface, you mad rogues ! " and so fell to.   They fed more hungrily
than if they had come from the siege of Jerusalem.   Not a word was
heard amongſt them for a long time, only their teeth made a noise, as
if so many mills had been grinding.   Rats going to the assault of a
Holland cheese could not more valiantly lay about them ; nay, my
Lord Mayor's hounds at the dog-house, being bidden to the funeral
banquet of a dead horse, could not pick the bones cleaner.   At length,
when the platters began to look lean, and their bellies grew plump,
then went their tongues.   But such a noise made they, such a confusion
was there of beggarly tales, some gabbling in their canting language,

others in their own, that the scolding at ten conduits,[7] and the gossipings of fifteen bakehouses was delicate music of it.   At the length, drunken healths reeled up and down the table, and then it would have made a physician himself sick, but to have looked upon the waters that came from them.   The whole room showed afar off (but that there was heard such a noise) like a Dutch piece of drollery ; for they sat at table as if they had been so many antics.   A painter's 'prentice could not draw worse faces than they themselves made, besides those which God gave them, no, nor a painter himself vary a picture into more strange and more ill-favoured gestures, than were to be seen in the action of their bodies ; for some did nothing but weep, and protest love to their morts, another swore daggers and knives to cut the throat of his doxy,[8] if he found her tripping ; some slept, being drowned so deep in ale dregs that they slavered again ; others sung bawdy songs ; another crew devised curses upon Justices of Peace, headboroughs and constables, grinding their teeth so hard together for anger, that the grating of a saw in a stone-cutter's yard, when it files in sunder the ribs of marble, makes not a more horrible noise.   In the end, one who took upon him to be speaker to the whole house, bidding the French and English pox on their yelping throats, cried out for silence, telling them it was his turn, according to the customs of their meeting, to make an oration in praise of beggary, and of those that profess the trade.   Hereupon, as if an owl had happened amongst so many birds, all their eyes did presently stare upon him, who thus began :

" My noble hearts, my old weather-beaten fellows and brave English spirits, I am to give you that which all the land knows you justly deserve —a roguish commendation ; and you shall have it.   I am to give beggars their due praise, yet what need I do that, sithence no man, I think, will take anything from them that is their due.   To be a beggar is to be a brave man, because 'tis now in fashion for very brave men to beg.   No, but what a rogue am I to build up your honours upon examples !   Do we not all come into the world like arrant beggars, without a rag upon us ?   Do we not all go out of the world like beggars, saving only an old sheet to cover us ?   And shall we not walk up and down in the world like beggars, with old blankets pinned about us ? "

" Yes, yes, we will," roared all the kennel, as though it had been the dogs of Paris Garden.

" Peace," cries the penniless orator and with a hem proceeds.

" What though there be Statutes to burn us i'th ears for rogues, to singe us i'th hand for pilferers, to whip us at posts for being beggars,

and to shackle our heels i'th ſtocks for being idle vagabonds, what of
this? Are there not other Statutes more sharp than these to punish
the reſt of the subjects, that scorn to be our companions? What
though a prating conſtable, or a red-nosed beadle say to one of us,
' Sirrah Goodman Rogue, if I served you well, I should see you whipped
through the town'? Alas! alas! silly animals! If all men should
have that which they deserve, we should do nothing but play the executioners and tormenters one of another.

" A number of tailors would be damned for keeping a hell[9] under
their shop-board ; all the brokers would make their Wills at *Tyburn,* if
the searching for ſtolen goods which they have received should like a
plague but once come amongſt them ; yea, if all were served in their
right kind, two parts of the land should be whipped at Bridewell for
lechery, and three parts, at leaſt, be set i'th ſtocks for drunkenness.
The life of a beggar is the like of a soldier. He suffers hunger and cold
in winter, and heat and thirſt in summer ; he goes lousy, he goes lame,
he's not regarded, he's not rewarded. Here only shines his glory :
the whole kingdom is but his walk, a whole city is but his parish ; in
every man's kitchen is his meat dressed, in every man's cellar lies his
beer, and the beſt men's purses keep a penny for him to spend.

" Since, then, the profession is ancient—as having been from the
beginning—and so general that all sorts of people make it their laſt
refuge ; since a number of artificers maintain their houses by it ; since
we, and many a thousand more, live merrily with it ; let us, my brave
tawny-faces, not give up our patched cloaks, nor change our copies,
but, as we came beggars out of our mothers' bellies, so resolve and set
up your ſtaves upon this, to return like beggars into the bowels of the
earth. *Dixi.*"

Scarce was the word *Dixi* belched out of his rotten aly lungs, but all
the bench-whiſtlers from one end to the other gave a ringing *plaudite*
to the epilogue of his speech in sign of approbation. Whereupon they
rose up as confusedly as they sat down, and, having paid so far as their
purses would ſtretch for what they had devoured, making O's in chalk[10]
for the reſt when they met there next, and every man with his mort
being assigned to their quarter ; which order given, at what following
fairs to shake hands, and what ale-bush to tipple, with items likewise
given where to ſtrike down geese, where to ſteal hens, and from what
hedges to fetch sheets, that may serve as pawns, away they departed.

Turba gravis paci, placidæque, inimica quieti.

LANTERN AND CANDLELIGHT

OR

THE BELLMAN'S SECOND NIGHT'S WALK

By Thomas Dekker

1608.

A table of all the matters that are contained in this book.

To the very worthy gentleman, Master Francis Mustian, of Peckham.

SIR,

IT may happily seem strange unto you that such an army of idle words should march into the open field of the world under the ensign of your name, you being not therewith made acquainted till now. You may judge it in me an error; I myself confess it a boldness. But such an ancient and strong charter hath custom confirmed to this printing age of ours, by giving men authority to make choice of what patrons they like, that some writers do almost nothing contrary to the custom, and some, by virtue of that privilege, dare do any thing. I am neither of that first order, nor of this last. The one is too fondly ceremonious, the other too impudently audacious. I walk in the midst, so well as I can, between both. With some fruits that have grown out of my brain, have I been so far from being in love, that I thought them not worthy to be tasted by any particular friend, and therefore have they been exposed only to those that would entertain them. Neither did I think the fairest that ever was mine so worthy, that it was to be looked upon with the eye of universal censure. Two sorts of madmen trouble the stationers' shops in Paul's Churchyard: they that out of a mere and idle vainglory will ever be pamphleting, though their books being printed are scarce worth so much brown paper; and this is a very poor and foolish ambition: of the other sort are they that being free of wit's Merchant Venturers, do every new moon (for gain only) make five or six voyages to the press, and every term-time upon booksellers' stalls lay whole litters of blind invention; fellows yet, if they do but walk in the middle aisle, spit nothing but ink, and speak nothing but poem. I would keep company with neither of these two madmen, if I could avoid them. Yet I take the last to be the wisest and less dangerous; for sithence all the arrows that men shoot in the world fly to two marks only (either pleasure or profit) he is not much to be condemned that having no more acres to live upon than those that lie in his head, is every hour hammering out one piece or other out of this rusty iron age, sithence the golden and silver globes of the world are so locked up that a scholar can hardly be suffered to behold them. Some perhaps will say, that this lancing of the pestilent sores of a kingdom so openly may infect those in it that are sound, and that in this our school, where close abuses and gross villainies are but discovered and not punished, others, that never before knew such evils, will be now instructed by the book to practise them. If so, then let not a traitor or a murderer be publicly arraigned, lest the one laying open to the world how his plots were woven to contrive a treason, or the other, what policies he was armed with for the shedding of blood, the standers-by, that are honest, be drawn by their rules to run headlong into the same mischief. No, our strong physic works otherwise. What more makes a man to loath that mongrel madness, that half English, half Dutch sin, drunkenness, than to see a common drunkard acting his scenes in the open street? Is any gamester so foolish to play with false dice, when he is assured that all who are about him know him to be a sworn cheater? The letting therefore of vice blood in these several veins, which the Bellman hath opened, cannot by any judicial rules of physic endanger the body of the commonwealth, or make it feeble, but rather restore those parts to perfect strength, which by disorder have been diseased.

Give me leave to lead you by the hand into a wilderness, where are none but monsters, whose cruelty you need not fear, because I teach the way to tame them. Ugly they are in shape, and devilish in conditions. Yet to behold them afar off may delight you, and to know their qualities, if ever you should come near them, may save you from much danger. Our country breeds no wolves nor serpents, yet these engender here, and are either serpents or wolves, or worse than both. Whatsoever they are, I send unto you not the herd of the one, or the bed of the other, but only a picture of either. View them, I pray, and where the colours are not well laid on, shadow them with your finger. If you spy any disproportion, thus excuse it: such painting is fit for monsters. How rudely soever the piece is drawn, call it a picture. And when one more worth your view lies under the workman's pencil, this bad one shall bring you home a better. In the meantime, I cease, and begin to be, if you please,

All yours,

THOMAS DEKKER.

To my own nation.

Readers,

After it was proclaimed abroad that, under the conduct of the Bellman of London, new forces were once more to be levied against certain wild and barbarous rebels, that were up in open arms against the tranquility of the weal public, it cannot be told what numbers of voluntaries offered themselves daily to fight against so common, so bold, so strange, and so dangerous an enemy. Light horsemen came in hourly, with discovery where these mutineers lay entrenched ; delivering, in brief notes of intelligence, who were their leaders, how they went armed, and that they served both on horse and foot. Only their strengths could not be descried, because their numbers were held infinite. Yet instructions were written and sent every minute by those that were favourers of goodness, showing what military disciplines the foe used in his battles, and what forts, if he were put at any time to flight, he would retire to; what stratagems he would practise and where he did determine to lie in ambuscado. They that could not serve in person in this noble quarrel sent their auxiliary forces, well armed with counsel. So that the Bellman, contrary to his own hopes, seeing himself so strongly and strangely seconded by friends, doth now bravely advance forward in main battalion. The day of encounter is appointed to be in this Michælmas Term. The place, Paul's Churchyard, Fleet Street, and other parts of the City. But before they join, let me give you note of one thing, and that is this.

There is an usurper, that of late hath taken upon him the name of the Bellman, but being not able to maintain that title, he doth now call himself the Bellman's brother. His ambition is, rather out of vainglory than the true courage of an experienced soldier, to have the leading of the van, but it shall be honour good enough for him (if not too good) to come up with the rear. You shall know him by his habiliments, for, by the furniture he wears, he will be taken for a beadle of Bridewell. It is thought he is rather a neuter than a friend to the cause. And therefore the Bellman doth here openly protest that he comes into the field as no fellow in arms with him.

Howsoever it be struck, or whosoever gives the first blow, the victory depends upon the valour of you that are the wings to the Bellman's army ; for which conquest he is in hope you will valiantly fight, sithence the quarrel is against the head of monstrous abuses, and the blows which you muſt give are in defence of law, juſtice, order, ceremony, religion, peace, and that honourable title of goodness.

Saint George ! I see the two armies move forward : and behold, the Bellman himself firſt chargeth upon the face of the enemy. Thus :—

To the Author.

Howe'er thou may'ſt by blazing all abuse
Incur suspect, thou speak'ſt what thou haſt proved,
Though then to keep it close it thee behoved ;
So, Reason makes for thee a juſt excuse.
Yet of thy pains the beſt may make good use ;
Then of the beſt, thy pains should be approved,
And for the fame of them shouldſt be beloved ;
Sith thou of Falsehood's flood doſt ope the sluice,
That they at waſte continually may run,
By showing men the reaches that they have,
That honeſt men may so o'er reach a knave,
Or sound their swallowing deeps, the same to shun.
But if from hence a knave more cunning grows,
That spider sucks but poison from thy rose.
                    Thy friend if thine own,

                                        Jo. Da.

To his friend.

Of vice, whose counter-mine a ſtate confounds,
Worse than sedition ; of those mortal wounds
Which, throughly searched, do kingdoms' hearts endanger ;
Of plagues that o'errun cities ; of those ſtranger
Big-swoln impoſtumes, poisoning the ſtrong health
Of the moſt sound, beſt dieted commonwealth,
Thou tell'ſt the causes, and doſt teach the cure,
By medicine well-compounded, cheap, and sure :
And, as one read in deep chirurgery,
Draw'ſt of these evils, the true anatomy.
Then on thy plainness let none lay reproof,
Thou tak'ſt sin's heighth, as men do ſtars, aloof.

                                        M. R.

To my industrious friend.

In an ill time thou writ'st, when tongues had rather
Spit venom on thy lines, than from thy labours,
As druggists do from poison, medicine gather ;
This is no age to crown desert with favours.
But be thou constant to thyself, and care not
What arrows malice shoots.   The wise will never
Blame thy loud singing, and the foolish dare not.
None else but wolves will bark at thine endeavour.
When thou in thy dead sleep liest in thy grave,
These charms to after-ages up shall raise thee.
What here thou leav'st, alive thy name shall save,
And what thou now dispraisest, shall then praise thee.
Though not to know ill be wise ignorance,
Yet thou by reading evil dost goodness teach,
And, of abuse the colours dost advance
Only upon abuse to force a breach ;
The honour that thy pen shall earn thereby
Is this : that though knaves live, their sleights here die.
                                                    E. G.

LANTERN AND CANDLELIGHT

OR

THE BELLMAN'S SECOND NIGHT'S WALK.

CHAPTER II

THE BELLMAN'S SECOND NIGHT'S WALK

IT was term-time in Hell[2]—for, you must understand, a lawyer lives there as well as here—by which means Don Lucifer, being the Justice for that county where the brimstone mines are, had better doings and more rapping at his gates, than all the doctors and empirical quack-salvers of ten cities have at theirs in a great plague-time. The hall where these termers were to try their causes was very large and strongly built, but it had one fault : it was so hot that people could not endure to walk there. Yet to walk there they were compelled, by reason they were drawn thither upon occasions ; and such jostling there was of one another, that it would have grieved any man to be in the throngs amongst them. Nothing could be heard but noise, and nothing of that noise be understood, but that it was a sound as of men in a kingdom when on a sudden it is in an uproar. Every one brabbled with him that he walked with, or, if he did but tell his tale to his counsel, he was so eager in the very delivery of that tale, that you would have sworn he did brabble. And such gnashing of teeth there was when adversaries met together, that the filing of ten thousand saws cannot yield a sound more horrible. The Judge of the Court had a devilish countenance, and as cruel he was in punishing those that were condemned by law, as he was crabbed in his looks, whilst he sat to hear their trials. But albeit there was no pity to be expected at his hands, yet was he so upright in justice, that none could ever fasten bribe upon him, for he was ready and willing to hear the cries of all comers. Neither durst any pleader at the infernal bar, or any officer of the Court, exact any fee of plaintiffs and such as complained of wrongs and were oppressed ; but only they paid that were the wrongdoers ; those would they see damned ere they should get out of their fingers ; such fellows they were appointed to vex at the very soul.

The matters that here were put in suit were more than could be bred in twenty vacations, yet should a man be despatched out of hand. In one term he had his judgment, for here they never stand upon Returns[3], but presently come to trial. The causes decided here are many; the clients that complain, many; the counsellors, that plead till they be hoarse, many; the attorneys, that run up and down, infinite; the clerks of the Court, not to be numbered. All these have their hands full: day and night are they so plagued with the bawling of clients that they never can rest.

The ink wherewith they write is the blood of conjurers: they have no paper, but all things are engrossed in parchment, and that parchment is made of scriveners' skins flayed off, after they have been punished for forgery: their standishes are the sculls of usurers; their pens, the bones of unconscionable brokers, and hard-hearted creditors, that have made dice of other men's bones, or else of perjured executors and blind overseers[4], that have eaten up widows and orphans to the bare bones: and those pens are made of purpose without nibs, because they may cast ink but slowly, in mockery of those who in their lifetime were slow in yielding drops of pity.

Would you know what actions are tried here? I will but turn over the records, and read them unto you as they hang upon the file.

The courtier is sued here, and condemned for riots.

The soldier is sued here, and condemned for murders.

The scholar is sued here, and condemned for heresies.

The citizen is sued here, and condemned for the city-sins.

The farmer is sued here upon penal Statutes, and condemned for spoiling the markets.[5]

Actions of battery are brought against swaggerers, and here they are bound to the peace.

Actions of waste are brought against drunkards and epicures; and here they are condemned to beg at the grate for one drop of cold water to cool their tongues, or one crumb of bread to stay their hunger, yet are they denied it.

Harlots have process sued upon them here, and are condemned to howling, to rottenness, and to stench. No Acts of Parliament that have passed the Upper House* can be broken, but here the breach is punished, and that severely, and that suddenly. For here they stand upon no demurrers,[6] no *Audita querela*[7] can here be gotten, no writs of errors,[8] to reverse judgment: here is no flying to a Court of Chancery

* Heaven.

for relief, yet every one that comes hither is served with a *subpœna*. No, they deal altogether in this Court upon the *Habeas Corpus*,[9] upon the *Capias*,[10] upon the *Ne exeat regnum*,[11] upon rebellion,[12] upon heavy fines (but no recoveries),[13] upon writers of outlawry, to attach the body for ever, and last of all upon Executions after judgment, which being served upon a man is his everlasting undoing.

Such are the customs and courses of proceedings in the offices belonging to the Prince of Darkness. These hot doings hath he in his term-times. But upon a day when a great matter was to be tried between an Englishman and a Dutchman, which of the two were the foulest drinkers, and the case being a long time in arguing, by reason that strong evidence came in reeling on both sides—yet it was thought that the Englishman would carry it away, and cast the Dutchman—on a sudden all was stayed by the sound of a horn that was heard at the lower end of the hall. And everyone looking back, as wondering at the strangeness, " Room ! room ! " was cried and made through the thickest of the crowd, for a certain spirit in the likeness of a post, who made a way on a little lean nag up to the bench where Judge Radamanth with his two grim brothers, Minos and Æacus, sat. This spirit was an intelligencer sent by Beelzebub of Batharum into some countries of Christendom, to lie there as a spy, and had brought with him a packet of letters from several lieges that lay in those countries for the service of the Tartarian their Lord and Master, which packet being opened, all the letters, because they concerned the general good and state of those low countries in Hell, were publicly read. The contents of that letter stung most, and put them all out of their law-cases, were to this purpose :

That whereas the Lord of Fiery Lakes, had his ministers in all kingdoms above the earth, whose offices were not only to win subjects of other princes to his obedience, but also to give notice when any of his own sworn household, or any other that held league with him, should revolt or fly from their duty and allegiance ; as also discover from time to time all plots, conspiracies, machinations, or underminings, that should be laid (albeit they that durst lay them should dig deep enough) to blow up his great infernal city : so that if his Horned Regiment were not suddenly mustered together, and did not lustily bestir their cloven stumps, his territories would be shaken, his dominions left in time unpeopled, his forces looked into, and his authority which he held in the world contemned and laughed to scorn. The reason was, that a certain fellow, the Child of Darkness, a common night-walker, a man that had no man to wait upon him but only a dog, one that was a disordered person, and at midnight would beat at men's doors, bidding them in mere mockery to look to their candles, when they themselves were in their dead sleeps, and albeit he was an officer, yet he was but of light carriage, being known by the name of the Bellman of London, had of late not only drawn a number of the Devil's own kindred into question for their lives, but had also, only by the help of the lantern and candle, looked into the secrets of the best

Plate XIII.

WESTMINSTER HALL IN 1647.

[*face p. 320*

THE BELMAN
OF LONDON.

Bringing to light the moſt notorious
villanies that are now practiſed
in the K I N G D O M E.

Profitable for Gentlemen, Lawyers, Merchants, Citizens, Farmers,
Maſters of Houſholds, and all ſortes of ſeruants, to marke,
and delightfull for all men to Reade.

Lege, Perlege, Relege.

Printed at London for NATHANIEL BVTTER. 1 6 0 8.

Plate XIV.

[*face p. 321*

trades that are taught in Hell, laying them open to the broad eye of the world, making them infamous, odious, and ridiculous; yea, and not satisfied with doing this wrong to his Devilship, very spitefully hath he set them out in print, drawing their pictures so to the life, that now a horse-stealer shall not show his head, but a halter with the hangman's noose is ready to be fastened about it; a foist nor a nip shall not walk into a fair or a playhouse, but every crack will cry, " Look to your purses "; nor a poor common rogue come to a man's door, but he shall be examined if he can cant. If this bawling fellow, therefore, have not his mouth stopped, the light angels that are coined below will never be able to pass as they have done, but be nailed up for counterfeits. Hell will have no doings, and the Devil be nobody.

This was the limning of the letter, and this letter drave them all to a nonplus, because they knew not how to answer it. But at last advice was taken, the Court brake up, the term was adjourned, by reason that the hell-hounds were thus plagued, and a common council in Hell was presently called how to redress these abuses.

The satanical synagogue being set, up starts the Father of Hell and Damnation, and, looking very terribly with a pair of eyes that stared as wide as the mouth gapes at Bishopsgate,[14] fetching four or five deep sighs (which were nothing else but the smoke of fire and brimstone boiling in his stomach, and showed as if he were taking tobacco, which he oftentimes does), told his children and servants, and the rest of the citizens that dwelt within the freedom of Hell, and sat there before him upon narrow low forms, that they never had more cause to lay their heads together, and to grow politicians. He and they all knew that from the corners of the earth some did every hour in a day creep forth to come and serve him; yea that many thousands were so bewitched with his favours and his rare parts that they would come running quick to him. His dominions, he said, were great and full of people; emperors and kings, in infinite numbers, were his slaves; his court was full of princes; if the world were divided, as some report, but into three parts, two of those three were his; or if, as others affirm, into four parts, [in] almost three of that four had he firm footing.

But if such a fellow as a treble-voiced Bellman should be suffered to pry into the infernal mysteries and into those black arts which command the spirits of the deep, and, having sucked what knowledge he can from them, to turn it all into poison, and to spit it in the very faces of the professors, with a malicious intent to make them appear ugly and so to grow hateful and out of favour with the world; if such a conjurer at midnight should dance in their circles and not be driven out of them, Hell in a few years would not be worth the dwelling in. The great Lord of Limbo did therefore command all his Black Guard, that stood

N

about him, to bestir them in their places, and to defend the Court wherein they lived; threatening, besides, that his curse, and all the plagues of stinking Hell should fall upon his officers, servants, and subjects, unless they either advised him how, or take some speedy order themselves to punish that saucy intelligencer, the Bellman of London. Thus he spake, and then sat.

At last, a foolish devil rose up, and shot the bolt of his advice, which flew thus far, that the Black Dog of Newgate should again be let loose, and afar off follow the bawling Bellman, to watch into what places he went, and what deeds of darkness every night he did. *Hinc risus.* The whole synodical assembly fell a laughing at this wiseacre, so that neither he nor his Black Dog durst bark any more.

Another, thinking to cleave the very pin with his arrow, drew it home to the head of wisdom, as he imagined, and yet that lighted wide too. But thus shot his counsel, that the ghosts of all those thieves, cheaters, and others of the damned crew, who by the Bellman's dis-covery, had been betrayed, were taken, and sent westward, should be fetched from those fields of horror, where every night they walk, dis-puting with Dr. Story,[15] who keeps them company there in his corner cap; and that those wry-necked spirits should have charge given them to haunt the Bellman in his walks, and so fright him out of his wits. This devil, for all his roaring, went away neither with a *plaudite*, nor with a hiss. Others stepped up, some pronouncing one verdict some another. But at the last, it being put into their devilish heads that they had no power over him farther than what should be given unto them, it was concluded and set down as a rule in court, that some one strange spirit, who could transport himself into all shapes, should be sent up to London, and, scorning to take revenge upon so mean a person as a Bellringer, should thrust himself into such companies as, in a warrant to be signed for that purpose, should be nominated; and, being once grown familiar with them, he was to work and win them by all possible means to fight under the dismal and black colours of the Grand Sophy, his Lord and Master. The fruit that was to grow upon this tree of evil would be great, for it should be fit to be served up to Don Lucifer's table, as a new banqueting-dish, sithence all his other meats, though they fatted him well, were grown stale.

Hereupon Pamersiel, the messenger, was called, a passport was drawn, signed and delivered to him, with certain instruments how to carry himself in this travel. And thus much was openly spoken to him by word of mouth:

" Fly, Pamersiel, with speed to the great and populous city in the west; wind thyself into all shapes; be a dog to fawn, a dragon to confound; be a dove, seem innocent; be a devil, as thou art, and show that thou art a journeyman to Hell. Build rather thy nest amongst willows, that bend every way, than on tops of oaks, whose hearts are hard to be broken. Fly with the swallow close to the earth, when storms are at hand; but keep company with birds of greater talents, when the weather is clear; and never leave them till they look like ravens. Creep into bosoms that are buttoned up in satin and there spread the wings of thine infection; make every head thy pillow to lean upon, or use it like a mill, only to grind mischief. If thou meetest a Dutchman, drink with him; if a Frenchman, stab; if a Spaniard, betray; if an Italian, poison; if an Englishman,—do all this.

" Haunt taverns, there thou shalt find prodigals. Pay thy twopence to a player; in his gallery mayest thou sit by a harlot. At ordinaries mayest thou dine with silken fools. When the day steals out of the world, thou shalt meet rich drunkards under welted gowns search for threescore in the hundred. Hug those golden villains, they shine bright, and will make a good show in Hell. Shriek with a cricket in the brewhouse, and watch how they conjure there. Ride up and down Smithfield, and play the jade there. Visit prisons, and teach jailers how to make nets of iron there. Bind thyself 'prentice to the best trades. But if thou canst grow extreme rich in a very short time— honestly—I banish thee my kingdom: come no more into Hell. I have read thee a lecture; follow it. Farewell."

No sooner was farewell spoken, but the spirit to whom all these matters were given in charge vanished. The cloven-footed orator arose, and the whole assembly went about their damnable business.

CHAPTER III

GULL-GROPING

How gentlemen are cheated at ordinaries.

THE Devil's footman was very nimble of his heels, for no wild Irishman could outrun him, and therefore in a few hours was he come up to London; the miles between Hell and any place upon earth being shorter than those between London and St. Albans to any man that travels from thence thither, or to any lackey that comes from hence hither on the Devil's errands ; but to any other poor soul that dwells in those low countries, they are never at an end, and by him are not possible to be measured.

No sooner was he entered into the City, but he met with one of his master's daughters called Pride, dressed like a merchant's wife, who, taking acquaintance of him, and understanding for what he came, told him that the first thing he was to do, he must put himself in good clothes, such as were suitable to the fashion of the time, for that here men were looked upon only for their outsides ; he that had not ten pounds' worth of wares in his shop, would carry twenty marks on his back ; that there were a number of sumpter-horses in the City, who cared not how coarsely they fed, so they might wear gay trappings ; yea, that some pied fools, to put on satin and velvet but four days in the year did often-times undo themselves, wives and children ever after ! The spirit of the Devil's Buttery, hearing this, made a leg to Pride for her counsel, and, knowing by his own experience that every tailor hath his hell[16] to himself under his shop-board, where he damns new satin, amongst them he thought to find best welcome, and therefore into Birchin Lane[17] he stalks very mannerly, Pride going along with him, and taking the upper hand.

No sooner was he entered into the ranks of the linen-armourers, whose weapons are Spanish needles, but he was most terribly and sharply set upon. Every 'prentice boy had a pull at him. He feared they all had been sergeants, because they all had him by the back. Never was poor devil so tormented in Hell as he was amongst them. He thought it had been St. Thomas his day[18], and that he had been called upon to be constable. There was such bawling in his ears, and no strength could shake them off, but that they must show him some suits of apparel, because they saw what gentlewoman was in his company, whom they all knew. Seeing no remedy, into a shop he goes, was fitted bravely, and beating the price, found the lowest to be unreasonable, yet paid it, and departed, none of them, by reason of their crowding about him before, perceiving what customer they had met with. But now the tailor spying the devil, suffered him to go, never praying that he would know the shop another time, but, looking round about his warehouse if nothing were missing, at length he found that he had lost his conscience. Yet remembering himself, that they who deal with the Devil can hardly keep it, he stood upon it the less.

The fashions of an ordinary.

The Stygian traveller being thus translated into an accomplished
gallant, with all accoutrements belonging, as a feather for his head,
gilt rapier for his sides, and new boots to hide his polt-foot (for in Bedlam
he met with a shoemaker, a mad slave, that knew the length of his laſt),
it reſted only that now he was to enter upon company suitable to his
clothes ; and knowing that your moſt selected gallants are the only
tablemen that are played withal at ordinaries, into an ordinary did he
moſt gentlemanlike convey himself in ſtate.

It seemed that all who came thither had clocks in their bellies, for
they all ſtruck into the dining-room much about the very minute of
feeding. Our cavalier had all the eyes that came in thrown upon him,
as being a ſtranger ; for no ambassador from the Devil ever dined
amongſt them before. And he as much took especial notes of them.
In observing of whom and of the place, he found that an ordinary was
the only rendezvous for the moſt ingenious, moſt terse, moſt travelled,
and moſt fantaſtic gallant ; the very exchange for news out of all countries ; the only bookseller's shop for conference of the beſt editions ;
that if a woman, to be a lady, would caſt away herself upon a knight,
there a man should hear a catalogue of moſt of the richeſt London
widows ; and laſt, that it was a school where they were all fellows of
one form, and that a country gentleman was of as great coming as the
proudeſt Juſtice that sat there on the bench above him ; for he that had
the grain of the table with his trencher, paid no more than he that
placed himself beneath the salt.

The Devil's intelligencer could not be contented to fill his eye only
with these objects, and to feed his belly with delicate cheer ; but he
drew a larger picture of all that were there, and in these colours.

The voider having cleared the table, cards and dice for the laſt mess[19]
are served up to the board. They that are full of coin, draw ; they
that have little, ſtand by and give aim ; they shuffle and cut on one side ;
the bones rattle on the other. Long have they not played, but oaths
fly up and down the room like hail-shot. If the poor dumb dice be
but a little out of square, " the pox " and " a thousand plagues " break
their necks out at window. Presently after, the four knaves are sent
packing the same way, or else, like heretics are, condemned to be
burnt.

In this battle of cards and dice, are several regiments and several
officers.

They that sit down to play are at first called leaders.
They that lose are the forlorn hope.
He that wins all is the eagle.
He that stands by and ventures is the woodpecker.
The fresh gallant that is fetched in is the gull.
He that stands by and lends is the gull-groper.

The gull-groper.

This gull-groper is commonly an old moneymonger, who, having travelled through all the follies of the world in his youth, knows them well, and shuns them in his age. His whole felicity being to fill his bags with gold and silver, he comes to an ordinary to save charges of housekeeping, and will eat for his two shillings more meat than will serve three of the guard at a dinner, yet swears he comes thither only for the company, and to converse with travellers. It's a goldfinch that seldom flies to these ordinary nests without a hundred or two hundred pound in twenty shilling pieces about him. After the tearing of some seven pair of cards, or the damning of some ten bale of dice, steps he upon the stage, and this part he plays: If any of the forlorn hope be a gentleman of means, either in *esse* or in *posse*—and that the old fox will be sure to know to half an acre—whose money runs at a low ebb, as may appear by his scratching of the head, and walking up and down the room, as if he wanted an ostler, the gull-groper takes him to a side window and tells him, he's sorry to see his hard luck, but the dice are made of women's bones, and will cozen any man; yet for his father's sake, whom he hath known so long, if it please him, he shall not leave off play for a hundred pound or two. If my young ostrich gape to swallow down this metal, and for the most part they are very greedy, having such provender set before them, then is the gold poured on the board, a bond is made for repayment at the next quarter-day, when exhibition is sent in.[20] And because it is all gold, and cost so much the changing, the scrivener, who is a whelp of the old mastiff's own breeding, knows what words will bite, which thus he fastens upon him, and in this net the gull is sure to be taken howsoever. For if he fall to play again, and lose, the hoary goat-bearded satyr that stands at his elbow, laughs in his sleeve; if his bags be so recovered of their falling-sickness that they be able presently to repay the borrowed gold, then Monsieur Gull-groper steals away of purpose to avoid the receipt of it: he hath fatter chickens in hatching: 'tis a fairer mark he shoots at. For the day being come when the bond grows due, the withinnamed Signor Avaro will not be within ; or, if he be at home, he hath wedges enough in his pate to cause the bond to be broken ; or else a little before the day, he feeds my young master with such sweet words, that surfeiting upon his protestations, he neglects his payment, as presuming he may do more. But the Law having a hand in the forfeiture of the bond, lays presently hold of our young gallant with the help of a couple of sergeants, and just at such a time when old *Erra Pater,* the Jew that lent him the money, knows by his own prognostication that the moon with the silver face is with him in the wane. Nothing then can free him out of the fangs of those bloodhounds, but he must presently confess a judgment for so much money, or for such a manor ot lordship, three times worth the bond forfeited, to be paid or to be entered upon by him, by such a day, or within so many months after he comes to his land. And thus are young heirs cozened out of their acres, before they well know where they lie.

The woodpecker.

The woodpecker is a bird that sits by upon a perch too. But is nothing so dangerous as this vulture spoken of before. He deals altogether upon returns, as men do that take three for one, at their coming back from Jerusalem, etc., for having a jewel, a clock, a ring with a diamond, or any such like commodity. He notes him well that commonly is best acquainted with the dice, and hath ever good luck. To him he offers his prize, rating it at ten or fifteen pound, when haply 'tis not worth above six ; and for it he bargains to receive five shillings or ten shillings, according as it is in value, at every hand, second, third, or fourth hand, he draws. By which means he perhaps in a short time makes that yield him forty fifty pound, which cost not half twenty. Many of these merchant venturers sail from ordinary to ordinary, being sure always to make saving voyages, when they that put in ten times more than they, are for the most part losers.

The gull.

Now if either the leaders, or the forlorn hope, or any of the rest, chance to hear of a young freshwater soldier that never before followed these strange wars, and yet hath a charge newly given him by the old fellow *Soldado Vecchio* his father, when death had shot him into the grave, of some ten or twelve thousand in ready money, besides so many hundreds a year, first are scouts sent out to discover his lodging ; that known, some lie in ambush to note what apothecary's shop he resorts to every morning, or in what tobacco-shop in Fleet Street he takes a pipe of smoke in the afternoon. That fort which the puny holds is sure to be beleaguered by the whole troop of the old weather-beaten gallants, amongst whom some one, whose wit is thought to be of a better block for his head than the rest, is appointed to single out our novice, and after some four of five days spent in compliment, our heir to seven hundred a year is drawn to an ordinary, into which he no sooner enters, but all the old ones in that nest flutter about him, embrace, protest, kiss the hand, congee to the very garter ; and in the end, to show that he is no small fool, but that he knows his father left him not so much money for nothing, the young cub suffers himself to be drawn to the stake. To flesh him, Fortune and the dice, or rather the false dice, that cozen Fortune and make a fool of him too, shall so favour him that he marches away from a battle or two, the only winner. But afterwards, let him play how warily soever he can, the damned dice shall cross him, and his silver crosses shall bless those that play against him ; for even they that seem dearest to his bosom shall first be ready, and be the foremost to enter with the other leaders into conspiracy how to make spoil of his golden bags. By such ransacking of citizens' sons' wealth the leaders maintain themselves brave, the forlorn hope, that drooped before, does now gallantly come on. The eagle feathers his nest, the woodpecker picks up his crumbs, the gull-groper grows fat with good feeding, and the gull himself, at whom every one has a pull, hath in the end scarce feathers enough to keep his own back warm.

The postmaster of Hell, seeing such villainies go up and down in cloaks lined clean through with velvet, was glad he had such news to send over, and, therefore, sealing up a letter full of it, delivered the same to filthy-bearded Charon, their own waterman, to be conveyed first to the porter of Hell, and then by him to the master-keeper of the devils.

CHAPTER IV

OF FERRETING.

The manner of undoing gentlemen by taking up of commodities.

HUNTING is a noble, a manly, and a healthful exercise ; it is a very true picture of war, nay, it is a war in itself ; for engines are brought into the field, stratagems are contrived, ambushes are laid, onsets are given, alarums struck up, brave encounters are made, fierce assailings are resisted by strength, by courage, or by policy ; the enemy is pursued, and the pursuers never give over till they have him in execution ; then is a retreat sounded, then are spoils divided, then come they home wearied, but yet crowned with honour and victory. And, as in battles there be several manners of fight, so in the pastime of hunting, there are several degrees of game. Some hunt the lion, and that shows as when subjects rise in arms against their king ; some hunt the unicorn for the treasure on his head, and they are like covetous men, that care not whom they kill for riches ; some hunt the spotted panther and the freckled leopard ; they are such as to enjoy their pleasures, regard not how black an infamy sticks upon them. All these are barbarous and unnatural huntsmen, for they range up and down the deserts, the wilderness and inhabitable mountains.

Others pursue the long-lived hart, the courageous stag, or the nimble-footed deer. These are the noblest hunters, and they exercise the noblest game. These, by following the chase, get strength of body, a free and undisquieted mind, magnanimity of spirit, alacrity of heart, and an unwearisomeness to break through the hardest labours : their pleasures are not insatiable but are contented to be kept within limits, for these hunt within parks enclosed, or within bounded forests. The hunting of the hare teaches fear to be bold, and puts simplicity so to her shifts, that she grows cunning and provident : the turnings and cross-windings that she makes are emblems of this life's uncertainty : when she thinks she is furthest from danger, it is at her heels, and when it is nearest to her, the hand of safety defends her. When she is wearied and has run her race, she takes her death patiently, only to teach man that he should make himself ready when the grave gapes for him.

All these kinds of hunting are abroad in the open field, but there is a close city hunting only within the walls, that pulls down parks, lays open forests, destroys chases, wounds the deer of the land, and make[s] such havoc of the goodliest herds, that by their wills, who are the rangers, none should be left alive but the rascals. This kind of hunting is base and ignoble. It is the meanest, yet the most mischievous, and it is called ferreting. To behold a course or two at this did the light horseman of Hell one day leap into the saddle.

City hunting.

This ferret-hunting hath his seasons as other games have, and is only followed at such a time of year when the gentry of our kingdom by riots, having chased themselves out of the fair revenues and large possession left to them by their ancestors, are forced to hide their heads like conies in little caves and in unfrequented places ; or else, being almost windless by running after sensual pleasures too fiercely, they are glad, for keeping themselves in breath so long as they can, to fall to ferret-hunting, that is to say, to take up commodities. No warrant can be granted for a buck in this forest, but it must pass under these five hands.

1   He that hunts up and down to find game is called the tumbler.
2   The commodities that are taken up are called purse-nets.
3   The citizen that sells them is the ferret.
4   They that take up are the rabbit-suckers.
5   He upon whose credit these rabbit-suckers run is called the warren.

How the warren is made.

After a rain, conies use to come out of their holes and to sit nibbling on weeds or anything in the cool of the evening, and after a revelling when younger brothers have spent all, or in gaming have lost all, they sit plotting in their chambers with necessity how to be furnished presently with a new supply of money. They would take up any commodity whatsoever, but their names stand in too many texted letters already in mercers' and scriveners' books. Upon a hundred pounds' worth of roasted beef they could find in their hearts to venture, for that would away in turning of a hand. But where shall they find a butcher or a cook that will let any man run so much upon the score for flesh only ?

Suppose, therefore, that four of such loose-fortuned gallants were tied in one knot, and knew not how to fasten themselves upon some wealthy citizen. At the length it runs into their heads that such a young novice, who daily serves to fill up their company, was never entangled in any city lime-bush. They know his present means to be good, and those to come to be great. Him, therefore they lay upon the anvil of their wits, till they have wrought him like wax, for himself as well as for them. To do anything in wax, or, indeed, till they have won him to slide upon this ice—because he knows not the danger—is he easily drawn; for he considers within himself that they are all gentlemen well descended, they have rich fathers, they wear good clothes, have been gallant spenders, and do now and then still let it fly freely. He is to venture upon no more rocks than all they. What then should he fear? He therefore resolves to do it, and the rather because his own exhibition runs low, and that there lack a great many weeks to the quarter-day, at which time, he shall be refurnished from his father.

The match being thus agreed upon, one of them that has been an old ferret-monger, and knows all the tricks of such hunting, seeks out a tumbler, that is to say, a fellow who beats the bush for them till they catch the birds, he himself being contented, as he protests and swears, only with a few feathers.

The tumbler's hunting dry-foot.

This tumbler, being let loose, runs snuffing up and down close to the ground in the shops either of mercers, goldsmiths, drapers, haberdashers, or of any other trade where he thinks he may meet with a ferret; and though upon his very first course he can find his game, yet, to make his gallants more hungry, and to think he wearies himself in hunting the more, he comes to them sweating and swearing that the City-ferrets are so coped (that's to say, have their lips stitched up so close) that he can hardly get them open to so great a sum as five hundred pounds which they desire. This herb being chewed down by the rabbit-suckers, almost kills their hearts, and is worse to them than nabbing on the necks to conies. They bid him, if he cannot fasten his teeth upon plate or cloth or silks, to lay hold on brown paper or tobacco, Bartholmew babies, lutestrings[21] or hobnails, or two hundred pounds in St. Thomas's onions, and the rest in money. The onions they could get wenches enough to cry and sell them by the rope, and what remains should serve them with mutton. Upon this, their tumbler trots up and down again, and at last, lighting on a citizen that will deal, the names are received, and delivered to a scrivener, who, enquiring whether they be good men and true, that are to pass upon the life and death of five hundred pounds, finds that four of the five are wind-shaken, and ready to fall into the Lord's hands. Marry, the fifth man is an oak, and there's hope that he cannot be hewed down in haste. Upon him, therefore, the citizen builds so much as comes to five hundred pounds, yet takes in the other four to make them serve as scaffolding till the farm be furnished, and if then it hold, he cares not greatly who takes them down. In all haste are the bonds sealed, and the commodities delivered ; and then does the tumbler fetch his second career, and that's this :

The tumbler's hunting counter.

The wares, which they fished for, being in the hand of the five shavers, do now more trouble their wits how to turn those wares into ready money, than before they were troubled to turn their credits into wares. The tree being once more to be shaken, they know it must lose fruit, and therefore their factor must barter away their merchandise, though it be with loss. *Abroad* is into the City. He sails for that purpose, and deals with him that sold to buy his own commodities again for ready money. He will not do it under 30 *l.* loss in the hundred. Other archers' bows are tried at the same mark, but all keep much about one scantling. Back therefore comes their carrier with this news, that no man will disburse so much present money upon any wares whatsoever. Only he met by good fortune with *one* friend— and that friend is himself—who for 10 *l.* will procure them a chapman. Marry, that chapman will not buy unless he may have them at 30 *l.* loss in the hundred. "Fuh!" cry all the sharers. "A pox on these fox-furred curmudgeons ! Give that fellow your *friend* 10 *l.* for his pains, and fetch the rest of his money." Within an hour after it is brought, and poured down in one heap upon a tavern table, where, making a goodly show as if it could never be spent, all of them consult what fee the tumbler is to have for hunting so well, and conclude that less than 10 *l.* they cannot give him, which 10 *l.* is the first money told out. Now let us cast up this account. In every 100 *l.* is lost 30 *l.*, which, being five times 30 *l.*, makes 150 *l.* That sum the ferret puts up clear, besides his overpricing the wares ; unto which 150 *l.* lost, add 10 *l.* more which the tumbler gulls them of, and other 10 *l.* which he hath for his voyage, all which makes 170 *l.* ; which deducted from 500 *l.* there remaineth only 330 *l.* to be divided amongst five ; so that every one of the partners shall have but 66 *l.* Yet this they all put up merrily, washing down their losses with sack and sugar, whereof they drink that night profoundly.

How the warren is spoiled.

Whilst this fair weather lasteth, and that there is any grass to nibble upon, these rabbit-suckers keep to the warren wherein they fattened. But the cold day of repayment approaching, they retire deep into their caves ; so that when the ferret makes account to have five before him in chase, four of the five lie hidden, and are stolen into other grounds. No marvel then if the ferret grow fierce and tear open his own jaws, to suck blood from him that is left ! No marvel if he scratch what wool he can from his back ! The purse-nets that were set are all taken up and carried away. The warren therefore must be searched. *That* must pay for all : over *that* does he range like a little lord. Sergeants, Marshals-men,[22] and bailiffs are sent forth, who lie scouting at every corner, and with terrible paws haunt every walk. In conclusion, the bird that these hawks fly after is seized upon ; then are his feathers plucked, his estate looked into ; then are his wings broken, his lands made over to a stranger ; then must our young son and heir pay 500 *l.*, for which he never had but 66 *l.*, or else lie in prison. To keep himself from which, he seals to any bond, enters into any statute,[23] mortgageth any lordship, does anything, says anything, yields to pay anything. And these City storms which will wet a man till he have never a dry thread about him, though he be kept never so warm, fall not upon him once or twice ; but, being a little way in, he cares not how deep he wades : the greater his possessions are, the apter he is to take up and to be trusted : the more he is trusted, the more he comes in debt : the farther in debt, the nearer to danger. Thus gentlemen are wrought upon ! thus are they cheated ! thus are they ferreted ! thus are they undone !

CHAPTER V

FALCONERS.

Of a new kind of hawking, teaching how to catch birds by books.

HUNTING and hawking are of kin, and therefore it is fit they should keep company together. Both of them are noble games and recreations, honest and healthful ; yet they may so be abused that nothing can be more hurtful. In hunting, the game is commonly still before you, or i'th hearing, and within a little compass ; in hawking the game flies far off, and oftentimes out of sight.   A couple of rooks, therefore, that were birds of the last feather, conspired together to leave their nest in the City, and to flutter abroad, into the country. Upon two lean hackneys were these two Doctor Doddypols horsed, civilly suited, that they might carry about them some badge of a scholar.

The Devil's rank rider, that came from the last City-hunting under-standing that two such light-horsemen were gone a hawking, posts after and overtakes them.   After some ordinary highway talk, he begins to question of what profession they were.   One of them, smiling scorn-fully in his face, as thinking him to be some gull (and, indeed, such fellows take all men for gulls who they think to be beneath them in quality), told him they were falconers.   But the fox that followed them, seeing no properties belonging to a falconer about them, smelt knavery, took them for a pair of mad rascals, and therefore resolved to see at what these falconers would let fly.

How to cast up the lure.

At last on a sudden says one of them to him : " Sir, we have sprung a partridge, and so fare you well ! "   Which words came stammering out with the haste that they made, for presently the two foragers of the country were upon the spur. Pluto's post, seeing this, stood still to watch them, and at length saw them in main gallop make toward a goodly fair place, where either some knight or some great gentleman kept.   And this goodly house belike was the partridge which those falconers had sprung.   He, being loath to lose his share in this hawking, and having power to transform himself as he listed, came thither as soon as they, but beheld all which they did, invisible.   They both, like two knights errant, alighted at the gate, knocked and were let in. The one walks the hackneys in an outward court, as if he had been but squire to Sir Dagonet ; the other, as boldly as St. George when he dared the dragon at his very den, marcheth undauntedly up to the hall, where, looking over those poor creatures of the house, that wear but the bare blue-coats, for *Aquila non capit muscas*, what should a falconer meddle with flies ?   He only salutes him that in his eye seems to be a gentlemanlike fellow.   Of him he asks for his good knight or so, and says that he is a gentleman come from London on a business,

which he muſt deliver to his own worshipful ear. Up the ſtairs does
brave Mount Dragon ascend. The knight and he encounter, and with
this ſtaff does he valiantly charge upon him.

How the bird is caught.

" Sir, I am a poor scholar, and the report of your virtues hath drawn
me hither, venturously bold to fix your worthy name as a patronage to
a poor short discourse which here I dedicate, out of my love, to your
noble and eternal memory." This speech he utters barely.

The hawking pamphleteer is then bid to put on, whilſt his miscellane
Mæcenas opens a book fairly apparelled in vellum, with gilt fillets
and fourpenny silk ribbon at leaſt, like little ſtreamers on the top of a
marchpane caſtle, hanging dandling by at the four corners. The
title being superficially surveyed, in the next leaf he sees that the author
he hath made him one of his gossips ; for the book carries his worship's
name, and under it ſtands an epiſtle juſt the length of a henchman's
grace before dinner, which is long enough for any book in conscience,
unless the writer be unreasonable.

The knight, being told beforehand that this little sunbeam of Phœbus,
shining thus briskly in print, hath his mite or atomy waiting upon him
in the outward court, thanks him for his love and labour, and considering
with himself, what coſt he hath been at, and how far he hath ridden
to come to him, he knows that patrons and godfathers are to pay scot
and lot alike, and therefore to cherish his young and tender muse, he
gives him four or six angels, inviting him either to ſtay breakfaſt, or if
the sundial of the house points towards eleven, then to tarry dinner.

How the bird is dressed.

But the fish being caught (for which our Heliconian angler threw
out his lines), with thanks, and legs, and kissing his own hand, he
parts. No sooner is he horsed, but his oſtler, who all this while walked
the jades, and travels up and down with him, like an undeserving player
for half a share, asks this queſtion : " Straws or not ? "—" Straws "
cries the whole sharer and a half.—" Away then," replies the firſt.
" Fly to our neſt." This neſt is never in the same town, but commonly
a mile or two off ; and it is nothing else but the next tavern they come to.
But the village into which they rode being not able to maintain an ivy-
bush, an ale-house was their inn ; where, advancing themselves into the
faireſt chamber, and bespeaking the beſt cheer in the town for dinner,

down they sit, and share before they speak of anything else. That done, he that ventures upon all he meets, and discharges the paper bullets (for, to tell truth, the other serves but as a sign, and is merely nobody) begins to discourse how he carried himself in the action, how he was encountered, how he stood to his tackling, and how well he came off. He calls the knight " a noble fellow," yet they both shrug and laugh, and swear they are glad they have gulled him.

More arrows must they shoot of the same length that this first was off, and therefore there is trunkful of trinkets, that's to say, their budget of books, is opened again, to see what leaf they are to turn over next ; which, whilst they are doing, the ghost, that all this space haunted them, and heard what they said, having excellent skill in the black art, that's to say, in picking of locks, makes the door suddenly fly open, which they had closely shut. At his strange entrance they, being somewhat aghast, began to shuffle away their books, but he knowing what cards they played withal, offered to cut, and turned up two knaves by this trick.

" My masters," quoth he, " I know where you have been, I know what you have done, I know what you mean to do. I see now you are falconers indeed, but by the —— (and then he swore a damnable oath), unless you teach me to shoot in this birding-piece, I will raise the village, send for the knight whom you boast you have gulled, and so disgrace you. For your money I care not."

The two freebooters, seeing themselves smoked, told their third brother he seemed to be a gentleman and a boon companion. They prayed him, therefore, to sit down with silence, and sithence dinner was not yet ready, he should hear all.

" This new kind of hawking," quoth one of them, " which you see us use, can afford no name unless five be at it, viz.

" 1. He that casts up the lure is called the falconer.

" 2. The lure that is cast up is an idle pamphlet.

" 3. The tercel-gentle that comes to the lure is some knight, or some gentleman of like quality.

" 4. The bird that is preyed upon is money.

" 5. He that walks the horses, and hunts dry-foot is called a mongrel.

The falconer and his spaniel.

" The falconer, having scraped together certain small parings of wit, he first cuts them handsomely in pretty pieces, and of those pieces does he patch up a book. This book he prints at his own charge, the mongrel running up and down to look to the workmen, and bearing likewise some part of the coſt, for which he enters upon his half share. When it is fully finished, the falconer and his mongrel, or it may be two falconers join in one, but, howsoever, it is by them devised what shire in England it is beſt to forage next. That being set down, the falconers deal either with a herald for a note of all the knights' and gentlemen's names of worth that dwell in that circuit which they mean to ride, or else by inquiry get the chiefeſt of them, printing off so many epiſtles as they have names, the epiſtles dedicatory being all one, and vary in nothing but in the titles of their patrons.

" Having thus furnished themselves and packed up their wares, away they trudge like tinkers, with a budget at one of their backs. Or it may be the circle they mean to conjure in shall not be out of London, especially if it be term-time, or when a Parliament is holden, for then they have choice of sweet-meats to feed upon. If a gentleman seeing one of these books dedicated only to his name, suspeἀ it to be a baſtard, that hath more fathers besides himself, and, to try that, does defer the presenter for a day or two, sending in the meantime, as some have done, into Paul's Churchyard amongſt the ſtationers, to inquire if any such work be come forth, and if they cannot tell, then to ſtep to the printers, yet have the falconers a trick to go beyond such hawks too, for all they fly so high ; and that is this. The books lie all at the printers, but not one line of an epiſtle to any of them—those bugbears lurk in Tenebris. If, then, the spy that is sent by his maſter ask why they have no dedications to them, Monsieur Printer tells him the author would not venture to add any to them all, saving only to that which was given to his maſter, until it was known whether he could accept of it or no.

" This satisfies the patron ; this fetches money from him ; and this cozens five hundred besides. Nay, there be other bird-catchers that use ſtranger quail-pipes. You shall have fellows, four or five in a country, that, buying up any old book (especially a sermon, or any other matter of divinity) that lies for waſte paper and is clean forgotten, and a new-printed epiſtle to it, and, with an alphabet of letters which they carry about them (being able to print any man's names for a dedication on the sudden), travel up and down moſt shires in England, and live by this hawking."

" Are we not excellent falconers now ? " quoth three-half-shares.
" Excellent villains," cried the Devil's deputy.

By this the meat for dinner came smoking in, upon which they fell moſt tyrannically, yet, for manners' sake, offering firſt to the bailiff of

Beelzebub the upper end of the table. But he, fearing they would make a hawk or a buzzard of him too, and report they had ridden him like an ass, as they had done others, out a doors he flung with a vengeance as he came.

O sacred learning, why dost thou suffer thy seven-leaved tree to be plucked by barbarous and most unhallowed hands? Why is thy beautiful maiden-body polluted like a strumpet's, and prostituted to beastly and slavish ignorance? O thou base brood, that make the Muses harlots, yet say they are your mothers! You thieves of wit, cheaters of art, traitors of schools of learning, murderers of scholars! More worthy you are to undergo the Roman *furca* like slaves, and to be branded in the forehead deeper than they that forge testaments to undo orphans.[24] Such do but rob children of goods that may be lost: but you rob scholars of their fame, which is dearer than life. You are not worth an invective, not worthy to have your names drop out of a deserving pen, you shall only be executed in picture, as they use to handle malefactors in France, and the picture, though it were drawn to be hung up in another place, shall leave you impudently arrogant to yourselves, and ignominiously ridiculous to after ages. In these colours are you drawn.

The true picture of these falconers.

> There be fellows
> Of coarse and common blood; mechanic knaves,
> Whose wits lie deeper buried than in graves,
> And indeed smell more earthy; whose ambition
> Was but to give a boot or shoe good fashion.
> Yet these, throwing by the apron and the awl,
> Being drunk with their own wit, cast up their gall
> Only of ink; and in patched, beggarly rhymes,
> As full of foul corruption as the times,
> From town to town they stroll, in soul as poor
> As th'are in clothes. Yet these at every door
> Their labours dedicate. But, as at fairs,
> Like pedlars, they show still one sort of wares
> Unto all comers (with some filed oration)
> And thus to give books, now's an occupation.
> One book hath seven score patrons. Thus Desert
> Is cheated of her due: thus noble Art
> Gives Ignorance, that common strumpet, place,
> Thus the true scholar's name grows cheap and base, etc.

Chapter VI.

Jacks of the Clock-house.

A new and cunning drawing of money from gentlemen.

There is another fraternity of wandering pilgrims who merrily call themselves Jacks of the clock-house, and are very near allied to the falconers that went a hawking before. The clerk of Erebus set down their names too in his tables, with certain brief notes of their practices. And these they are.

The Jack of a clock-house goes upon screws, and his office is to do nothing but strike. So does this noise, for they walk up and down like fiddlers, travel with motions; and whatsoever their motions get them is called striking.

Those motions are certain collections, or witty inventions, sometimes of one thing, and then of another—there is a new one now, in rhyme, in praise of the Union[25]. And these are fairly written and engrossed in vellum, parchment, or royal paper, richly adorned with compartments, and set out with letters, both in gold and in various colours.

This labour being taken, the master of the motion hearkens where such a nobleman, such a lord, or such a knight, lies, that is liberal. Having found one to his liking, the motion, with his patron's name fairly texted out, in manner of a dedication, is presented before him. He receives it, and, thinking it to be a work only undertaken for his sake, is bounteous to the giver, esteeming him a scholar, and knowing that not without great travail he hath drawn so many little straggling streams into so fair and smooth a river; whereas the work is the labour of some other, copied out by stealth, he, an impudent ignorant fellow, that runs up and down with the transcripts, and every ale-house may have one of them, hanging in the basest drinking room, if they will be but at the charges of writing it out. Thus the liberality of a nobleman or of a gentleman is abused! Thus learning is brought into scorn and contempt! Thus men are cheated of their bounty, giving much for that, out of their free minds, which is common abroad, and put away for base prices! Thus villainy sometimes walks alone, as if it were given to melancholy, and sometimes knaves tie themselves in a knot, because they may be more merry, as by a mad sort of comrades, whom I see leaping into the saddle, anon it will appear.

CHAPTER VII.

RANK RIDERS.

The manner of cozening inn-keepers, poſtmaſters and hackney-men.

THERE is a troop of horsemen that run up and down the whole kingdom. They are ever in a gallop, their business is weighty, their journeys many, their expenses great, their inns everywhere, their lands nowhere : they have only a certain freehold, called Tyburn, situate near London, and many a fair pair of gallows in other countries besides, upon which they live very poorly till they die, and die for the moſt part wickedly, because their lives are villainous and desperate. But what race soever they run, there they end it, there they set up their reſt, there is their laſt halt, whithersoever their journey lies. And these horsemen have no other names but rank riders. To furnish whom forth for any journey, they muſt have riding-suits cut out of these four pieces.

1. The innkeeper or hackney-man, of whom they have horses, is called a colt.

2. He that never alights off a rich farmer or country gentleman, till he have drawn money from him, is called the snaffle.

3. The money so gotten is the ring.

4. He that feeds them with money is called the provender.

These rank riders, like butchers to Romford market, seldom go under six or seven in a company, and these careers they fetch. Their purses being warmly lined with some purchase gotten before, and they themselves well booted and spurred and in reasonable good outsides, arrive at the faireſt inn they can choose, either in Weſtminſter, the Strand, the City, or the suburbs.

Two of them who have clothes of purpose to fit the play, carrying the show of gentlemen. The other aćt their parts in blue coats, as they were their serving-men, though, indeed, they be all fellows. They enter all dirtied or duſtied, according as it shall please the highway to use them, and the firſt bridle they put into the colt's mouth (that's to say, the innkeeper's) is at their coming in to ask aloud if the footman be gone back with the horses. 'Tis answered, Yes. Here the rank riders lie three or four days, spending moderately enough, yet abating not a penny of any reckoning to show of what house they come ; in which space their counterfeit followers learn what countryman the maſter of the house is, where the oſtlers and chamberlains were born, and what other country gentlemen are guests to the inn. Which lessons being presently gotten by heart, they fall in study with the general rules of their knavery; and those are, first to give out that their master is a gentleman of such and such means, in such a shire (which shall be sure to stand far enough from those places where any of the house, or of other guests, were born), that he is come to receive so many hundred pounds upon land which he hath sold, and that he means to inn there some quarter of a year at least.

This brass money passing for current through the house, he is more observed and better attended, is worshipped at every word; and the easier to break and bridle the colt, his Worship will not sit down to dinner or supper, till the master of the house be placed at the upper end of the board by him.

In the middle of supper, or else very early in the following morning, comes in a counterfeit footman sweatingly, delivering a message that such a knight hath sent for the headmaster of these rank riders, and that he must be with him by such an hour, the journey being not above twelve or fourteen miles. Upon delivery of this message, from so dear and noble a friend, he swears and chafes, because all his horses are out of town, curseth the sending of them back, offers any money to have himself, his cousin with him, and his men, but reasonably horsed. Mine host, being a credulous ass, suffers them all to get up upon him, for he provides them horses either of his own, thinking his guest to be a man of great account (and being loath to lose him, because he spends well); or else sends out to hire them of his neighbours, passing his word for their forthcoming within a day or two. Up they get, and away gallop our rank riders as far as the poor jades can carry them.

The two days being ambled out of the world, and perhaps three more after them, yet neither a supply of horsemen or footmen, as was promised, to be set eye upon. The lamentable innkeeper, or hackney-man, if he chanced to be saddled for this journey too, loose their colt's teeth, and find that they are made old arrant jades; search then runs up and down like a constable half out of his wits upon a Shrove Tuesday[26], and hue and cry follows after, some twelve or fourteen miles off, round about London, which was the farthest of their journey as they gave out. But, alas! the horses are at pasture four score or a hundred miles from their old mangers. They were sold at some blind drunken thievish fair, there being enow of them in company to save themselves by their toll-book.[27] The serving-men cast off their blue coats, and cried, "All fellows!" The money is spent upon wine, upon whores, upon

fiddlers, upon fools, by whom they will lose nothing, and, the tide being
at an ebb, they are as ready to practise their skill in horsemanship to
bring colts to the saddle in that town, and to make nags run a race of
three score or a hundred miles off from that place, as before they did
from London.

Running at the ring.

Thus, so long as horseflesh can make them fat, they never leave
feeding. But when they have beaten so many highways in several
countries, that they fear to be overtaken by tracers, then, like soldiers
coming from a breach, they march fair and softly on foot, lying in garrison, as it were, close in some out towns, till the foul rumour of their
villainies, like a stormy dirty winter, be blown over ; in which time of
lurking in that shell, they are not idle neither, but like snails they venture
abroad, though the law hath threatened to rain down never so much
punishment upon them. And what do they? They are not bees, to
live by their own painful labours, but drones that must eat up the sweetness, and be fed with the earnings of others. This therefore is their
work. They carelessly inquire what gentleman of worth, or what rich
farmers, dwell within five, six or seven miles of the fort where they
are ensconced—which they may do without suspicion—and, having got
their names, they single out themselves in a morning, and each man
takes a several path to himself ; one goes east, one west, one north,
and the other south, walking either in boots with wands in their hands,
or otherwise, for it is all to one purpose. And note this by the way,
that when they travel thus on foot, they are no more called rank riders
but strollers, a proper name given to country plaiters, that, without
socks, trot from town to town upon the hard hoof.

Being arrived at the gate where the gentleman or farmer dwelleth,
he boldly knocks, inquiring for him by name, and steps in to speak with
him. The servant, seeing a fashionable person, tells his master there
is a gentleman desires to speak with him. The master comes and
salutes him, but, eying him well, says he does not know him.

" No sir, " replies the other, with a face bold enough. " It may be
so, but I pray you, sir, will you walk a turn or two in your orchard or
garden ; I would there confer."

Having got him thither, to this tune he plays upon him :

How the snaffle is put on.

"Sir, I am a gentleman, born to better means, than my present fortunes do allow me. I served in the field, and had command there, but long peace—you know, sir—is the canker that eats up soldiers, and so it hath me. I lie here not far off, in the country, at mine inn, where, staying upon the despatch of some business, I am indebted to the house in moneys ; so that I cannot with the credit of a gentleman leave the house till I have paid them. Make me, sir, so much beholden to your love as to lend me forty or fifty shillings to bear my horse and myself to London ; from whence within a day or two, I shall send you many thanks with a faithful repayment of your courtesy."

The honest gentleman, or the good natured farmer, beholding a personable man, fashionably attired, and not carrying in outward colours the face of a cogging knave, gives credit to his words, is sorry that they are not at this present time so well furnished as they could wish, but if a matter of twenty shillings can stead him, he shall command it, because it were a pity any honest gentleman should for so small a matter miscarry. Happily they meet with some chapmen that give them their own asking ; but howsoever, all is fish that comes to net. They are the most conscionable market folks that ever rode between two panniers, for from forty they will fall to twenty, from twenty to ten, from ten to five : nay, these mountebanks are so base that they are not ashamed to take two shillings of a plain husbandman, and sometimes sixpence, which the other gives simply and honestly of whom they demanded a whole fifteen.

In this manner do they dig silver out of men's purses all the day, and at night meet together at the appointed rendezvous, where all these snaffles are loosed to their full length, the rings which that day they have made are worn. The provender is praised or dispraised, as they find it in goodness ; but it goes down all, whilst they laugh at all.

And thus does a commonwealth bring up children that care not how they discredit her, or undo her. Who would imagine that birds so fair in show, and so sweet in voice, should be so dangerous in condition ? But ravens think carrion the daintiest meat, and villains esteem most of that money which is purchased by baseness.

The under-sheriff for the county of the Cacodæmons, knowing into what arrearages these rank riders were run for horse-flesh to his master, of whom he farmed the office, sent out his writs to attach them, and so narrowly pursued them, that for all they were well horsed, some he sent post to the gallows, and the rest to several jails ; after which, making all the haste he possibly could to get to London again, he was waylaid by an army of a strange and new-found people.

Chapter VIII.

Moon-men.

A discovery of a strange wild people, very dangerous to towns and country villages.

A moon-man signifies in English a madman, because the moon hath greatest domination, above any other planet, over the bodies of frantic persons. But these moon-men, whose images are now to be carved, are neither absolutely mad, nor yet perfectly in their wits. Their name they borrow from the moon, because, as the moon is never in one shape two nights together, but wanders up and down Heaven like an antic, so these changeable-stuff-companions never tarry one day in a place, but are the only, and the only base, runagates upon earth. And as in the moon there is a man, that never stirs without a bush of thorns at his back, so these moon-men lie under bushes, and are indeed no better than hedge-creepers.

They are a people more scattered than Jews, and more hated ;[28] beggarly in apparel, barbarous in condition, beastly in behaviour, and bloody if they meet advantage. A man that sees them would swear they had all the yellow jaundice, or that they were tawny Moors' bastards, for no red-ochre-man carries a face of a more filthy complexion. Yet are they not born so, neither has the sun burnt them so, but they are painted so ; yet they are not good painters neither, for they do not make faces, but mar faces. By a by-name they are called gypsies ; they call themselves Egyptians ; others in mockery call them moon-men.

If they be Egyptians, sure I am they never descended from the tribes of any of those people that came out of the land of Egypt. Ptolemy king of the Egyptians, I warrant, never called them his subjects ; no, nor Pharaoh before him. Look what difference there is between a civil citizen of Dublin and a wild Irish kern, so much difference there is between one of these counterfeit Egyptians and a true English beggar. An English rogue is just of the same livery.

They are commonly an army about four score strong, yet they never march with all their bags and baggages together, but, like boot-halers, they forage up and down countries, four, five or six in a company. As the Switzer has his wench and his cock with him when he goes to the wars, so these vagabonds have their harlots, with a number of little children following at their heels ; which young brood of beggars are sometimes carted, like so many green geese alive to a market, in pairs of panniers, or in dossers, like fresh fish from Rye that comes on horse-back, if they be but infants. But if they can straddle once, then as well the she-rogues as the he-rogues are horsed, seven or eight upon one jade, strongly pinioned and strangely tied together.

One shire alone and no more is sure still at one time to have these Egyptian lice swarming within it, for, like flocks of wild-geese, they will evermore fly one after another. Let them be scattered worse than the quarters of a traitor are, after he's hanged, drawn and quartered, yet they have a trick, like water cut with a sword, to come together instantly and easily again. And this is their policy, which way soever the foremost ranks lead, they stick up small boughs in several places, to every village where they pass which serve as ensigns to waft on the rest.

Their apparel is odd and fantastic, though it be never so full of rents. The men wear scarfs of calico or any other base stuff, hanging their bodies like morris-dancers with bells and other toys, to entice the country people to flock about them, and to wonder at their fooleries, or rather rank knaveries. The women as ridiculously attire themselves, and, like one that plays the rogue on a stage, wear rags and patched filthy mantles uppermost, when the undergarments are handsome and in fashion.

The battles these outlaws make, are many and very bloody. Whosoever falls into their hands never escapes alive, and so cruel they are in these murders, that nothing can satisfy them but the very heart-blood of those whom they kill. And who are they, think you, that thus go to the pot ? Alas ! innocent lambs, sheep, calves, pigs, etc. Poultry-ware are more churlishly handled by them than poor prisoners are by keepers in the Counter i'the Poultry. A goose coming amongst them learns to be wise that he never will be goose any more. The bloody tragedies of all these are only acted by the women, who, carrying long knives or skenes under their mantles, do thus play their parts. The stage is some large heath, or a fir-bush common, far from any houses ; upon which, casting themselves into a ring, they enclose the murdered till the massacre be finished. If any passenger come by, and wondering to see such a conjuring circle kept by hell-hounds, demand what spirits they raise there, one of the murderers steps to him, poisons him with sweet words and shifts him off with this lie, that one of the women is fallen in labour. But if any mad Hamlet, hearing this, smell villainy, and rush in by violence to see what the tawny devils are doing, then they excuse the fact, lay the blame on those that are the actors, and perhaps, if they see no remedy, deliver them to an officer, to be had to punishment. But by the way a rescue is surely laid; and very valiantly, though very villainously, do they fetch them off, and guard them.

The cabins where these land-pirates lodge in the night are the out-barns of farmers and husbandmen, in some poor village or other, who dare not deny them, for fear they should ere morning have their thatched houses burning about their ears. In these barns are both their cook-rooms, their supping-parlours and their bedchambers; for there they dress after a beastly manner whatsoever they purchased after a thievish fashion. Sometimes they eat venison, and have greyhounds that kill it for them, but if they had not, they are hounds themselves, and are damnable hunters after flesh, which appears by their ugly-faced queans that follow them, with whom in these barns they lie, as swine do together in hogsties.

These barns are the beds of incests, whoredoms, adulteries, and of all other black and deadly-damned impieties; here grows the cursed tree of bastardy, that is so fruitful; here are written the books of all blasphemies, swearings and curses, that are so dreadful to be read. The[29] simple country people will come running out of their houses to gaze upon them, whilst in the meantime one steals into the next room, and brings away whatsoever he can lay hold on. Upon days of pastime and liberty, they spread themselves in small companies amongst the villages : and when young maids and bachelors (yea, sometimes old doting fools, that should be beaten to this world of villainies, and forewarn others) do flock about them, they then profess skill in palmistry, and, forsooth, can tell fortunes, which for the most part are infallibly true, by reason that they work upon rules, which are grounded upon certainty. For one of them will tell you that you shall shortly have some evil luck fall upon you, and within half an hour after you shall find your pocket picked or your purse cut.

These are those Egyptian grasshoppers that eat up the fruits of the earth, and destroy the poor corn fields. To sweep whose swarms out of this kingdom, there are no other means but the sharpness of the most infamous and basest kinds of punishment. For if the ugly body of this monster be suffered to grow and fatten itself with mischiefs and disorder, it will have a neck so sinewy and so brawny, that the arm of the law will have much ado to strike off the head, sithence every day the members of it increase, and it gather new joints and new forces by priggers, anglers, cheaters, morts, yeomen's daughters, that have taken some by blows, and, to avoid shame, fall into their sins, and other servants both men and maids that have been pilferers, with all the rest of that damned regiment, marching together in the first army of the Bellman,[30] who running away from their own colours, which are bad enough, serve under these, being the worst.

Lucifer's lanceprisado, that stood aloof to behold the musterings of these hell-hounds, took delight to see them double their files so nimbly, but held it no policy to come near them, for the Devil himself durst scarce have done that. Away therefore he gallops, knowing that at one time or other they would all come to fetch their pay in Hell.

Chapter IX.

The Infection of the Suburbs.

THE infernal promoter being wearied with riding up and down the country, was glad when he had gotten the City over his head ; but the City being not able to hold him within the freedom, because he was a foreigner, the gates were set wide open for him to pass through, and into the suburbs[31] he went. And what saw he there ? More ale-houses than there are taverns in all Spain and France ! Are they so dry in the suburbs ? Yes, pockily dry. What saw he besides ?

He saw the doors of notorious carted bawds like Hell-gates stand night and day wide open, with a pair of harlots in taffeta gowns, like two painted posts, garnishing out those doors, being better to the house than a double sign. When the door of a poor artificer, if his child had died but with one token of death[32] about him, was close rammed up and guarded, for fear others should have been infected[33], yet the plague that a whore-house lays upon a city is worse, yet is laughed at ; if not laughed at, yet not looked into ; or if looked into, winked at.

The tradesman having his house locked up, loseth his customers, is put from work and undone ; whilst in the meantime the strumpet is set on work and maintained (perhaps) by those that undo the other. Give thanks, O wide-mouthed Hell ! Laugh Lucifer at this ! Dance for joy all you devils !

Beelzebub keeps the register-book of all the bawds, panders and courtezans ; and he knows that these suburb sinners have no lands to live upon but their legs : every 'prentice passing by them can say, " There sits a whore." Without putting them to their book they will swear so much themselves. If so, are not constables, churchwardens, bailiffs, beadles and other officers, pillars and pillows to all the villainies, that are by these committed ? Are they not parcel bawds to wink at such damned abuses, considering they have whips in their own hands, and may draw blood if they please ? Is not the landlord of such rents the grand-bawd, and the door-keeping mistress of such a house of sin, but his under-bawd, sithence he takes twenty pounds rent every year for a vaulting school, which from no artificer living by the hardness of the hand could be worth five pound ? And that twenty pound rent, he knows must be pressed out of petticoats. His money smells of sin : the very silver looks pale, because it was earned by lust.

How happy therefore were cities if they had no suburbs, sithence they serve but as caves, where monsters are bred up to devour the cities themselves ! Would the Devil hire a villain to spill blood, there he shall find him ; one to blaspheme, there he hath choice ; a pander that would court a matron at her prayers, he's there ; a cheater that would turn his own father a begging, he's there too ; a harlot that would murder her new-born infant, she lies in there !

What a wretched womb hath a strumpet, which being, for the most, barren of children, is notwithstanding the only bed that breeds up these serpents ! Upon that one stalk grow all these mischiefs. She is the cockatrice that hatcheth all these eggs of evils. When the Devil takes the anatomy of all damnable sins, he looks only upon her body. When she dies, he sits as her coroner. When her soul comes to Hell, all shun that there, as they fly from a body struck with the plague here. She hath her door-keeper, and she herself is the Devil's chamber-maid. And yet for all this, that she's so dangerous and detestable, when she hath croaked like a raven on the eaves, then comes she into the house like a dove. When her villainies, like the moat about a castle, are rank, thick, and muddy, with standing long together, then, to purge herself, is she drained out of the suburbs, as though her corruption were there left behind her, and as a clear stream is let into the City.

What armour a harlot wears coming out of the suburbs to besiege the City within the walls.

Upon what perch then does she sit? What part plays she then? Only the puritan. If before she ruffled in silks, now is she more civilly attired than a midwife. If before she swaggered in taverns, now with the snail she ſtirreth not out of doors. And where muſt her lodging be taken up, but in the house of some citizen, whose known reputation she borrows (or rather ſteals), putting it on as a cloak to cover her deformities? Yet even in that hath she an art too, for he shall be of such a profession, that all comers may enter, without the danger of any eyes to watch them. As for example, she will lie in some scrivener's house, and so, under the colour of coming to have a bond made, she herself may write *Noverint universi.* And though the law threaten to hit her never so often, yet hath she subtle defences to ward off the blows. For, if gallants haunt the house, then spreads she these colours: She is a captain or a lieutenant's wife in the Low Countries, and they come with letters, from the soldier her husband. If merchants resort to her, then hoiſts she up these sails: She is wife to the maſter of a ship, and they bring news that her husband put in at the Straits, or at Venice, at Aleppo, Alexandria, or Scanderoon, etc. If shopkeepers come to her, with " What do you lack? " in their mouths, then she takes up such and such commodities, to send them to Rye, to Briſtol, to York, etc., where her husband dwells. But if the ſtream of her fortunes run low, and that none but apronmen launch forth there, then keeps she a politic sempſter's shop, or she ſtarches them.

Perhaps she is so politic that none shall be noted to board her. If so, then she sails upon these points of the compass: So soon as ever she is rigged, and all her furniture on, forth she launcheth into those ſtreets that are moſt frequented; where the firſt man that she meets of her acquaintance, shall, without much pulling, get her into a tavern; out of him she kisses a breakfaſt and then leaves him. The next she meets, does upon as easy pulleys draw her to a tavern again. Out of him she cogs a dinner, and then leaves him. The third man squires her to a play, which being ended, and the wine offered and taken, for she's no recusant to refuse anything, him she leaves too. And being set upon by a fourth, him she answers at his own weapon, sups with him, and drinks upsy-Freeze till the clock ſtriking twelve, and the drawers being drowsy, away they march arm in arm, being at every footſtep fearful to be set upon by the band of halberdiers, that lie scouting in rug-gowns to cut off such midnight ſtragglers ; but the word being given, and " Who goes there ? " with " Come before the conſtable " being shot at them, they vail presently and come, she taking upon her to answer all the billmen and their leader, between whom and her suppose you hear this sleepy dialogue :

" Where have you been so late ? "

" At supper forsooth with my uncle here (if he be well bearded), or with my brother (if the hair be but budding forth), and he is bringing me home."

" Are you married ? "

" Yes forsooth."

" What's your husband ? "

" Such a nobleman's man, or such a Juſtice's clerk." And then name[s] some alderman of London, to whom she persuades herself one or other of the bench of brown bills are beholden.

" Where lie you ? "

" At such a man's house."

Sic tenues evanescit in auras[34]. And thus by ſtopping the conſtable's mouth with sugar-plums, that's to say, whilſt she poisons him with sweet words, the punk vanisheth. O Lantern and Candlelight, how art thou made a blind ass, because thou haſt but one eye to see withal ! Be not so gulled, be not so dull in underſtanding. Do thou but follow aloof those two tame pigeons, and thou shalt find that her new uncle lies by it all that night, to make his kinswoman one of mine aunts ; or if she be not in travail all night, they spend some half an hour together. But what do they ? Marry, they do that which the conſtable should have done for them both in the ſtreets, that's to say, *commit, commit*.

You guardians over so great a princess as the eldeſt daughter of King Brutus[35] : you twice twelve fathers and governors over the nobleſt city, why are you so careful to plant trees to beautify your outward walks, yet suffer the goodlieſt garden within to be overrun with ſtinking weeds ? You are the pruning knives that should lop off such idle, such unprofitable, and such deſtroying branches from the vine. The beams of your authority should purge the air of such infeetion ; your breath of juſtice should scatter those foggy vapours, and drive them out of your gates as chaff tossed abroad by the winds.

But ſtay ! Is our walking spirit become an orator to persuade ? No, but the Bellman of London with whom he met in this perambulation of his, and to whom he betrayed himself and opened his very bosom, as hereafter you shall hear, is bold to take upon him that speaker's office.

CHAPTER X.

OF JINGLERS.

Or the knavery of horse-coursers in Smithfield discovered.[36]

AT the end of fierce battles, the only rendezvous for lame soldiers to retire unto is an hospital ; and at the end of a long progress, the only ground for a tired jade to run in is some blind country fair, where he may be sure to be sold. To these markets of unwholesome horseflesh, like so many kites to feed upon carrion, do all the horse-coursers that roost about the City fly one after another. And whereas in buying all other commodities, men strive to have the best, how great soever the price be, only the horse-courser is of a baser mind, for the worst horseflesh, so it be cheap, does best go down with him. He cares for nothing but a fair outside, and a handsome shape, like those that hire whores, though there be a hundred diseases within : he, as the other, ventures upon them all.

The first lesson, therefore, that a horse-courser takes out, when he comes to one of these markets, is to make choice of such nags, geldings, or mares especially, as are fat, fair, and well-favoured to the eye. And because men delight to behold beautiful colours, and that some colours are more delicate even in beasts than others are, he will, so near as he can, bargain for those horses that have the daintiest complexion, as the milk-white, the grey, the dapple-grey, the coal-black with his proper marks (as the white star in the forehead, the white heel, etc.) or the bright bay with the like proper marks also. And the goodlier proportion the beast carries or the fairer marks or colour that he bears, are or ought to be watchwords as it were to him that afterwards buys him of the horse-courser, that he be not cozened with an overprice for a bad pennyworth ; because such horses, belonging for the most part to gentlemen, are seldom or never sold away but upon some foul quality, or some incurable disease, which the beast is fallen into. The best colours are therefore the best cloaks to hide those faults that most disfigure a horse. And next unto colour, his pace doth oftentimes deceive and go beyond a very quick judgment.

Some of these horse-hunters are as nimble knaves in finding out the infirmities of a jade, as a barber is in drawing of teeth ; and albeit, without casting his water, he does more readily reckon up all the aches, cramps, cricks, and whatsoever disease else lies in his bones, and for those diseases seems utterly to dislike him. Yet if by looking upon the dial within his mouth, he find that his years have struck but five, six, or seven, and that he proves but young, or that his diseases are but newly growing upon him, if they be outward, or have but hair and skin to hide them, if they be inward, let him swear never so damnably that it is but a jade, yet he will be sure to fasten upon him.

So then a horse-courser to the merchant that out of his sound judgment buys the fairest, the best-bred, and the noblest horses, selling them again for breed or service, with plainness and honesty, is as the cheater to the fair gamester. He is indeed a mere jadish monopolitan, and deals for none but tired, tainted, dull and diseased horses. By which means, if his picture be drawn to the life, you shall find every horse-courser for the most part to be in quality a cozener, by profession a knave, by his cunning a varlet, in fairs a haggling chapman, in the City a cogging dissembler, and in Smithfield a common forsworn villain. He will swear anything, but the faster he swears, the more danger 'tis to believe him. In one forenoon, and in selling a jade not worth five nobles, will he forswear himself fifteen times, and that forswearing too shall be by equivocation. As for example, if an ignorant chapman coming to beat the price, say to the horse-courser, " Your nag is very old "—or thus many years old, and reckon ten or twelve, he claps his hand presently on the buttock of the beast, and prays he may be damned if the horse be not under five, meaning not that the horse is under five years of age, but that he stands under five of his fingers, when his hand is clapped upon him. These horse-coursers are called jinglers, and these jinglers having laid out their money on a company of jades at some drunken fair, up to London they drive them, and, upon the market day, into Smithfield bravely come they prancing. But lest their jades should show too many horse tricks in Smithfield before so great an audience as commonly resort thither, their masters do therefore school them at home after this manner.

How a horse-courser works upon a jade in his own stable to make him serviceable for a cozening race in Smithfield.

The glanders in a horse is so filthy a disease, that he who is troubled with it can never keep his nose clean ; so that when such a foul-nosed jade happens to serve a horse-courser, he hath more strange pills than a 'pothecary makes for the purging of his head : he knows that a horse with such a quality is but a beastly companion to travel upon the highway with any gentleman.

LANTHORNE
and Candle-light.
Or
The Bell-mans second Nights walke.

In which

Hee brings to light, a Broode of more ftrange Villanies,
then euer were till this yeare difcouered.

--Decet nouiſſe malum; feciſſe, nefandum.

LONDON
Printed for *Iohn Busbie*, and are to be fold at his fhop in
Fleet-ftreet, in Saint Dunftans Church-yard.
1608.

Plate XV.

[*face p. 352*

O per ſe O.

LONDON:
Printed for *Iohn Buſbie*, and are to be ſould at his ſhop in
Fleeteſtreet in S. Dunſtans Church-yard.
1612.

Plate XVI.

[*face p. 353*

Albeit therefore that the glanders have played with his nose so long that he knows not how to mend himself, but that the disease, being suffered to run upon him many years together, is grown invincible, yet hath our jingling mountebank Smithfield-rider a trick to cure him five or six ways, and this is one of them.

In the very morning when he is to be rifled away amongst the game-sters in Smithfield, before he thrust his head out of his master's stable, the horse-courser tickles his nose, not with a pipe of tobacco, but with a good quantity of the best neezing powder that can be gotten ; which with a quill being blown up into the nostrils to make it work the better, he stands poking there up and down with two long feathers plucked from the wing of a goose, they being dipped in the juice of garlic, or in any strong oil, and thrust up to the very top of his head, so far as possibly they can reach, to make the poor dumb beast avoid the filth from his nostrils ; which he will do in great abundance. This being done, he comes to him with a new medicine for a sick horse, and mingling the juice of bruised garlic, sharp biting mustard, and strong ale together, into both the nostrils with a horn is poured a good quantity of this filthy broth ; which by the hand being held in by stopping the nostrils close together, at length with a little neezing more, his nose will be cleaner than his master's the horse-courser, and the filth be so artificially stopped that for eight or ten hours a jade will hold up his head with the proudest gelding that gallops scornfully by him, and never have need of wiping.

This is one of the comedies a common horse-courser plays by him-self at home, but if when he comes to act the second part abroad, you would disgrace him, and have him hissed at for not playing the knave well, then handle him thus : If you suspect that the nag which he would jade you with be troubled with that or any other suchlike disease, grip him hard about the weasand-pipe, close toward the roof of the tongue, and, holding him there so long and so forcibly that he cough twice or thrice, if then after you let go your hold his chaps begin to walk as if he were chewing down a horse-loaf, shake hands with old Monsieur Cavaliero Horse-courser, but clap no bargain upon it, for his jade is as full of infirmity as the master of villainy.

Other gambols that horse-coursers practise upon foundered horses, old jades, etc.

Smithfield is the stage upon which the mountebank English horse-courser, advancing his banner, defies any disease that dares touch his

O

prancer ; insomuch that if a horse be so old as that four legs can but carry him, yet shall he bear the marks of a nag not above six or seven years of age.   And that counterfeit badge of youth he wears thus : The horse-courser with a small round iron made very hot burns two black holes in the top of the two outmost teeth of each side the outside of the horse's mouth upon the nether teeth, and so like wise of the teeth of the upper chap, which stand opposite to the nether, the quality of which marks is to show that a horse is but young.   But if the jade be so old that those teeth are dropped out of his head, then is there a trick still to be fumbling about his old chaps, and in that stroking his chin, to prick his lips closely with a pin or a nail, till they be so tender, that, albeit he were a given horse, none could be suffered to look him in the mouth, which is one of the best calendars to tell his age.   But a reasonable-sighted eye, without help of spectacles, may easily discover this juggling, because it is gross and common.

If now a horse, having been a fore-traveller, happen by falling into a cold sweat to be foundered, so that (as if he were drunk or had the staggers) he can scarce stand on his legs, then will his master, before he enter into the lists of the field against all comers, put him into a villainous chasing, by riding him up and down a quarter or half an hour, till his limbs be thoroughly heated.   And this he does, because so long as he can discharge that false fire, or that, being so cholerically hot, he tramples only upon soft ground, a very cunning horseman shall hardly find where his shoe wrings him, or that he is foundered.   And to blind the eyes of the chapman, the horse-courser will be ever tickling of him with his wand, because he may not by standing still like an ass show of what house he comes.

If a horse come into the field like a lame soldier halting, he has not crutches made for him as the soldier hath, but because you shall think the horse's shoemaker hath served him like a jade, by not fitting his foot well, the shoe shall be taken off purposely from that foot which halts, as though it had been lost by chance ; and to prove this, witnesses shall come in, if at least twenty or thirty damnable oaths can be taken that the want of the shoe is only the cause of his halting.   But if a horse cannot be lusty at legs, by reason that either his hoofs be not good, or that there be splints, or any other eyesore about the nether joint, the horse-courser uses him then as cheating swaggerers handle novices : what they cannot win by the dice, they will have by foul play.   And in that foul manner deals he with the poor horse, riding him up and down in the thickest and the dirtiest places, till that dirt, like a ruffled boot drawn upon an ill-favoured gouty leg, cover the jade's infirmity from the eyes of the buyer.

How a horse-courser makes a jade that has no stomach to eat lamb-pie.

Albeit lamb-pie be good meat upon a table, yet it is so offensive to a horse's stomach that he had rather be fed a month together with musty oats than to taste it. Yet are not all horses bidden to his lamb-pie breakfasts, but only such as are dieted with no other meat ; and those are dull, blockish, sullen and heavy-footed jades. Whensoever therefore a horse-courser hath such a dead commodity as a lumpish slow jade, that goes more heavily than a cow when she trots, and that neither by a sharp bit nor a tickling spur he can put him out of his lazy and dogged pace, what does he with him then? Only he gives him lamb-pie. That is to say, every morning when the horse-courser comes into the stable, he takes up a tough round cudgel, and never leaves fencing with his quarterstaff at the poor horse's sides and buttocks, till with blows he hath made them so tender that the very shaking of a bough will be able to make the horse ready to run out of his wits. And to keep the horse still in this mad mood, because he shall not forget his lesson, his master will never come near him, but he will have a fling at him. If he do touch him, he strikes him ; if he speaks to him, there is but a word and a blow ; if he do but look upon him, the horse flings and takes on, as though he would break through the walls, or had been a horse bred up in Bedlam amongst mad folks. Having thus gotten this hard lesson by heart, forth comes he into Smithfield to repeat it, where the rider shall no sooner leap into the saddle but the horse-courser giving the jade, that is half scared out of his wits already, three or four good bangs, away flies Bucephalus as if young Alexander were upon his back. No ground can hold him ; no bridle rein him in. He gallops away as if the Devil had hired him of some hackney-man, and scuds through thick and thin, as if crackers had hung at his heels. If his tail play the wag and happen to whisk up and down—which is a sign that he does his feats of activity like a tumbler's 'prentice by compulsion and without taking pleasure in them—then shall you see the horse-courser lay about him like a thrasher, till with blows he made him carry his tail to his buttocks, which in a horse, contrary to the nature of a dog, is an argument that he hath metal in him and spirit, as in the other it is the note of cowardice.

These and such other base jugglings are put in practise, by the horse-courser. In this manner comes he armed into the field. With such bad and deceitful commodities does he furnish the markets. Neither steps he upon the Devil's stage alone, but others are likewise actors in the self-same scene, and sharers with him. For no sooner shall money be offered for a horse, but presently one snake thrusts out his head and stings the buyer with false praises of the horse's goodness; another throws out his poisoned hook and whispers in the chapman's ear that upon his knowledge so much or so much hath been offered by four or five, and would not be taken. And of these ravens there be sundry nests, but all of them as black in soul as the horse-courser with whom they are yoked is in conscience. This regiment of horsemen is therefore divided into four squadrons, *viz.*

1. When horse-coursers travel to country fairs, they are called jinglers.

2. When they have the leading of the horse and serve in Smithfield, they are drovers.

3. They that stand by and cony-catch the chapman, either with out-bidding, false praises, etc., are called goads.

4. The boys, striplings, etc. that have the riding of the jades up and down are called skipjacks.

CHAPTER XI.

JACK-IN-A-BOX.

Or a new kind of cheating, teaching how to change gold into silver, unto which is added a map by which a man may learn how to travel all over England and have his charges borne.

How many trees of evil are growing in this country! How tall they are! How mellow is their fruit! And how greedily gathered! So much ground do they take up, and so thickly do they stand together, that it seemeth a kingdom can bring forth no more of their nature. Yes, yes, there are not half so many rivers in Hell, in which a soul may sail to damnation, as there are black streams of mischief and villainy, besides all those which in our now-two voyages we have ventured so many leagues up for discovery, in which thousands of people are continually swimming, and every minute in danger utterly to be cast away.

The horse-courser of Hell, after he had dirtied himself with riding up and down Smithfield, and having his beast under him, galloped away amain to behold a race of five miles by a couple of running-horses, upon whose swiftness great sums of money were laid in wagers. In which school of horsemanship, wherein for the most part none but gallants are the students, he construed but strange lectures of abuses. He could make large comments upon those that are the runners of those races, and could teach others how to lose forty or fifty pound politically in the forenoon, and in the afternoon with the self-same gelding to win a thousand marks in five or six miles riding. He could tell how gentlemen are fetched in and made younger brothers, and how your new knight comes to be a cousin of this race. He could draw the true pictures of some fellows, that diet these running-horses, who for a bribe of forty or fifty shillings can by a false die[t] make their own masters lose a hundred pound a race. He could show more crafty foxes in this wild goose chase than there are white foxes in Russia, and more strange horse-tricks played by such riders than Bankes his curtal[37] did ever practise—whose gambols of the two were the honester.

But because this sort of birds have many feathers to lose before they can feel any cold, he suffers them to make their own flight, knowing that prodigals do but jest at the stripes which other men's rods give them, and never complain of smarting till they are whipped with their own.

In every corner did he find serpents engendering: under every roof some impiety or other lay breeding. But at last, perceiving that the most part of men were by the sorcery of their own devilish conditions transformed into wolves, and being so changed, were more brutish and bloody than those that were wolves by nature, his spleen leapt against his ribs with laughter, and in the height of that joy resolved to write the villainies of the world in folio, and to dedicate them in private to his lord and master, because he knew him to be an open-handed patron, albeit he was no great lover of scholars.

But having begun one picture of a certain strange beast called Jack-in-a-box, that only (because the City had given money already to see it) he finished. And in these colours was Jack-in-a-box drawn. It hath the head of a man, the face well-bearded, the eyes of a hawk, the tongue of a lapwing, which says *Here it is* when the nest is a good way off; it hath the stomach of an ostrich, and can disgest silver as easily as that bird doth iron. It hath the paws of a bear instead of hands, for whatsoever it fasteneth upon, it holds. From the middle downwards, it is made like a greyhound, and is so swift of foot that if it once get the start of you, a whole kennel of hounds cannot overtake it. It loves to hunt dry-foot, and can scent a train in no ground so well as the City, and yet not in all places of the City. But he is best in scenting between Ludgate and Temple Bar ; and 'tis thought that his next hunting shall be between Lombard Street and the Goldsmiths' Row in Cheapside. Thus much for his outward parts. Now you shall have him unripped, and see his inward.

This Jack-in-a-box, or this devil in man's shape, wearing, like a player on a stage, good clothes on his back, comes to a goldsmith's stall, to a draper's, a haberdasher's, or into any other shop where he knows good store of silver faces are to be seen. And there, drawing forth a fair new box, hammered all out of silver plate, he opens it, and pours forth twenty or forty twenty-shilling pieces in new gold. To which heap of worldly temptation thus much he adds in words, that either he himself, or such a gentleman, to whom he belongs, hath an occasion for four or five days to use forty pound. But because he is very shortly, nay, he knows not how suddenly, to travel to Venice, to Jerusalem or so, and would not willingly be disfurnished of gold, he doth therefore request the citizen to lend upon those forty twenty-shilling pieces so much in white money but for four, five or six days at most, and for his good-will he shall receive any reasonable satisfaction. The citizen, knowing the pawn to be better than a bond, pours down forty pound in silver. The other draws it, and, leaving so much gold in hostage, marcheth away with bag and baggage.

Five days being expired, Jack-in-a-box, according to his bargain, being a man of his word comes again to the shop or stall, at which he angles for fresh fish, and there casting out his line with the silver hook, that's to say, pouring out the forty pound which he borrowed, the citizen sends in, or steps himself for the box with the golden devil in it. It is opened, and the army of angels being mustered together, they are all found to be there. The box is shut again and set on the stall, whilst the citizen is telling of his money. But whilst this music is sounding, Jack-in-a-box acts his part in a dumb show thus : he shifts out of his fingers *another* box of the same metal and making that the former bears, which second box is filled only with shillings, and being poised in the hand, shall seem to carry the weight of the former, and is clapped down in place of the first. The citizen in the meantime, whilst this pitfall is made for him, telling the forty pounds, misseth thirty or forty shillings in the whole sum, at which the Jack-in-a-box ſtarting back, as if it were a matter ſtrange unto him, at laſt making a gathering within himself for his wits, he remembers, he says, that he laid by so much money as is wanting of the forty pounds to despatch some business or other, and forgot to put it into the bag again. Notwithſtanding, he entreats the citizen to keep his gold ſtill ; he will take the white money home to fetch the reſt, and make up the sum. His absence shall not be above an hour or two ; before which time he shall be sure to hear of him ; and with this the little devil vanisheth, carrying that away with him, which in the end will send him to the gallows, that's to say, his own gold, and forty pound besides of the shopkeeper's, which he borrowed, the other being glad to take forty shillings for the whole debt, and yet is soundly boxed for his labour.

This Jack-in-a-box is yet but a chicken, and hath laid very few eggs. If the hangman do not spoil it with treading, it will prove an excellent hen of the game. It is a knot of cheaters but newly tied, they are not yet a company. They fly not like wild geese in flocks, but like kites, single, as loath that any should share in their prey. They have two or three names, yet they are no Romans, but errant rogues, for sometimes they call themselves Jack-in-a-box, but now that their infantry grows ſtrong, and that it is known abroad that they carry the philosophers' ſtone about them, and are able of forty shillings to make forty pound, they therefore use a dead march, and the better to cloak their villainies, do put on these masking suits, *viz.*

1. This art or sleight of changing gold into silver is called trimming.
2. They that praċtise it term themselves sheep-shearers.
3. The gold which they bring to the citizen is called Jason's fleece.
4. The silver which they pick up by this wandering is white wool.
5. They that are cheated by Jack-in-a-box are called bleaters.

O Fleet Street ! Fleet Street ! How haſt thou been trimmed, washed, shaven and polled by these dear and damnable barbers ! How often haſt thou met with these sheep-shearers ! How many warm flakes of wool have they pulled from thy back ! Yet if thy bleating can make the flocks that graze near unto thee and round about thee to lift up their eyes, and to shun such wolves and foxes when they are approaching, or to have them worried to death before they suck the blood of others thy misfortunes are the less, because thy neighbours by them shall be warned from danger.

Many of thy gallants, O Fleet Street, have spent hundreds of pounds in thy presence, and yet never were so much as drunk for it. But for every forty pound that thou layest out in this Indian commodity of gold, thou hast a silver box bestowed upon thee, to carry thy tobacco in, because thou hast ever loved that costly and gentleman-like smoke. Jack-in-a-box hath thus played his part.

There is yet another actor to step upon the stage, and he seems to have good skill in cosmography, for he holds in his hand a map, wherein he hath laid down a number of shires in England, and with small pricks hath beaten out a path, teaching how a man may easily, though not very honestly, travel from country to country and have his charges borne ; and thus it is :

He that undertakes this strange journey, lays his first plot how to be turned into a brave man, which he finds can be done by none better than by a trusty tailor. Working therefore hard with him, till his suit be granted, out of the City, being mounted on a good gelding, he rides upon his own bare credit, not caring whether he travel to meet the sun at his rising or at his going down. He knows his kitchen smokes in every county, and his table covered in every shire. For when he comes within a mile of the town where he means to catch quails, setting spurs to his horse, away he gallops, with his cloak off (for in these besiegings of towns he goes not armed with any), his hat thrust into his hose as if it were lost, and only an empty pair of hangers by his side, to show that he has been disarmed. And you must note, that this Hotspur does never set upon any places but only such, where he knows by intelligence there are store of gentlemen, or wealthy farmers at the least. Amongst whom, when he is come, he tells with distracted looks, and a voice almost breathless, how many villains set upon him, what gold and silver they took from him, what woods they are fled into, from what part of England he is come, to what place he is going, how far he is from home, how far from his journey's end, or from any gentleman of his acquaintance, and so lively personates the lying Greek (Sinon) in telling a lamentable tale, that the mad Trojans (the gentlemen of the town), believing him, and the rather because he carries the shape of an honest man in show, and of a gentleman in his apparel, are liberal of their purses, lending him money to bear him on his journey ; to pay which he offers either his bill or bond, naming his lodging in London, or gives his word as he's a gentleman, which they rather take, knowing the like misfortune may be theirs at any time.

And thus with the feathers of other birds is this monster stuck, making wings of sundry fashions, with which he thus basely flies over a whole kingdom. Thus doth he ride from town to town, from city to city, as if he were a landlord in every shire, and that he were to gather rent up of none but gentlemen.

There is a twin brother to this false galloper, and he cheats innkeepers only, or their tapsters, by learning first what countrymen they are, and of what kindred ; and then bringing countefeit letters of commendations from such an uncle, or such a cousin, wherein is requested that the bearer thereof may be used kindly, he lies in the inn till he have fetched over the master or servant for some money (to draw whom to him he hath many hooks), and when they hang fast enough by the gills, under water our shark dives, and is never seen to swim again in that river.

Upon this scaffold also might be mounted a number of quack-salving empirics, who, arriving in some country town, clap up their terrible bills in the market-place, and filling the paper with such horrible names of diseases, as if every disease were a devil, and that they could conjure them out of any town at their pleasure. Yet these beggarly mounte-banks are mere cozeners, and have not so much skill as horse-leeches ; the poor people not giving money to them to be cured of any infirmities, but rather with their money buying worse infirmities of them.

Upon the same post, do certain straggling scribbling writers deserve to have both their names and themselves hung up, instead of those fair tables which they hang up in towns, as gay pictures to entice scholars to them. The tables are written with sundry kinds of hands, but not one finger of those hands, not one letter there, drops from the pen of such a false wandering scribe. He buys other men's cunning good cheap in London, and sells it dear in the country. These swallows brag of no quality in them so much as of swiftness. In four-and-twenty hours they will work four-and-twenty wonders, and promise to teach those that know no more what belongs to an A than an ass, to be able in that narrow compass to write as fair and as fast as a country vicar who commonly reads all the town's letters.

But wherefore do these counterfeit masters of that noble science of writing keep such a flourishing with the borrowed weapons of other men's pens? Only for this, to get half the birds which they strive to catch, into their hands, that's to say, to be paid half the money which is agreed upon for the scholar, and his nest being half filled with such goldfinches, he never stays till the rest be fledged, but suffers him that comes next to beat the bush for the other half. At this career the rider that set out last from Smithfield, stopped, and, alighting from Pacolet, the horse that carried him, his next journey was made on foot.

Chapter XII.

The Bellman's Second Night-walk.

Sir Lancelot of the infernal lake, or the knight errant of Hell, having thus, like a young country gentleman, gone round about the City, to see the sights, not only within the walls, but those also in the suburbs, was glad when he saw Night, having put on the vizard that Hell lends her (called Darkness) to leap in to her coach, because now he knew he should meet with other strange birds and beasts fluttering from their nests and crawling out of their dens. His prognostication held current, and the foul weather which he foretold, fell out accordingly. For Candlelight had scarce opened his eye, to look at the City, like a gunner shooting at a mark, but fearfully, their feet trembling under them, their eyes suspiciously rolling from every nook to nook about them, and their heads, as if they stood upon oiled screws, still turning back behind them, came creeping out of hollow trees, where they lay hidden, a number of cozening bankrupts in the shapes of owls, who, when the marshall of light, the sun, went up and down to search the City, durst not stir abroad, for fear of being hooted at and followed by whole flocks of undone creditors.

But now, when the stage of the world was hung in black, they jetted up and down like proud tragedians. Oh, what thanks they gave to Darkness ! What songs they balladed out in praise of Night, for bestowing upon them so excellent a cloak wherein they might so safely walk muffled ! Now durst they, as if they had been constables, rap aloud at the doors of those to whom they owed most money, and brave them with high words, though they paid them not a penny.

Now did they boldly step into some privileged tavern, and there drink healths, dance with harlots, and pay both drawers and fiddlers after midnight with other men's money, and then march home again, fearless of the blows that any shoulder-clapper durst give them.

Out of another nest flew certain murderers and thieves in the shapes of screech-owls, who, being set on by the night, did beat with their bold and venturous fatal wings at the very doors whereas, in former times, their villainies had entered.

Not far from these came crawling out of their bushes a company of grave and wealthy lechers in the shapes of glow-worms, who with gold jingling in their pockets, made such a show in the night, that the doors of common brothelries flew open to receive them, though in the day-time they durst not pass that way, for fear that noted courtezans should challenge them of acquaintance, or that others should laugh at them to see white heads growing upon green stalks.

Then came forth certain infamous earthy-minded creatures in the shapes of snails, who, all the day-time hiding their heads in their shells, lest boys should with two fingers point at them for living basely upon the prostitution of their wives' bodies, cared not now, before Candlelight, to shoot out their largest and longest horns.

A number of other monsters like these were seen as the sun went down to venture from their dens, only to engender with darkness: but Candlelight's eyesight growing dimmer and dimmer, and he at last falling stark blind, Lucifer's watchman went strumbling up and down in the dark.

How to wean horses.

Every door on a sudden was shut; not a candle stood peeping through any window; not a vintner was to be seen brewing in his cellar; not a drunkard to be met reeling; not a mouse to be heard stirring. All the City showed like one bed, for all in that bed were soundly cast into a sleep. Noise made no noise, for every one that wrought with the hammer was put to silence. Yet notwithstanding when even the Devil himself could have been contented to take a nap, there were few innkeepers about the town but had their spirits walking. To watch which spirits what they did, our spy that came lately out of the lower countries, stole into one of their circles, where, lurking very closely, he perceived that when all the guests were profoundly sleeping, when carriers were soundly snorting, and not so much as the chamberlain of the house but was laid up, suddenly out of his bed started an ostler, who, having no apparel on but his shirt, a pair of slip-shoes on his feet, and a candle burning in his hand like old Hieronimo[38], stepped into the stable amongst a number of poor hungry jades, as if that night he had been to ride post to the Devil. But his journey not lying that way till some other time, he neither bridled nor saddled any of his four-footed guests that stood there at rack and manger, but, seeing them so late at supper, and knowing that to over-eat themselves would fill them full of diseases (they being subject to above a hundred and thirty already), he first, without a voider, after a most unmannerly fashion took away, not only all the provender that was set before them, but also all the hay, at which before they were glad to lick their lips.

The poor horses looked very ruefully upon him for this, but he, rubbing their teeth only with the end of a candle, instead of a coral, told them, that for their jadish tricks it was now time to wean them. And so wishing them not to be angry if they lay upon the hard boards, considering all the beds in the house were full, back again he stole to his coach, till break of day : yet, fearing lest the sun should rise to discover his knavery, up he started, and into the stable he stumbled, scarce half awake, giving to every jade a bottle of hay for his breakfast ; but all of them, being troubled with the greasy toothache, could eat none, which their masters in the morning espying swore they were either sullen or else that provender pricked them.

This ostler for this piece of service was afterwards preferred to be one of the grooms in Beelzebub's stable.

Another night-piece drawn in sundry colours.[39]

Shall I show you what other bottoms of mischief Pluto's beadle saw wound upon the black spindles of the night in this his privy search ? In some streets he met midwives running, till they sweat, and, following them close at heels, he spied them to be let in at the back doors of houses, seated either in blind lanes, or in by-gardens ; which houses had rooms builded for the purpose, where young maids, being big with child by unlawful fathers, or young wives, in their husbands' absence at sea or in the wars, having wrestled with bachelors or married men till they caught falls, lay safely till they were delivered of them. And for reasonable sums of money, the bastards that at these windows crept into the world, were as closely now and then sent presently out of the world, or else were so unmannerly brought up, that they never spake to their own parents that begot them.

In some streets he met servants in whose breast, albeit the arrows of the plague stuck half way, yet by cruel masters were they driven out of doors at midnight and conveyed to garden-houses, where they either died before next morning, or else were carried thither dead in their coffins, as though they had lain sick there before, and there had died.

Now and then at the corner of a turning he spied servants purloining fardels of their masters' goods, and delivering them to the hands of common strumpets.

This door opened, and Lust with Prodigality were heard to stand closely kissing, and, wringing one another by the hand, softly to whisper out four or five good-nights, till they met abroad the next morning.

A thousand of these comedies were acted in dumb show, and only in the private houses; at which the Devil's messenger laughed so loud that Hell heard him, and for joy rang forth loud and lusty plaudits. But being driven into wonder why the night would fall in labour, and bring forth so many villainies, whose births she practised to cover (as she had reason), because so many watchmen were continually called and charged to have an eye to her doings, at length he perceived that bats, more ugly and more in number than these, might fly up and down in darkness. For though with their leathern wings they should strike the very bills out of those watchmen's hands, such leaden plummets were commonly hung by sleep at all their eyelids, that hardly they could be awakened to strike them again.

On, therefore, he walks, with intent to hasten home, as having filled his table-books with sufficient notes of intelligence. But, at the last, meeting with the Bellman, and not knowing what he was because he went without his lantern and some other implements—for the Man in the Moon was up the most part of the night and lighted him which way soever he turned—he took him for some churlish hobgoblin, seeing a long staff on his neck, and therefore to be one of his own fellows. The bell-ringer smelling what strong scent he had in his nose, soothed him up, and questioning with him how he had spent his time in the City, and what discovery of land-villainies he had made in this island voyage, the mariner of Hell opened his chart, which he had lined with all abuses lying either east, west, north or south. He showed how he had pricked it, upon what points he had sailed, where he put in, under what height he kept himself, where he went ashore, what strange people he met, what land he had discovered, and what commodities he was laden with from thence. Of all which the Bellman drawing forth a perfect map, they parted; which map he hath set out in such colours as you see, though not with such cunning as he could wish. The pains are his own, the pleasure, if this can yield any pleasure, only yours, on whom he bestows it. To him that embraceth his labours, he dedicates both them and his love. With him that either knows not how, or cares not to entertain them, he will not be angry, but only to him says thus much for a farewell:

Si quid novisti rectius istis,
Candidus imperti ; si non, his utere mecum.

Finis.

O PER SE O

By Thomas Dekker (?)

1612.

AND so good morrow Goodman Bellman of London. Your night-piece is drawn, and my day-work is now to begin. Let my morning therefore, I pray you, be your midnight, and now when all others rise to go to their labours—who could scarce sleep by reason of the noise you made with your clapper—get you to your bed, and dream upon your pillow upon some new discovery. In that map of villainies, which you have drawn in print already, I like the handling of your pencil, but not the laying on of your colours. They are smooth enough, but you have not given them their true sweetening, heightening and shadowing. But I cannot blame you, because *nocte latent mendæ*[1] : women, horses and colours are not to be chosen by candlelight. And you, Gaffer Bellman, having no better guide, it is a wonder you stumbled no more, considering you walked i'th dark. If, therefore, by my spectacles being clearer than yours I have discovered more nests of blackbirds—I mean more villainies of the Devil's own hatching—than ever flew to your fist, and were sold afterwards to sing in shops in Paul's Churchyard, it ought not to raise up your collar an inch higher for all that, sithence in both our land-discoveries our sails are hoisted up only to do good to the commonwealth, and because the notes which I sing may appear to be of mine own setting, and not either borrowed or stolen from any other. You shall know that, serving in the late Queen's time many years together in the office of an High Constable, in that county wherein I now dwell, I drew from the examination of such lewd persons as came before me the truth of all those villains which here I publish.

In the mustering of this damned regiment, I found, that whether they were rogues taken in romboyles, that is to say, in watches or wards, by the petty harman beck, who in their company signifies a petty constable, or whether they were such as in the canting tongue are called maunderers (of begging or demanding), whether they lived in bousing kens (ale-houses) or what other coarse thread of life soever any of them all spun, it was ever wound in a black bottom of the most pernicious making up that the Devil could teach them ; insomuch that, albeit the

366

very sunbeams could possibly have written down the discovery of any gross villainies by them committed, they would as easily venture upon damning, in denial of it with oaths, as if there had been no hell for such offenders.

For my better painting forth these monsters, I once took one of them into my service, being a sturdy, big-limbed young fellow. Of him I desired some knowledge in their gibberish, but he swore he could not cant, yet his rogueship seeing himself used kindly by me, would now and then shoot out a word of canting, and being thereupon asked why with oaths he denied it before, he told me that they are sworn never to disclose their skill in canting to any householder, for, if they do, the other maunderers or rogues mill them (kill them), yet he for his part, he said, was never sworn, because he was a clapperdudgeon, that is to say, a beggar-born. This clapperdudgeon stayed with me so long as he durst, and then binged a waste in a darkmans (stole away from me in the night-time). So that what intelligence I got from him, or any other trained up in the same rudiments of roguery, I will briefly, plainly and truly set down, as I had it from my devilish schoolmaster, whom I call by the name of *O per se O*.

Of him I learned that the cause why so many of this wicked generation wander up and down this kingdom is the free command, and abundant use they have of women; for if you note them well in their marching, not a tatterdemalion walks his round, be he young, be he old, but he hath his mort, or his doxy, at his heels (his woman, or his whore); for in hunting of their rascal deer this law they hold, when they come to strike a doe, if she will not wap for a win, let her trine for a make. (If she will not —— *O per se O* for a penny, let her hang for a halfpenny.)

And this liberty of wenching is increased by the almost infinite numbers of tippling-houses, called bousing kens, or of stalling kens, that is to say, houses where they have ready money for any stolen goods; unto which nests birds fly of the same feather that the owner is of; for if the ale-seller be a horse-stealer, a cutpurse, a robber by the highway, a cheater, etc., of the same coat are his guests. These houses are the nurseries of rogues and thieves. For how could they bestow cloaks, sheets, shirts and other garments, being stolen, if they had not stalling kens to receive them? Why should grunters (pigs) go whining out of the world, having their throats cut by rogues, if they had not bousing kens to eat them in? In the ceremony of whose ragged assemblies, the Bellman a little mistook himself, for priggers, filchers and cloyers (being all in English, stealers) use neither roast meat, nor spits in their feaſtings, as he furnisheth them, but when they intend to ſtrike a hand, they levy their damnable troops in the day, but they sally forth and share the spoils in the night. For some one ſturdy hell-hound above the reſt undertakes to be the miller, that is to say, the killer. (I hope this can be no disgrace to any honeſt miller, who is no thief with a false hopper.) And this killer brings to the slaughter-house of the Devil (viz., a bousing ken) a bleating-cheat (a sheep) ; another mills a crack-mans (breaks a hedge), and that wood heats the oven, whilſt the sheep is dressed, cut in pieces, and put into earthen pots made for the purpose to bake their victuals in. The oven's mouth being thus daubed up, out fly the little devils more damned than the oven, either to break an house some two or three miles off, or to do as bad a villainy. The piece of service being performed, a retreat is sounded, and about midnight they return merrily, fall to their good cheer manfully, and then divide the spoils of ſtolen shirts, smocks or anything else moſt thievishly. In which partnership the hoſt and hoſtess are chief sharers, but such subtle shopkeepers are these haberdashers of the devil's small wares, that they never set out to sell but when the coaſt is clear, and that (as thieves do among brokers) the hue and cry's throat be ſtopped that went bawling after them. For about a seven night after, when all is hushed, to the ſtalling ken goes the duds for lour (to the thieving house are the ſtolen clothes sent roundly for money), which being told out and divided, awⱥy fly these ravens scatterringly, the next prey that they light upon being ever at some fair, or else a market.

And now that we talk of fairs, let my pen gallop over a few lines, and it shall bring you, without spurring, swiftlier into Glouceſtershire than if you rode upon Pacolet[2]. There if you please to alight near Tewkesbury, at a place called Durreſt Fair[3] (being kept there upon the two Holy Rood Days), you shall see more rogues than ever were whipped at a cart's arse through London, and more beggars than ever came dropping out of Ireland.[4] If you look upon them, you would think you lived in Henry the Sixth's time, and that Jack Cade and his rebellious ragamuffins were there muſtering. Dunkirk cannot show such sharks.[5] The wild Irish are but flocks of wild geese to them. And these swarms of locuſts come to this lousy fair from all parts of the land within an hundred miles' compass. To describe the booths is loſt labour, for, let the hangman show but his wardrobe, and there is not a rag difference between them. None here ſtands crying, " What do you lack? " for you can ask for nothing that is good, but here it is lacking. The buyers and sellers are both alike, tawny sun-burned rascals, and they flock in such troops, that it shows as if Hell were broke loose. The shopkeepers are thieves, and the chapmen rogues, beggars and whores; so that to bring a purse-full of money hither were madness, for it is sure to be cut.

But would you know what wares these merchants of eel-skins utter? Only duds for the quarroms, that is to say, clothes for the body, which they have pilfered from hedges or houses. And this filthy fair begins before day, and endeth before nine in the same morning. At which breaking up, they do not presently march away with their bags and their baggages, but he who is chosen the Lord of the Fair, who is commonly the lustiest rogue in the whole bunch, leads his tattered footmen and footwomen from ale-house to ale-house, where, being armed all in ale-of-proof, and their bene bouse (the strong liquor) causing them to have nase nabs (drunken coxcombs), up fling they the cans, down go the booths about fly broken jugs. Here lies a rogue bleeding, there is a mort cursing, here a doxy stabbing with her knife. And thus this fair, which begins merrily, ends madly; for knaves set it up, and queans pull it down.

Yet to meet at this assembly, how far off soever they be, they will keep their day, though they hop thither upon one crutch. And it is for seven causes that thus they bestir their stumps to be at this upsitting, which are these, viz.

1. Every one, as his rogueship is of bulk, or can best swagger, desireth to be chosen Lord of the Fair; or, if he lose his lordship, yet to be a retainer at least, and to fight under his tattered colours.

2. To meet with the sisterhood and brotherhood of whores and wallet-mongers.

3. To share such money as is taken for duds and cheats won (clothes and things stolen).

4. To know how the world goes abroad, what news in the dewse-a-vill (the country), and where is beneship (good), or where queer (naught).

5. To be bousy (drunken) for company.

6. To bandy their tawny and weather-beaten forces of maunderers, being of their own fraternity, against any other troop of mountebanks, at any other fair or market, where the lowest rendezvous is to be made.

7. Lastly, to enact new-warm orders for fresh stealing of clothes, etc., with all manner of armour for the body, but especially stamps (shoes) because, being beggars, they are seldom set on horseback.

These are the seven halters that draw these hell-hounds to this fair, for the least of which seven they will venture a hanging.

The fair is broken up, and because it is their fashion at the trussing up of their packs to trudge away merrily, I will here teach you what *O per se O* is, because nothing else but the burden of a song, set by the Devil, and sung by his choir ; of which I will set no more down but the beginning, because the middle is detestable, the end abominable, and all of it damnable.

Thus it sounds :

> Wilt thou a begging go ?
>   *O per se O.   O per se O.*
> Wilt thou a begging go ?
>   Yes verily, yea.
> Then thou must God forsake,
> And to stealing thee betake.
>   *O per se O.   O per se O.*
> Yes verily, yea, &c.

This is the music they use in their libkens (their lodgings) where thirty or forty of them being in a swarm, one of the master-devils sings, and the rest of his damned crew follow with the burden. In which midnight caterwaulings of theirs nothing is heard but cursing and profanation, and such swearing as if they were all knights of the post. Jews did never crucify Christ with more dishonour, than these rake-hells, who with new-invented fearful oaths tear Him in pieces. And no marvel, for most of those who are beggars born, are never christened. Besides, they have in their canting a word for the Devil, or the plague, etc., as Ruffin for the one, and cannikin for the other ; but for God they have none : only they name Him, but it is not in reverence, but abuse, all their talk in their nasty libkens, where they lie like swine, being of nothing but wapping, niggling, prigging, cloying, filching, cursing, and such stuff. Who therefore would pity such impostors, whose faces are full of dissembling, hearts of villainy, mouths of curses, bodies of sores, which they call their great cleyms—but laid upon their flesh by cunning—; whose going abram (that is to say, naked) is not for want of clothes, but to stir up men to pity, and in that pity to cozen their devotion. Now, whereas the Bellman in his privy search found out the nests of these screech-owls, pulling off some of their feathers, only to show their ugliness, but for want of good and perfect eyesight, not flaying off their skins, as I here purpose to do, and so to draw blood. I will finish that which the Bellman, by being over-watched, left lame, and show those abuses naked to the world which he never discovered.

First, therefore, shall you behold the abram-man in his true colours, his right shape, his own rags, and then shall you hear the phrase of his maund or begging.

Next him comes marching the counterfeit soldier, with his maunding note too. At his tail follow bene-fakers of gybes, that is to say, counterfeiters of passports.

Then dummerers.

Then clapperdudgeons in their true habiliments, and their true beggarly rhetoric they use in begging.

Then will I show you how they hang together in fraternities, and what articles of brotherhood they are sworn to, with a note (as good as any rogue's mark they carry about them) how to know these knots of knaves, or these brotherhoods, their names, their libkens, or lodgings, their stalling kens, to which all stolen goods are brought.

And lastly, to show you that even in their mirth they are devils, you shall hear their true canting songs now used among them.

In setting down all which hidden villainies, never till this day discovered, you shall find a mixture not only of all those detestable subtleties used in making those sores which eat into their flesh, but also the tricks and medicines they have, without help of surgeons, to cure them. I will besides in their descriptions here and there stick words and phrases of their gibberish or beggarly language, giving them the stamp presently of true English, which labour I take of purpose to procure delight to the reader.

Of the abram, his description.

The abram cove is a lusty strong rogue, who walketh with a slade about his quarroms (a sheet about his body) trining (hanging) to his hams, bandolierwise, for all the world as cutpurses and thieves wear their sheets to the gallows, in which their trulls are to bury them. Oftentimes, because he scorns to follow any fashions of hose, he goes without breeches ; a cut jerkin with hanging sleeves in imitation of our gallants, but no satin or camlet elbows, for both his legs and arms are bare ; having no commission to cover his body, that is to say, no shirt ; a face staring like a Saracen ; his hair long and filthily knotted, for he keeps no barber ; a good filch (or staff) of grown ash, or else hazel, in his famble (in his hand), and sometimes a sharp stick, on which he hangeth ruff-peck (bacon). These, walking up and down the country, are more terrible to women and children, than the name of Raw-head and Bloody-bones, Robin Goodfellow, or any other hobgoblin. Crackers tied to a dog's tail, make not the poor cur run faster than these abram ninnies do the silly villagers of the country, so that when they come to any door a begging, nothing is denied them.

Their marks.

Some of these abrams have the letters E and R upon their arms ; some have crosses, and some other mark ; all of them carrying a blue colour. Some wear an iron ring, etc. Which marks are printed upon their flesh, by tying their arm hard with two strings three or four inches asunder, and then with a sharp awl pricking or razing the skin to such a figure or print as they best fancy. They rub that place with burnt paper, piss and gunpowder, which being hard rubbed in, and suffered to dry, sticks in the flesh a long time after. When these marks fail, they renew them at pleasure. If you examine them how these letters or figures are printed upon their arms, they will tell you it is the mark of Bedlam,[6] but the truth is, they are made as I have reported.

And to colour their villainy the better, every one of these abrams hath a several gesture in playing his part. Some make an horrid noise, hollowly sounding ; some whoop, some hollow, some show only a kind of wild distracted ugly look, uttering a simple kind of maunding, with these addition of words : " Well and wisely." Some dance, but keep no measure ; others leap up and down, and fetch gambols. All their actions show them to be as drunk as beggars ; for, not to belie them, what are they but drunken beggars ? all that they beg being either lure or bouse (money or drink).

Their maund, or begging.

The first begins : " Good urship, master (or good urships, rulers of this place), bestow your reward on a poor man that hath lain in Bedlam without Bishopsgate three years, four months and nine days. And bestow one piece of your small silver towards his fees, which he is indebted there, the sum of three pounds, thirteen shillings, seven pence halfpenny (or to such effect), and hath not wherewith to pay the same, but by the good help of urshipful and well-disposed people, and God to reward them for it."

The second begins : " Now dame, well and wisely, what will you give poor Tom now ? one pound of your sheep's feathers to make poor Tom a blanket ? or one cutting of your sow side, no bigger than my arm ? or one piece of your salt meat to make poor Tom a sharing horn ? or one cross of your small silver towards the buying a pair of shoes—well and wisely. Ah, God bless my good dame, well and wisely, give poor Tom an old sheet to keep him from the cold, or an old doublet or jerkin of my master's, God save his life."

Then will he dance and sing, or use some other antic and ridiculous gesture, shutting up his counterfeit puppet-play with this epilogue or conclusion : " Good dame, give poor Tom one cup of the best drink—well and wisely. God save the King and his Council, and the governor of this place, etc."

Of counterfeit soldiers.

These may well be called counterfeit soldiers, for not one (scarce) among the whole army of them ever discharged so much as a caliver : nothing makes them soldiers but old mandilions, which they buy at the broker's. The weapons they carry are short crab-tree cudgels ; and these, because they have the name of soldiers, never march but in troops two or three in a company. Of all sorts of rogues these are the most impudent and boldest, for they knock at men's doors as if they had serious business there, whereas, the door being opened to them, they begin this parle.

Their maunding.

" Gentle rulers of this place, bestow your reward upon poor soldiers, that are utterly maimed and spoiled in her Majesty's late wars, as well for God's cause as her Majesty's and yours. And bestow one piece of your small silver upon poor men, or somewhat towards a meal's meat, to succour them in the way of truth, etc., for God's cause."

These fellows go commonly hurt in the left arm, beneath the elbow, having a gybe jerked (that is to say, a passport sealed), with licence to depart the colours (under which, if you rightly examine them, they never fought) ; yet wheresoever the wars are, and how far off soever, thus can they wound themselves at home.

Their making of their sores.[7]

Take unslaked lime and soap, with the rust of old iron. These mingled together, and spread thick on two pieces of leather which are clap upon the arm, one against the other ; two small pieces of wood, fitted to the purpose, holding the leathers down, all which are bound hard to the arm with a garter ; which in a few hours fretting the skin with blisters, and being taken off, the flesh will appear all raw. Then a linen cloth being applied to the raw blistered flesh, it sticks so fast, that, upon plucking it off, it bleeds : which blood (or else some other), is rubbed all over the arm, by which means, after it is well dried on, the arm appears black, and the sore raw and reddish, but white about the edges like an old wound. Which if they desire to heal, a brown paper with butter and wax being applied, they are cured. And thus, without weapon, do you see how our maundering counterfeit soldiers come maimed.

Of placing their sores.

The soldier hath his sore always on his left arm (unless he be left-handed, for then, because of the better use of that hand, it is upon the right), betwixt the elbow and the wrist, and is called by the name of soldier's maund.

When a sore is placed on the back of the hand, and that he saith he was hurt by an horse, then it is called footman's maund.

When the sore is above the elbow, as if it were broken or hurt by falling from a scaffold, it is called mason's maund. And thus the altering the place of the sore altereth the maund.

Of these counterfeit soldiers, some of them being examined will say they were lately serving-men, but their master being dead, and the household dispersed, they are compelled to this baseness of life for want of means. Some of them can play the abram (be mad Toms), or else beg rum-maund (counterfeit to be a fool), or else that his tongue is tied, and cannot speak, and suchlike.

Of bene-fakers of gybes.

They who are counterfeiters of passports are called bene-fakers, that is to say, good makers. And these makers, like the Devil's hackney-men, lie lurking in every country, to send his messengers post to Hell. The best passports that ever I saw were made in S——shire, with the hand of one M. W. subscribed unto them. There was another excellent bene-faker about P——, a town in G——shire. In S—— dwelt another, who took two shillings and sixpence (two bords and six wins, or two bords and a flag) for every passport that went out of his beggarly office ; he counterfeited the seal of L. D.

Of these bene-fakers I could say much more, if I would be counted a blab. But now the very best of them are made in L—— to carry men from thence unto W——.

How to know counterfeit passports.

The seals of noblemen, gentlemen, Justices, or any other who have authority to use seals, are graven in silver, copper, or some hard stuff: and those things which are so graven seal the arms or suchlike with sharp edges, and with a round circle enclosing it, as if it were cut with an instrument of steel, and it maketh a neat and deep impression. But these counterfeit jarks (or seals) are graven with the point of a knife, upon a stick's end, whose roundness may well be perceived from the circle of a common turned seal; these for the most part bearing the ill-favoured shape of a bugher's nab, or a prancer's nab (a dog's head, or a horse's), and sometimes an unicorn's, and suchlike; the counterfeit jark having no circle about the edges. Besides, in the passport you shall lightly find these words, viz., *For Solomon saith: Who giveth the poor, lendeth the Lord,* etc., and that constables shall help them to lodgings, and that curates shall persuade their parishioners, etc.

Another note is, let them be in what part of the land soever they will, yet have they an hundred miles to go at least: every one of them having his doxy at his heels. And thus much of bene-fakers.

Of dummerers.

The Bellman took his marks amiss in saying that a dummerer is equal to the crank; for of these dummerers I never met but one, and that was at the house of one M. L. of L——. This dummerer's name was W——. He made a strange noise, showing by fingers across that his tongue was cut out at Chalk Hill. In his hand he carried a stick, about a foot in length, and sharp at both ends, which he would thrust into his mouth, as if he meant to show the stump of his tongue. But in doing so, he did of purpose hit his tongue with the stick to make it bleed, which filling up his mouth, you could not for blood perceive any tongue at all, because he had turned it upwards, and with his stick thrust it into his throat. But I caused him to be held fast by the strength of men, until such time that, opening his teeth with the end of a small cudgel, I plucked forth his tongue, and made him speak.[8]

Of clapperdudgeons.

A clapperdudgeon is in English a beggar born. Some call him a palliard ; of which sorts there are two : first, natural ; secondly, artificial. This fellow (above all other that are in the regiment of rogues) goeth best armed against the cruelty of winter. He should be wise, for he loves to keep himself warm, wearing a patched caster (a cloak) for his upper robe ; under that a togmans (a gown) with high stampers (shoes), the soles an inch thick pegged, or else patches at his girdle, ready to be clapped on ; a great skew (a brown dish) hanging at his girdle, and a tassel of thrums to wipe it ; a brace of greasy night-caps on his head, and over them, lest he should catch a knavish cold, a hat, or nab-cheat, a good filch, or staff, in his hand, having a little iron peg in the end of it ; a bugher (a little dog) following him, with a smug doxy, attired fit for such a roguish companion. At her back she carryeth a great pack, covered with a patched safe-guard, under which she conveyeth all such things as she filcheth. Her skill sometimes is to tell fortunes, to help the diseases of women or children. As she walks, she makes balls or shirt-strings—but now commonly they knit—and wears in her hat a needle with a thread at it. An excellent angler she is ; for when her cove maunds at any door, if any poultryware be picking up their crumbs near them, she feedeth them with bread, and hath a thread tied to a hooked pin, baited for the nonce, which the chicken swallowing is choked, and conveyed under the caster. Chickens, linen or woollen, or anything that is worth the catching, comes into her net.

Under this banner of the patched clapperdudgeon do I levy all palliards, as well those of the great cleym (or sores) as others, whom I term artificial clapperdudgeons, albeit they are not beggars born.

Of their maund.

This palliard, or artificial clapperdudgeon, who carryeth about him the great cleym to stir compassion up in people's hearts, thus acteth his part. He slides to the earth by his staff, and lying piteously on the ground, makes a fearful horrid strange noise, through an hoarse throat uttering these lamentable tunes :

" Ah, the urship of God look out with your merciful eyne ! One pitiful look upon sore, lame, grieved and impudent (for impotent) people, sore troubled with the grievous disease, and have no rest day nor night by the canker and worm, that continually eateth the flesh from the bone ! for the urship of God, bestow one cross of your small silver, to buy him salve and ointment, to ease the poor wretched body, that never taketh rest ; and God to reward you for it in Heaven."

These palliards walk two or three together, and as one gives over this note, the second catcheth it at the rebound, using the self-same howling and grunting ; which ended, they say the Lord's Prayer, and in many places the *Ave*, never ceasing till something be given them.

How they make their great sores, called the great cleym.

They take crowfoot, spearwort and salt, and, bruising these together, they lay them upon the place of the body which they desire to make sore. The skin by this means being fretted, they first clap a linen cloth, till it stick fast, which plucked off, the raw flesh hath ratsbane thrown upon it, to make it look ugly ; and then cast over that a cloth, which is always bloody and filthy ; which they do so often, that in the end in this hurt they feel no pain, neither desire they to have it healed, but with their doxies will travel, for all their great cleyms, from fair to fair, and from market to market, being able by their maunding to get five bords, that is, five shillings, in a week, in money and corn. Which money they hide under blue and green patches ; so that sometimes they have about them six pound or seven pound together.

The clapperdudgeons that have not the great cleym, are called farmerly beggars.

Of their fraternities.

There is no lusty rogue but hath many both sworn brothers and the morts his sworn sisters ; who vow themselves body and soul to the Devil to perform these ten articles following, viz.

Articles of their fraternities.

1. *Thou shalt my true brother be, keeping thy faith to thy other brothers as to myself if any such thou have.*

2. *Thou shalt keep my counsel, and all other my brother's, being known to thee.*

3. *Thou shalt take part with me, and all other my brothers in all matters.*

4. *Thou shalt not hear me ill spoken of without revenge to thy power.*

5. *Thou shalt see me want nothing, to which thou canst help me.*

6. *Thou shalt give me part of all thy winnings whatsoever.*

7. *Thou shalt not but keep true 'pointments with me for meetings, be it by day or night, at what place soever.*

8. *Thou shalt teach no householder to cant, neither confess anything to them, be it never so true, but deny the same with oaths.*

9. *Thou shalt do no hurt to any maunder but with thine own hands ; and thou shalt forbear none that disclose these secrets.*

10. *Thou shalt take clothes, hens, geese, pigs, bacon, and suchlike for thy winnings, wherever thou canst have them.*

How to know their brotherhoods.

When at the end of a town, wherein a fair or market is kept, you see an assembly of them together chiding and brawling, but not fighting, then those coves are sworn brothers. If likewise two doxies fall together by the ears, whilst the rogues themselves stand by and fight not, that also is a brotherhood ; for it is one branch of their laws to take part with their doxies in any wrong.

Of their names.

Every one of them hath a peculiar nickname proper to himself, by the which he is more known, more enquired after by his brothers, and in common familiarity more saluted, than by his own true name. Yea, the false is used so much that the true is forgotten. And of these nicknames, some are given to them for some special cause : as Olli Compolli is the byname of some one principal rogue amongst them, being an abram ; being bestowed upon him, because by that he is known to be the head or chief amongst them. In like manner these surnames following belong to other grand Signors and commanders, viz., Dimber Damber, and Hurly Burly, General Nurse, the High Shrieve, the High Constable, and suchlike. And some nicknames are either upon mockery, or upon pleasure given unto them : as the Great Bull, the Little Bull, and many other suchlike. The Great Bull is some one notable lusty rogue, who gets away all their wenches ; for this Great Bull by report had in one year three and twenty doxies, his jockey was so lusty. Such liberty have they in sinning, and such damnable and moſt deteſtable manner of life do they lead.

As the men have nicknames, so likewise have the women ; for some of them are called the White Ewe, the Lamb, etc.   And, as I have heard, there was an abram who called his mort Madam Wap-apace.

Of their libkens or lodgings.

As these fugitive vagabonds have nicknames to themselves, so have they libkens, or lodgings, and places of meeting : as one of the meeting places, as I have heard, being a sheep-cote, is by the queſt of rogues who nightly assemble there, called by the name of *Stophole Abbey*. So likewise another of their lodgings is called by the same name.   Then have they others, as, the *Blue Bull*, the *Prancer*, the *Bull's Belly*, the *Cow's Udder*, the *Green Arbour*, the *Blazing Star*, etc.   Suchlike by-names give they also to their ſtalling kens.   And note this, that after a robbery done, they lie not within twelve miles at the leaſt of the place where they do it, but having eaten up their ſtolen mutton, baked as aforesaid, away they trudge through thick and thin, all the havens of Hell into which they put in being always for the moſt part of an equal diſtance one from another.   For look how far as the one *Stophole Abbey* ſtands from the other, and juſt so far is the *Bull's Belly* from the *Cow's Udder*, and so of the reſt.   So that what way soever these night-spirits do take after they have done their deeds of darkness, they know what pace to keep, because, what ſtorms soever fall, they are sure of harbour, all their journeys being but of one length.   Yet dare they not but let their morts and their doxies meet them at some of these places, because how cold soever the weather be, their female furies come hotly and smoking from thence, carrying about them glimmer in the prat (fire in the touch-bore) by whose flashes oftentimes there is glimmer in the jockey (the flask is blown up too), of which dangerous and deadly skirmishes the fault is laid upon serving-men dwelling thereabouts, who like freebooters are so hungry of flesh, that a doxy, if she have a smug face, cannot peep out, but she is taken up for hawk's meat.   And it is no wonder there is such ſtealing of these wild bucks, because there is such ſtore of them.   Nor is it a marvel there is such ſtore, sithence he is not held worthy to walk, or to be counted one of the four-and-twenty orders, but to be banished as a silly animal and a ſtinkard from all good fellowship, society, and meetings at fairs, markets, and merry bousing kens, who when the trumpet sounds, that is to say, when the cuckoo sings, thrusts not out his head like a snail out of his shell, and walks not abroad about the dewse-a-vill (the country), with his spirit of lechery and thieving, his doxy, at his heels.

Why the staff is called a filch.

Thus much for their fraternities, names, lodgings, and assemblies, at all which times everyone of them carries a short staff in his hand, which is called a filch, having in the nab, or head, of it, a ferme (that is to say, a hole) into which, upon any piece of service, when he goes a filching, he putteth a hook of iron, with which hook he angles at a window in the dead of night, for shirts, smocks, or any other linen or woollen. And for that reason is the staff termed a filch. So that it is as certain that he is an angler for duds, who hath a ferme in the nab of his filch, as that he is a thief who upon the highway cries " Stand," and takes a purse. This staff serveth to more uses than either the cross-staff or the Jacob's, but the uses are not so good nor so honest ; for this filching-staff being artificially handled, is able now and then to mill a grunter, a bleating-cheat, a redshank, a tib of the buttery, and suchlike, or to fib a cove's quarroms in the Rome-pad, for his lour in his bung, that is to say, to kill a pig, a sheep, a duck, a goose, and suchlike, or to beat a man by the highway for the money in his purse.

And yet for all these base villainies and others, of what blackness soever they be, you shall at every Assises and Sessions see swarms of them boldly venturing amongst the prisoners. One cause of their tempting their own danger so, is, that being sworn brothers in league, and partners in one and the same thievery, it behoves them to listen to the prisoner's confession, which they do secretly, and so to take their heels, if they spy a storm coming. Another cause is, to learn what lime-twigs caught the bird i'th cage, and how he was entangled by the Justice in his examination,[9] that thereby he abroad may shun the like. But the Devil is their tutor, Hell their school, thievery, roguery and whoredom the arts they study, before Dr. Story[10] they dispute, and at the gallows are made graduates of Newgate and other jails, the hangman's colleges. To shut up this feast merrily, as sweetmeats are best last, your last dish which I set before you to digest the hardness of the rest, is a canting song, not feigned or composed as those of the Bellman's were, out of his own brain,[11] but by the canters themselves, and sung at their meetings.

The Canting Song.

1 *Bing out bene morts, and tour, and tour,*
  Bing out bene morts and tour ;
 For all your duds are binged a waſte ;
  The bene cove hath the lour.

2 *I met a dell, I viewed her well ;*
  She was beneship to my watch :
 So she and I did stall and cloy
  Whatever we could catch.

3 *This doxy dell can cut bene whids,*
  And wap well for a win,
 And prig and cloy so beneshiply,
  All the dewse-a-vill within.

4 *The boil was up, we had good luck,*
  In frost for and in snow.
 When they did seek, then we did creep,
  And plant in ruffmans low.

5 *To stalling-ken the mort bings then,*
  To fetch lour for her cheats :
 Duds and ruff-peck, romboyled by harman-beck,
  And won by maunders' feats.

6 *You maunders all, stow what you stall,*
  To Rome-coves watch so queer :
 And wapping dell, that niggles well,
  And takes lour for her hire.

7 *And gybe well jarked, tick rome comfeck,*
  For back by glimmer to maund :
 To mill each ken, let cove bing then,
  Through ruffmans lage or laund.

8 *Till cramp-rings queer tip cove his hire,*
  And queer-kens do them catch :
 A cannikin mill Queer Cuffin,
  So queer to bene coves' watch.

9 *Bene darksmans then, bouse, mort and ken,*
  The bene cove's binged a waſte :
 On chats to trine, by rome-cove's dine,
  For his long lib at last.

10 *Bing out bene morts, and tour, and tour,*
  Bing out of the Rome-vill :
 And tour the cove that cloyed your duds
  Upon the chats to trine.

FINIS.

Thus for satisfaction of the readers, Englished.

1   Go forth brave girls, look out, look out,
       Look out, I say, good conies,
    For all your clothes are stolen, I doubt,
       Mad shavers share the monies.

2   I met a drab, I liked her well :
       My bowls did fit her alley.
    We both did vow to rob pell-mell,
       And so abroad did sally.

3   This bouncing trull can rarely talk,
       A penny will make her—— :
    Through any town which she doth walk,
       Nought can her filching 'scape.

4   The house being raised, aside we stepped
       And through the mire did wade :
    To avoid hue and cry to a hedge we crept,
       And under it close were laid.

5   To th' broker's then my hedge-bird flies,
       For stolen goods bringing coin ;
    Which, though the constable after hies,
       Our tricks away purloin.

6   You maunding rogues, how you steal beware
       For privy search is made :
    Take heed thou too, thou hackney-mare,
       Who ne'er art ridden, but paid.

7   A licence got with counterfeit seal
       To beg as if undone
    By fire : to break each house and steal,
       O'er hedge and ditch then run.

8   Till shackles soundly pay us home,
       And to the jail compel us.
    Ill may the Justice ever thrive,
       So cruel to good fellows !

9   Sweet   punk, beer-house and beer, good-night,
       The honest rogue's departed
    To hanging, by the Justice' spite :
       To his long home he's carted.

10   Away sweet ducks, with greedy eyes,
       From London walk up Holborn :
    Sue him who stole your clothes : he flies
       With hempen wings to Tyburn.

FINIS.

MARTIN MARKALL

BEADLE OF BRIDEWELL

His Defence and Answers to the Bellman of

LONDON

Discovering the long-concealed Original and Regimen of Rogues, when they first began to take head, and how they have succeeded one the other successively unto the six-and-twentieth year of King Henry the Eighth, gathered out of the Chronicle of Crackropes, and (as they term it) the Legend of Losels.

By S.R[ID?].

1610

Oderunt peccare boni virtutis amore :
Oderunt peccare mali formidine poenae.[1]

To the Courteous Reader.

GENTLEMEN, a preface to a pamphlet is as foolish as fancied, and verses *in laudem authoris* are far worse than a horse-courser's commendation of a Smithfield jade, the one too, too common, the other frivolous. For mine own part, if the inside of my labour cannot win your content, let the outside of the subject show his author's intent. I know I shall be contemned of some for being too forward, controlled of others who, perhaps, are rubbed on the fore, and condemned of a third sort for a loose style and lame phrase. Indeed, Gentlemen, this I do confess : I shall bring upon this great stage of fools (for *omne sub sole vanitas*) a piece of folly. If such as count themselves wise dare venture the reading of it over, I cannot let them ; but when they have perused it, and find therein nothing but folly, let them reprehend neither the work nor workmaster, but rather themselves, in that they would spend their time so foolishly, being before warned of so foolish and idle a subject.

Yours in love,
S.R.

MARTIN MARKALL

His Apology, to the Bellman of London.

THERE hath been of late days great pains taken on the part of the good old Bellman of London[2] in discovering, as he thinks, a new-found nation and people. Let it be so for this time. Hereupon much ado was made in setting forth their lives, order of living, method of speech, and usual meetings, with divers other things thereunto appertaining. These volumes and papers now spread everywhere, so that every jack-boy now can say as well as the proudest of that fraternity : " Will you wap for a win, or trine for a make ? "

The gentle company of cursitors began now to stir and look about them, and, having gathered together a convocation of canting caterpillars, as well in the north parts, at the Devil's Arse A-peak*, as in the south, they diligently enquired, and straight search was made whether any had revolted from that faithless fellowship. Hereupon every one gave his verdict. Some supposed that it might be someone that, having ventured too far beyond wit and good taking-heed, was fallen into the hands of the magistrate and carried to the trining-cheats, where, in show of a penitent heart and remorse of his good time ill spent, turned the cock and let out all. Others thought it might be some spy knave, that, having little to do, took upon him the habit and form of an hermit, and so, by daily commercing and discoursing, learned in time the mystery and knowledge of this ignoble profession. And others, because it smelt of a study, deemed it to be some of their own company, that had been at some free school, and belike because he would be handsome against a good time, took pen and ink and wrote of that subject[4]. Thus, *tot homines, tot sententiae* : so many men, so many minds. And all because the spiteful poet would not set to his name ! At last up starts an old cacodemical academic with his frieze bonnet and gives them all to know that this invective was set forth, made, and printed above forty years ago ; and being then called *A Caveat for Cursitors*, is now newly printed and termed *The Bellman of London*, made at first by one

---

* Where at this day the rogues of the north part once every three years assemble in the night, because they will not be seen and espied, being a place to those who know it very fit for that purpose, it being hollow and made spacious underground, at first by estimation half a mile in compass, but it hath such turnings and roundings in it that a man may easily be lost if he enter not with a guide.[3]

Master Harman, a Justice of Peace in Kent in Queen Mary's days, he being then about ten years of age.

At this news the whole company of clapperdudgeons were indifferently well resolved, yet their minds were not fully satisfied, because they knew not by whom this book was set out. Hereupon for this time the Synagogue of Satan was dismissed, and the whole regiment of ragamuffins betook themselves to their usual occupations, expecting that this villainous ill-willer of theirs, at one time or other, would be known and brought to light. Not long after this, this perverse persecutor of poor pilgrims, not content with the former injury done against them, but seeking by all means to root out and scatter them, if it were possible, out of the land, raises new forces and persecutes them with fire and sword and deadly war.

The fury and malice of the Bellman once again bruited abroad, and they, not knowing the author of the first, now grow outrageous, begin to curse with bell, book, and candle ; that, if he were to be known, they would spare neither cost nor labour for the search, and enquire of him forth.

Meantime the rogues of the north, that had before met at the Devil's Arse A-peak, hearing of this unexpected news, with rage inflamed, trot on their lusty ten toes with bag and baggage toward the southern regiment, who, being entertained with such welcomes and compliments as are used among themselves, they presently send to the beadle of the hall to summon and warn all of that company and fraternity to make his personal appearance at the *Swan with Five Necks* in King's Street[5] as the fittest place to receive so ignoble a court of crack-ropes.

The congregation of caterpillars gathered together, and the court of cozeners now set, up starts a ragged over-roasted Jack of the clock-house, with his crutch in his hand instead of a tipstaff, makes three solemn Oyez, which done with a fiery face and filthy throat, he proclaims as followeth :

" All manner of people that were summoned to appear here this day before Corporal Fize, Chief Commander of the Regiment and Corporation of Good Fellows and Maunders, let them draw near and give their attendance, for the court is set."

As soon as ever the proclamation was ended, Lord ! what a company of petitioners pressed to the bar to prefer their papers of injuries, that were offered and done among themselves ! Here one complains that he could not travel safely, nor carry any money, without danger of the upright-man and tinker, but that they would rob and spoil them of all

that was ought about them ; here another, that they could not quietly
take their rest in the night, nor keep his autem, or doxy, sole unto
himself, but that the ruffler, padder, or any upright-man would take
them away perforce ; and others, that they could not converse and keep
company with those that they met, but that in the night they are sure
to be clied in the night by the angler, or hooker, or suchlike pilferers
that live upon the spoil of other poor people.

These were generally the effect of their petitions ; but oh, if a man
were there to hear the noise, the clamour and bawling that was there
among them, you would sure think that all the dogs in Paris Garden[6]
were broke loose, and came thither on purpose to yawl ! Yea, I think
in my conscience Cerberus, that three-throat[ed] horrible hell-hound,
never kept a more doleful nor horrid noise than those kennel of clapperdudgeons did at that time. But after that proclamation was made for
silence, Corporal Fize, Chief Commander of that court, began as
followeth :

" My friends and fellows, our meeting here at this time is not to
discuss and determine of matters between party and party ; but our
assembly now is to find out, judge, and determine of one that of late
hath published two malicious and injurious pamphlets concerning us
and our whole course of life. Therefore, I would request you forbear
until the Court have fully finished and ended this matter ; and, if we
have any spare time afterward, we will be ready to redress any wrongs
you, or any of you, have sustained."

At this motion the wind was calm. Then they proceeded to call
forth the grand jury, or quest of enquiry, who being called they did
appear, and then the charge was given them as followeth :

The names of the Grand Jury, or Quest of Enquiry of Crack-ropes.

Anthony ap Hugh, the Apple-squire of Apesbury.
Bartholomew Barfilching, the Bottlemaker of Bristol.
Christopher Chafelitter, the Chimneysweeper of Knoctivergos.
Demetrius Dingethrift, the Dorsermaker of Dorneby.
Edwin Evesdropper, the Eel-pie-eater of Elton.
Friskin Fitz-Fizler, my Lady Brach[7] Gent. Usher of Faversham.
Gregory Greenwinchard, the Gunfounder of Goggleton.
Haunce Haltersick, the Harnessmaker of Hornchurch.
Jeffrey Jobbernall, the Jerkinmaker of Jorley.
Kenrick Coleprophet, the Cockle-taker of Canterbury.
Lecherous Lousycoat, the Lark-taker of Laleham.
Martin Mark-a-knave, the Millstone-cutter of Marbury.
Nunquam Neverthrive, the Nutcracker of Newbury.
Owen Overthwart, the Onion-seller of Ockingham.

Peter Poundkarlick, the Pouchmaker of Pendlebury.
Quinton Corrifavell, the Quacksalver of Quanton.
Rowland Rinceprichard, the Ratcatcher of Ramsey,
Stephen Stink-a-pace, the Sow-gelder of Stamford.
Timothy Hol-hazard of Tritrace, the Tilemaker of Tonbridge.
Vincent Veryknave, the Vintner of the Vintry.
Wilkin Wiredrawer, the Welsh Wizard of Wickham.
Hextus Sextus, the Sexton of Sexbury.
Yanikin Yanner, the Yarn Spinner of Yarmouth.
Nicholas Chatborne, the Bousy Bag-bearer, or Clerk of the Snapsack ; good men
   in nothing, but true in villainy.   Stand near and hear your charge.

"My masters of the jury, and you, my good friends : the cause of
our unexpected and unaccustomed meeting at this time is not unknown
unto you all, how an upstart pamphlet-maker and a most injurious and
satirical libeller hath of late days done as much as in him lieth, not
only to disgrace and defame so ancient and long continuing profession ;
but also [to] extirp and overthrow all our customs, acts, and ceremonies,
which time out of mind have been accustomed, and now are daily in
use and custom among us.   The cause of this his muddy humour, I
cannot guess otherwise than this, that being weary of his good name
and reputation, if ever he had any, is now contented to disburden himself
thereof, and give the whole world to understand that, delighting in
roguery more than honesty, he would show himself to be little better
than a tame rogue.   The matter that he busyeth himself about savoureth
only rancour and malice.   The end whereat he aimeth, tendeth to death
and desolation, subversion of our state and fashion.   And therefore,
my masters, it behoveth you, as at all other times, so especially at this
time, wisely and considerately to weigh and ponder of this fact.   For
it is not an offence against one or two private men, but it toucheth the
whole company in general, and therefore a thing not to be passed slightly
over.

"You, therefore, that have the managing of this business, without
whom we of ourselves can proceed in nothing, you being our right
hand herein, bend all your care for the good of this little commonwealth.
And as you are elected and chosen to suborn and uphold this small
regiment, so I pray you show yourselves, as I hope you will, the true
supporters and pillars of the same.   But briefly to make an end, because
I purpose not to use many words, you shall not need to enquire and
search for the author, or his name, of this invective, for he is known,
and in his second round,[8] as he calls it, hath set to his name ; and
therefore you may save that labour.   Your charge is only to find of
the slander and scandal comprised in the indictment, or no.   If you

find him guilty, you shall return on the backside of the indictment that he is guilty, and so give it in court, that we may proceed against him accordingly. Meantime, because it is fit to proceed with equity and justice, and not to give judgment rashly and hastily against any man, before he have made his apology or purgation, our pursuivant shall be speedily sent to him, to bring him before us, that he may answer to the objections and crimes laid against him."

Straight was a stout sturdy and bigbone knave sent in embassage to Signor the Bellman to appear, who as soon as his message was delivered—he needed not to be bid make haste—speedily hastens to the Bellman's house, where he finds him at home by the fire-side, mumbling a piece of bread and cheese. The Bellman, seeing this rude and unmannerly fellow come in puffing without any God-speed, was ready to choke for fear. But after they had parle[ye]d on the matter and delivered his message, the Bellman locks fast his door, and puts the key under the still, and away they go together toward the Court of Crack-ropes.

In the meantime the jury gave up their verdict. They made not a long harvest of a little corn, but suddenly they laid their knaves' heads together and concluded that the Bellman was guilty of the slander comprised in the indictment; and thereupon delivered up again the indictment into the court, and so for that time they all departed to dinner.

By this time the gentlemen of the ragged order had almost dined; and now come in all haste the Bellman and his keeper, who, as soon as they were now come, word was carried in to the Masters of Misrule that the Bellman was in the hall ready to avouch what he had published. At this word they all straight rose, although scarce well dined, as all moved with a covetous and greedy desire to see the confusion of the poor Bellman.

As soon as the benchers of the ragged robes were set, in was called the Bellman to make his apology, where, after he had made his appearance, the Chief Commander of Crack-ropes began thus as followeth:

"Signor Bellman, I marvel what madness hath bewitched you, or what fury hath made you so fantastic, thus to rail on us poor vagrants, penniless pilgrims. Hath your nightly watchings and continual disorder of your brains so worried your senses that you can let fly at none other but on us, poor forlorn wretches, that trouble you not? no, not so much as once in seven years.

"Methinks it should have been your part rather to have told of domestical affairs and household matters; what good rule is kept among your watch; how here lies one drunk when he should stand sentinel;

there, another lying along asleep upon a bench complaining how his back aches with carrying the tankard and burthens in the daytime, so that he were more fit to have been at home in bed asleep than busied with any service for the City abroad at night ; how you found this door left open by 'prentices, either to let in their whores when their maſters be asleep, or to purloin their maſters' goods to maintain their trulls ; here to find out a knave picking open a lock by the help of his black art, and there in a tailor's ſtall, hot luxury making riot. These and many more might you have busied your brain about, and not thus scandalously and satirically to tyrannize over us as your crossbiters do over their simplers. No, no, Goodman Bellman ! Though we are of the contemned sort, yet we have supporters, and those that will fight in our quarrel, were you never so ſtrong.

" But to the matter. Surely you think you have done a noble exploit, thus to descry and declare to the world our manner of living and cuſtomary laws, our inns, feaſts and meetings ; and that herein you have done the part of a good subjeċt, thus to anatomize and piċture out such kind of people as you term base, that live by the sweat of other men's brows, as you say. This I scent your reason. Indeed I will say as you say. But shall I tell you : your praise had been much more the greater, if you had searched into the particular enormities and palpable villainies committed daily in your city. Let us poor folk live as we do. We do no man hurt but ourselves, nor no man's foe but our own ; we have nothing but what other men can spare ; other men's leavings are our refreshings ; and if it were not for us, much good meat would be in danger of fly-blowing, or caſt to the dogs. If there be any in our vocation or calling, that live disorderly and out of compass, what trade can you name that do not the like ? If we sometimes lie with our neighbours' wives, is it not usual elsewhere ? Nay, herein, by your favour, we do beſt paint out the Family of Love,[9] who do not ſtick but to have all things in common. If in boaſting we overdrink ourselves, do not some of the beſt in your city do the like ? If some make little conscience in lying, swearing, and ſtealing, I think few of your tradesmen go free. If then it be all one in city as in country, among the rich as amongſt us poor, and generally in all trades and occupations deceit and abuses (sith it is so that he that cannot dissemble cannot live), why then should you be so spiteful, Goodman Sans-bell, to inveigh againſt us poor souls above the reſt, who, of all others, in shifting are the moſt simpleſt souls in this overwise world.

" But you, good sir, like a spider to entrap only the smalleſt flies,

suffer the great ones to fly through ; you scour the ditch of a company
of croaking frogs, when you leave behind you an infinite number of
venomous toads ; you decipher and paint out a poor rogue, or a doxy
that steal and rob hedges of a few ragged clothes, which you can
make but petty larceny, and never speak of those vultures that ruin
whole lordships and infect the commonwealth by their villainous living,
to the discredit of some and ill example to all.

" Sir reverence on your mastership, good Master Bellman, had you
such a mote in your eye that you could not see those fox-furred gentlemen, that harbour more deceit under their damask cassocks, than is
in all the poor rogues in a country, brokers I mean, and usurers, that
like vultures prey upon the simple, those that are moths in a commonwealth, living upon the spoil of young gentlemen, as thirsty as a horse-
leech, that will never leave drinking until he burst ; a knave that hath
the interest in the leases of forty bawdy-houses, and a receiver of lifts,
and a dishonourable supporter of cutpurses, sleeping with his neighbours'
pledges all night in his bosom, and feeding upon forfeits and penalties
as ravens do upon carrion ; one that is a bousy bawdy miser, good for
none but himself and his trug, the scum of your seven deadly sins, and
an enemy to all good minds ?

" What say you to these now, good Signor Bellman ? Had you not
been better occupied to have discovered and lain open these kind of
caterpillars, than thus at random to rail on us poor harmless pilgrims ?
These are within your precinct and liberty, with whom you are daily
conversant. But you will verify the old saying, ' Where the ditch is
lowest, there men go over thick and threefold.' But it seems you durst
not make any mention of these, because they be your good masters
and benefactors. But for my part I care for none of them, no more
than they care for me.

" The nearest to our profession that I know, you are most like to the
whip-jack, who, as you say, being an idle fellow and a freshwater soldier,
never sailing further than Gravesend, will talk and prate of the Low
Countries, of this battle and that skirmish that he fought in, whereas,
indeed, he never durst say so much as bo to a mouse ; so you, never
going further out of town than a farthing candle will light, you will talk
and prate, and make a flourish of a number of things done both out of
your precinct and capacity. Say you are acquainted with all the damned
crew about the City, must it needs follow that you have the insight
and mystery of our calling and profession likewise ? No, good sir,
know you are wide by the length of your nose, yea, and so wide that

you shall never know the full depth thereof, until you have undertaken the sublime habit and shape of a poor pilgrim and humble hermit. And so *Benedicite!* "

After this profound orator had thus bespoken, licence was granted to the Bellman to make his answer and purgation, where, when he had cleared his throat with a hem, and made himself ready for that purpose, he proceeded thus :

" My masters, and you that are here present to hear me, I take no care how to answer you, knowing my cause to be just and honest. It hath been ever known that those that have guilty consciences will think that every thing that is said is spoken against themselves. And now I find it too true that it is not good meddling with galled jades, lest they winch and kick. For mine own part, what I have said, I dare avouch, and I am fully resolved to stand to my tackling, come what tempest will. And since you have given me leave freely to speak my mind without interruption, I will begin with your lives, and show you how vile and base it is before God and the world. For I think there be none here but such as you call maunders, clapperdudgeons, and a few padders, and those of the meanest sort, all of which I may rightly term you, and give you this one name drowsy drones and lousy loiterers. And what is a loiterer or drone ? Nothing but a sucker of honey, a spoiler of corn, a destroyer of fruit, a waster of money, a spoiler of victual, a sucker of blood, a breaker of good orders, a seeker of brawls, a queller of life, a basilisk of a commonwealth, which by company and sight doth poison a whole country and staineth honest minds with the infection of his venom, and so draweth the commonwealth to death and destruction. And such is the end of your lives and commanding ! When we see a great number of flies in a year, we judge it to be a great plague. And having so great a swarming of loitering vagabonds and sturdy rogues, ready to brawl and swagger at every man's door, doth it not declare a greater infection ready to ensue ?

" Who therefore can otherwise deem but that this pestilence, wherewith this our flourishing commonwealth is so plagued with, is above all other most pestilent, yea, and so pestiferous that indeed there can be no more hurtful a thing to a well-governed estate ? And therefore it is not only most odious, but also pestilent, in that it hath spotted the whole country with such a stain and blot of idleness.

" What say you to a number of vagabonds and sturdy rogues, that, after the overthrow of the enemy and breaking-up of the camp, will swarm in every corner of the realm, and not only lie loitering under hedges, but also stand sturdily in cities, and beg boldly at every door, leaving labour which they like not, and following idleness which they should not?   For after wars it is commonly seen that those that went out honest, return home again like roisters ; and as they were brent to the war's bottom, they have ever after all their days an unsavoury smack thereof, and smell still towards day-sleepers and hedge-creepers, purse-cutters, padders, quarrellers and blood-shedders.

" Is it not seen commonly after wars, more robbing, thieving, begging and murdering than before, and those to stand in highways to ask alms, whom men are afraid to say Nay unto honestly, lest it be taken away from them violently, and have more cause to suspect their strength, than to pity their need?   Men cannot safely ride in the highway, unless they ride strong ; work is left at home undone, and loiterers laze in the street, lurk in ale-houses, and range in the highways ; sturdy knaves play in towns, and complain of need, whose filchman or staff, if it be once warm in their hands, or sluggishness bred in their bosom, they will never be allured to work, according to the saying that you have among yourselves—If you can cant, you will never work : showing, that if they have been rogues so long that they can cant, they will never settle themselves to labour again.   And what more noisome beasts in a commonwealth can there be, than you loiterers are?   Divers vermin destroy corn, kill pullen, and engines and snares are made for them.   But for yourselves, although you are made men that should have reason, yet nothing will serve to bridle you or keep you in compass, until your neck be compassed with a with or halter.

" And what a grief is it to an honest man, to labour truly in youth, and to gain painfully by labour, wherewith to live honestly in age, and to have this, gotten in a long time, to be suddenly caught and rapt away by violence ! "

Here the Bellman would have said more, and scarce hitherto could they refrain themselves, but with indignation and choler were ready to tear the poor Bellman in pieces amongst them ; for, the sun being in Cancer, and the mid-summer moon at full, their minds were imbrued with such follies, and their heads carried away with such vanities, that, as men of Athens, they could hear no man speak but themselves, and thought nothing well said, but what came out of their own mouths. But after the storm was passed, and an Oyez was made for silence, in comes a post and messenger in all haste from Don Purloiningo of Thievingen to the masters and governors of this wicked rabblement, in this fashion :

" Room, my masters ! I bring you news ; not common tidings of old matters, but an answer of your letters of complaint, sent to my master, Don Purloiningo. They came to his hands. He hath perused them, and sent you his general protection, to defend you from the hands of the impatient and severe people. Now you may be of good comfort, and pull up your hearts. If you offend again, you need fear no punishment, but swagger till your guts crack. You shall have all at your own wills to the full. Nay, 'tis true as I tell you. If you will not believe, you shall see his letters of comfort and writing consolatory, which he hath granted in favour to you. Dispatch ! get up all your trumpery ! For the ships will be ready for you at the next wind."

With that he pulled forth of his pocket the protection sent from Don Purloiningo, which followeth.

But before we go any further, you shall hear the copy of the letter sent by them to this new-found knight ; the indorsement of which is thus :

To the Thrice-renowned Potentate, Don Purloiningo, Chief Governor of the Region of Thievingen.

Creeping at your unreverend feet, your suppliants,[10] the Gentlemen of the Ragged Order.

That, whereas in all places we are daily persecuted by all sorts of officers, as marshals, beadles, sergeants, bailiffs, constables and such other officers, lying continually as spies to entrap and catch us poor souls as we are following our callings in markets, fairs, frays, throngs and assemblies, wherein heretofore we have lived reasonable well, though not with any great credit, yet void of suspicion or apprehension ; and, being so taken, have been carried to places of correction, there woefully tormented by blue-coats, cowardly fellows that durst not let us have our hands at liberty, but, without all humanity, have so scourged us, that flesh and blood could hardly endure it. And whereas our predecessors before, for the good of this commonwealth of ours, took great pains in devising a new speech or language, to the end we might utter our minds freely, and speak boldly without controlment one to another, which no doubt was a great help to us and our predecessors heretofore ; yet such is the malice of some envious ill-willer of ours, that hath, we know not how, not only discovered our manners and fashions, but also this our language and speech, whereby we are oftentimes overheard, and taken and sent to prisons and tortures, and only by our own confessions, which we have uttered in this our language, and which we have trusted unto us boldly, as if we had been safe bolted in a castle or stronghold.

Now, forasmuch as we have not any friend to whom we may have access that will hear or tender our causes in these affairs, we know not whither to resort for aid, but to your good worship, who, we assure ourselves, love and favour us, and will stretch yourself to the uttermost of your power, for our enlargement and delivery from these perplexities by your mediation to Papa Beelzebub the Black Prince ; for whose sake we have endured many bitter storms, cursings and revilings, contrary to our expectation when we first began to practise our trade and occupation.

Besides the loss of many good booties, as silver, plate, jewels, apparel and such-like things, which, when we have fingered to do us credit, have been taken as way-fees to our great impoverishments, when we have been driven to yield to the officers, by which we, finding ourselves to grow so weak in purse, dare hardly adventure to get to discharge our daily consummations and expenses ; nay, although we would, we cannot ; for the very vulgar are grown so crafty, that we are known so well as the beggar knows his dish, although we dissemble our habits and estates never so much.

Therefore, presuming you will ungratiously consider of our hardness, and speedily fetch us away from these places which in torture [are] to us more hot than hell, we lie thick and threefold under stalls, bulks and hedges, praying for your worship, whose good word we make no question of, knowing well the pity remaining in your good head and often extended in love to us, expecting your answer, we leave you.

                    Yours in the basest fashion,
                              The Derrickman's.

Don Purloiningo, at the receipt of these woeful letters, having an extraordinary tender care over them, as being of one stock and kindred, hath first invented a course for their transportation and conveyance into his territories and dominions, considering how they are likely to decrease, and their trade like to fail, through the proditions and betrayings of the people which are contrary to them and of another sex, hath appointed them a place, set and being in the plain-country of Thievingen near Knavesborough Plain, for their more quiet and peaceable living ; which place and whose manners I think good to describe, being that it was never heard of until of late days* ; to the intent that such as shall, by Don Purloiningo his patent, have right and title there in the confines of the same land, may make a preparado to have passage when the wind shall sit fair for that place and voyage.

The description of the state and situation of Thievingen, with the nature and disposition of the people there inhabiting.

The land of Thievigen is a country bordering upon the famous and thrice-renowned city, Gazophylacium†. It is a country vast, full of deserts and thick woods ; and although the land be mightily replenished with all sorts of nations and people, yet is it turned to no use at all, neither for pasture nor arable, but only a mere wilderness. It hath been a country inhabited from the beginning, although not discovered so plainly heretofore as of late days. People from all countries daily resort and flock thither for ease and quietness, as the Proditorians, Curtatoriences, *Vagabundi Piratorii*, Jesuits, seminaries, and generally

* By Master I.H.[11]

† Signifying a close and strong place to keep treasure in.

all of the Pope's sectaries, all murderers, outlaws and fugitives, bankrupts and brokers to the Devil's grace, parasites, day-sleepers, and generally all that have fought in defence of Lecheritania. These are naturally given and inclined to idleness and lazy lives, insomuch that it cometh to pass, that being hungry they will steal one from another, and often cut one another's throats. They never take pains for anything they have, and yet they have all things without money. Their beer is of that force, and so mighty, that it serveth them instead of meat, drink, fire and apparel; which they learn of their neighbour Drinktalians to brew. And they have the praise above all other, far beyond the Darbalians, the Labourinvainalians or the Pimliconians.[12]

Close upon this country eastward is situate a goodly, fair and most rich city, called, as I said before, Gazophylacium. This city is very strongly defenced, for it is environed about with a wall of silver beaten out with the hammer; and yet, for all this, the inhabitants are very covetous and fearful to lose that which they have got together. And for that it is so rich and opulent, all the whole world are daily plotting how to surprise the same, sometimes with policy and sometimes by force. But above all the rest they are troubled and pestered with the Thievingers, that they are forced day and night to keep continual watch; and yet, for all that, do what they can, they are so pilled and robbed by them, upon the sea-coasts, called *Mare Discontentaneum*, that oftentimes they are driven into great ecstacies and perplexities.

These are altogether bent to melancholy and given much to be malcontent, for that the sea, *Mare Discontentaneum*, floweth often over the banks of this country at every full moon; as also because this land, being full of creeks and small rivers, which run out and in this sea, and the inhabitants using to live thereof (having little or no water for their sustenance and contentation), doth so work within their bodies such a distemperature, that thereof proceedeth a marvellous lumpishness and melancholy blockishness in their wills and dispositions, some to cruel murders, others to plot treason, some to burn houses, and others to run mad for revenge; so that the inhabitants round about them are wonderfully plagued with them, as the Eatalians*, the Drunkalians*, Lecheritanians†, and especially the Foolianders, who oftentimes are cozened and cheated of so much silver and riches in an hour as they have been gathering and raking together in ten years before.

* Not so much with the recited misdemeanours as in the cozening and deceiving them of victuals and beer, which, by long running on the score, often is seen.

† Making fair promises but no deeds.

They are of a strange religion, for they fear neither God nor the Devil. Their first father was Cain from whence proceeded the race of Runagates, for after that Cain had murdered his brother, I suppose he ran away* out of his native country into this new-found land to hide himself, wherein he lived some years and died, whose posterity from age to age have possessed the same. And at this day there is a monument, called in times past Canabel's† Pyramids, to blot out the remembrance of which, they have invented long cans and stone pots in form of that monument, still retaining the form, but altering the matter or substance.

They have an imperial seat of black and brittle substance, and therefore subject to moulding. As fast therefore as that consumes away, there are workmen daily appointed to maintain and repair the same. There are seven wise‡ masters of his Council, the wisest whereof once in four-and-twenty hours, declares himself openly a notorious fool by custom. All their counsel, plotting and devising is to surprise that goodly city, Gazophylacium; their minds are as brave as Cæsar's, for their wills must stand for laws; they are possessed with a very humorous disposition of flattery, for they will look you in the face smilingly, and in the meantime pick your pocket; and for their apparel they are so fantastic, that to-day they will go in a suit of satin and to-morrow in tattered rags, to-day a pound and to-morrow ne'er a penny.

They have a language among themselves, composed of *omnium gatherum*; a glimmering whereof one of late days hath endeavoured to manifest as far as his author is pleased to be an intelligencer; the substance whereof he leaveth for those that will dilate thereof—enough for him to have the praise, other the pains, notwithstanding Harman's ghost continually clogging his conscience with *Sic vos non vobis*.[13]

Upon their banners they display an owl in an ivy-tree with this motto proceeding out of his mouth: *Defertis defertus*. Their houses are made cursory like our coaches with four wheels, that may be drawn from place to place, for they continue not long in a place; and although this country be their own by inheritance, yet now it is peopled and inhabited by the Eatalians, Drunkalians and people of other nations,

---

* Which is as much to say, the remembrance of our great-grandfather Cain, who was a runagate for killing his brother Abel.

† Now called Canabello, *quasi* can-and-a-bell; because cans with bells are there altogether used. Such a one is in Houndsditch with us, but it is a Polony shoe with a bell, that will not be left for ten pound, because he hath it by inheritance. But Ingle Bells at the upper end of Whitecross Street comes very near this country fashion.

‡ Superbrains.

who do dwell and have increased marvellously since the late discovery of this country by Master I. H.[14] Yea, sometimes like to the snail they carry their houses about them, like good husbands which are made and tempered of such fine stuff that when they are hungry they may feed thereof; insomuch oftentimes it comes to pass that, having eaten up their lodging, they are fain to lie in stubble for want of feather-beds.

They, above all other people, observe that ancient command, Care not for to-morrow, for to-morrow will care for itself—imitating the men of the old world, who, taking upon them the habit of pilgrim and friars, carry neither wallet nor scrip, nor yet oftentimes any money in their purses.

In a large and spacious plain called Knavesborough Plain doth Don Purloiningo keep his court, which many men of sundry nations and trades have desired to see and behold; who, when they have had their desire, and remained but some small time there, have so fashioned themselves to the manners and conditions of those people that many have thenceforth turned Turks, smelled of the country and savoured of their detestable and vicious kind of life all their days after. And most of your travellers hitherto are your vain and curious tailors, milliners, tirewomen, sempsters, St. Martin's Observants, shuttlecock- and farthingale-makers and twenty other occupations, who, to fill the world full of vanities and toys, care not whither they travel, so they may find out new fashions and fooleries to cozen and deceive the whole country again.

In this plain are situate divers petty villages and hamlets, as Filchington, Foistham, Nimington, Liftington, Swearinghampton, the great and the little. These towns at first were made to entertain and lodge all such travellers as came to see that ancient seat of Don Purloiningo, who were so named, as the Pharaohs in Egypt, the Ptolomies in Greece, the Cæsars in Rome. Now people, strangers, finding the country very pleasant to inhabit, take up their abode and content themselves there to live and die. The end of their travel is not so much for curiosity, necessity or pleasure, as for their experience and learning.

The ready highway to this palace, and the chief places of abode and lodging in this journey, I will briefly set down, as fitting most directly for the latitude of Great Britain, and generally for the whole world.

The first day then that they leave their own native country, and begin to enter the dominions of Don Purloiningo, they pass along a very fair meadow, passing pleasant to the eye, which is in the confines and uttermost part of Foolania the Less. But, after half a day's journey they come to bogs and quagmires, much like to them in Ireland, of which, unless they be very careful, they may quickly slip up over head and ears in mire.

Having passed the pikes of the first day's danger, they enter into a goodly fair palace, but inhabited by few, having this superscription over the gates, *Æthiopem lavas*, whereupon our English travellers call it the " Labour-in-vain." Here many at the first are purposed to remain and abide ; but seeing the place very spacious and without any inhabitants, and used only as a tap-house for travellers, they take it for their lodging the first night, and away they haste in the morning forward on their journey.

The second day, after three or four mile, they ascend very high and craggy mountains, far passing the Clee or Malvern hills in Wales, where, when they come down again, at the foot of these hills standeth yet at this day the image of the Vicar of Saint Fools, to which every passenger, before he can pass, must offer upon his knees for his pass and safe-conduct through the country of Foolania the Great, thirty bord.

In the middle of this country is built a very fair city, called Vanita, beautiful to the eye, but of no permanence, for it is built after such a slight manner, that they are fain to re-edify their houses, walls and temples every year anew. This city is governed by a woman called Madonna Instabilita, sitting upon an imperial throne, far excellent beyond the seat of Rome. She wears upon her head seven imperial diadems*. She is of that power and command, that she makes the proud Pope to be at her obeyance ; yea, and so rules in his dominions that his land is altogether governed by her and her Council.

Their city walls seem to be made of changeable taffeta ; their houses, of painted papers of sundry colours. They are busied all day about nothing but inventing of new fashions, of tires, garments, behaviours, speeches, words and oaths ; in their apparel, fantastical ; their hats sometime of the Italian block, another-while of the French, and another time of the Spanish ; their doublets with great bellies with the Dutchmen, and small skirts ; sometimes with small skirts, and sleeves seamed, and quartered as if they were to put on armour of proof, to fight under the bloody ensign of the Duke of Shoreditch ; their hose sometimes Spanish, like to shipmen's hose, and sometimes close to the buttock like the Venetian galligaskin. Lord ! it would ask a whole ream of paper to describe their fashions ! It were tedious likewise to speak of the variety of their shoes, and of their shoe-strings, garters, cuffs, ruffs,

* Noting the seven deadly sins.

hat-bands, and all things they wear—not one month, nay, scarce a week, do they continue in one fashion. For their lives, they are dissolute in behaviour, apish, doggish, and swinish, according to the disposition of their bodies ; flattering in speech, deceitful in words ; and in oaths not a devil can surpass them. In all sin they abound, because with them they have a toleration, like to Rome—*Omnia venaliae Romae.* Our gallants in England come most near them in fashion and behaviour— too near them, more is the pity.

Through this city thou mayest pass along. But see thou tarry not long there : only, mark them and their fashions as superficially as thou art able, lest too much desiring their company, thou art forced in the end to cry out thus : " O pain, thou art come, pain, too nigh ! "

Among the rest, this is to be noted, that in the midst of this city there issueth out of the earth a spring in great abundance, which is walled about with marble, and serveth the inhabitants to bathe and wash themselves, much like to our baths here in Europe, only it is of another operation. The people there call this bath *Tribulamenti Fons* ; and it runneth from thence with a swift course along the fields and ways with a thousand turnings and windings, until it come to a steep promontory that overlooketh all the country of Thievingen, Lecheritania, and the rest, and there maketh so great and violent a fall, that it spreadeth itself and runneth round about the countries by divers small creeks and rivers, where, meeting with other small springs of the same nature [they] run altogether, as by one consent, into the sea called *Mare Discontentaneum.*

Leaving this city as well as you can, you pass a whole day along towards Thievingen, crossing this river twenty times over straight and narrow bridges, until you come to this steep and high mountain before spoken of ; upon the edge whereof, dwelleth an old hermit called Father Advisal, a man aged and of long continuance, and therefore well experienced in the world ; a hater of flattery, and a lover of truth. As soon as you come to that place, this new well-willer of yours will straight be in hand with you to know from whence you came, whither you mean to go in so dangerous a place, and in mere love and pity will be inquisitive how you durst travel without a warrant from the magistrate of your country, persuading you by all means to return back, and not venture your life in so dangerous a country as that is, telling you that few return back the same men they were when they first entered that land, but that some returned maimed and lame, others sick of one disease or other, and others, of frenzy and madness, so contaminate a place, so loathsome the manners, so despised a country, that a man, unless he were half beside himself would never once desire to behold that place. Thus, and to this effect, will he speak, and many good persuasions will this good old man use, and many motives he will urge you with to retire, but all in vain, for when men feel the reins of liberty on their necks, and may take a course without controlment, such, whose lust is law, and whose will must not be controlled for a world, little regarding all wise admonitions or sayings of the aged, do with the untamed colt, and fat-fed steed, let fly their heels into the air, and with the extravagant and erring libertine run headlong into a thousand eminent dangers; then, when the black ox hath trod upon their feet, and have been well beaten with their own rod, in the end they come home by Weeping Cross, and cry *peccavi*; when their ambitious conceits gain them nought but this to comfort them in their destruction, that when by their aspiring brain, they have procured their own overthrow, men may say after their death, This fellow carried a brave mind and shot at mighty matters.

But to return. Leaving Father Advisal with his good advice behind, and following vice now before you, you must down this hill (you need no help down), at the bottom whereof you shall be at a trice. And albeit it be ten days' journey up, yet so is the steepness thereof, that you shall be conveyed to the bottom in half an hour. At the foot of this mountain are two great portways, the one on the right hand leading to the countries of Lecheritania, Drunkalia and Eatalia, and the other on the left hand, leading toward Thievingen and the neighbour countries thereabout. To leave the right-hand way for such as have travelled thither to discourse on, we will take our journey toward Don Purloiningo's palace. This only by the way: about ten miles from the foot of this hill in Lecheritania standeth the temple of Venus, and there is the goodly picture of Venus framed of silver in her chariot, drawn by two swans and two doves, her head bound with myrtle-leaves, a burning star on her breast, a globe representing the earth in her right hand, and three golden apples in her left; behind her were the three Graces back to back, hand in hand, and apples in their hands. Not far off that place is likewise to be seen the story of Venus her original, lively painted out; how Saturn deprived his father, Celus, of those parts which were fittest for generation, and, throwing them into the sea, by wonderful power Lady Venus was made; the blood whereof falling short, fell into the land of Thievingen (which country we are now about), of which sprang fierce, hot and cruel people, with which at this day the land is mightily replenished and pestered.

Concerning the original and beginning of these people, historiographers do differ and disagree. Leo Hebraeus out of the ancient poet Pronapides reports that Demogorgon perceived that a dangerous and pernicious tumult was breeding in the bowels of Chaos; wherefore of very love and pity he stretched out his hand and opened her womb, whence presently issued forth a most deformed issue called Litigium, which no sooner appeared, but presently it bred brabbles, and made such a foul stir that it waxed proud, and strove to mount up to Heaven; but Demogorgon, foreseeing what would ensue, threw him down with his neck forward into this country.

But others, more likely, report that they came of Neptune and Iphimedia; which very well may be, for Neptune's brood is furious and unruly, by reason of the superabundant store of unbridled humours; and Iphimedia is nothing else but an obstinate and self-willed conceit and desire, grounded in the mind, and not removable; such as your idle vagabonds that after war will betake themselves to no honest course of life to live in, but be robbers by the highways, cozeners and cony-catchers, that live by their wits, and will not betake them to honest trades, but especially seditious and rebellious subjects in a commonwealth, schismatical and heretical seducers in the Church, as Brownists, Papists, Jesuits and suchlike. And for this cause as there was a school erected for villains in times past called Cacodemica Lycaon,[15] so called because he was the first that did violate the laws of truce and league, by killing and sacrificing unto Jupiter a certain hostage, sent from the Molossi, whereof came the fable that he set man's flesh before Jupiter, to try whether he were a god or no. So the Pope now hath erected another, because this was not large enough, called *Satani Senatus*, wherein is taught the art of stabbing, poisoning, betraying, perjury, treason in all degrees, blowing-up and consuming by gunpowder, witchcraft and sorcery, sodomitry and buggery, torments for innocents, and, in truth, for the achieving and bringing to pass of all mischief. So that now, if any be so minded to murder his Prince, father or mother, friend, wife or any else, he shall be here protected, holpen, backed, encouraged, and pardons granted for them and their children for ever.

After a day's journey, you shall come into deserts and solitary woods, wherein you shall see very strange and fearful sights and apparitions. There will appear to you monsters that have faces and bodies comely like to women, ready to allure and to entice you with them, but their lower parts are ugly and deformed, having upon their hands and feet sharp clasping claws, that, if they once grasp you, you shall hardly escape their clutches. And if they seize on you, they will bring you out of the way, through diſtraught and fear, until you meet another company more horrid and terrible, their hair all of crawling snakes, their garments down to the heels, close girt with a snaky girdle, serpents in the one hand and fire-brands in the other, their eyes, face and teeth portending malice and vengeance. These are the miniſters of death. They dwell in dark dens thereabout. Their office is to bring such passengers as travel that way to a moſt unspeakable horrid den, out of which proceeds so noisome an exhalation, that birds as they fly over the same are poisoned with the very breath and air thereof. This is that place which in the old world was called Avernus, round about which, and at the entrance of which cave Virgil (*VI Æneid*) placeth a rabblement, as woe, vengeance, wrath, sickness, old age, fear, famine, penury, death, labour, sleep, war, discord and suchlike. In the midſt of this cave is seated an imperial throne, whereon sits the black prince, with a crown on his head, a sceptre in his hand, and his great dog Cerberus between his feet, fawning on those that come in, but devouring those that seek to go out. But to leave this way, if thou be wise, take heed of the firſt insinuating flatterers, leave their pretended friendship and keep on thy way.

In this country nothing is worthy of praise or commendation, for in all this solitary travelling, you shall find no comfort but the screeching of owls, croaking of ravens, and such uncouth and baleful echoes. The beſt part of your food will be herb-rue, a bitter herb to feed on ; but after, when you have better looked into your lives and carriages you will call it herb-grace. Your drink is altogether of the water of that country, called throughout *aqua discontentanea*.

After two or three days thus travelling, you shall come into a fair plain, called Knavesborough Plain, wherein Don Purloiningo keeps his court. You shall at the firſt be made very welcome, yet so that they will narrowly spy into your carriage and behaviour ; and, although they pretend never so great love and friendship unto you, yet will they not ſtick to cozen and deceive you, if they can, of all you have.

And thus much for the description of the ſtate and situation of Thievingen, with the disposition of the people there inhabiting. And now, to give over this tedious journey, you shall hear the protecſtion of Don Purloiningo, sent to Corporal Fize, Chief Commander of Rogues, and his assiſtants ; the copy whereof is as followeth :

The copy of the Commission and Grant, sent from Don Purloiningo to Corporal Fize and his assistants.

I Don Purloiningo, Great Commander over the Province of Thievingen, have received divers woeful and pitiful letters from sundry nations and people, but especially from those under the government of Corporal Fize, chief commander of the poor persecuted pilgrims in Europe, wherein they lay open to me their woeful sorrows, vexations and troubles, that they endure by sundry persons in sundry places where they abide. Now forasmuch as it is not only a charity to redress their foresaid griefs, by sending for them into a country where they shall be at quiet and heart's-ease, but also a pleasure to people of better fashion, that cannot by any means disgest their idle and untoward lives, which may prove hurtful both to king and people.

Be it therefore known that I have granted to all persons whatsoever, that will take the benefit of this my Grant and Commission, free leave and licence to come and inhabit within my country of Thievingen, and the profits of my land to use and enjoy as freely without contradiction as if they were there bred and born.

Now for the more speedy execution of the same, we command all sailors, as well within our jurisdiction as without, that they make present search for all old boats, hoys, ships and barks, which have long rested to be ready for this voyage ; and that all things be in readiness, to the end that, when they are in a good mind, they may be gone, that never after any good land be troubled and cumbered with so filthy and noisome a people ; and that all carmen, coachmen and carters have their charge in readiness at a day, that they may be carried in pomp to the water-sides ; and that all trumpeters, bagpipers, fiddlers and drummers be ready with their music to bring them onward of their journey. Moreover, we command all jailers to open their prison doors, and let them all out that mean to see my dominions, and that never, hereafter, they once suffer any to come within their hold or jurisdiction.

And, further, upon their departure we will all inventions for punishments appointed for the torturing of such persons be immediately pulled down, cut in pieces, and be made in bonfires, for joy that the land is disburthened of so loathsome a people.

And, further, we expressly command that the sailors and mariners (because we know them to be hasty and surly) to use them kindly, and not by any means to cross them, lest they take snuff in the nose and so fall together by the ears ; for they being very choleric, as we have heard, are subject to disagreeing.

And that, at their arrival, they be presently placed every one according to his degree, and that with quietness they receive the profits of my land, without the let of those that have been dead five hundred years before. Further that no man mock or delude them, or so much as bid them farewell, for fear that a little famili-arity cause them to have a desire to remain and tarry rather than to walk ; but let them have quiet passing, because they go to a land better for their turns, for they desire only ease, which there they shall have, if once they can arrive and get to the borders thereof.

These our Letters and Commission now at your request granted, our desire is, that you may do well. If otherwise betide you than well, look to yourselves, and use your own discretions. And so fare you well !

At this news the whole fraternity of vagabonds hooted for joy, as glad at the heart to think what a swaggering and domineering they should keep in this new-found land, and wherein they made account to be young lords and masters; so that the poor honest Bellman had licence without any controlment or contradiction to depart; and if he would spit out any more of his malice against them, let him spit till he were dry for them, for they would little regard what he did, and cared not two chips, because they were determined to travel, and meant to be out of the walks and dangers of the honest.

Now, Gentlemen, by my troth, I could find in my heart to have spent a bottle of ale that you had been there with me to have seen the concourse of these caterpillars, and heard the confused noise of these cozening crack-ropes, singing, hollowing and whooping, dancing and whistling. At this time there you should have seen one that had been lame near forty years, and gone on his crutches fifteen to my knowledge, throw away his stilts, and dance the round morris; there another that puts on a foul cloth on his head, counterfeiting the falling sickness, throw it away in a corner, and falls to swagger with his doxy; here another with pitiful forelegs and arms to see to, can now leap and wrestle as well as the best; and divers with scald-pates and other diseases, going before double in the streets, to cause and move pity, can now for joy stand on their heads, fetch frisks about the house, pull one another by the ears, and, indeed, what did they not do? None could perceive but that they were all youthful and lusty.

*All took all pleasure, and all for joy to be sailing.**

Suppose now, by this the greatest part of them are sailing on the black sea. What will become of them, how they arrived, how entertained by the inhabitants there, and of their prosperous voyage, you shall hear at the next boat-post. In the meantime because the Bellman entreateth any that is more rich in canting to lend him better or more with variety, he will repay his love double.

I have thought good not only to show his error in some places in setting down old words, used forty years ago before he was born, for words that are used in these days—although he is bold to call me an usurper (for so he hath done in his last round), and not able to maintain the title—but have enlarged his dictionary (or Master Harman's) with such words as I think he never heard of, and yet in use too, but not out of vainglory, as *his* ambition is, but, indeed, as an experienced soldier that hath dearly paid for it. And therefore it shall be honour good enough for him, if not too good, to come up with the rear—I do but

* Hoist up, sailors. The drummers and pipers are at hand. Make ready. They come, they come, a jolly crew! God send they want no shipping! A fair company! I promise you when they are gone we shall have corn good cheap. 'Ware your purses, ho!

shoot your own arrow back again—and not to have the leading of the van as he means to do, although small credit in the end will redound to either.

You shall know the words not set in either his dictionaries by this mark (*) ; and for showing the error in his words, and true Englishing of the same and other, this mark (†) shall serve.

* *Abram,* mad.
* *He maunds abram,* he begs as a madman.
  Autem, the Church.
  Autem-mort, a married woman.
† *Bung* is now used for a pocket, heretofore for a purse.
  Bord, a shilling.
  Half-a-bord, sixpence.
  Bouse, drink.
  Bousing ken, an ale-house,
  Bene, good.
  Beneship, very good.
  Bufe, a Dog.
  Bing a waste, get you hence.
* *Budge a beak,* run away.
* *A bite, secreta (   ) mulierum.*
  Caster, a cloak.
* *Crackmans,* the hedge.
  Commission, a shirt.
* *To castle,* to see or look.
* *A room-cuttle,* a sword.
* *A cuttle-bung,* a knife to cut a purse.
* *Chepemans,* Cheapside Market.
  To cut, to tell or call.
† *Cut me bene whids,* tell me truth.
† *To cut queer whids,* to lie.
  Crashing-cheates, apples.
† *Chates,* the gallows. Here he mistakes both the simple word, because he so found it printed, not knowing the true original thereof, and also in the compound. As for *chates* it should be *cheats,* which word is used generally for things, as, *Tip me that cheat,* give me that thing ; so that if you will make a word for the gallows, you must put thereto this word, *trining,* which signifies hanging ; and so *trining-cheat* is as much to say " hanging-things," or the gallows, and not *chates.*
  Cove, a man.
† *Couch a hogshead,* to lie down and sleep. This phrase is like an Almanac that is out of date : now the Dutch[16] word to *slope* is with them used," to sleep" and *liggen,* " to lie down."
* *Crank,* the falling sickness : and thereupon your rogues that counterfeit the falling sickness are called *counterfeit cranks.*
  To cly the jerk, to be whipped.
  Drawers, hosen.
  Duds, clothes.
  Darkmans, the night.
  Dewse-a-vill, the country.
  Dup the jigger, open the door.

* *A flick*, a thief.
 Fambles, hands.
 Fambling-cheats, rings.
* *Famblers*, a pair of gloves.
* *To filch*, to beat.
* *A filchman*, a cudgel or staff.
 Flag, a groat.
* *To fence* property, to sell anything that is stolen.
* *To foist*, to pick a pocket.
* *A faker of loges*, one that beggeth with counterfeit writings.
 Glaziers, eyes.
* *Greenmans*, the fields.
 Gan, a mouth.
 Gage, a quart pot.
 Granmer, corn.
 Glimmer, fire.
 Jigger, a door.
* *Gilks for the jigger*, false keys for the door or picklocks.
* *Gracemans*, Gracious Street[7] Market.
 Gentry mort, a gentlewoman.
 Gentry cove's ken, a gentleman's house.
 Harman-beck, the constable.
 Harmans, the stocks.
* *Jockam*, a man's yard.
* *Jan*, a purse.
* *Jere*, a turd.
 Ken, an house.
 Stalling-ken, a house to receive stolen goods, or a dwelling-house.
* *Lugs*, ears.
 Lag of duds, a buck of clothes.
* *Loges*, a pass or warrant.
 A faker of loges, one that beggeth with false passes.
 Libbeg, a bed.
 Lour, money.
 Libkin, a house to lodge people.
 Lage, water or piss.
 Lightmans, the day.
 Mint, gold.
 The muggill, the beadle.
 Make, an halfpenny.
 Maunding, begging.
* *What maund do you beak?* What kind of begging use you?
* *I'll mill your maund.* I'll spoil your begging.
* *To nip a jan*, to cut a purse.
* *Nab*, a head.
* *Nab-cheat*, an hat.
* *Numans*, Newgate Market.
† *Niggling*, company keeping with a woman. This word is not now used, but *wapping*, and thereof comes the name *wapping-morts*, whores.
 Prat, a buttock.
* *Your prat whids romely*, you fart lustily.
† *Peck*, meat. *Peck* is not meat, but *peckage*. *Peck* is taken to eat or bite : as, *the bufe pecks me by the stamps ;* the dog bites me by the shins.
 Ruff-peck, bacon.

* *Peckage*, meat ; or scruff, scraps.
* *To plant*, to hide.
* *Stow your whids and plant ;*
* *The cove of the ken can cant.*
  Prancer, a horse.
  Prigging, riding.
  Patrico, a priest.
  Pad, a way.
* *Padder*, an highway robber or purse-taker.
* *Queer* : this word is always taken in ill sense for naught.
* *Queer-ken*, a prison house.
* *Queer bouse*, bad drink.
* *What a queer whidding keep you !* What a scolding keep you !
  Quarroms, the body, or arms, or back.
  Room-vill, a great town, commonly taken for London.
  Room-bouse, wine. This word [*room*] is always taken in the best sense, to show
    a thing extraordinary or excellent.
* *Room bousing ken*, a tavern.
  Room mort, a Queen or Gentlewoman ; and so *room cove*, a gentleman.
† *Ruffmans*, not the hedge or bushes as heretofore ; but now the eavesing of houses
  or roofs. *Cragmans* is now used for the hedge.
  Ruffan, the Devil.
* *Scraps, fat and glorious bits* : sound blows and bangings.
* *The muggill will tip you fat scraps and glorious bits* : the beadle will well bombast
  you.
  Stamps, legs.
  Stampers, shoes.
  Slate, a sheet.
  Scew, a cup or glass, a dish or anything to drink in.
  Skipper, a barn.
† *Solomon*, the mass. Now, when many do press the poor rogues so earnestly to
  swear by the *Solomon*, do not blame them though they refuse it. For
  although you know not what it means, yet they very well know. Many men
  I have heard take this word Solomon to be the chief commander among the
  beggars. But to put them out of doubt, this is not he. Marry, there was
  one Solomon in King Henry the Eighth's time that was a jolly fellow among
  them, who kept his court most an end at Foxhall[18] at the upper end of Lambeth
  —if it be true as their records make mention—who was successor to Cock
  Lorel. Of him and his successors much is to be spoken, if licence may be
  granted, and of whose runagate race I could frame a whole treatise : but here
  enough.
* *A stander*, he that stands sentinel upon the pad or highway to rob.
  Strummel, the straw.
* *Spreader*, butter.
† *Smeller*, a garden, not *smelling-cheat*, for that's a nosegay.
* *Trining*, hanging.
* *Trining-cheat*, the gallows.
* *To tip*, to give.
* *Tip a make, bene room cove*, give a halfpenny, good gentleman.
  To tour or castle, to see.
* *To whid*, to speak.
* *A win*, a penny.
* *Whittington*, Newgate.
  Yarrum, pottage or milk.

And thus have I run over the Canters' Dictionary. To speak more at large would ask more time than I have allotted me ; yet in this short time that I have, I mean to sing song for song with the Beliman, ere I wholly leave him.

> Tour out bene morts and tour,
> Look out bene morts and tour,
> For all the rome coves are budged a beak,
> And the queer coves tip the lour.
>
> The queer coves are budged to the bousing ken,
> As romely as a ball,
> But if we be spied, we shall be clied,
> And carried to the queer-ken hall.
>
> Out budged the cove of the ken,
> With a bene filch in his quarrom,
> That did the prig good to binged in the Risome,
> To tour the cove budge alar'me.

But now I will show you what I heard at Knock-ver-gos, drinking there a pot of English ale, two maunders born and bred up rogues in their native language.

> O bene mort, wilt thou pad with me ?
> One bene slate shall serve both thee and me ;
> My caster and commission shall serve us both to maund ;
> My bung, my lour, and fambling-cheats,
> Shall be at thy command.
>
> O bene cove, that may not be,
> For thou hast an autem-mort, who ever that is she,
> If that she were dead and binged to his long lib,
> Then would I pad and maund with thee,
> And wap and for thee fib.
>
> O bene mort, castle out and tour
> Where all the room coves slopen, that we may tip the lour.
> When we have tipped the lour and fenced away the duds,
> Then bing we to the bousing ken,
> That's cut the Robin Hood.
>
> But, O bene cove, what if we be clied ?
> Long we cannot foist and nip : at last we shall be spied.
> If that we be spied, Oh then begins our woe,
> With the harman-beck out, and, alas !
> To Whittington we go.
>
> Stow your whids and plant, and whid no more of that,
> Budge a beak the crackmans, and tip lour with thy prat.
> If trining thou dost fear, thou ne'er will foist a jan.
> Then mill and wap and trine for me ;
> A jere peck in thy gan !

As they were thus after a strange manner a wooing, in comes by chance a clapperdudgeon for a pint of ale, who, as soon as he was spied, they left off their roguish poetry, and fell to mock the poor maunder thus.

> The clapperdudgeon lies in the skipper ;
>   He dares not come out for shame,
> But when he bings out he du[p]s budge to the jigger ;
>   Tip in my skew, good dame.

And thus hath the Bellman through his pitiful ambition caused me to write that I would not. And whereas he disclaims the name of brotherhood, I here utterly renounce him and his fellowship, as not desirous to be resolved of anything he professeth on this subject, knowing myself to be as fully instructed herein as ever he was. But hereof enough, if not more than enough. I mean now to show the original and beginning of these people, when they began to gather to an head, and how they first came up.

THE RUNAGATES' RACE, OR THE ORIGINAL OF THE REGIMENT OF ROGUES, WHEN THEY FIRST BEGAN TO TAKE HEAD, AND HOW THEY HAVE SUCCEEDED ONE THE OTHER SUCCESSIVELY, UNTIL ABOUT THE SIX-AND-TWENTIETH YEAR OF KING HENRY THE EIGHTH, COLLECTED OUT OF THE LEGEND OF LOSELS.[19]

At what time King Henry the Sixth of famous memory bear rule over the Britons, there was one John Mendall, *alias* Jack Cade, an Irishman, that named himself by the name of John Mortimer, cousin to the Duke of York ; whereupon, he, gathering together a great company out of Kent, assured and persuaded them that the enterprise he took in hand was both honourable to God and the King, and profitable to the whole realm. The Kentishmen, moved with these persuasions and other fair promises, marched to Blackheath, where they lay for a month pilling the country round about.

At the same time, which was about 1450, two unruly fellows, the one named Bluebeard, the other Hugh Roberts, which were lately come over from France, who had been soldiers under the Duke of Somerset and the Earl of Shrewsbury in the winning and losing of Constance, Guines, Rouen, and divers other cities in France ; the which Bluebeard, in a commotion shortly after he came over, being made their captain, before he had attempted any thing at all was taken and executed ; but

Roberts, keeping in Kent, gathered a number of rakehells and vagabonds together to the number of an hundred in that country, to whom likewise masterless men, after they heard of his fame, came cluttering on heaps, so that he had in a short space to the number of five hundred followers.

These sturdy vagabonds, joining with Jack Mendall in this rebellion, march toward London and enter Southwark, and there lodged at the *White Hart* for a night or two, prohibiting all from rape, robbery and murder, the more to allure the hearts of the people to favour his enterprise. After, they came into London, and there they play Rex, and return back into Southwark again, where, after many conflicts between them and the citizens, the King's pardon was proclaimed : at which hearing, the poor people were so glad, and so ready to receive it, that without bidding farewell to their captains, withdrew themselves every man towards his own home.

Jack Mendall, despairing of succours, and fearing the reward of his lewd dealings, fled away into the woods ; but proclamation made, that whosoever could bring Jack alive or dead to the King, should have a thousand marks for his pains, was after slain by a gentleman in Kent, and so brought to the King.

But Roberts kept himself in the woods closely a long time after, although not with so great a company as he had before, and there lived by robbing and spoiling in the night, keeping themselves close in all the day. And thus by the space of a twelve month they passed their time in villainy, robbing and spoiling the country people of their poultry, pigs, and other sustenance, wherewith they sustained themselves and their families. In which time he set down laws and customs to be kept and observed among them, and to keep them in awe and fashion, who are prone of themselves to live out of all rule and fashion.

1. First, he appointed that of everything that they got, he had first the taking and leaving of the best thereof at his pleasure.

2. That if any of their fellows could not purchase any victuals or necessities for food that night, that then they should be in commons with the rest the day following.

3. That no robbery or violence be used upon any man within four miles of the wood, or the place of their abode.

4. That none be so hardy as to run to the wood for succour or relief after he hath perpetrated any thing, lest that hue and cry follow, and so descry the whole company.

Thus, after a year and upward was spent by them in this sort, they brake up their camp, and proclamation was made, to meet there in that place every three years for a memorial, if they then lived. In the meantime they spread themselves abroad in the country, some remaining there, others travelling northward and join themselves with the Duke of York, and generally in all commotions and rebellions. These in memory of their first acquaintance and love to their new-found captain, called themselves by the name of Roberdsmen, as the servants of Hugh Roberts, their commander.[20]

This Roberts lived roving up and down the country for the space of ten years, in which time he kept his court days as himself listed, and in which time there came to him divers new followers, and, as some decayed and died, some hanged and dead of the pox (for to that end they all come), so others succeeded in their places.

In the first year of Edward the Fourth, this Roberts in the wars against Henry the Sixth in the north parts (who was deposed) was there slain, besides 36,776 persons, all Englishmen.[21]

Hereupon presently (their late captain now dead) all that were left alive of this company hie themselves to their wonted place of meeting, where by the general assent they chose one Jenkin Cowdiddle to be their ring-leader.

This Jenkin Cowdiddle was a man given much to swearing, drunkenness and lechery. He was never out of England as soldier or traveller, but from his first beginning he continued a wandering rogue. He was stout of stomach, audacious and fierce ; he was known to all the damned crew for a boon companion, and therefore chosen as fittest for their captain. He first ordained that none were so hardy as to have the undoing of a maid wanderer, or anything to do with her, unless first she were brought to him to be broken up, or to some of his assigns, that could obtain the same of him by friendship or bribery.

He commanded likewise that all beggars should spend all their gettings in the day past in good beer or ale at night, or, at the farthest, by Saturday night ; and if any were found or known to have above twopence halfpenny in his purse on Monday morning, he should forfeit a dozen of beer to any whatsoever of their company would challenge it. He exercised his command about ten years, until the time that the great rebellion and uproar was in the western parts, as Somersetshire, Wiltshire, Dorsetshire and Cornwall, about the crowning of Prince Edward, son to King Henry VI, who had been all this time in France. And this fell out about the eleventh year of Edward IV. Then this Jenkin Cowdiddle, accompanied with 300 tattered knaves, joined in battle against the King, with the western men, in which battle at Tewkesbury he was slain, and buried there with the rest of the dead bodies.

The battle ended, these Roberdsmen (for so they were termed a long time after) hie them to their rendezvous, their usual and known place, and there, with the full consent of the whole company, they chose one Spising to be his successor.

And now, whenas the feast and solemnizing of this new-made squire was newly ended, news was brought to this Spising, how that one Thomas Neville (son to Faukenbridge),[22] who had been at sea as a pirate and robbed divers merchants, was newly arrived in England, and got a great company of mariners out of all parts of the land and many traitors and misgoverned people to follow him, whereunto, as fitly for his turn, this Spising accompanies and enters into league and familiarity, besides divers also forth of other countries, that delighted in theft and robberies.

And now his strength increased daily, for having been at Calais and brought from thence into Kent many evil-disposed persons, he began to gather his power in that country, meaning to attempt some great and wicked enterprise against King Edward and his kingdom, but his quarrel, he pretended, was to have King Henry the Sixth out of the Tower, and to restore him to his sceptre again. Thus, accompanied with seventeen thousand men, they marched into London by ships which lay between Blackwall and Redriff. And then came Spising[23] with his band at Aldgate, who behaved themselves so stoutly, that they won the bulwark there, and drave the citizens back within the portcullis, and entered the gate with them to the number of a dozen. But some of them were slain with the fall of the portcullis, that was let down upon them to keep the residue out ; but those that were within the walls were suddenly dispatched.

To be short, at last the Bastard was vanquished and utterly despaired ; for, hearing the King coming with thirty thousand men, durst stay no longer, but brake up and dispersed themselves, some one way, and some another. The Bastard with his mariners and such rebels, robbers and wicked persons as sought nothing but spoil, got them to shipboard as fast as they could. Those that were left behind and those of Spising's company lurked a day or two about the country secretly in woods, until they thought the coasts to be clear, and after met at their wonted place, where they, as merry as pot and can, pass their time in villainy and robbery.

This Spising was a man given to voluptuousness and pleasure, delighting in bousing and venery. He ordered that every one that professed himself a wanderer and taking upon him the occupation of begging, shall be stalled to the order of rogues; that is, he shall be brought to the Chief Commander then being, and there he shall show the cause of his going abroad and what countryman he is; which done, he pays a dozen of beer as a fine for his freedom and instalment, and so is permitted to live and die a rogue; but if he be born a rogue, that is, if his grandfather were one, and his father one, so that consequently he must be one also, such a one shall be freely discharged from such instalment, as being made free by his father's copy.[24]

This Spising about the first year of King Edward the Fifth, committed a robbery and murder near Highgate in Middlesex, whereafter he fled and took sanctuary at Westminster[25]; for these places in that time were wonderfully abused by wicked men. Rabblements of thieves, murderers and traitors would thither flock when they had achieved any villainy; unthrifts riot and run in debt upon boldness of these places; rich men run thither with poor men's goods. There they build and there they spend, and bid their creditors go whistle. Men's wives run thither with their husbands' plate, and say they dare not abide with their husbands, for fear of beating. Thieves bring in thither their stolen goods, and there live upon them till all is spent; and when nothing is left, they again in the night range abroad to seek other booties; there they devise new plots to rob and kill, and then to come in again at their pleasure. So those places did not only give them safeguard for their villainies, but a licence also to do more. Such a one was this Spising for a year or two before he was hanged; for being taken the second time at Wombourn in Staffordshire, for killing a man in a drunken humour, was presently apprehended and carried to the jail, and after hanged, all save the head; he domineered about eleven years.

Not long after, when certain news was blazed abroad of their captain's confusion, they chose a notable swaggering rogue called Puffing Dick to revel over them, who played revel-rout with them indeed. In this squire there were no villainies left unattempted, but he was still at the one end.

He first gave terms to robbers by the highway, that such as rob on horseback were called high lawyers, and those who robbed on foot, he called padders. The difference of these two sorts of villains is this: The first sort are called gentlemen robbers, or thieves, and these ride on horses well appointed, and go in show like honest men. The other rob on foot, and have no other help but a pair of light heels and a thick wood. Concerning the first sort, that delight in the credit of a high lawyer, that with their swords freeboot abroad in the country like cavalieros on horseback, are commonly such men, that either are younger brethren who, being brought up in idleness and gaming, when their friends are dead, do fall to this kind of life to maintain the main chance ; others, again, being left well by their friends, having no government of themselves, but banqueting with whores, and making late suppers, do greatly impoverish and beggar themselves ; and when all is spent after this manner, and their money wasted like snow against the sun, they, for their *ultimum refugium,* are[26] forced to undertake this wretched and abhorred profession, robbing honest poor men, and taking all their money from them, yea, and often more than is their own, to the utter undoing of the poor man, his wife and children for ever ; who, when they have it, waste it as vainly as they wickedly purchased it ; and others, that, having been soldiers, when they come from the wars, either by breaking up of the camp, or by running away from their colours to see their friends, or what way soever, cannot betake themselves to any honest trade of life, but, loving to live in idleness, betake themselves to robbing and stealing, until they be taken and carried westward, there to make their rehearsal.

These fellows, first, that they may not be known, bespeak and get such artificial beards and heads of hair, that although you ride, dine, and sup with them from day to day, you shall not be able to discern them, nor espy their falsehood. And in this practice all their villainy consists ; for I have heard, and partly know, a highway lawyer rob a man in the morning, and hath dined with the martin, or honest man, so robbed, the same day at an inn, being not descried, nor yet once mistrusted or suspected for the robbery.

Their knavery is on this manner. They have always good geldings and trusty, which they can make curtals when they list, and, again, set to large tails, hanging to the fetlocks, at their pleasure, yea, and so artificially that it shall not be perceived or spied of the ostler that dresseth them ; besides they have cloaks tormosant, as they call them, made with two outsides, that wear them howsoever the right side will be always outwards. Now their artificial beards and heads of hair withal will make them seem to dance in a net a long time ere they be espied. Now, how easy it is for them to escape all dangers, all hues and cries, it may easily be perceived, for the complexion of the man, and his beard, the garments that he wears, and the making of his horse, [are] three things which are the especial marks whereby notice is taken to make enquiry; which being changed and altered, they may escape as safely as they did the robbery.

The other sort of robbers, that having no means to relieve them, instead of swift courses to eschew danger fly away upon their trusty ten toes into woods and close places, there to continue until hue and cry be passed. These fellows wear counterfeit beards and heads of hair as the other sort do, using not many words but, *Stand and deliver !* Some will have curs and mankind masties following them, to further and help them in this enterprise. Some, under the name of the upright-man or soldier, as they go through towns, beg the charitable devotion of people. They will go also strongly, with three or four in a company, to a farmhouse, where oftentimes they are relieved more for fear than devotion. But, when they can come in [a] place where they may conveniently take a purse, it shall go hard but that they will either win the horse or lose the saddle, although their hardy adventure be payed home with a crack of the best joint they have after.

But to return again to Puffing Dick. This devil incarnate, as he was bold to attempt any wicked enterprise, so he wanted not wit first to lay the plot to achieve it and to bring it to pass. He used first the cozenage at dice and to invent for that purpose false dice, whereby he got much money. But as it was ill got, so was it as ill spent in all manner of vice that could be named, wherein he excelled all before him. Yet this by the way: It is reported of him that he was free from murder, and commanded that whosoever, under his conduct, was so cruel as to murder any man or woman in the attempt of robbing them should forthwith be discovered to be apprehended. He likewise ordered that all high lawyers, padders, lifts, foists, cheaters or cony-catchers shall not presume to purchase any lands or revenues, nor hoard up their money to the hindrance of good fellowship, maintenance of good-natured damsels and impeachment of the fraternity; but that they shall heartily spend it among good company and fellows, such as themselves are, and, as they came lightly by it, so lightly to let it fly. He was a man crafty and bold; yet he died miserably. For, after he had commanded now fully eight years, he had the pining of the pox and Neapolitan scurf. And here an end of Puffing Dick !

In his place was chosen by the consent of the rabblement one not much inferior in vice to the former, but in regard of manhood a mere cravant, called Laurence Crossbiter, or Long Laurence. This Laurence had been brought up all his days a serving-man, and now, being about fifty or three score, at what time serving-men are past the belt, and

Q

commonly grow lazy, and cast out of service, and so was fain to live among the wicked, sometimes a stander for the padder, sometimes a verser for the cony-catcher, sometimes a stale for a foist, but most commonly an applesquire for a trugging-house. He first used that art which now is named crossbiting, and from whose name this damned art (crossbiting) took her first call, as of Laurence Crossbiter, that first invented the same. The manner in brief is thus : Some base rogue without the fear of God or man, that keepeth a whore as a friend, or marries one to be his maintainer, consents or constrains those creatures to yield the use of their bodies to other men, that so, taking them together, they may strip the lecher of all the money in his purse or that he can presently make. He commanded about six years, and then, as he lived in filthiness, so was his end, for it was reported that his bowels were eaten out with the pox whilst he was yet alive, so miserable was the end of this wretch.

All these six years that this Laurence lived in his controlment, he durst never be so hardy as once to aid Perkin Warbeck in the attempting of the crown ; slavish was his mind, and given to cowardice, for all the time that he bear rule among his companions, which was 1491 until 1497, did Perkin Warbeck essay to win the kingdom, feigning himself to be the Duke of York, son to King Edward IV deceased ; to the bringing to pass of which device, he essayed many ways, plotted divers devices and attempted mighty matters, and yet all in vain, for after almost six years, all which time he was busied about this enterprise, he was taken prisoner, after he had taken sanctuary at Beaulieu, not far from Southampton.

To set down the whole story of this Perkin Warbeck it would be long, and, besides from the matter now in hand. But because the sequel of the story a little concerneth us, I will briefly run it over ; and thus it was : He was a man base of stock, a Fleming by birth, and provoked to feign himself the son of King Edward IV by the Duchess of Burgundy, sister to King Edward IV.

He first went into Ireland out of France, to entice the Irish to rebel ; after, called back by the French king to go against King Henry the Seventh, then invading France. After this, he lands in Kent, purposing to prove the people, how they were affected towards him. Hereupon he sends some of his men out of the ships to know their minds ; but they were suddenly taken by the Sheriff of Kent, and, railed in ropes like horses in carts, were adjudged most to be hanged. But Perkin hoists up his sails at these tidings, and away sails he again into Ireland, where he stays not long, being a place not fit for his turn, the people being poor and naked. He sails into Scotland, where, after a smooth long oration to the king, he is royally entertained by the said king. Afterward the king, to persuade the world that all was true, espouseth the Lady Catharine, daughter to Alexander, Earl of Huntly, his nigh kinsman, to him. Then go they both against England, wasting all Northumberland, and committing many outrages and enormities; but, when they saw no aid come from England, they retire. After, Perkin (upon the truce between England and Scotland) with his wife sail into Ireland again: from thence, cuts over into Cornwall, where he gathered to him above 3,000 persons, all promising him to take his part and follow him till death.

First then by the advice of his counsellors, John Heron, mercer, a bankrupt, Richard Skelton, a tailor, and John Asteley, a scrivener, they essay the winning of Exeter, where, for lack of munition for war and ordnance to break open the gates, they endeavoured by casting of stones, lifting with iron bars, and kindling of fires under the gates, to bring to pass their purpose. Much ado there was here about this enterprise. But, when he heard the King coming with his power, he removes to Taunton, and the King after him. Upon this he flies to Beaulieu, and there takes sanctuary, but after yields himself to the mercy of the King; who, being delivered to the King's Guard carefully to be kept, notwithstanding escapeth, and thought to get over into Flanders; but the sea-coasts being all laid that he could not pass, he was in great perplexity, came back to the prior of Sheen besides Richmond, and there entreats the prior, even for God's sake, to beg his life of the King.

The King, at the request of the prior, pardoned him; but [he] was set in the stocks at Westminster Hall door a whole day, and so likewise the next day was he set on a scaffold at the standard in Cheapside[27], with many mocks and revilings cast against him; being now in hold again, by false persuasions and great promises, corrupted his keepers and would have fled away, but his purposes being known, he was at last apprehended, taken, and executed at Tyburn, he and his keepers. And this is the end of Perkin Warbeck.

Laurence Crossbiter now dead, and Perkin Warbeck, with two of his counsellors, Heron and Asteley, fled to sanctuary, it booted not the company to stay there, but, their chief leaders fled, everyone threw away his armour as people amazed, and betake themselves to their heels, among the rest, Skelton, a notable knave, one of Perkin's counsellors before mentioned, being well known among the rascality, was led to the wonted place of meeting, and there solemnly was ſtalled a rogue and made their general.

This Skelton was sometimes a tailor in Taunton in Somersetshire, who, being blown down with an unfortunate blaſt, was forced and ready for any commotion or rebellion. He was of a proud and haughty disposition. He lived in this new government until about the fourth year of King Henry the Eighth, which was in the year 1501.

This fellow, among other decrees and orders, confirmed this : That if any one, using the necessary help of his crutches (although indeed he hath not any need or use of them but only to deceive people there-with), shall at any time forsake them for a time, either to run for a wager with another, or to play at nine-holes[28], loggats[29], or bowls, or any other game, so that he be seen and marked by some that have seen him else-where with his crutches halting, and by them so challenged for a counterfeit rogue, he shall forfeit for every such offence two dozen of beer, as a fine for disgracing so ancient a trade as peregrination.

After him succeeded by the General Council one Cock Lorel[30], the moſt notorious knave that ever lived. By trade he was a tinker, often carrying a pan and a hammer for a show ; but when he came to a good booty, he would caſt his profession in a ditch, and play the padder, and would then away, and, as he passed through the town, would cry " Ha' you any work for a tinker ? " To write of his knaveries it would ask a long time. I refer you to the old manuscript, remaining on record in Maunders' Hall[31].

This was he that reduced and brought in form the Catalogue of Vagabonds, or Quartern of Knaves, called the five-and-twenty orders of knaves ; but because it is extant and in every man's shop[32], I pass them over.

And now about this time, whenas wars abroad and troubles domeſtical were ended, swarmed in every part of the land these caterpillars, like flies againſt a plague.

In the northern parts another sort of vagabonds (at the Devil's Arse A-peak[33] in Derbyshire) began a new regiment, calling themselves by the name of Egyptians. These were a sort of rogues that lived and do yet live by cozening and deceit, praǄising the art called legerdemain, or faſt-and-loose, whereby they got to themselves no small credit among the country people by their deep dissembling and deceitful praǄices, feeding the common people, wholly addiǄed and given to novelties, toys, and new fangles, delighting them with the ſtrangeness of the attire of their heads, and practising palmistry to such as would know their fortunes.

The first that invented this new fellowship was one Giles Hather. He carried about with him his whore, called Kit Callot, which was termed the Queen of Egypties[34]. They go always never under an hundred men or women[35], causing their faces to be made black, as if they were Egyptians. They wander up and down the country as it pleaseth them best, with their horses to carry their bastards and baggage after them ; and when they come into any country town, they pitifully cozen the poor country girls, both of money, silver and the best linen, only in hope to hear their good fortunes told them.

After a certain time that these upstart losels had got unto a head the two chief commanders of both these regiments met at the Devil's Arse A-peak, there to parley and entreat of matters that might tend to the establishing of this their new-found government. And first of all they think it fit to devise a certain kind of language, to the end their cozenings, knaveries, and villainies might not so easily be perceived and known in places where they come. And this their language they spun out of three other tongues, viz., Latin, English and Dutch—these three especially, notwithstanding some few words they borrowed of the Spanish and French. They also gave names to such persons of their company according to the kind of life that he undertook, as for example : a common beggar or rogue, they termed a clapperdudgeon ; one that counterfeited the falling sickness, they termed him the counterfeit crank, for *crank* in their language is the falling sickness, and so counterfeit crank is the false falling sickness ; and so of the rest.

This Cock Lorel continued among them longer than any of his predecessors before him or after him ; for he ruled almost two-and-twenty years, until the year A.D. 1533, and about the six-and-twenty year of King Henry the Eighth.

1. He made, among other, these statutes among them : that whosoever he be, that being born and bred up in the trade of maunding, nipping and foisting, for the space of ten years, and hath not the right dexterity in his fingers to pick a pocket, but is fain to cloy his fellows, and cowardly to demand scrappage—such a one is to be known and brought hither to be fined for his faint-heartedness ; and if such a one after venture and be taken upon the first fault, let him know that he is going the highway to perdition without pity, as a just punishment for his folly, that he betook himself so soon to the occupation.

2. *Item.* We think it meet that none eat meat, as pigs, capons, geese or suchlike, unless he purchase it by privy pilfery and cleanly conveyance ; neither shall they be merry in every bousing-ken or ale-house as they list, but in some odd outhouse remote from dwellers, a stalling-ken that is known of purpose to be trusty, yea, and that in the night too, lest they be notified and suspected to be scandalizing of the profession ; neither shall they be merry out of measure, lest, by their extraordinary noise, the constable and watchmen take them, and so carry them to ward, as a just punishment for their presumptuous and unordinate proceedings : for which some of late days have woefully felt the smart.

Captain Giles Hather first began in A.D. 1528, concerning whom there is nothing made mention of, but of his cozenage and deceit, for these kind of people lived more quietly and out of harm in respect of the other sort, making themselves as strangers, and would never put forth themselves in any tumult or commotion, as the other sort did. But what vice they exercised not one way, they were not inferior to them in the like, or rather worse, another way. So that, what between them both, they were two pestiferous members in a commonwealth. But I will leave them both, and pray for a prosperous wind to bring my bark to the wished port of her desire, which is to be favoured and well liked of in your sight ; which, if good fortune favour me so much, I shall be boldened once more to play the merchant venturer ; at whose second arrival I will present you with things more strange, not far-fetched but dearly bought, and wherein, if licence may be permitted, I will proceed and set down the successors from Cock Lorel until this present day, and who at this day bears the greatest sway amongst them[36].

Finis.

THE

COUNTER'S

COMMONWEALTH

OR

A VOYAGE MADE TO
AN INFERNAL ISLAND

discovered by many Captains, Seafaring
Men, Gentlemen, Merchants,
and other Tradesmen

But the conditions, natures, and qualities of the people
there inhabiting, and of those that traffic with
them, were never so truly expressed
or lively set forth as

By
WILLIAM FENNOR
HIS MAJESTY'S SERVANT.
1617.

AD LECTOREM :

Sufficit scire locum esse in carcere :

It is enough to know, too much to see,
That in the Counter there is room for thee.

To all cashiered captains, or other their inferior officers, heedless and headless young gentlemen, especially elder brothers, forsaken serving-men, roaring boys, broken citizens, country clients, or any other of what art or fashion soever that shall by chance, rather mischance, be unresistably encountered, and so become tenants against their will, within the territories of this ensuing commonwealth, greeting and meeting —rather at an ordinary than here.

WORTHY Gentlemen, I rest assured this small volume (being no elephantine load of Mogulian story, compiled by the wandering pawn-knight of Troy) will be bought and read over by many. How it will be censured I know not, or how I shall be reputed for publishing it. To deal plainly I care not, so it bring future benefit to my country, and content to the judicious, to whom I commend it for two especial reasons. The first stands grounded on these three points, a prospective glass, an instructive book and a suspective blow. For as [a] prospective, set to the sight of a man's eye, will draw the object so near the sense, that he may discern whether his opposite be friend or foe, and make haste too, either to embrace the one, or shun the other, before he come near him; so in this glass a young gentleman may plainly perceive the folly that reigns in others, and seek to eschew them before they take hold, which will hurry him into these inconveniences. It is a book to instruct young heirs to keep out of books and bonds, which oftentimes are the main cause of their overthrow, and brings that long-suspected blow upon their shoulders, which, if it chance to light here, they may clearly discover the keepers' large conscience, and be thoroughly instructed to shun their extortion.

My second reason is an apology, to shield me from those wounding tongues that may perhaps tax me for writing so harshly against citizens, prodigals, sergeants and other officers. To such I answer: let the galled jade winch till he break his heels against my buckler, which thus I advance. How much I reverence and respect the right worshipful order of this famous city in their just proceedings, let my best and utmost service be a true witness. Neither seem I to carp at the bounty or large expense of young gentlemen, whose means and birth are correspondent. No, no; I rather encourage and commend their worths, for of such there are too few, and for their sakes only I have discovered what traps and snares are daily set by careless unthrifts, to wind them into the like ruin they themselves are in.   They have ſtrange devices, and a certain kind of longing to caſt their eſtates in a consumption, by which their persons may lie languishing under that infeċtious disease, wherewith they themselves are poisoned by the incurable plague of poverty.   Concerning sergeants, I hope there are none so shallow conceited to think my pen so full of vinegar to write againſt their mere profession, which in a well-governed ſtate is so necessary.   I rather wish they were as free from abusing their place and office, as I am from disliking of it, and then a shorter chapter would serve to discover their siniſter devices and treacherous dealings, which I have observed so carefully, that if any of the fraternity of the macemongers chance to fall sick at the conceit, let them but diligently view it over and they shall find as comfortable cordials to refresh the heart, as I did from that cold caudle when they firſt arreſted me, which I willingly beſtow upon them in requital.

But methinks I hear some curious critic murmur, before he hath read over half the preamble, because I entitle it a commonwealth, and begin it so singly with myself.   To such I answer : my unwilling experience, and not reports of that they shall read hereafter, emboldened me to write the truth.   That I have tried, which may beget belief in those that read ; if not, I wish it may be their good fortunes to go the voyage, and let them confute me if they can.   If any shall objeċt, what reason I have to discourse of the four branches, before I come to the main body of the commonwealth, and ſtand so long on them, deferring their expeċtations, let them reſt satisfied with this answer : A building cannot be raised without a groundwork, or a tree will seem naked without branches, and a man wanting limbs to support him is but a decrepit body ; which I considering, have adorned this ocean with complete rivers, which are indeed the beſt benefaċtors that belong to it. The firſt three chapters show how diſtress and oppression joined hands to wound my weak and unprovided eſtate, by which single example all other may discern the true usage they shall receive from the kind keepers if their means once fail or their friends forsake them.   The four chapters following lay open the four arms or currents, with their several natures, that bring supply to this body, or main ocean, which in the laſt three chapters is lively anatomized : the cruelty of keepers and the misery of prisoners.   For the truth of which, I have quoted an authority in the margin[1] and for your delight mingled it with many pleasant dis-courses, which I freely send abroad to all, either to those that have been passengers through this troublesome ocean and know the danger, or

to any that shall hereafter, upon special occasion, be forced to make proof of this relation ; laftly, to those that have no desire to venture this voyage, but will rather be contented to sit at home and read the discovery.   I commend it with as much love as keepers bear to prisoners' purses when they have money in them, wishing it might prove as delightful to them, as their ill dealings were hateful to me.   And so farewell !
From the Counter in Wood Street, 1616, October 23.

Yours in what he may, thus beftraited and diftraded,

WILLIAM FENNOR.

THE COUNTER'S COMMONWEALTH,

or a voyage made to an infernal island, long since
discovered by many captains, seafaring-men,
gentlemen, merchants, and other tradesmen.

The Penner

WILLIAM FENNOR

His Majesty's Servant.

CHAPTER I.

*Containing : 1. The manner of my arrest. 2. The description of a brace
of sergeants. 3. Their counsel to me. 4. My coming into prison.
5. The description of a jailer. 6. And my entertainment into the
Master's side.*

WALKING not long since in an evening through the City, when the
heavens were muffled up in clouds, as many of our modern gallants'
faces are in their cloaks, and being in a fixed meditation with myself,
a Trinobantine[2] burgher, coming in haste, ran full butt at me with his
head, so that he had nigh gored me into the kennel. I took him to be
some complete harnessed bench-beleaguerer, for he had a wrought
nightcap on his head to keep the broth of his wit warm, satin sleeves,
a taffeta jerkin to cover his canvas back, and a pair of velvet hose. I,
for his unexpected courtesy, not forgetting to give him the good time
of the night, up with my sword, scabbard and all, and took him a sound
knock o'erthwart the pate, that if the most headstrongst ox that ever was
sacrificed in St. Nicholas Shambles[3] had received but half such a blow,
it would have staggered him. But he, like a valiant and provident
tradesman, bare it off with his sinciput and shoulders and ran away.

I, as glad I was rid of him as he of me, posted as fast to my lodging
as a released prisoner (heigh-ho a prisoner !) from the jail, for fear he
should run to the Counter and enter an action against me. But, having

428

escaped the Charybdis of this danger, I instantly fell into the Scylla of a more deep and dreadful than the first, for, as I was making homewards, a brace of bandogs belonging to one of the Counters, most cowardly came snarling behind me and fastened on my shoulder, giving me this salutation : " Sir, we arrest you in the King's Majesty's name, and we charge you to obey us."

These ravens had no sooner croaked out this ominous message, but I looked as blank as those that sold all their estate and ventured it at a lottery and drew blank, or an old usurer when he hears of a Privy Seal[4], or a copyholder ploughholder when he is served with a *subpoena*. But all could not prevail. I was forced to obey them for fear of further inconvenience, so rendered my weapon into their hands, and my body to the laws of my Sovereign, telling them the thunder I so much feared, was now fallen on mine head. Yet the thought of my arrest did not so much affright me as the countenances of those pewter-buttoned, shoulder-clapping catchpoles that seized on my body.

The one had a face ten times worse than those Jews that are pictured in arras-hangings whipping Christ. His black hair hung dangling about his ears like elf-locks, that I cannot be persuaded but some Succubus begot him on a witch ; his nose was precious, richly rubefied, and shined brighter than any summoner's snout in Lancashire[5].

The other of these pagans had a physiognomy much resembling the Saracen's Head without Newgate, and a mouth as wide-vaulted as that without Bishopsgate[6]. I was in a great doubt whether he were an Englishman or no, for I was certified a Dane begot him on a Switzer's wife. And, to make him show the more like himself, his ill-favoured visage was almost eaten through with pock holes (the " grand " I hope), so that half a parish of children might easily have played at cherry-pit in his face.

These furies had no sooner fastened their sharp flesh-hooks on my shoulders, but they, as their fashion is, began to exhort me to patience, telling me I ought not to be incensed against them, for they were but the ministers and executioners of the law ; and that the mace, which they held in their clutches, was put into theirs by the hand of Justice ; that they were both for the good of the commonwealth and the discharge of their own consciences, sworn to execute their office, though it were upon their own father ; that I, being so gracious in the Court, could not long be detained in the Counter ; that, after I had been resident there but one quarter of a year (if it should be my ill fate to stay there so long), I would not lose the rich experience I should learn there for ten times so much debt I was arrested for ; and, lastly, swore as they were Christians, they would do me what kindness lay'in their power, either persuading my creditor to come to a reasonable composition, or provide me bail. The cormorants told me true, for they swore " as they were Christians " they would do me good, but, being contrary to them, played the Jews and falsified their oaths with me, for I never saw them after I was mewed up in the Counter. But before I was matricu-lated in one of these City universities, by persuasion they got me into a tavern not far from the enchanted castle—the prison—and there milked me out of all my money, to stuff their paunches with wine and good cheer. But, their guts and garbage being full-gorged, they told me it was time to repair to the Counter, for if the Sheriff, their master, should be certified of their detaining a prisoner so long after an arrest, it would be a great prejudice to them, and small good to myself. So I, discharging the reckoning, wishing them choked, and all their fellow varlets that ever after should taste of my bounty (when I began to scent their roguery), came over with them, so bid them farewell and be hanged.

But here is one serious point not to be slipped over : for the Cerberus that turned the key of the counter-gate[7] no sooner saw those hell-guides bringing me in, but he set the door as wide open to receive me, as West-minster Hall is in the term-time to country clients, which put me in mind of that odd old verse in the poet :

Noctes atque dies patet atri janua ditis.

I no sooner was entered into this infernal island, where many men lie wind-bound sometimes four or five years together, but a fellow (whom at first sight I took to be a gardener, because he had somewhat a reddish beard and turned-up withal) called me to a book—no Bible or divinity, but rather of necromancy, for all the prisoners called it the Black Book. Coming to it, he demanded my name. I told him. And then he set it down, as horses are in Smithfield at the toll-booth[8]. This ceremony being ended, he asked me whether I would go to the Master's side, the Knights' Ward, or any other place of a cheaper rate. I answered, the best, though it were the dearest ; for I did hope to get my liberty before a week was expired. Upon this determination, there was one called to show me the way to my lodging, who, upon the first call, made no delay, but instantly came waddling downstairs. He was a gross fellow, one that had a fat body though a lean brain, a face of a sanguine complexion, and an heart correspondent to the same. He had a motley beard cut round like a rubbing brush, so that if all the skin of his body had been like that of his face, it would have served excellent well, when he had been dead, to make cloakbags of. This lump of man's flesh (that like a foreman of a jury could speak nothing so well as guilt) conveyed me up a pair of stairs and so to a door, where another Fury like himself sat, telling me that if I meant to have entrance there, I must pay my fees, or else I could have no farther passage that way. A shilling was his demand, which he would have, or else I must return the same way I came. I, seeing nothing but a silver key would open this lock, gave him his fee, wishing the weight of that twelve pence in aqua fortis or mercury-water in his neck, but, having shot this gulf, my corpulent conductor brought me through a little gallery, which led us to a spacious room, and then into a hall hung round about with the story of the Prodigal Child, a very edifying piece of workmanship for the guests of that place.

Being come into this uncouth and strange place, my guide, with a countenance as sour as any mustardmaker in the City, bade me welcome, and told me that there was a garnish to be paid. But I, that understood the Hebrew, the Syriac or Chaldean language as well as his speech, asked him what that was. He told me two shillings would discharge it. I mildly certified him I was not at that unhappy present so well furnished; besides, I was ignorant whether any such thing were due to him, or no. At this answer he roused himself up like an angry mastiff, and being in choler, in a currish manner barked out these words to me:

" Sir, if you mean to lie on this side, you must and shall pay me my fees, or, though you be no alderman, I will be so bold as to uncloak you."

I, seeing him so resolute, and myself loath to lie without a bed because it was late, put mine arm into my pocket, which was so sore with the sergeants' gripping that I had much ado to pull two shillings out of it. That being discharged, like a base viol he went grumbling upstairs with me and brought me to my lodging, richly hung with cob-web-lawn. So having showed me my bed, whereon he clapped a pair of sheets, that never came nigh Holland by three hundred mile[9], left me a piece of candle scarce so long as his nose, locked up the door, bid me goodnight, went down jingling his keys, and left me to my repose.

CHAPTER 2.

1. Mine acquaintance with my fellow-prisoners. 2. Mine entertainment at dinner-time the next day. 3. The character of a prison. 4. The keepers' kindness to me while I had money. 5. Their unkindness to me when I had none. 6. Lastly their transporting me from the Master's side to the Knights' Ward.

But, what with change of my lodging and meditating of mine entertainment, I slept not at all, but, like a true malcontent, made my brains the minutes to every clock I heard, betwixt whose several sounds the watch of mine invention beating up my panting heart hammered forth a hundred strange cogitations. Thus lay I longing for day, at whose approach I might discern the manner of my new distasteful lodging, which looked so confused, rasty, and ominous that every object presented new grief and struck me into further consideration of this worse than woeful purgatory, wherein I lay plunged by the froward will of Fate, dreading the danger I was in, and doubting how long this unwelcome affliction might continue.

In the midst of my musing my chamber-fellows awaked, whom I conjectured to be of the same fellowship of affliction that I myself was. I saluted them with a *Bon jour*. They, perceiving me to be a stranger, gratified my good-morrow with a *Bien*, asking of me whether I came in upon an arrest or a command. I answered, with a deep sigh and sad voice : "Faith! gentlemen, I am arrested, to my grief. God help me!" At which words I could scarce refrain from tears, which caused my kind chamber-fellows to pity my present sorrows and apply some words of comfort to expel them. In the same chamber lay an attorney, who began to be more busy than the rest; who, perceiving I was apt to give ear to any new conceited hope, slipped on his black suit (which was worn bare for want of brushing) and, coming to my bedside, whispered in mine ear and told me if I would rise he could tell me something for my good. These words possessed each part with more than haste to hear this unexpected kindness ; so being with speed apparelled, down the stairs posted I and my attorney, who, taking me by the hand, demanded of me whether I were in upon action or execution[10]. I answered : "An action of a hundred pound"; to which he replied he would have me out presently, and with an *Habeas Corpus*[11] remove my cause to the King's Bench, and so farewell!

I, thinking the doors had been blown open already by his breath, stood in amaze, considering with myself whether he were mortal or no, yet marking that his crabbed countenance accorded with his counsel, for which he greedily gaped for ten groats. I began to pause with myself, and asked him what the charge would amount to. He told me for forty shillings he would undertake to set me free. I told him I would consider a little of it, and then he should hear my resolve. And so we transcended to our former lodging chamber, where we found all our associates upon their legs, some buttoning, some trussing, others taking tobacco to expel noisome savours. They all kindly saluted me, and so from complimenting and talking, we fell to drinking, the only remedy to drive away melancholy, and bring strangers acquainted. Thus we passed away the morning, while service-time, which being spent in devotion, the table was covered, and up came our dinner, at which each man sat down without respecting of persons, for he that first comes is first seated like those that come to see plays or go to dinner at an ordinary, but I, being the youngest prisoner as their fashion is, sat at the upper end of the table, to which preferment by much entreaty I was advanced; short grace served for sharp stomachs, and so to it they fell without circumstance. But I, seeing all their teeth labouring so hard, thought foul shame, mine should stand idle, began to accompany my quick shavers; but as I was about to put meat into my mouth, one with his mouth half full, mumbled out an ill tuned speech of a garnish. The vintner's boy that waits for such purposes was ready with a pottle of claret, who, filling a bowl brim full, set it on my trencher; and so I was entreated to drink to all the society, and compelled to pay for it when I had done. These plagues dived deeper into my pockets than Gravesend Searchers[12] do into ships, to find out uncustomed commodities.

Thus, having finished our feast, and waiting for no banquet, we rose, every man disposing of himself as he pleased, only myself, guided by the evil Fate walked into the foreroom, where the fraternity of keepers and other servants of the house were feeding on the fragments that were reserved from our table. I with a common salutation bade much good do them; but [they], when they had emptied their crammed jaws, told me there was certain garnish to be paid. I, now being too well acquainted with that language, told them plainly I would pay no more; to which they replied and said, that then I should have my liberty no more, for all the rest of my fellow-prisoners had paid it, and, except I would be their imitators and come off roundly, I should be barred of that privilege the rest of my associates had. I, loath to be pent up like a lion in the Tower and have no more liberty than to look through an iron grate, demanded the sum. They told me sixpence, to send for a quart of claret wine, which was the last tester that remained in my peaceful pockets. At last, flinging it to them, I walked up to my lodging again, and there by chance espied a standish and a sheet of undefiled paper, which being fit for my purpose, I made bold with, and in the midst of melancholy writ this character of a prison :—

It is a fabric built of the same stuff the keepers of it are made of, stone and iron. It is an unwholesome, full-stuffed, humorous body, which hath an Hole in the posteriors of it, whence it vents many stinking, noisome and unsavoury smells, which is the only cause there is such a perpetual sickness and disease in it. It is a book where an honest man may learn and read a lesson of bettering himself, and where a bad man may study to be ten times worse. It is a costive creature, that surfeits almost all the year long, yet very seldom doth purge itself ; and when it doth, it leaveth abundance of ill humours behind. When Epimetheus opened Pandora's box, there did not more mischiefs and maladies fly out of it into the world than there is in this cursed place, for it hath more sicknesses predominating in it than there are in twenty French hospitals, or at the Bath[13] in the spring or fall of the leaf. It is a bankrupt's banquetting-house, where he sits feasting himself with dishes borrowed from other men's tables, without any honest determination to repay them again. It is a prodigal's purgatory and a sickness that many young gentlemen and citizens' sons and heirs are incident to be troubled with at the age of one-and-twenty or much thereabout. It is a dicing-house, where much cheating is used ; for there is little square dealing to be had there, yet a man may have what bail he will for his money.

This being finished, I viewed it over ; but as I was reading of it, I was called down to speak with a friend that came to visit me in my new transformation, and after some formal gossipping discourses, as, " I am sorry to see you here," " How were you met withal and what hard hap had you ? " and suchlike, lent me a brace of angels, the sight of which two fair creatures made me courageous and a companion for the best. I then roused my heart up to a strain of mirth, which caused the gentlemen to delight in my company. The keepers began to wax diligent. I could no sooner name a bottle of ale, but it was ready to fly into my face ; the vintner's boy was ready at mine elbow, that if I called but for a quart of sack or claret, would forget his errand by the way, and for his own profit present me with a pottle. In this jovial vein I wasted my money and time, never desiring to deal with mine attorney for my liberty, because I understood by others that it was only a trick to worm me out of my money. Many such supplies I had to uphold my mirth, but none to discharge my debts, which began to increase, for every day brought in a new action, till the total sum of my debts had drawn ahead and joined their forces in the Paper-house.

But at the end of the week when they use to call for their reckoning (which is for diet and lodging), they willingly trusted me, telling me there was no such haste. Thus I frolicked out three weeks on the Master's side, thinking my credit stood built on the firm rock of their kindness, whereas, indeed, as the sequel shall unfold, it was sunk in the quicksands of their cruelty. For having run myself into a month's arrearages, my friends began to wax weary of supplying my wants, and the keepers, knowing of it, unwilling to trust me any farther ; thus both my friends and hopes shook hands with me, and bade me farewell ; to be brief, the month being ended, my fat fellow (before mentioned) like a watchman came with a bill in his hand to make a privy search in my purse, but finding it altogether unprovided for his purpose, returned the bill to the book without any cross language. Upon the view of these unsatisfied figures, there arose a thunderclap of conspiracy against me for my present transportation over from the Master's side to the Knights' Ward, but I that scorned to be frighted with the first flash of false fire, defended myself with good words that night, and so went to bed, determining with myself, rather than be offensive to them, which might more incense them against me, the next day to go quietly over myself, and not to discredit myself so much as to be forced over by compulsion. So the next morning, as soon as I was ready, I took my leave of all my fellows on that side, and instantly went over, writing these few verses in a little piece of paper, and left them to the perusing of my kind comrades :—

> To all my friends that hear this single story,
> If you to try their kindness have occasion,
> Being possessed i' th' Counter's Territory ;
> Whilst money last they'll please thee with persuasion ;
> But being spent, they change their first evasion
> To their own shapes ; when they your wealth have won,
> With you they'll deal as they with me have done.

Thus leaving the Master's side, I kindly entreat your patience to walk over to the Knight's Ward with me and partake of the fruits of my new society and strange unexpected entertainment.

CHAPTER 3.

1. Mine entrance into the Knights' Ward. 2. My rough usage. 3. The description of a commanding officer in that place. 4. My strange acquaintance with a company of gentlemen, being all prisoners. 5. The occasion of this ensuing discovery. 6. And, lastly, the entrance into this discovery.

I NO sooner came down the Master's side stairs, but a key was turned for me ; so up went I into the Knights' side, but did go as heavily (howsoever I laid a brave and gilded outside upon my heavy and leaden discontent) as those poor prisoners that go up Newgate stairs after they come condemned from the sessions house. At first I went through a long dark gallery, that represented the place it was most like—Hell. For it was as gloomy as if the ravenlike wings of night did continually cover it. Having passed through this Egyptian fog, on a sudden I stepped into the Hall, where men were walking up and down, as thick as merchants do on the Exchange between twelve and one in the afternoon. Being entered, I began to play my part as well as I could, and thus to salute them :

" Gentlemen, God save you all ! May that you all long for happen unto you all—Liberty." Courteously they returned the like to me, and bade me welcome, holding me in discourse concerning my forsaking the Master's side. But as I was making an apologetical defence for my poverty and a true narration of their cruelty that turned me over, I was interrupted by a fellow, whose character I thus will describe unto you : He was a tall rawboned thing, and might very well at midsummertime have served instead of a maypole, had he been in a country town, for all the hobnail wearers in the parish to dance about. His face was much like a withered warden, and wrinkled all over like an apple-John of a year old. He was chapfallen, and looked like the picture of Famine ; the hair that grew upon his muzzle was so black, that I thought he had a couple of black puddings round about his chaps. Besides all these exterior endowments, his internal virtues were as many, for he was as proud as a new made constable, and would move his hat no more to any man that came within his jurisdiction, than a lawyer will to a poor client, though he stand two hours together bare before him. This compound of ill qualities (I say) very roughly came to me, when Heaven knows I never dreamt of such a mischief, and thus accosted me : " Sir, are you a prisoner ? "

"Yea sir," said I. "Fortune and the world have been my heavy adversaries, who, conspiring together, have concluded that I muſt lie here while the divine providence doth break the adamantine bond of my dull and Saturnine mishaps."

"But sir," said he, "have you any money?"

"If I have none," said I, "make no doubt but my supplies will come in tomorrow, and then what is fit to be done, I will see satisfied."

"Nay," said he, "I muſt not be procraſtinated, prorogued or demurred withal; I muſt have a garnish of you, a parcel of eighteen-pence; I will not spare you if you were my father."

I believed him, therefore gave him fair words, desiring him to be calmer, and the next money that I was blessed withal he should participate of.

At this answer he began to look as scurvily on me as a whore on a conſtable, a beggar on a beadle or whipping-poſt, as a cheater on a juſtice; and began to rent out three or four three-piled huge basilisco oaths, that would have torn a roaring boy's ears in a thousand shatters, telling me that the quality of my usage should be according to the quantity of my money; which I found true, for when it drew near bedtime, he brought me to a privy lodging—or, indeed, a lodging neighbouring nigh the privy, for the chamber ſtinks worse all the year long than a jakes-farmer's clothes doth at twelve o'clock at night. But day's roseate finger had no sooner bored out the eyes of night, but I got up, and began in a solitary and sad manner to mourn and pity myself, being more amazed than those that dreamed they saw Hell and had felt the tortures thereof, or those that drunk of Circe's cups and felt themselves turning monſters.

Being thus drenched in a boundless sea of melancholy (for the space of a fortnight or three weeks together) I resolved to walk into the yard to see if I could espy any of my friends that were in the Maſter's side, purposing to spend the day away in discourse, but I walked there an hour or more, and saw none but such as were as melancholy as myself, so I determined to walk up again. But by chance I turned my head aside, and saw the cellar door ſtanding open, gaping to swallow any prisoner that drew near; so, hoping to find some of mine old acquaintance there, I ſtepped down, and being no sooner descended but I beheld a company of gentlemen, all prisoners, sitting at a square table, making themselves exceeding merry with the music the cans made, being as brimful of beer [as] mine heart was of melancholy, or theirs of mirth, some having the pipes never out of their mouths, who puffed more smoke out of their noses than ever came out of Coldharbour chimneys[14], or any brewhouse in St. Katherine's[15]; some again singing as merrily as if they had been as free as the mountain air. I, seeing them in these Bacchanalial rages, fain would have slipped by them; but one that sat at the upper end of the table, having a can in one hand and a pipe in the other, desired me to approach and be one of their society (protesting more kindness to me than a Dutchman will when he is drunk), so proffered me half a can.

I told him I could not pledge him so much, but I would drink a whole one in conceit.

"Why!" quoth he, "not drink! Foot, man, it is the soul of good fellowship, the marrow of a poet's Minerva; it makes a man as valiant as Hercules, though he were as cowardly as a Frenchman when he is sober. Besides, I will prove it necessary for a man to be drunk sometimes, for suppose you should kill a man when you are drunk, you should never be hanged for it while you are sober, therefore I think it is good for you to be always drunk. Again, it is the kindest companion and friendliest sin of all the seven, for whereas most sins leave a man (by some accident) before his death, this trusty Trojan drunkenness will never forsake him while the breath is out of his body. And lastly, a full bowl of sack or claret, or a can of strong beer, will drown all sorrows."

"Indeed, sir," said I, "whether it will drown all sorrows or no, I am not greatly experienced in, but I am sure it will drown our souls. Yet, sir, for your kindness I will bestow the courtesy of the cellar upon you." And so I called for half a dozen, and drank a little to them all.

Another that was opposite against me, asked me if I would drink tobacco, so proffered me the pipe, which I denied, telling him that I would not be conversant with that Indian whore, that not only the lords and gentry of the land had committed adultery with, but also every tinker, cobbler and drayman of the City.

"Why," said he, "it is an excellent purge for the head."

"True," said I, "but it is a vile purge for the purse," and that for mine own part I had rather have a piece of pudding of an inch long for mine own eating, than twenty yards of pudding tobacco for my drinking.

They, seeing my fixed and solid resolution, let me alone to have mine own humour, as they had theirs; so that we sat exceeding merry without any melancholy fit, and, at the last, I began to give them a touch of my quality. But after we began to be more familiar together, he that first entertained me whispered me in the ear and told me, if he thought I would be secret, he would reveal that to me which should not only for ever gain me a never-dying memory, but also would be an unknown profit to the commonwealth. I promised him to be as secret as any surgeon. Then he called me aside from the rest of the company and told me, if I would repair to him in the morning, he would unbowel the hugest bulk of villainy that ever was burthensome to the world, that he would anatomize vice, and lay the ulcers and sores of this corrupted age, so apparant to the sight of this kingdom that the most osprey- and owl-eyed spectator should not choose but confess, there never was a more necessary and commodious discovery revealed.

"Why sir," said I, "there is a book called *Greene's Ghost haunts Cony-catchers*, another called *Legerdemain*, and *The Black Dog of Newgate*—but the most wittiest, elegantest and eloquentest piece, Master Dekker (the true heir of Apollo) composed, called *The Bellman of London*—have already set forth the vices of the time so vively, that it is unpossible the anchor of any other man's brain can sound the sea of a more deep and dreadful mischief."

"These, indeed," said he, "have done—especially the last—most exquisitely, both for their own reputation and their country's good; but I have that locked up in the closet of my breast, that, when it is opened and made apparent to you, will amaze you. Therefore I admire that the fabric of the earth is not continually shaken with earthquakes, that the earth itself (as she is a mother to bear all kind of fruit) doth not engender all kind of murdering and killing creatures, as harpies, cockatrices, wolves and hyenas, to destroy those that are continually trampling on her teeming womb; that the air is not choked with fogs; and that black pitchy mists doth not perpetually mask the face of Heaven, and leave the world in obscurity, putting us in mind of our sins, a thousand times blacker than that eclipse; and, lastly, that the sea is not turned all to blood to put us in mind of the cruelty and unconscionable usage of one man toward another, for there are vices in this sin-drowned age that are able to pull the two-edged sword of vengeance on our heads, and pluck fire from the forge of Heaven. I admire that we have not lean-faced famine, meagre mortality, pale sickness, and grim-faced war, tyrannizing in this land, as once it did in Jerusalem in the time of Titus and Vespasian, when the glorious *Sanctum Sanctorum* was set on fire, when the fields were filled with slaughtered carcases, and when the mother, for want of food, was driven to kill her own child, to quench her own hunger."

He would have proceeded farther in his discourse, but that I entreated him to contain himself while the morning, telling him, I would rather fail of my liberty than to meet him to hear this discovery.

Upon this resolve we both went to our former seats, and fell to our former familiarity, but, on a sudden, the keepers broke off our mirth and commanded every man to his lodging. So, not daring to displease their authority, we payed the shot, in a friendly and kind manner took our leaves one of each other, went upstairs and every man to his several ward and lodging. But my brains, like the wandering stars or clocks on Shrove-Tuesdays, were never at quiet, but all night I lay wondering and musing what discovery this should be. Therefore I longed more to see the day than an hungry courtier will a table groaning underneath the weight of well-filled dishes. But the Day-star no sooner began to cherish the world with his all-reviving light, but I sprung from mine hard couch, made me ready, and when the doors were open, by much entreaty, got into the yard, where, having not walked half a dozen turns, but I made my repair into the cellar, more athirst to have my mind's pallate quenched with his discourse, than my mouth with the best liquor in all the barrels, but, having called for two cans of beer, I sent for a quart of sack to whet the point of his wit, that it might wound vice the deeper. That being come, I sent for my friend, who lay in the Hole, who was forthwith let out, being an old prisoner, and, being come down, thus I began to salute him :

" Ingenious friend, as welcome to me as this fair day is to the world, this night hath seemed long ; but the burning desire I had to confer with you concerning the discovery you, out of your love, promised to reveal, made it more tedious, and, if you will but disclose the main body, let me alone to unmask the face, and lay every member open to the world's eye."

" Sir," quoth he, " you seem so complete in your quality that I hope you will publish what I shall relate. If you should smother it, I rather would keep it to myself than impart it ; but, not doubting of your diligence in this matter, I will venture my discourse, and, good sir, give a diligent attention."

I, as glad to hear as he to speak, took up a room in a private place, and, loath to hold myself in delays, first of all swept clean the channel of mine attention with a cup of sack, drunk an health to him, and the liberty of all poor distressed prisoners that lay labouring underneath the burthen of misery, which, being pledged in this (or such a) manner, he began :

" As the main ocean is nourished by the arms and rivers, that pay hourly tribute to him with the silver ſtreams, and especially, out of our land, by swan-blessed Thames, swift Severn, dangerous-passing Humber, and smooth-faced Trent, so is this turbulent sea, the Counter, by these four currents hereafter mentioned: firſt, unconscionable citizens; secondly, politick prodigals, *alias* engineers; thirdly, catchpoles; fourthly and laſtly, conſtables and their adherents, as the beadle and his watchmen: all whose abuses I will ſtrip naked, and jerk with my tongue, till I fetch blood. The firſt of whom have been the only cause of my detaining in prison this four years; yet let no man think that I speak againſt all citizens. No! as I hope for eternal happiness, I reverence that worshipful, ancient, and fameworthy order, I mean, such as maintain themselves and their families. I touch not those that care not who look and pry into their consciences, because their dealings have been so square and honeſt; but such as enrich themselves by fraud, deceit and siniſter means, working upon the infirmity of youth and green-witted gallants, to increase their own ſtore, caring not how much they decrease other men's eſtates. Such there are in the moſt flourishing and religious commonwealths in the world. In the moſt famous universities in Chriſtendom there are some dunces resident, that not only disgrace themselves, but also their fellow-ſtudents. It is impossible, but that in the moſt virtuous court there will be some parasites, so in the moſt goodly and glorious city under Heaven's canopy there are some asps lurking, that ſting the reputation of their brethren by their poisonous and corrupt dealings. Such as these I will portray and limn forth to you; and firſt of all I will discourse unto you the extreme abuse of gain-greedy citizens, and in order will touch the politic prodigals, *alias* engineers, and, I think, soulless sergeants, and conſtables and beadles. But firſt of the firſt."

CHAPTER 4.

Containing: 1. *The subtlety of many unconscionable citizens that entangle young gentlemen and lap them into bonds.* 2. *The craft and cunning of their confederates, gentlemenlike brokers, by whose wicked and unChriſtian-like dealing many elder brothers and brave gentlemen are undone.*

" I HAVE read that Italian mountebanks, before they speak in their drug-tongue and fuſtian language to the auditory of innocent and ignorant people, furnish out the play, where they sing their own encomiums, with vials, painted boxes, and bills of all the famous cures they pretend to have done in many foreign parts of Chriſtendom, which base and usual jugglings are only to enrich themselves and defraud the general rout that flock about them. Many mountebank citizens have we in this moſt sumptuous, but moſt subtle and sinful, city of London, that when they would ravish the mind and take the intuitive sense of many profuse prodigals, and, melting heirs with their siren-like seducings, lay open their wares, as satin, velvets, gold and silver lace, or any other braided commodities (or rather, indeed, discommodities) which though they show rich, yet are out of fashion or not saleable. These are springes to catch young country woodcocks or our City dottrels, that had rather be out of the world than out of the fashion ; who will be brave for the present time, though their gallantry coſt them all their future fortunes ; who with more fervency and proteſtation woo the citizen for his trash and trumpery, than many decayed knights will rich widows to inherit their possessions.

"But our tradesman, perceiving their forwardness and follies, plays the ropemaker and will be extreme backward, and will not be brought to truſt them with any of his Bartholomew-Fair ſtuff upon any condition. Bonds he refuseth, recognizances he disdaineth, judgments he will not hear of, ſtatutes he scorneth, and tells them in a puritanical fashion, that he had rather truſt a gentleman on his word, than his bond or oath. 'For,' saith he, 'they that will not have a care to keep their words, will not ſtick to have so large a conscience as to break their day, and slight the payment of their bonds.' Again, he tells them the danger he is in of losing of his debt. 'For,' saith he, 'when the bonds come to be due, and pay-day at hand, may not they ſtraight fly over into the Low Countries, or take sanctuary in Milford Lane[16], Duke Humphrey's Ordinary[17], or get a Protection Royal[18] from the King, and so defraud me of my debt ; and many such collops as these have been cut from the body of mine eſtate since I have been a tradesman. Therefore good gentlemen,' saith he, 'I cannot dare truſt any longer, for my kindness hath bred mine own calamity. Then set up your resolutions and trouble me no more, for I have given you your answer.'

"Thus are my young novices ſtruck to the heart at the firſt venny, and dare come no more for fear of as sharp a repulse.

"Alas! alas! this is but to grind the blunt appetite of my commodity-taker into a sharper edge, and make them more greedy of their own ruins, imitating the cunning and deceit of pretty but petulant and close courtezans, that are nice when a sick-brained young gallant

importunes them upon any kindness, only to make him more fierce
upon his own confusion, holding him off, like a fencer, at distance a
month or two, because he shall come up the roundlier to her purpose.
But to the matter.

"But some or one of my young gallants, that never gives over
plodding with himself how he might get into the books of some goldsmith, haberdasher, silkman, woollen- or linen-draper, hath some
broker or other coming early in a morning and certifies him that, if it
pleased him, he should have a commodity that lay ready to be carried
away, if he would enter into bond for it, nominating the same man that
gave him the former repulse. My young heir, whose heart knocks
against his ribs for joy, kindly bids the broker welcome, sends for a
cup of wine, and drinks to him with all his heart, resolving to entertain
his proffer upon any condition, protesting rather than he will let such
a blessed opportunity slip, will set his hands to more parchment than
a whole flock of sheep are able to furnish a scrivener with. But my
broker, before-instructed by the commodity-letter, tells him that,
though he heard him speak something doubtful of him, yet, if he would
be ruled by him, he would undertake to make his credit pass as firm as
any farmers' or yeomen in Kent. 'For,' saith he, 'I am a great friend
of this tradesman's, and make no doubt but may prevail as much with
him as any man in this town, especially if you will be ruled by me.
You must not be too importunate, but as scornful as he is disdainful.
Tell him that you are your father's heir, and that such lands he hath
you must inherit, and that the entailment cannot be cut off, though he
were never so heinous an enemy of yours. Besides you must tell him
you are about to marry some rich widow which you know you might
win, so that you could but have a hundred pound or two to put yourself
in good clothes.'

"These spells charms my poor prodigal. So at last he and the wolf
that came as legate from the tiger, go together and find my citizen busy
in his shop, not taking any notice of their coming, but, as to other
passengers, at first asks them what they lack, and what they would buy.
But boldly they come into the shop, and, after acquaintance taken,
the broker unfolds the matter and the occasion of their coming to him,
telling him that he came with a friend of his about a commodity, and
if he were a friend, as he always took him to be, as to condescend to the
gentleman's request, and let him have an hundred pound. 'For,'
saith he, 'I know his friends are of fair possessions. He is his father's
eldest son. Besides, on my conscience, he would not trouble you at

this present, if he were not to marry with a rich widow, whom he may lose for want of setting forth, and then no doubt, when the match is made up, but he will have an honest care to pay in your money, with a million of thanks for your kindness.'

" Now all the while the broker is pleading, mine innocent doth second him, and will, rather than go without his trinkets, bind whatsoever the broker saith with half a score oaths.

" The citizen begins to hearken after this, and protests to my green gosling that he would be glad to do any man a pleasure, but that he hath had so many losses already, and that he would be willing to let him have an hundred pounds' worth of commodities, if so be he thought it would redound to his good, and that he might be sure at the six months' end to have his money paid in. The young gallant protests, the broker warrants it, and at last, though very loath, the citizen condescends; but how, thus, that if he could procure as good a man as himself to be bound with him, he should have what ware he could desire. ' For,' saith he, ' man's life is frail and brittle, and you may die a fortnight or a week hence for ought that I know, nay, tomorrow, or soon at night, and then where is mine hundred pound? Therefore, good sir, look out some of your most especial and endeared friends, and get one of them to be bound with you, and you shall have the wares at a quarter of an hour's warning.'

" The tide now is turned, and Signor Unthrift put to his nonplus, and at last falls to entreat Master Broker to be the man; who for two or three days together, will by no means or persuasions be won to enter into bond with him, except he must share half.

" Is not this extreme and almost incredible villainy, and most unconscionable dealings, thus to snare in the gentry of the land, and ruin his fortunes but newly in the spring, knowing that he will rather let him have three-quarters of the commodity than go without it, because, as many others do, he would go gallant, have money in his purse, and keep company with satin and velvet outsides?

" But suppose the commodities are delivered, after they have both sealed the bonds (you must suppose the heir always to be the principal), how must these hobby-horses, reams of brown paper, Jew's-trumps and baubles, babies and rattles be sold? The gentleman is ashamed to proffer them to sale himself; no, he trusts the other that shares half with him to put them off; who must be hired to sell them, and, perhaps, when they are all sold outright, will have to his own share three-quarters of them. Are not these dealings worthy of the sharpest rod Justice ever did hold in her righteous hands? They are and have been soundly lashed and severely punished by that most noble, grave, wise and provident statesman, the Right Honourable the Lord High Chancellor of England[19]. Yet, for all this, there will such false play be acted, though the Sword of Justice continually were hanging over their heads.

"But I will return to our former subject. Let us now suppose my young gallant revelling in a tavern or ordinary. You may be sure the broker is triumphing, that he plucked the feathers of this young gull, and means ere long to leave him as bare of means as he is of brains. Now my usurious citizen dreams of nothing but his day, which he hopes my novice will break; which is no sooner expired, but instantly, by some stratagem or other, gets him within the liberty, then invites him to supper, by giving him fair words, either to his own or some of his neighbours' houses; and, when they have almost made an end, instead of a mess of fruit, or a piece of Banbury cheese to close up their stomachs, a brace (or more) of sergeants are not far from his shoulder, and, except he presently pay, he must presently to prison.

"Are these worthy the names of citizens? No, no, such may be citizens of London, but never of Heavenly Jerusalem!"

At this period I began to speak to him, saying: "Sir, I protest you have revealed a strange and monstrous abuse to the gentry of this land. If I did not take you to be (what I think you are) an honest man I should stand in a great doubt whether your discourse did taste of truth or no. But, good sir, proceed."

"Sir, as I hope for salvation," said he (an oath not for a Christian to dally with), "I relate no untruth, but what is as nigh akin to truth as I am to misery, for what I have spoken, I find by mine own woeful experience to be true, and what hath been practised on myself by these city cormorants. These tricks have been put on me, and for which I have suffered a long imprisonment; and yet they will have no compassion on me, but rather see me starve than relieve me, and either have my carcase or their coin. Yet their consciences know what I had from them was nothing but rotten, base and moth-eaten commodities, an hundred pounds' worth, of which, according to their rate, I never made fifty of; yet they stick not to demand an hundred of me, beside the interest and all their charges.

"Again, mark the policy they have to keep a poor prisoner in fetters of adversity. If they suppose the prisoner goeth about to sue out an *Audita querela*[20], forthwith they either put their debt over to some alderman, or else agree with some officer in the Exchequer, and so put their debt over to the king, feigning they owe him so much money, knowing that the Chancery will not, or cannot, allow anything, in such a case as this, to proceed against his Majesty. This is a speeding trick, and such a one I am now trounced with, and many besides myself.

" I have read, when Jews have bought a red haired boy, at first they will clothe him in silks and taffetas, ravish him with all delights that can be thought on, never have music from his ears or banquets from his taste, and thus use him until such time they know he is plump, fat, and fit for their purpose ; but when the poor Christian least thinks of his imminent ruin, he is taken by a brace of slaves, and tied up by the heels, so by degrees beaten to death with cudgels, having mummy made of his brains. Such as these are unconscionable citizens, that at first will clothe our young prodigals in silks and velvets, gold and silver lace, invite him home to dinner, use him very courteously, but when his bonds are due, and that he least dreams of his misfortunes, a couple or two of sergeants are set upon him, and hurry him to the Counter, where perhaps he shall lie two, three, four or five year, nay, a dozen or twenty years together, before he can get himself released ; or, if he chance to prevail so much with his creditors as to enfranchize him, it must be upon some unreasonable, unconscionable condition, as to give [them] five hundred pound for an hundred at the death of his father. Vulcan fell from Heaven into the isle of Lemnos, and by that fall lost the use of one of his feet. Let all such unconscionable citizens take heed they fall not from the earth to Hell, and lose their souls !

" These are the boars that plough up whole acres, nay, whole fields, of gentlemen's lands with their snouts ; these are swine that eat up whole orchards, and these are they whose fiery consciences drink up whole fish-pools at a draught. Their usurious dealings make so many cornutos in the City as there are ; for, when young gentlemen have been beggared by their extortion, they have no other means than to fall in with their wives and seek to them for supply. It is this that makes Newmarket Heath[21] and Royston Downs[22] about Christmas-time so full of highwaymen that poor country people cannot pass quietly to their cottages, but some gentleman will borrow all the money they have— only, indeed, they will make them take their bonds. This makes Tyburn and Wapping[23] have so many hangers-on ; and this is the cause so many such citizens' sons are plagued after their fathers' deaths, as their fathers when they were living have plagued others ; for most commonly some knave or debauched fellow lurch the fools their sons as cunningly after their fathers' decease as *they* did others only to make their sons gentlemen, who at last may as miserably die in the Hole for want of sustenance[24] as some of his father's debtors have done before him."

Upon this I began to interrupt him, saying, " Sir, in this short time that I have been here I have seen some creditors bring their debtors both meat, drink and money, when they have been sick and ill at ease."

" 'Tis true, sir," said he. " I acknowledge it ; but did you never hear that when a lion hath got a pretty bleating lamb or kid in his paws, he will play and tumble up and down with them a little while ; but you must not think it is for any love he bears them, but only to chafe their blood and make them eat more sweet and tender. Such are these kind of unkind citizens that, when they have got young gentlemen into prison, will, if the sum be anything weighty, relieve him with meat, drink, and money, if they see him begin to droop. But do you think this is in love to him ? No ! If you do, you wander a thousand leagues from a true construction. He doth it to keep him alive, that he may have his money if any means should fall to him, and that the world may take notice of his charity. Alas ! alas ! this is but a feigned holiness, which is a double iniquity. This kindness is but like Alchemy, or St. Martin's rings[25], that are fair to the eye, and have a rich outside, but if a man should break them asunder and look into them, they are nothing but brass, and copper. The apples of Gomorrah have glorious rinds, but infectious cores.

" It is an extreme misery for a prisoner to be indebted to a rich man, or a very poor man ; for the first, most commonly, will have all or none, for if his debtor chance to die, the loss he may well spare, but if it is his fortune to live and pay him, it adds to his estate ; the other, that is, the poor man, will have no pity, because it may be the debt is all he is worth.

" Thus do many gentlemen perish under the hands of cruel creditors ! Nay, a father that hath brought up his child with care and pain, grief and heartbreaking, and thinks to leave him such fair possessions, after his decease, that he may live in his country like a gentleman (as his ancestors have done before him), either in his lifetime doth see his son lie rotting in prison, or is not able to show his face out of his father's gates, or, after his decease, his brothers, sisters, friends and kinsfolks see his lands extended on, his woods felled down before his face, those legacies and portions he should pay to his brothers and sisters, paid away to satisfy his debts (being base commodities), and so beggars a whole worshipful family, who before that cursed time had lived a hundred years or more in grace and favour in his country. Alas! alas!"

With that, the tears fell from his eyes, and he could speak no more for weeping; yet I desired him to proceed. But he craved my pardon, and told me that he was at the farthest end of that discourse. "And thus," quoth he, "have I showed you the nature, property and quality of this main arm that hourly pays tribute to the ocean, the Counter. Now will I go to the second arm, which is concerning Gentlemen-cheaters."

CHAPTER 5.

1. *The true nature and quality of many of our modern spent gallants.*
2. *Their tricks to fetch in young heirs to set their hands to bonds.*
3. *And a true narration of their vicious and lewd course of life.*

"How can those tyrants flourish in their kingdoms, when the foundation of their reign is built on the sepulchres of the right and lawful heir they have murdered? And how can those men prosper whose raisings are reared upon other men's ruins? Many such there are in these most sinful days, who being gulled themselves when they were ignorant sots by knaves, turn knaves themselves, and study to cheat, defeat and cozen young heirs. Is not this a strange metamorphosis? It is better to be a poor fool than a rich knave. Many of these unlucky and ominous stars wag and wander perpetually, reigning in the sphere of this City, that hunt after young heirs as greedily as the Devil doth after usurers' souls when they be upon their death beds, for these, like pirates or bandits, live only upon the spoil.

"These soldiers, having been beaten to the world, or, indeed, beaten by the world, begin to summon up their senses, and call their idle brains to a strict reckoning how to get that up again their riot and follies have spent, and, thinking there is no way to recover themselves but by that they have ruined themselves, cast about them and begin to fish after this order:

"They prepare their lines, provide their baits, make ready their hooks, which shall have such constant and firm barbs that, after they have struck a gudgeon in the gills, shall be sure to hold him, though they suffer him to play a little in the stream. When they have all these things in readiness, they seek into divers floods, as the Temple, Inns of Court, citizens' houses, as wealthy merchants and goldsmiths, pry into ordinaries, and inquire if there be any in that place worthy a bait. If these fail, then they repair into Paul's Church, to playhouses, cockpits, brothels and taverns, and leave no place unsearched, but, like the air, visit all parts, rather than they will go without their prey ; and if they have found any that is agreeable to their minds, or that they think may easily be wrought upon, in this fashion they use him :

"Like his shadow, they will never be from his heels, but dog him into what place soever he goes, especially if he be a young country gentleman, whom his father hath sent up to the City to see fashions ; and, rather than he shall go out of town as raw as he came in, they will season him, and give him a little of the City powdering. They will first seek what means his father doth allow him, then of what nature he is, either merry or melancholy, mild or dogged, and, according to the garb and fashion he is of, bear themselves toward him. He shall not go into a tavern, ordinary, or almost any friend's house, but they will be as nigh his body as his sins are his soul, and by some sinister way cement and glue themselves into his familiarity, whatsoever it cost them. This being brought to perfection, and themselves grown something familiar—as in much company-keeping a man shall join himself to much society—they never will be from his elbow, but seem to be his bosom friend, his masculine sweetheart, and that, like Hippocrates' twins, they must live and die together.

"The golden-leaved marigold never opens her leaves while the sun doth rise, and never closeth herself while he doth set. So these politic prodigals never will be stirring while my heir is rising, and never sleep while they see him inclining that way—because they would be sure to have him in their sight. But having by much industry and sweat apted and fitted him to their humour and purpose, and wrought him to such a soft and waxen temperature (that they may cast him into what mould they list), bring him to their rendezvous, an ordinary, where this decayed knight salutes him, that poor esquire doth embrace him, the other beggarly gentleman kindly entertains him, and all their servants vail bonnet to him, none use him discourteously, but all most lovingly. They will have him to playhouses, invite him to a tavern to supper, and as yet let him not pay a penny, what company soever he comes in. And if he chance to borrow forty or fifty shillings of them, nay, three or four pound, they will not ask a penny. Yet all this while he runs but on that unconscionable score, which they will make him discharge to the last farthing before they leave him.

R

" This young innocent, scarce having scented the City air, all this while thinks himself in a heaven upon earth ; that he is in Elysium, and sees more delights than the Turk's paradise affords ; thinks himself much graced (as to be so much beholden to them), as to be entertained among gallants, that were wrapped up in satin suits, cloaks lined with velvet, that scorned to wear any other than beaver hats, and gold bands, rich swords and scarfs, silk stockings and gold fringed garters, or russet boots and gilt spurs, and so complete cap-à-pie that he almost dares take his corporal oath the worst of them is worth at least a thousand a year, when, Heaven knows, the best of them all for a month, nay, sometimes a year together, have their pockets worse furnished than chandlers' boxes that have nothing but twopences, pence, halfpence, and leaden tokens in them. Yet he still is confidently persuaded the country he was born in yields not such a man as the worst he hath associated himself with.

" Alas ! alas ! I truly pity them, and would as truly relieve them if it lay within my poor power ; but, when youth is in the height and full vigour of their desires, neither wholesome counsel or lamentable examples can give them sufficient warning of their future falls. But they hurt themselves, not me."

" Why, sir," said I, " this discourse tends not to a young gentleman's hurt, but, as I suppose, rather to his good ! "

" Sir," said he, " you as much err from the true conceiving of this business, as my young gentleman from a true course of life ! This is but the *preludium*, or prologue, to the play that is to come after, for my country novice being honeyed with these sweet and nectar delights, that these false brethren serve him with, thinks that all the kindness he can return them is not able to give them a true and due satisfaction ; and, if at any time these practitioners perceive my fresh gallant to droop or languish, with these or the like speeches (which are as wholesome as a whore in the dog-days), will strive to shake off his melancholy : ' Why how now, my noble spirit ! What is it that lies within the reach of our abilities that we can supply you with ? Speak. You shall not want it. It may be you mourn because you are not so well accoutred as those you keep company with. Come, our tailor shall furnish you. We will have you strip off this Devonshire-kersey suit, and put on satin. You shall cast off this course cloth cloak, and be furnished with one lined with velvet, your four-shillings Dutch felt shall be converted to a three-pound beaver, your worsted stockings and neat's-leather shoes to russet boots and gilt spurs. Then courage, man ! Is it not better to live in the City among a brave society of gallants, than in the country with a herd of gulls? What man is so stupid and blockish as to drink the running streams when he may quaff Greek wines? Who will feed on coarse cates when he may hourly taste of delicates? Who will wear poor serge D'bois when he may go in satins? And who will live in a smoky country cottage, when he may lead his life in a brave ordinary in the City? You are your father's heir. Therefore lay it on while you may. If it should be your fortune to be clapped up, do you think your friends will see their only son and heir, the sole hopes of their house, perish in a prison? No. Therefore play the lion and rouse yourself up, and be not so lamblike and still, but freely unfold your thoughts to us, and, as we are gentlemen and your sworn friends, we will endeavour with our utmost strength and ability to redress you, or in any other fashion to pleasure you.'

" This draught of poison, administered to him in a golden bowl, swells his heart up with such hopes, that he is ready to burst. He refuseth not their proffered kindness, but takes them as willingly as they treacherously meant them, and thinks that a rich suit will immortalize him. But yet these clothes are but like the shirt Deianira sent to Hercules, which, being poisoned with a Centaur's blood, wrought his death. So these rich trappings in short time after, either cost four or five years' imprisonment—if his friends are not the more affectionate to him—or pay four or five hundred pound or more to ransom him out ; for, after he is thus invested, it may be he revels it up and down the City with his familiars, drinks, domineers, and declares in every company he comes in how much he is beholden to such gentlemen ; and, having his brains thoroughly warmed with wine, vows to do them any kindness that lies in his power. But mark the sequel.

" At last, as a whole congregation of these caterpillars (that eat up some of the chiefest fruit that grow in the garden of this commonwealth) are carousing healths to some strumpet or other, there must enter— having his cue given him—a scrivener, with a bond of five or six hundred pound ready made for one of these gallants my prodigal doth most of all dote on, telling him if he can procure some gentleman, either of present means or future hopes, to be bound with him, he might instantly, upon the sealing of the bonds, have so much money he lately spake for, laid down to him. My politician, being in a counterfeit maze, at first begins to fret, fume and swear, saying that his credit was never before this time so slighted as not upon his own bond to be trusted for so small a matter. Then he begins to try his consorts about him, desiring them to ſtand bound with him. They tell him plainly they will not enter into bonds for their brother, but, if he had need of a hundred or six score pound, they would make it up among them and lend him. ' Pox of it,' saith he, ' I am to purchase such a lordship of such a knight, and two or three hundred pound will not serve my turn, for I have some two thousand pound ready, and if I had this full sum, the lordship were mine own ; which, if I should miss, I might lose three or four hundred pound, which easily I may get if I were furnished. Besides, if I could ſtay while next term, I should have a thousand pound paid to me upon a bond, and then I could easily cancel this.'

" At this, Simon Sandbox, the scrivener, is about to depart, and Signor Shift chafes, frets, and is ready to tear his hair for grief that he cannot be furnished. At laſt he comes to Corkbrain my country novice, desiring him to ſtand his friend, and ſtand bound with him for that sum of money, and that he should ſtand only for a cipher, and that he rather would lose all his lands (you may believe him !) than prejudice him in the leaſt thing the world might tax him with. Now, my young gallant— that never before this time was lapped up in lambskin, and would rather set his hand to his own undoing than displease him—takes it as a kindness that he would entreat him to do him such a courtesy ; so, without any reading over the bond, to see how the condition runs, seals and delivers it to Signor Security, the scrivener, never dreaming that he is put principal, or of the after-claps that will fall heavy on him about six months after, or that this bond he sealed to, was for some base commodities to furnish his supposed friend, or, laſtly, that it is some old debt that now he hath shifted from himself and laid on the novice's back ; but ſtill holds him as dear to him as his life blood is to his heart, and ſtill they will revel together, when, all this while, my cousin never looks into the ensuing danger, because he never considers of the day, or what the penalty of forfeiting a bond is. So, to be short, when the time is expired that the money should be paid in, the scrivener and the cheat plot to arreſt him, knowing him the beſt able to pay ; and, on a sudden, when they have him within the City, with the help of half a dozen puttocks belonging to one of the Counters, lay their claws on him, and seldom ſtay, except he be able to discharge the debt, while they have incarcerated him.

" Thus is this poor gentleman's fortunes, by his own kindness and this villain's policy, utterly overthrown, who never comes at him, sends to him, nay, or so much as once thinks on him ! Many of these moſt deteſtable and dishoneſt tricks have I known praċtised on young gentlemen, newly come to the Temple, Inns of Court and other places, that now my heart bleeds to think on."

" Sir," said I, " I have heard much of those that lie in privileged places being in debt, daring not show themselves, but I never heard they practised such abuses."

" Sir," said he, " if what I speak taste of untruth, may I never inherit eternal happiness. What good would it do me to wrong them, and do myself no good, only to hold you in a discourse ? Yet these are not half the vices that are daily practised among them. For, let a gentleman come into their company, you shall hear some cursing and damning for money they have lost either at cards or dice ; others chafing and swearing they have lost twenty pound, when their conscience knows they have won as much more ; others stabbing one another about some trivial word passing between them, so that there will be such a confused Babylonian language of blasphemy among them, that none (but their truchman the Devil) can interpret it. And when they have lost that in a quarter of an hour at cards, dice, tables, or bowls they have borrowed of some raw freshman, that lately was admitted into their worse than Jesuitical college, what will they do, but start out, some this way, and the rest another, some betake themselves to their geldings, pistols, and a good sword, and not stick to bid a traveller good morrow, and for that courtesy lighten him of his purse, because he might ride the easier, and then return home again.

" Others lie in their beds, musing—having their tutor the Devil, not far from them—where they may find out some easy gull of whom they must borrow some money for a day or two. But whatsoever they borrow for one hour is borrowed for one age ; for though they bind it with a thousand Damme's that they will repay it again within the space of a week, you may as well never bestow lip-labour to demand your money, for you shall be sure never to have it again.

" Others lie penning bawdy letters to citizens' wives, enticing them to let them have money or wares ; but if they will not be instructed by their devilish doctrine, as to deceive their husbands to supply their wants, what will they do, but raise causeless scandals and imputations against them ; and so, contrary to the will of God, go about to part man and wife. These are they that care for nobody but themselves, nay, not themselves, for, if they did, they would not so often hazard their lives in the field upon the refusal of some drunken health, or in speaking against some painted, prostituted courtesan ; and he that kills the most men is accounted the bravest man.

"These are they that like owls dares not show their faces into the City in the day-time; but as the dogs of Egypt, when they come to drink of the stream of Nilus, lap here and there, and dare not stay long in one place, for fear the crocodiles, that lie lurking within the banks, should pull them into the current; so these, when they chance to skulk out of their dens to some tavern to be merry, dare not stay long there, but straight shift to another for fear some sergeants, that lay watching about the stalls, should fasten on them and pull them into one of the Counters.

"These are they that go brave by running in debt, and never care how to pay, so they have it. I once read a pretty tale of a popinjay, that, against the time he should appear before the eagle, who had summoned all the birds to come before him, borrowed of everyone of his acquaintance a feather. The peacock lent him one of his plumes, bravely shining with variety of colours; the parrot lent him one of his green feathers, the goldfinch one of his yellow; so that, as soon as he was dressed and had presented himself before the royal and princely bird, and dismissed, he flew up and down the woods so proudly, that every inferior bird, as the titmouse, the hedgesparrow and wren, began to adore him. At last these birds that he had been so much beholden to, came to challenge their feathers of him, and, though very loath, he was constrained to render them back again, that when he was bare and naked he looked ten times worse than those poor birds that lately did admire him. Such popinjays are these that borrow of every citizen to make them show glorious in the world's eye; but when the goldsmiths, merchants, silkmen, and haberdashers come to claim their own and get it, they will seem ten times more foul than lately they did fair and glorious.

"These are the instrumental causes that many fathers disinherit their right heirs, and put in their second sons; who at last are forced to marry some whore, for want of means, or fly into the Low Countries and, for half-a-crown a week, serve in some garrison town; for, if they are caught (being by their means run into debt), they will be clapped into prison, and there lie and rot, where in process of time, when these cheating gallants grow old, and their tricks fail, [the latter] may lie themselves and fatten a prison, and end their days in the Hole, in poverty, famine and extreme wretchedness.

"Thus have I described to you the nature of the second arm that continually runs to the main ocean, the Counter. Now will I haste to the third, which is—Villainous Sergeants."

Chapter 6.

Containing : 1. The condition of sergeants.   2. Their nature and property.   3. A paradox in praise of them.   4. Their abuses, their tricks and sleights in arresting of men.   5. In what garb and fashion they oftentimes apparel themselves ; and, lastly, their unsufferable extorting from his Majesty's subjects, and their cruelty toward them.

" In Heaven there are many times engendered meteors, exhalations and fiery comets. In many countries there are many monsters ; as in Russia, rugged bears ; in Germany, tusked boars ; in Clenoma, tail-strong lions ; in Ireland, cruel blood-sucking back-biting six-footed creepers. But the most ravening and cruel monsters in *our* land are the shoulder-clapping purse-biting mace-bearers ; a necessary evil and plague-sore in the body of an infected City, and a disease that the most of the gentry is sick of. For, as in the most medicinable physic there is most infectious poison (which else would not be forcible or have any virtue), so in the most peaceful and populous commonwealth there must be such necessary instruments or else it would not long continue. These are they that strike with the axe of law and justice deeper cuts than they have authority for, so that sometimes they murder a whole family at a blow, and have no more mercy when they strike than a Spanish army when they are upon the execution or slaughter of their enemy. Yet thus much I will say for them, when a gentleman's fortunes begin to be sick and crazy, most commonly they will apply him with caudles and cordials, which only have but this fault, they taste something too much of the mace, a spice more familiar in England than in the East Indies ! For the most base sort of people in the land are never without it in their pockets.

" But now I think on it, I will not be invective against them, because no subject plays his part to the life so well as these do. Then, what kind of vocation is more necessary in a commonwealth ? I hold them very religious men, for they will continually watch and prey—watch a whole day together to catch young gentlemen, and after they have clutched them, prey upon them. They are very valiant men, for they will strike the bravest spirit that walks in the street. I have known many knights run away at the sight of them. They are men of great respect and reverence, for I have seen many gentlemen give them the wall, and, rather than they will jostle with them, let them have the whole street at their command. They are men of good consciences, for they will do nothing without warrant unless it be now and then for their advantage. They are very loving creatures, for I have seen them come running to a gentleman and hang about his neck and not leave him to the death. They are very familiar, and as sociable as any whore, for they will be drunk with any man, so it be not of their own cost. And, lastly, very kind and affable, for they will promise a young gentleman more courtesy than a courtier will a citizen. Why then should we not think well of sergeants?"

"Sir," said I, "I am sure you speak this paradox only to make yourself and me merry, for, on my conscience, what you now speak is rather in an ironical kind of fashion than serious or true; for, if you will have my opinion of them, they are the excrement that proceeds from the body of a commonwealth, whose vile doings have been so unsavoury to me that (for ever, as all the world else beside do) I shall hate them worse than a butcher doth Lent, or a fishmonger Christmas or Easter weeks. Therefore, good sir, be not partial in your proceedings, but lash them at the whipping-post of justice and equity, while you fetch as much blood from their ribs as they have tears from many poor men and women's eyes."

"Faith, sir," said he. "Indeed, to tell you true, I am like a kind mother that, having seen her child do some witty unhappy trick, stands in doubt whether she shall laugh at him and let him escape, or frown at him and correct him. So I, having seen the cleanly and smooth practices of these fellows, know not whether I shall smile at them and let them escape the scourge of my tongue, or grieve at them and correct their enormities; but, howsoever I have so brave and constant a champion on my side as Truth, I will go on, though all the sergeants belonging both to Poultry and Wood Street Counter were within earshot of me. Therefore thus I will charge upon them with a volley, shall wound some of their consciences—if it is possible for them to have any.

"In ancient Rome the lictors, or sergeants, went always with their staves of office in their hands, and in such apparel that the whole city knew them, and, yet to this day, in this form and fashion they continue, or carry about them some mark of difference. So in many other countries they are so markable that they are no sooner seen than known. But here in England, where they once went in pied coats, and white rods in their hands, as a badge of infamy, they will alter their fashion of habit oftener than a whore doth her lodging, or a French count his shirts in summer-time. Proteus never changed shapes oftener than these fellows, for sometime they will go accoutred like a scholar, then like a merchant, sometime like a counsellor, then a butcher, porter, or country gentleman, with their boots and spurs as dirty as if they had rid five hundred mile through the deepest sloughy way that ever was travelled; but this is, most commonly, when they go to arrest some farmer or yeoman of the country, that is either but newly come into his inn, or going out of town. And a hundred more such stratagems have they in their heads when they are well greased in the hand, or when the arrest is something dangerous. Therefore, first of all I will relate the manner they oftentimes arrest a man, to make you a little merry, and then proceed to the manner of their usage of a man after they have arrested him.

" A Norwich man being exceedingly indebted to certain Londoners, who often laid wait to arrest him, came to the City so private, that they knew not how to come at him, though sometime they had intelligence where he was; and when, as it was very seldom, the citizens came to parley with him, it was out of a window, but he could by no means be drawn nigh their forces, for he was too subtle for them, and always left word with the servants in the house where he lay, that none should have access to him before such time he himself had seen them, especially if they were in satin doublets, cloaks faced with taffeta, and ruffs of a merchant's set. At last his creditors, being incensed against him (caring not what cost they were at so they might encounter him), came to the Counter in Wood Street and feed half a score sergeants, promising them, if they could take him, they should have a Jacobus apiece besides. One of these, scenting the business, straight forged a device, which was in this manner: He was certified that this Norwich man had weekly some letters come to him out of Norfolk, and that the porter that brought them had free access to him. This sergeant instantly provided a frock, a red cap, a rope about his shoulders—which would have become his neck better—and, with letters in his hand directed to the same party, trudges to his lodging being just on that day the porter was accustomed to come to him; knocking at the door and being demanded his business, told them that he had letters out of Norfolk for such a gentleman. Upon this he was directed upstairs to the chamber door, who no sooner knocked but the gentleman did start up from his bed to the chamber door, peeping before through the key-hole, and, seeing him to be a porter, let him in. As soon as he was entered, he bid his worship good-morrow, vails his bonnet, and delivers him a letter that should come from a gentleman of his acquaintance. But, as he was opening of it, what doth my porter do, but pulls his mace out of his pocket—the gentleman not dreaming of such a breakfaſt—and laid on his shoulders, and arreſted him, telling him that he was not what he seemed to be (a porter) but what he was (a sergeant) and that there was no way with him but either to give satis-faction to his creditors, or—to prison. 'Therefore make yourself ready, and along.' So he, seeing how he was betrayed and arreſted, went quietly with him to the Counter, and died in execution.

"As pretty a prank as this the same sergeant played by another gentleman that ſtood upon his guard, who, having his creditors with him the day before, seemed to grow to a composition with him upon the sealing of certain bonds, promising to release him while a farther day, telling him that the next day they would be with him, and bring a counsellor and a scrivener; a counsellor to give them direction for the managing of the business on both sides, and the scrivener to make and write what they should determine. The creditors having taken their leave, ſtraight plotted together overnight how they might arreſt the gentleman in the morning, and, having invented the project, forthwith went to the Counter and there did fee these sergeants and half a dozen more with them, to despatch this business. The sergeants, being well oiled in the hand with *aurum potabile*, were as hot upon the exploit as an Italian on a wench of fifteen; and did long to put their device in practice. The sergeant would needs take upon him to be the counsellor, and his yeoman, the scrivener; who had attired themselves so quaint that they who had never seen them before would have sworn they had been the same they counterfeited; for the sergeant had a barriſter's gown on his back (that ever after could not choose but infect the true owner with knavery), a double ruff about his neck, and his beard cut as close as a ſtubble-field; his yeoman, that had as villainous a look as any scrivener between Charing Cross and Paul's, had his inkhorn at his girdle, his pen in his ear, and his parchment and wax in his hand; and away they go with a score more of their comrades, whom they had appointed not to be far from them, but to come and relieve them when they heard a piſtol discharged (which lay in the gentleman's window ready charged to guard himself with). The citizens led the way, and my counsellor and scrivener trot after, until they came to the house; so the folks, seeing there was nobody but such as had been there the day before—except a counsellor and a scrivener—conducted them up into the gentleman's chamber, where were half a dozen of his men about him for fear of the worſt. So the gentleman and the creditors began to lay open the matter to the counsellor, who desired the gentleman to dismiss his servants for half an hour; for it was not fit they should hear any of their proceedings. They were so. Then the counsellor begins to utter his opinion, while the scrivener began to sneak nigh the window, and, when he saw his time, discharged the pistol, and then instantly arrested him. The other sergeants, hearing the watchward given, straight ran up into the chamber with their swords drawn, and laid hold on him, telling him their intent and what they were. So the poor gentleman, seeing himself thus caught, rather than go to prison paid the debt; so sent the sergeants and citizens away.

"Other such dog-tricks as these have they played, as upon a merchant, that (either upon policy or poverty) broke, and having made all his goods ready to go into the Low Countries, wanted nothing to despatch, but to mend three or four dry-vats, which he meant to put his goods in, and gave order to his maid to provide two or three coopers to mend them, but she, being bribed by his creditors, betrayed her master's purpose to them, so they provided half a dozen sergeants to go like coopers the next morning to mend this merchant's dry-vats, and were let in to despatch it, and had direction from the merchant himself how to finish it. But as he was busy about them, instead of hooping the barrels, they hooped *him* in their arms, and arrested him; so that, before they left him, they made him pay the executions they had to charge him withal, and was glad to give them a fee beside, that they should lay no more actions on him.

"An hundred such stratagems they have been fortunate in, and came off without dread or danger, but now I have related to you the manner of their arresting many men, now will I tell you how they use many, or most, men they have arrested. If they perceive the party whom they have seized on to be a country gentleman, they will be busy with him to know whether this were the first time he was arrested. If it be, they have the better subject to work on, and know, as they term it, how to milk them the better. First they will carry him to some tavern—but it shall be nigh one of the Counters—where they will call for pottle after pottle, and such meat as the house affords, holding him in delays, while their guts are full; telling him they will do him what pleasure they can for him, and that they only keep him there, because they would have his adversaries come to him and despatch him with all expedition, swearing to him that they were sorry to do their office upon him, and that, if his creditor had not been with them, they had rather have given a crown to another to arrest him, than take a twenty-shilling piece to execute their office. Upon this, one of them will make as though he goes to fetch his adversary, when, God knows, he goes up and down Cheapside and other places of the City, enquiring among the tradesmen whether such a gentleman be indebted to him or no. If he be, then he will tell them, if they[26] will give him a piece of money he will undertake to arrest him, for he, by chance, had intelligence where he supped ; and when he hath his fees, what will he do but go to the Counter, enter an action, takes his warrant out of the office, and comes to the tavern again, telling him, he hath been with his adversary, and that he could not possible come to him this three or four hours yet, and that if he would give them any money, they would stay with him ; if not, they must have him to the Counter, for they had other businesses to despatch that they might get five pound by. If he offer them an angel or a mark for two or three hours waiting with them, [they] account it nothing, and scorn to stay so long for so small a matter, knowing the poor gentleman will rather disburse the value of twenty shillings, than go to prison, still expecting his adversary's coming, of whose approach there is no more hope than of the King's. Little thinking of the villainy they are practising against him, yet still he expects his adversary ; but, when it begins to be late, they call for something to supper, and, according to the lining of the poor man's purse, will sauce him. If they see he hath good store of crowns, they will counsel him to go and lie in their house a day or two, telling him it is a thousand to one whether his adversary will come or no, for though he promised he would not fail, yet he seemed very unwilling. ' Besides,' say they, ' if you fear any other actions, we can keep you so safe in our house that none of them shall know where to find you ; whereas, if you were in prison, they would all come thundering upon you, so it may be you may be laid up for two or three winters.' These speeches terrifies my poor gentleman, and still, rather than he would go to prison, would give all the money in his purse. At last, having discharged all the reckoning at the tavern, away he goes with them, and lies in some of their houses a day or two, which is enough—for it will cost him at least twenty shillings, day and night—and yet the poor man is farther from his liberty than when he was first arrested, and when these purse-leeches have sucked him dry, then they bring him to prison."

" Why sir," said I, " when I was arrested I never saw any such abuses among them."

" It may be so," said he. " Then they perceived you had no money, or that you were too wise to be cheated ; for I have seen divers gentlemen come into prison, after they have lain a fortnight or three weeks at some of their houses, at an excessive rate, without either cloak, sword, or hat (which the sergeants have got from them, only bearing them in hand that they will get them bail).

" Again, if he be a poor simple fellow, as some serving-man, or country tradesman, they will carry him to some blind ale-house, and there practise on him, telling him that, if he go to prison, it will cost him at first entrance a mark or fourteen shillings, and that he must have irons put on his legs as soon as he comes in, and put into a place where he shall neither see foot or hand, while he hath discharged the debt, and that he would give them so much money, they ought to have for arresting him, and something to drink besides, they would if it should be his fortune to go thither speak to the keepers to use him kindly. This trick I have known them serve a poor country-fellow, and brought him to prison with never a penny in his purse. Once they served a friend of mine so, but I think I made them render the money back again and be glad they could be rid so quietly of him.

" If I should but repeat but half their abuses, I should fill a ream of paper. I have seen them come dragging in a poor man by the heels, that his head hath knocked against the stones for a quarter of a mile together, and so battered and martyred that a man could scarce know whether he were a man or no. Sometimes, when they know a man in fear of arresting, they will, without warrant from the creditor, give him a cast of their office, only to get some money out of him, and so let him go again. Sometime, when they are feed to arrest a man, they will send the party word to keep out of their way, hoping to have a gratitude from him. Sometime when they have arrested a man, if the creditors be not by, will not stick to take a brace or two of angels and let him go, telling his adversary the next time he meets him, he cannot set eye of him. And, whereas a sergeant's fee from the creditor is no more than one shilling for an arrest, they scorn to step from the gate under a crown, a noble, or an angel. And, whereas there is a statute[27] that none of them shall take above a groat of him that is arrested, they will not stick to milk him out of all his money, and turn him into prison without either hat, cloak or sword.

" They have other tricks as bad as these, as for example, when they have arrested any man, either upon an execution or action, and if any gentleman or tradesman, or of what fashion soe'er he be, by chance do but jostle them as they are bringing their prisoner to the Counter, [or] if they call them by their right names, ' Varlets,' they, without warrant or any authority from some superior power, as justice or con-stable, but by the virtue of their own office, will carry him to prison, and either lay my Lord Mayor's command on him, or clap some heavy action on him, that, except he have good friends or a fat purse to compound with them, he may lie and rot there for all them.   I know a poor man* that did but offer to rescue his friend, was clapped up by them, and could never get free from them while he was worth a tester, and if the judge, before whom he was bailed, had not been more pitiful than they were conscionable, he had been in prison all his lifetime.

" If any man they arrest, in his struggling to make an escape from them, chance to hit any of them, either on the legs, face or breast, so that they have no hurt at all, they will grip, beat and pinch the poor man so miserably that he shall not be able to lift his arm to his head, and then enter an action of battery against him, which will more vex and disturb him than all the rest.   I myself have been eyewitness of the like, for in the beginning of August, 1616, they arrested a poor serving-man†, who had an action entered against him by them, because he offered to make an escape from them, and when he had all his other actions withdrawn he could by no means get free from them.   They were so unreasonable in compounding with him, that he took a strong conceit, and the nineteenth of the same month ended his life.

" Thus have I portrayed forth in my freshest colours the abuses and wrongs his Majesty's subjects daily sustain by these sergeants, for which they can have little or no remedy, and, as well as I could, waded through the third arm that pays tribute to the main ocean, the Counter.   Now will I proceed to the fourth and last."

CHAPTER 7.

Containing :   1. The nature of a constable's office.   2. An objection concerning the abuses his Majesty's subjects suffer by beadles and watchmen that understand not the virtue of their office.   3. And, lastly, an answer in their defence.

" REASON, the soul of Law, and Law, the life of a commonwealth, should shine and be translucent in those that bear the office of a constable[28], for he, being the King's deputy for the night, is the king of the night, therefore, being so, he should impartially with his staff, which representeth Justice, beat down disorder, and defend Equity, Peace and

* One Atkinson, now dwelling at Highgate.
† John Rogers.

Innocence. But there are many constables in these days, that through their own negligence, not wilfulness, do contrary to the nature of their office ; for very often the beadle and watchmen in his absence commit that which the constable himself is much blamed for, who under the pretence of seeing good order kept, as I have heard, are the first that breed disorder. But for mine own part I never was eyewitness of any of their misdemeanours, but only as I have heard it reported ; therefore I dare nor will go no further than truth doth guide me. For first, I should wrong that worthy office, in relating what I have no probability for, and secondly, myself, in making myself a dishonest man in print."

"Why sir," said I, " I have often heard it reported, that the beadles and watchmen are in fee with the keepers of both the Counters, and that for every man they commit they receive a groat, and, therefore, only for gain, will, upon any light or slight fault, carry any man that comes in their way to prison, or if any man fee them, they will, if he be never so drunk, unruly or disordered, convey him to his lodging ; or otherwise, if he be unfurnished, convey him to one of the Counters. And to mine own knowledge I have known a beadle committed to the Gate House[29] for committing a nobleman's servant, who went upon special business for the lord his master. Therefore, if he had not first wronged this gentleman, and secondly the force and nature of his office, why should he, being an officer, be committed for his misdemeanour ? Again, I have seen many men come into prison since I came hither, that have been extremely hacked and maimed with their halberds ; which in my opinion they cannot answer, for though they have authority to commit, they have none to kill or wound. Therefore in my judgment these abuses are unsufferable, and only are upholden by their head the constable."

"Sir," said he, " you must understand that a constable is but an island brook that pays but small tribute to the ocean the Counter, he is but *causa accidentalis*, an accidental cause, and by chance fattens the gross and vast body of it ; for, after his watch is set, he is bound by oath to perform his office both for the discharge of his own conscience, and the good of his Prince and country, in which duty every good subject is bound in duty to assist him. For a constable is the preserver of peace, the attacher of vice, and the intelligencer of injuries, and hath as strong and forcible power to commit offenders in the night as any Justice of Peace hath in the day ; nay, if any lord, knight, or gentleman, of what degree or fashion soever he be, coming in the night-time through the watch in an unruly fashion, is as subject to his command and authority as the poorest subject that walks the streets. And, if he should not sometimes, nay, many times, clap up such personages, they would be thought very slack in their office and not worthy of that authority and power the King hath given them. For many men, though they have brave outsides, may commit or act as great or more heinous mischief than those that are of a poor rank; for, if the constable should not stand sentinel, how many men would be robbed in the space of one week, nay, of one night, which by his industry and care he preserves.

"But here it is objected that the beadle and watchmen have for every man they commit, a groat. Whether it be true or false I never could confidently speak of. If they have, it is fit that for so many nights as they sit up for the good of the commonwealth, they should have something allowed. And who is the fittest to allow it, but such as have offended and they have been troubled with the night before?

"Again you say they will commit such as have no money to give them, though it be upon a slight occasion; and let such pass though their fault be never so heinous, so they will grease them in the fist. This objection I will thus answer: If this abuse is offered, it cannot enter into my mind that the constable hath any hand in it, for there are many occasions that may call him away after his watch is set, and he that is his deputy may commit the offence—knowing not what truly belongs to his office or place—and if sometimes they let a drunkard escape without going to prison, it is a thousand to one but they that conduct him to his lodging will have the housekeeper pass his word for his coming forth in the morning to answer what shall be laid to his charge before the Justice. And I think a tester or a shilling is well bestowed upon them for such a courtesy. Again, if they chance to let any unruly gallant pass, it is either upon his submission to the constable or his deputy, or else he must allege some firm and constant reason what the occasion is of his being so late out of his lodging. And though there are many men hurt in the watch, the fault lies most of all in themselves and not in the watchmen, for when a company of gallants come from some tavern, or worse place, high gone in wine, and will not render an account of their walking at such an untimely season, but draw their swords and fall to hacking them, therefore they are bound first of all by the King's law to apprehend them, and secondly by the law of nature to defend themselves, and rather offend then to be offended. Thus have I answered your objections, desiring to draw to an end, for this is a subject I have no firm or solid ground to work on. If constables, beadles and watchmen, are conscious or guilty of these objections I have defended, I desire they may amend and correct them and give no occasion to have any pen busy itself in describing the abuses. Thus have I set forth in order the four arms that pay tribute to the ocean the Counter. Now will I come to the Counter itself."

CHAPTER 8.

Containing : 1. A resemblance between the sea and the Counter ; 2. With the true nature and conditions of such as live in it.

" Now I have crossed the arms of this main ocean the Counter, I will sail in the ocean itself. And well may the Counter hold similitude with the sea ; for as the sea is oftentimes disturbed with storms, gusts and tempests, so is the Counter with continual storms of grief, gusts of sorrow, and tempests of tribulation, which are continually beating upon the head and heart of many a poor prisoner. The sea, as philosophers hold, is ruled by the moon, and, according to the nature of her four quarters, she doth ebb and flow, rise or fall. So is the Counter maintained by the Law and the four Terms, and, according to their nature and property, it is full and empty. The sea hath many fearful and hideous monsters in it ; so hath the Counter an abundance of sergeants. In the sea the great ones eat up the little ones ; so in the Counter the jailers and officers feed upon the poor prisoners. In the sea there are many rocks and quicksands ; so in the Counter is the book where many poor men pay their fees, and the paper-house where he hath his discharge : in the sea there are many ships cast away by wracks and tempests, so in the Counter are many men, by extortion and cruel creditors. And, lastly, as in a storm at sea a brave ship royal-well manned, that hath store of skilful mariners and a good pilot, may ride out the fury and rage of the tempest, when a poor, rotten, weather-beaten pink, destitute of anchor, sails, munition, men, and skilful pilots, is soon drowned. So in the Counter, in the most horridest wrack of affliction, a rich man, well-friended, well-moneyed (his chiefest pilot), may make way through the fearfullest storm of adversity, and come again to the port and haven of Liberty ; while the poor man, destitute of friends and money, is soon cast away in a small brunt and shock of adversity. But now to the matter.

" In Noah's ark there were some of all sort of creatures ; so in the Counter, some of all kind of people, for to say the right of it, it is a commonwealth, though very little wealth be common there. There lies your right worshipful poor knight, your worshipful beggarly esquire, your distressed gentleman, your mechanic tradesman, your prating pettifogger, and juggling (*liars*, I would say) lawyers—all these, like so many beasts in a wilderness, desire to prey one upon the other, for I think there are as many sins looking through the grates of a prison as there are walking through the gates of a city. For though we are all prisoners, yet the causes of our restraint are divers. Some are in for debt ; some for other more heinous and criminal actions. Some there are that are in upon constraint, and such are they that come in for debt and can no way shun what they suffer, or have no means to give satisfaction to their creditors. Others there are that are voluntary and such are they that come in of purpose, who, if it please themselves may keep themselves out ; of which I find four kind of people, that are good subjects to this commonwealth the Counter, and they are these : the first, your subtle citizen ; the second, your riotous unthrift ; the third, your politic highwayman ; and the fourth and last, your crafty mechanic.

" The first of these is the firmest leg the body of this commonwealth doth stand upon, for after he hath been a tradesman some five or six years or longer, having borne up his head as high as his neighbours, hath had good credit on the Exchange among the merchants and continually paying them at the day appointed, may if it please him (having kept his word so faithfully with them) have what goods he pleaseth at half a year or year's day of payment. At last, when he finds his best opportunity, what doth he, but gets five hundred pounds' worth of wares of one merchant, as much more of another, and so runs over all those he hath had doings with ; and, when he hath got the quantity of four or five thousand pounds' worth of goods into his hands, a month or six weeks before the day of payment, my citizen in private sells all these commodities by wholesale for ready money at the best rate, and having all this cash in his purse straight flies into the country among his friends, and lies there perhaps a summer together for his own pleasure ; and when he hears of any writs that are out for him, returns again to the City, and lies close, making none acquainted with his lodging but some man he knows will break before the next quarter, and employs this party to go to his creditors to certify them of the misery he is in, and that, by trusting young gentlemen, he hath undone himself, desiring them to be good to him, protesting that they shall have all that is left

among them if they will be content to let him walk the streets quietly
to use some means to raise his fortunes once again. His creditors,
perhaps, gives his friends good words, telling him they will not be rough
with him, hoping with this bait to catch my citizen abroad and so clap
him up ; which my bankrupt little cares for, knowing that, after he hath
lain in prison a year or two, they will be glad to take a quarter of their
debts and let him out. What cares he for actions, executions, judgments,
statutes, or any other writs ! He hath enough to keep himself in prison,
and will make them come to composition with him as he list himself,
or they get none at all. So his creditors at last, seeing his resolution
so fixed and settled, will, though very loath, take one quarter of their
debts rather than lose all—and, it may be, not half of that in money,
but young gentlemen's bonds, and desperate debts that God knows
whether they shall ever recover one penny. Thus do many bankrupts
lie in divers prisons about this town, enriching themselves ; and by their
policy are good for nothing but to defraud his Majesty's subjects, and
fatten a loathsome prison. And this is the first of these voluntary
soldiers.

" The second of these are such that will compound with a brace of
sergeants to arrest them—and such are many young gentlemen that
want money to supply some vicious use or other—knowing they have
kind friends, will voluntarily have an action entered against them and
be arrested ; so perhaps will lie there a day or two, while their friends
hear of it, who, if it be but a matter of four or five pound, will not stick
to discharge it ; which being no sooner done but straight they go to the
party to whom the money was paid and there give the sergeant an angel,
and share the rest among themselves. Many tricks of this kind have I
seen put in practice since I came hither. But one thing I will not forget,
which was this. One of these fellows that had used this trick three or
four several times, and been fetched out by his friends for several sums
of money, did once more put it in practice, which his friends at last
perceiving, let him lie there some two or three years together—and
the most part of his imprisonment was in the Hole—and if at last he had
not got off clear by his own industry he might have been a prisoner
there while this time, for all them. How say you, sir ? Was not this
a pretty trick ? "

" Yes, faith, sir," said I. " I would all such voluntary prisoners
might be served so ; but, good sir, to the third of these voluntaries."

" The third sort of these are such that having been in prison, and
lying in the Hole, have been released by legacies ; but being freed,

and feeling the sweetness of it, will purposely once a year (as about Christmas or Easter, when they know legacies come in), get some friend of theirs to arrest them for a matter of thirty or forty shillings, and then make suit to the merchants that yearly come and release prisoners, if their debts be not above that value ; which if they get, they have so much money clear to be merry with. These base tricks are usual, though they be not looked into or corrected, for it is an extreme wrong, first to the party that gives it, in cheating of him, and, secondly, in defrauding other poor prisoners that lie in for due debts.

" The fourth and last sort of these are young gallants that now and then will make a step to Newmarket Heath or some such place, and after they have that they long looked for, come posting to London, and if the hues and cries come too hotly after them, instantly get themselves arrested into one of the Counters, and lie there while the matter cools. For who will look into such a place for any such offenders ? Thus have I laid down in my best method the nature of these voluntary prisoners that fatten this commonwealth the Counter."

" Sir," said I, " these reports strike me into amazement. I protest I thought there could not have been such villainy extant in a realm, much less in a prison. But I hope, sir, you are come to treat of the keepers."

" I am, sir," said he ; and thus began.

CHAPTER 9.

Containing :   1. A character of a jailer.   2. Their true nature and disposition.   3. Their cruelty and extortion.   And fourthly and lastly, such abuses that have been discovered, lively displayed.

" DARE you write ? "

" Why not ? My door is shut. They that pinch me see not how I pinch them."

" But when your discourse comes out the keeper will hold you in the faster."

" Tush, my book must help me out. I hope to see Paul's Church-yard as soon as it. If I do not, the worst censure that can pass will be a railer against a jailer. Bold Muse, hold on thy pace."

" If the world is a body, then I cannot be persuaded but jailers and keepers of prisons are the nails of it, for they scratch exceedingly, and like sick men possessed with lunacy snatch at anything. These kind of fellows are as nigh akin to sergeants as brokers are to usurers. Both of them are inseparable purse-leeches, and are men that, having run through their trades as they have their estates, at last are forced to take upon them this most base and odious kind of life; which they no sooner have obtained but are as proud of it as a lousy prisoner of a fresh suit, or a beggarly rhymer of twelvepenny dole when he oweth ninepence for ale. They are men that have no quality in them but one, and that is to ask money, and, like lawyers, without their fees will do nothing. They imitate ravens, kites and crows, that feed upon the corruption, stinking garbage, and guts of any carrion lying in the fields, and leave that part that is most wholesome untouched; so these feed upon the follies and vices of the age, and have nothing to do with anything that is good. If a gentleman come into their confines, that hath his purse well lined with crowns they will have no more mercy over him than a dog-killer hath over a diseased cur in the plague time. Which makes me call to mind that motto I have often seen and read, *homo homini lupus*, man is to man a wolf. If a man should travel into the wilderness or some vast desert, and be devoured by some bear, or boar, or suchlike savage creature, it were but their kind to do so, being pricked and stung with hunger. But for one man like a cannibal to feed upon the other, what more monstrous and worse than cruelty is this, which every day is seen in this place! Yet in their cruelty they will use deliberation, and feed upon a man while he hath money, and make as dainty of him as a Spaniard will of a piece of beef or mutton, and make many sweet meals of him; or, like some cruel surgeons, that have a rich man in cure of some dangerous disease, will not at first send him to purge in another air, but let him by lingering, and, as they call them with their compounding plasters make him smart while they have got more money from him; and, while they have drawn his life to the last thread, and think there is no more to be got out of him, straight post him to his grave; so jailers when a man's money is spent turn him into the Hole."

"Sir," said I, "I have seen some of their doings since I came hither, and have admired they should be so hardened that their hearts cannot be mollified with the oil of compassion, no, nor cut with the diamond of compunction, or that they have no sense or feeling of their own inhumanity and hard-heartedness, nor once think that God may one day make them in as wretched a plight as those they thus tyrannize over."

" Sir," said he, " you shall seldom see a butcher's dog that continually lies in the shambles without a bloody mouth, and those officers that live in this place, having once their finger dipped in the blood-bowl of cruelty, seldom or never can be reduced to a milder kind of usage. Custom is a second nature with them, and because they daily do it, they think it is as natural with them as their meat and drink.

" But I will leave their strict dealing with old prisoners while another time, and come to their usage and behaviour to new-come prisoners at their first entrance.

·" At the first entrance of any man into this Daedalean labyrinth, after they have viewed him and know his name, then according to the fashion of his clothes, but most especially the weight of his purse, they bear themselves towards him. Flies never come to painted gallipots for their gay outsides, but their sweet insides, as suckets, sugars, and other preserves ; so these rather respect the purse than the person ; for they had rather know he hath a silver inside than see him to have a golden outside. If they know he hath good friends that will not see him want, or that he hath means of his own correspondent to their expectation, they will fawn and flatter him in every respect, more than a funeral sermon will a dead man. He shall want nothing while he wants not money ; every officer will have a cap and a knee for him ; every time they see him, he shall command all the house be *Dominus factotum* ; what abuse soever he offers, shall be smothered, suffering him to do any wrong, yet take none, when a poor man for the least offence shall be clapped into irons, and cast into the Hole, and there shall remain while such time he submits himself in all humility to Master Keeper.

" If they see a young novice come in, who liberally and freely will pay all the large fees of the house without much asking, and sometimes grease their perpetual dry palms with a tester or a shilling, he shall not only command their hats, but also their hearts. A covert parasite will not be more submiss[ive] to his best patron than these Counter spaniels will be before such profuse prodigals. But if a gentleman of a rectified and solid understanding chance to be arrested, and, being demanded the fees and garnish, stand upon interrogatories with them, asking them what warrant they can show for the taking of such money (being loath to cast away his money), they will instantly answer, it is a custom. A custom ! O heavens ! Is custom become law, and must it, because it is usual with them, be lawful for them to grind the faces of his Majesty's subjects, who will not for the most part stand and capitulate with them, but rather condescend to them, so they may get good usage of them, and when they are discharged never think of their abuse, but are glad they have got from them, and will rather leave their cruelty to be punished by God's hand than the Law's?

" I desire to know the reason, why, when a gentleman comes to the Master's side he must, before he is suffered to come into the dining room, pay twelvepence for turning the key, which not long since was but a groat. By what authority or warrant are they now to take two groats more than their due? Nay, indeed, why should they have any at all? Because I never read in any place in the statutes of England that such fees are due; therefore, having no warrant from thence, I admire they dare venture to take that which may turn to their undoing, if any informer should prosecute this extortion against them.

" Again, suppose a man pays the shilling is demanded of him by the porter, why should he pay for his bed the first night two shillings, which extortion is divided between the Chief Keeper and the chamberlain, his servant? They can yield none other reason but this, that it is a custom : and if they be hardly put to it, they will say that is the pleasure of the Sheriffs. On my conscience, they do belie their worshipful master ; for though they are masters of the house where prisoners are, yet they are not masters of their purses.* Besides, no man can be so ignorant and simple, to believe that they will devise laws of themselves, for which they have no warrant out of the statutes. Besides, the statutes of the Counter were wont five years since to hang in the yard, that every man might see what was due to the house and every officer ; but now they are cut down and buried in oblivion, that they may demand what they list, which they cannot justify, for if they could, they would, when they are put to it, stand to the virtue of their authority and office ; which not long since I saw tried, which ever since made me confidently believe that no such large fees, they usually take, are due to them.

" For a gentleman they afterward clapped into the Hole, because he plainly and boldly told them of their abuses, being arrested came into the Master's side, and being demanded his fees and garnish, which he very well had been acquainted with—because he often, by his own confession, had been a prisoner—told them there was none due and none he would pay. ' For,' said he, ' howsoever you may fetch over young gulls for their money, I will not be so soon caught. What I call for, I will make a shift to see discharged. Otherwise, I determine to pay nothing. And so resolve yourselves.'

" The chamberlain (the chiefest officer on that side) began to take

* Prisoners worse used than slaves, whose price appeareth written on their backs.

the repulse very heinously, and thought he would one way or other be even with him, making no account that he should lose his fees by him. Early the next morning, before the gentleman was up, came into his chamber, where he found him sleeping, and his cloak, the mark he shot at, lying on the table by him ; so took it up and went downstairs again. But when the gentleman was awake, and began to make himself ready, he found his cloak missing ; so that he began to enquire of his chamber-fellows if they saw it not ; but they denied it. At last he had intelligence that the chamberlain had got it for his fees. Upon this, he first went and demanded his cloak of him, who refused to deliver it, unless he would pay him his garnish. ' For,' quoth he, ' you have met with no fools.'—' No, faith,' said the gentleman, ' I rather think I am come among a crew of cunning knaves ; and unless you redeliver me my cloak again, I will make some of you appear so before yours and my betters.' And so forthwith sent his letter by a friend of his to the next Justice, demanding his warrant for the apprehending of such a fellow, naming of him, that the same night had robbed him, so laid flat felony to his charge. The Justice hearing the matter could do none other, seeing he purposed to swear against him, and, being for the King, granted him his warrant for the attaching of the same chamberlain, and to bring him before him to be examined. He, seeing how he was served with this warrant, would have given the gentleman his cloak again, which he refused. But at last by much persuasion he was entreated to take it again, if so be he might hear no more of the matter, and with all his heart forgave him all such fees he before demanded of him, and was glad he escaped so well. And that the world may know this is no fiction of mine own invention that I have related, I will tell the name of him that did this, who was one Mr. Vennard, that went by the name of England's Joy,[30] that afterward died here in misery, plagued by the keepers, being more guilty of his death than his cruel adversaries. For after he began to tell them of that they were loath to hear of, they thrust him into the Hole, being in winter, where, lying without a bed, he caught such an extreme cold in his legs that it was not long before he departed this life.

" Now I would know of them, if their fees had been due, why did they not stand to the maintaining of their due ; or if the Sheriffs did appoint such fees to be taken, why did they not appeal to him, and desire his aid in the matter ; and since that time why did they not procure of him that the articles might be hung up by the gate, that all prisoners, as soon as they are brought in upon an arrest or command, may read them, and not stand in contention, but pay what the right worshipful Sheriffs and Court of Aldermen think fit to be paid?

" That the extortion[s] of these jailers are extreme, look into the statutes of Henry the Sixth, where it was appointed by act of Parliament* that a jailer should take of any prisoner committed to ward but a groat. In this injunction there is not set down any due belonging to the door-keeper; there is no shilling mentioned for him; no two shillings for the chamberlain; no sixpence for the porter; or large fees for the book-keeper; but here is only mention made of a groat for the jailer, and no more. This is the injunction, after which follows the penalty, which is this (mentioned in the same statute):

And if any jailer shall anyways do contrary to this aforesaid ordinance, he shall lose to the party thus endamaged or grieved his treble damages, and forfeit forty pound at every time that any of them do contrary in any point of the same, whereof the Queen shall have one half to be employed only to the use of her house, and the party that will sue, the other half; only the Warden of the Fleet and of the Queen's Palace at Westminster for the time being, shall not be prejudiced by this ordinance in the duty of his office.[31]

" Thus you have heard the injunction and penalty of this statute, which was made in King Henry the Sixth's time, which were in force in Queen Elizabeth's time, and which now is of virtue and efficacy in our Sovereign James his time. For these statutes never since they were first made in the honourable house of Parliament were repealed. Therefore I admire they, knowing the statutes, will endanger themselves so much every day as to infringe this ordinance, by the breaking of which they reap an infinite gain yearly; for of so many thousands that come into their jurisdictions, they let none 'scape, but have five times more than this statute allows them, nay, sometimes ten times, nay, twenty times, more than they can answer. For I have seen some men pay ten groats for his fees at book; some ten shillings; some, a mark; some, twenty shillings. Nay, I have noted it, they have not been ashamed to ask forty shillings for his fees—besides garnish, and other charges which will amount to the matter of a noble or seven shillings if he lie here but one night, let him go the nighest way to work he can. Therefore I have many times wished a promotor at some of their backs to see their unconscionable dealing, that he might serve them out of the Exchequer with a *subpoena* for their horrible extortion; and make some of the worst of them (if there can be one worse than another) examples for the rest; for no jailer will stand to trial if he be wise, but will rather

* 23rd of his reign.

confess it, and plead guilty, which if he do, he confesseth his extortion ; but if he be so valiant as to stand to a justification, he hath no warrant to exceed his limitation.   Therefore whether he pleads guilty, or stands to his justification, he cannot choose but show himself an extorter, as one Carman*, that lay in the Counter of the Poultry two or three year, had like to prove one of his keepers, if he had stood to the trial, but he was glad to compound with him and give him a piece of money to let his suit fall, which if many other prisoners would take example by this fellow, and call their good doings in question, it would be a great ease to many poor men's purses.   For what extreme extortion is it when a gentleman is brought in by the watch for some misdemeanour com- mitted, and stays but while the next morning, that must pay at least an angel before he be discharged !   He must pay twelvepence for turning the key at the Master's side door, two shillings to the chamberlain, twelvepence for his garnish for wine, tenpence for his dinner, whether he stay or no ; and when he comes to be discharged at the book, it will cost at least three shillings and sixpence more, besides sixpence for the book-keeper's pains, and sixpence for the porter.   But this abuse was once complained on by one that had been wronged in this nature, and my Lord Mayor sent word, and commanded that no man coming in by the watch should be received into the Master's side.   Yet within six or seven weeks after, they could not forget their old wont, but fell to it again, imitating the fox that was commanded by the lion, for killing many geese and hens, to go a pilgrimage for his sins, yet he could not choose but cast his eye on every flock of geese he saw grazing on every green he travelled through ; and at last, for all the lion's command, cast off his pilgrim's weed before he had gone half his journey, and fell to his old trade again.

" But they have other tricks as bad as these, which are as followeth : When a gentleman that hath been long resident in the Master's side, and hath paid all their demand there, and chanceth to be turned over to the Knight's Ward for want of means, he must be forced to pay all the fees over again, or else they will either pull his cloak from his back, or his hat from his head, and the steward of that ward will stand as peremptorily upon it as if it were confirmed to him by act of Parliament, or had it under all the Privy Councils' hands.   And if a gentleman stay there but one night, he must pay for his garnish sixteen pence, besides a groat for his lodging, and so much for his sheets ; and still he that

* *Carman* and *Bud*, secundo of the King in Michaelmas Term ; and *How* and *Bud*, quarto of the King in Trinity Term.[32]

receives it says, it is a custom, and that it is toward the buying of such things he wants. Why, if it be so I think every prisoner is of understanding sufficient to buy these things himself, and not to trust his money in other men's hands, and stand to their kindness for such things he shall want. But these are only tricks to get money. For I have seen them put to their nonplus, and dared by gentlemen that understood their dealings to pull their cloaks from their backs, telling them that there was no such exactions due. At which hot repulse they have been as calm as midnight. But if they meet with some raw young fellow that will swallow and digest such wrongs, they will triumph over him, and not let him pass, while they have made him open his purse and give them their demand.

" When a gentleman is upon his discharge, and hath given satisfaction for his executions, they must have fees for irons, three halfpence in the pound, besides the other fees. So that if a man were in a thousand or fifteen hundred pound execution, they will, if a man is so mad, have so many three halfpence ! But I think the keeper of one of the Counters that took such unlawful fees was forced to pay back again what he had received, with a thousand thanks, as soon as he perceived he had a *subpœna* was served upon him out of the Exchequer. Thus if some men would but take this order with them, and jerk them with such rods, they would learn a better and honester lesson.

" To mine own knowledge I saw a promotor that was arrested used more kindly and respect[ful]ly than a gentleman of five hundred pound a year. He had what in reason he called for in the cellar, and might have broth and meat out of the kitchen at any time whensoever he would call for it. But will any man think that this was in love to him ? No, it was in fear. For, not many years since, he had informed against them for extortion. Therefore, this considered, unless they knew themselves guilty of such faults they did suspect he would scent out, why should they stand so much in fear of him ? And if they had took nothing but their due, they might have let him gone, like an informing knave as he was, and scorn his worst of malice, for Truth is a brasen tower and will retort the shot of malice into their own faces that shoot them. Virtue is like a bed of camomile. The more it is trodden on, the more it flourisheth ; the more she is depressed the more she expresseth herself. What a strange thing is it when a man is arrested and puts himself to the Knight's Ward must pay a groat a night for his lodging, and a groat for every pair of sheets he lies in ! What conscience have they, to exact so much, when the best bed in that side is not worth a serving-man's yearly wages ! But I have heard their due is but twopence a night, if a man lie alone, and a penny a night if he have a bedfellow ; and that in the twopenny-ward, where they receive fourteen pence a week, their due is but seven-pence. Then what excessive gains is this in a year, when I have heard it credibly reported that within the circuit of one year there is committed and discharged, both upon command and arrest, at the least five thousand prisoners ! What might this amount to, besides their fees at the book and their garnishes ? But no more of this ! For if any keeper should eavesdrop us, and be witness of what I relate, I perpetually should be locked up into the Hole, or never have a good look of the well-favouredst of them all*. Therefore my pen shall sleep in silence, and reveal no more of their abuses, that lie hid from most men."

" Sir," said I, " I perceive you are either loath to proceed in your discourse, or else you grow weary with discoursing. Therefore I will give you some expansion and breathing time, and unfold unto you what I heard of others, since I came in, concerning them. And if in any point I err in the relation, I desire you to be my guide and put me into the right way, for I am loath to wrong them, though they wrong most men they have power over, but would have the body of my discourse stand upon the feet of truth.

" I have heard it reported, when any legacies[33] come into the house, towards the release of the poor people of the Hole, the keepers sometimes takes them into their hands, promising those that deliver them, that they shall be laid forth toward the discharge of the poor ; but, contrary to the will of the benefactor deceased, relieve not only the poor in the loathsome dungeon of the Hole, to whom it was solely given, but help those out with them that lie in the twopenny ward, because they owe them money for their lodging, and so, not for any good will to them, help them to a legacy, that they might be paid themselves out of it, or else they might lie there like the rest of their fellows. Thus they first wrong the charitable benefactors, that on their death-beds bequeath their bounty to the poor, and, lastly, the poor themselves, in depriving them of that which is due to them, in making them stay—it may be two months or a quarter of a year before they can be released—expecting other legacies, whenas half a score or more of them may die before they come in. Again, I have heard some murmur at their plots, in keeping men in by policy that have store of money, letting them not go before such time their money is almost spent ; and when their creditors come

* I hope my book shall meet with a printer that never married jailer's daughter.

to hear of them, will not ſtick to tell them that they have money enough
in their pockets, and that it was fit they should have their due before
they withdrew their actions ; yet when they see his coin begin to waſte,
will not ſtand out to persuade their adversaries to take pity of them,
and come to some reasonable composition : for what should they do
with them when they have no more cash—dealing with them as some
dainty lady will with a woodcock, cares not what becomes of the body,
when she hath eaten up his brains ; or as huntsmen do with foxes, fling
the carcase into some ditch or on some dunghill, after they have ſtripped
his skin over his ears. Besides these tricks I have heard that when a
young gentleman is arreſted, and hath competent allowance from his
friends (as weekly his diet and his lodging discharged), they continually
will certify his friends or his father of the leaſt misdemeanour he shall
commit—nay, rather than fail to relate all, will add more to it, to make
it more heinous, so that he might be incensed againſt his child, and ſtill
keep him in prison—which policy is only for this cause, that they might
ſtill have so good a gueſt as he is, knowing his friends will see such
things he calls for truly discharged.

" These things, say they, are common with them, and when a tradesman is arreſted upon several actions, they will give (being feed well)
intelligence to their adversaries whether they mean to put in bail or no
to them, or what they determine to get their release by, caring not what
becomes of the poor man, wife and children, so they themselves gain
but twelvepence. Some, say they, will not ſtick to take fees of dead
men, and scarce let the coffin go out of their gates before his friends hath
paid his fees. Therefore, if these reports be true, it is firſt moſt abominable for them to act, and moſt lamentable to hear. Therefore, good
sir, let me have your advice and opinion in this matter, and truly, without
any fallacy or equivocation, whether these things I lately was certified
of are true or no."

After a little pausing, he began to resolve me in this manner :

" Indeed sir, some of these devices I have found practised upon
myself, but for some others, that you have made mention of, I will not
boldly warrant to be true, but you have heard no more reported than I
have heard spoken. But this I can juſtify to be true, as a true token
and sign of their wolfish disposition, and ingluvious appetites, there
cannot a dish of meat come into the gates, but they muſt, and will, have
a share of it, nay, and think that the poor prisoners are much beholden
to them, that they are so much graced, or have so much favour, as to
have them partake with them. But if any man, hating their society,

will neither give them entertainment, or invite them to any piece of meat, he shall be sure to be locked up all that week that keeper waits, and do him some villainous mischief whensoever he conveniently can contrive it. Or, on the contrary, if any young novice that hath no execution against him, be pliant to their humour, they will use him with as great a respect as any nobleman's heir. If they see him profuse and riotous, they will not leave urging him to go abroad with them to take some composition with his creditors, when Heaven knows, it is not for any good they purpose to *him* but *themselves*. For they use him as anglers do the fish, give him a bait, but it is for his bane ; so these are kind, but it is for some benefit they expect from him, for they will never go abroad with any of these under two shillings or half a crown, if they stay but an hour with them. Besides, in what company soever they come in, and stay at dinner and supper, either at an ordinary or tavern, or any friend's house, they pay not a penny ! Thus do they persuade many a broad with them, that else would stay at home, I mean in prison, first that they might furnish their purses with money, and their bellies with good cheer, and bring them home at night, as bare of money as a sheep is of wool that all day long hath been feeding among bushes and briers.

" But suppose this man from whom they have received so much kindness as good diet, money and other favours, fall into want and distress, do you think they will relieve him ? No, they will let him lie and break his heart with his own sighs, wash his couch with his own tears, grind his teeth into powder, and make himself bread of it to eat, before they will relieve or help him, or, if by chance they *do* relieve any poor man (as it is very seldom), they will in a pharisaical ostentation report it to any friend that comes to visit him.

" I have seen an emblem, where the picture of Charity held in one hand loaves of bread, distributing it to the poor standing round about her, and in the other, a trumpet to report to the world her benevolence. Such are these jailers, that upon the least taste of friendship or kindness showed to a man, will be sure to have all the people in the house know of it, yet these courtesies come as seldom from them, as virgins out of Picthatch[34], or sound horses out of Smithfield.

" But for one good quality they have ten bad, and what injury or wrong soever they do a man he must not complain ; a rugged behaviour towards them prevails not. If a man rush through a quickset hedge in haste, he cannot choose but have his face scratched, whereas if he temperately did divide the bushes with his hands, he might go through without any hurt. When a poor man comes nigh a churlish mastiff he must not spurn at him if he mean to go quietly by him, but flatter and stroke him on the back, and spit in his mouth. So[35] prisoners, if they mean not to be pricked with a jailer's thorny disposition, must use him gently, or, if he will not be bitten with his currish and dogged usage, let him give fair words, and sometimes, if he be able, fling a sop or two into his gaping and all-devouring jaws.

" They do, as all the world else, more for money than merit, for I have seen a fellow come in with scarce a rag on his back, being some cheat or decoy, that hath been preferred to the Master's side, because the keepers knew they of his trade would fetch him out speedily, and pay all the fees. When, on the contrary, I have known a gentleman of good reputation whose behaviour and outward habiliments showed his desert, clapped up into a dark room, without any light, among half a score men ; and, if there were no spare bed for him to lie on, let him take up his lodging on the boards, which he must pay for before he and they part. Other men's miseries makes them merry, and the more prisoners they have committed, the more is their gain, for I have often heard them, when my Lord Mayor's officers have brought in bakers for making their bread an ounce or two too heavy,[36] whisper in their ears, telling them they have had but a few prisoners that week, which is an instigation to them to bring as many as they can possible. Besides, the book-keepers do not much stand upon it to give sometime a pint or a quart of wine to a beadle that he might not forget him the next night following, but wake the watchmen if they should chance to nod, so by that means might lose a night-walker.

" Their cruelty is as great as their policy, for I have heard since I have been a prisoner a poor sick man, that not half an hour before he died, called about midnight for water to quench his thirst, yet none of these hard-hearted keepers would rise to relieve him, but were deaf to his lamentable and sad complaints ; so that the poor soul before day took his leave of the world. But what comes all the dirt and dross to, they thus scrath and scrape together ? Most commonly to nothing, for what they are getting in three or four year, they may lose in an afternoon, so that it is as rare to see a rich jailer, as a drove of fat oxen in Spain. For sometimes when they go abroad with prisoners for twelvepence or eighteen pence gain, may loose them before they come in again, and so are forced to compound with their creditors. And that I may recreate your spirits (too much dulled I fear with my tedious discourse), I will tell you three or four pretty tricks three or four several prisoners served those keepers that went abroad with them.

" A poor man having been two or three winters in the Hole, and
a long time frost-bitten with calamity and want, desiring to free himself
because neither his friends nor his cruel adversaries would do so much
for him, came to a keeper desiring him to go abroad with him, telling
him he had a firm hope to make a small agreement with all his creditors.
For he was going to a friend of his to receive so much money—naming
the sum to him—as would release him.   And if he would take the pains
to go out with him he would, before he stepped one foot out of the gates,
give him content.   The keeper, that had as excellent a gift in taking
money as any leaking boat hath in taking water, vouchsafed to receive
his fees, and, to be short, went abroad with him.   The best part of the
day they spent in walking up and down the City from friend to friend,
yet they could not get so much as one sixpenny piece from any.   At
last, to prolong the time, the prisoner desired the keeper but to go with
him to one friend more, and there he made no doubt but to speed.
Well, away they go together, but they found no more money there than
they did at divers places they had been at before, so that they were
coming home again as empty of money as they went out.   For the
keeper would not stay a minute longer, when he saw there was *non
larjohn* to be had.   So he hastens his charge to go a little faster, that
they might be at home betimes.   ' Nay, faith,' said the prisoner, ' seeing
you have been so good as to stay out with me so long, I desire you to
do me that honest office as to go into a barber's shop, and stay while I
am trimmed, which I have not been this twelvemonth.   And to recom-
pense you for your pains, I will give you your shaving.'   The keeper
not refusing this courtesy, thinking to save a groat or sixpence in his
purse by the bargain, went with him into the next barber's shop they came
to, where the barber, after a cynical congratulation, bids them welcome,
and provides his chair and his napkins, his combs, and his scissors, his
balls and his sponges, and falls first about the prisoner's ears ; who,
being dispatched, gave him a tester and went to the window to put on
his band.   The keeper instantly upon his rising began to fall into his
room, and being set, fell a talking with the barber about what news he
heard in the City.   But they had not discoursed long, but Cutbeard
stopped his mouth with a washing-ball, desiring him to shut his lips
for fear the suds should come into his mouth, and to close his eyes,
for he was trimming him with a stinging-ball.   The keeper did so.
Now in this time the prisoner had made himself ready, slipped out of
doors, went quite away, and was never heard of again.   Now the barber
had no sooner took the basin from the keeper's chin, and was carrying

it to the window, but the keeper, admiring he could not hear his prisoner's tongue walk all this while, opened his eyes, venturing a smarting, to see whether the prisoner were in the shop or no, whom he no sooner missed, but up he ſtarts, runs out of doors bearing the barber over and over, that came with his razor in his hand to shave him, and ran into the ſtreets with the barber's cloths about his shoulders, with his chops all white with the froth and suds that hung about them, so that he looked like a boar that foamed at mouth, or a well-travelling horse, and in this order runs he madding up and down the ſtreet inquiring for his prisoner.   The barber follows him for his cloths, and money for his trimming ; while every man, woman, and child that met him gave him way, thinking he had newly broke out of Bedlam.   But my barber at laſt overtook him, laid hold on him, and got his cloths and his money of him before he would let him go.   And so my keeper was forced to turn back to the Counter without his prisoner, so that when all his fellows heard the conceit they almoſt laughed him out of countenance, besides the plague he was put to in compounding with the prisoner's adversaries.

" But in my conceit the beſt jeſt was of a fellow who was committed to the Counter for getting a wench with child, by a Juſtice, who sent this proviso to the keepers, that they should not permit him to go abroad until such time he had put in sufficient bail to discharge the parish of the burden.   Now the wench was not yet delivered, but looked every hour.   In the meantime this fellow made continual suit to go abroad to seek bail.   At laſt one of the book-keepers let him go to some of his friends, having for his keeper one of the messengers belonging to the house.   Now the prisoner being abroad and seeing his time and oppor-tunity, moſt nimbly and like an Irish footman betook himself to his heels, and ran quite away—I cannot say *clean* away, for he was in such a fright that a man might have smelt him a furlong.   But to conclude, the messenger went home to the Counter as like an ass as he went out, and brought home the sad tidings, which was as welcome to the book-keeper as a prisoner that had never a penny in his purse.   Well, to be short, the parish complained of the keeper's negligence, who laid the fault on the messenger's head.   At laſt it fortuned so, that the wench was brought abed.   But with what, in the name of God ?   By my troth, with two chopping boys ; which the Juſtice hearing of, to ease the parish of such a charge, sent for the book-keeper and the messenger, and made the book-keeper keep one of them, and the messenger the other. And this was their juſt and righteous doom.

S

" Thus with my beſt art and induſtry according to my promise I have compiled in as brief a method as I could the ſtate of the Counter's Commonwealth, rehearsing the beſt and chiefeſt subjeɕts belonging to it, as *subtle citizens, politic prodigals, villainous sergeants,* and *officious conſtables and beadles,* which are the four main pillars that support it. Then I discoursed to you of the nature of the place itself and the inhabitants, their extortion, and cruelty.   I could now relate to you the villainy of the messengers that are members of the same body, who inſtead of going to men's friends with letters which concerns their liberty or relief, will sit drinking in some ale-house, and negleɕt their business, which it may be is a perpetual undoing to the poor man.   I could display the abuses of drunken tapſters, that poison poor prisoners with their ſtinking sour beer, which they sell as dear as if it were as good as ever dyed any nose in grain.   For the moſt we have is, as you see, scarce a wine-pint for a penny ; and they will not suffer us to send for it out of doors, where we may have far better, and better measure ; but will break such bottles our friends send in, too, for our relief ; and will neither truſt us when we have no money, nor suffer us to send for it where we may be truſted, but serve us with drink that the worſt jailer among them will scorn to taſte of ; but when we are all locked up into our wards, will send for better out of doors, and will be drunk when many a poor soul is so dry that they are ready to choke.   I was entreated to have a jerk at the paper-house, which I could not be won to, because I know nothing in their office worthy of displaying ; for if I should express more than I know, both the wrong and disgrace would redound to myself ; therefore if there be any corruption or double dealing among them, I will leave it to their own consciences.   And thus will I leave of this discourse, desiring you, if you mean to put these observations in print I have delivered, not to nominate me, or reveal from whom you have had this discovery."

" Sir," said I, " I will be as close as an alderman's door at dinner-time.   Yet, good sir, let it not seem tedious or troublesome to you to acquaint me with one secret more, and I shall reſt your friend in the higheſt degree of love and affeɕtion, which is that you, though concisely, would express to me the nature of the Hole, what place it is, and what government they have there, for I have heard much of the authority among themselves."

At this he began to smile, telling me he was one of the chiefeſt in that place, and if it should be known that he revealed any of their secrets, he should not only have a fine put upon his head, but also

should be put out of share.   I, seeing his backwardness, drunk a cup of
sack to him, and at laſt, though very loath, he began to me once more
as followeth :

CHAPTER 10.

*Containing : 1. The misery of such as live in the Hole.   2. A resemblance
between Jerusalem and it.   3. An answer to certain objeƈtions.   4. A
resemblance between the Hole and a well-governed city.   5. The
authority of the ſteward and the twelve oldeſt prisoners.   6. Their
manner of sitting in council.   And, laſtly, their juſtice, law, and
equity.*

" He that would see the ſtrange miracles of God, let him take some long
voyage to sea, and he that would see the miseries of man, let him come
into this place the Hole, that ſtinks many men to death, and is to all
that live in it as the dog-days are to the world, a causer of diseases,
except a few whom I have seen so ſtout and tough (ſtink-proof, nay,
plague-proof I think), that no infeƈtion could pierce their hearts.
Jerusalem when it was sacked had not more calamities feeding upon
her heart than this place, and I think it was the true idea and shadow
of this loathsome dungeon we live in, for as there was pinching famine
in Jerusalem, so in this place there are many men that for want of
suſtenance utterly perish.   In Jerusalem there was sickness, so in this
place a man shall not look about him but some poor soul or other lies
groaning and labouring under the burthen of some dangerous disease ;
the child weeping over his dying father, the mother over her sick child ;
one friend over another, who can no sooner rise from him, but he is
ready to ſtumble over another in as miserable a plight as him he but
newly took his leave of.   So that if a man come thither he at firſt will
think himself in some churchyard that hath been fattened with some
great plague, for they lie together like so many graves.   In Jerusalem
the wars ruined millions of souls ; so in this place the continual war
that hard-hearted creditors make againſt the lives of their poor debtors
deſtroy many wretched and moſt miserable creatures.   And as in
Jerusalem a mother was forced through hunger to eat her own child
to save her own life, so in this place one man is ready to prey upon the
other, so that they walk up and down like so many ghoſts for want of
food to relieve them.   Laſtly in Jerusalem were inteſtine seditions,

so here innumerable assaults of our home-bred friends descended from
our own flesh [and fighting against us in our own clothes]."[37]

"But sir," said I, "I have heard it reported for truth that there are
many living in that place that go gentlemanlike, have money continually
in their purses, eat good meat, live as merrily as the best of the house.
If this be true it cannot choose but hinder them from such charity that
else would be sent unto them; for what need charitable benefactors
send them means, when so many of them go so neat and handsome;
for it is not given them to lay on their backs, but to put into their bellies,
for in such a place the coarsest garments are the best. Again, they say
there is a certain company of them that take what they list themselves
of what relief soever comes in, and the rest, as the poorest, have their
leavings. So then this is objected to be one of the chief causes that
there is such continual sickness, poverty and famine there. And, lastly,
that what means or money soever comes in to them, in the space of an
hour after will either in wine, beer or tobacco make themselves drunk
for the present time, which is the cause they fast a week after. Therefore, good sir, resolve me these doubts, and I shall cease to trouble you
any more."

He instantly condescended, and thus began to answer me:

"Sir," said he, "it is granted that there be some in this place that
go decent and handsome, but you must not be persuaded that they get
it from such charities as are sent in to them. Their own endeavours
and labours procures it them, and it may be some of them, as they have
lived like gentlemen abroad, so they would be glad to show themselves
still, though they be in prison. Besides, their friends sometimes
furnish them with such necessaries as are fit to keep them clean and
handsome. Again, whereas you say that there are some of them have
what they list, and leave what they dislike to the poor, is not to be credited,
for there is nothing that comes in, but the youngest hath as great a share
as the eldest, ay, as Master Steward himself. Therefore whosoever
informed you of this, spake it out of envy towards us. Yet we confess,
at Easter or Christmas, when any good legacy comes in, it is fittest that
those prisoners that have been of five or six years standing should have
the profit of it before such as have been there but two or three months;
and this breeds a mutiny many times among them, because the youngest
hath not that privilege the eldest ought to have. And lastly, whereas
you allege how riotous they live there when they have money, may be
very well denied; for they have no money delivered into their hands,
but into the steward's disposing, who carefully provides them such

necessaries as they want.   Only at Christmas and Easter or such times,
when the liberality of the City is more ample than at any other time of
the year else, they, though unwillingly, may fall into some error, being
kept from a full diet so long time as many of them are.   And now, sir,
I hope I have cleared your doubts.   Therefore now I will proceed to
the government of the place.

  " This little Hole is as a little city in a commonwealth ; for, as in
a city there are all kinds of officers, trades and vocations, so there is in
this place, as we may make a pretty resemblance between them.   Instead
of a Lord Mayor we have a Master Steward to oversee and correct all
such misdemeanours as shall arise.   He is a very upright man in his
dealings, though he stoop in his body.   But the weight of the office he
bears is the cause he bends, which is a great sign of humility.   And as
the City hath twelve companies that exceed all the rest for authority,
antiquity and riches, so hath this place twelve old prisoners that help
the Steward in his proceedings, who by the general voice of the house
rule and bear sway over all the rest.   And here as in a city is divine
service said every evening and morning.   Here as in a city is a commanding constable, that upon any misdemeanours offered by any man
either to the steward or the twelve, shall be bravely mounted and have
ten pounds with a purse, that the print of their justice shall stick upon
his buttocks four-and-twenty hours after.   And, lastly, as in a city
there is all kinds of trades, so is there here ; for here you shall see a
cobbler sitting, mending old shoes, and singing as merrily as if he were
under a stall abroad.   Not far from him you shall see a tailor sit cross-
legged like a witch on his cushion, threatening the ruin of our fellow-
prisoners the Egyptian vermin.   In another place you may behold a
saddler, empanelling all his wits together how to patch this Scotch pad
handsomely, or mend the old gentlewoman's crupper, that was almost
burst in pieces.   You may have a physician here, that for a pottle of
sack will undertake to give you as good a medicine for melancholy as
any doctor will for five pound, and make you purge upward and downward as well as if you had taken down into your guts all the drugs in
Lothbury.   Besides, if you desire to be removed before a judge, you
shall have a tinker-like attorney not far distant from you, that in stopping
up one hole in a broken cause will make twenty before he hath made
an end, and at last will leave you in prison as bare of money as he himself is of honesty.   Here is your choleric cook, that will dress our meat,
when we can get any, as well as any greasy scullion in Fleet Lane or
Pie Corner.   And twenty more than these there are, which for brevity

sake I will leave out, because I would discourse unto you the majesty and state of these officers, when every Saturday at night they sit in counsel about their affairs, and thus it is :

"About the time that Bow bell summons the toast-and-butter eaters to shut up their shops, the council begin to flock together, and then the youngest man of the Twelve provides a broom and makes the little cockloft as clean as any citizen's wife's chamber in the town ; then spreads a green carpet on the board not much bigger than a horse's saddle-cloth, just before the place the Steward sits in ; and then takes three or four stoups in his hands and trudges down to the cellar, calling for the best liquor, telling Froth the Tapster that it is for Master Steward and the rest of his brethren, who gives them of the best, because they are his best customers. When he hath his full load of drink—I mean his *arms* and not his *head* full—away he goes to the council-chamber, not forgetting to carry with him half a dozen papers of tobacco. Having ascended the ladder in a most comely order, he places the cans on the table, and fills half a score pipes of tobacco. Thus having all things in readiness he requests the Steward and the rest of the Twelve to come up, who being ascended begin to suck out the brains of the barrels to add to their own, and light the pipes and let them go merrily round. The reason that they drink so much before they determine of any thing is this, that they may the easier cast up their reckonings ; and why they drink so much tobacco is, that if any man be brought before them for any abuse committed, they might smoke him soundly. When they have devoured all their drink and Trinidado, they sift and boult out what expenses they have been at that week, what pepper, salt, vinegar, faggots and candles they have spent, how many dozen of bread, sheep's gathers and barrels of four-shillings' beer they have had brought in that week. This business of moment despatched, the youngest of the privy council calls up all such as have had wrong done them any time that week, and prefers their bills of complaint up to the whole body of the council, or else are permitted to relate, but with all modesty and deliberation, the nature of the offence ; and so, producing their witnesses, shall without all partiality have the law pass upon the offender, who must either fine for the fault, or, if he be not worth so much, will make his posteriors pay for it. If any man be known to be a common drunkard he shall, if he be able, fine for it, or else his punishment shall be to go adry while he can get money to quench his thirst, or else must either drink water or choke. If any man steal any of his fellows' meat, if it be known, he shall fine for it ; but if he be not able, the Twelve will take such order with him that he gets not a penny loaf three days after. Whosoever forswears himself, if he be able, he shall fine for it ; if he be not, shall go and be damned as long as he stays in the house, and never have so much credit as run one penny on the tapster's score.

" Again, if they chance to fall together by the ears themselves about anything they enact, so that they beat the cans about each other's ears, they will not long bear envy in their hearts, but at the approach of the other half dozen quench that fire of debate, drink a health to some of their best benefactors, shake hands, be sworn friends, break up council for that night, and go to their beds—if they have any.

" Thus have I beguiled the time and, I fear, myself, in relating to you the true nature of the Hole, the misery of it, my defence to the slanderous objections, and the authority and justice of the Steward and the Twelve. Therefore I will touch one point more and draw to a conclusion. . . ."

But as he was going forward in his discourse the bell of the Master's side rang to dinner, and by this means we were both called up. So I promised him secrecy as he entreated me, made an end of our sack, put a small token of my love into his hand. So he went to his Hole, and I to my ward, but I no sooner was entered into my chamber, but with all expedition I took pen, ink and paper, writing what I could remember of his discourse, which I have made bold to publish to the world, hoping that those that read it will not think amiss of me for setting it forth ; for I doubt not but if it be seriously perused, it will give true content to them. So, remembering my best love and service to all those that affect me and my willing labours, I rest theirs to be commanded, and remain their poor and then imprisoned friend,

WILLIAM FENNOR.

Finis.

THE SONG OF A CONSTABLE:

Made by JAMES GYFFON, Constable of Albury, *Anno 1626.*

To the tune of *Jump to me, Cousin.*

I A CONSTABLE[1] have took mine oath,
   By which shall plain appear
The truth and nothing but the truth,
   Whos'ever my song will hear.
One Great Constable of England was,
   Another late should have been,[2]
But little ones now 'tis found will serve,
   So they be but honest men.
A constable must be honest and just,
   Have knowledge and good report,
And able to strain with body and brain,
   Else he is not fitting for't.

Some parish puts a constable on,
   Alas! without understanding,
Because they'd rule him when they have done,
   And have him at their commanding;
And if he commands the poor, they'll grutch,
   And twit him with partial blindness;
Again, and if he commands the rich,
   They'll threaten him with unkindness.
To charge or compel 'em he's busy, they'll tell 'im;
   In paying of rates they'll brawl;
Falls he but unto do that he should do,
   I'll warrant you displease them all.

Whip he the rogues, they'll rail and they'll curse,
   Soldiers as rude 'cause they are,
Sent to the treasurer with their pass,
   And may not beg everywhere.
If warrants do come, as often they do,
   For money, then he it demands;
To everyone with 's rate he does go
   Wherein they are levied by lands.
They'll say then, he gathers up money of others
   To put to use for increase;[3]
Else gathers it up to run away w'it:
   What terrible words be these!

Hearing a press for soldiers, they'll start,
  Else hide themselves when we come.4
Their wives then will say, " To press we ye may :
  Our husbands are not at home."
Coin for magazines, sent for in haste,
  Much ado was ere they yielded.
Yet's gathered and paid, and I am afraid
  They will not in haste be builded.5
The Justices will set us by the heels,
  If we do not as we should ;
Which if we perform, the townsmen will storm ;
  Some of them hang 's if they could.

The constable's warned to th' Sessions then :
  Unwilling some goes, alas !
Yet there may wit and experience learn,
  If that he be not an ass.
There shall he see the Justices set,
  Hear three of *Oyez'es*, and
Then shall he hear the Commission read,
  Though little he understand.
[Fo]ur free-landed men are called for in then,
  To be of the Great Inquest ;6
The chief of our towns with hoar on the crowns,
  That what should be done knows best.

Choice men of every town in the Shire,
  Three juries there must be more,7
Called unto the book with " Here, sir, here,"
  The wisest of twenty before.
Then there shall he see whom hath transgressed
  Punished for his offence ;
There shall he hear a number amerced
  Along of their negligence.
What things are amiss, what doings there is,
  Justices charge them enquire,
'Fore Clerk of the Peace, and bailies at least
  A dozen, besides the crier.

Verdicts must come from these juries then,
  But howsoe'er they indict them,
They'll not be took till next day at ten,
  Unless that their clerks do right them.
Rough words or smooth are all but in vain ;
  All courts of profit do savour ;
And though the case be never so plain,
  Yet kissing shall go by favour.
They'll punish the leastest, and favour the greatest,
  Nought may against *them* proceed ;
And who may dare speak 'gainst one that is great ?
  Law with a powder indeed !

Thus now my constableship's near done ;
  Mark, hearers, sayers and singers :
Not an officer under the sun,
  But does look through his fingers !
Yet where I see one willing to mend,
  Not prating nor making excuses,
Such a one, if I can, I'll befriend
  And punish the gross abuses.
My counsel now use, you that are to choose ;
  Put able men ever in place ;
For knaves and fools in authority do
  But themselves and their country disgrace.

FINIS.

NOTES TO THE TEXT

THE HIGHWAY TO THE SPITAL-HOUSE.

This poem in dialogue form is the best known original work of Robert Copland, who was described in 1547 as the " eldest printer in England." The little book is undated, but references to the statute concerning beggars of 1531 (p. 9) and to the false popery of proctors (p. 12) suggest that we may accept the date 1535-6 with a fair certainty. As Mr. J. M. Berdan has demonstrated (*Early Tudor Poetry*, chap. 3), the poem may be divided into two sections. The first part (to p. 13) deals in a realistic way with the types of applicant seeking relief at a London hospital—in all probability St. Bartholomew's. Copland presents to us the beggars and impostors whom he himself must have had dealings with in the course of his duties as watch,

> " when that we go about,
> Under the stalls, in porches, and in doors."

If Copland's inspiration is to be sought in the works of earlier writers, the closest resemblance to this first part will be found in Alexander Barclay's *Ship of Fools* (1509), a free adaptation of the *Narrenschiff* (1494) of Brandt, which describes a shipload of fools, classified in groups. The second half of the present poem is less vivid than the other, dealing as it does with various classes of unfortunates, who through their own foolishness or the wickedness of others sink from comfort to beggary. It is an instructive commentary on the social life of England at the time of the dissolution of the monasteries. Mr. Berdan points out the close similarity between this section and the earlier satirical poem, *Cock Lorel's Boat* (c. 1500), which catalogued the knaves and fools of the kingdom in a grotesque setting. Had it not been for the difficulties of modernizing the English of *Cock Lorel's Boat*, I should have included it in the present collection. The version of Copland's *Highway* here given follows the text of the copy, printed by the author, in the British Museum. Reprints have previously been made by E. V. Utterson in 1817 and W. C. Hazlitt in 1866.

[1] Vulg, Matt. iii, 3-8.

[2] The Barbican became later a quite respectable street ; the Spanish Ambassador was living there in 1618. Turnmill Street continued to have an evil reputation into Jacobean times (see p. 509, note 2). Houndsditch, once part of the city moat, was paved in 1503, and became a popular place of business for small dealers and vendors of second-hand clothes ; it was regarded as a dirty quarter. By the Fleet we are to understand the prison which stood on the east bank of the Fleet ditch and north of Ludgate Hill.

[3] The place-names are those of encounters and sieges in Henry the Eighth's campaign of 1513 in Flanders and Picardy—*twenty-two* years earlier !

[4] The act referred to is 22 Henry VIII, c. 12 (1531). Copland's failure to notice that the " valiant " mendicant and the idle person found begging without licence were also liable " to be tied to the end of a cart naked, and be beaten with whips . . . till his body be bloody by reason of such whipping," and to be sent to the place of birth or settlement, suggests that the full provisions of the act were not generally carried out.

[5] i.e., is still in force.

[6] It was already unlawful in Copland's time to practise medicine or surgery without a licence. The ordinary of the diocese was the licensor under 3 Henry VIII, c. 11. But 14-15 Henry VIII, c. 5 exempted physicians from ecclesiastical control ; those who were not qualified university graduates must get permission to practise from the London Society of Physicians.

[7] The activities of itinerant pardoners were already curtailed by the beggar's act of 1531 (22 Henry VIII, c. 12, § 4). The religious legislation of the Reformation Parliament (1529-36) stopped the efficacy of indulgences in England ; but licences to proctors to collect money for charitable purposes—with a proviso against the practices of the bishop of Rome—were issued during many years after this.

8 *sic* orig.

9 Vulg. Ecclesiaſticus xxiii. 12.

10 ? mixed.

11 The ship-maſter Cock Lorel, a famous character in Elizabethan rogue books, was, thinks *The Camb. Hiſt. Engl. Lit.*, " probably a historical personage." But no one has yet discovered any foundation for such a belief. The name simply means " chief rascal " (*lorel* and *losel* being the same thing). Cock Lorel firſt makes his bow in *Cock Lorel's Boat* (c. 1500)—see introductory note above—as the leader of a band of low-class characters drawn from the workshops and gutters of London, and sails the land of England through and through. He reappears from time to time in Tudor literature, always as a mythical anti-hero, leading great arrays of beggars and robbers, hatching conspiracies againſt the State, and entertaining the Devil to dinner. We shall meet him again in Awdeley's tract (p. 51), and as a rogue-captain, placed and dated, in *Martin Markall* (p. 42off). For further references consult Chandler, *Literature of Roguery*, 110, and J. M. Berdan, *Early Tudor Poetry*, 222-5.

A MANIFEST DETECTION OF DICE-PLAY.

This pamphlet is almoſt as important to the ſtudent of sixteenth century manners as it was in the creative development of Elizabethan rogue literature. Not only does it present to us an early and, to all appearances, genuine picture of the London cony-catcher who preyed upon the upper classes of society, with an account of the devices and tricks of the trade obviously founded on personal knowledge; it becomes a quarry from which the writers of the next generation draw their material. Robert Greene, who finds the temptation ſtrongeſt when writing *The Notable Discovery* (p. 119), is guilty of lifting whole passages, scarcely changing a word. Six years later an anonymous pamphlet, *Mihil Mumchance*, goes so much farther in this direction that it contributes nothing original at all, being in fact a copy of the *Detection* with a few slight alterations, and one omission—the ſtory of the misadventure with the surfling water—which may indicate a change in public taſte. *Mihil Mumchance* in its turn serves as a source-book for others. The descent of one passage, having its original in the *Detection* (p. 39), through three later rogue books is fully shown by Dr. Aydelotte (*Elizabethan Rogues*, App. B).

Four copies only of this exceedingly rare work are known to the *Short Title Catalogue* (24961). One of these, in the Bodleian Library, provides the text for the present version. There has been no opportunity of comparing this work with other copies, but it seems to be eſtablished that two editions, if not three, were issued about 1552. The Bodleian copy bears the printer's name, Abraham Veale, without date, and appears to be identical with that mentioned in J. O. Halliwell's preface to his Percy Society reprint (1850) of the Veale text. In the volume from which this came an apparently contemporary MS. note gave the authorship to Gilbert Walker, of whom nothing else is known. Richard Tottyl printed a dated edition in 1552 (Hazlitt, *Handbook*, 1867, p. 639), not 1532, as ſtated with confusing results by Lowndes' *Manual* (1834) and followed by Halliwell. The date of the Veale text is eſtablished in any case as about 1552 by the reference to James Ellis the pickpocket (p. 48), who perished in that year; but there may have been an earlier edition of 1544 or 1545, for the writer speaks of the taking of Boulogne (p. 31) as if it had juſt happened, and the campaign ſtill in progress. If this be so all copies have disappeared. Halliwell's reprint, itself rare, is spoilt by a number of misreadings of the original, but it has made a few obvious corrections, which I have adopted.

1 The campaign in France in 1544 was not a very successful one. Boulogne was captured in September after a siege of two months. At this point the conclusion of a separate peace with France by Henry's ally the Emperor forced the English to withdraw from the interior of Picardy and cancel plans for active military intervention. The present passage seems to refer to the events of the early autumn of 1544 and to have been written at this time.

2 No more is known about this pioneer than is ſtated in the text.

3 *Cheator* : this form, which is out of use at the present day, has been retained here to preserve the sense of the author's etymological argument. Elsewhere in the present text the uniform spelling *cheater*, one who plays falsely, is employed.

4 The meaning of this sentence is that these cheating fellows differ from other people in their behaviour, not so much in the choice of an object, as in the dissimilation practised in pursuing it.

⁵ *scil.* " of land."

⁶ The passages which follow on the dicing sharp's technique will become clear if the reader will consult the glossary under " dicing terms," and bear in mind certain essential points. The opposite numbers of a true die always total seven. There are three pairs of faces : cater-trey (3-4), sice-ace (6-1), cinque-deuce (5-2). A bias can be imparted to the die in various ways : (a) by giving it more than its due length along one dimension (*langret* or *barred* die) ; (b) by making it shorter along one dimension (*flat*) ; (c) by hollowing or weighting (*gourd* and *fullam*); (d) by attaching a bristle. *High men* and *low men* have one face, or more, falsely numbered. The procedure of the game of novem-quinque is described at some length. Here the advantage went to those who could avoid throwing 9 or 5 with two dice. With fair dice one of these totals would be thrown up on an average once in four throws. The cheat used *barred cater-treys* (longer in the 3-4 axis), a pair of which never threw up any but combinations of 1, 2, 5 and 6. Thus with these in play totals of 5 and 9 were impossible. Suspicion was allayed by " foisting in " from time to time a *flat cater-trey* in place of one of the *barred* dice. The temporary combination (one of *contraries*) would produce a total of 5 or 9 on an average every second cast. The cheat would stake little or nothing on such throws, but his victim would be deceived nevertheless into thinking that all was well with the dice.   The chief skill of the rogue consisted in hiding the dice which were waiting in reserve, holding them perhaps in the hollow between first finger and thumb, perhaps under the table where he would " let the true dice fall, ...   and so take up the false " (Ascham). Having mastered the sleight-of-hand he would still need to learn the signs by which he might know what his confederates were doing. In modern practice a sharp will recognise the peculiar falseness of a die by the presence of a small nick on one edge of it or by noticing that the numbers on the faces are not arranged in the conventional order. R.s' friends employed a less dangerous, if more elaborate, method of informing one another : they used certain recognised expressions in the flow of their professional patter to explain what men " were walking on the board," and those in the secret would throw or stake accordingly. But the " young scholar " of the craft did not learn everything ; for his master was careful to keep tricks in reserve which would break him should he fail in pliability. Much curious information on dicer's trickery will be found in J. N. Maskelyne's *Sharps and Flats* (1894). R. F. Foster, *Dice and Dominoes* (1901), pp. 13, 14, discusses scoring probabilities with high and low loaded dice.

⁷ Orig. reads " 10 " for " 9 ", but this is obviously a printer's error.

⁸ The author is evidently using words well-known to sharps ; he is not inventing ; nor does he employ terms loosely as a writer might have done who was only acquainted with Roger Ascham's catalogue of false dice (published in 1545): " I trow, if I should not lie, there is not half so much craft cursed in no one thing in the world as in this cursed thing. What false die use they ? As dice stopped with quicksilver and hairs, dice at a vantage, ' flats ', ' gourds ' to chop and change when they list ; . . . .   and, if they be true dice, what shift will they make to set the one of them with sliding, with cogging, with foisting, with quoiting as they call it ! . . . .   Now, sir, beside all these things, they have certain terms (as man would say) appropriate to their playing, whereby they will draw a man's money but pay none, which they call ' bars ', that surely he that knoweth them not may soon be debarred of all that he hath afore he learn them " (*Toxophilus*, ed. Giles, 1864, pp. 43, 44).

⁹ passage = Ital. *passa-dieci*, Fr. *passe-dix*, i.e. pass-ten. " Passage is a game at dice to be played at by two, and it is performed with three dice. The caster throws continually till he hath thrown doublets[two alike] under 10, and then he is out and loseth ; or doublets above 10, and then he *passeth* and wins " (C. Cotton, *Complete Gamester*, 1680, p. 119, qu. *N.E.D.*, s.v.) High men are dice which may have a high number substituted for a low on one or more faces. With two high men on the board the cheat could be certain of reaching doublets above 10. Two low men would presumably be foisted on the opponent.

¹⁰ i.e. the clothiers of the " west of England " cloth-making counties, Wilts, Gloucestershire, N. Somerset and Oxfordshire. At the time when this little book was written the west country was entering on the period of its greatest prosperity as the producing area of the finest heavy white cloth in Europe. The clothier, a typical figure in this industry, was the entrepreneur who financed the various stages of production and marketed the cloth in London.

¹¹ Of the cheating gamester's devices mentioned here, " pinching the cards privily with the nails " is a method which will have suggested itself to many players. " Playing upon the prick " may mean that the surface of a card was pricked beforehand with a pin. Five spots of ink are also mentioned. " Cutting by a bum card " was the finding of a card having

a slightly raised surface amongst the others when dividing the " pair " or pack.   " Cutting at the neck " eludes explanation, but may mean using a pack which of some of the cards had been trimmed or nicked at the edges.

[12] In Callot's etching, reproduced in *Elizabethan Rogues*, 89, by F. Aydelotte, this kind of cheating is depicted.

[13] i.e. handed over for arbitration.

[14] orig. " Jon ".

[15] For Greene's clever elaboration of this cony-catching device see pp. 123ff below.

[16] See note 2, p. 499.

[17] This is one of the earliest references to bear-baiting in Paris Garden.   It has been argued that this bear-garden was never farther west than the Liberty of the Clink, which stretched along Bankside between Paris Garden and London Bridge.   Whatever may have been the exact point occupied by the bear-pit in our author's time a favourite approach certainly led from the river up Paris Garden Stairs opposite the west end of St. Paul's ; hence perhaps the popular association of bears with Paris Garden.   Sir Edmund Chambers refers to an interesting passage in Foxe's *Book of Martyrs* which perhaps locates the baiting-place in 1539 (*Elizabethan Stage*, ii, 460).   See also *Review of English Studies*, I, 461.

[18] 30 April 1552—" the same day was sessions at Newgate for thieves, and a cutpurse specially was one James [Ellis], the great pickpurse and cutpurse that ever [was] arraigned, for there was never a prison and the Tower but he had been in them . . . . The 11 day of July hanged was James Ellis, the great pickpurse that ever was, and cutpurse, and seven more for theft, at Tyburn (*Machyn's Diary* 1550-63, pp. 18, 21, Camden Soc.).   Ellis' conviction in 1552 must have been the talk of the town, and the reference here helps to date the publication of the book.   (See Aydelotte, *Elizabethan Rogues*, 120).

[19] St. Thomas's Waterings, where the gallows were set up for the felons of Surrey (and elsewhere).   The site, which was beside the Kent Road, near the boundaries of Newington and Camberwell, was chosen for its purpose because past it must go the pilgrims to Canterbury and much of the ordinary traffic into Kent.   Chaucer's Prologue to the *Canterbury Tales* refers to the place but not to the gallows :

> " And forth we riden a litel more than pace,
> Unto the waterynge of seint Thomas,
> And there our ost bigan his hors areste."

THE FRATERNITY OF VAGABONDS.

This tract was probably first printed in 1561 by John Awdeley, who is usually regarded as the author.   It is a very slight little work, chiefly interesting by reason of its service as a kind of model for Harman's classic, *A Caveat for Common Cursitors* (p. 61), published a few years later.   Until Furnivall established its prior date *The Fraternity* was thought to be a pilfering from the *Caveat*, but apart from the evidence of the Stationers' Register, Harman's knowledge of, and debt to, Awdeley's work can be established by reference to the introduction to the *Caveat*.   Only the first and longer of the two sections of *The Fraternity* is here printed. We are given a short dictionary of country rogue types followed by three sketches describing the activities of their urban cousins.   In the second section, omitted because it departs altogether from reality, there are short descriptions under fanciful names of the knaves of the twenty-five orders mentioned on the title page.   The treatment is artificial.   A specimen may be offered :

" 11.   Green Winchard is he that when his hose is broken and hang out at his shoes, he will put them into his shoes again with a stick, but he will not amend them.   This is a slothful knave that had liefer go like a beggar than cleanly."

Furnivall issued reprints of Awdeley's tract for the Early English Text Society (1869) and the New Shakspere Society (1880), under the title *Rogues and Vagabonds of Shakspere's Youth*.   He uses the Bodleian Library text of 1575.   The present modernised version follows Furnivall's very reliable text with only a few slight modifications.

[1] See p. 492, note 11.

[2] Mr. O'Donoghue thinks that the name may be connected with the Abraham ward, a long gallery in Bethlehem Hospital with cells for twenty patients leading out of it (*Story of Bethlehem Hospital*, 142).

³ Harman (p. 93) denies the existence of Awdeley's jarkmen and patriarch coes as separate professional classes.

⁴ Apparently a gypsy word and a gypsy custom. See note 3 above and Aydelotte, *Elizabethan Rogues*, 19-20, citing Simson and Borrow.

⁵ Throughout the later Tudor period the aisles of St. Paul's were the most popular resort in London for the lounger and the man who was seeking a private or business acquaintance. It is here that the first episode of *The Manifest Detection* is set (p. 28). The cony-catchers of Greene's day wait here for their victims; respectable folk come here to do business, exchange news, examine the posters and bookstalls and hire servants; lovers keep appointments with their mistresses; and men in a hurry slip through from door to door to save a journey around the churchyard. John Earle in his *Micro-cosmography* (1628) thus characterises Paul's: " The whole world's map, which you may here discern in its perfectest motion, justling and turning; . . . and were the steeple not sanctified, nothing liker Babel. The noise in it is like that of bees, a strange hum, mixed of walking tongues and feet; it is a kind of still roar or loud whisper. It is a great exchange of all discourse, and no business whatsoever but is here striving and afoot. It is the synod of all parties politic, jointed and laid together, in most serious position, and they are not half so busy at the parliament. . . . It is the general mint of all famous lies . . . All inventions are emptied here, and not a few pockets ! The best sign of a temple in it is, that it is the thieves' sanctuary, which rob more safely in a crowd than in a wilderness " (qu. Milman, *Annals of St. Pauls*, 287-8). Elizabeth's Council tried to prohibit by proclamation the making of business agreements within the church, but failed to enforce the rule. On the activities of the public within the building see Kingsford's notes to his edition of Stow's *Survey*, 1908, ii, 316, 348-9.

⁶ In Awdeley's time Christ's Hospital was a new institution; it had been founded by Edward VI in 1552-3 on the site of the Greyfriars Monastery by Newgate Street, as a school for orphan children and others.

⁷ This reference to the Royal Exchange must have been inserted in the 1575 edition. The building had not been erected at the time the first was printing.

⁸ Here follows in original *The Twenty-five Orders of Rogues*.

A CAVEAT FOR COMMON CURSITORS.

Thomas Harman, the author, was a country magistrate with a house at Crayford near Dartford in Kent. Ill health prevented his taking an active part in the affairs of the county. Spending most of his time at home, he turned his disability to account by keeping close observation on the travellers upon the neighbouring highroad, the Watling Street of the old maps. Many of the pedlars and tramps passing through the locality called at his door for charity or advice. He interviewed them himself. Few appear to have left the house without imparting some bit of information which would go to swell the body of miscellaneous knowledge upon which Harman drew when writing his book. It became a survey of the moving population of the Kentish roads, and has proved to be the best sixteenth-century account of vagabondage and roguery. Harman has all the deftness of the trained sociologist; he compares, classifies, notes the significant detail; he keeps a record of individual names and activities; he draws a few obvious morals, and presents his work to the public that it may learn the lesson. The book was destined to become, not, as he might have hoped, a handbook for the magistrate, but a rich quarry to be plundered by subsequent writers on roguery. Nearly all the later tracts printed in this collection owe something to its stimulus, even where they do not borrow outright. Harman had no axe to grind in the composition of his work; his account may be accepted as genuine and in most particulars correct (see Aydelotte *Elizabethan Rogues*, 122-3, and App, A.5). The *Caveat* was first published in 1566, the second and third editions appeared early in 1568, the second being dated 8 Jan. 1567-8. The first edition is not known, but would seem to have contained less material than the later ones (see p. 67). The version here printed follows in the main the reprint made by Viles and Furnivall for the Early English Text Society, which employed the third edition, and which I have checked with the original in the British Museum. In a few places I have accepted alternative readings from the second and fourth (1573) editions, and have inserted in the text the later episodes in the story of Nicholas Jennings, *alias* Blunt, which are given in full only in the fourth edition. A discussion of the dates of the several issues will be found in Furnivall's introduction to *Rogues and Vagabonds of Shakspere's Youth* (E.E.T.S., 1869, New Shakspere Soc., 1880), p. iv, ff. These volumes also contain further material added by an unknown hand to a new edition of the *Caveat* called the *Groundwork of Cony-Catching* issued in 1592.

¹ The celebrated " Bess of Hardwick " who had once been a noted beauty. About the time of Harman's 1568 editions she was married for the fourth time, and became the second wife of George Talbot, sixth earl of Shrewsbury. She was a shrewd, hard-hearted woman and a bad wife. But Harman's picture of her as a careless giver, the fit subject for the remonstrances of a charity organisation society, is not altogether out of keeping with what we know of the character of this lady of great estates. See *D.N.B.* for mention of her alms-house at Derby.

² The small volume referred to appears to be Awdeley's *Fraternity of Vagabonds* (first edn. 1561).

³ 17 May, 1521.

⁴ At the funerals and marriage feasts of the gentry it was customary to allow all and sundry to flock in and partake of hospitality. When wealthy Jack Winchcomb married the daughter of the poor man of Aylesbury, " the wedding endured for ten days, to the great relief of the poor that dwelt all about " (T. Deloney, *Jack of Newbury*, chap. ii).

⁵ The pious hope was not destined to be fulfilled. Four years earlier the third gypsy act went on to the statute book, prescribing the penalty of death not only for those who were actually " Egyptians " or pretended to be such, but also for those found in the company of vagabonds calling themselves " Egyptians ".

⁶ See pp. 109-13.

⁷ See pp. 113-7.

⁸ He is referring to a criticism of the first edition of 1566. No copy of this exists. Dr. Aydelotte states that it was " dated Nov. 11, 1566 by Robert Burton (who evidently knew it well) in a manuscript note in his copy of the *The Bellman of London* now in the Bodleian."

⁹ The earliest use of the word *vagabond* noticed by the *New English Dictionary* occurs in 1404 in a letter preserved in the Cotton collection (printed in Ellis, *Original Letters*, ser. ii, vol. i, 37).

¹⁰ 27 Henry VIII, c. 25 § 3. " . . . all and every idle person and persons, rufflers calling themselves serving-men, . . . " etc.

¹¹ i.e. Bermondsey Street ; Barmesey or Barmesé being an old spelling (W. Rendle, *Old Southwark*, 277). The district referred to was one in which stolen goods, especially those made in metal and leather, could be disposed of ; for Southwark was a suburb of dealers and small workshops, which generally escaped the supervision of the authorities across the river. Kent Street retained its evil name for centuries, but rather as the haunt of disreputable people than as a place of industry. See below, p. 503, note 29.

¹² Irish beggars appear to have been as troublesome to the Tudor justice as they were to his successors at certain periods in the nineteenth century. References to them abound. In the beggars' act of 1572 (14 Eliz., c. 5, §§33-34) special provision was made for their re-transportation at the cost of the county which first received them. This had no noticeable effect. Thirteen years later " one of the chronic rebellions in Ireland swept a horde of [them] into Bridewell by way of Bristol " (O'Donoghue, *Bridewell Hospital*, 203). The corporation thought £10 well invested to get rid of them.

¹³ Cf. pp. 373-4, 377.

¹⁴ See note 17 below.

¹⁵ The hospital was contained in the old priory buildings of St. Mary of Bethlehem with-out Bishopsgate, founded in 1247 and coming under the protection of the City in the following century. By 1403 " it had already become an asylum, principally, though not exclusively, for the insane, and at that time there were six lunatics and three sick persons there " (*V.C.H.*, *London*, i, 496). Perhaps, as Stow suggests, the distraught people were transferred from an earlier asylum at Charing Cross, too near the palace for the king's comfort (*Survey*, ed. Kingsford, ii, 98). In 1546, on the petition of the City, the dissolved convent was handed over to it as a hospital, and in 1557 it was placed for administrative purposes under the control of the governors of Bridewell. They paid very little attention to their annex of Bedlam, and it remained throughout our period a foul place where the inmates supported life, if they could, between two open sewers. " It was so loathsomely and filthily kept that it was not fit for any man to come into " (Visitation of 1598, qu. O'Donoghue, *Bethlehem Hospital*, 144). A keeper had the place in farm. Some of the twenty inmates in 1598 were supported by their

parishes ; the others were private patients kept at a weekly charge of 1s. 4d. to 5s.   The less dangerous people wandered about the buildings and yards, and warmed themselves in winter at the kitchen fire ; refractory patients were chained up on beds of straw, and alternately humoured and thrashed

> " They must be used like children, pleased with toys,
> And anon whipped for their unruliness."
>
> *Honest Whore*, Pt. I, V, ii,

Privileged visitors would come to make sport of them, and members of the general public on paying for admission could stroll in and look round.   It is not easy to determine whether there ever were regular out-patients.   Certainly the Poor Toms and Abram-men described themselves as such, and showed medals, or marks branded in their skin (see p. 372) in earnest of their good faith.   But there is reason to believe that most of these wandering mad folk were impostors.   Some credit must, however, be given to John Aubrey, who, writing during the reign of Charles II, stated that " till the breaking out of the civil wars Tom o' Bedlam did travel about the country ; they had been poor distracted men, but had been put in Bedlam, where, recovering some soberness, they were licentiated to go a-begging, i.e., they had on their left arm an ampulla of tin about four inches long ; they could not get it off. . . .   Since the wars I do not remember to have seen any of them " (*Nat. Hist. of Wilts*. qu. Wheatley and Cunningham, *London Past and Present*, i, 276).

[16] The Stourton murder case, judging by the impression it made on the western country-side, caused considerable public excitement towards the end of Queen Mary's reign. Harman's readers would be familiar with the circumstances.   Charles Stourton, Baron Stourton, was brought to trial at Westminster Hall in February 1557 and convicted of the murder of William Hartgill and John Hartgill his son, who were close neighbours of his. The murder was foully conceived and cruelly carried out by Stourton's servants ; but there were extenuating circumstances ; for although Lord Stourton was a bully, the elder Hartgill was "a surly, dogged, cross fellow," who had been quarrelling with his neighbour over lands for some time.   In spite of certain obligations to the convicted nobleman under which the queen's government rested, the sentence of hanging was carried out at Salisbury on March 6, 1557.   Tradition has it that a silken cord was used.   (See Colt Hoare, *Modern Wilts*, Hundred of Mere, 1822, pp. 152-7 ; art. by Rev. J. E. Jackson in *Wilts. Archaeol. Mag.*, 1864, pp. 242-336).   The Stradling mentioned by Harman may well have told a true story, for he went under a common west-country surname.

[17] In 1551 one of these forged commissions came into the hands of the Lord Admiral, who was surprised to find what appeared to be his own signature upon it.   The Council had the two rogues put in the pillory (*Acts P.C., N.S.* iii, 389).   For particulars of the way in which the false seals were made see below p. 375.   The device of requiring members of the poorer classes to carry official papers when travelling dates back to the labour legislation of Richard II (12 Ric. II, c. 3 & 7).   In the Tudor period the system was elaborated, and supervision became stricter.   Licences must be obtained from the proper authority by proctors and others begging as representatives of a charity (p. 81), by discharged sailors and soldiers returning home (p. 373), by labourers proceeding to new employment, by vagabonds who have been whipped and are being returned to their home parish.   In the last case the existence of a passport would exempt the holder from further punishment.   Before the end of the century pedlars and other travelling salesmen found the law tightened around them ; letters of authorisation had become an essential part of their equipment.   Among the Lansdowne MSS. is a forged passport, with the aid of which a vagabond travelled from Cumberland to Somerset where he was apprehended ; it is reproduced in *Shakespeare's England*, ii, 488, and Aydelotte, *Elizabethan Rogues*, 41.   See also the honest specimens, *ibid*, App.A.9.

[18] It was from the borders of Shropshire and Cheshire that ninety vagabonds obtained their counterfeit licences, " whereof some were of the Great Seal of England ", in 1576. The authorship was traced to a certain Massie, a schoolmaster of Whitchurch, who was duly apprehended and dealt with by the Council (Acts P.C. ix, 304, 321, 341).   Some veiled references to manufacturers are made by the author of *O per se O* (p. 374-5).

[19] See note 8 above.

[20] The precinct of Whitefriars, to the south of Fleet Street and east of the Temple, was before the Reformation occupied by the church and buildings of the White Friars.   Stow reports that after the dissolution " in place of this friars' church be now fair houses builded, lodgings for noblemen and others " (*Survey*, ed. Kingsford, ii, 47).   The precinct retained its immunities from City jurisdiction.   In Harman's day it seems still to have been a rich

residential quarter. It was later to become a sanctuary for what Strype vaguely describes as a " loose kind of lodgers."

[21] There is, so far as I can discover, no extant record of the keeper's name at this time.

[22] An open space between Southwark and Lambeth ; they took their name from St. George's Church in Southwark.

[23] Newington was then an isolated village separated from Southwark by a stretch of fields. The cage mentioned was the village lock-up. Newington was regarded as a disorderly neighbourhood.

[24] For the various readings here see Furnivall's text (E.E.T.S., *Rogues and Vagabonds of Shakspere's Youth*, 1869 and 1880), 55.

[25] The remainder of the sentence is from the edition of 1573.

[26] The remainder of the chapter is from the edition of 1573, which continues the story in the light of further knowledge.

[27] The context does not make it clear whether this individual is the ward alderman's deputy, an official who does much of his chief's routine work, or the deputy-constable. We hear very little of deputy-constables in Tudor London. Probably the former is indicated.

[28] The disaster which befell Jennings is again referred to on pp. 117-8 and below. Of the jails mentioned in this paragraph, the Counters, besides being prisons for debtors, also served for the detention of misdemeanants awaiting a magistrate's decision ; the old palace of Bridewell was a receptacle for the scourings of the streets ; once the scene of state functions, it was handed over to the City by the king in 1553 after the preaching of an eloquent sermon by Bishop Ridley. Its use was part of an ambitious programme for the checking of abuses, and it was allocated as a house of correction and workhouse for the poor. It became the model for scores of buildings raised all over the country. By 1557 it was in working order, and the governors were beginning to set up crafts for the occupation and training of prisoners of the vagrant type. Whipping as well as compulsory labour was the common lot of the able-bodied entrant. The court-books give much information about procedure and the types of inmate during Elizabeth's reign. A volume which would give particulars of Nicholas Jennings' arrest in 1567 is unfortunately missing. See O'Donoghue, *Bridewell Hospital*, chap. xxi, where this and similar cases are mentioned.

[29] See above, p. 55.

[30] Le Havre.

[31] Not the famous inn in Thames Street to which belonged the original of this title. The author is here referring to a barn outside the walls.

[32] *Thistleworth* commonly did duty for Isleworth in the sixteenth century. See Furnivall's introduction to *Rogues and Vagabonds of Shakspere's Youth*, xxix-xxx, where also will be found conjectures as to others of the places mentioned in this paragraph.

[33] Northall is in Bucks ; Harman probably means Northolt.

[34] Probably Kidbrooke, as Furnivall suggests.

[35] Richard Hilton and Will Pettyt were probably gypsies (*Journal of Gypsy Lore Soc.*, 3rd ser., vii, 37-8.)

[36] A private war between the Earls of Desmond and Ormonde issued in a pitched battle at Affone in 1565.   The struggle created a great disturbance on the countryside of Munster. See note 12 above.

[37] This paragraph is omitted in the 1573 edition, the subject matter being fully dealt with on pp. 89-90 above.

[38] These verses are embellished with woodcuts in the original.

A NOTABLE DISCOVERY OF COZENAGE.

Robert Greene, poet, dramatist, story-teller and pamphleteer, appears to have been born at Norwich in the summer of 1558.   In 1592 at the age of 34 he died in London in extreme poverty ; a man with few friends, miserable at the thought of a life which his troublesome conscience described as ill-spent, as indeed it was if we are to believe half the accusations he makes against himself in his *Repentance*. In his travels abroad, undertaken between courses of study at Cambridge and Oxford, and in his later life in London, his inclinations led him into vicious companionship. " What durst not he utter with his tongue, or divulge with his pen, or countenance with his face ?   Or whom cared he for, but a careless crew of his own associates ?   . . .   Lo, a wild head, full of mad brain and a thousand crotchets ; a scholar, a discourser, a courtier, a ruffian, a gamester, a lover, a soldier, a traveller,   . . .

a cozener, a railer, a beggar, an omnigatherum, a gay nothing !" writes the spiteful Harvey (*Four Letters*, iii) ; and he remarks elsewhere, in support of accusations of moral turpitude, that Greene substituted for the wife he had deserted, the sister of a certain Cutting Ball, a ruffian whom he employed—" till he was intercepted at Tyburn "—to levy a crew of bravos as a precaution against arrest (*ibid*, ii). This is happily not a typical contemporary sketch ; yet neither Greene's behaviour nor his literary work was held in high esteem by his fellow craftsmen. He was, it seems, admired more for the quantity than the quality of his output ; there could be no denying that he had a genius for catching the favour of the public. The five pamphlets reprinted in this collection were written and published during the last year of the poet's life. They show the author's gift for effective vivid narration, his style at last purged of the euphuistic elegances which in his earlier prose romances impede the flow of the story. These brightly written tracts set a model for numerous imitators of Greene's work in the realistic school of the end of the century, and introduce the city rogue into the popular literature of the day. Greene's intentions in opening up this new field have been widely discussed. The pamphlets have generally been regarded as evidence of a sincere desire on the part of the author to emancipate himself from the evil career he was at no pains to avoid disclosing to the public, and as an earnest of his plans for a reformed life now to be devoted to the national service—" *Nascimur pro patria.*" Without doubt he was remorseful, and, in his own peculiar fashion, repentant. But doubts as to his sincerity arise when one watches with the development of the series into a journalistic success, the abandonment of the high moral tone of the opening introduction (itself partly cribbed from Gilbert Walker's *Manifest Detection* !), and the intrusion of short stories with the rogue always prominent as " anti-hero." Greene exploits all the devices of the preliminary announcement and the follow-up ; he deliberately excites the reader's interest by references to the threats made by members of the cony-catching fraternity as tract follows tract in the process of exposure ; and he is guilty at one stage (April, 1592) of producing an anonymous reply to his own attacks, a reply which he seems to hint, in advance of its appearance, is the work of a scholar employed by enemies to make an invective against him (p. 162). The problem of the authorship of the *Defence of Cony-catching* is discussed by J. C. Jordan in *Robert Greene*, 1915, Chap. iv. The reader will be able to form his own views upon the quality of disinterest after a perusal of the pamphlets themselves. A short note is provided for each title giving dates and bibliographical information. For full discussions see A. B. Grosart, *Life and Letters of Robert Greene*, M.A. (*Huth Library*), introd. vol., J. C. Jordan, *op. cit.*, and H. C. Hart in *N. and Q.*, ser. X, vols. iv and v. The present version of the *Notable Discovery* follows the text of the British Museum copy of the first edition printed by T. Nelson in 1591. Previous reprints have appeared in Grosart's collected edition (1881-6) and in the " Bodley Head Quartos " (1923, etc.). Mr. G. B. Harrison's excellent little editions of this and other pamphlets has been of the greatest help to me in the preparation of this volume.

[1] Referring to the *Manifest Detection of Dice-play*, 1552 (pp. 47-8). Greene would like his readers to believe that the account which follows has only been gained by diligent enquiry. But it will be observed that from this point to the end of the paragraph he actually uses Gilbert Walker's words, condensing here and there, and making now and again a verbal improvement. Rowlands in *Greene's Ghost haunting Cony-catchers* (1602) notices the set form the Barnard's Law has taken, and denies that the names or the practice mentioned here have ever existed.

[2] This is an instance of Greene's careless methods in copying from other writers. When Walker wrote these lines in 1552 (above p. 47), the overture, or expansion, of prices was a burning question. It was a case of sudden inflation following a depreciation of the coinage. There was no similar phenomenon in the forefront of discussion in 1591.

[3] Orig. reads, " What shall I *cut* ?" but this is obviously a mistake, for the verser has already cut off the top cards. The procedure is somewhat obscure. After the cards have been shuffled, the cony's " confederate " lifts off four or five cards from the pack and lays them down. He then transfers the remainder on top of them, thus completing the cut, whilst giving the cony a glimpse of the bottom card in the large pack. The cony calls the card which he has seen ; it is now fifth or sixth from the bottom. The opponent calls his choice. Greene omits to mention the manner in which the cards in the pack are now shown in turn. We get the impresssion that the pack is laid face downward and the cards turned over one by one ; but this is evidently a wrong notion, for it would give the opponent a ten to one chance of winning. The pack must have been laid on its back, and the cards lifted

off face upward.   A few minutes later, when the barnacle joins in a game, he wins by inserting the card of his choice between the cony's card and the face of the pack.

⁴ Cf. above p. 35.

⁵ See p. 509, note 2.

⁶ Cf. *Manifest Detection*, above p. 38 Greene again adopts a speech from Walker's book.

⁷ Evidently a jailer in Newgate.

⁸ His only reason is that he has no personal experience in the matter ; he could but paraphrase the *Manifest Detection* or *Mihil Mumchance*, and it is to be doubted whether he understood all the dicing expressions there employed.

⁹ *Si quis*, i.e. " if anyone—the commencement of advertisements put up in St. Paul's, etc., by persons seeking for employment " (Grosart).

¹⁰ Elizabeth put religious nonconformists and captured Spanish sailors in Bridewell. As early as 1591, if not before, it was also used as a prison of arrest for miscellaneous criminal charges.   After the turn of the century it was employed regularly as a common jail for prisoners arrested in the neighbourhood.   Thus in 1613 the sheriffs heard that some apprentices were giving a semi-private performance in the Whitefriars of a play called *The Hog hath lost his Pearl*, an attack on the mayor.   The sheriffs surprised them at it, " and carried some six or seven of them to perform the last act at Bridewell ; the rest are fled " (Pearsall Smith, *Sir H. Wotton*, ii, 13, qu. Chambers, *Eliz. Stage*, iii, 496).

¹¹ An information relating to adultery would bring the accused before one of the Courts Christian, and, besides involving possible excommunication, would necessitate vexatious waste of time and money.   Such a case coming within London jurisdiction would normally go to the bishop's consistory court, unless it arose in one of thirteen parishes under the direct control of the Archbishop, when the Dean of Arches, sitting in the Court of Peculiars at Bow Church, would hear it.   A threatening informer could extort a heavy bribe for his silence.   It was alleged that apparitors carried about with them blank processes *Quorum nomina*, signed or unsigned, with a place ready for the victim's name (Cotton's Articles for Exeter, pr. in W. P. M. Kennedy, *Elizabethan Episcopal Administration*, iii, 329).   The fees of proctors, apparitors, registrars, etc. had to be paid whether or no innocence was proved.

¹² i.e., she had been whipped.

¹²ᵃ The colliers acted as middlemen between the charcoal burners of Kent, Surrey, Herts, etc., and the London public, which used great quantities of wood coal for domestic purposes.

¹³ Bull was the Tyburn hangman at this time (1591).   Greene makes him brother-in-law to Laurence Pickering the foist.   Afterwards came Derrick, whose name occurs elsewhere in this collection.   Derrick's successors were Gregory and Richard Brandon, Dun, and Jack Ketch.

¹⁴ St. Mary Hill : running up from Billingsgate Wharf to Little Eastcheap.

¹⁵ i.e. of womankind.

THE SECOND PART OF CONY-CATCHING.

This must have reached the public within a few days of the appearance of *A Notable Discovery* if not simultaneously with it, for both were registered in December, 1591 and both published in 1591, though from different offices.   It is not unreasonable therefore to suppose that no interval passed between the composition of the first and the second tract.   Greene tries to persuade us that the first had already created a considerable impression before he got to work again, and that the professors of cony-catching are " greatly impoverished by the late edition of their secret villainies " (p. 159) ; but he is only trying to hoodwink a gullible public.   As a third instalment was entered on February 7, 1591/2 it is evident that he lost no time in exploiting a promising situation.   Dr. Grosart reprinted the first edition of the present tract (December, 1591).   The version here presented follows the text of the second edition (1592), a copy of which is in the Bodleian Library.   This edition is in part revised by Greene, and adds the " Tale of a Nip " (p. 153).   One story which was in the first edition is now omitted.   I refer to this in note 14 below.   The second edition was re-entitled *The Second and Last Part of Cony-catching*, but I have preserved the shorter title of the first edition to save confusion with *The Third and Last Part* (p. 179).

¹ *Quetries* orig.

² i.e. *A Notable Discovery* (p. 119).

³ See note 11 below.

⁴ *breake* orig.

⁵ Mithridate : an antidote against all poisons ; after Mithridates, king of Pontus, who successfully resisted every poison by prudent anticipation.

⁶ Ovid, *Metam.* i, 190.   Greene has *resecandum* in orig.

⁷ Elizabeth, the widow of Robert Baron Rich and mother-in-law of Penelope Rich, Sidney's Stella, died in December, 1591 and was buried at St. Gregory's by St. Paul's.

⁸ i.e. cancel the contract which bound an apprentice to his master.   No indenture of course existed in this case.

⁹ See previous note and p. 500, note 13.

¹⁰ The hue and cry would generally be called by a constable on an information given by an aggrieved person.   A justice's warrant would be sought.   Armed with this the constable could insist on the whole neighbourhood turning out, whether it were night or day, to help in the pursuit.   One's impression is that the hue and cry was valuable to the police authorities, rather because it gave them—especially constables—fuller powers of arrest, than because the participation of the public was of much assistance.   See Holdsworth, *Hist. of English Law*, iii, 599ff. ; Blackstone, *Commentaries*, iv, 293-4.   As late as 1735 legislation was passed to stimulate police officers in the performance of hue and cry, but by this time it was an old-fashioned remedy in London (P. Colquhoun, *Treatise on Police of Metropolis*, 1796, p. 218).

¹¹ The statute referred to is 31 Eliz., c. 12 (1588-9), which although it does not, as Greene suggests, make the buying of a stolen horse a felony, yet strictly enjoins that all purchases of horses at fairs and markets shall be certified before the toll-taker by the seller, who must produce a substantial witness to his own honesty and *bona fides*.   The owner of a stolen horse discovering it in the possession of another man who has bought it from the thief, can reclaim his beast within six months on handing over the purchase price.

¹² Grosart conjectures that a *shore* is "a slant stroke that reaches its mark by a curve." This would explain the difficulty, but it is questionable whether the word *shore* would bear this interpretation.   I have found no other use of it in this sense, and enquiry among present-day authorities on the game has only produced the information that the word, now almost obsolete, is applied to a rod for measuring the distance of the players' bowls from the jack. For a further description of the tricks of bowling-alley cheats see below p. 300.

¹³ The law sessions of the higher courts attracted large numbers of litigants and others from the provinces.   During the short period of the term, lodging-houses were full, and the ways leading to Westminster Hall packed with wide-eyed strangers.   The courts met four times in the year.   Sir Thomas Smith, writing early in Elizabeth's reign, says that Michaelmas Term lasted for five or six weeks from about October 8 ; Hilary, three weeks, starting a month after Christmas ; Easter, a little more than three weeks, beginning seventeen days after Easter ; Trinity, two weeks and a little over, from about the seventh day after Trinity Sunday (*De Republica Anglorum*, bk. ii, chap. 11).

¹⁴ The second edition, which furnishes the text, omits a cony-catching story occurring at this point in the first edition.   The narrative is similar to the tavern tale of *A Notable Discovery* (p. 137ff.), but the details are different, and the trick is described as having actually been played on an Exeter merchant.   He is cony-caught by an old acquaintance, whose associate plays the barnacle.   Greene then goes on to say : " Not long after this the cony chanced to come to my chamber to visit me for old acquaintance, where he found a book on cony-catching new come out of the press, which when he had smiled at for the strangeness of the title, at last began to read it, and there saw how simply he was made a cony and stripped of his crowns.   With that he fetched a great sigh, and said : ' Sir, if I had seen this book but two days since it had saved me nine pound in my purse.'   And then he rehearsed the whole of the discourse, how kindly he had been made a cony."   The author proceeds to argue that his cony-catchers are the lowest of the low, sparing not their best friends with their devices.   " The very nips . . . desire to smoke them, and have them in as great contempt as they themselves are despised of others. ' For,' say the nips, ' I disdain to use my occupation against any friend, or to draw a purse from him that I am familiarly acquainted with.' " (Grosart's *Greene*, x, 95-96).

¹⁵ Where a criminal could escape the death penalty by pleading benefit of clergy, he would prove his qualifications by reading a verse of the Bible, which was kept printed and at hand. As the test piece was usually the first verse of the fifty-first Psalm, a preliminary coaching provided the necessary equipment even for men who were quite unable to read, and the procedure was a mere farce.

¹⁶ See note 10 above.

[17] " All and every person and persons, whatsoever they be, being above the age of fourteen years, being hereafter set forth by this act of parliament to be rogues, vagabonds or sturdy beggars, . . . duly convict, . . . shall be adjudged to be grievously whipped and burnt through the gristle of his right ear with a hot iron of the compass of an inch about " (14 Eliz., c. 5, § 2, 1572). Branding-irons were kept in town jails, some with initial letters such as V and M to indicate the offence. The corporation of Fordwych paid the jailer a fee of 2s. for " burning ". W. Andrews in *Bygone Punishments* quotes an anonymous authority on the procedure at Lancaster at a somewhat later period. The " iron is attached to the back of the dock ; it consists of a long bolt with a wooden handle at one end and the letter M at the other. In close proximity are two iron loops for securing firmly the hand of the prisoner whilst the long piece of iron was heated red hot, so that the letter denoting ' malefactor ' could be impressed. The brander after doing his fiery task examined the hand, and, on a good impression being made on the brawny part running from the thumb, would turn to the judge and exclaim—' A fair mark, my Lord ! ' "

[18] This is probably a fiction. See my introductory note to *A Notable Discovery* (p. 498-9).

[19] The Royal Exchange in Lombard Street (built 1566-7), besides being a place of business for merchants, was also frequented by women of fashion who came there to buy toys and trifles.

[20] The bear-gardens were on the Southwark bank in the open space behind the houses lining the waterside, and at this time (1591-2) there seem to have been at least two places there at which bear-baiting enthusiasts were on certain days indulged. The actual positions occupied by the Hope Theatre and the other spots where animals were baited have been the subjects of a hot controversy into which I have not the courage to plunge. These and other questions relating to the sport are discussed at length by Sir Edmund Chambers (*Eliz. Stage*, ii, 448ff.). The whole area in question was a holiday place for London crowds, and being within the bounds of the Clink and Paris Garden liberties it sheltered actors, bear-wards and cony-catchers alike from the inquisitive interference of the City authorities. See above p. 494, note 17.

[21] Greene's law is not very sound on this point. He is evidently thinking of an act of 1566 (8 Eliz., c. 4), which left a thief free to plead benefit of clergy—and so not coming within " compass of life "—except when the theft is " from the person privily." The law knew no distinction between stolen goods on the person of the thief and on the ground or elsewhere. See Hawkins, *Pleas of the Crown*, ii, c. 33, s. 25.

[22] Felons taken to the place of execution would often be permitted, with halter round neck, to address the crowd from the cart's end, on the wickedness of their past deeds, and, if so disposed, to make a public repentance. Then the cart would be driven on.

[23] The Great Hall of Westminster is all that remains to-day of the buildings which once housed the central administration of the law. The Great Hall itself was used for some centuries as the place for trials, but, with the growing complexity of the central jurisdiction, it became impossible to find places for all the courts in one room. In Greene's day some of the queen's judges were accommodated in rooms to the west of Westminster Hall proper, the great structure of Richard II serving for three of the courts and as ante-room and lobby for litigants and their advisers. We hear much of the rows of booksellers' stalls along the walls, and the toy-dealers' and sempstresses' shops. There was a conflagration in the hall in 1621 when these caught fire. During term-time one came here to pick up gossip and to meet one's friends from the country ; young lawyers waited on the look-out for possible clients ; and all classes alike were preyed upon by a numerous band of shady characters, many of whom were hangers-on of officialdom. When the courts were in session a member of the public entering the north door of the hall would find the Common Pleas on the right— probably in a kind of bay—and, facing him, on either side of the great stairway leading up to St. Stephens, the King's Bench and the Chancery court. The courts of Requests and Exchequer were housed in the buildings to the west destroyed by fire in 1834. Reconstructions of the old plan will be found in Brayley and Britton, *Ancient Palace of Westminster* (1836), p. 464, and A. F. Pollard, *Evolution of Parliament* (2nd. edn.), p. 332.

[24] The best contemporary guide to this fair, which was held in the precinct of the old priory of St. Bartholomew, West Smithfield, is Ben Jonson's *Bartholomew Fair* (acted 1614). The saint's day was August 24. The fair began two days earlier and lasted for about a fortnight. Once important as a cloth fair, by 1591 its principal fame was that of an annual carnival, with all the delights of puppet shows, roast pork and sweetmeats, monster rarities and fortune-tellers. The fair was a happy hunting ground for pickpurses. " While we were

at the show, one of our company, Tobias Salander, doctor of physic, had his pocket picked of his purse with nine crowns *du soleil*, which without doubt was cleverly taken from him by an Englishman who always kept very close to him that the doctor did not in the least perceive it " (Paul Hentzner's *Itinerarium*, c. 1598, qu. Wheatley and Cunningham, *London Past and Present*, i, 112).

[25] See p. 508, note 11.

[26] Cf. the fictitious set of rules drawn up by Rid, pp. 421-2, and preamble to 8 Eliz., c. 4 (1566).

[27] An illustration of the way in which such cutpurses as were known to the authorities were sometimes made to pay for an associate's misdeeds is given by Luke Hutton, below p. 289.

[28] A large house in Bishopsgate opposite Bethlehem Hospital and within fifty yards of Houndsditch, where perhaps the meetings were actually held.

[29] Kent Street, Southwark, a rough quarter; it is now Tabard Street. It was " very long, but ill-built, chiefly inhabited by broom-men and mumpers [superior beggars] " (Strype's *Stow*, 1720, iv, 31).

[30] See p. 500, note 13.

[31] The *Three Tuns* in Newgate Market is mentioned also by Jonson. There were several inns of this name in London.

[32] A somewhat different version of this story is given by Greene in *The Third Part of Cony-catching* (p. 193).

[33] i.e., change.

[34] *adamant* : an occasional sixteenth century meaning, as here, is loadstone or magnet.

[35] In 1591, Moorfields, a stretch of marshy low ground north of the city wall, was still undrained and uncared for. In 1606-7 the fields were cleared, put in order, and laid out in walks. There are many allusions to the laundresses who bleached their washing here.

[36] A warrant to a jailer to keep a specified person in close custody until delivered by process of law.

THE THIRD AND LAST PART OF CONY-CATCHING.

Of this tract of Greene's only one edition is known. It was entered 7 February, 1592, scarcely two months after the first and second members of the series. Greene now frankly sets himself to please his readers with more stories of rogue behaviour, using only the transparent device of ascribing the authorship of the " notes " to an experienced magistrate, in order to connect the new book up with the rest of the series as part of a serious sociological investigation. The version here printed follows the text of the Bodleian Library copy.

[1] Whittington College was an alms-house founded under the will of Sir Richard Whittington (d. 1423), the hero of the legendary tale. Greene may here be referring, not to the college, but to the prison of Newgate, which also was erected on money set aside under the will of the Lord Mayor, on the site of the older gate-house which, " because it was feeble, over little, and so contagious of air that it caused the death of many men, was thrown down " (*Rot. Parl.*, iv, 370-371). Elsewhere Dekker also uses the name in the same sense.

[2] The two earlier tracts printed above.

[3] St. Laurence (Jury) Lane is meant. The party does not seem to have taken the shortest route to Finsbury Fields, which would have been through Moorgate and Moorfields to the present site of Finsbury Square, beyond which there were open fields and the famous windmills (see above, note 35). They went along Aldermanbury, through Cripplegate and into Fore Street.

[4] Orig., perhaps correctly, reads *owes*.

[5] Gracechurch Street.

[6] In his first brush with the magistrate the arrested person was certainly at a disadvantage. Two acts of Mary's reign (1 & 2 Phil. and Mary, c. 13 ; 2 & 3 Phil. and Mary, c. 10) revised the law in the favour of the prosecution by definitely permitting the justice of the peace to ally himself with the antagonists of the prisoner. He becomes an inquisitor as well as a judge. In fact, by interrogating witnesses and cross-examining the prisoner for the purpose of preparing a written proof of the offence at the preliminary examination, the Tudor justice becomes a party to the case ; and, that he may have every facility, he is entitled to take

statements from witnesses for the prosecution in the absence of the accused. Police officials do this kind of thing to-day, but they exercise a special rôle, which has been taken over from the magistrate ; and there are certain safeguards.

⁷ At the end of Ivy Bridge Lane ; it passed over a road running down to the river from the Strand.

⁸ See above p. 503, note 32.

⁹ One of the London inns turned into theatres in Elizabeth's reign ; used for plays and prizes (i.e. contests) at arms. See Chambers, *Eliz. Stage*, ii, 380-1 ; Malone Soc., *Collections*, I (i), 55ff.

¹⁰ A lane to the south of the cathedral running to Carter Lane. It got its name from a chain which was hung there to keep the open space free from traffic during service time.

A DISPUTATION BETWEEN A HE CONY-CATCHER AND A SHE CONY-CATCHER.

Greene's *Disputation* was written and published between February and August, 1592 ; it forms the fifth (or, if the *Defence of Cony-catching* be not accepted as his, the fourth) of the series of rogue books which began with the *Notable Discovery*. Probably the present tract came out in May, June or July, in any case before the appearance of the next, and last, of the series, *The Black Book's Messenger* (p. 248), which was entered on August 21—see the preliminary puff, p. 226. The *Disputation* is in two parts : the first treating of subjects already familiar to readers of the earlier tracts ; the second telling the story of the seduction and ruin of a girl of gentle breeding, and of her final redemption. Greene's ability in narration is demonstrated in his treatment of the last incidents in the story, and we can sense a deeper human understanding than the rest of his cony-catching books give evidence for. The text of the Bodleian Library copy of the *Disputation* was consulted in preparing the present version.

¹ Master Huggins is John Higgins, who in 1574 brought out a new edition of *The Mirror for Magistrates*—the first published in 1559 as a collection of nineteen legends in verse about famous characters in English history. Higgins added a new series of sixteen legends, of which the story of King Mempricius is one. The quotation is made from stanza 16 (Hazlewood's edn., 1815, i, 102).

² Possibly a misprint for *sirens*. Grosart suggests alternatively *hyena*, a beast fabulously endowed with a voice which allured and entrapped men and women.

³ Cf. p. 19.

⁴ Orig. *not*.

⁵ We are evidently intended to believe that this Laurence is none other than Laurence Pickering described in *The Second Part of Cony-catching* (p. 165) as " one that hath been, if he be not still, a notable foist. A man of good calling he is, and well allied, brother-in-law to Bull the hangman." At his house in Kent Street the association of pickpockets has its feasts and weekly meetings. Bull is again referred to in the present tract (p. 220) as the brother-in-law of Laurence, Nan's interlocutor. Does this complete the identification ? It may be objected that it does not ; for Nan's Laurence himself, in the story of the country farmer (p. 214) speaks of Pickering as of a third person. But this is probably Greene's carelessness ; the story was perhaps written at another time and inserted in the dialogue without correction.

⁶ In the Middle Temple : an obscure allusion.

⁷ " If the name ' Pierce Penilesse ' was the invention of Nashe—and I have failed to find an earlier example of it—it is evident that this is a reference to the book [of that name, by Nashe], which Greene probably saw in manuscript " (R. B. McKerrow in *Works of Nashe*, iv, 80).

⁸ i.e. the author's *Notable Discovery*.

⁹ See introductory note above.

¹⁰ The action for trespass was freely used when the real subject of the action was debt. By obtaining a writ of trespass the complainant could get his adversary arrested and held in restraint until trial came on in the King's Bench, when the complaint of trespass would be dropped, and the action for debt proceeded with.

¹¹ St. Paul's and its precincts still retained some claim to furnish protection from arrest ; but I do not know whether Greene is correct in saying that the sheriffs could not make arrests within the liberty. For general police purposes there can be no doubt that the Lord Mayor's writ did not run there. Of course an officer would be wise to hesitate before making an arrest in the cathedral building itself.

¹² *Clubs !* the cry with which London apprentices called their fellows to their aid in a street brawl.

¹³ See note 2, p. 509.

¹⁴ The bars were at the northern exit from West Smithfield to the unsavoury quarter round Turnbull Street, and, says Strype, they were " there set up for the severing of the City liberty from that of the county [of Middlesex]."

¹⁵ Hogsdon is our modern Hoxton. In Elizabethan times it was the Londoner's gateway into the country, and here holiday crowds would come to play in the fields and drink at the Pimlico tavern. Greene selects Hoxton because it had a special notoriety as the place of habitation of loose women. Cf. Gosson, *School of Abuse*, 1579 (Arber reprint, 1869, p. 37).

¹⁶ I can find no other reference to this inn. Lambeth Marsh as a district was not respectable. Stow seems to imply that there were a few dwellings there ; but the Marsh was for the most part swampy open country.

¹⁷ See introductory note above, and, for Bull, p. 500, note 13. R. G., of course, is Robert Greene.

¹⁸ *Ale Peria :* " an error for Alopecia, the medical name for sickness or mange, leading to baldness " (Grosart). Greene seems anxious to suggest to readers who know R. B.'s identity that whatever may be the accepted explanation of his indisposition, its real nature is such that it would be libellous to publish it without better proof.

¹⁹ Spilsby in Lincolnshire. The fair was held annually at Whitsuntide.

²⁰ Fowler must have been an officer of Bridewell. Whippings of prostitutes were frequent. They were carried out with great formality before members of the court of governors. At the time when Ned Ward was writing *The London Spy* (1698-1703) the prisoner was beaten at the whipping-post until the president's hammer fell. " Pray, good Sir Robert, knock ! " became a cry of derision when a woman of the streets went by.

²¹ See below, p. 519, note 17.

²² An obscure passage. The proper names that follow are probably references to taverns.

²³ The well of Dame Annis a Cleare was in Hoxton (see note 15) near Shoreditch, and was supposed to be the place where Annis, an alderman's wife, had drowned herself. See Sugden, *Topographical Dictionary*, p. 20, for references which suggest that the place had a certain notoriety.

²⁴ A tavern of great note which stood on the north side of the present Ludgate Hill.

²⁵ This incident may possibly have occurred, but it may equally well be an invention of Greene's. He never hesitates to magnify the resentment created among the cony-catchers by his revelations.

²⁶ Ovid, *Ars Amat.*, i, 99.

²⁷ *ibid.*, ii, 113, 114.

²⁸ *Ecclesiasticus*, xxvi, 13, 14.

²⁹ *ibid.*, xliii, 9-11.

³⁰ Orig. *her.*

³¹ *a* omitted.

³² Ovid, *Ars Amat.*, ii, 280.

THE BLACK BOOK'S MESSENGER.

This tract, the last in Greene's cony-catching series, was entered 21 August, 1592 under the title : *The Repentance of a Cony-catcher, with the life and death of [   ] Mourton and Ned Browne, two notable cony-catchers : the one lately executed at Tyburn, the other at Aix in France* (see Mr. G. B. Harrison's introduction in the *Bodley Head Quartos*, X, p. vii). Less than a fortnight later the author died. Presumably the tract had already appeared in print, or we should have had a reference somewhere in it to his death. His plans in regard to it had evidently undergone a change. Originally it was conceived as a considerable work, to be entitled *The Black Book,* and to contain exposures of the most revealing kind of the names and habits of London criminals (see above p. 226). One may be allowed to doubt whether Greene had the requisite knowledge ; for elsewhere he is mysteriously shy of giving intimate details concerning actual personages ; it was not delicacy that made him withhold confidences. His illness towards the end may have suggested the postponement of the larger work and the publication of *The Messenger* here reprinted. Even so the full promise of the entry in the Stationers' Register is not fulfilled ; only Ned Browne makes his appearance, and Mourton is reserved for a later tract. Whether *The Black Book* was ever written is uncertain. I am inclined to question its existence. Mr. Harrison, relying on a passage in Chettle's *Kind-hartes Dreame*, thinks that the MS. was in being at the time of Greene's death (*loc. cit.*, p. viii). The text here employed is that of the Bodleian Library copy.

[1] Marshal-men were employed under the Knight Marshal, the great disciplinary officer of the royal court ; their duties included the mastership of ceremonies and the keeping of good order about the palace and in processions (J. H. Round, *The King's Serjeants*, 86, 87). London also had its marshal-men under the City Marshal.

[2] Grosart's not altogether convincing comment : " As the daisy was the accepted emblem of dissembling, and as Greene so calls it in his *Quip*, this probably means, that fortune played him false and that he got into difficulties."

[3] A garden on the south side of Fenchurch Street, near the church of St. Katherine Coleman (Sugden, *Topog. Dict.*, 125).

[4] Probably refers to a famous series of plates engraved by Raimondi seventy years earlier and published with sixteen of Aretino's sonnets.

[5] Grosart conjectures : " famous courtezans."

[6] *sic.*

[7] Amasis II was king of Egypt from 570 to 526 B.C. The author gets the story from Herodotus, *History*, ii, 187.

[8] Statute merchants were contrived in the thirteenth century for the convenience of merchants who required security for debts due to them. In 1531-32 the privilege was extended to non-merchants. The borrower acknowledged his debt before a magistrate. If the sum due were not paid at the appointed day the lender could get judgment upon the borrower, have him thrown into prison until the amount was paid, and, after three months without satisfaction, secure possession of the lands and goods to recover his loss out of them. In the present case the borrower is a man of no substance ; he has no property to pledge, but he risks imprisonment, and will have to disappear before the six months is ended.

THE BLACK DOG OF NEWGATE.

Luke Hutton, who died a felon's death at York, appears to have combined the pursuits of highwayman and pamphleteer. Despite the interest taken in his career and trial, to which the ballad printed below (pp. 292-5) testifies, a very slight account indeed of his doings has come down to us. Although he belonged to the family which produced Matthew Hutton, Archbishop of York (1595-1606) his parentage is uncertain. Sir John Harington (*Additions to Godwin*) said that Luke was the archbishop's own son, and in this is supported by *Athenae Cantabrigienses* (1861, ii, 540-1), which remarks that the popular belief expressed by Harington was not questioned till more than fifty years after the archbishop's death, and suggests that Luke's name was intentionally left out of the family pedigree. Another possible claimant to the parental honour is Dr. Robert Hutton, brother of the archbishop, and a prebendary of Durham (Fuller, *Church Hist.*, ed. Brewer, 1845, v, 356). Two publications can with some probability be ascribed to Luke Hutton : (1) His *Repentance* (1595 ?), of which no printed copy is known. Ralph Thoresby, the antiquarian, had it in manuscript (Thoresby, *Vicaria Leodiensis*, 1724, p. 140). The title was entered in the Stationers' Register, 3 November, 1595 ; a passage relating to it in *The Black Dog* (see p. 266) clearly indicates that it had passed the press. (2) The present work (c. 1596) is written by one who knows London and its police system intimately. There is little reason to suppose that the author is any other person than the Yorkshire criminal, except that we should expect to have heard something of the highwayman's activities in the metropolis if he had had time to make a careful study of cony-catchers and magistrates there. The work may have been written in Newgate, if we are to read the author's remarks to Zawny (p. 291) as referring to the time of composition. In addition to the above-mentioned pamphlets there is (3) *Luke Hutton's Lamentation*, which follows the present reprint, being a ballad " which he wrote the day before his death." Condemned criminals do not write ballads on the eve of their execution. In any case, had Hutton written this confession it would have contained more exact information about his life. Evidently it was a fabrication. The date of entry in the Stationers' Register is 22 December, 1595. The entry might seem to throw doubt on the generally accepted date of Luke Hutton's death, which is three years later. The probable explanation is that Hutton was pardoned after conviction for a capital crime in 1595; and it may even be suggested that the dedication of *The Black Dog* (which appeared shortly after the *Lamentation*) to Chief Justice Popham was an act of gratitude for his intercession on the criminal's behalf. Hutton finally closed his career on the gallows at York for a robbery committed on St. Luke's Day, 1598. The present version of *The Black Dog* follows the text of the copy (without date) in the British Museum.

¹ Sir John Popham was Chief Justice of the King's Bench from 1592 to 1607, " a sound lawyer and severe judge." The story that when a child he was stolen by gypsies is now discredited; but there is no denying that, whether because he came from the lawless county of Somerset, or for some other reason, he earned a great reputation as the scourge of vagabonds and thieves. " The deserved death of some scores preserved the lives and livelihoods of more thousands; travellers owing their safety to this judge's severity many years after his death " (Fuller's *Worthies*, qu. Foss, *Judges of England*, vi, 184). Popham helped to draft the beggars' act of 1597 (39 Eliz., c. 4). He played a prominent part in the founding of Virginia, and desired to use part of it as a penal colony. Whether or not he succeeded in sending out a shipload of malefactors is uncertain.

² The author is using a trick invented by Robert Greene. He quickens the reader's interest by posing as a public-spirited man, cheerfully endangering his life in daring to disclose the secrets and identity of rogues. This device has an obvious value in giving an authentic stamp to the details of the exposure.

³ The 1638 edition, which appeared under the name of *The Discovery of a London Monster*, has some additional notes at the beginning. Three explanations are offered of the currency of the name Black Dog in Newgate jail (Sig. A. 4 verso and B. 1 recto): (1) " It was a walking spirit in the likeness of a black dog gliding up and down the streets a little before the time of execution, and in the night while the sessions continued; and his beginning thus: In the reign of King Henry the Third there happened such a famine throughout England, but especially in London, that many starved for want of food, by which means the prisoners in Newgate eat up one another alive, but commonly those that came newly in, and such as could make small resistance. Amongst many others cast in this den of misery, there was a certain scholar, brought thither upon suspicion of conjuring, and that he by charms and devilish witchcrafts had done much hurt to the king's subjects; which scholar, maugre his Devil's Furies, sprites and goblins, was by the famished prisoners eaten up, and deemed passing good meat. This being done, such an idle conceit possessed the minds of the poor prisoners, that they supposed nightly to see the scholar, in the shape of a black dog, walking up and down the prison, ready with his ravening jaws to tear out their bowels, . . . and withal they hourly heard, as they thought, strange groans and cries, as if it had been some creature in great pain and torments; whereupon such a nightly fear grew amongst them, that it turned to a frenzy, and from a frenzy to desperation, in which desperation they killed the keeper; and so many of them escaped forth, but yet whithersoever they came or went they imagined the black dog to follow, and by this means . . . the name of him began." (2) " A great black stone standing in the dungeon called Limbo, the place where the condemned prisoners be put after judgment, upon which they set a burning candle in the night, against which I have heard that a desperate condemned prisoner dashed out his brains." (3) " The Black Dog is a black conscience, haunting none but black-conditioned people, such as Newgate may challenge to be its guests. Yet this ragged cur has his several abidings, as in the bosoms of traitors, murderers, thieves, cutpurses, cony-catchers and such like." The Black Dog made two appearances under other auspices than Hutton's: (1) a ballad entitled *The Black Dog of Newgate's Lamentation for all his knavery* was entered 9 February, 1596 (was this a reprint of *Hutton's Lamentation* ?); (2) In 1602/3 the Earl of Worcester's Company bought a play in two parts called *The Black Dog of Newgate*, by Day, Hathaway, Smith, and another, of which the second part was produced in February, 1603. The text has not survived (Chambers, *Eliz. Stage*, ii, 227). No very reliable historical sketch of Newgate exists. Official records of one kind and another have been drawn upon by C. Gordon, *The Old Bailey and Newgate* (1902).

⁴ Orig. *now*.

⁵ If there was a big scandal at Newgate at this time (c. 1596) it is not on record. In 1582-3 complaints had been made about the malpractices of Crowther the jailer and his subordinates, but Crowther was able to defend himself (*Index to Remembrancia*).

⁶ The punctuation here hazarded may perhaps be rejected by those who feel bold enough to offer an explanation of the meaning. The line reads in the original : " Worlds euils, wracke then, sheepes cloth, Wolues pray concluding."

⁷ As general warrants mentioned no party by name, it was not unnatural that they were sometimes abused in the manner here described. Coke held that a justice was not empowered to issue a warrant to arrest on suspicion (4 *Inst.*, 176) ; but the practice was common enough, and generally condoned ; and, indeed, where the discretion of the arresting officer could be relied upon, it enlarged his powers in a very necessary manner.

⁸ Robert Greene died 3 September, 1592.

⁹ Terence.

¹⁰ There is a pun here. *Gallows* is an obsolete word in printers' usage which applies to the frame supporting the packing apparatus on an old press.

¹¹ *Coronation Day* in Elizabeth's reign usually means Accession Day—17 November. It was an almost annual occasion from the middle of the reign onwards for joustings in the Tiltyard in Whitehall (see Chambers, *Eliz. Stage*, i, 18, 141ff. ; Stow, *Survey*, ed. Kingsford, ii, 101). These anniversary celebrations, which were sometimes held on or about the real Coronation Day—16 January—drew together enormous crowds. In January, 1581, " through the great concourse of people thither repairing, many of the beholders, as well men as women, were sore hurt, some maimed, and some killed, by falling of the scaffolds overcharged " (Holinshed, *Annals*, 1587, ii, 1315).

¹² See above p. 502, note 23.

LUKE HUTTON'S LAMENTATION.

The authorship of this ballad is discussed in the introductory note to Luke Hutton's *Black Dog of Newgate* (above p. 506). The text here given follows that of the original copy in the Bagford Collection in the British Museum (c. 40. m. 10. 72)—of date about 1660, judging from the imprint. A few modifications have been suggested by the text printed in *The Roxburghe Ballads*, viii, 55. The earliest extant copy was printed in 1598, but there were probably earlier impressions (see H. L. Collmann, *Ballads and Broadsides at Britwell Court*, Roxburghe Club, 1912).

¹ Orig. has *receive* ; apparently a printer's error.

² Not the sheriff ; it would have been beneath his dignity. Probably one of his bailiffs came.

THE LAST WILL AND TESTAMENT OF LAURENCE LUCIFER.

The Black Book (entered 22 March, 1604 and published in the same year), by T. M., contains two sections ; the first being an account of the visit of the Devil to Pierce Penilesse in his lodgings ; the second consisting of the Devil's Will and Testament. Only the second is here given. T. M. is probably Thomas Middleton (1570 ?-1627), the dramatist and friend of Dekker. The latter may have had a hand in the production of *The Black Book* (F. P. Wilson, *Dekker's Plague Pamphlets*, xix-xx). Both poets were intimately familiar with London ; both were probably anxious to write sequels to Thomas Nashe's very successful tract, *The Supplication of Pierce Penilesse* (1592). Dekker accomplished this to some degree in *News from Hell* (1606). *The Black Book* is no doubt Middleton's effort. In *The Supplication of Pierce Penilesse* Nashe, in the person of Pierce, sends a petition to the Devil by the hand of a knight of the post, setting out in a very racy and readable prose the abuses of contemporary life, where those who have a talent for seizing prosperity have an unfair advantage over the handicapped poor scholar. None of Nashe's imitators in the Devil-and-sulphur school have succeeded in reproducing his vigorous treatment of topical questions ; but in T. M.'s continuation we have something which is quite excellent in its way. The thing was to lash the key-figures in London's underlife, and lash them hard. No one will deny that T. M. is vigorous, and what is more important for our purpose, informative. A. H. Bullen was confident enough of Middleton's authorship to include the tract in the collected works of that dramatist (1885). I have taken the present text from the black-letter copy of *The Black Book* in the British Museum (E2 recto to F3 recto).

[1] Orig. *Frig-beard*, apparently a misprint.

[2] The testator is merely cataloguing the quarters of London in which vice flourished. *Shoreditch*, lying outside the City, had a bad name. " 'Tis easier to find virginity in Shoreditch than to hear of my mistress " (*Jack Drum's Entertainment*, 1600, ii, 359). *Turnbold Street* is T. M.'s name for Turnbull (or Turnmill) Street, which lay outside the walls to the east of the Fleet Ditch, or Turnmill Brook as it was called at this point. The Elizabethan drama is full of references to this quarter, famous throughout England as a centre for prostitutes and thieves (see Donald Lupton, *London and the Country Carbonadoed*, 1632, s. 13). *Whitefriars* is discussed elsewhere. *Westminster* harboured dubious characters, because of its traditional immunities, but references to this side of its life seldom particularize the exact neighbourhood (see Sugden, *Topog. Dict.*, 560). The Strand had along its north side a string of lodging-houses, some of them clean and reputable, but many of them tightly packed with thieves and women of easy virtue.

[3] *Mazard* (drinking vessel) was sometimes used, as in this case, to mean *head*. The London trained bands used to be mustered at Mile End.

[4] " *Picked-hatch* : a hatch or half-door, surmounted by a row of pikes or spikes to prevent climbing over ; *spec.* a brothel " (N.E.D.). Lucifer in the first part of *The Black Book* is searching for Pierce Penilesse, and proceeds " toward Picthatch, intending to begin there first, which (as I may fitly name it) is the very skirts of all brothel-houses " (Bullen's *Middleton*, viii, 11). Bullen describes Picthatch as a notorious bawdy-house in or near Turnmill Street (see note 2 above) ; but it should probably be placed farther east, near the Charter-house, and in the angle between Old Street and Goswell Road. See Wheatley and Cunningham, *London Past and Present*, iii, 92 ; and *N. and Q.*, ser. I, i, 484. Pinks in his *Hist. of Clerkenwell* (edn. 1881, p. 696), assumes from the passage quoted above that " Nashe, the rude, railing satirist," died in Picthatch ; but this is mere conjecture. No one knows where Nashe died.

[5] Authorship uncertain ; first produced probably in 1603.

[6] By Thomas Heywood ; acted 1603, printed 1607.

[7] Coombe, to the south of Richmond Park, was well known as a haunt of highwaymen. In 1576 it is thus described : " a perilous bottom, compassed about with woods ; too well known for the manifold murders and mischiefs there committed " (Fleming's transl. of Caius' treatise *Of English Dogs*, qu. Bullen). Middleton in *Your Five Gallants* has a scene laid there.

[8] See p. 500, note 13.

[9] A red lattice guided the steps of the thirsty to an ale-house.

[10] Peter Bales was the author of a book on calligraphy and the prizewinner in a public competition in penmanship. What captured the interest of his contemporaries was his alleged feat of transcribing the Bible within the limits of a walnut. The misspelling of his name here has an obvious intention.

[11] " a play on the meaning of the word—a false piece of money used for reckoning, and a prison " (Dyce).

[12] Cornhill is clearly meant here. Cp. Dekker, *The Meeting of Gallants* : " . . . they ran through Cornewell just in the middle of the street, with such a violent trample as if the Devil had been coachman."

[13] A dig at Barnabe Rich, author of *A Looking-glass for Ireland* (1599), and an enemy of tobacco-taking. His most vigorous denunciation of smoking appears in *The Irish Hubbub* (1617).

[14] James the First's *Counterblast to Tobacco* (1604) can only just have been published. The first recorded importation of tobacco into England was that made in 1565 by Sir John Hawkins. In other European countries it was known and smoked even earlier. During the later Elizabethan period " tobacco-drinking " became a fashion among rich and poor, and was the subject of bitter controversy. A bishop of London is said to have died of tobacco-poisoning. Barnabe Rich says that early in James' reign there were at least seven thousand tobacco-shops in London. There were certainly a good many. A smoker on entering a shop would be offered a pipe and could indulge his weakness on the premises. See *Shakespeare's England*, i, 28-29.

[15] It should be borne in mind that for the purpose of this pamphlet Pierce Penilesse *is* Nashe. But there is no particular reference to the poor scholar at this point, and it seems a poor sort of joke anyhow.

[16] See introductory note above.

[17] *Heigh pass ! Come aloft !* : words used by the juggler and bear-ward respectively.

THE BELLMAN OF LONDON.

The authorship of this little book, which appeared anonymously and ran through four editions in 1608, is established by Dekker's signature to the epistle of the companion volume, *Lantern and Candlelight* (2nd edn.), which was published later in the same year. Thomas Dekker (1572 ?-1641 ?) left few traces of his life for future biographers (references and clues alike are brought together by Mary L. Hunt in *Thomas Dekker : a study*, 1911). Born in London, he became the City's poet and ardent eulogist, using even the sins and vices of his birthplace, the " nurse of his being," as material for tolerant and sympathetic studies of the ways of her citizens. From Dekker's plays and pamphlets may be learnt more about contemporary life in London than from any other of the Elizabethan men of letters. How he acquired his miscellaneous knowledge it is not always easy to say. In his obscure youth he contrived somehow to pick up all but a professional knowledge of linen-drapery, shoe-making, and the shadier aspects of the solicitor's practice. He was acquainted with the Low Countries, could read Dutch, and possibly fought in the Spanish wars in his youth. In 1598 or earlier he started upon the active career of a dramatist. Most of the plays which have survived were written in collaboration with others, although some which have disappeared must have been his sole work, produced during the early years of his maturity. It was " in all probability a hard, hand-to-mouth sort of existence, whose only incident was an occasional visit to a debtors' prison " (McKerrow). Whilst assisting Henslowe (who helped to get him out of the Poultry Counter in 1598) in the dramatic field, Dekker turned to the writing of prose pamphlets. Here he found a medium where his peculiar talent for descriptive writing could find full opportunities. Three short publications on the plague in London, of which one, *The Wonderful Year, 1603*, has become deservedly famous, and a few other works of journalistic quality, were followed by the first of the rogue pamphlets, *The Bellman of London*, in 1608. Dekker does not show the same originality as Greene in the selection of subjects. He is, in fact, less familiar with the subject-matter than his great predecessor in the art of rogue portraiture. In *The Bellman* we meet once more our old friends of Harman's beggar world, anglers, upright-men, palliards, and the rest. They are now drawn with more skill, but less accuracy, than the characters of the *Caveat*, and the plagiarism is obvious throughout the section that discusses them. Greene's pamphlets and *Mihil Mumchance* are also quarried. This wholesale borrowing (discussed fully by F. W. Chandler, *Literature of Roguery*, i, 106-7, and Aydelotte, *Elizabethan Rogues*, 130, 176) detracts from the value of a pamphlet which in other respects makes excellent reading. The author, finding himself in a wood, is moved first of all to write several pages in praise of the country life. There is a change in tempo when a cottage has been discovered and the narrator hides himself to watch the antics of the beggarmen who have rallied there. Their meal is finished, and they go. So far the work is original. There follows a listing of rogue types, drawn from Harman, undertaken by the woman of the cottage. Dekker is now disgusted with the country. " I have heard of no sin in the city, but I met it in the village, nor any vice in the tradesman, which was not in the ploughman." He returns to town, and meets the Bellman, " a man with a lantern and a candle in his hand, a long staff on his neck, and a dog at his tail." " He called himself the sentinel of the City, the watchman for every ward, the honest spy that discovered the 'prentices of the night." His experience enables him to tell Dekker about the cozeners and cheats of London and their ways, which he proceeds to do at considerable length until the book reaches its end. The part of the book printed in the present collection is that which describes the beggars' banquet in the wood. Apart from its value as showing Dekker in his best vein of prose narration, it has some importance as indicating a revival of interest in the countryside and its types and problems. This may have been caused by the agrarian troubles in the midlands in the spring of 1607, when the rioters, led by " Captain Pouch," " violently cut and broke down hedges, filled up ditches, and laid open all such enclosures of commons, . . . which of ancient times had been open and employed to tillage " (Stow, *Annals*, 1615, p. 889). It has been argued (K. L. Gregg, *Thomas Dekker*, 1924, pp. 89, 90) that the author is alluding to the rioters of the previous year when he describes the guests at the old woman's table, but this is hard to sustain. The present version relies principally upon the editions made from the second impression (1608) by A. B. Grosart (Huth Library, 1884-5) and O. Smeaton (1904), both of which have been used to check doubtful readings in the carelessly printed first impression in the British Museum. The extract begins sig. B2 recto, and ends C3 recto (1st impr.).

¹ i.e. misanthrope, like Timon of Athens.

² They live on the threshold of an ale-house.

³ Personally acquainted with the inside of the prison there.   It was a privilege (dating back to 1382) of freemen of the City, being householders and paying scot and lot, who were arrested for debt or contempt, to be incarcerated in this gatehouse, where the accommodation was reasonably decent, and the charges of the jailers were kept within bounds (Stow, *Survey*, ed. Kingsford, i, 39-40 ; Hist. MSS. Comm., *4th Rep.*, 83).   The prison appears later to have lost its special attractiveness (Webb, *Manor and Borough*, 667).   There were ninety freemen there in 1644 (Petition in British Museum at E. 21.23).

⁴ i.e. beggars ; cf. *Hungarians* above.

⁵ With the list which follows compare pp. 67-108 above.   Harman's *Caveat* in one of its several editions was Dekker's source here.

⁶ Probably misprint for *doxies*.

⁷ Conduits in this sense were watercocks set up in streets and market places to provide the people of the neighbouring houses, etc.

⁸ Orig. *dopye*.

⁹ *hell* : the current name for the dark hole beneath a shopman's counter into which remnants and rubbish were thrown.

¹⁰ *scil.*, on a board.

LANTERN AND CANDLELIGHT.

The Bellman of London (1608) met with a more than satisfactory reception. Seven months later Dekker followed it up with *Lantern and Candlelight*, adopting as title a popular phrase perhaps suggested to him by a ballad of the same name (entered 1569-70) ; and again introducing the Bellman as a character. But already there is a rival in the field, " that hath of late taken upon him the name of the Bellman ; but being not able to maintain that title, he doth now call himself the Bellman's brother. You shall know him by his habiliments, for by the furniture he wears, he will be taken for a beadle of Bridewell." The first appearance of the Beadle has left no record. The author of his being was no doubt the S. R. (to be identified probably with Samuel Rid, see p. 514-5) who returned to defend the Beadle with *Martin Markall* in 1612 (see p. 383ff). S. R. gave back more than he received. His ragged debaters in the opening section are indignant at the calumnies of the Bellman and his exposure of their language and tricks. It was a foul thing, they say, to attack them anonymously, although " in his second round, as he calls it, [he] has set to his name " (p. 389). It is pointed out by one of their number that the " invective was set forth, made and printed above forty years ago, and, being then called *A Caveat for Cursitors*, is now newly printed and termed *The Bellman of London*—made at first by one Master Harman, a Justice of the Peace in Kent in Queen Mary's days, he being then about ten years of age ! " (p. 386). The rogues send for the Bellman, and their messenger " finds him at home, mumbling a piece of bread and cheese." On arrival at the court of Crack-ropes he is assailed with violent words. He defends himself sturdily, but is in danger of being torn in pieces when a diversion is provided. S. R. returns to the attack later in the book when he enlarges and amends Dekker's canting dictionary, " or Master Harman's ! with such words as I think he never heard of, and yet in use too, but not out of vainglory as *his* ambition is " (p. 406). S. R. may be more deeply versed in the ways of rogues, but there is more realism in Dekker's work. *Lantern and Candlelight* introduces us to many cunning fellows not to be met with in earlier works. It is to be feared that some of them are more at home in Dekker's pages than they would be in real life ; but others are convincing enough, notably the ferret-hunters and falconers. Dekker probably invents some of the fancy names. In preparing the present text, the second edition (1609), as used by A. B. Grosart (Huth Library, 1884-5) and O. Smeaton (1904), has been employed ; the reprint is complete but for the omission of Chapter I, which is composed of material familiar enough to those who know Harman's *Caveat* ; it is, in fact, an unblushing plagiarization of Harman. The excision would not have been made were there anything of value in the chapter in question. In a few cases doubtful points have been resolved by reference to the first edition, which differs but little from its successor. The copy used (British Museum, c. 38. d. 24) has furnished the title-page here reproduced. The side-notes of the original are omitted.

¹ Chapter I omitted as explained in note above.

² The setting of scenes in hell or among its denizens is a familiar device much employed

in this type of literature in Dekker's period. " Visions of Heaven, Purgatory and Hell had originated in paganism, had flourished all through the Middle Ages in a Christian form, and still retained their popularity. . . . After the Reformation, these legends, like the sins, lost their theological significance, but . . . literary free-lances were only too glad to avail themselves of the spell which visions still exercised over the popular imagination " (H. V. Routh in *Camb. Hist. of English Literature*, iv, 353). Cf. Nashe, *Pierce Penilesse*, Middleton's *Black Book*, Rid's *Martin Markall*, and Dekker's own *News from Hell*.

[3] The sheriff made his returns when he sent reports to a court on the writs directed to him. By *returns* here we ought probably to understand *return-days*, the appointed days for the receipt of the sheriff's reports. This would explain the reference to the law's delays.

[4] An overseer's task was to assist the executors of a will.

[5] It was a statutory offence, under certain conditions, to purchase market provisions before they were offered for public sale and to " engross " commodities such as corn with a view to forcing up the price.

[6] " The defendant who *demurs* admits the facts as stated by the plaintiff, but contends that these facts give the plaintiff no cause of action " (Holdsworth).

[7] See p. 519, note 20.

[8] Procedure by *writ of error* was in some respects equivalent to an appeal to a higher court against judgment already given. The plaintiff in error complained to the Crown of certain mistakes in the written record of the trial, and thus, even where he could not get the decision reversed, he could delay execution of the original judgment.

[9] The process by which a prisoner could be delivered from custody under one of the writs of *habeas corpus* had not yet become famous as the protector of the liberty of the subject. In the early seventeenth century the writs were employed as a rule, not with the primary intention of giving an imprisoned person a speedy trial, but rather with that of asserting the powers of one court as against another.

[10] i.e. *Capias ad respondendum* : a writ directed to the sheriff, instructing him to arrest the defendant to an action.

[11] Or *Ne exeat regno* ; a writ employed to prevent a man from leaving the kingdom to avoid some legal process, or for any other reason.

[12] The *Commission of Rebellion* was another method of securing the arrest and attendance in court of a defendant who failed to put in a spontaneous appearance. See Blackstone, III *Commentaries*, 444.

[13] *Fines and Recoveries* were devices employed (until 1833) by way of fictitious legal actions to convey interests in real property. The author is punning ; cf. *Hamlet*, V, i.

[14] The face painted or carved at the *Saracen's Head* inn. Cf. p. 518, note 6.

[15] The life and death of John Story (1510 ?-1571) were remembered long after he had met a traitor's end. At one time a regius professor at Oxford, he became under Bishop Bonner a zealous persecutor of the reformers. After two spells of imprisonment in 1560 and 1563, he escaped to Flanders and worked for the overthrow of Protestantism with a pension from Philip II. He was kidnapped by an English skipper in 1570, while searching the ship for forbidden books, and, to the great joy of many ardent Protestants, butchered at Tyburn in the following year. His beatification was pronounced at Rome in 1886 (see Foxe, *Acts and Monuments*, 1839, viii, 743 ; and also *D.N.B.*).

[16] See p. 511, note 9.

[17] Birchin Lane was the street to which the visitor in London went to buy ready-made clothes. Stow says it was inhabited by wealthy drapers and hosiers ; but it was the second-hand trade, among provincial people, that really flourished there. The present passage is influenced by a description of a similar incident in T. M.'s *Black Book*, 1604 (Bullen's *Middleton*, viii, 29).

[18] i.e. 21 December. The constables of the twenty-six London wards were nominated on St. Thomas's day (Giles Jacob, *City Liberties*, 1732, p. 43).

[19] As a final dish.

[20] The creditor, without notice to the gull, sends in a formal statement of the debt for production in court.

[21] Possibly means *lustring*, a silk fabric, though this is rather an early use in that sense.

[22] See p. 506, note 1.

[23] i.e. a statute merchant or statute staple. For the operation of the former see p. 506, note 8.

[24] The penalty for forging wills and other important documents was imprisonment for life and a horrible mutilation and burning of the face (5 Eliz., c. 14, § 1).

²⁵ The question of engaging with Scotland in a legislative and commercial union was before the English parliament in 1606 and 1607. The matter was not followed up owing to the precipitation of James I and the violent opposition of the London merchants.

²⁶ Shrove Tuesday was a day when a special licence among the London apprentices was tolerated as of long custom. Sometimes a crowd would get out of hand and cause damage to life and property. In the theatres the players might be compelled to act the parts which were popular with the mob. " Shrove Tuesday falls on that day on which the 'prentices plucked down the Cockpit [in Drury Lane], and on which they did always to use rifle Madame Leake's house [a bawdy-house] at the upper end of Shoreditch " (*The Owl's Almanac*, 1618, qu. Chambers, *Eliz. Stage*, i, 265). " This was not Puritanism but a traditional Saturnalia," says Sir Edmund Chambers (*loc. cit.*). Cf. *The Honest Whore* (II), IV, iii.

²⁷ There are enough of them to vouch for one another as substantial people in the toll-keeper's book at the market. See note on the law relating to horse-stealing, p. 501, note 11.

²⁸ This is the first discussion in English general literature of the habits of gypsy vagrants.

²⁹ Sentence in original begins, *That the* . . .

³⁰ i.e. the orders of rogues described by Dekker in *The Bellman of London*, 1608.

³¹ See note 39 below.

³² The pustules of bubonic plague perhaps resembled traders' tokens of tin and brass.

³³ The author was an authority on London's pestilences. " A red cross, 13 inches in length and breadth, was painted in oil colours upon infected houses. On the lintel was fastened a paper with the inscription *Lord have mercy upon us!* . . . The plague of 1603, like that of 1625, began in the suburbs " (F. P. Wilson, *Dekker's Plague Pamphlets*, 224-5).

³⁴ Cf. Virgil, *Aeneid*, ii, 791.

³⁵ London is Dekker's birthplace. He frequently seizes opportunities of exalting the origins and history of his beloved city. London mythology, drawing upon Geoffrey of Monmouth, ascribed the foundation of the city to Brutus, great-grandson of Aeneas. The city was then called New Troy, which became corrupted into Trinovantium. The Trinovantes were found by Cæsar north and north-east of the site of London.

³⁶ London's permanent horse and cattle market at West Smithfield; it remained until 1835, and is described by Dickens in *Oliver Twist* in words which would apply almost equally well to the early seventeenth century. Smithfield drovers had a bad reputation as deceivers; but in this great market all kinds of beasts were sold, good as well as bad.

³⁷ A famous performing horse. It " would restore a glove to the due owner, after the master had whispered the man's name in his ear: would tell the just number of pence in any piece of silver coin newly showed him by his master " (Kenelm Digby, qu. *Shakespeare's England*, ii, 409).

³⁸ There is a scene in Kyd's *Spanish Tragedy; or Hieronimo is mad again* (II, iv) in which Hieronimo, Marshal of Spain, enters his garden and finds the body of his murdered son Horatio hanging in an arbour.

³⁹ No Elizabethan writer has a good word to say for the suburban quarters outside the city where the garden-alleys were. At the end of Elizabeth's reign we find Stow complaining that the open fields beyond Bishopsgate have been covered with huts and bowling-alleys and tenter-yards; and outside Aldgate, " in some places it scarce remaineth a sufficient highway for the meeting of carriages . . ., much less any wholesome way for people to walk on foot " (*Survey*, ed. Kingsford, i, 127; ii, 72). Stubbes really lets himself go about the evils of the suburbs (1583): " They have gardens, either palled or walled round about very high with their arbours and bowers fit for the purpose. And lest they might be espied in these open places, they [the proprietresses] have their banquetting houses with galleries, turrets and what not else, sumptuously erected, wherein they may, and doubtless do, many of them, play the filthy persons. . . . Some of them have three or four keys apiece, whereof one they keep for themselves; the others their paramours have to go in before them . . . Then to these gardens they repair when they list, with a basket and a boy, where they, meeting their sweethearts, receive their sweet desires " (*Anatomy of Abuses*, E.E.T.S. edn., 1879, p. 88); and Whetstone, speaking of " alleys, gardens, and other obscure corners, out of the common walks of the magistrate. The daily shifts of these privy houses are masterless men, needy shifters, thieves, cutpurses, unthrifty servants. . . . Here a man may pick out mates for all purposes, save such as are good " (*Mirror for Magistrates, Touchstone for the Time*, 31). Cf. *Nobody and Somebody*, I, 1 verso, and above p. 348, where Dekker speaks of the high rent the landlord of a place used for improper purposes can charge.

T

O PER SE O.

The book was published anonymously in 1612, and consists of two parts. The first is merely a reprint of Dekker's *Lantern and Candlelight*; the second is a not altogether success-ful attempt at continuation. We leave the city rogue, and return to the abram-man, the clapperdudgeon, and their colleagues of the country highway, types already discussed at some length by Dekker in *The Bellman* in a section of that pamphlet which has been omitted in the present collection. *O per se O* escapes the criticism of plagiarism in a way in which the earlier work cannot, and offers fresh and interesting information on beggar life. There are for instance two useful receipts for the production of artificial sores. It has not been established definitely as the fruit of Dekker's industry—it is inferior in literary quality to most of his prose publications—and may well have been the work of one of his hack-writing contemporaries. The curious title is difficult to explain. Dr. Chandler hazards the sugges-tion : " In *Greene's News both from Heaven and Hell*, the ghostly paper delivered to the author begins, ' It is I, *I per se I*, Robert Greene, in Artibus Magister,' to which Dekker's *O per se O* may be an allusion " (*Literature of Roguery*, i, 109). The section of the book printed above comprises the new matter only of the 1612 volume, and the text is based upon that of the British Museum copy (c. 27. b. 19), which also furnishes the title page for reproduction.

¹ Ovid, *Ars Amat.*, i, 249.
² *Pacolet* : the name of the horse ridden by the Devil's messenger (see p. 361).
³ This fair must be an invention of the author's.
⁴ See p. 496, note 12.
⁵ It was from Dunkirk that privateers were constantly sailing out under the colours of the Spanish regent to prey upon merchant shipping.
⁶ See p. 512, note 15.
⁷ Cf. Harman's receipt (p. 81), and further instructions below (p. 377).
⁸ Cf. Harman's story of how a dumb man was made to speak (p. 91).
⁹ Another reference to the inquisitorial procedure of the examining magistrate. See p. 503, note 6.
¹⁰ See p. 512, note 15.
¹¹ Dekker, in *Lantern and Candlelight* (chap. i, " Of Canting "), gives, in addition to a dictionary, two canting rhymes. The first, beginning " Enough, with bousy cove maund nase," is lifted from Copland's *Highway to the Spital-house* (p. 24) ; the second opens with the line, " The Ruffin cly the nab of the harman-beck," and is " composed . . . out of his own brain " by Dekker from phrases given in Harman's *Caveat* (pp. 115-7). The new canting song here printed has fewer artificial elements, and is probably an improved version of an authentic song, though it still seems to have the literary flavour of Harman's period. It is taken over later by *The English Rogue* (1665, etc.), and turns up again in Mark Twain's *Prince and the Pauper*.

MARTIN MARKALL, BEADLE OF BRIDEWELL.

The authorship of this little book, published over the initials S. R. in 1610, is customarily given to Samuel Rowlands (1570?-1630 ?), whose work often appeared with initials only. It was reprinted by the Hunterian Club (1880), and bound up with Rowland's works. No special grounds exist for this attribution beyond the fact that there is some certainty that Rowlands wrote another rogue book, *Greene's Ghost haunting Cony-catchers* (1602), by S. R. ; and we know that he specialised in low London life. Dr. Aydelotte argues convincingly that *Martin Markall* is by another hand (probably Rid's) ; for had Rowlands written it he must have mentioned Dekker's plagiarism in *The Bellman* of certain passages in *Greene's Ghost*. While omitting to do this, the author takes Dekker to task for pilfering from Harman's *Caveat* (Aydelotte, *Elizabethan Rogues*, 134. See also *Journal of Gypsy Lore Soc.*, N.S., ii, 271). The rencontre between our S. R. and Dekker is discussed on p. 511 above. Samuel Rid is almost certainly the author of the present tract. In 1612 he published a small vagabond book, *The Art of Juggling*, which not only fulfils part of the promise made by the Beadle at the end of our text " once more to play the merchant venturer," but actually continues the discussion of the gypsy life and of Giles Hather and Kit Callot, the gypsy king and queen.

At the conclusion, moreover, of *The Art of Juggling*, we are exhorted to " take heed of the Beadle." There are other passages in *Martin Markall* which suggest Rid's authorship—and yet others, it may be added, which show that he is as much to be condemned for wholesale pilfering as Dekker whom he attacked. There is some probability that the book appeared in an earlier form in 1608 between the publication of *The Bellman* and *Lantern and Candlelight*. No copy of such an impression has survived. In its present shape *Martin Markall* was entered in the Stationers' Register 31 March, 1610.

[1] Cf. Horace, *Epist.*, I, 16, 52.

[2] For a note on the rivalry of S. R. and Dekker see above p. 511.

[3] The Peak Cavern, or Devil's Hole, at Castleton was famous as a sheltering place for wandering beggars, gypsies and lawless men. Cf. the jackman's song at the beginning of *Gypsies Metamorphosed*; and S. Rid, *The Art of Juggling* (1612), 1614 edn., sig. B recto, where the Peak and " Ketbrooke by Blackheath " are mentioned as two of the gypsies' rendezvous. (Ketbrooke is probably taken from Harman.) From Camden's description the place seems to have been safe enough for visitors; no reference is made to vagabonds.

[4] See p. 511.

[5] King Street ran from Charing Cross to the royal palace of Westminster, and was noted for its taverns. The *Swan with Five Necks* is not mentioned elsewhere by this name—*Necks* should of course be *Nicks*—but is possibly the Swan in King Street visited by Pepys (*Diary*, ed. Wheatley, ii, 32; vi, 3).

[6] i.e. the dogs used in teasing the bulls and bears. For Paris Garden see p. 494, note 17, and p. 502, note 20.

[7] *brach* here means bitch-hound. For similar usage cp. *I Henry IV*, III, i; *King Lear*, I, iii.

[8] See p. 511.

[9] The Family of Love was a sect founded by Henrick Niclaes, a German mystic, who visited England in the early fifties of the sixteenth century. Niclaes and his elders made some very exalted claims touching their own impeccability. Current slander grew busy with the doings of some of the Familists, who were said to interpret *love* as licence; but the persecution of the society by the Council appears to have been caused not by these, probably unfounded, rumours, but by the Family's religious unorthodoxy. A play called *The Family of Love* by Middleton (publ. 1608), deriding the sect, seems to have had a success similar to that achieved by certain productions ridiculing psycho-analysis and spiritism in our own day.

[10] This epistle is written in clever imitation of the style of petitions drawn up by small traders' associations complaining of unfair treatment.

[11] S. H. J. Herrtage conjectures that this mention of Master I. H. (? J. H.), which recurs on p. 399 below, is a reference to Thomas Harman's *Caveat* (see *Works of Rowlands*, Hunterian Club, 1880, iii, Notes, p. 53). But it is unlikely that the same error in the printing of the initial would occur twice. No other candidates are forthcoming.

[12] Not the Pimlico in Westminster, but the pleasure resort near Hoxton, " famed for its cakes, custards and Derby ale. The name is still preserved in ' Pimlico Walk ' by Hoxton church " (Wheatley and Cunningham, *London Past and Present*, iii, 96).

[13] Dekker in his *Lantern and Candlelight*, 1608, ch. I, printed a dictionary of thieves' slang, but this was only a copy, with a few not very intelligent modifications, of the list of words given by Harman in his *Caveat* (see pp. 114-5). The author is here comparing Dekker with Bathyllus, who claimed the authorship of some verses written by Virgil, but was found out when the latter added the lines beginning :

> Hos ego versiculos feci, tulit alter honores ;
> Sic vos non vobis . . . .

[14] See note 11 above.

[15] Lycaon, king of Arcadia, who served human flesh to Jupiter when the god visited him (Ovid, *Metam.*, i, 217-39).

[16] *Dutch* : meaning German.

[17] i.e. Gracechurch Street; a market for corn and other goods was held upon the pavement.

[18] Foxhall was the common name for Falk's Hall, now Vauxhall. In 1610 the riverside had not yet been laid out in pleasure gardens, but the place was already a common resort for thieves and masterless men.

[19] The chronological narration given in the section which follows consists of a clever admixture of invention with fact, as gleaned from the historical works available to writers of the time. Among other accounts the author has made use of Fabyan's *Chronicle*, Polydore Vergil's *History*, and Hall's *Chronicle*, especially the last named, from which he takes over whole sentences. As far as I can discover, the account of the continuous development of a society of rogues with a shifting headquarters, etc., proceeds from the fertile imagination of the writer himself. Some of the rogue names mentioned are fictitious, as their names suggest, e.g., Jenkin Cowdiddle and Laurence Crossbiter ; but Bluebeard had a pseudonymous existence in the Cade rising. The story of this rogue society is interwoven with the actual details of rebellions and disorders in the past. The orders and regulations said to have been issued by the captains and leaders are of course an invention ; but some of them ring true enough, and S. R. may be credited with having picked up a knowledge of thieves' conventions. J. J. Jusserand's *English Wayfaring Life*, pt. I, ch. ii, should be consulted by those who seek to get an idea of the dangers of the road in the later Middle Ages.

[20] S. H. J. Herrtage points out that this derivation is quite fanciful. " Roberdesmen " are mentioned in an act of 1331 (5 Edward III, c. 14). The author errs in famous company, for the scrupulous Coke thinks they were followers of Robin Hood.

[21] The battle of Towton, 1461. The number of deaths is as given by Hall.

[22] Thomas Neville, the Bastard of Fauconberg, " had sometime been made admiral by the Earl of Warwick, to keep the passage between Calais and Dover, that none of King Edward's side might freely pass ; after that, being become needy and offensive, as well to friend as foe, he began openly to play the pirate . . . He robbed and spoiled all about the coast. At the last, arriving in Kent, he came a-land, and, having gathered no small power of Kentish people, he marched right to London, and at his first coming made great spoil." The mayor " assembled a good number of soldiers, and, giving charge upon Fauconbridge, rescued the spoil and put him to flight, killing and taking many of the Kentish folk in the chase. The Fauconbridge sped him speedily into his ships, but soon after, arriving unadvisedly at Southampton, he was taken and beheaded " (Polydore Vergil's *History*, Camden Soc., 1844, pp. 153-4). Cp. R. R. Sharpe, *London and the Kingdom*, i, 314-6.

[23] Spising, according to Fabyan, was one of the Essex leaders in the attack on London led by the Bastard of Fauconberg (see note 22) in 1471. He was executed, and his head set up on Aldgate. Nothing is known about his heading a band of robbers (Fabyan, *Chronicles*, 1811, p. 662 ; Kingsford, *Chronicles of London*, p. 185).

[24] The author here pushes the comparison between his society of rogues and an organised trade to the extreme limit, and makes the sons of qualified rogues free of their trade by patrimony ; they become master rogues without payment of a fine, just as the trained son of a qualified weaver might be accepted as a master weaver.

[25] What follows is part of the famous speech put into the mouth of the Duke of Buckingham in More's *Life of Richard III*, and copied by some of the later annalists, e.g. Hall (edn. 1809) 354 ; Stow (1614) 442. The large sanctuary privileges then claimed by the Abbey are discussed by Dean Stanley in *Historical Memorials of Westminster Abbey* (5th edn.), Ch. v ; and J. C. Cox, *Sanctuaries and Sanctuary Seekers*, ch. iii.

[26] Orig. *as*.

[27] This was a water-standard opposite Honey Lane, a place for popular gatherings, where joustings were held, and men were put in the pillory and sometimes executed. See Stow, *Survey*, ed. Kingsford, ii, 251.

[28] A game played with small balls and nine holes numbered in a series ; three variations are mentioned in *The English Dialect Dictionary*, iv, 274.

[29] " A stake is fixed in the ground ; those who play throw loggats [small sticks] at it, and he that is nearest the stake wins " (Gomme, *Games*, qu. *Engl. Dialect Dict.*, iii, 641).

[30] See p. 492, note 11.

[31] The author bestows on his beggars a hall, bringing them into line with the craftsmen's companies.

[32] Seems to refer to Awdeley's *Fraternity of Vagabonds* (above p. 51) or some reprint of it ; a side-note at this place has " The quartern of knaves made by Cock Lorel ", a close approximation to Awdeley's sub-title.

[33] See note 3 above.

[34] The traditional names of the first gypsy king and queen in England. There is no ground for supposing the corporeal existence of either. Giles Hather appears as the nickname of a rogue (No. 14) in the last section of Awdeley's *Fraternity* (1561). Kit and Callot

appear as type-names of females, separately and together, in English literature before the coming of the " Egyptians." Thus :

> " . . . and with that ich awakened,
> And called Kytte my wife, and Kalote my daughter,
> ' Arys and go reverence godes resurreccion'."
>   (*Piers Plowman*, Skeat's edn., 1886, C passus 21, 472-4.)

[35] It cannot be established that the gypsies went about in bands of any standard size. Dekker says they went in an army four-score strong, throwing out raiding detachments of six or less. Contemporary constables' accounts show that a party might be of any number from six to twenty (T. W. Thompson in *Journal of Gypsy Lore Soc.*, 3rd ser., vii, 34).

[36] The writer tried to carry out this promise : see p. 514.

THE COUNTER'S COMMONWEALTH.

The known facts of the life of the author are scanty. William Fennor was a rhymester and a pamphleteer. He came of a Worcestershire family. By 1614 he was married and had children. He was connected with the stage, and on one occasion he gave a one-man show. In 1616 he published a collection of indifferent verse ; and, in October of the same year, the present book, written in the Wood Street Counter, was entered in the Stationers' Register. On coming first to London Fennor is said to have been bound apprentice to a blind harper, who, like the sightless master of Lazarillo de Tormes, quarrelled with the boy about the distribution of their scanty victuals. About 1614 he came into the public eye. In that year he seems to have presented an entertainment by Richard Vennard (with whom he has been confused). A contest of wits to take place on the stage of a theatre between Taylor the Water Poet and Fennor was much advertised by the former with bills and announcements ; at the appointed time Fennor excused himself and failed to appear. Taylor was furious, and at once published a scurrilous attack on the rival rhymester, describing him as the companion of thieves and scoundrels. Fennor replied, likewise in verse, but with much less vigour :

> " If I at Gravesend rhymed for fourteen pence,
> For twelve pence thou hast rowed that voyage since," etc.

The Water Poet's rejoinder to this finally accused him of purloining manuscript poems in the possession of (and by ?) the Richard Vennard referred to above (see too note 30 below), and of presenting these as his own to eight knights of the Garter ! These broadsides, together with *The Counter's Commonwealth*, are our only sources of information (see *Taylor's Revenge* ; *Fennor's Defence* ; *A Cast over the Water given gratis to William Fennor the Rhymer*, all 1615). *The Counter's Commonwealth* was reprinted twice in Fennor's own day, first as *The Miseries of a Jail* (1619) ; secondly as *A True Description of the Laws of a Counter* (1629). The present modernized version follows the text of the original of 1617 in the British Museum.

[1] A few of Fennor's marginal notes are here reprinted as foot-notes. Where they add nothing material they have been omitted.

[2] See p. 513, note 35.

[3] Originally a church so named from its proximity to the butchers' shambles on the north side of Newgate Street ; it was pulled down at the Reformation, but the name survived.

[4] A privy seal demand note was usually a printed form requesting the loan of a sum of money to the government. Collectors were employed to present these to possible lenders, and if a sum were forthcoming, the amount was entered in the blank, and the " privy seal " became apparently a negotiable instrument to be cashed in due course at the Exchequer. The system was not at all popular ; for the Council would use pressure to secure loans in cases where alacrity was absent. See R. D. Richards, " The Evolution of Paper Money in England," *Quart. Journ. Econ.*, May, 1927 ; and the political histories of the period.

[5] Lancashire was a county of many papists, and this perhaps explains the reference ; for the summoners would be active in presenting them for non-attendance at church, and in the course of their duties qualify with the many fees, bribes, and free drinks for the distinction in question.

⁶ The *Saracen's Head* without Newgate was to become a coaching inn of considerable fame ; it was removed when the Viaduct was built. For a description of the signs see *Nicholas Nickleby*, Chap. iv. The site of the inn of the same name without Bishopsgate in now occupied by Saracen's Head Yard, Aldgate.

⁷ The present tract gives us the best account that is known of life in the Counters. There were two of these debtor's prisons north of the river ; and one across the bridge within the structure of the old parish church of St. Margaret, Southwark, where it shared quarters with the Court of Admiralty and the assizes (Stow, *Survey*, ed. Kingsford, ii, 59). In Elizabeth's day those in the City were the more famous—" the unlucky cranks about Cheapside." The prison in the Poultry (destroyed 1817) was very ancient ; the sister building in Wood Street was first used in 1555-6, when a predecessor in Bread Street had its inmates transferred, because the keeper, who had once before been punished for ill-treating his prisoners, continued in his cruelty, cheated them of their victuals, and gave shelter to thieves and strumpets for fourpence a night. (Stow himself was one of the jury which took these complaints ; *ibid.*, i, 350.) The Counters were the sheriffs' prisons ; and to these jails of theirs were committed most of those arrested in London in action for debt. A man of means could live in comfort in either ; indeed, for some people they served as a favourite retreat from the vengeance of enemies and even of the law (cf. Chap. 8). An apartment on the Master's Side of the prison was the best accommodation provided. The Knights' Ward was not so good, but comfortable as prison usage went. The Twopenny Ward and the Hole were no better than common jails—in some respects worse, for prisoners could count on no public assistance of any value in the provision of food, and a penniless man might actually starve to death in the Hole if he failed to secure relief or help from one of the citizens' legacies or the Christmas-treat funds provided for the very poor. There are references to these charities and their frequent misuse in the text. Life in the Counters and the Fleet appears to have been comparatively free. Having satisfied the jailers' fees and extortionate supplementary demands, the prisoner could move about as he liked within the walls, dine and gamble with his acquaintances, or gather material for a social enquiry like Fennor and his grief-stricken companion. He could receive friends ; he could bribe a jailer to escort him out of doors— and, if he were quick-witted enough, escape down a side street into oblivion, to the great discontent of his creditors, keepers and sureties. Within the walls he could set up a trade and earn a sort of livelihood. Social degredation was not necessarily involved by a period of incarceration in the Counter. Men of respectability do not appear ashamed to confess that they have suffered in this way. Contemporary literature has frequent references to the Hole and the Twopenny Ward and the other apartments.

> " Bedlam cures not more madmen in a year
> Than one of these Counters does ; men pay more dear
> There for their wit than anywhere. A Counter !
> Why, 'tis an university ! . . .
>   . . . With fine honey'd speech
> At's first coming in he doth persuade, beseech
> He may be lodg'd with one that is not itchy,
> To lie in a clean chamber, in sheets not lousy ;
> But when he has no money, then does he try,
> By subtle logic and quaint sophistry,
> To make the keepers trust him."
>   *The Roaring Girl*, III, iii.

⁸ See p. 501, note 11.

⁹ Some of the best linen came from the province of Holland.

¹⁰ The question is : before or after trial and judgment ? The answer is : before. Therefore the lawyer is able to promise his client to have him removed from the jurisdiction of his creditor's court, and perhaps also to free him from custody.

¹¹ See p. 512, note 9.

¹² Junior officers of the Customs.

¹³ Bath in the early seventeenth century was already popular as a bathing resort. According to the description published by Tobias Venner, M.D. (1628), who did much to spread the fame of the place, it contained four principal baths, varying in the intensity of heat and in their efficacy in the treatment of various disorders. The hot waters (applied externally) were of singular force against diseases gotten by cold, of the head and sinews (apoplexies,

cramps, forgetfulness, trembling), and also greatly profited the owners of windy and hydropic bodies, those that feared obesity, and the victims of diseases of the skin. Bodies naturally hot and dry did not respond well to the treatment (*Harl. Miscell.*, 1809, ii, 311ff.). Camden has an interesting description of the baths and bathers in his *Britannia* (see edn. 1695, p. 79), but would shake the confidence of the enquirer when he observes that only at certain hours are the waters wholesome. " From eight in the morning till three in the afternoon they are extreme hot and boil up violently, by which they are muddled and throw up a filthy sort of stuff from the bottom." Gibson (*loc. cit.*) says that this is an exaggeration.

[14] A district of small tenements in Dowgate Ward, built on part of the site of an ancient house called Poultney's Inn, which was pulled down in 1593. This quarter was outside the ordinary jurisdiction of the City, and became a sanctuary of evil reputation. Heywood and Rowley also remark on the number of chimneys. A historical note and the reproduction of an engraving of 1650 appear in *The London Topographical Record*, x, 94ff.

[15] The precinct of the church of St. Katherine by the Tower. The hospital was suppressed at the Reformation, and the neighbourhood became a low haunt of sailors and their companions. The district was famous for its breweries.

[16] Milford Lane, like the near-by streets of Whitefriars, afforded shelter to men wanted by the law and other doubtful characters.

" In Milford Lane, near to St. Clement's steeple,
There lived a nymph, kind to all Christian people."

(Henry Savile.)

[17] The reader who knew the ways of London would understand this to mean taking sanctuary in St. Paul's. Humphrey, Duke of Gloucester, was buried at St. Albans, but there was a monument in one of the aisles of St. Paul's to Sir John Beauchamp which was popularly supposed to be the good Duke Humphrey's. Dining with the Duke was understood to mean loitering in the aisle in question, known as Duke Humphrey's Walk, in the hope of receiving an invitation to dinner.

[18] A debtor could get a writ of protection against his creditors if he could show that he himself was a creditor of the Crown. See Blackstone, III *Commentaries*, ch. xix.

[19] The practice of lending in commodities in lieu of cash was a recognised abuse, and was generally condemned, not only as a particularly offensive method of evading the usury laws, but also because the borrower attracted by this type of loan was of the kind that fell an easy dupe to underhand practitioners. The Lord Chancellor mentioned here is probably Lord Ellesmere who resigned 3 March, 1617, after the book was entered. If publication were delayed beyond this date Ellesmere's successor, Bacon, may be indicated, although his titular address was Lord Keeper until January, 1618. Bacon is known to have held strong views about " commodity loans "; and among his papers was preserved a draft bill against this " usurious shift of gain ", which would have the effect of making bonds for such dealings void (*Works*, 1854, i, 641). A complaint by the parent of the young dupe of a commodity-lending London mercer was sent in to parliament in 1641 (*Hist. MSS. Comm.*, 4th *Rep.* 83b).

[20] When a judgment had been given upon a man for debt, and he had been imprisoned as a consequence of his default, he could sometimes have his case brought before a court on suggesting some just cause for his release. When they learn of his intention to get a writ for this purpose his creditors take measures to strengthen their position.

[21] Newmarket Heath was already a highwayman's haunt before the racecourse began to be used (temp. James I). " Were ye all three upon Newmarket Heath, Sir John would quickly rid you of that care [money] " *Sir John Oldcastle*, Pt. I, I, ii (1598); " Newmarket Heath that makes thieves rich " *Maidenhead well lost* (1633).

[22] At Royston, Herts. James I was often in residence there; and at such times the traffic to and from London was considerable. This early reference to highwaymen there seems to have passed unnoticed by antiquarians. See *V. C. H., Hertford*, i, 258 for mention of highway robbery at a later date.

[23] There are numerous references in the literature of the period to the fatal end of criminals on the gallows at Wapping-in-the-Woze. In Stow's day and for two centuries afterwards this was the place of execution " for hanging of pirates and sea-rovers, at the low water-mark, there to remain till three tides had overflowed them." Highwaymen also suffered there; see, for example, mention of the execution of the professional robber Sir George Sandys in S. P. Dom. James I, xcvi, 58; *Cal.* 1611-18, p. 527. The place of execution was moved somewhat farther down the river towards the end of Elizabeth's reign, and in

the low open space was built a street of ships chandlers' shops and slum tenements (Stow, *Survey*, ed. Kingsford, ii, 70, 71).

[24] " Where shall the wretched prisoners have their baskets filled every night and morning with your broken meat ? These must pine and perish. The distressed in Ludgate, the miserable souls in the Holes of the two Counters,   .   .   .   how shall these be sustained ? " (*A Rod for Runaways, Dekker's Plague Pamphlets*, 148-9). The poorest prisoners depended on gifts of food from the charitable placed in the baskets hung outside the prison. They seem also to have been given the scraps from the sheriffs' tables (Mayhew and Skeat, *Dictionary* s.v. *basket*. See, too, petition of prisoners in the Hole at Wood Street Counter, qu. in *Shakespeare's England*, ii, 508). At Christmas, 1644, the Hole of the Poultry Counter had about seventy inmates (Petition in British Museum at E. 21/32).

[25] Imitation gold rings and other counterfeit objects were made in the district of St. Martin-le-Grand on and around the site of the old collegiate church.

[26] Orig. *he*.

[27] See note 31 below.

[28] A short note on the duties of a village constable will be found on p. 521. The prescribed activities of his London cousin were much the same, although some of the technicalities with regard to appointment and eligibility differed. The City had twenty-five wards on the north bank and one over the bridge. The ratepayers of each of the twenty-five appointed a constable from their number annually in December. A wealthy citizen who did not relish the prospect of a year in Dogberry's office could, with the confirmation of the wardmote, nominate and pay a substitute, or even purchase temporary exemption with a big fine. The setting of the nightly watch was the responsibility of the Inquest of the ward ; the householders served as watchmen by rotation, probably under the constables' supervision. There were also bellmen, beadles and other junior officers ; but the constable, working in co-operation with the Inquest, was the man from whom the enforcement of law and order was expected. The present chapter, which is not unsympathetically written, gives some idea of the common trials of the police officer of the early seventeenth century.

[29] The reference appears to be to the Gate House at the Abbey end of Tothill Street. This, of course, was beyond the boundaries of the City, and served as a prison for Westminster. It has been suggested that the term may have been used as an alternative name for Newgate jail (Harben, *Dict. of London*, 251.)

[30] This Richard Vennard (or Vennar) was described by John Manningham in his *Diary* (qu. Chambers, *Eliz. Stage*, iii, 501) as " the grand cony-catcher with golden spurs and a brazen face," a man " with some metal in him." He had an adventurous career among the theatres and about the court ; more than once he was imprisoned in London and, as Fennor tells us, he died in the Wood Street Counter owing to the keeper's neglect. Vennard " was universally regarded as an impostor, and dubbed ' England's Joy ' " from the fact of his having advertised the production of a play of that title in 1602 (*D.N.B.*). " And when he had gotten most of the money into his hands, he would have showed them a fair pair of heels, but he was not so nimble to get up on horseback but that he was fain to forsake that course and betake himself to the water, where he was pursued and taken, and brought before the Lord Chief Justice, who would make nothing of it but a jest and a merriment, and bound him over in five pound to appear at the sessions " (Chamberlain to Carleton, 19 November, 1602).

[31] 23 Henry VI, c. 9. Fennor has paraphrased in places.

[32] I have not been able to find a report of either of these cases.

[33] For examples of legacies for the relief or feeding of prisoners in the Counters, Ludgate and elsewhere, see *Hist. MSS. Comm., 4th Rep.*, 16 ; Stow, *Survey* (ed. Kingsford), i, 106ff. A special instance of this kind of charity is the action of Robert Dowe (d. 1612), who created a trust to provide £20 annually for paying the debts of the poorest inmates of the London prisons, and also a fund which would provide for the ringing of bells and for other measures calculated to bring to repentance the condemned felons of Newgate just before their departure on the Tyburn carts (C. M. Clode, *Early History of Merchant Taylors' Company*, i, 159f.).

[34] See p. 509, note 4.

[35] *must* omitted.

[36] An intentional misstatement perhaps ; every reader would know that a baker offended against the assize of bread by making his loaves light.

[37] The bracketed words appear as a side-note in the original.

THE SONG OF A CONSTABLE.

The original of this song, or ballad, is in manuscript in Harleian MSS., 367, at folio 159. Although it was apparently written out for the press, I can find no trace of a contemporary printed copy; nor do I follow Professor Rollins in his arguments (*Old English Ballads, 1553-1625*, p. 379) for its having been circulated in printed form—unless the words *per me Jacob. Gyffon de Albury predic.*, written in looking-glass hand at the foot of the sheet, can be construed into evidence for publication. For a note on the tune " Jump to me, Cousin," see H. E. Rollins, *loc. cit.*

[1] An idea of the manifold responsibilities of the constable of a township may be gathered from the handbooks on local government published during our period, e.g. Lambarde's *Duty and Office of Constables* (various edns.). This is not the place in which to set them out in detail. But it may be remarked that the petty constable, or borsholder, was an unpaid and untrained officer, who was chosen annually, by the Court Leet if one existed, or by the vestry, or even, as in a few recorded cases, by the justices (e.g., Fordwych, where a short list of householders was sent up at the time of the presentation of the grand jury). Historically speaking, the constable was the agent and mouthpiece of the township. In actual practice many of his duties were imposed and regulated from above; in fact, he was the local factotum of the shire authorities. He must see that the peace was kept; arrest rioters and those who " go armed offensively "; pursue wrong-doers; apprehend eavesdroppers, night-walkers and " vagrom men," and put them in the village cage pending a magistrate's investigation; see that the watch was kept and that the petty officials of the parish were appointed; collect assessments and fines; and inflict minor punishments, such as flogging and branding, if no local tormenter existed. At sessions time he must make a particular report of all that had happened in his area touching the operation of the law. Certainly the most arduous, and generally the least well executed, of his duties were those connected with the arrest and punishment of the vagrant folk of the types pictured in the present collection.

[2] The third Duke of Buckingham, executed in 1521, was the last High Constable of England who made pretensions to play a special part in public affairs. With him the hereditary character of the office perished and thereafter the Constable performed his duties only on Coronation Days. See J. H. Round, *The King's Serjeants and Officers of State*, 78, etc.

[3] i.e., to put out at interest.

[4] At this time (1626) public feeling was high on the question of the government's right to impress substantial citizens for the army, especially as the disputed right was being used as a political weapon to enforce payment of a forced loan (S. R. Gardiner, *History*, vi, 148, 155, etc.). For the legal side see E. P. Cheyney, *History of England from Defeat of Armada*, II, ch. xxvi.

[5] An interesting commentary on the public granary scheme put forward by the Privy Council, 1620-23. Large towns and shire centres were to build storehouses for corn with the idea of steadying prices. Professor Gras (*English Corn Market*, 248-9) thinks that nothing came of these plans; but in Surrey funds for building were evidently collected.

[6] i.e. the grand jury of the county, which contained the principal men, freeholders, of all hundreds of the shire. The nominal number summoned was twenty-three. The writer makes it clear that the practice in Surrey was to call four men from each hundred in which a defendant resided. The general purpose of the whole machinery was, of course, to bring in bills of indictment against alleged criminals before they were brought before a jury of trial.

[7] The constable evidently had his hands full with the duty of nominating men qualified to serve on these various bodies at Quarter Sessions. In addition to the grand jury, there were three others drawing upon the personnel of the parish of Albury. One of these must have been the petty, or felons' jury, which took part in the trial of the prisoners presented by the former; another must have been the jury of the hundred, which made presentments on miscellaneous local matters; the fourth may have been the jury of constables which existed in some counties. (See discussion on this last in Webb, *English Local Government, Parish and County*, bk. II, ch. iv.) Alternatively Cowell's *Interpreter* (Edn. 1727, I, i, 4), may give the true explanation. "In the general assize there are usually many juries, because there be store of causes both civil and criminal commonly to be tried; whereof one is called the Grand Jury, and the rest Petty Juries, whereof it seemeth there should be one from every hundred."

GLOSSARY

(Words in canting use are printed in italics)

abject	to cast out, reject.
abram, abraham	mad ; naked.
abram-man	one of a class of vagrants who excited sympathy or terror in beholders by feigning madness.
abroach, to set	to let the liquid out of a cask.
admiration	a marvel.
advoutery	adultery.
affect	to regard affectionately.
affiance	confidence, trust.
after-clap	subsequent and unexpected stroke.
afterdeal	disadvantage.
aim, to give	to guide or encourage the archers.
alate	of late.
ale-bush	inn sign, inn.
All Hallows	toll-collector's office at market.
altham	wife of a vagabond.
amerce	to fine (as legal punishment).
amort, all	out of spirits.
angel	a gold coin, value 10s. to 11s.
angler	thief who uses a hook on a line.
antic	clown, merry-andrew.
apple-squire	a pimp.
apt	to make fit, adapt.
apronman	workman, mechanic.
armour of proof	strong armour of tested quality.
arrant	(subs.) errand ; (adj.) itinerant, downright.
a-swame	fainting.
ataunt	see " taunt."
atomy	an atom, tiny being.
autem	a church.
autem-mort	a married female vagrant.
bailie	bailiff, sheriff's officer.
bale (of dice)	set required for any game.
band	the flat collar which began to replace the ruff in men's dress about the end of the sixteenth century.
bandog	a fierce watchdog, mastiff, hence a " bloodhound of the law."
bandore	stringed musical instrument like a lute or guitar (Stanford).
barnard, barnacle	member of a group of swindlers ; he first appears to be the victim of a joke, in which the dupe takes part.
barnard's law	a special department of the cony-catcher's craft. The dupe is persuaded to think that he is cheating others.
barred dice	see " dicing terms."
Bartholomew babies	dolls like those sold at Bartholomew Fair.
bash	to be put out of countenance.
basil	a fetter.
basilisco	a piece of heavy ordnance.
bate	strife, discord.
bat-fowling	cony-catching at cards.
batteler	a rank among poor students at Oxford.
bauer	beaver, the lower face-portion of a helmet.
bawdy-basket	name for peddling woman.
bawker	roguish player in bowling-alley who has confederates in the crowd.
beak	magistrate.
beaupere	companion.
beater	taker-up (*q.v.*).
bell-brow	place of receiver of stolen property.
bellman	watchman or town-crier.
belly-cheat	apron.
bench-whistler	idler.
bene	good.
beneship	very good ; goodness.
bene-faker of gybes	one who manufactures false passes, licences, etc.
beray	befoul.
bestraited	distraught.
bett	past tense and past participle of " beat."
bing	to go.
bing a waste !	go you hence !
bird	cozeners' dupe.
bit, bite	coin or money.
black jack	a leathern jug for beer, tarred outside (Skeat and Mayhew).
bleater	victim of a Jack-in-a-box (*q.v.*).

bleating-cheat	calf or sheep.
blue-coat	beadle, servant in livery.
bob	to steal (from a person); to make game of.
boil	to betray. The boil is up: the alarm is given.
boll	to drink.
bolt	a roll of textile fabric.
bolt, boult	to sift.
bolsterer	? one who shares another's bolster. See N.E.D., s.v. "bolster" v. 6.
bombast	cotton wadding.
boon	represents (in such phrases as "boon voyage") a sixteenth century attempt to anglicise the French "bon."
boot-haler	freebooter, brigand.
booty	(i) play, at bowls, etc., which begins with intentional losses in order to encourage the opponent, who finally comes to grief; (ii) play which ends in loss, the "booty" coming to the loser's friends, who have laid their bets against him.
bord	a shilling; half-a-bord, sixpence.
borsholder	petty constable.
boun	to get oneself ready.
bouse	liquor; to drink. Rome bouse: wine.
bousing ken	ale-house.
brabble	to quarrel.
brach	bitch-hound.
brack	a flaw in cloth (N.E.D.).
braid	to assault, reproach passionately.
brast	burst.
brazil	brazil-wood, used for making dyes, also for walking-sticks, clubs, etc.
bribering	stealing.
bristle dice	see "dicing terms."
broach	to spit (in cooking); to stab.
broker	middleman; second-hand dealer; often employed to mean receiver of stolen goods.
broom-man	street-sweeper, scavenger.
brunt	a blow, onset.
buck	clothes prepared for washing; the liquid; the action of washing them.
budge a beak	to flee from justice.
budget	a bag, wallet.
bufe, bugher	dog.
bung	a purse, pocket.
buy	a purse.
cackling-cheat	cock or capon.
cacodaemon	evil spirit.
caliver	light musket.
callet	a drab.
Candlemas	February 2nd, the Feast of the Purification of the Virgin.
cannikin	the plague.
cant	the secret language of thieves and beggars; to speak this language; to beg in a whining tone.
cantle	the protuberant part at the back of a saddle (N.E.D.).
cap-case	travelling-bag.
carcanet	a collar of jewels.
carl	common fellow, countryman.
cassan	cheese.
cast	condemn; overthrow an opponent.
caster	a cloak.
castle	to see or look.
catchpole	officer employed for making arrests.
cater	one who buys provisions.
cates	victuals.
caul	spider's web.
cautel	precaution, wariness.
cent, sant	game at cards with winning score a hundred.
chafer	saucepan.
chapman	trader, bargainer, salesman.
charm	one who picks a lock.
chats, cheats	gallows.
cheap	to trade, bargain.
cheaped	had at a bargain.
cheat	anything (usually qualified by preceding word, thus, "bleating-cheat," sheep).
cheat	a false die.
cheat	fine, forfeit, reversion, etc. which falls to a landlord.
Chepemans	Cheapside Market.
chip	worthless thing.
chop	to buy and sell.
chop a card	to change its place in the pack secretly.
chopping	vigorous, strapping.
clapperdudgeon	a beggar born; also as term of reproach.
clewner	chief man among the rogers (*q.v.*).
cleym	a sore.
clinker	to cause to shrink.
cloth-man	clothier.
cloy	a snap (*q.v.*).
cloy	to steal; to obstruct, encumber.
cloyed	intruded upon by others claiming a share (Grosart).
cly	seize, steal.

cly the jerk	to be whipped.
cog	a coin.
cog	to cheat at dice or cards, to practice deceit; see "dicing terms."
cole, colt	a cheating knave.
colt	innkeeper who becomes victim of rank-riders (*q.v.*).
colour	pretence, false appearance of correctness.
commission	shirt.
commodity	advantage, profit; parcel of goods handed over by money-lender to a needy client instead of money (sometimes called a "commodity of brown paper"); a whore.
conceit, to take a	to sicken of some morbid affection.
congee	to make a ceremonious bow.
conject	to devise, plot.
contraries	see "dicing terms."
conveyance	a trick, piece of roguery.
cope	to fasten up a ferret's mouth.
copesmate	associate, comrade.
copy, to change one's	to alter one's behaviour.
cornuto	a cuckold (lit. furnished with horns).
corporal oath	corporale juramentum, taken while touching a sacred object.
corsie	a corrosive.
cote-card	court-card.
couch	to embroider (rare).
couch a hogshead	to lie down to sleep.
counsellor	advising barrister.
country	a word often employed to mean county. Thus, "a countryman of mine": a man from my county.
couples	pair of leashes holding together two hunting dogs.
courtesy-man	spokesman of a company of beggars pretending to be ex-soldiers.
courtlax	cutlass.
cousin	a dupe.
cove	person, fellow.
covert	protection, shelter.
covetise	covetousness.
crack	talk big, boast, brag (Skeat and Mayhew).
crackmans	a hedge.
cramp-rings	fetters.
crank, the	the falling sickness. A "counterfeit crank" is one who pretends to be a sufferer.
crashing-cheats	teeth.
crassing-cheats	apples, pears, and other fruit.
cravant	craven.
creeping law	the craft of those who follow petty thievery in the suburbs.
crome	stick furnished with a hook at the end.
cross	coin (colloquial).
crossbiter	swindler, trickster; often with a special sense, meaning one who extorts money by threats from a man found compromising himself with a woman of easy virtue.
cross-lay	a wager meant to deceive the company as to the caller's intentions.
cue	=Q, half a farthing.
cuffin	man, fellow.
curb	the curber's hook.
curber	one who steals from open windows.
cursitor	wanderer, tramp.
curtal	small piece of artillery; horse with docked tail (term of abuse).
curtal	vagabond who wears a short cloak.
cushnet	a little cushion.
cut	to speak, say.
cut benely, to	to speak gently.
cut bene whids, to	to speak properly, truly.
cuttle	knife.
cuttle-bung	cutpurse's knife.
darkmans	the night.
dell	young woman of the vagrant type.
decoy	a card game of which no particulars have survived.
demanders for glimmer	beggars who seek relief on the plea that their houses and goods have been burnt.
demi	see "dicing terms."
denier	Fr. one-twelfth of a sou; colloquially, "penny."
derrick	hangman; gallows. From the name of a Tyburn hangman (c. 1600).
deuce-ace	two and one (i.e. a throw that turns up deuce with one die and ace with the other); hence a poor throw, bad luck, mean estate, the lower class (N.E.D.). See "dicing terms."
Devonshire kersey	a rough cloth conforming to the Devon standard; mostly made in that county.

dewse-a-vill	the country, as opposed to town.
dicing terms	ace=1 ; deuce=2 ; trey=3 ; cater=4 ; cinque=5 ; sice =6.
	Kinds of dice : (i) *squariers* are fair dice ; (ii) *langrets* or *barred dice* are not perfect cubes, but have greater length along one axis. Thus *barred cater-treys* are longer in the 3-4 direction and will seldom turn up these numbers ; so with *barred sice-aces, cinque-deuces* ; (iii) *flats* are dice shorter in one dimension ; a *flat cater-trey* will therefore normally throw up a 3 or 4 ; (iv) *fullams* are weighted, and will throw up the side farthest from the weight ; (v) *gourds* and (?) *graviers* are hollowed near one face and produce a contrary result ; (vi) *bristle dice* have a short bristle attached to one face or edge ; (vii) *high men* and *low men* are wrongly numbered on one face ; usually 5 is substituted for 2 in a *high man*, and 2 for 5 in a *low man* ; (viii) a *demi* or *demi-bar* is apparently a false die with only half the usual bias ; (ix) *contraries* are false dice with an opposite tendency to those already in play, and will thus " crossbite " them ; (x) the *vantage* is the tendency of a die ; (xi) *cogging* is the manipulation of the die in the dice-box.
dicker	half-score.
diddering and doddering	shaking and shivering.
diet	course of life ; board.
disgest	to digest.
dispense	heavy spending.
diver	house-thief who employs small boy to slip through windows.
doddypol	foolish person.
dodkin	" doit," a Dutch coin ; any small coin.
dorsermaker	maker of panniers.
dosser	basket.
dottrel	kind of plover, an easy prey.

doxy	female vagabond, travelling usually with a man.
draw	to pick a pocket.
draw-latch	petty thief.
drift	a scheme.
drigger	a thief.
drink tobacco	to draw in or inhale the smoke.
drover	a cheating horse-dealer in Smithfield Market.
drug	drudge.
dry-vat	box or cask for dry goods.
duds	clothes, things in general ; *lag of duds*, wash-bundle.
dummerer	beggar who feigns dumbness.
dup	to open (door or gate).
dure	to endure.
eagle	member of a group of confederates cheating at cards or dice. He it is who ultimately wins.
ensample	an example.
even and odd	a simple game of chance that can be played with dice and other pieces.
exigent	an emergency, critical moment or state.
extirp	extirpate.
face, to show a brave	to speak deceitfully.
faculty	trade, occupation.
fadge	to fit in with.
fairing	a present, generally understood as having been bought at a fair.
faitour	early name for vagabond or cheat.
faker (or *feager*) of loges	one who makes or begs with false papers.
fallows, to come over his	to come over the ground that he had neglected—a rural metaphor (Grosart).
famblers	gloves.
fambles	hands.
fambling-cheat	a ring.
farce	to break open or pick a lock.
fardel	a bundle.
farmerly beggars	beggars who carry no artificial sores.
feager	see *faker*.
fence	to buy or sell stolen goods.
ferme	hole.
ferret	tradesman who lends commodities to *ferret-hunters* and their victims.
ferret	to cheat.
ferret-beat, ferret-claw	to strip a man of money by cheating him.

ferreting, ferret-hunting	the practice followed by presentable rogues who join their credit, which is worthless, with that of their dupe, and borrow money, or goods in lieu thereof, from a tradesman, with whom they are sometimes in league
fet	to fetch.
fettle	to make ready.
fib	to beat.
fig-boy	pickpocket.
figging law	the art of the cutpurse.
filch	to beat, strike, steal.
filch, filchman	cudgel; a hooked staff used by window-thieves.
fillock	a wanton girl.
fingerer	one of a gang of card-cheats.
flag	a groat.
flankard	the meaning is doubtful. See N.E.D., *s.v.*
flasket	basket.
flick	a thief.
fleece	booty when shared out.
foin	a pickpocket.
foist	cheat, rogue, pickpocket; piece of roguery.
foist	to pick a pocket; palm or conceal dice.
footman's maund	artificial sore on back of hand.
footpack	pedlar's bag.
forestalling	buying up goods before they come to market with intention of selling again.
forlorn hope	player at cards or dice, who plays to lose so that his confederates may win.
frater	beggar armed with forged authorisation who pretends to collect money for a charity.
French marbles	the pox.
fresh-water mariner	beggar pretending to be a discharged sailor.
fridge	to fidget.
frieze	a kind of cheap woollen cloth.
frisk, to fetch a	to dance a jig.
frumenty	seasoned dish of wheat boiled in milk.
furca	gallows (L.).
fustian	pretentious, without worth.
gage	quart pot.
galligaskins, gallyslops	wide hose.
gan	a mouth.
garbage	shoplifter's spoil; stolen goods.
gathers	the various organs plucked from the inside of a carcase.
gawl	to bawl out (N.E.D.).
Gazophylacium	orig. box for Temple offerings; treasure chest, strong-box.
gear	dress, equipment; trash, stuff.
geason	rare, scarce.
gentry cove	man of the upper class.
gentry mort	woman of the upper class.
gilks	skeleton keys.
gillot	a wanton.
gin	mechanical contrivance, trap.
ging	troop, company, rabble.
Gip !	exclamation of derision.
gittern	a cithern.
give the wall	to give the courtesy of the pavement.
glaziers	eyes.
glimmer	fire.
glimmerers	demanders for glimmer (*q.v.*).
glimpsing	glimmering.
gloried	adorned.
goad	the accomplice of a cozening dealer at a horse fair.
gore	to charge like a horned animal.
gossip	familiar friend; godparent.
Gracemans	Gracechurch Street Market.
grain, to dye in	to dye in permanent colour (often scarlet).
grain of the table, to have the	to sit at the head, preside.
gran	gaffer.
grannam, granmer	corn.
grate	prison.
greenmans	the fields.
gripe	a griffin.
gripe	rogue in bowling-alley who lays bets with the crowd.
gripe	to grip, obtain extortionate hold upon.
grief	a wound, sore.
groat	a coin value 4*d*.
grunter, grunting-cheat	a pig.
grutch	to complain, repine.
guard	an embroidered edge, ornament; " guarded " (adj.).
gudgeon, to swallow the	to be caught, trapped.
gull	to swallow greedily.
gull	a dupe, victim of dishonest card- or dice-players.
gull-groper	money-lender in alliance with cheats.
gybe	a false pass; any writing.
gybe jarked	a sealed passport.
hackster	cut-throat, bully.
haggard	one who resists enticements of professional cony-catchers.

haggard	wild, disorderly.
handsel	first fruits ; good luck.
hard-meat	dry fodder.
harlot	a rogue, vagabond.
harman-beck	a parish constable.
harmans	the stocks.
haskard	base, dirty fellow.
hazard	(i) a group of games at dice ; (ii) a game in which cards were turned up in succession from the pack.
headborough	parish constable, or officer, or his assistant.
hearing-cheats	ears.
heave a bough or *booth*	to rob a stall.
hent	to seize.
herbeger	lodging-house keeper ; lodger.
high law	the art of highway robbery.
high-pad	the highway.
hippocras	a cordial of spiced wine.
hornbook	a card or paper, often shaped like a hand-mirror, with the letters of the alphabet, the Lord's Prayer, etc., the paper portion having a transparent horn covering.
horse-courser	jobbing dealer in horses (N.E.D.).
hostage	inn, board.
hostry	hostelry.
hugger	to lie concealed.
Hungarian	joc., needy, hungry person.
hurl	to rush.
hurkle	to shudder, contract.
imbraid	to upbraid.
impostume	an abscess.
ingluvious	gluttonous.
inkle	linen thread or tape.
Irish toyle	kind of pedlar.
ivy-bush	tavern-sign, inn.
jack-boy	boy employed in menial capacity, stable-boy.
Jack (or John) Drum's entertainment	a rough reception, turning an unwelcome guest out of doors (N.E.D.).
Jack-in-a-box	one who *trims*, i.e. steals money by substituting one box for another.
Jack of the clock-house	small figure which strikes the bell of a clock.
Jacobus	the gold " sovereign " of James I, value 20s. to 24s.
jakes-farmer	one employed, usually under contract, to clean privies.
jan	a purse.
jark	a seal ; to seal.

jarkman	educated beggar, who makes a living by forging licences.
Jason's fleece	name for the gold coin employed in the trick of *trimming* (*q.v.*).
javel	a low fellow.
jerk	to whip.
jig	joke, contrivance.
jigger	door.
jingler	dishonest horse-dealer.
jugging law	the mode of thievery followed by those who make dishonest gains at certain games of chance, such as nine-holes.
ken	a house.
kennel	a gutter.
kenning	range of vision.
ketler	a tinker.
kinchin, kitchin	a child.
kinchin co or *cove*	a vagabond boy.
kinchin mort	a vagabond girl.
knap	a rogue.
knap of the case, the	the villain of the piece.
knight of the post	person hired to give evidence of a man's respectability ; perjurer.
lag of duds	bundle of washing, clothes.
lage (*g* hard)	water ; to wash.
lamback	to flog.
lambskin, lapped up in	bound by a legal document.
lance-man	mounted thief.
lance-prisado	lance-corporal.
lap	buttermilk, whey.
larjohn	largesse (?).
lask	a laxative ; disturbed condition of digestive organs.
laund	a glade.
law	branch of the rogue's art.
lazar	leper ; miserable diseased person.
leader	one of a group of cheats at cards or dice.
leese	to lose.
leet	police-court which was normally part of private jurisdiction of local landlord.
leg, to make a	to make obeisance.
let	to prevent, obstruct.
lewd	base, common, worthless.
lib	sleep.
libbeg(e)	a bed.
libbet	a stick.
libken	a place to lie in.
licentious	lacking in self-restraint.
lickerish	self-indulgent, lecherous

lift	to steal.
lifter	thief, cheat.
lifts	stolen goods.
liggen	to lie down.
lightly	usually.
lime-twigs	playing-cards.
limiting law	the art of thieves who practise their craft at assize-towns and fairs.
linen-armourer	orig. maker of adjuncts to armour ; became jocular term for " tailor."
lither	lazy, demoralised.
loges	counterfeit papers.
lorel, losel	rogue, ragamuffin.
lour	money.
lour	a scowl.
lowing-cheat	a cow.
lugs	ears.
lurch	a high score in various games.
lurch	to deceive, leave in the lurch.
lurch, to have on the	to have a man at a disadvantage.
lurcher	one who cheats at bowls.
lusk	a worthless fellow.
macemonger	nonce-word for police officer.
make	companion, mate.
make	a halfpenny.
male	portmanteau (Utterson).
mammering	muttering.
mandilion	kind of overcoat worn by soldiers and servants.
mankind	fierce, furious.
Margery-prater	a hen.
mark	13*s*. 4*d*., not a coin.
marker	shop-thief's accomplice.
marter	receiver of stolen goods.
martin	a dupe.
Marymass	one of the festivals of the Virgin.
mason's maund	artificial sore on arm above the elbow.
masty	mastiff.
maund	begging ; to beg.
maund abram, to	to beg in the manner of the *abram-man*.
maunder(er)	a beggar.
meschant	miserable, bad.
metely	moderately.
meuse	a hare's form.
micher	sneak, petty thief.
mill	break up, rob, spoil, kill.
minion	a loved one, mistress.
mint	money.
mistress	the jack (in bowls).
moly	a herb ; Ulysses armed himself with it against Circe.
monopolitan	monopolist.
moon-man	night-walker, gypsy.

morris-pike	sixteenth century weapon, said to have had a Moorish origin.
morrow-mass	first mass of the day.
muffling-cheat	napkin.
muggill	beadle.
mummy	medical preparation originally extracted from the substance with which mummies were embalmed.
myrabolan	dried fruit, formerly in repute for its astringent properties (Stanford Dict.).
nab	a head.
nab-cheat	a hat or cap.
nase	drunken.
nappy	fresh, strong, " heady " (E.D.D.).
Neapolitan scab, scurf, etc.	the pox.
neat's leather	oxhide.
neeze	sneeze.
neezing-powder	taken to cause sneezing.
new-cut	a card game.
niggling	venery ; the word is said to have died, except in literary usage, by 1610.
nigh	to approach.
nip	a cutpurse.
nip a bung, to	to cut a purse.
noble	a gold coin minted in several values in sixteenth century.
nosegent	a nun.
novel(s)	news.
novem, novemquinque, novum	a game at dice ; the principal throws are 4 and 5. Five or six persons play.
Numans, Newmans	Newgate Market.
oak	he that standeth to watch in *high law* (Greene).
one-and-thirty	a round (?) game at cards, said to have resembled vingt-et-un.
ordinary	eating-house supplying a set meal. Some London ordinaries were notorious gaming houses.
ought	owed.
pad	soft padded saddle.
pad	road.
padder	highway robber.
pair of cards	a pack.
palliard	vagrant beggar (wearing a patched cloak).
paltry, peltry	rubbish, worthless stuff.
pannam	bread.

pantofles	slippers ; "to be upon one's pantofles," to stand upon one's dignity.
Paper-house	office of the Counter.
parcel	in some degree, partially.
parle	a talk, discussion.
passage	game with three dice in which the first player to throw two numbers alike, totalling more than 10, wins.
patching	knavish.
patrico, *patriarch co*	priest, hedge-priest.
patrico's kinchin	pig.
peasant	clown, rascal.
peck, peckage	food.
peck	to eat.
peevish	mischievous, perverse.
peld	bald, shorn.
pelfry	goods pilfered ; housebreaker's spoils.
pelting	petty, mean.
penner	pen-case.
pettilashery, petulacery	petty larceny.
petty bribery	petty larceny.
picking	stealing.
picklock	skeleton key ; one who picks a lock.
pigeon-holes	stocks.
pikes, to pass the	to pass through dangers successfully.
pill	to plunder.
pillow-bere	pillow-case.
pink	sailing-vessel (usually small).
placard, placket	petticoat, pocket in woman's skirt.
plant	to hide.
plaudite	chorus of applause.
point	tagged lace for fastening clothes.
poke	bag or pocket.
poll	to plunder, fleece, extort.
Polony	Polish.
polt-foot	club-foot.
poplars	porridge.
port	state, sumptuous way of living.
port-sale	sale at auction.
portway	main road from town to town.
possede	to possess.
pot-hunter	*barnard (q.v.).*
pottle	half-gallon.
poynado	poniard.
prancer, pranker	horse ; one who robs on horseback ; horse-thief.
prank	to deck out.
prat	buttocks.
prattling-cheat	tongue.
prease	to press.
preparado	preparation.
pretty	clever, ingenious.
prick	mark in the centre of a target.
prick-song	song pricked out in musical notation ; part of song or accompaniment which supports principal melody.
prig	to ride ; steal.
prigger	horse-thief.
prigman	tramp who subsists by stealing clothes hanging on bushes, etc., catching hens and so on.
prima-vista	game at cards, by some identified with primero (N.E.D.).
primero	game at cards ; four cards were dealt to each player, each card having thrice its ordinary value (N.E.D.). Introduced shortly before 1530.
proctor	licensed representative begging on behalf of almshouse, etc.; indulgence-seller (rare).
prodition	treachery.
proditorian	fanciful name for traitor.
proface !	a word of salutation at a meal or drinking party.
promit	to promise.
promoter	common informer.
prospective	optical instrument, as telescope, microscope.
provant	provisions ; ammunition ; mercenary service.
pull	to strip, fleece.
pullen	poultry.
purchase	winnings.
purse-nets	commodities lent to a borrower in lieu of money.
puttock	kite-like person, catchpole.
quacking-cheat	a duck.
quarroms	body, arms, back.
quartered	(of clothes) cut in quarters like a heraldic garment.
quartern	quarter of a hundred.
queer	worthless, bad, having evil associations.
queer-bird	jail-bird.
Queer-cuffin	Justice of the Peace.
queer-ken (hall)	prison.
querry	see *quittery.*
quire	pamphlet, small book.
quit	to acquit.
quittance	to cancel, repay.
quittery, querry (i.e. equerry)	confederate of horse-thief, will go surety for his honesty.

rabbit-suckers   impecunious rascals who bor-
                    row on the credit of a
                    richer companion.
rakehell   out and out rascal.
rank rider   highwayman, moss-trooper.
rank riders   rogues who get credit from inn-
                    keepers under pretence of
                    being important personages.
rapt   caught up.
rastly   rancid.
ray   to befoul.
raze   to slash.
rebate   to reduce in strength.
rede   counsel.
redshank   a duck.
retriever   " *verser* " (*q.v.*).
revie   see " vie and revie."
rew   row, rank.
rifle   to raffle ; gamble at dice.
rifler   toll-collector.
ring-faller,   one who plays on the greed
    ring-chopper of street passengers by
                    letting fall a ring falsely
                    made to look like gold.
risse   past tense of " rise."
roaring-boys   young bloods and rascals who
                    amused themselves by an-
                    noying respectable citizens.
roberdsman   member of one of the vagrant
                    bands numerous in England
                    in the fourteenth century.
roger   beggar pretending scholarship.
roil   to wander about.
romboyle   (subs.) watch and ward ;
                    (v.) to seek after with a
                    warrant.
rome, room,   great, good ; usually found
    rum   in combination with some
                    other word, as, *rome-bouse,*
                    wine, good drink ; *room-*
                    cuttle, sword ; *rome-cove,*
                    gentleman ;   *rome-mort,*
                    queen,   gentlewoman ;
                    Rome-vill, London, or a
                    big town.
rubber   see " *rutter.*"
Ruffin, Ruffian   the Devil.
ruffler   lusty rogue who has, or
                    pretends to have, seen
                    service in the wars ; his
                    trade is robbery, open or
                    disguised.
ruffmans   woods, hedges ; eaves (Rid).
ruff-peck   bacon.
rug-gown   coat made of coarse woollen
                    material, worn by beadles
                    and others.
runagate   vagabond.
russet   (of boots, etc.) tan, unblack-
                    ened.

rutter, rubber   the last of a gang of card-
                    playing cony-catchers to
                    appear on the scene. If
                    need be he provokes quar-
                    rels and confusion.
sacking law   the craft of the brothel-
                    keeper.
safe-guard   outer petticoat worn to protect
                    the skirt.
sand-eyed   purblind.
Sans bell   Sanctus bell.
sant   see " cent."
santar   third member of shoplifting
                    gang, who carries away the
                    goods.
sapient   travelling quack.
sauce, to pay   to pay dearly.
scald   scabby.
scald-pate   diseased scalp.
scantling   (in archery) the distance from
                    the mark within which a
                    shot was not recorded as a
                    miss (N.E.D.).
scelerous   wicked.
scour the cramp-
    rings   to wear fetters.
scrappage   scraps of food (?).
scrath   to scratch.
scrip   beggar's wallet.
scripper   he that setteth the watch in
                    high law (Greene).
scrivener   notary, one who drafts legal
                    documents and performs
                    many of the functions of a
                    modern solicitor, including
                    the arrangement of loans,
                    mortgages, etc.
scruff   scraps (of meat, etc.).
seminary   short for seminary priest.
sennight   period of seven days.
setter   see " *taker-up.*"
shadow   to protect, screen.
shark-shift   shady character.
shave   to fleece.
shaver   swindler, extortioner.
sheep-shearing   one who practises trimming
                    (*q.v.*).
shells   money, stolen money.
shend   to reproach, humiliate.
shift   expedient, contrivance.
shot   a payment, tavern reckoning.
shrap   wine.
shrieve   sheriff.
shrive   relieve of burden, rob.
shruff   cinders, combustible refuse.
simpler   victim of " *crossbiter* " (*q.v.*).
sinciput   front half of skull.
sith   since.
sithence   afterwards ; seeing that.

skene	dagger.
skew	beggar's dish; vessel for drinking.
skipjack	horse-dealer's lad.
skipper	barn.
slade, slate	sheet.
slip	counterfeit coin; counter.
slope	to sleep.
slops	wide breeches or hose.
slouch	lout.
smeller	garden.
smell-feast	one who smells out the coming feast, the uninvited guest.
smelling-cheat	garden; orchard; nosegay.
smoke	to suspect, detect.
snaffle	one who gets money by false pretences from country gentlemen and farmers.
snap, snapper	thief; one who claims a share in the spoil of other thieves.
snap, snappage, snappings	the gains of the snap (above).
snout-fair	handsome.
soaker	an old, experienced hand.
sod	boiled.
soldier's maund	artificial sore on the forearm.
Solomon	mass; altar.
sound	swoon.
Spanish pip	the pox.
speeder	one who helps, or one who prospers, in a suit.
spet	to spit.
spill	to destroy, waste.
spital-house	hospital, infirmary.
splint	malady attacking the legs of horses.
spoil	damage, destruction.
stall	to fix, appoint a place; induct, ordain.
stall, stale	decoy, one who entices the dupe, or occupies a person's attention while the colleagues steal.
stalled to the rogue	admitted by ceremony to the order of thieves.
stalling-ken	place of receiver of stolen goods.
stamps	legs.
stampers	shoes.
stand	housebreaker's mate who watches.
stander	highwayman, or highwayman's mate and look-out man.
standish	inkstand.
starting-hole	hiding-place; loophole for escape.
stew	brothel; (plur.) quarter of town in which brothels abound.

stigmatical	infamous.
stoop	to swoop down like a hawk; to humble oneself; to hazard money at cards, etc.
stop dice	false dice.
stopper	one who performs certain part in a game at tennis. See N.E.D., s.n.
storing of the rogueman	the procedure of the hedge-thief.
stow you !	hold your peace !
strait	narrow, limited.
straw, there lay a	here I will desist.
strike	to rob or steal.
striking	the action of picking a pocket.
stripping law	the art of robbery practised by extortionate jailers.
strummell	straw.
stroller	one who lives by his wits, borrowing from country people.
suborn	to give support to.
sucket	candied fruit, sweetmeat.
sue	to follow.
suffier	rogue who feigns drunkenness (in versing law).
surfling water	preparation of sulphur water or other cosmetic.
surpress	to weigh down, suppress.
surview	to survey.
swadder	pedlar.
swigman	a peddling vagabond.
table-book	note-book.
tag	to cheat (?).
taker, taker up	the first of a group of cony-catchers to introduce himself to the dupe.
tarmosind	coat so made that when turned it would reveal a good outside.
tatterdemalion	ragged, beggarly person.
taunt	to the full, thoroughly. " To drink ataunt," to drink immoderately.
tercel-gentle	(literally, the male of the falcon) gentleman from whom money is cheated by rogue who pretends to have dedicated book to him.
termage	gains of a cheating gambler in a bowling-alley.
termer	" one who resorts to London in term-time only for the sake of gain or for intrigue; a frequenter of the law-courts" (Skeat and Mayhew).
tester	i.e. teston, a 6d. or 1s. piece.
texted letters	letters in an engrossed document.

throng — crowded.

tib (of the buttery) — goose.

tine — prong, spike.

tinkard — tinker.

tip — to give.

tire — attire.

tire — (of a bird of prey) to feed on, tear at.

togman(s) — coat or cloak.

toll-booth — office and lock-up in markets for the detention of defaulters and others.

toller — toll-collector.

tour — to see, look, peep.

trace — way, path.

tracer — one who follows up traces, a detective.

trade up — to train up.

traffic — whore.

train — to draw on.

trammel — hobble for tying up a horse.

treacher — a cheat.

tricker — thieves' instrument for forcing windows and cutting metal.

trimming — the trick of changing gold for silver, getting away with both.

trine — to go; to hang. *Trine to the cheats*, to be hanged.

trining-cheats — gallows.

Trinidado — Trinidad tobacco.

triumph — public procession, pageant, tilting match

truandise — idleness, vagabondage.

truchman — interpreter.

trug — light woman.

trugging-house — brothel.

trump — game resembling whist.

truss — to pack close, fasten up.

trussed — (of a horse) well-knit.

tumbler — one employed to draw a person into a swindler's net.

unbolish — abolish.

uneath — scarcely, hardly.

upright-man — a sturdy fellow; one of the aristocracy of the vagabond world.

upsy-Frieze — excessively, in the Frisian fashion.

vade — to go away.

vail — to lower, stoop, bow.

vantage, with the — with a little over.

vaulting-house — brothel.

venery — lechery.

venny — to thrust or wound in sword-play.

verse — to introduce oneself to a stranger.

verser — cheat, cozener; is one of a group of sharpers and poses as the well-to-do friend of the taker-up (*q.v.*).

vie and revie — to vie is to hazard a stake on a card; to revie (by the opponent) is to cover the first stake with a larger; to revie again is to raise the original stake.

vigliacco — rascal.

vincent — victim of bowling-alley cheats.

voider — one who clears the remains of a meal from the table.

vouchsafe — to grant or condescend graciously.

wanion, with a — with a vengeance.

walking mort — vagrant unmarried woman travelling with a male companion.

wapping — venery.

wapping-mort — whore.

warp — curber's look-out man.

warren — victim of ferret-hunter (*q.v.*).

washing-ball — cake of soap.

washman — a kind of palliard (*q.v.*).

weasand-pipe — windpipe.

ween — to suppose, imagine.

welted — fringed.

western pug — a bargee on a Thames craft above London.

westward, to be carried — to be taken to Tyburn gallows.

whet — to urge on.

whid — a word; to speak.

whip-jack — beggar who pretends to be a sailor, using a forged licence to travel.

white money — silver money.

white wool — name for the silver coin stolen in the trick of trimming (*q.v.*).

Whittington — Newgate.

whittled — drunk.

win — penny.

winch — (of a horse) to start, kick out.

with — cord of twisted willow.

wood — mad.

woodcock — simpleton.

woodpecker — card- or dice-player's confederate who stands by and bets.

wrester — lock-picking instrument.

yarrum — milk.

yede — went.

Index

Places now within the London area are indexed under London

M